HUNTERS, FISHERS AND FORAGERS IN WALES

*This volume is dedicated to my daughter Lian
and granddaughters Paige and Mya*

HUNTERS, FISHERS AND FORAGERS IN WALES

Towards a social narrative of Mesolithic lifeways

Malcolm Lillie

Oxbow Books
Oxford & Philadelphia

Published in the United Kingdom in 2015 by
OXBOW BOOKS
10 Hythe Bridge Street, Oxford OX1 2EW

and in the United States by
OXBOW BOOKS
1950 Lawrence Road, Havertown, PA 19083

Paperback Edition: ISBN 978-1-78297-974-6
Digital Edition: ISBN 978-1-78297-975-3

A CIP record for this book is available from the British Library

Library of Congress Cataloging-in-Publication Data

Lillie, Malcolm, author.
  Hunters, fishers and foragers in Wales : towards a social narrative of Mesolithic lifeways / Malcolm Lillie.
-- Paperback edition.
     pages cm
  Includes bibliographical references and index.
  ISBN 978-1-78297-974-6 (pbk.)
  1. Mesolithic period--Wales. 2. Wales--Antiquities. I. Title.
  GN774.22.G7L55 2015
  936.2'9--dc23
                      2015030009

Printed in the United Kingdom by Hobbs the Printers Ltd, Totton, Hampshire

For a complete list of Oxbow titles, please contact:

UNITED KINGDOM
Oxbow Books
Telephone (01865) 241249, Fax (01865) 794449
Email: oxbow@oxbowbooks.com
www.oxbowbooks.com

UNITED STATES OF AMERICA
Oxbow Books
Telephone (800) 791-9354, Fax (610) 853-9146
Email: queries@casemateacademic.com
www.casemateacademic.com/oxbow

Oxbow Books is part of the Casemate Group

Front cover: A small waterfall in the Elan Valley, Powys © Malcolm Lillie
Back cover: Waun Fignen Felin, Llywel, Breconshire, Powys © Malcolm Lillie

CONTENTS

LIST OF FIGURES

LIST OF TABLES

Acknowledgements

This is a book that I had wanted to write since I first got hooked on the Mesolithic period when studying as an undergraduate at Nottingham University in the late 1980s. I was fortunate enough to be taught by the late Roger Jacobi, and it is to him that I offer this first acknowledgement as he was directly responsible for igniting my interest in Mesolithic archaeology. I also have to thank James Kenworthy who not only taught me that prehistoric archaeology was the most interesting subject to study as an undergraduate, but who also helped me considerably by editing my early efforts at essay writing, enthusiastically and with a bright red pen, I quickly began to realise how bad my early attempts at essay writing were! Unfortunately both Roger and James succumbed to cancer in 2009 aged 62 and 2011 aged 61 respectively. Inspirational lecturers who are engaging and enthusiastic about their subject are always sorely missed.

My desire to write this book is also inspired by the fact that I grew up in south Wales, not knowing (or being taught) anything about the diverse and rich cultural heritage that was all around me in Wales, I was actually surprised to discover that I had grown up only a few miles from the Roman fortress at Caerleon; where I began my commercial archaeology career with the Glamorgan and Gwent Archaeological Trust (GGAT). Despite the (apparent) paucity of the Mesolithic record for Wales, I have always felt that the Mesolithic is a period that warrants a considered and integrated approach. Unfortunately, the Mesolithic is not always easily interpreted in a British context, due in no small part to the lack of direct physical evidence for Mesolithic individuals, and a general lack of stratified sites with secure contexts (with one or two notable exceptions).

There have been a number of recent volumes that have considered, in detail, some of the key elements of Mesolithic lifeways in Wales, to a greater or lesser degree, e.g. *Prehistoric Wales* (Lynch *et al.* 2000), *Prehistoric Coastal Communities: The Mesolithic in Western Britain* (Bell 2007a) and *Palaeolithic and Mesolithic Settlement in Wales: with Special Reference to Dyfed* (David 2007). These volumes cover key aspects of the available evidence, often with exception detail and clarity, and as such, the current volume is aimed at contributing to the available literature through an holistic consideration of the ways in which the evidence for people in the Mesolithic in Europe, in general, can allow for a nuanced consideration of Mesolithic lifeways and the generation of data that moves towards a social narrative for this period in Wales.

It is hoped that the use of primary data sources held at the regional HERs of Dyfed, Clwyd-Powys, Gwynedd and Glamorgan-Gwent enhances the discussion of Wales in the Mesolithic and ensures that the dataset that has been generated provides a robust basis for the analysis undertaken in this volume. The various HER managers and their colleagues are thanked for all of the help and advice that was proffered when I visited. In this context Marion Page (DAT) in particular, along with Nina Steele and Angharad Stockwell at Gwynedd Archaeological Trust, Sophie Watson, Charlotte Baxter, Jeff Spencer and Bob Silvester at Clwyd-Powys Archaeological Trust and Sue Hughes and Neil Maylan (GGAT) are all thanked for their generosity in helping me negotiate the HER databases.

In addition, a number of colleagues have been kind enough to forward me copies of their more recent papers as I trudge through the academic quagmire; I have also been extremely fortunate to be able to call on a number of colleagues and friends for information, help and advice, both in general, and during the production of this book. In no particular order these individuals include Paul Buckland, Chelsea Budd, Christopher Meiklejohn, Inna Potekhina, Paul Bahn, Paul Pettitt, Lars Larsson, Andrew David, Helen Fenwick, Nigel Page, Marion Page, John Grattan, Marek Zvelebil, Christine Rawson, Peter Halkon, Nicky Milner, David Williams, Jenny Moore, Clive Waddington and Mickle Zhilin; apologies to any others I have neglected to mention.

The Cefn Estate is thanked for allowing access to view the Cefn Cave.

John Garner (GEES, University of Hull) produced the North Sea bathymetry maps used in Figures 1.2 and 2.1. Professors Mark Bateman and Paul Buckland (and co-workers) are thanked for permission to use Figure 1.1. Paul Bahn provided a copy of the Creswell Cave art used in Figure 1.9 and both Paul and the British Cave Art Research Team are thanked for permission to use this image. Thanks to Paul Bahn for comments on Chapter 1, and Paul Buckland is also thanked for his considerable help with the editing and sourcing of the material that is discussed in Chapters 1 and 2 as his encyclopaedic knowledge far exceeds my own limited range. Obviously, as a corollary, special thanks must go to Professor Paul Buckland for his advice in relation to Chapters 1 and 2 of this book, and for all of his help in general since I graduated from the masters programme in environmental archaeology at Sheffield in 1991. Professor J. R. L. Allen is thanked for permission to use his images in Figures 2.6 and 2.7. Whilst the detail of these two chapters is perhaps wide-ranging in setting the scene for the Palaeolithic and Mesolithic periods, I hope the reader appreciates the need for such a level of detail in a volume that endeavours to consider human-landscape interactions across the Pleistocene-Holocene transition.

Figure 3.2 was provided by Lars Larsson and photographed by Arne Sjöström to whom I am grateful for permission to use this image. Figure 4.1 is used with the permission of Bruce Hardy and ANU E Press, and I would like to thank both for permission to use this image. Similarly I would like to thank George Nicholas for permission to use Figure 4.4 and Mike Zhilin for permission to include Figure 4.2. Clive Waddington provided Figure 4.5. Figure 5.5 was produced by Chelsea Budd, again many thanks for this. Figures 4.7 and 4.8 were provided by Professor Nicky Milner, York University and the Star Carr Project. Figures 6.4 and 6.5 were provided by Lennart Larsen, Nationalmuseet Arbejdsmark, Denmark. I would like to thank Helga Schütze for sending these, and Lars Larsson for letting me know who to contact regarding access.

After Martin Bell pointed me in the right direction both Victor Ambrus and the Council for British Archaeology were kind enough to give me permission to use the artist's impression of the activity at Goldcliff that appears as Figure 4.9. The reader is guided to Victor's book *Drawing on Archaeology: Bringing History Back to Life* (Tempus 2006) for more reconstructions of life in the past. Catrina Appleby and Julia at the CBA are thanked for their quick response to my query about the use of this particular image.

In addition to the above, other direct assistance with this book, in terms of images for use in illustrating important parts of the text, and details in relation to his own work in Wales, was received from Andrew David. Furthermore Helen Fenwick took the database of Mesolithic sites that I created from the available literature and HER's and made it make sense in terms of mapping within the GIS platform. These maps form the basis of the sites distributions in Chapter 3 and the distribution maps in Chapter 1 and 2. There are limitations in the dataset, but it is, on the whole, representative of the archive for Wales.

For permission to use the Author's Prologue by Dylan Thomas I would like to thank Marigold Atkey at David Higham Associates (London) and Christopher Wait at New Directions Publishing (New York) for all their help in obtaining copyright access to this work.

Finally, I would like to thank Clare Litt and Julie Gardiner at Oxbow for their patience as this project has developed.

Any omissions in this list of colleagues and friends are, of course, purely the responsibility of the author.

The reader is directed to the new Historic Environment Record database for the Welsh Archaeological Trusts at http://www.archwilio.org.uk/ where a searchable database exists for all archaeological periods and site types in Wales. As mentioned above the four Welsh trusts were extremely helpful when I was researching the background data for this work, and the reader might like to follow the activities of the trusts at their respective websites; Gwynedd (http://www.heneb.co.uk/), Clwyd-Powys (http://www.cpat.org.uk/), Glamorgan-Gwent Archaeological Trust (http://www.ggat.org.uk/) and Dyfed Archaeological Trust (http://www.dyfedarchaeology.org.uk/) where their work, activities and events, and downloads of a range of reports can be accessed (see Figure 0.1 for current, and past, county boundaries and unitary authority areas).

This volume was produced during my time at the University of Hull while I was also involved in teaching and various research endeavours, some of this work can be accessed online at http://www2.hull.ac.uk/science/waerc.aspx. My focus on teaching proved to be a factor that limited the time I was able to put into the production of this volume, but the long gestation period proved useful in allowing me time to reflect on each chapter as it developed. As ever, I hope this reflective approach proves to be a strength in the volume that has resulted from this process.

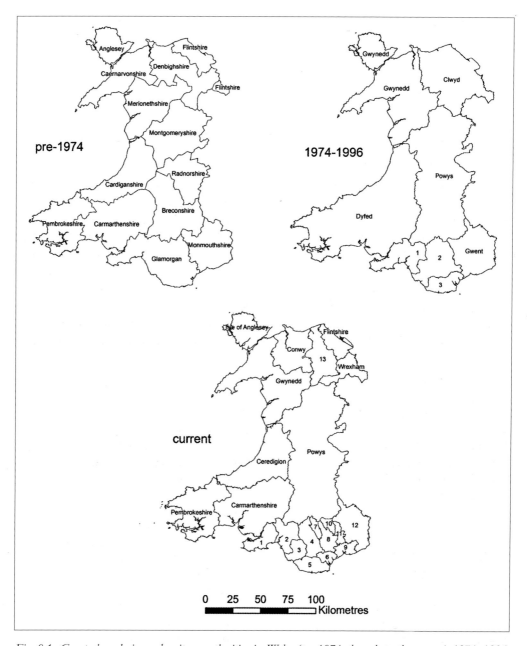

Fig. 0.1: County boundaries and unitary authorities in Wales (pre-1974 through to the present) 1974–1996:
1 = West Glamorgan; 2 = Mid Glamorgan; 3 = South Glamorgan. B. Current Map (from April 1996) –
1 = Swansea; 2 = Neath Port Talbot; 3 = Bridgend; 4 = Rhondda Cynon Taff; 5 = Vale of Glamorgan;
6 = Cardiff; 7 = Merthyr Tydfil; 8 = Caerphilly; 9 = Newport; 10 = Blaenau Gwent; 11 = Torfaen;
12 = Monmouthshire; 13 = Denbighshire.

DYLAN THOMAS: AUTHOR'S PROLOGUE

I had, of course, heard of Dylan Thomas as a child growing up near Newport in South Wales in the 1960s and '70s, but I had never read any of his work; and did not do so until I was in my 30s. My recollection of the education system in south Wales in the 1970s is that I only learnt about English history and the only poetry that I recall is the Wilfred Owen poem with the lines Dulce et decorum est pro patria mori (although, whilst born in Shropshire, Owen apparently had a mix of English and Welsh ancestry and the borders town has both Welsh and English speakers). Unfortunately as a young student in secondary school it was generally assumed that all of the boys would end up working at Llanwern Steelworks, and there was no real encouragement to aspire to anything beyond this (perhaps "they" were right). Of the Dylan Thomas poems that I have read the following Author's Prologue is the one that speaks to me the most in relation to the key focus of my academic interests, i.e. landscapes, people and the hunter-fisher-foragers of the Mesolithic and the incipient farmers of the Neolithic. I hope it speaks to the reader in a similar fashion …

This day winding down now
At God speeded summer's end
In the torrent salmon sun,
In my seashaken house
On a breakneck of rocks
Tangled with chirrup and fruit,
Froth, flute, fin, and quill
At a wood's dancing hoof,
By scummed, starfish sands
With their fishwife cross
Gulls, pipers, cockles, and snails,
Out there, crow black, men
Tackled with clouds, who kneel
To the sunset nets,
Geese nearly in heaven, boys
Stabbing, and herons, and shells
That speak seven seas,
Eternal waters away
From the cities of nine
Days' night whose towers will catch
In the religious wind
Like stalks of tall, dry straw,
At poor peace I sing

To you strangers (though song
Is a burning and crested act,
The fire of birds in
The world's turning wood,
For my sawn, splay sounds),
Out of these seathumbed leaves
That will fly and fall
Like leaves of trees and as soon
Crumble and undie
Into the dogdayed night.
Seaward the salmon, sucked sun slips,
And the dumb swans drub blue
My dabbed bay's dusk, as I hack
This rumpus of shapes
For you to know
How I, a spinning man,
Glory also this star, bird
Roared, sea born, man torn, blood blest.
Hark: I trumpet the place,
From fish to jumping hill! Look:
I build my bellowing ark
To the best of my love
As the flood begins,

Out of the fountainhead
Of fear, rage red, manalive,
Molten and mountainous to stream
Over the wound asleep
Sheep white hollow farms
To Wales in my arms.
Hoo, there, in castle keep,
You king singsong owls, who moonbeam
The flickering runs and dive
The dingle furred deer dead!
Huloo, on plumbed bryns,
O my ruffled ring dove
In the hooting, nearly dark
With Welsh and reverent rook,
Coo rooing the woods' praise,
Who moons her blue notes from her nest
Down to the curlew herd!
Ho, hullaballoing clan
Agape, with woe
In your beaks, on the gabbing capes!
Heigh, on horseback hill, jack
Whisking hare! who
Hears, there, this fox light, my flood ship's
Clangour as I hew and smite
(A clash of anvils for my
Hubbub and fiddle, this tune
On a tongued puffball)
But animals thick as thieves

On God's rough tumbling grounds
(Hail to His beasthood).
Beasts who sleep good and thin,
Hist, in hogsback woods! The haystacked
Hollow farms in a throng
Of waters cluck and cling,
And barnroofs cockcrow war!
O kingdom of neighbors, finned
Felled and quilled, flash to my patch
Work art and the moonshine
Drinking Noah of the bay,
With pelt, and scale, and fleece:
Only the drowned deep bells
Of sheep and churches noise
Poor peace as the sun sets
And dark shoals every holy field.
We will ride out alone and then,
Under the stars of Wales,
Cry, Multitudes of arks! Across
The water lidded lands,
Manned with their loves they'll move,
Like wooden islands, hill to hill.
Huloo, my proud dove with a flute!
Ahoy, old, sea-legged fox,
Tom tit and Dai mouse!
My ark sings in the sun
At God speeded summer's end
And the flood flowers now.

Dylan Thomas

INTRODUCTION

... Human niches are defined to a large extent by technology, even among foragers. There are horse-mounted, bow-and-arrow hunters of bison, harpoon hunters of walrus who travel in kayaks, salmon weir-fishers, and spear, blowgun, and net hunters... (Marlowe 2005: 54)

As the above quote from Marlowe highlights, there is no single "type" of hunter-fisher-forager society in the present, and as such, we would be in error to suppose that there would be a single "type" in the past. In the Mesolithic period, throughout Europe, hunter-fisher-forager communities occupied a diverse range of ecological zones, exploiting resources from coastal, lacustrine and riverine contexts and from lowland to upland areas. The nature of the archaeological evidence for this activity is as diverse as the environments that were exploited, but unfortunately it is often ephemeral in nature. In general, the archaeological record for past hunter-fisher-foragers is complex, difficult to disentangle, and often fragmentary, at best. With this in mind, this volume will endeavour to characterise past hunter-fisher-forager settlement, subsistence and economic activity during the Mesolithic period in Wales, with reference to the remainder of Europe, between *ca.* 10,200 and 6000 years ago.

In order to ensure that an holistic overview is generated it will be necessary to link the discussion of the welsh evidence throughout the text with examples from the wider regional context, as the welsh evidence is fragmentary and relatively limited in terms of directly dated, well excavated stratified activity sites and burials (Grimes 1951). As such, the discussion throughout this volume will include a diverse range of examples from other areas of Europe (and further afield) in order to illustrate the dynamic, complex and vibrant nature of Mesolithic society. In this respect the author believes that the study is not weakened by the use of examples from outside of the modern political boundary of Wales as, during earlier prehistory, such artificial boundaries have no significance. Furthermore, throughout the Mesolithic period, the land area currently under the North Sea formed a dryland plain linking Britain to the rest of northwest Europe, and whilst the North Sea is a natural barrier today, this was not the case during the earlier part of the Mesolithic period. As a consequence, we are in effect simply studying an area of land that was originally joined to, and on, the northwestern edge of the European landmass. In a similar manner, around the coasts of Wales, the "submerged forests" that we see at low tide, attest to the fact that the landscapes exploited by earlier Holocene hunter-fisher-foragers was more extensive than the landscape that we see/use in the present, although these coastal landscapes were changing across the Mesolithic as sea levels rose. As a consequence we need to attempt to visualise an extensive, rich and diverse lowland landscape that was exposed by much lower sea levels, and which has subsequently been submerged as the ice sheets of the later Pleistocene have receded and released their melt waters into the earth's oceans, raising them by >100m in certain areas of the world (see discussion in Chapters 1 and 2). Our modern perceptions of landscape are markedly different to those of our hunter-fisher-forager ancestors, and as we know, our subsistence strategies are markedly different as well! Fortunately, we have reliable evidence, dredged up from the bed of the North Sea, that indicates that hunter-fisher-forager groups in the later Pleistocene would have been able to cross the North Sea plain from as early as *ca.* 21.8–11.8 thousand years ago (kyBP), and indeed that much earlier traverses would/ could have been undertaken. As the Devensian ice sheets retreated and climate ameliorated human groups would have explored and travelled in search of new environments, from which, a diverse range of resources, habitation sites and focal points were integrated into their experiences of the world; and where these new experiences could be both engaged with and used to expand the groups knowledge and shared commonality. The fundamental needs of hunter-fisher-forager societies, e.g. food, shelter, warmth, companionship, social, economic and ritual interactions, would have differed across the Mesolithic period (these are considered in Chapters 3–6 of this volume). We should always remember that whilst a relatively small group size was often the optimal way to exploit the environment prior to the adoption of agriculture (see discussion in Chapter 7), this would have necessitated a considerable degree of co-operation in order to ensure group continuity, but also that whilst co-operation was important, it is likely that both intra- and inter-group conflicts would have occurred. Individual choice could, and undoubtedly would have influenced socio-political, economic and ritual actions, and as with society today a single individual's actions could have a profound influence on the group's internal and/or external dynamic.

Returning to the finds from the bed of the North Sea, these include both archaeological artefacts and environmental evidence, often encountered as net snags by the many trawlers that exploit the rich, albeit still threatened, resources that the sea has to offer (NSPRMF 2009). These finds include flints, harpoons and re-worked or carved fossil mammal bones, alongside unmodified finds, dredged up from areas such as the Dogger, Brown, Leman and Ower Banks, and German Bight – the former and latter areas might be recognisable from BBC4's shipping forecast as produced by the UK Met Office. As the term bank might suggest, these areas, whilst currently submerged, would have been areas of higher ground in the North Sea plain prior to its inundation. As discussed below, recent studies have sought to illustrate and characterise the archaeo-environmental potential of the lands beneath the North Sea (e.g. Coles 1998; 2000; Flemming 2002; 2004a; Ward *et al.* 2006; Gaffney *et al.* 2007) and other areas such a Liverpool Bay and the Bristol Channel (e.g. Dyfed Archaeological Trust 2011). Furthermore, there is also palaeoenvironmental evidence for the presence of birch, pine and willow recovered from freshwater peats at a depth of –46m MSL on the southeastern slope of Dogger Bank, which are dated to *ca.* 9.9–9.0 kyBP[1] (Ward *et al.* 2006: 209, and references therein).

The archaeological remains from the North Sea include a barbed antler point that was dredged up in 1931, in a lump of peat, from *ca.* 36m depth, in between the Leman and Ower Banks (Godwin 1960; Ward *et al.* 2006). Other finds include human remains recovered from the southern Bight, which confirm Mesolithic occupation in the southern areas of the North Sea between 11.6 and 9.2 kyBP (Glimmerveen *et al.* 2004), and which were found in association with bones of wild boar and red deer. Flemming (2002) has reported the fact that, quite literally, hundreds of finds of fossils and artefacts are dredged up from the North Sea annually, although unfortunately as noted by Ward *et al.* (2006: 215) it is only recently that a concerted effort has been made to accurately record the locations and depths of such find spots. Furthermore, the accurate dating of finds and palaeoenvironmental remains is still lacking.

As noted above, in the context of the current study of hunter-fisher-forager groups in Wales during the Mesolithic period, it should always be remembered that the changes in sea level affecting the North Sea Basin are also influencing the nature of the coastline, along with the landscapes and seascapes, around Wales throughout the latter part of the Pleistocene and into the Holocene period. This situation is of fundamental importance to our understanding of this period as the biases that are introduced by rising sea levels appear to be considerable, and of course, human groups would have consistently been negotiating and renegotiating their landscape interactions across this period.

The situation during the earlier part of the Holocene is diverse in terms of landscape developments (Chapter 2) and human responses to these changes are equally diverse (Chapters 3–7). The land area currently occupied by the modern country of Wales is topographically varied, and as such would also have supported a wide range of fauna and flora, available to the hunters, fishers and foragers of the Mesolithic period. Wales is in excess of 20,700 sq kilometres (8,000 sq miles) in area, and *ca.* one-third of this area lies above the 244m (800ft) contour, i.e. is classed as upland (Silvester 2003; Caseldine 1990). However, by contrast, this obviously means that *ca.* two-thirds of this land area is, by definition, lowland. It is also immediately apparent that a significant proportion of the landscape is intimately linked to coastal, estuarine or riverine environments. This diversity in relation to landscape features would have produced an extremely rich mosaic of environments for exploitation by human groups throughout the earlier Holocene period.

It should also be noted, however, that Wales itself is not an island (Silvester 2003), and that during the earlier Mesolithic period hunter-fisher-forager populations would have moved around the landscape of Britain, and the North Sea Basin, interacting with other forager groups and exploiting the wide, and developing, range of environments and species (of both plants and animals) that they would have encountered as the ice sheets of the Pleistocene retreated. Subsequently, warmth adapted species expanded into those northerly areas of Europe that were previously covered by the Devensian ice-sheets and the permafrost zones that extended beyond them. The gradual replacement of open grasslands by warmth-adapted plants and animals at the start of the Holocene period (i.e. *ca.* 10,200 or so years ago) is a shift that would have occurred at other times in the Pleistocene as the glacial (and stadial) cold periods were interspersed with warmer interglacials (and interstadials).

The nature of climate change and human-landscape interactions is complex, and in order for us to be able to generate realistic interpretations of the Mesolithic period we therefore need to use all of the evidence that is available to us. In this context, many researchers endeavour to generate meaningful interpretations of past hunter-fisher-forager activity through analogy with anthropological and ethnographic studies (Marlowe 2005); albeit with the caveat that these studies and the societies they discuss need to be considered with caution when using them as analogies for the past. Obviously, a hunter-fisher-forager group in the present is unlikely to represent a direct analogy to a prehistoric hunter-fisher-forager group, but there are many activities that can provide important and meaningful insights into past human activity.

Overall, when we study the past we attempt to generate holistic and meaningful approaches to the analysis and interpretation of settlement, ritual, social interactions, diet and subsistence (Clark 1976); our aim is to evaluate the links between these and other aspects of hunter-fisher-forager social life, and to consider both the empirical and more theoretical elements of the archaeological record when generating hypotheses about the past. No easy task in a period where there are no written records and only a fragmentary archaeological record from which to construct our social narratives!

Furthermore, it is often easy to forget that humans have been hunters, fishers and foragers (and at certain times scavengers) for the majority of their existence (>99% of the time that humans have been on the earth), and that, by contrast farming has only been the main subsistence strategy during the current warm period (the Holocene – an interglacial) (Malone 2001). In fact, in Britain elements of farming have only been part of subsistence strategies for *ca.* 6000 years, at best, and hunting, fishing and foraging is embedded in subsistence activities throughout prehistory. With this in mind it is perhaps difficult for us to conceive of the fact that we have subsisted as farmers for only a fraction of human history, yet in the present day there are very few individuals, or groups, who are capable of surviving from the exploitation of wild resources alone. Indeed, we only have to look at the modern landscape of Britain to see that the domestication of plants and animals is intimately linked to the domestication of the landscape, and that the environments exploited by humans at the start of the Holocene are, with relatively few exceptions, vastly different to those that currently dominate. Being a hunter-fisher-forager today would necessitate the knowledge and application of a very different set of skills to those used at a time when, at the start of the Holocene, farming was still *ca.* 4 or 5 millennia away from being integrated into subsistence strategies in Britain. As mentioned above, the earlier Holocene was also a time when the environment of Britain was being reshaped as the climate improved and sea levels continued to rise, after the removal of the ice sheets.

With the above thoughts in place, this volume will endeavour to illustrate just how different these landscapes/environments were, and also to highlight how, in many respects, our hunter-fisher-forager ancestors were very similar to us in their immediate needs. These include their social relations, treatment of the dead, rites of passage (such as birth, the shift from childhood to adulthood, and death), tool production and subsistence strategies, the need for clothing, warmth and shelter, and even decoration and ornaments, and the myriad everyday interactions that characterise the human condition. In attempting to provide an overview of the hunter-fisher-foragers of Wales, this volume will begin with a summary of what went before. This is the evidence for human-landscape interactions across the Pleistocene period, and the Palaeolithic (Old Stone Age) human groups that exploited our region as the climate shifted between glacial and interglacial stages over the past *ca.* >650,000 years or so.

As might be expected, the further back we go, the greater the impact of the glaciations and other factors on the landscape. Given the low population densities during the Palaeolithic in Britain the archaeological evidence is relatively sparse, and as this has been subjected to a considerable degree of destruction and reworking during successive glaciations, the archaeological record is often limited to the margins of the ice sheets and the coastal regions of Wales (Caseldine 1990: 23). The available evidence for this period in Britain is considered below in Chapter 1.

In order to set the entire Mesolithic period into its context, the chapters follow a sequence from the palaeoenvironmental background (Chapter 2), through a consideration of the use of stone tools (Chapter 3) and settlement patterning in the Mesolithic (Chapter 4). Fundamental to a group's existence of course is the procurement of food and the exploitation of a viable subsistence strategy. During the Mesolithic period the expanding deciduous woodlands offered a wide range of possibilities in terms of resources, although the large fauna is more dispersed in this period than it would have been during the preceding Palaeolithic period. A consideration of the range of available resources is presented in Chapter 5.

One final point of note in outlining the scope of the current volume relates to the less obvious aspects of hunter-forager and subsequent hunter-fisher-forager groups; these are the arenas of symbolism, ritual and spirituality that would have been embedded in everyday life (Chapter 6). To make these more understandable it is worth remembering that symbols are fundamental elements of modern life. For instance, there are symbols that tell us where to obtain "fast" food or logo's that tell us that our phone or computer is cutting edge technology, or the emblem's on the front of a car that tells you that it probably cost the owner a lot of money, and by extension suggests affluence. In the past the symbols would have obviously been very different, but it is probable that they would have imbued a similar level of meaning, information dissemination and importance, through their collective social meaning/significance; just as our modern symbols do.

Similarly, we see a church, cathedral or mosque as places where everyday spiritual matters are engaged with, whilst in the Mesolithic period spirituality may have been embedded in special places such as a lake, a rocky outcrop, a tree or a shaman's hut. Rituals may have been mundane everyday occurrences, such as formally acknowledging an elder or making an offering to the spirits of the animals that you hunt, they may also have been significant rites of passage such as the point at which a teenager becomes an adult or a novice becomes a hunter. In modern society these rites of passage revolve around milestones such as passing your driving test, reaching your 18th or 21st birthday, getting married or leaving home. All of the symbols, rituals and spiritual aspects embedded in modern life are in place and not necessarily always consciously engaged with, in the past whilst these symbols, rituals and spiritual elements may have been more proscribed and visible, they were also not necessarily always consciously engaged with by all levels of society. However, as noted by Zvelebil (2003: 4) knowledgeable social actors could have affected deliberate changes and manipulated social symbols in order to innovate, transmit knowledge or change their structural content, thereby embedding change into existing rules and conventions. This is an area where a greater degree of consideration of the meaning embedded within the archaeological record is warranted. As such, the current volume will endeavour to integrate an evaluation of these aspects of Mesolithic society in developing a social narrative of Mesolithic lifeways throughout the text from Chapter 2 onwards. This is undertaken in an effort to bring the past to life in a meaningful and considered way.

Finally, one thing that we should keep in mind as we move through this volume is the fact that there is no universal standard for the Mesolithic, or indeed for what went before and what was to follow (Kozłowski 2003). We cannot simply tick a list of essential requirements for defining hunter-fisher-forager populations, and in actual fact the term "hunter-fisher-foragers" implies a particular combination of subsistence activities, but whilst some groups may well have integrated this range of economic activities into their subsistence strategies, others may not have. The situation in coastal areas of Wales, in relation to subsistence, settlement and even spiritual matters would not necessarily be the same as in upland areas, even when the same groups move between these zones in the landscape. Furthermore, the groups that exploited the Late-glacial environments of Europe formed the basis for the populations that expanded into the newly developing post-glacial (Holocene) environments of northern Europe as the ice sheets melted and new plant and animal species (including the humans themselves) re-colonised the landscape from the glacial refugia; it is these Holocene groups that the current study focuses upon.

The volume concludes with a discussion of the theoretical basis for the shift away from the exploitation of wild resources towards the integration of domesticates into subsistence strategies (Chapter 7), i.e. the shift from food procurement to food production. This concluding section does not *per se* consider the character of the Neolithic period itself, but it assesses the context of the changes that occur as human groups re-orientate their socio-economic, political and ritual beliefs in light of the newly available resources, influences from the continent, and ultimately their social condition at the time of "transition".

Note
1   See appendix 1 for calibration chart for dates from 10,200 BP to the end of the Mesolithic period at *ca.* 5200 BP

1

SETTING THE SCENE: THE PALAEOLITHIC AND THE LATE-GLACIAL OF BRITAIN, ADAPTATION AND SUBSISTENCE IN A CHANGING ENVIRONMENT

Cultural Man has been on earth for some 2,000,000 years; for over 99 percent of this period he has lived as a hunter-gatherer...of the estimated 150 billion *people* who have ever lived on earth, over 60 percent have lived as hunters and gatherers; about 35 percent have lived by agriculture, and the remaining few percent have lived in industrial societies ... (Lee and Devore 2009a: 3)

Introduction

In geological terms the Quaternary period covers the last 2.4 million years up to the present, with the geological epochs comprising the Pleistocene (*ca.* 2.4 mya through to *ca.* 11,700 years ago) being sub-divided into the Lower Pleistocene (2.4 mya to *ca.* 780,000 years ago), and the Middle and Upper Pleistocene (*ca.* 780,000 to 126,000 and 126,000 to 11,700 years ago respectively), followed by the current interglacial period, the Holocene (*ca.* 11,700 years ago up to the present). However, as noted by Lowe and Walker (1997: 1) the past 11,700 years or so simply represent another warm period within the sequence of glacial/interglacial cycles of the Pleistocene, and as such should really simply be considered to be the most recent part of the Pleistocene. As indicated, during the Pleistocene numerous cold periods (glacials), were interspersed by warmer periods (interglacials), and shorter, often more unstable stadial and interstadial periods. In archaeological terms this period is termed the Palaeolithic (Old Stone Age), and from *ca.* 1.9–1.6 mya hominins of the *Homo erectus* group were producing flaked stone tools. By the end of the Early Pleistocene, there were tool-using hominins around the North Sea Basin (Parfitt *et al.* 2010) and tools, most frequently recognised in the handaxes, indicate their intermittent presence through much of the Middle and Late Pleistocene. From the Middle Palaeolithic (*ca.* 200,000–40,000 years ago) *Homo sapiens*, our ancestors, evolved in Africa and migrated outwards, being evidenced in Britain towards the end of this period.

The Middle Palaeolithic in Britain has been sub-divided by White and Jacobi (2002) into two stages, an Early British Middle Palaeolithic (equivalent to Marine Isotope Stages[1] [MIS] 8–7, starting at *ca.* 300,000 years ago; discussed below), when a new flintworking technology, the Prepared Core or Levallois technique was introduced (Stringer 2006), and a Late British Middle Palaeolithic (beginning in terminal MIS 4/early MIS 3). Recently, White and Pettitt (2011) have suggested that the Early Middle Palaeolithic should be equated to MIS 9–7 (*ca.* 330,000–180,000 BP), and the Late Middle Palaeolithic correlated to MIS 3 (*ca.* 60–35,000 BP).

These stages are separated by a period of human absence between the penultimate glaciation and the Middle Devensian (MIS 6–3) lasting some 120,000 years (White and Jacobi 2002: 111, White and Pettitt 2011: 26). Recolonisation by Neanderthals occurred during the late Middle Palaeolithic (MIS 3) at around 60,000 years ago, *Bout coupé* handaxes appear in the artefact record in significant numbers, and Levallois technology is rare at this time (White and Jacobi 2002: 123–8, White *et al.* 2006: 526). By *ca.* 40,000 years ago anatomically modern humans (*Homo sapiens sapiens*) were in Europe and probably Britain (Stringer 2006). It is likely that the anatomically modern humans that occur in Europe after *ca.* 40,000 years ago, during the Aurignacian period, encountered and interacted with the Neanderthals (White and Pettitt 2011), but the precise reasons for the demise of the latter lineage is still open to debate, with climate change and competition with modern humans being considered as possible factors in their extinction (Mellars 2004; Stewart 2007; Banks *et al.* 2008). However, a reconsideration of the evidence for Britain by White and Pettitt (2011: 59) has led to the suggestion, or as they state "the falsifiable hypothesis", that *Homo sapiens* (Aurignacian culture) arrived only after a considerable occupation gap following regional Neanderthal extinction.

Neanderthal morphological characteristics appear to have entered the *Homo* lineage at some point around 250,000 years ago, with the fully developed *Homo neanderthalensis* entering the record at around 125,000 years ago (during the Ipswichian interglacial; although there is no evidence for a human presence in Britain during this Marine Isotope Stage [5e]). The use of oxygen isotope records from microfossils contained in marine cores, and their designation as Marine Isotope Stages, works because the marine oxygen isotope balance is controlled by fluctuations in land ice volume; as such the variations in evidence in the oxygen isotope record reflect glacial/interglacial fluctuations during the Pleistocene (Lowe and Walker 1997: 9; for an overview of the various dating techniques used to produce an absolute chronology for the Pleistocene epoch see Walker 2005).

All of our distant relatives subsisted as hunters and gatherers (occasionally probably scavengers as well, especially in the Lower Palaeolithic), and hunting and gathering continued to be the main subsistence strategy for human groups into the Holocene period (at *ca.* 10,200 years ago). Whilst the main evidence for the exploitation of marine resources occurs in the last *ca.* 50,000 years or so (Gaudzinski-Windheuser and Niven 2009: 101), there are sites that date back to 115–60,000 years ago e.g. at Moscerini cave in Italy (i.e. Middle Palaeolithic age), and at Grotte Vaufrey in France at least six different fish species were probably exploited. An even earlier date exists for marine resource exploitation at 160,000 years ago, at Pinnacle Point in South Africa (although in this example the evidence consists of just 79 shells) (Bailey and Flemming 2008). For freshwater resource exploitation the evidence is primarily confined to the last 20,000 years or so (Richards *et al.* 2001), and by the late Middle Palaeolithic period hominin exploitation of small game, birds and fish becomes more visible in the archaeological record (Gaudzinski-Windheuser and Niven 2009: 101). Despite these observations, it is only at (or just prior to), the start of the Holocene period that the nature of subsistence strategies orientated more visibly towards a strategic combination of hunter-fisher-forager lifeways, with these gradually shifting to the domesticating of wild grasses and animals in certain locations around the globe. Ultimately agriculture is adopted, the timing of which again differs depending on a myriad of influencing factors globally.

In trying to disentangle the nature and impact of the various glacial/interglacial cycles during the Pleistocene, it is worth noting that, when writing in 2004, Clarke *et al.* reported that there were some 2,000 academic papers written in the past 150 years that considered the nature of (solely) the last glacial period (the Devensian; after *ca.* 75–70,000 years ago, although progressive cooling had been occurring across marine oxygen isotope stages 5d–a, i.e. from around 110,000 years ago) in Britain, and many more papers have been written on this subject since this date. Even with a GIS (Geographical Information System) database that included some 20,000 features, when attempting to produce a glacial map of the Devensian ice sheet, Clarke *et al.* (2004) note that the database was still not fully comprehensive (see also Lowe and Walker 1997: fig. 2.12). Given this observation, and the complex nature of glacial/interglacial cycles up to the last glacial period, it is perhaps unsurprising that the *ca.* 18 or 19 glacial/interglacial (stadial/interstadial) cycles that are known to have characterised the Pleistocene period have had a huge and complicating impact on the archaeological and environmental evidence for the past, such that we have only a limited, fragmentary record prior to the Last Glacial Maximum in Britain (and even this latter period remains partial in certain respects) (e.g. Clark *et al.* 2004; Murton *et al.* 2009). However, before we consider the Late-glacial period in detail (i.e. the period between *ca.* 14,000–10,200 BP) it is worth remembering that during the Palaeolithic period in Wales and England the available evidence appears to indicate intermittent hominin activity in the landscape from at least *ca.* 0.66 mya (or *ca.* 660,000 years ago) until 11,700 years ago, during both the colder and warmer phases of global climate change. Although Stringer (2006) notes that between *ca.* 200,000 and 60,000 years ago, Britain was abandoned.

In Britain as a whole, we now have evidence that appears to suggest that some of our pre-human ancestors visited this northwestern part of the European landmass, possibly from as early as *ca.* >9–800,000 years ago (Parfitt *et al.* 2010), and very probably pre-*ca.* 700,000 years ago (Stringer 2006). Two key English sites, Pakefield in Suffolk (at *ca.* >700,000 years ago) and Happisburgh in Norfolk (pronounced Haysborough – Stringer 2006) (*ca.* 970–814,000 years ago, or younger – see below) apparently demonstrate the ability of early hominins to exploit the differing environments at the southern edge of the Boreal zone at a very early date (Parfitt *et al.* 2010; Coope 2006). The material at Happisburgh comprises 78 flint artefacts used as tools by these early hominins (which included hard-hammer flakes, notches, retouched flakes and cores), and which on the basis of the geological evidence, were deposited at an activity site located in the upper estuarine zone of the Thames river during an interglacial stage in the earlier Pleistocene period (>0.78 Myr). However, Westaway (2011: 384) has inserted a note of caution in relation to the dating of a number of earlier sites, such as Pakefield and West Runton, arguing that "sites with distinct biostratigraphy do not necessarily represent different MIS (Marine Isotope Stage) sub-stages or even different MIS stages". Indeed, Westaway has argued that Happisburgh 3 and West Runton (Norfolk) and Pakefield (Suffolk), eastern England, all appear to fit in MIS 15 (*ca.* 600–550,000 years ago), and that the earlier dating of Happisburgh to MIS 25 or 21 should be treated with some caution on the basis of a re-assessment of the stratigraphy, pollen, faunal and geomagnetic evidence from this location (2011: 394). Despite questions relating to the dating of this site, which is clearly pre-Anglian glaciation, Marine Isotope Stage 12, in age (pre *ca.* 450,000 years ago), the finds of sturgeon, pike and carp bones from Happisburgh might provide a very early indication for the opportunistic exploitation of these species in the Palaeolithic period. More detail on the evidence from the earlier activity sites from Britain can be found in Stringer (2006) and White *et al.* (2006).

In general, interglacial deposits correlated to MIS 9 (Purfleet on Thames – *ca.* 340–300,000 years ago), MIS 11 (*ca.* 400,000 years ago – Hoxnian interglacial/Swanscombe skull [Stringer 2006]), and MIS 13 (*ca.* 500,000 years ago – Boxgrove and Westbury [*ibid.*]), and more recent MIS 7 (*ca.* 200,000 years ago) and MIS 5 (*ca.* 125–70,000 years ago), are in evidence in Britain, but, as might be anticipated, the further back in time we go, the less precision we have in the dating of the chronological boundaries. This situation is not simply due to problems of dating, but also due to limitations in the evidence, and occasionally, debate about what characterises the shift from glacial to interglacial conditions, and back again. Despite these limitations, the evidence from ocean cores has indicated that the cold-warm alternations extend back beyond the Middle Pleistocene, although the terrestrial evidence for earlier glaciations is poor (e.g. Lee *et al.* 2004). In addition, pre-human and human groups in the Palaeolithic were considerably fewer in number than those that characterise the early Holocene period (Smith 1992a; 1992b), thus making the recovery of direct evidence for human-landscape interactions a more fortuitous and often tenuous endeavour, as the above discussion indicates.

An additional complication lies in the fact that, in general, the material that has survived down the millennia is often derived from its original depositional context, sometimes being re-worked over significant distances, and through reworking, the associations between artefacts, human and faunal remains and depositional sequences are often difficult to determine with any degree of certainty, and as a consequence, are often poorly dated. There are exceptions to this general rule, as the sites at Hoxne in Suffolk, Swanscombe in the Thames Valley and Boxgrove, on the south coast of England attest (e.g. Roberts *et al.* 1994; Stringer *et al.* 1998; Stringer 2006). At these locations, and others, it is frequently the lack of any clear spatial patterning to the activity areas that confuses the evidence, for as Gamble (2001: 26) notes, despite their antiquity "these are some of the best preserved sites in the whole of European prehistory". The exceptional preservation at these locations is attested by the presence of the footprints of extinct deer in the soft silts that contain the stone tools at Swanscombe (*ibid.*); at Boxgrove over 300 handaxes have been excavated, locations where people (*Homo heidelbergensis*) crouched down to produce their stone tools, and butchery marks on the bones of giant deer, red deer, bison, horse and rhinoceros indicate that these people had primary access to large game animals during the Middle Pleistocene (Stringer 2006).

The environmental evidence

We are fortunate enough to have the evidence from deep-ocean sediment records and ice cores from the Greenland and Antarctic ice sheets (with their record of changing oxygen isotope and other signals) to provide a relatively detailed picture of the various warm and cold stages during the Mid-Later Palaeolithic periods (e.g. Green and Walker 1991; Lowe and Walker 1997; Alley 2000a; Mayewski and White 2002), and for more recent periods there are detailed palaeoenvironmental records that provide a much greater resolution for use in interpreting environmental change. The evidence that we have for reconstructing the past includes macroscopic evidence (>1mm in size which can be seen with the naked eye), e.g. bones (human and animal), plant material, seeds, fruits and leaves, wood and charcoal, and insect remains etc.; and microfossil evidence such as pollen, diatoms, fungal spores etc. which require analysis under the microscope (as the name might imply) (for an overview of environmental techniques see Berglund 1986; Lowe and Walker 1997: 162–236; Mackay *et al.* 2003).

As the ice sheets spread across the landscape, scouring out and mixing up the evidence from earlier periods, away from the ice sheets reworking of archaeo-environmental material occurred through additional factors such as the action of frost, rivers flowing across the landscape, and wind etc., all of which erode, mix and damage the archaeological record. However, despite the taphonomic mixing that occurred during the Pleistocene, there are tantalising glimpses into the past. These "glimpses" are provided by the exceptional sites such as Happisburgh in Norfolk, where the plant taxa recorded by Parfitt *et al.* (2010: 466) included hemlock and hop-hornbeam type (which were thought to only occur in the Early Pleistocene between 2.52 and 0.78 Myr), along with a fauna which included southern mammoth, extinct equid (horse), extinct elk, red deer, and at least two species of extinct vole, and also "advanced" forms of voles. Taken together the dating, plant and animal evidence are thought to bracket occupation at this site sometime between 0.99 and 0.78 Myr ago (i.e. 990–700,000 years ago), although see discussion above, and Westaway (2011).

Other environmental evidence at Happisburgh includes pollen, seeds, pine cones and wood alongside foraminifera, marine molluscs, barnacles, beetles and vertebrates (a very rare suite of environmental evidence for this early period). The environment immediately preceding the deposition of the flint artefacts (stone tools) at Happisburgh (i.e. immediately preceding hominin activity at this site) was characterised by deciduous oak woodland with hop-hornbeam, elm and alder in evidence; the earliest stage of artefact deposition occurred in a heathland dominated environment (Ericaceae-type), with pine and spruce in evidence (Parfitt *et al.* 2010: 231). These two tree species dominated the environment during the main phase of hominin activity at Happisburgh, although the conifer forest did have a minor deciduous component and grassland habitats were clearly present in the vicinity. This exceptional range of environmental evidence indicates that the river at this location was large and slow-flowing, with adjacent reed-swamp, alder carr, marshy areas and pools, and sturgeon swimming in the river; average summer temperatures (as indicated by the beetle evidence) were 16–18°C, not too dissimilar to southern Britain in the present; whilst winter temperatures were slightly lower than experienced in the present at 0 to –3°C (*ibid.*: 232).

The evidence from Happisburgh provides us with an exceptionally vivid insight into the sort of environments that our distant ancestors exploited, whilst highlighting the fact that, in reality, we would easily recognise these landscapes, and also those that existed to the south of 45°N where steppe, tropical forest and Mediterranean habitats all persisted (Parfitt *et al.* 2010). The past may be distant, but it is not as unfamiliar as we might first think!

Environmental evidence for the period *ca.* 425,000–375,000 years ago (or 423–360,000 cal BC; as outlined in Stringer 2006 and Jones and Keen 1993) has been recovered from a number of MIS 11 sites, including during excavations in the 1970s in the vicinity of a flintworking site located on the edge of an ancient river channel at Hoxne in Suffolk. This location has provided the basis for discussion of this interglacial stage, hence its designation as the Hoxnian Interglacial. Lower Palaeolithic, Acheulian handaxes from Hoxne were first discussed by John Frere in 1979; who wrote a brief illustrated account of bifacial flaked stone tools from this location (Gamble 2001: 10–11). Faunal remains from this site include elephant, rhinoceros and lion, along with fish, vole, beaver, fallow deer and macaque monkey. The palaeoenvironmental sequences, recovered from an ice wasting hollow (known as a "kettle hole"), which was subsequently entrained within a river channel system, indicate that four phases of landscape change are attested as occurring towards the end of the Hoxnian interglacial (a warm period) at this location. The early part of the sequence indicates birch and pine dominated forests, which were replaced by more temperate vegetation of oak, hornbeam, elm and lime, with colder conditions at the end of the interglacial being attested by the return of pine and birch, before the onset of the subsequent glaciation. Stringer (2006) notes that recent re-investigation of the Hoxne sequences has shown that the human activity at this location occurs towards the upper part of the depositional sequences, after the main Hoxnian interglacial sequence, at a time when the environment was cooler and the landscape more open than during the full warm interglacial stage of landscape development.

During the warmer parts of the Hoxnian, other tree species, such as hazel, yew and alder are also attested, and the archaeological evidence for a human presence in the landscape is strong, being indicated by numerous sites and findspots (Singer *et al.* 1993; Stringer 2006), although after this date, down to *ca.* 100,000 years ago, the archaeological record is less robust in relation to the number of sites and finds indicative of a human presence (Stringer 2006). Some debate continues as to the actual users of the two distinct flint industries in evidence in Britain at this time, termed the Clactonian and the Acheulian, with some seeing these industries as representing discrete culture groups, and others viewing the differences in tool types as representing the same people undertaking different activities (Stringer 2006). In support of the latter assertion, re-evaluation of the depositional contexts of Clactonian and Acheulian assemblages at East Farm, Barnham, Suffolk, by Ashton *et al.* (1994), has shown that the main flint knapping area (*ca.* 10m^2), where cores had been processed for the production of flakes (Clactonian), lies some 50m west of a small (*ca.* 3m^2) area where bi-face manufacturing flakes (Acheulian) were produced. A third, stratigraphically higher, flintworking area was also investigated. The evidence from this site has been used to suggest that it is erroneous to infer that the two industries are culturally distinct, and that it is the complexity of human-landscape interactions that has produced the "seemingly" distinct technologies that are in evidence (*ibid.*: 589).

Sites containing Clactonian stone tool assemblages have been investigated at Clacton-on-Sea, Swanscombe, in Kent, Little Thurrock in Essex, and Barnham St Gregory in Suffolk, all from what would have been riverside locations, whilst Acheulian activity is attested at both riverside and cave locations at sites such as Kent's Cavern, Torbay, Devon, Fordwich in Kent, Stoke Newington in Hackney, Hitchin, Hertfordshire, Foxhall Road in Ipswich and Elveden in Suffolk, alongside Swanscombe in Kent and Hoxne (Stringer 2006; Darvill 2010). Interestingly, another site of this age (>400,000 years ago), Beeches Pit near West Stow in Suffolk, provides us with the first good evidence for the use of fire in Britain (Preece *et al.* 2006), as at this location the identification of discrete hearths, knapping areas and finished handaxes, and burnt bone, gives this impression of a settlement or camp site where early humans were undertaking day-to-day activities such as cooking and eating, making and perhaps repairing or trimming their tool kits, and engaging in the social interactions necessary for group cohesion and co-operation.

An important, post-Hoxnian (MIS 11) location is that of Purfleet in Essex (MIS 9) around 320,000 years ago. Stringer (2006) notes that temperate woodland species such as fallow deer are in evidence early in the stratigraphic sequence, and that fish (carp and pike), birds, amphibians, small mammals (such as white-toothed shrew and water vole), and large mammals such as roe deer, beaver, macaque monkey and straight-tusked elephant are all attested. The environment comprised oak forests with open areas, and importantly, macaque monkey is not attested in subsequent periods. Other sites in Essex, such as Grays Thurrock and Belhus Park, near the Thames and Cudmore Grove, near the Blackwater river, can all be assigned to the same interglacial as Purfleet, at *ca.* 320,000 years ago (Stringer 2006).

Whilst the above evidence demonstrates that we do have a number of important sites with archaeological and palaeoenvironmental evidence for the Pleistocene, as might be anticipated there appear to be major "gaps" in our records, and after 320,000 years ago, the next significant location in the record is Pontnewydd (Bont Newydd) Cave, Elwy Valley, North Wales, which is dated to *ca.* 225,000 years ago (MIS 7). Other sites dating to the period include West Thurrock, Ilford, and Aveley in Essex, all dated to the Aveley interglacial at 250–200,000 years ago. After this date the record of a human presence in Britain is relatively sparse, especially for the period between *ca.* >225,000–100,000 years ago, during MIS 6 (Wolstonian), and the earlier part of the Ipswichian interglacial MIS 5, and there is also limited evidence due to the Devensian glacial stage.

For MIS 6, Aldhouse-Green (1998: 142) has suggested that there may be evidence for activity at Pontnewydd at *ca.* 175,000 years ago, during a temperate climatic phase. The Wolstonian glacial period has been shown to comprise three cold periods separated by two warmer periods, with some continuation of Hoxnian traditions in evidence in the human activity (Jones and Keen 1993; Stringer 2006). In terms of the range of available indicators of past environments, the fossil insect record for Britain during the Wolstonian glacial period, and in particular the record from 14 sites recovered from freshwater deposits in southern England (Coope 2001), is important. These records date to the period immediately preceding the earliest known site in Wales, that of Pontnewydd Cave (Green 1984), or they may, perhaps overlap with the human occupation at this site. Furthermore, the material from these sites also provides some evidence for the subsequent interglacial periods, thereby providing an important resource from which to enhance our reconstructions of the environment of Britain.

As indicated, these sites and their contained assemblages provide important insights into the nature of the environment after *ca.* 245,000 years ago, and also after *ca.* 128,000 years ago (MIS 8, 7, and 5e). Significantly, beetles have not changed morphologically for the entire Quaternary period (i.e. the last 2.4 million years), and physiologically there is also little evidence for change, meaning that entomologists can identify very specific temperature and environmental preferences from their study of the beetle remains (albeit with caveats) (Coope 2004). The species found in the earlier deposits (after *ca.* 245,000 years ago), at sites such as Tattershall Thorpe, Lincolnshire, Strensham, Worcestershire and Stanton Harcourt in Oxfordshire, include a restricted beetle fauna (i.e. there are fewer species in evidence when compared to the later Ipswichian period). These faunal assemblages include a staphylinid beetle that is now probably restricted to the Caucasus Mountains and a weevil that is now primarily confined to south-eastern Europe (*ibid.*: 1721). As such, the species identified from the earlier chronological deposits appear to indicate that temperatures were lower than those of the later Ipswichian, being more temperate in character (all of this data, together with the habitat data on individual species is collated at www.bugscep.com). Stringer (2006) notes that Stanton Harcourt is an important site at 200,000 years ago as bones from bison, bear, lion, horse, hyena, elephant and mammoth occur alongside the pollen, seeds and nuts from oak, hornbeam, alder, hazel, and willow, and shellfish, snails and insects.

Flint procurement, flintworking and hunting are all attested during the MIS 8 cold stage, at locations such the open air campsite in the lower Thames Valley at Baker's Hole, Northfleet, Kent, and other sites at South Woodford, Redbridge and Red Barns near Porchester, indicating that although cold, the environment was not so hostile as to preclude a human presence. The introduction of the new flintworking (Levallois) method appearing during this time (MIS 8), or perhaps slightly earlier towards the end of MIS 9 at *ca.* 320,000 years ago (White and Jacobi 2002: 125; White *et al.* 2006), has been suggested as possibly representing local developments in stone tool manufacturing (Stringer 2006). The artefact types found in Mousterian assemblages include blades, scrapers, handaxes, points, and the Levallois flakes, which could have been used as spear tips (e.g. White *et al.* 2006: 538). Whilst Pontnewydd represents one of only a limited number of Aveley Interglacial (located roughly at the transition between MIS 8 and 7) sites from Britain, it is a very important site for a number of reasons (discussed below), and it may well represent one of the only British sites where the "earlier" handaxes overlap with an incipient stage of the new "Levallois" (or Tortoise core) technique; although the derived nature of the depositional sequences does limit the veracity of the available evidence (White *et al.* 2006: 534; Stringer 2006).

Coope (2001: 1718) notes that the post-MIS 5e interglacial beetle assemblages (post *ca.* 128,000 to *ca.* 115,000 years ago) indicate open landscapes with deciduous woodland at some distance from the sampling sites he summarises. During the Ipswichian interglacial period, the warmer climate caused melting of the glaciers, to the point where Britain was an island, hippopotamus swam in the Thames, lions and elephants roamed where Trafalgar Square is now located in central London, and mean annual temperatures in Britain were 1–2°C higher than at present (Coope 2001). The sampling sites considered by Coope are usually ponds or abandoned river channels with reedswamp and/or grassy vegetation in close proximity, and with grazing herbivores such as elephant, mammoth and rhinoceros attested throughout the faunal record. The temperature preferences of one of the groups of beetles studied by Coope indicates that they favoured mean July temperatures that were *ca.* 4°C higher than at present in southern England (2001: 172). The sites with these beetle assemblages in evidence include Trafalgar Square, London, Woolpack Farm, Fenstanton in Cambs, and Deeping St. James in Lincolnshire. Strangely, despite the favourable conditions during the Ipswichian interglacial, there does not appear to be any secure evidence to support a human presence in the landscape at this time (David 2007: 4–5).

As we move through the Pleistocene the extent and as a consequence, impact, of the successive glacial periods lessens, so that during the earlier Devensian glacial period (after *ca.* 75–70,000 years ago), the British and Irish Ice Sheet (BIIS) only extended as far south as the Vale of York in England, and in the North Sea Basin the ice extended down the eastern side of the British landmass (over Lincolnshire) and down to the Wash, and blocked the Humber Gap. This blocking of the Humber Gap ultimately resulted in the creation of a lake at the front of the ice sheet which, perhaps unsurprisingly, has been called Lake Humber (Bateman *et al.* 2008).

On the western side of Britain the ice sheet appears to have extended in a southerly direction from the west of the Pennines, with ice from Scotland and the Lake District streamed southwards through Lancashire and Cheshire to coalesce with local Welsh ice and extend southwards to Wolverhampton. To the south and west, the Welsh glaciation extended southwards across the Severn Estuary reaching its most southerly limit in the Irish Sea and on the Isles of Scilly, *ca.* 45km WSW of Land's End (Hiemstra *et al.* 2006), and it extended westwards to cover the whole of Wales, with the exception of the southern margins of the country in the far west and east (Clarke *et al.* 2004). Detailed mapping of the margins of the ice-sheet, especially around the Welsh Borders, have proven difficult due to conflicting lines of evidence (see Fig. 1.1), not least of which is the difficulty associated with the accurate dating of the glacial deposits as recorded (*ibid.*). During the Devensian cold period, widespread periglacial activity impacted upon the Welsh landscape, with ice entering the levels in the Carmarthen bay, Swansea and Cardiff bay areas at the glacial maximum (*ca.* 23–19,000 years BP) (Allen 2000a: 17).

As noted by White and Pettitt (2011: 29), the majority of Neanderthal activity in Britain occurs during the period of MIS 3, *ca.* 59–25,000 BP. Whilst MIS 3 represents a time of re-colonisation, the climate is actually relatively cold, and characterised by fluctuations in climate. White and Pettitt (2011: 29) note that during MIS 3, the ice core data indicate that fifteen abrupt warming and slower cooling events are in evidence, making this period neither a glacial or interglacial period in conventional terms.

As indicated above, interglacials are the long sustained warm periods between glacials which produced temperatures that were as high, or even higher, than those we have experienced over the past 10,000 years or so (Lowe and Walker 1984: 8). Furthermore, the interglacial periods resulted in increases in global sea levels as the glaciers melted and retreated (Lambeck and Chappell 2001). In reality however, the dominant sea level condition throughout the Pleistocene was for sea levels that were much lower than experienced in the present (Bailey and Flemming 2008); up to a maximum of *ca.* 120m lower at certain times in fact, and as such, the landscape that early hominins encountered were very different to those of today (Fig. 1.2). Britain, far from being an island, was a peninsula of the northeastern European landmass throughout much of the Pleistocene epoch. As the past 10,000 years (the Holocene) are an interglacial period, and as *generally* these interglacials last around 10–15,000 years or so, we may soon (in geological terms) be fortunate enough to see the nature of the transition to glacial conditions globally, especially if the general trend of glacial-interglacial cycles continues in sequence. The resulting lowering of global sea levels, as more water is taken up into ice, would have the potential to expose significant areas of coastal lowland and allow us first hand insights into the changing landscapes of a glacial period, and potentially even, some access to the submerged sites around the Welsh coast and the North Sea Basin. However, it is also possible that current anthropogenic warming may delay, but not necessarily abort this process.

It is perhaps worth noting at this point that contrary to the general assumption that interglacials were characterised by relative climatic stability, the new data from the Greenland ice cores indicates that climatic instability was in fact occurring, and that abrupt oscillations during which temperatures fell by as much as 14°C in a matter of decades are in evidence (Lowe and Walker 1997 327). Given that, as mentioned above, we are currently in an interglacial period, it is perhaps salutary to remember (as also noted by Lowe and Walker) that the earth's climate systems are not controlled by humans; it is entirely possible that the sort of dramatic climate shifts recorded in past interglacials could occur in the current one. In actual fact, Alley (2000a: 4) has noted that the current stable climatic interval is amongst the longest in evidence in the Greenland ice core record.

Turning to the environmental record for the Pleistocene period in Wales, we are fortunate that Caseldine (1990) and Aldhouse-Green (2000a) both provide overviews of the environmental evidence from depositional sequences containing palaeoenvironmental material (e.g. West Angle Bay and Marros, Pembrokeshire, and Pen-y-Bryn, Caernarfon), and the Limestone caves in Wales; with most of the palaeoenvironmental evidence coming from pollen analysis (*ibid.*). There are only three sites with pre-Devensian (i.e. pre-*ca.* 75,000 years ago) environmental indicators, with the majority of sites dating to the Late Devensian and later periods (Caseldine 1990: 24–6). Caseldine (1990: 27) lists 19 cave sites with Pleistocene faunas (two of which also have pollen evidence and four of these have molluscan evidence), and in addition nine sites that only contain a pollen record are listed. Not all sites contain evidence for Palaeolithic human activity or occupation however, and

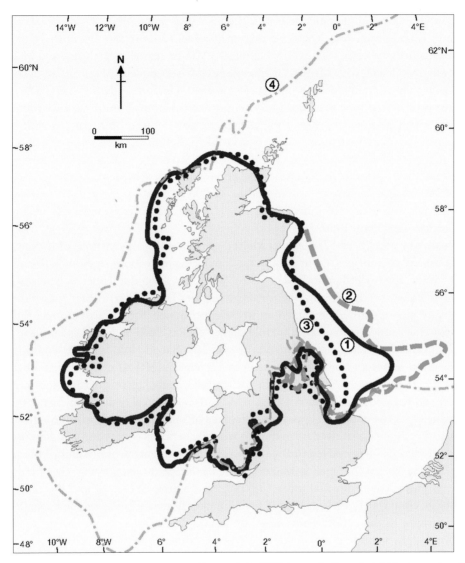

Fig. 1.1: Map showing selected maximum glacial limits of the BIIS during the Late-glacial Maximum, in order to highlight the uncertainty associated with the eastern sector of the ice sheet (after Bateman et al. 2011, modified and used with permission). 1: after Boulton et al. 1977, 2: after Balson and Jeffrey 1991, 3: after Bowen et al. 2002, 4: after Scourse et al. 2009. (see Bateman et al. 2011 for references).

the reader is directed to Caseldine (1990, and David 2007) for a comprehensive overview of the evidence; the following represents a summary of some of the more informative sites discussed by Astrid Caseldine.

At Pontnewydd Cave, dated to sometime around 225,000 years ago, and with *direct* evidence for a human presence, the fauna is indicative of open steppe environments, which were neither fully temperate nor fully glacial (Caseldine 1990: 26; Aldhouse-Green 2000a: 6). Long Hole cave, West Glamorgan (Caseldine 1990: 28) has both faunal and pollen evidence, the earliest of which belongs to MIS 5e (early Ipswichian), and indicates temperate woodland, with bison/*Bos* in evidence. A subsequent phase of arctic tundra development is interrupted by boreal conifer forest, which may date to *ca.* 65,000 years ago. The presence of pine marten and elk support the identification of a coniferous forest stage, although it should be noted that recent records indicate that pine marten is not restricted to conifer forest habitats (Lovegrove 2007). Returning to Pontnewydd, a further stage of tundra and steppe (open) environmental conditions, with abundant juniper and willow, with hyena, woolly rhinoceros, horse and reindeer in evidence is suggested as being of Late Middle Devensian age (at around *ca.* 40,000 years ago). However, there is some debate in relation to the reliability of the chronologically later environmental evidence at this location (Caseldine 1990: 28).

White and Pettitt (2011: 57) note that whilst there are no clear associations of humans with MIS 5e faunal assemblages, there are also no convincing indications of Middle Palaeolithic activity in the early glacial period (MIS 5d–b). When assessing the faunal assemblage from Bacon Hole Cave on the Gower Peninsula, Currant and Jacobi (2001: 1707) argued that the absence of hippopotamus precluded an MIS 5e attribution for this assemblage; this was determined by comparison of Bacon Hole to the "classic" MIS 5e faunal assemblage from Joint Mintor Cave, Buckfastleigh, Devon. As such, the Bacon Hole faunal assemblages are considered to represent both MIS 5a and early Devensian (MIS 4) material (Campbell and Bowen 1989; Caseldine 1990: 28), with the MIS 5a fauna including northern vole, mammoth, roe deer and red deer, all of which are again indicative of Boreal conditions. Again, there is no archaeological evidence to support the presence of humans in the landscape at this time. The MIS 5a assemblage is overlain in the sequence by deposits containing wood mouse and red deer, indicative of more temperate oak forest environments. Currant and Jacobi (2001: 1709) have attributed the open character of the landscape during parts of this interglacial to the sustained environmental impact of megaherbivores. These authors use the faunal assemblage from Bacon Hole as one of their "marker horizons" in assigning a mammalian biostratigraphy to the Late Pleistocene of Britain (*ibid.*: 1707).

Interestingly, according to Caseldine (1990: 24), after the Ipswichian Interglacial there is actually very little in the way of direct evidence for the environment of Wales before the Late Devensian period (Upper Palaeolithic), prior to *ca.* >40,000 years ago, and there is in general also relatively little evidence for a human presence between *ca.* 40,000-18,000 years ago, with notable exceptions, e.g. Paviland Cave.

Despite the absence of a human presence, there is evidence for a limited fauna (in terms of species diversity) in Britain during MIS 4 (after *ca.* 87,000 years ago), with species such as bison and reindeer dominating, and wolf, wolverine, mountain hare, a very large species of brown bear, and northern vole all in evidence (Currant and Jacobi 2001: 1710). The mammalian assemblages attributed to this stage are classified as the Banwell Cave Mammal Assemblage Zone by Jacobi and Currant (2001), and generally indicate cold environmental conditions at this time.

The key reasons for the lack of a human presence may include the Devensian glacial period (from *ca.* <110,000 years ago), during which time mean July temperatures rarely exceeded *ca.* 10°C, with winter temperatures as low as –25°C occurring (Lowe and Walker 1997: 336). The resulting lack of carrying capacity, and consequent reduction in large mammal species (as outlined above), may have restricted human exploitation of the environment. Additionally, the continual cooling trend after MIS 5e (after *ca.* 110,000 years ago), alongside climatic fluctuations, may have been sufficient to make this northwestern area of the European landmass sufficiently inhospitable so as not to warrant exploitation by humans across the period *ca.* 110–60,000 years ago; or to make any activity very ephemeral in nature and as such difficult to identify in the archaeological record. Furthermore, the nature of the ice sheets during MIS 4 and 3 meant that sea level fluctuated considerably from lows down to –100m in MIS 4 rising to –50m at the onset of MIS 3, fluctuating around –60 to –80m below modern sea level after *ca.* 50,000 years ago (White and Pettitt 2011: 33).

Stringer (2006) has also noted that the channel river may have formed a significant barrier to human movement, and particularly the northward dispersal of Neanderthals, during both glacial and interglacial periods, as the combined southerly flow of the Thames, Rhine and Seine produced a significant river valley in what is now the English Channel (see also White and Pettitt 2011: 33–4). The return of humans to Britain occurs during MIS 3, at *ca.* 60-38,000 years ago, and is associated with Currant and Jacobi's Pin Hole Cave Assemblage Zone, named after Pin Hole Cave, Creswell, Derbyshire, which is located at the Creswell Crags S.S.S.I. (2001: 1711). The Pin Hole Cave assemblage is used by Currant and Jacobi to replace the Coygan Cave (Carmathenshire) assemblage, as this site was destroyed by quarrying. Faunal species in evidence during the Middle Devensian include wolf, brown bear, lion, woolly mammoth, wild horse, woolly rhinoceros, giant deer, reindeer, bison, red deer, Arctic fox, spotted hyena, the species in evidence are indicative of extreme continental "Mammoth Steppe" conditions (*ibid.*: 1711–12). White and Pettitt (2011: 33) note that for much of MIS 3, much of Britain was free of ice, and ice advance does not occur until the onset of MIS 2, at *ca.* 34,000 BP, during this time Britain formed a peninsula of the northern European landmass.

Research at Lynford, in Norfolk indicates that at *ca.* 60,000 years ago an early river channel meandered across the landscape, fluctuating between periods of flow and still water. The archaeological record has shown that mammal, fish, birds and amphibians, along with 160 species of beetle were deposited in the area at a time when average summer temperatures were *ca.* 13°C and winters were extremely cold at –10°C (Stringer 2006). The environment would have been dominated by open steppe grassland, possibly with some trees, and faunal remains of mammoth, woolly rhino, reindeer, horse, bison, fox, wolf, hyena and brown bear are associated with the stone tools that are related to Neanderthal activity at this site (*ibid.*). Whilst the stone tool assemblage comprises some 2,700 finds, including 47 handaxes, Shreeve (2006) has reported a considerable degree of taphonomic disturbance, such as trampling and reworking, to the faunal material, and has shown that there is no evidence for butchery on the mammoth bones at this location; although Shreeve

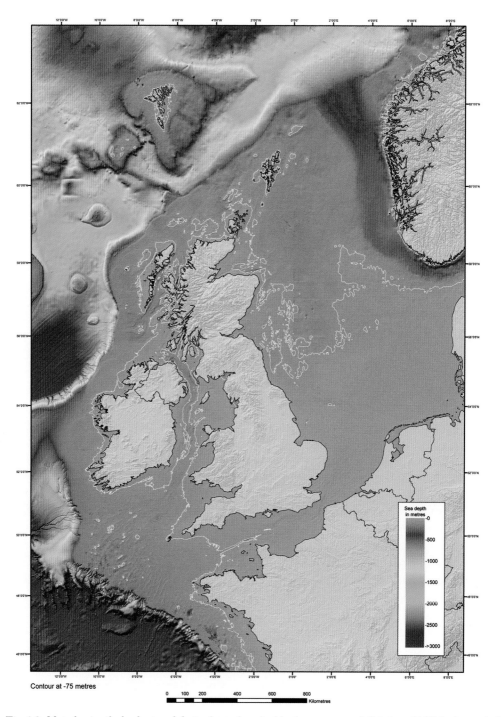

Contour at -75 metres

0   100   200   400   600   800
Kilometres

Fig. 1.2: Map showing the land exposed during lowered sea level in the areas around Britain to highlight the marked changes in landscape during glaciations (white line marks the –75m OD contour). © WAERC, University of Hull.

argues that given the size and thickness of the meat on mammoths this is probably not surprising (*ibid.*: 551) The main evidence for butchery occurs in relation to other species such as horse, reindeer and woolly rhinoceros, and the assemblage shows clear evidence for the splitting of bone to recover the marrow. Whilst there are significant gaps in the evidence at Lynford, there is little doubt that this site provides important insights into Neanderthal exploitation strategies during MIS 3, not least as the circumstantial evidence for the removal of meat-bearing limb-bones hints at the selective removal of these elements (*ibid.*: 553). Other sites at this time (MIS 4–3) include Pin Hole and Robin Hood caves, Creswell, Derbyshire, Kent's Cavern, Torquay in Devon, Hyena Den, Wookey, Somerset, Coygan Cave, Carmarthenshire and Paviland, West Glamorgan (discussed below) (Stringer 2006). Two of these sites, Kent's Cavern and Hyena Den have also produced (very) limited pollen evidence that suggests the presence of trees during MIS 3, and more recent work appears to reinforce this presence (see White and Pettitt 2011: 44).

There is both ice core and coleopteran evidence to suggest that MIS 3 was climatically unstable, with rapid oscillations in evidence during this period. Coope (2002) analysed 27 beetle assemblages from central and southern England, plotting maximum and minimum inferred temperature ranges for MIS 3 and the early part of MIS 2. The data show that there was a "temperate interlude between about 43,000 and 41,000 ^{14}C yr BP, during which the summer temperatures were at least as warm as those in southern Britain today, with winter temperatures which need not have been much colder than those of today" (*ibid.*: 403). The data also show that there were few, if any, trees in Britain during this warm period (in fact it has been suggested that there are no trees evidenced during the entirety of MIS 3), a fact that reflects the lack of soil development immediately following the arctic conditions, and the lack of nutrients and humus in the soils that were present (Coope 2002), and as noted by Currant and Jacobi (2001) the presence of grazing herbivores would no doubt have inhibited woodland development. After this warm interlude, there is some data to suggest a second, short-lived warm period at *ca.* 34,000 ^{14}C yr BP, but the overall climate signal from the coleopteran record indicates cold conditions with summer averages of 10°C and winter temperatures that were as low as –20°C, continuing to *ca.* 25,000 ^{14}C yr BP (Coope 2002: 404).

At Little Hoyle, Pembrokeshire indirect evidence of a climatic downturn after *ca.* 30,000 years ago is indicated by the presence of a breeding population of Barnacle geese, a species that does not breed further south than eastern Greenland in the present (Aldhouse-Green 1996: 70, 2000a: 10). Immediately prior to the Late-glacial period Wales experienced a maximum glacial advance *ca.* 24,000–18,000 years ago, after which deglaciation progressed until *ca.* 14,500 years ago (the Dimlington Stadial, or Last Glacial Maximum [LGM]) (Bateman *et al.* 2008). The landscape of the northwestern European landmass at the time of maximum glaciation is (fortunately) unparalleled in modern terms, however, in her speculative 1998 study, Bryony Coles sought to assess the influence of two major ice sheets; in general, the weight of the British and the Scandinavian ice sheets caused a forebulge, or ridge, running northwest to southeast across the North Sea plain, with the effect that the nature of river drainage was changed, and pro-glacial lakes were formed at the ice margins.

It is perhaps difficult for us to envisage an ice sheet some 1.5km in thickness covering large areas of what is now Britain, or the existence of an even greater ice sheet to the north and east covering Scandinavia, but it should not be too difficult to understand the effect that such a huge weight of ice could have had in terms of compression of the underlying landmass, or that to the south of the ice sheet a bulging effect would have occurred. This is a very simplistic outline of what were a very complex set of processes, but it serves to illustrate just how different the environment was both during the Pleistocene and towards the end of the last (Devensian) glacial period in northwest Europe.

It is also worth remembering at this point that when global ice sheets expanded a significant amount of the earth's water was locked up in the ice. This resulted in a significant lowering of global sea levels such that large expanses of land that are currently submerged formed extensive low-lying grassy plains that animal (and human groups) exploited. Interestingly, investigations of the cave deposits at Little Hoyle Cave near Tenby (Green 1986: 40), whilst not producing direct evidence for human activity, have produced ^{14}C and U-series determinations that cluster around 18,000 years ago. The animals attested in the landscape at this time include bear, reindeer, red fox, collared lemming, narrow-skulled vole, and water vole, all at a time when the Devensian ice sheet was only *ca.* 20 miles (30km) away. There is an hiatus in the evidence for human activity in Britain during the coldest stages of the Devensian, and given the new dates from Goat's Hole cave, Paviland, it is currently possible to suggest that the environment was of sufficient severity to preclude a human presence *ca.* 28–15,400 cal BP (Barton *et al.* 2003), or perhaps even as late as the GISP2 Late-glacial interstadial date of 14,700 cal BP (Blockley *et al.* 2000; 2006), although the initial warming phase may have begun as early as 16,500–15,000 cal BP in Britain (Walker *et al.* 1993).

Despite the inherent gaps in the evidence there is little doubt that the variations in climate during the Pleistocene had a marked influence on the human presence in Britain, and that these changes influenced the nature of the environment, the available plant and animal biomass, and consequently subsistence activities. Hunting would have been easier in the open grasslands away from the ice sheets (Aldhouse-Green 2000a, although see discussion in O'Shea 2006 in relation to Europe), and as might be anticipated, hunting in dense forest (if this was undertaken) before the bow and arrow were developed in the Upper Palaeolithic (Rozoy 1990a; Nuzhnyi 1989; 1990; 1993) could be a very dangerous activity when spears were the main hunting weapon!

It should be noted at this juncture, out of interest, that O'Shea (2006) has recently assessed the dimensions of European Middle and Upper Palaeolithic flint points, asserting that for the Middle Palaeolithic in mainland Europe the dimensions of the points indicate that they would have functioned best if used on thrusting spears or hand-thrown spears but not as projectile points. It is not until *ca.* 38–32,000 years ago that the Châtelperronian points found in northern Spain, southern France and northern Italy, exhibit dimensions that would suggest their use as spearthrower dart tips, and from this point onwards (until *ca.* 17,000 years ago) there is no evidence to indicate the use of Upper Palaeolithic points as arrow heads (*ibid.*: 838–9). Whatever the technique used to bring down large game, it is apparent from the available faunal assemblages that hominins (whether Neanderthals or *Homo heidelbergensis or Homo sapiens*) were exploiting both large and small game animals during the Middle to Upper Palaeolithic. An embedded theme in studies of stone tools and their function is that a degree of regional variability occurs, and that specialised tools were produced for specific tasks. Clearly then, whilst some tools would have been used for dismembering and processing carcasses, cleaning hides and even cutting human hair?, the points had an important function in Palaeolithic tool-kits, as being able to kill or fatally wound the animal being hunted was a first priority for Palaeolithic hunters. The range of the animals being exploited by Palaeolithic groups is expanded upon below in the discussion of the evidence from cave sites in Britain.

For Wales, during the latter part of the Upper Palaeolithic we have four key cave sites, Paviland, Hoyle's Mouth, Nanna's Cave and Cathole with evidence for Creswellian (European Late Magdalenian) occupation (thirteenth millennium) and four sites with Final Palaeolithic (12th millennium) activity attested (Paviland, Priory Farm, Nanna's cave and Potter's Cave) (Aldhouse-Green 2000: 12; David 2007). The environmental record provides evidence for wolf, red fox, arctic fox, bear, wild cattle, elk, horse, red deer and mammoth, alongside smaller mammals, birds and rodents in the environment of Britain (*ibid.*: 11; David 2007), and as there has not been a subsequent glacial period, the evidence for a human presence in the landscape is considerably enhanced.

The evidence from caves

As early as 1951 W. F. Grimes noted that the earlier evidence for human occupation in Wales was more abundant during the so-called "cave period", when human activity was "confined to the Carboniferous Limestone areas, of which … Pembrokeshire and Gower in the south and the Vale of Clwyd in the north" were key foci of activity (1951: 3, and Murphy 2002). In this context, Davies (1989) has discussed the archaeological evidence from 32 caves (with activity dating to a range of Pleistocene and Holocene ages) in the Gower Peninsula, extending from Bacon Hole in the east to Ogof Garreg Hir in the west (Fig. 1.3).

Whilst a number of the caves in southwest Wales contain Late Upper Palaeolithic, Creswellian material (see section on the Late-glacial period below), e.g. Hoyle's Mouth and Little Hoyle in the Tenby area, and Potter's Cave, Nanna's Cave, Ogof yr Ychen and New Cave on Caldey Island, many of the archaeological and faunal remains from these caves remain undated in absolute terms, and the relationships between the fauna and the evidence for human activity at many locations requires greater resolution. Where preserved, these sites are in need of more detailed study along the lines of the work undertaken at Paviland by Stephen Aldhouse-Green and co-workers (Aldhouse-Green 2000a, 2000b; Aldhouse-Green *et al.* 2011).

Fortunately, whilst there are currently no exceptionally early sites in Wales, to match Happisburgh and Pakefield, there are a number of sites that provide us with important insights into early human activity in our region during the Palaeolithic period. Significantly, one of these sites provides the earliest *direct* evidence for a human presence in Wales, and as a corollary, in the most westerly part of this northwestern region of Europe. Sites such

Fig. 1.3: Distribution Map showing locations of key caves with Palaeolithic activity in Wales. Caves in the Elwy Valley, North Wales are Pontnewydd, Cae Gronw and Cefn Cave. 1 – Priory Farm Cave, Monkton, Pembs, 2 – Hoyle's Cave, 3 – Potter's Cave, Caldey Island, 4 – Nanna's Cave, Caldey Island, 5 – Paviland Cave, Gower, 6 – Cathole Cave, Ilston, Gower, 7 – Pontnewydd Cave, St Asaph, 8 – Cefn Cave, Elwy Valley.

as Boxgrove in Sussex (human left tibia and two lower incisors) (Stringer *et al.* 1998) and Swanscombe in Kent (skull fragments) provide *direct* evidence for a human presence at times that are significantly earlier than the Welsh evidence, however, the fossil record is greatly enhanced by the finds from Pontnewydd, Clwyd, as, at Pontnewydd, the oldest human remains in Wales were found during excavations between 1978 and 1985 (Green 1986).

For the Lower Palaeolithic period in Wales the evidence from Pontnewydd Cave in the Elwy valley may attest an age of *ca.* 245,000 yrs ago (or 225,000–186, 000 yrs ago) (Aldhouse-Green 2000a) for a warm stage fauna that includes brown bear, horse, roe deer, wood mouse and beaver; whilst a lower Breccia layer has a fauna that suggests a colder, more continental type of climate, indicated by the presence of Norway lemming

Fig. 1.4: Cefn Cave (west entrance) in the Elwy Valley (SJ 0207053), located high up the valley on the opposite side to Pontnewydd Cave, Cefn commands extensive views of the valley (© Author).

and northern vole (Caseldine 1990). Butchery marks on a number of the horse and bear bones provide a direct link to the Neanderthal activity at this site, although, as mentioned above, the dating and stratigraphic resolution requires work. Pontnewydd is one of three cave sites investigated by Green (1986), in the Elwy valley area. These sites, Pontnewydd, Cae Gronw and Cefn (Figs 1.3 and 1.4), have all produced Palaeolithic material in the form of faunal remains, but only Pontnewydd has produced significant human remains in the form of eight fragmentary fossils (including; three lower premolars, a fragment of right maxilla from a child, with the dm^2 and M^1 preserved, a possible M^2, a further fragment of right maxilla, additional teeth and a thoracic vertebra) representing at least three individuals, being an adult, sub-adult and child aged *ca.* 9 years of age (Stringer 1986: 60).

Pontnewydd Cave is clearly very early, at *ca.* >225,000 years ago, and has important evidence for the physical presence of early Neanderthals. Similarly, a much later, but equally significant site is recorded at Paviland, West Glamorgan (*ca.* 34–33,000 years ago; discussed below), where anatomically modern human activity is attested in the form of a burial, and as a result, this is a site where we can identify a number of the traits that today we would consider as "markers" of what it is to be a modern human.

At Coygan Cave, Carmarthen Bay (now destroyed) Middle Palaeolithic period (at *ca.* 180,000–*ca.* 40–38,000 years ago) Mousterian artefacts (including two *bout coupé* handaxes associated with Neanderthal activity), and an hyena den fauna were identified (Green, 1986: 39; Davies 1989: 86; Aldhouse-Green *et al.* 1995). Consequently these finds provide us with *indirect* evidence for Neanderthals at *ca.* 50,000 years ago; again, whilst dating and other issues are still a problem, the material does enhance our understanding of human-landscape interactions between the Lower and Upper Palaeolithic periods. Whilst this site was primarily used as a hyena den, Aldhouse-Green (2000a: 8) notes that the artefacts at Coygan Cave probably predate the carnivore activity. The Neanderthals that used Coygan Cave re-colonised the landscape in an environment that comprised arid grasslands which supported a wild fauna with species such as mammoth, woolly rhinoceros, horse and spotted hyena in evidence (*ibid.*). As noted above, there appear to be some overlaps in Europe between the late Neanderthals and anatomically modern humans (*Homo sapiens sapiens*) who are responsible for a new and diverse range of flintworking technologies designed for use in specific tasks in hunter-gatherer subsistence strategies (Mellars 2004).

The fact that Coygan Cave has been destroyed by quarrying led Currant and Jacobi to re-assign their mammal assemblage zone for this period (MIS 3: *ca.* 50–38,000 years ago) to Pin Hole Cave, Creswell, Derbyshire (2000: 1711), this latter site has an extensive faunal list which includes small mammals, birds and fish, along with pollen from the cave sediments and spotted hyena coprolites. Currant and Jacobi (2000) report that red deer, which is not represented at Pin Hole, and arctic fox which is unstratified at this site, are both common components of other Middle Devensian faunas in Britain. The Pin Hole fauna is indicative of a "Mammoth Steppe" environment with species such as woolly mammoth, woolly rhinoceros, wild horse, red and giant deer, reindeer, bison, lion and spotted hyena (a very common MIS 3 species, found at a number of cave sites including Little Hoyle and Coygan Cave, Carmarthenshire) in evidence (a detailed species list is provided in Currant and Jacobi 2000: table 5). According to White and Pettitt (2011: 46) this mix of cold and warm adapted species may indicate factors such as seasonal variation, the impact of millennial scale climatic variability (which would be essentially invisible given the poor resolution of the site), or a non-analogous community.

During the Devensian cold stage, at Goat's Hole cave, Paviland (now more commonly referred to as Paviland Cave) stone artefacts and the partial remains of a skeleton (lacking the skull and most of the right side of the skeleton) thought to date to the Middle–Upper Palaeolithic period (i.e. after *ca.* 59,000 years ago) were originally investigated by William Buckland in 1823, and excavated completely by W. J. Sollas in 1912. The transition from the Middle to Upper Palaeolithic occurs at *ca.* 40–30 ka BP (see Stringer 2006; Lynch *et al.* 2000: fig. 2 for a list of boundary dates for the Lower Palaeolithic through to the Neolithic transition). Paviland cave is located to the east of Port Eynon on the southern coast of the Gower Peninsula, and due to its location, *ca.* 9.15m (30ft) above the high tide mark, the site is currently only easily accessible at low tide (Grimes 1951; Jacobi and Higham 2008). Grimes (1951) described objects of ivory and bone from Goat's Hole, with the finds including ivory rods and armlets, and teeth of wolf and reindeer pierced for stringing together in necklaces (although see discussion below), and bone awls and spatulae.

Grimes (1951: 5) asserted that the associated finds and the ubiquitous application of red ochre left little doubt that the individual interred at Paviland was of Palaeolithic date. The "Red Lady" is in actual fact a modern human male, part of the populations known as Cro-Magnons (Stringer 2006). He was *ca.* 25–30 years old, with an averaged stature of 1.735m (*ca.* 5ft 8in), and he weighed about 71.3kg (*ca.* 11st 2lb), when he was buried (Trinkaus and Holliday 2000). A wide range of faunal material was found at Paviland, and although the association of these finds to discrete periods of human occupation is not possible due to the lack of secure stratigraphic context, it is worth noting that horse, red deer (although see cautionary note in Jacobi and Higham 2008: 901), reindeer, brown bear, aurochs, woolly rhinoceros and reindeer were common finds. In addition, Irish elk, wolf, mammoth, red fox, arctic fox, and hyena are in evidence in the faunal assemblage.

Re-excavation of the Paviland caves in 1997 (Goat's Hole, Hound's Hole, Foxhole Cave and Ogof-y-Môr) produced evidence for both Upper Palaeolithic and Mesolithic human activity that is relevant to the current study, whilst also confirming that no deposits associated with the burial of the "Red Lady" were preserved at Goat's Hole (Aldhouse-Green 2000b: 1). Radiocarbon dating of finds from Paviland (Pettitt 2000) has shown that activity occurs at this location from >31,000 through until 21,000 years ago, with phases of carnivore activity (between >31–24,000 and at *ca.* 17,000 years ago), dates for herbivores (pre-27,000 for woolly rhino, reindeer and *Bos* sp./Bison sp.), and at 24–21,000 years ago for mammoth. There is a lot of human activity associated with this later period, which can be pushed further back in time to *ca.* 26,000 years ago, if the dates for the worked ivory are included (Pettitt 2000).

As noted above, the evidence for human activity comes in the form of worked ivory and bone, including spatulas, a mammoth ivory pendant and a lissoir-like object, along with the burial of the "Red Lady". The span of human activity identified by Pettitt's dating program (2000) included the periods >29–21,000 years ago, and also at 7000 years ago during the Holocene (considered in more detail in Chapter 6). On the basis of the dating of the ivory and bone objects Pettitt (2000: 66) states that "it is clear, at the 95% level of confidence that the 'Red Lady' is not associated with any of the worked ivory and bone dates here". This latter observation might appear to contradict the evidence from Buckland's reporting of the burial, and also the reporting by Aldhouse-Green (2000b: 115–32), but in actual fact they reinforce the observation that human activity at this site occurs in the form of a series of occupations over time. In fact, Pettitt (2000: 66) observed that the dating evidence supported the suggestion that during the Pleistocene period (*ca.* 35–15,000 years ago) human and animal activity at Paviland (particularly hyena, bear and human) was characterised by several brief occupations over several millennia, and that the working of ivory occurred across the period *ca.* 26–21,000 years ago at this location. Unfortunately, despite what appears to be a diverse range of faunal remains from Paviland, Turner (2000: 133–40) notes that whilst a number of possibilities exist for the accumulation of this assemblage (e.g. hyena and bear den's and human use for processing of material from kill events and ivory/bone working), the assemblage is difficult to interpret in its current state, but it does indicate that at times during the colder stages of the last glaciation Wales was a favourable place for occupation.

Other finds associated with the burial are reported as including perforated shells of common periwinkle (*Nerita littoralis*) which Aldhouse-Green (2000: 115–6) suggests could have been collected from the contemporary coastline, which was some 100km away in the Bristol Channel at this time. Ivory rods (>40–50 nearly cylindrical items of around 10mm mean diameter and 53.4mm mean length) were found near the ribs of the "Red Lady". Whilst these are of uncertain function, they may have been blanks for bead making or "magical wands" (Aldhouse-Green 2000b: 117). Finally, the ivory "bracelets" attributed to the burial (*ca.* 10–12.5cm in diameter) are reported as having a number of possible typological affinities to chronological period, but their actual function is unknown, and the term bracelets is used generically (Aldhouse-Green 200b: 117) due to the form of the objects. The range of objects found at Paviland is extensive given the dating of the cave, and whilst a full overview is beyond the scope of the current chapter, the reader is directed to the aptly titled (at the time) "definitive report" by Stephen Aldhouse-Green (2000b).

There has, since the publication of the Paviland report (Aldhouse-Green 2000b), been a more recent re-analysis of the evidence from this site by Jacobi and Higham (2008). These authors have integrated a detailed consideration of the lithic (stone tool) evidence, from the *ca.* 5000 artefacts recovered to date, with new Accelerator Mass Spectrometry (AMS) radiocarbon dating of organic finds, in order to attempt a re-consideration of the timing of human occupation at this location. The assessment of the leaf-points from the assemblage led Jacobi to suggest an early Upper Palaeolithic date of *ca.* 38–36,000 ^{14}C BP for these artefacts, and to also suggest that they may have been produced by the last Neanderthals to occupy this area of Europe (*ibid.*: 899). It is also worth noting that, with the exception of Gough's Cave, Cheddar Gorge in Somerset, the stone tool assemblage from Paviland is the largest from a British Pleistocene cave, with Aldhouse-Green (2000b:

table 2.2) listing some 4928 artefacts recovered by eight different collectors between 1823 and 1922.

The majority of the lithic assemblage at Goat's Hole (Paviland) is considered to be late Aurignacian (Swainston 2000, referenced by Jacobi and Higham 2008: 899), and ages for this colonisation by modern humans range between *ca.* 31,700 and 29,000 ^{14}C years ago, with the earlier date being considered to be a more realistic age for an Aurignacian presence in Britain (*ibid.*). Higham (2011: 238–9) also asserts that the age of 31,550±340 BP for a bone or antler point from Hyena Den (Wookey Hole, Somerset) is realistic and fits well with other evidence for osseous (bone) point manufacture during the Aurignacian of Europe.

The new AMS ultrafiltration dating of two fragments of human bone from the "Red Lady", a rib fragment and part of the left scapula, has shown that the age of the skeleton is now placed between 34,050 and 33,260 cal BP (the ^{14}C ages are 29,490±210–28,400±120 BP), earlier than suggested by Pettitt's (2000: 64) determinations (26,350±550 and 25,840±280 [OxA-1815 and OxA-8025]). On the basis of the new dates, and problems associated with obtaining secure dates for a number of artefacts from Paviland, Jacobi and Higham (2008: 906) suggest that the earliest activity at the cave was during the Initial Upper Palaeolithic period. This period has previously been assigned to *ca.* 38–32,000 BP and correlated to "leaf-point" technology; this observation is possibly supported by an AMS date on a hyena mandible from Bench Cavern near Brixham, which was associated with a leaf point and dated to *ca.* 34,500 BP (David 2007: 6). This earlier phase of activity is followed by the human occupation during the Aurignacian, during which fires were lit in the cave and the majority of the lithic artefacts were made. The "Red Lady" is attributed to a later cultural stage, the early Gravettian age, and he *is* associated with the ivory artefacts from the cave.

The ages obtained by Pettitt (2000) on the ivory artefacts have also been called into question by the work of Jacobi and Higham (2008) who suggest that a ^{14}C age of 26,170±150 BP (OxA-13656) should perhaps be considered as a *minimum* age for the bone knives at Paviland. These authors are of the opinion that it is unlikely that human activity continued at Paviland after the burial, and that it is unsafe to conclude that this site provides evidence for a human presence in Wales down to 21,000 ^{14}C years ago as conditions worsened towards the glacial maximum. Despite this new evidence, as noted by Stephen Aldhouse-Green (2000b), the "Red Lady" is the oldest *Homo sapiens* skeleton in Wales, and in actual fact the new dating undertaken by Jacobi and Higham (2008) confirms this by moving the skeleton further back in chronological terms.

Finally, some insights into the subsistence activities of the male interred at Paviland have been forthcoming from the work of Richards (2000: 73) who has used stable isotope analysis (δ^{13}C and δ^{15}N) to investigate the potential range of dietary proteins exploited by this individual. The analysis produced a δ^{13}C ratio of −18.4‰, which suggests that marine proteins made up about 10–20% of this person's diet (for more information into the technique of stable isotope analysis see Chapter 4). The δ^{15}N ratio of 9.4‰ is considered by Richards to indicate that animal proteins made up a significant proportion of the diet, but that plant proteins were not significant. The limited faunal material with which to compare diets is problematic, but it is interesting to note that the δ^{15}N ratio for the Paviland burial is very similar to the *Bos/Bison* sp. (8.8‰ and 7.9‰) that were analysed, suggesting that these animals were not the main meat species exploited. The reason for this observation is that we are what we eat, plus some, as there is a trophic level shift between the animals being consumed and the person consuming the animals. Therefore if *Bison/Bos* sp. were being eaten the human $\delta^{15}N$ values should be elevated by 2–4‰ from the animal ratios, so they would be at least *ca.* 10-11‰ if these species were a significant part of the man's diet at Paviland.

The human remains from a range of other sites in Europe, e.g. in the Czech Republic at Brno-Francouzká and Dolní Věstonice, and in Russia at Kostenki and Mal'ta, dated to a slightly later period at *ca.* 26–20,000 years ago, have provided evidence for the consumption of a significant freshwater resource component, such as fish and fowl, in human diets (Richards *et al.* 2001: 6529). In the case of Kostenki, Richards *et al.* (2001) suggest that freshwater resources would have made up *ca.* 50% of the dietary protein intakes, whilst at Sungir in Russia the stable isotope evidence indicates that herbivore protein made up the main portion of the diet. Combined with Paviland, the data indicate that an increasingly broad range of resources are being exploited in Europe towards the end of the Palaeolithic as anatomically modern groups enter the archaeological record.

At the time of the burial at Paviland (MIS 3), the Devensian ice sheet had locked up significant amounts of water, reducing sea levels to *ca.* –80m OD (and even as low as –100m OD at the height of glaciation), and as noted by Aldhouse-Green (2000a: 6–8) not only was Britain a peninsula of the European landmass, but even during the early Mesolithic period, as sea levels were rising, sea levels around Carmarthen Bay would have been lowered to around *ca.* –35m OD at the start of the Holocene (Figs 1.2 and 2.1). In fact, during the Palaeolithic period many of the cave sites that have produced evidence for the fauna and occasional direct evidence for humans in this period would have been located at a significant distance from the contemporary coastline. As such, the exploitation of marine resources would have necessitated relatively long-distance forays to the coast, from Paviland, or perhaps as the groups using Paviland were returning to this "persistent" place in the landscape the seasonal exploitation of marine resources constituted one element of a much broader resource procurement strategy.

Evidence from elsewhere in Europe, e.g. sites such Dolní Věstonice I and II, Pavlov I and Předmostí in the Czech Republic, has shown that Upper Palaeolithic human groups had a high level of mobility in the landscape, with stone sources for tool production being non-local, and necessitating importation from distances up to 200km away from the occupation sites (Trinkaus *et al.* 2001). Whilst trade and exchange would no doubt have figured in the long-distance movement of these materials, the evidence indicates that Upper Palaeolithic humans were regularly moving over considerable distances during hunting, raw material procurement and foraging activities, such that the regular movement between the coast and Paviland cave would not appear to represent unusual levels of activity for the human groups exploiting the changing environments of Wales at this time.

As noted by David (2007), Paviland is not the only site to produce Early Upper Palaeolithic artefacts in Wales; additional sites include Ffynnon Bueno and Cae Gwyn in Clwyd, and The Hoyle's Mouth in Dyfed (Fig. 1.5). The Hoyle has a radiocarbon date on an unidentified, unstratified bone of 27,800±600 BP (OxA-1024) (this date is quoted as 27,900±900 BP in

David 1990: 148), although whilst hyena, cave bear, fox, wolf, mammoth, woolly rhinoceros, reindeer, red deer, giant deer and "ox" are reported from the numerous excavations at this site, this fauna represents both cold (Devensian) and warm (Late-glacial) adapted species. Whilst the majority of the lithic finds appear to be Late-glacial (Creswellian) in date (see Fig. 1.6), and as such are discussed below (David 2007: 12), there is also an unambiguous identification of a burin busqué of Aurignacian age at this location (David 1990: 148, 2007: 45).

Overall, the evidence for human activity in Wales is relatively sparse, but the Welsh cave sites can be linked into wider networks of activity; for instance at Creswell Crags, Derbyshire, Gough's Cave, in Somerset and Kent's Cavern, Torbay, Devon. A number of cave sites have provided significant data to compliment the evidence from Wales (see White and Pettit 2011 for a detailed overview of Middle Palaeolithic activity in Britain). The human maxilla from Kent's Cavern has been dated to *ca*. 31,000 ^{14}C years ago (*ibid*.: 7), although White and Pettitt (2011: 82, quoting Stringer 2006) caution that it is unclear whether this represents a late Neanderthal (*Homo neanderthalensis?*) or early *Homo sapiens* fossil, due to the lack of diagnostic characteristics.

As we move towards the latter part of the Palaeolithic period the occurrence of open air sites (as opposed to cave locations) increases, and there are a number of locations in England that have produced open air sites in older river gravels. Furthermore, the site of Badger's Hole, on the Mendip hills in Somerset, has been interpreted as a base camp, and there are a number of smaller scale occupations attested in the vicinity of this location which may have functioned as temporary activity sites in a wider hunting and gathering landscape setting (Darvill 2010: 44). Other Early Upper Palaeolithic sites in Wales (from *ca*. 40–24,000 years ago) with evidence for human activity, include, Cathole, Little Hoyle, Nanna's Cave, Potter's cave, Priory farm Cave, Kendrick's Cave, Ogof-yr-Ychen, Tan-y-Bryn, Cefn and Lynx caves (Aldhouse-Green 2000a: 12; David 2007: 5–14). One final point of note in relation to the Aurignacian and Gravettian activity in Britain needs to be made, Pettitt (2008: 28–33) has suggested that the very low numbers of artefacts and associated evidence for human activity could indicate that the British record is simply attesting the activities of a single seasonal trip by a forager group derived from the western French Aurignacian II groups, and that during the Gravettian, the evidence from eight sites only attests sporadic occupation, albeit with a much wider distribution of sites in Britain at this time.

As noted above, the available evidence indicates that the inhospitable nature of the environment from *ca*. <28–15,400 years ago results in a significant "gap" in the evidence for a human presence in Britain at this time, although a number of sites do provide evidence for a faunal presence (David 2007: 15). These sites include Ogof-yr-Ychen and Little Hoyle in Dyfed and Cae Gwyn in Clwyd (*ibid*.: 16). Pettitt (2008: 25) has suggested that in the context of the *ca*. 35,000 ^{14}C years of the Upper Palaeolithic, a human presence in Britain can only be demonstrated for *ca*. 5000 years of this time period, amounting to only five or so phases of occupation, and that a similar situation existed in northern France, Belgium and the Netherlands across the Upper Palaeolithic (the reader is directed to Pettitt 2008 for a detailed overview of the archaeological evidence for a human presence in Britain during the Upper Palaeolithic).

Fig. 1.5: The Hoyle (the Hoyle's Mouth); this cave can be seen, through the quite dense woodland foliage in front of it, from the road which curves around and below the site to the north (© Author).

In general, whilst a number of key interglacial periods are recognised during the Pleistocene, the evidence from ice cores has shown that over the last >250,000 years or so there were a significant number of temperate (warmer) stages interspersed with relatively rapid shifts back to colder conditions, and that these temperate stages themselves were often bracketed by much longer cold periods (see fig. 1.2 in Aldhouse-Green 2000a: 7, or fig. 1 in White and Pettitt 2011: 27). Consequently, the lack of fine dating resolution for the finds at sites like Pontnewydd, whilst unavoidable, does serve to slightly weaken the value of these finds in relation to the integration of this evidence for human activity and landscape interactions within the discrete warmer and cool stages occurring during

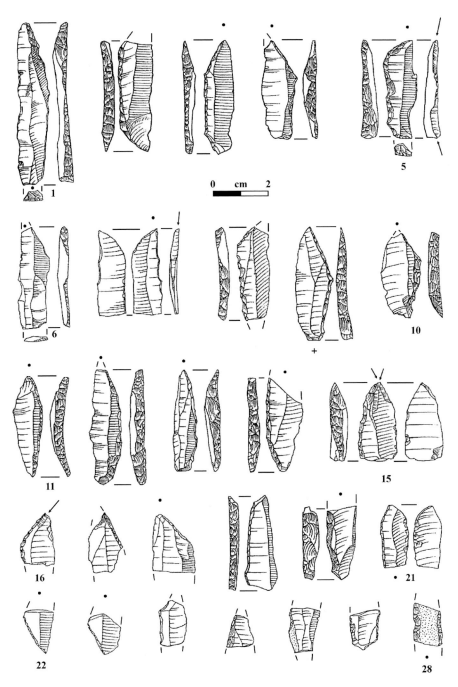

Fig. 1.6: The Hoyle's Mouth, Dyfed; backed blades and fragmentary backed blades: 1–5, "Cheddar Points"; 6 and 8, shouldered and truncated blades; 9–10, angle backed blades; 11–15, convex backed blades; 16–28, unclassified fragments; 5 and 7 have been reworked as burins (from David 2007: fig. 2: 20).

the Pleistocene. The problem, as already alluded to, is that even when combined with the evidence from elsewhere in England, the record of *direct* evidence for a human presence in Britain remains extremely sparse, a situation that will be re-visited to some degree when we consider the Mesolithic period in Wales.

Defining the Late-glacial

The Late-glacial period, which marks the shift from the ice dominated landscapes that characterise the Late Devensian (Last Glacial Maximum) period up to those of the warmer Holocene period (discussed in Chapter 2), occurs across a relatively short span of time (in geological terms at least), from about 13,200 to 10,200 ^{14}C BP (15,000–11,500 cal BP [Mayle *et al.* 1999]). At Glanllynnau, Caernarvonshire, the analysis of pollen and Coleoptera from kettle hole deposits has suggested that deglaciation was complete by *ca.* 14,500 years ago, and the beetle evidence indicates a marked thermal improvement, from average July temperatures of *ca.* 10°C to average July temperatures that were at least 17°C, with cold, dry conditions prevailing until *ca.* 13,200 BP (Coope and Brophy 1972; also Caseldine 1990: 25; David 1991, 2007). There are some complicating factors to consider when examining the Late-glacial period, not least due to the fact that different researchers have variously investigated the environment, climate, vegetation and landscape changes occurring across the Late-glacial, and have found that in many instances the onset of these changes exhibit some degree of asynchronicity throughout the British Isles (and northern Europe in general), and that not all sites produce a full Late-glacial record. The data is continually being refined as new sites are studied, such that some researchers think a longer Late-glacial sequence occurs in certain areas, i.e. between *ca.* 15–9,000 years ago, and that this longer timespan should be considered as being more realistic for the variations in climate that characterise the transition into the current interglacial period (Lowe and Walker 1997: 342).

Walker *et al.* (1994), defined the Late-glacial as comprising the Late-glacial interstadial between 13,000 and 11,000 uncal BP and the Younger Dryas (Loch Lomond) stadial, a time of pronounced cooling, between *ca.* 11,000 and 10,000 uncal BP (the start of the Younger Dryas is placed at roughly 13,000 years ago). At this time, these authors also noted that the interstadial had not been formally divided into the Bølling and Allerød periods because of confusions between climatostratigraphical and chronostratigraphical terminology.

The Late-glacial has been divided into four zones in Europe (the Bølling interstadial, 13,000–12,000 years ago; Older Dryas stadial (or Windemere) at 12000–11,800 years ago (a revertance episode (Walker *et al.* 1994: 114)); the Allerød interstadial, 11,800–11,000 years ago and the Younger Dryas stadial at 11,000–10,000 years ago) (Lowe and Walker 1997). The final zone of the Late-glacial (between *ca.* 11,000–10,200 years ago), the Loch Lomond Stadial (Younger Dryas in Europe), is characterised by a return to much colder conditions (when extreme winter temperatures may have been as low as –25°C (David 2007: 52), and a concomitant shift in the dominant regional vegetation types. Alley (2000b) has noted that the high resolution data recorded in the Greenland ice cores (GRIP – Greenland Ice Core Project and GISP2 – Greenland Ice Sheet Project II), indicates that the end of the Younger Dryas termination can be placed at around 11,500 years BP, with an error margin of about 1% (or 100 years). Problems exist with the absolute timing of the onset of the Younger Dryas due to the fact that it began in a series of steps, as opposed to the abrupt step at its termination (*ibid.*: 214), but the evidence indicates that the Younger Dryas persisted for between 1200 and 1300 years, probably ending *ca.* 11,660–11,625 BP. Caseldine (1990) has suggested that a simple way to view this entire period is as gradual climatic warming (the Windermere Interstadial), interrupted by a deterioration in climate during the Younger Dryas (Loch Lomond stadial). However, in light of subsequent research it is clear that this early assertion was somewhat generic, and whilst there are discrepancies in the timing of the various climate phases in the Late-glacial, it should be noted that the Allerød interstadial event is a worldwide event, although other interstadial events can be localised in northern regions, and in addition, the timing of the onset of these warm periods can differ depending on the region being studied (Walker *et al.* 1993; 1994).

The warming events that are identified during the Late-glacial, defined as interstadials (or oscillations) are relatively short lived events, as opposed to a full interglacial period (such as the current interglacial or Holocene period). In the earlier part of the Late-glacial higher summer and winter temperatures resulted in an expansion of vegetation cover and soil development (Walker *et al.* 1994: 111), with the landscape comprising open vegetation of grasses, sedges, sorrel or dock and mugwort, and perhaps a few trees such as Birch, and willow, juniper and birch scrub.

During the Late-glacial period there are a number of oscillations in climate, from cold to warm to cold and back again as we enter into the current interglacial period (Walker 2001). Mayle *et al.* (1999) and Mayewski and White (2002) have shown that the climatic shifts during the Late-glacial may have occurred over timescales of a decade or less. One of the sites analysed by these authors is Llanilid, a kettle hole section exposed in an open cast coal mine near Bridgend, Mid Glamorgan (Walker and Harkness 1990), where a Late-glacial through to earlier Holocene environmental sequence (*ca.* 13,200–9300 BP) was recorded. The work of Mayle *et al.* (1999) included three additional sites, Borrobol, northeast Scotland, Whitrig Bog in southern Scotland and Gransmoor, Holderness. These sites, along with Llanilid, were chosen in order to attempt to produce a coleopteran-based mutual climatic range model of Late-glacial climate, but only Gransmoor and Llanilid produced enough material to allow modelling. Focussing on Llanilid, for obvious reasons, the data generated has indicated that climate warming began as early as 16,000 cal BP (Blockley *et al.* 2004) with the highest temperatures, in excess of 18°C, occurring between 15,000–14,500 cal BP. Despite these high temperatures the response of trees to the climatic warming is delayed, such that the rise in juniper at this location only occurs at 14,500 cal BP (Mayle *et al.* 1999: 414). Interestingly, immediately at, or just after this climatic optimum temperatures fall by *ca.* 4°C, and as the climate cools, birch begins to dominate, peaking in abundance at 13,300 cal BP, and the climate continues to cool through until 13,100 cal BP when summer temperatures remain at *ca.* 12–11°C (*ibid.*), near to the thermal limit for tree growth (Walker *et al.* 2003: 512). The resolution of the data is difficult to interpret between 12,700 and 12,500 cal BP at Llanilid, but by 12,000 cal BP the climate is clearly deteriorating, with harsh tundra environments in evidence between 11,900 and 11,400 cal BP, succeeded by climatic amelioration in summer temperatures from 11.5°C to 20.5°C at 11,400 cal BP, which marks the onset of the Holocene (Mayle *et al.* 1999: 415, Walker *et al.* 2003: 513).

According to Lowe *et al.* (1988), the transition from organic stained silts to organic rich lake muds occurs at 12.2m depth in the profile at Llyn Gwernan, near Cader Idris, Gwynedd. The onset of this organic sedimentation, dated using AMS in order to verify the conventional radiocarbon method, is placed at 14,350–13,350 cal BC (SRR-1705: 13,200±120 BP) using conventional techniques and an average of six AMS determinations on the fractions of the deposit produces an age of 13,786±193 BP which calibrate to a slightly earlier range of 15,100–13,800 cal BC (Lowe *et al.* 1988: 366 give a slightly different date of 13,720±180 BP). This date marks the shift from open herbaceous landscapes towards a landscape in which juniper increases in frequency (the transition between local pollen assemblage zones [LPAZ] LGa and LGb). Juniper rises through the earlier part of LGb, to dominate the assemblage at 12m depth. Juniper peaks just below the dated horizon at *ca.* 11.9m depth, which is placed at 12,550–11,700 cal BC (SRR-1703: 12,120±130 BP). Summer temperatures were around *ca.* 17°C (similar to today) at the climatic optimum (Lowe *et al.* 1995), and immediately after the juniper peak, it begins to decline as birch pollen rises towards the end of this zone (LGb), at 11.6m depth. The end of this zone is undated in absolute terms, although Caseldine has indicated that the climate was deteriorating as birch was increasing in frequency, with colder wetter conditions prevailing. Soil instability is in evidence from *ca.* 12–11,000 BP, especially in upland areas (Walker *et al.* 1994).

At *ca.* 11,000 BP, there is a marked shift to cold conditions (the Loch Lomond stadial) which results in a return to periglacial conditions throughout northern Europe, although discontinuous permafrost may have occurred in Wales (Walker *et al.* 1994). The onset of the Loch Lomond stadial is identified in a change from organic lake muds to clay-rich minerogenic sediments at Llyn Gwernan, where this event is dated to 11,270–10,950 cal BC (SRR-1701: 11,160±90 BP). AMS dating of this transition (Lowe *et al.* 1988: 364) produces an average uncalibrated age of 11,783±121 BP (11,750±120 BP; *ibid.*: 366), which calibrates to 11,950–11,400 cal BC. The extreme cold conditions of the Younger Dryas (Loch Lomond) stadial continue through until *ca.* 10,200 BP, and during this period there is a replacement of woodland and heathland taxa by tundra and low alpine scrub plant communities such as grasses, clubmosses and *Artemisia* (Walker *et al.* 1994: 114).

The transition to the Holocene is visible in the Llyn Gwernan sequence at 10.6m depth, and is dated by conventional radiocarbon to 10,050–9300 cal BC (SRR-1700: 10,040±80 BP), and by an average of six AMS determinations to 10,950–10,150 cal BC (average 10,610±137 BP) (Lowe *et al.* 1988: 362), although Lowe *et al.* (*ibid.*) quote an age of 10,400±130 BP, which calibrates to 10,850–9850 cal BC. As can be seen from the above discussion, when comparing the use of conventional versus AMS radiocarbon dating techniques at Llyn Gwernan, the latter method appears to produce slightly older calibrated ages for the sequences analysed. In simple terms there is a general assumption that this situation is the result of the "bulking" of organic material in the conventional method when compared to the AMS techniques where the fine fractions of the sediment unit and a much smaller sample size, are used in the analysis. However, at Llyn Gwernan, Lowe *et al.* (1988: 367–8) outline a number of possible causes for the discrepancies in evidence, including the fact that the dates were obtained from two separate cores at this location.

When contrasted against full glacial periods, when major ice-sheets developed, stadials are cold periods of much shorter duration, during which localised expansion of ice sheets/ glaciers occur (Lowe and Walker 1984: 8), as in the western Grampian Highlands where a 2000km² icefield develops (Lowe and Walker 1997: 346) or in Snowdonia, on Cader Idris, and in the Brecon Beacons where localised glaciers develop (Hughes 2009). Hughes (2009) has reported on former cirque glaciers in the Aran and Berwyn mountains of north Wales, focussing on Llyn Lliwbran and Gwaun-y-Llwyni in the Arans and Cwm Llawenog, Llyn Lluncaws and Cwm Dwygo in the Berwyns, noting that estimations for glacier-climate reconstructions for the Loch Lomond Stadial suggest that in North Wales, a cold and wet climate characterises this period.

The dominant vegetation at this time is scrub tundra and tundra grassland communities, with woodland species representing only *ca.* 10% of the vegetation. Currant and Jacobi (2001) have allocated the Gough's Cave mammal fauna as the "type-assemblage" for the Late-glacial period. However, these authors note that there is a quite marked regionalisation in terms of the mammal species that are recorded during this period, with elk and mammoth exhibiting a northern distribution, steppe Pika, a temperate grassland mammal found in modern day Russia and Kazakhstan, occurs at Creswell Crags, Derbyshire, whilst red deer is well represented in southwestern Britain (*ibid.*: 1713).

The Gough's Cave fauna is considered to be representative of the Late-glacial (or Windermere Interstadial) and perhaps all of the Loch Lomond Stadial, with the radiocarbon dating indicating that this assemblage spans the period *ca.* 12,900–9900 ¹⁴C years ago (Currant and Jacobi 2001). The species that are represented in this assemblage zone include red deer, reindeer, aurochs, saiga antelope, wild horse (which dominates the assemblage), lynx, brown bear, red and arctic fox, wolf (although according to Stringer 2006: 209), these small animals are now considered to represent the earliest evidence for domestication, as these are actually dog bones), voles and lemmings, and arctic hare (Currant and Jacobi 2001: 1713–4). Stringer (2006: 209) notes that in addition to the exploitation of small mammals, birds such as black grouse, ptarmigan and partridge were being consumed when they were available. The environment at Gough's cave would have been similar to the conditions evidenced at Llanilid, and the faunal data at Cheddar suggests a combination of treeless moorland on top of the Mendips, with bushy scrub downhill, with possibly a narrow zone of trees on south facing slopes and in the sheltered valleys such as the Gorge (Stringer 2006: 210). In a similar manner to the landscape context at Creswell Crags in Derbyshire, the Cheddar Gorge provided and ideal location for hunter-gatherers in the Late-glacial.

As will be evident from the above discussion, the precise boundaries for each of the stadial/interstadial events differ slightly depending on the source being quoted, the location being studied, and the dating methods being used. A recent summary of the Late-glacial sequence as presented by Bell and Walker (2005) has the changing environmental conditions of the Late-glacial listed as; Older Dryas (Dimlington) stadial (up to 13,000 cal BC), the Bølling Oscillation (13,000–12,500 cal BC), the Older Dryas (Windermere) stadial (12,500–12,000 cal BC), the Allerød Oscillation (between 12,000–10,500 cal BC) and the final cold stage, the Younger Dryas (10,500–10,000 cal BC). The generic sequence is the same, but again, differences in approach mean that the timing of the boundary events differ slightly (Walker *et al.* 1994: 110; Saville and Ballin 2009: 37).

As outlined below, the fine-grained resolution of the warming and cooling events at the end of the Devensian is probably more complicated than this simple outline would imply. However, it is not until after *ca.* 10,200 BP that there is a progressive and sustained increase in temperature as we move into the current interglacial period, the Holocene, when birch, pine and hazel woodlands gradually re-colonise Britain. In recent years our attempts at understanding the nature of the changes occurring in the period immediately preceding the Holocene have been enhanced by sites such as Gransmoor in Yorkshire (Walker *et al.* 1993; Sheldrick *et al.* 1997; Dinnin 1995), and Llanilid, Mid Glamorgan (Walker *et al.* 2003), and with the integration of the evidence contained in ice cores recovered from the summit of the Greenland ice sheet (Mayle *et al.* 1999; Taylor *et al.* 1997). This evidence has shown that the transition from the preceding cold period (the Devensian) took *ca.* 1500 years, and occurred between 11,700 and 10,200 uncal BP (*ibid.*: 825). However, Taylor *et al.* (1997) have also shown that the high resolution data demonstrate that the shift to temperatures equivalent to our current interglacial took only 40 years to occur, albeit in short increments across a 200 year period in the earlier part of the Younger Dryas.

In general, there is a discrepancy in the evidence for the Late-glacial environmental changes as there appears to be a "lag effect" between the beetle evidence, the pollen data and geomorphological indicators (David 2007: 18), although as David notes, it is generally accepted that the beetle evidence provides the more realistic estimates for temperatures across this period due to their rapid re-colonisation when compared to the vegetation, and as a consequence, fauna (see e.g. Coope 1994; 2004; Coope and Brophy 1972). However, it should also be noted that the chironomid (non-biting midges) record (from Whitrig Bog, southeast Scotland) matches the ice core data even more closely than the beetle record (Brooks and Birks 2000). The data from this site indicates that although technically not a cold stage, the temperatures in evidence across the Late-glacial interstadial were only a maximum of 12.7°C, and that in general temperatures were below this across the interstadial, with four brief cold oscillations in evidence, and with temperatures falling from *ca.* 11.2°C to *ca.* 7.5°C at the onset of the Younger Dryas (Brooks and Birks 2000: 762). In general, the insect data indicate that at *ca.* 12,000 BP average temperatures were not too dissimilar to those of today, but that in the Loch Lomond (Younger Dryas) Stadial there is a return to glacial conditions, with minimum winter temperatures reaching *ca.* –25°C, and summer temperatures of only 9–10°C at their maximum (Coope and Brophy 1972).

Hunter-gatherers in the Late-glacial environment

Tolan-Smith (2003) outlined what he saw as three phases of human presence in Britain across the Late-glacial and early post-glacial (Holocene) periods. An initial phase of colonisation began around 12,500 BP, when human groups moved into lowland areas of central, southern and eastern England, whilst a second phase of immigration occurred during the Loch Lomond Stadial (Dryas III) and the Pre-Boreal (Pollen Zone IV), *ca.* 11,000–9000 BP (*ibid.*: 120-2). In this "consolidation" stage of colonisation (Tolan-Smith 2003: 122), the majority of England northwards up to a line extending from Newcastle in the east to Seascale on the west coast, and in the southwest of England to a point roughly between Bude on the north coast and Plymouth on the south coast, and all of Wales, have evidence for human occupation (Fig. 1.7).

The hunter-gatherer groups that entered Britain in the Late-glacial appear to have exploited the upland margins of western and central areas, along with major river catchment systems, which Nick Barton notes would have increased the resource spectrum available for exploitation at this time (Barton *et al.* 2003 Barton 2009). In addition, it is likely that river valleys may well have provided relatively easy access routes from the coast to inland areas, whilst also ensuring that early hunter-fisher-forager groups would have access to a broad range of reliable food resources and fresh water for drinking, cooking and washing. To date there is no evidence for a human presence in Ireland in the Late Upper Palaeolithic period.

Recent re-evaluation of the radiocarbon record for the Late-glacial re-colonisation of northern Europe (Housley *et al.* 1997: 43) has indicated that the majority of the evidence from cut marked bone occurs around 12,500–12,300 years ago, with an earlier date of *ca.* 12,800 years ago for the deer metapodial from Gough's Cave. Cut marks on the human remains from Gough's Cave have recently been examined by Bello *et al.* (2011), who have suggested that in three cases, skilled post-mortem processing of the head, with a high incidence of cut marks and the completeness of the vaults, could be indicative of their preparation for use as skull cups. Similar evidence for the preparation of skulls for use as skull-cups has been reported for two Magdalenian sites in France (*ibid.*). These authors also note that whilst there is evidence for skull-cup production, this is also accompanied by good evidence to suggest that the processing of the skeleton included the preparation of

Fig. 1.7: Map showing Tolan-Smith's second phase of recolonisation of the British Isles, which he dates to ca. 11,000–9000 uncal BP (redrawn by author from Tolan-Smith 2003: 121, fig. 7.2).

the cadavers for the consumption of body tissues and bone marrow (cannibalism), as the processing of the humans is the same as the animals at Gough's Cave (Bello *et al.* 2011). The warmer conditions of the Windermere Interstadial would appear to have proved favourable for human groups who migrated back into Britain at this time. Interestingly, Housley *et al.* (1997: 45) viewed the earlier date from Gough's Cave (12,800 ^{14}C years ago) as indicating pioneer re-colonisation by small specialised task groups, whilst the second phase of activity (12,500–12,300 ^{14}C years ago) was considered in terms of a more "semi-permanent" or residential camp phase of activity, although this was convincingly disputed by Blockley *et al.* (2000). In general, the available evidence after *ca.* 12,700 years ago indicates an increase in site visibility, with *ca.* >25 (and possibly as many as 35) find spots (both cave and open air sites) that have Creswellian activity in evidence (Barton *et al.* 2003).

The Creswellian is a stone tool industry, named after the "type-sites" at Creswell Crags in Derbyshire, and typified by the Gough's Cave assemblage in Cheddar, which include objects such as Cheddar points, scrapers, burins and piercers, and different forms of blades, but lacking the microlithic backed bladelets that typify Late Magdalenian industries on the continent around the North Sea Basin (for a summary see Barton *et al.* 2003: 633–4 and David 2007: 22–53). Interestingly, these authors disagree with the suggested phased re-colonisation advocated by Housley *et al.* (1997), arguing that from *ca.* 15,300–12,900 years ago there is direct evidence for a human presence, that was probably stimulated by improving climatic conditions towards the end of the Devensian cold stage (up to *ca.* 15,000 years ago). The data presented by Barton *et al.* (2003: fig. 1) show that human remains, artefacts of bone, antler and ivory, and modified animal bone indicates continuity in human activity across the period *ca.* 15,700–10,700 cal BP (the start and end of this range may be artificially extended by the ranges in the dating), and that, as mentioned below, there appears to be an hiatus in activity at the time of the final cold stage, the Loch Lomond (Younger Dryas) stadial event, although occasional finds in Eastern England do attest a limited human presence at this time (David 2007: 25).

In Wales there are a number of cave sites in the north and southwest that have produced evidence for human activity and subsistence activities at this time. Amongst these sites are the locations of Pontnewydd, Cefn and Cae Gronw in the Elwy valley, Clwyd, Kendrick's Cave at Great Orme's Head, North Wales, Little Hoyle in a tributary of the Retic near Tenby, Pembrokeshire, Potter's Cave, Nanna's Cave, Ogof yr Ychen and Daylight Rock, Caldey Island, the Coygan and Cathole Caves, Carmarthen Bay, Gower (Green 1986; David 1991, 2007: 22–53).

At Little Hoyle (Green 1986: 39–40), investigations outside the entrance to the cave have produced a Creswellian penknife point and a large flint blade, from a context containing pollen and fauna consistent with a Late-glacial context, wherein fox, bear, reindeer, collared lemming and hare existed alongside humans in a treeless tundra environment. As noted above, at the Hoyle's Mouth (David 2007: 44–50) has shown that a number of flint artefacts and the associated fauna's indicate both early to mid-Devensian and Late-glacial activity at this site (Fig. 1.6 above), with the Creswellian pieces at this site all having parallel's in the Gough's cave lithic inventory. David (1990: 148) noted that despite continued excavations at The Hoyle over a number of years, his research indicated that only 361 chipped stone artefacts could be accounted for from this location, with 52 of these finds representing tools of Late-glacial type. The close typological similarities between these sites, indicates that a date of *ca.* 12,800–12,000 BP can be assigned to the Welsh Late-glacial material (*ibid.*: 51).

Kendrick's Cave, Llandudno, Conwy, dated to *ca.* 13,500 years ago has finds that include a decorated horse jaw, the earliest example of portable art in Wales, along with human remains that indicate the presence of three adults and a child, and also nine decorated *Bos* and red deer teeth. David (2007: 20) reports that the age of the decorated horse mandible is 10,000±200 BP (OxA-111), which calibrates to 10,620–8,860 cal BC. In addition, David and Walker (2004: 299) note that Aldhouse Green (2000) has obtained a radiocarbon determination on a decorated bovid molar that calibrates to 11,000–10,160 calBC. Recent stable isotope analysis of three human individuals (including a child), a *Bos*/Bison and Roe Deer from Kendrick's Cave (Richards *et al.* 2005: 392) have suggested that the $\delta^{13}C$ ratios indicate that *ca.* 30% of the dietary proteins consumed by the individuals buried at this site was derived from marine protein. In addition, the $\delta^{15}N$ ratios indicate that terrestrial herbivores and marine mammals would have contributed the majority of the dietary proteins consumed. It should be noted though that the protein from plants is not readily identifiable with this method so these resources are underrepresented in this type of analysis.

At Gough's Cave, (Somerset) there is evidence for the making of pointed awls fabricated from the leg bones of arctic hare (*Lupus timidus*), and dates of 12,800±170 BP (13,800–12,300 cal BC) to 11,900±140 BP (12,100–11,450 cal BC) have been obtained from humanly modified horse and red deer bones, along with bones of mammoth and Bos/bison, at this location (David 2007: table 2.5). Important evidence for the techniques of bone point manufacture is also in evidence at Gough's Cave, where the groove and splinter technique has been identified. This is a technique that continues into the post-glacial period at Star Carr in the Vale of Pickering. Richards *et al.* (2000) have analysed human and faunal material from both Gough's Cave and Sun Hole Cave in the Mendips region and note that the dietary proteins appear to come from terrestrial herbivores, primarily red deer, bovines and possibly reindeer, with no indication of marine proteins in the diet. A recent re-assessment of the diet of these individuals (Stevens *et al.* 2010) has broadly confirmed the observations of Richards *et al.* (2000) in that the analysis of additional faunal samples (32 new analyses) from sites of a similar age to Gough's Cave has shown that the Sun Hole humans consumed red deer and bovines, and on first viewing it was concluded that the Gough's Cave individuals did appear to have consumed reindeer as their main prey (as observed by Richards *et al.* 2000).

Some modification of this latter observation is made in that it is considered more likely (Stevens *et al.* 2010: 59) that the human isotope signatures are in reality reflecting trophic level offsets for both $\delta^{13}C$ and $\delta^{15}N$, with red deer and bovines considered as the more likely prey species (and primary protein source) being exploited by three of the Gough's Cave individuals, and horse and red deer being exploited by the fourth individual from this site. Interestingly, in the context of exploitation strategies and the focus on a limited range of species, Jacobi (1987: 165) notes that Aveline's Hole in North Somerset was perhaps used as a "task-site" for the dismembering of horse and red deer during the

Late-glacial, between *ca.* 13,000–12,000 years ago. The significance of these observations is that variability in food consumption patterns is seen to be occurring during the Late-glacial period in Britain.

Mention must be made here of the exceptional finds made at Creswell Crags, Derbyshire, in particular the discovery of parietal art (images on walls or ceilings) in Church Hole cave on the 14 April 2003 (Bahn and Pettitt 2009: 1; Pettitt *et al.* 2007). Prior to this discovery, the engraving of a horse head made on a rib bone found in Robin Hood's cave in July 1876 by the Revd John Magens Mello (Bahn and Pettitt 2009: 9) (Fig. 1.8) was probably the most significant find of art from Britain, although the horse mandible from Kendrick's Cave in North Wales, decorated with an incised geometric pattern, also warrants mention.

The dating of the new discoveries (Pike *et al.* 2009: 92–3) using uranium-series disequilibrium dating on flowstones (created as water containing calcium carbonate in solution flows over the cave walls), have shown that the minimum age for the art, which has been covered over by thin flowstone deposits in some places, indicates that in Church Hole cave the age is greater than 12,630 years ago for "notches" in the wall, whilst the females/birds in this cave are more than 12,800 years old; in Robin Hood cave the "vulva" is more than 7320 years old. The dates obtained by Pike *et al.* (2009) are consistent with the dates obtained on humanly-modified arctic hare bones found with stone artefacts in Robin Hood, Church Hole and Pin Hole caves where calibrated radiocarbon ages between 15,700–13,200 BP have been obtained (*ibid.*: 93), and they are also consistent with the dates from Gough's cave in Cheddar.

Amongst the species depicted on the walls at Creswell are bison (Fig. 1.9), deer, horse and a number of birds (including an ibis?, a species unknown in Northern Europe at this time), in addition there are a number of incised geometric lines and drawings on the walls of the caves at Creswell Crags (Pettitt *et al.* 2007). Also see Yalden (2007: table 5.1) for a list of dated Late-glacial mammal finds from the UK. Amongst the species identified and dated are, woolly mammoth, giant Irish elk, reindeer, wild horse (tarpan), mountain hare, saiga, arctic fox, lynx, brown bear, wolf, elk, red deer and aurochs, indicating a mix of open ground and wooded environments during the Late-glacial.

Fig. 1.8: Horse head engraving on rib bone from Robin Hood's Cave, Creswell Crags, Derbyshire (©Trustees of the British Museum).

If we accept the reasoning put forward by Housley *et al.* (1997) that Late-glacial hunters followed animal communities, and chose locations with topographical advantages for hunting of prey, i.e. as at Cheddar Gorge or Creswell Crags, the hunters were (logically) following direct as opposed to random movements through the landscape (1997: 48–9). In addition, Aldhouse-Green (2000a: 11) has noted that there is evidence to suggest that Late Upper Palaeolithic hunters appear to have favoured spring and autumn hunting when animals formed large herds and migrated between upland/lowland pastures. Amongst the sites that Aldhouse-Green lists as possible intercept sites are Lanishen, Monmouthshire, Gwernvale, New Radnor and the Breiddin, Powys (*ibid.*). The exploitation of animals in herds has a logistic element, as herds migrate in a systematic manner, the more vulnerable or weaker herd members can be identified and targeted by the hunter, and at a simple level hitting an individual target is much more difficult than hitting a large group of animals that form the (much larger) target.

Finally, before considering the social aspects of hunter-gatherer lifeways during the Palaeolithic period, the observations made by Barton *et al.* (2003: 633) are relevant in summing up the end of the Late-glacial and the transition to the Holocene period in Britain, at around 11,500 years ago, in that these authors report "a clear hiatus between Late-glacial and post-glacial dates for a human presence ... which broadly can be equated to the Loch Lomond (Younger Dryas) chronozone, and the earliest part of the Holocene", although lithic traditions do appear to span this chronological transition.

Fig 1.9: Engraving of bison from Church Hole Cave at Creswell Crags (© British Cave Art Research Team: used with permission).

This position reflects the fact that across the final stages of the Upper Palaeolithic two phases of human activity are in evidence. The first of these stages is characterised by lithic assemblages that exhibit curve-backed points and blades, and the "Penknife" point which is a curved-backed blade with basal retouch, the appearance of which, as noted by Barton (1999: 24) coincides with the beginning of the forested part of the Late-glacial Interstadial, which is dated to *ca.* 12,000–11,000 uncal BP (the Allerød). There is increasing evidence for a human presence in the final cold stage of the Late-glacial, between *ca.* 11,000–10,000 uncal BP, and although rare, the Kendrick's Cave fauna has produced 11 pierced and incised red deer and bovid teeth, one of which is dated to 10,580±100 BP (OxA-4573), and calibrated to 10,900–10,200 cal BC, alongside the incised roe deer metapodia mentioned above (Pettitt 2008: 48). Although, it is possible that the red and roe deer artefacts represent imported personal possessions, as red and roe deer would be unusual species in the landscape at the height of the Loch Lomond cold stage. Again, as noted for earlier periods, Pettitt (2008) suggests that the evidence does not support anything more than intermittent seasonal forays by small hunting groups, and the typological similarities between the British material from the 28 known sites, and contemporary Ahrensburgian groups on the continent, might provide an indication of the origins of the hunting groups.

Social aspects of Pleistocene life

The archaeological evidence for the majority of the Pleistocene period is relatively sparse in Britain as a whole (although see discussion in White *et al.* 2006), but when coupled with the European evidence we are able to draw some important observations in relation to hominin and early modern human activity across the period *ca.* 900,000–10,200 years ago. In Wales and England the available evidence appears to indicate intermittent hominin activity in the landscape during both the colder and warmer phases of global climate change, although Stringer (2006) notes that between *ca.* 200,000 and 60,000 years ago, Britain was "abandoned". Sites such as Happisburgh 3 and West Runton (Norfolk) and Pakefield (Suffolk) apparently demonstrate the ability of early hominins to exploit the differing environments at the southern edge of the Boreal zone at a very early date (Parfitt *et al.* 2010; Coope 2006). The finds of sturgeon, pike and carp bones from Happisburgh (possibly at *ca.* 970,000–814,000 years ago, although see discussion above) might provide a very early indication for the opportunistic exploitation of these species in the Palaeolithic period. At Boxgrove (MIS 13: *ca.* 500,000 years ago) the available evidence indicates that *Homo heidelbergensis* crouched down to produce their stone tools and butchered animals such as giant deer, red deer, bison, horse and rhinoceros. This evidence indicates that these people had primary access to large game animals during the Middle Pleistocene (Stringer 2006).

Early hominins, certainly by the earlier Middle Palaeolithic period, appear to have been creating complex clusters of sites within a cultural landscape that may have influenced socially-embedded routine activities, and which coalesced to enhance social cohesion (White *et al.* 2006: 537). It is suggested that these hominins moved between upland flint procurement sites and lowland hunting grounds, and the differences in the artefacts discarded at various locations in the landscape suggest different taskscapes and resource procurement patterns. The problem that we face with this emphasis on "hunting grounds" is that, in general, we have extremely limited evidence for the plant portion of prehistoric diets, especially prior to the Holocene period. In general the fact that bone survives well in the archaeological record means that many earlier researchers placed and emphasis on meat as a resource when reconstructing past subsistence activities. White and Pettitt (2011: 72–3) discuss the lithic evidence for the Middle Palaeolithic in relation to hunting strategies, suggesting that:

> the technological organisation suggests a degree of planning, a versatile butchery kit being transported around the open landscape to counter the difficulties of predicting the distribution of mobile (animal) resources, and the possible spatial differentiation between (known) flint sources and the locations in which tools would be needed. (*ibid.*: 73)

Despite the above observations, it is unlikely that early hominins subsisted on meat alone, as there is an upper limit to the amount of meat that can be consumed. Research by Speth (1989; 1990) and Speth and Spielman (1983) has shown that meat protein alone would be insufficient in providing the range of nutrition required by human groups. As such, although meat consumption was clearly a very significant part of Palaeolithic diets, we need to remember that other resources would be required to ensure that an adequate diet was consumed. In this context it is worth noting that there is some (admittedly limited) evidence to suggest the consumption of plant foods by the earliest hominins, *Australopithecus afarensis*, from south Africa; although recent dietary studies on Neanderthals and Palaeolithic modern humans (*Homo sapiens sapiens*) appear to suggest that their diets were often similar to high level carnivores (Richards 2002). However, the main point of note here is that whilst the evidence appears to support meat-based diets, the samples analysed are limited in number, and given the nature of the environments that these individuals were exploiting, it seems unlikely that they did not experiment with different foods, even if these were initially just a few berries or even some herbs to flavour a meat dish! Given that during the Middle Palaeolithic period Neanderthals mainly used Britain as a summer hunting ground (White and Pettitt 2011: 53), it is probable that there were at least some edible plant species available for exploitation. It should also be remembered that plants and fish resources could have acted as "starvation foods" during periods of meat shortage, and the seasonal integration of these resources into hominin diets could lead to their gradual adoption as staple resources. One further point of note is that the stable isotope analysis of human diet places an emphasis on dietary proteins, due to the use of bone collagen in the analysis, and as such there is an inherent bias against the identification of the plant-based portion of the diet in studies that use this technique.

Furthermore, analysis of the plant macro-fossil remains from the site of Dolní Věstonice II in the Czech Republic, an early Gravettian site dated by analysis of a triple burial to 26,640±110 BP (Formicola *et al.* 2001), and also by dating of a hearth feature (Hearth D) to 26,390±270 BP (Mason *et al.* 1994), adds to the evidence from sites such as Klisoura Cave (Koumouzelis *et al.* 2001), Franchthi Cave in Greece and Mezhirich in Ukraine, in suggesting that root foods may have been exploited by the people that occupied these settlements.

Mason *et al.* (1994: 52) suggest that the fleshy root tissue of Asteraceae/Compositae found at Dolní Věstonice II may represent the remains of food discarded in the fire or material dropped accidentally during food preparation, along with material that may constitute a plant food "mush" that may have been processed to feed children. The problem is that plant foods only survive under certain extreme conditions such as charring, waterlogging, freezing or extreme aridity. Hearths are notoriously rare in British pre-Holocene contexts as they were usually constructed on the land surface (a similar situation pertains to the Mesolithic period as well), and as such they were prone to the vagaries of reworking and erosion. Cave deposits excepted, the nature of the glacial-interglacial cycles in Britain, and the peri-glacial environments that persisted through much of the Pleistocene mean that only in exceptional circumstances will we be fortunate enough to find the plant portion of Palaeolithic diets; however, this does not mean that we do not need to keep looking.

One further complicating factor, not really considered by many researchers to date, is how social necessities and obligations influenced human-landscape interactions in the past. Whilst it is easy to see the logistical structuring and technical organisation attested by the lithic evidence (White and Pettitt 2011), the role of children is ignored, as are the needs for group cohesion, and the role of women is still glossed over to some degree (Adovasio *et al.* 2007; Zihlman 1981). The general assumption is that man was the hunter, woman the gatherer, but reproductive success, and by extension group continuity and survival, was not simply predicated on meat procurement and consumption. The group dynamic provides numerous benefits, but within the group differing subsistence roles and the nature of social interactions, their mediation and articulation, would exert an influence on wider food procurement strategies, settlement patterning and the distances that a group could cover at certain times. The other option of course is that all of the evidence that we have for Palaeolithic activity in Britain is simply the result of men, hunting, away from the rest of the group, with no young or old individuals, no females or children and as such no restrictions on the areas that could be exploited; or of course that women went hunting and left the remainder of the group back at the base camp tending the fire!

In this context, whilst there were long periods during the Pleistocene when glaciers covered Scandinavia and the British isles, there are tantalising glimpses of hominin and early modern human activity in the landscape. Sites such as Happisburgh in Norfolk (*ca.* 970,000–814,000 years ago), and Pakefield in Suffolk (at *ca.* 700,000 years ago) demonstrate the fact that the environment was sufficiently attractive to warrant exploitation by early hominins. As with later interglacial periods the activities of these early individuals resulted in the production of activity sites or foci of activity, and at Happisburgh this activity occurred in the upper estuarine zone of the Thames, when the environment would not have looked too dissimilar to more northern latitudes in the present, with conifer forests of pine and spruce, areas of heathland, and stands of deciduous woodland in evidence. The river at this location was slow-flowing and flanked by reed swamp, alder carr, marshy areas and pools. The average summer temperatures of 16–18°C and winter temperatures of 0 to -3°C are not too dissimilar to those that we have experienced in recent years. These small groups of hunters and gatherers exploited the rich riparian environments, hunted the large herbivores that roamed in the grasslands, catching the fish that swam in the river, and perhaps swimming in the river themselves, gathered the fruits, berries, seeds and roots of the plants that grew in the vicinity of the site, perhaps told stories around the fire, and cared for their young in order to ensure group continuity. The evidence can seem idyllic, and in many respects the landscapes that were exploited would have had this element to them, but we must also recall that for much of the Pleistocene the early hominins were not at the top of the food chain, but were prey to large carnivores and they often scavenged for food; their existence could realistically have been hard, short-lived and traumatic.

Unfortunately, as the above discussion has highlighted, the successive glacial periods mean that there are significant gaps in the evidence for human exploitation of the environment in northern Europe, as hominin groups retreated to southerly regions away from the ice sheets at the height of glaciation (glacial refugia) along with the plants and animals that were not cold adapted. However, this does not mean to say earlier human groups were not able to cope with the colder environments of a glacial period. The evidence from Pontnewydd cave attests that there were milder periods during the glacials. As outlined above, Pontnewydd represents one of the few MIS 8–7 sites from Britain, but the *direct* presence of hominin activity at this time suggests that the cold stages of this glacial period were not so severe as to preclude a human presence, and that the subsequent warming associated with the Aveley interglacial allowed for a relatively rapid return of both humans and animals to Britain at this time. This observation is supported by the identification of an open air campsite in the lower Thames Valley at Baker's Hole, Northfleet, Kent, and other sites at South Woodford, Redbridge and Red Barns near Porchester (Darvill 2010: 37–9). Pontnewydd is also important as it provides evidence for the environment through analysis of the contemporary fauna, which is suggestive of open steppe like environments at *ca.* 225,000 years ago. In addition, there are butchery marks on a number of the horse and bear bones from this site which provide a direct link to the Neanderthal occupation and subsistence activities.

The evidence for humans in the landscape after Pontnewydd was occupied is lacking, and in general we only have faunal evidence between MIS 5e and *ca.* 40,000 years ago (Currant 1986). The evidence from Paviland Cave has proven to be of considerable importance in allowing us further insights into human activity during the Palaeolithic period, but there is no way to adequately "fill-in" the significant gaps in the evidence for a human presence prior to this. Paviland is an extremely significant site due to the occurrence of the "Red Lady" burial, which is a male *ca.* 25–30 years old, and the inclusion of grave goods, in the form of worked bone and ivory, with this interment. This burial, which is dated to *ca.* 34,050–33,260 cal BP has been analysed in order to determine the nature of the diet of this individual, with the analysis indicating that he probably consumed a diet in which the majority of the protein was from animals, but that *ca.* 10–20% of the protein component of the diet was from marine resources, and that plant proteins were perhaps not significant (Richards 2000, with the caveats outlined above). Other aspects of this burial that are worth considering relate to the fact that not only did people take the trouble to undertake a ceremony around the burial, but as is seen elsewhere in Europe during the Palaeolithic period, the inclusion of ochre and grave goods suggest that the individuals that were burying this individual may have had a sense of otherness, perhaps even a belief in the afterlife, and that death was not the end. We can only speculate on the significance of the structuring of interments at sites such as Paviland, but as will be outlined later in this volume, a belief in the spirit world and also a belief in an afterlife pervade the anthropological and ethnographic literature for hunter-gatherer groups around the globe.

Jacobi and Higham (2008: 898) note that at the time that Paviland cave was being used by humans during the later Pleistocene, the cave would have looked out over a grassy plain, and that the modern islands of Flat Holm, Steep Holm, Lundy, and Caldey would have been landlocked hills. There has been some discussion in relation to the activity at Paviland, with Jacobi and Higham (2008: 902), noting that that the suggestion has being forwarded that this site may have acted as a "special" or "unusual-place" over a period of about 5000 years (e.g. Aldhouse-Green and Pettitt 1998: 765). The succession visits were initially marked by the burial of the young adult male, the loss of whom to a small hunting and gathering group would have been very significant, as not only would this individual have been a son, partner, even father, but he would also have presumably been a hunter and provider for the members of the group. Whether the successive visits to the cave down to 21,000 ^{14}C yrs BP were made because of an embedded group memory of this individual, or whether the location became a persistent place for other reasons, it is apparent that Paviland was a significant place for the human groups exploiting the region of Wales during the Upper Palaeolithic period.

Similarly, the evidence from sites such as Gough's cave, Cheddar Gorge in Somerset adds to the record from caves, and open air sites, such as Hengistbury Head, located *ca.* 5 miles (*ca.* 8km) east of Bournemouth in Dorset, demonstrate that during the Late-glacial period human groups were exploiting both cave and open air locations. At this time they were operating with a developed stone tool (Creswellian), bone and antler technology, with evidence for the exploitation of horse, red deer, bear, arctic hare and aurochs. Gough's cave also has evidence for the production of pointed awls made from the leg bones of arctic hare, and bone needles have been found at a number of sites, including Gough's Cave, Kent's Cavern in Devon and Church Hole, Creswell. It is probable that arctic hare would have provided excellent furs for the production of clothes, and alongside the fact that they would have provided meat (albeit very lean meat), their bones were also used to produce the tools to prepare and sew the garments.

The above glimpses that we have had into the Palaeolithic past are sparse but illuminating, however, it is not until the later Upper Palaeolithic period that we get significant insights into the human condition through burials, such as those at Sungir in Russia (at *ca.* 25,000 years ago), or Dolní Věstonice in the Czech Republic (Formicola *et al.* 2001); or the exceptional cave paintings at sites like Lascaux, in the Dordogne, Chauvet Cave in the Ardèche region of southern France, or Altamira in Spain (at *ca.* 17,500–15,000 years ago); alongside the development of the complex tool kits that characterise the Aurignacian and Gravettian cultures across the period *ca.* <30,000 through to *ca.* 17,000 years ago. Similarly, it is not until the terminal Palaeolithic period that we have evidence for increased dietary breadth (Stiner *et al.* 2000). This is the period when modern humans, and many of the traits that we consider as "human", become more visible in the archaeological record. The period after *ca.* 40,000 years ago effectively provides the foundations for the subsequent Late-glacial and Mesolithic periods, although it is of course possible that any earlier art and ritual expression are less visible to us due to the vagaries of time. However, the available evidence suggests that by 40,000 years ago human groups have begun to exploit a wider range of environments, and there is evidence to suggest a different mindset in relation to human experience, with art (both portable and parietal) signifying an abstract expression of human thought. The exceptional burials of this period perhaps suggest that these humans had a concept of an afterlife, or that in death the individual did not "cease to exist". Paviland is important in this respect as the burial and the repeated subsequent visits might suggest a much deeper link to the ancestors and their memory than we might envisage for humans at this earlier date.

The Late-glacial evidence, from the sites in Wales, and Creswell and Cheddar in England (amongst others, and including Kilmelfort Cave, Argyll, Scotland (Saville and Ballin 2009)) indicates that human groups are now adept at all aspects of hunting-fishing and foraging in a wide range of environments. The tool-kits are complex, and the range of plant and animal species being exploited throughout Europe indicate that a broad spectrum subsistence strategy is being employed (Stiner *et al.* 2000; Richards *et al.* 2001).

Important evidence from the settlement sites of Meiendorf and Stellmoor in northern Germany (Grønnow 1985; Weinstock 2000; Street *et al.* 2002) has shown that during the Late-glacial, reindeer hunting was undertaken by the groups using these locations, and that the kill/butchery activities occurred as a series of discrete events at these base camps. Street *et al.* (2002, *after* Bratlund 1991) present an image showing the areas of the reindeer skeletons where impact damage from arrows was recorded (shown by embedded flint points in the bones) (Fig. 1.10).

Of interest in this context is the reanalysis undertaken by Grønnow (1985: 142). This work suggests that the animals found at Stellmoor represent the result of seasonal hunting activities (probably towards the late summer/autumn migrations), and the sorting of the more nutritionally rich animals from the poorer quality animals (such as calves and subadults), with the poorer quality animals being discarded. Grønnow (1985) suggests that this sort of activity usually occurs after a mass kill event, where more animals are killed than can realistically be processed and consumed by the hunters. Further selection in relation to nutritional quality is evidenced in the discarding of the front quarters of the animals, with a preference for the haunches and rear elements. Meat drying probably took place, and there is evidence of splitting of the bones for marrow. The remains from the processing of the animals were dumped into the lake at Stellmoor, probably in order to ensure that carrion feeding insects did not infest the location; but it may also be relevant that the ethnographic record suggests that the animals themselves would not return to an area where the rotting carcasses of other reindeer were left exposed (*ibid.*: 144). One final observation in relation to this site is the caching of raw antler blanks in the lake, this observation is important as it is likely that these items were being stored for future processing into harpoon points for use in fishing activities (Grønnow 1985: 147). In the British context, the technique used

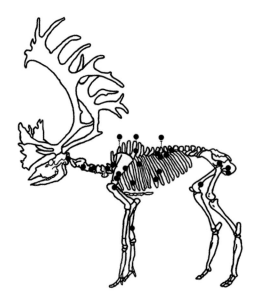

Fig 1.10: Locations of embedded fragments of flint arrowheads on the skeletal remains of reindeer from the Late-glacial site at Stellmoor, Germany (redrawn by author from Street et al. 2002).

in the manufacture of barbed antler points (the groove and splinter technique) is similar at the Late-glacial site of Gough's Cave to the techniques that are in evidence at Star Carr in the subsequent Mesolithic period.

In addition, the use of the bow and arrow is also in evidence from a Late-glacial date in Ukraine, at three sites, Voloshkoe, Vasilyevka I and III, in the Dnieper Rapids region (Lillie 2004). Interestingly, these sites are cemeteries that are dated to *ca.* 10,400–9200 cal BC (Jacobs 1993), and they have evidence for violent conflict, with a number of individuals having been killed by impact damage from arrows (Nuzhinyi 1989; 1990; 1993; Balakin and Nuzhinyi 1995). This evidence might suggest that as human groups are expanding their resource base, preferred locations such as the rapids along the Dnieper, where fish can be easily caught, are now considered to be important locations in the hunting territory of discrete groups. These are amongst the new "persistent places", where reliable resources such as fish are now worth fighting for, the ancestors are being buried, and in all probability seasonal aggregations of hunter-fisher-forager groups, perhaps extended family or groups with differing allegiances, meet to trade and exchange information, goods, marriage partners and to interact socially.

The end of the Palaeolithic is marked by the abrupt shift from the changing environmental conditions of the Late-glacial to the onset of more stable, sustained warm conditions as we enter the next interglacial stage, the Holocene period. It is this period, or rather the first 6,000 years or so of it, that form the basis of the remainder of this volume.

Note

1   Marine Isotope Stages are based on the early work of Cesare Emiliani who based his research on the analysis on the carbonate shells or tests of marine microorganisms from deep ocean cores, the composition of which was used to determine warm-cold ocean conditions in the past (Stringer 2006: 55–8). Using 16oxygen and 18oxygen ratios, Emiliani identified seven cold stages in Caribbean cores and fifteen in Pacific cores. The sequence starts at the top with current warm period (MIS 1) and goes back through alternating warm-cold cycles, with warm periods denoted by odd numbers and cold periods denoted by even numbers (*ibid.*). Subsequent work determined that the ice caps were important in determining the 16O/18O ratios in marine microorganisms as at times of extensive ice cover 18O ratios are higher as isotopically light (16O-rich) water is held in glaciers where it has fallen as rain, hail or snow. See Stringer (2006) for a more detailed summary of the development of this area of study.

2

THE VIEW FROM THE HILLS: SEA LEVEL RISE, POST-GLACIAL CLIMATE CHANGE, LANDSCAPE CHANGE AND CHANGING ENVIRONMENTS

The tem landscape is a generic term for the expression of particular ways of seeing the world ... the concept of landscape embraces much more widely applicable themes about relationships between people, the realm of ideas and values, and the worlds they have created for themselves to live in... (Darvill 1999: 104)

Our current perception of the Mesolithic masks important variation in the organisation of post-glacial hunter-gatherer communities, and obscures continuity between the Mesolithic and Neolithic ... (Marek Zvelebil 2008: 58)

Prologue

In archaeological terms the Mesolithic marks the start of the current interglacial, the Holocene (or Flandrian) period. Throughout this, and subsequent periods, sea levels were rising as glacial meltwaters were added to the world's oceans and seas. The Mesolithic period spans the Pre-Boreal to Atlantic periods (from *ca.* 10,200 uncal BP or *ca.* 9900 cal BC through to *ca.* 3800 cal BC) (Table 2.1), and as such extends for well over five millennia. As will be outlined in detail below, this period saw considerable changes in the vegetation cover of Wales as warmth-loving species re-colonised the British landmass after the retreat of the glaciers (as discussed above). During this period the vegetation cover changed from open grassland habitats, comprising varying percentages of grasses, herbs and mosses, to the more closed canopy deciduous woodlands that would characterise the later Mesolithic period. In coastal areas the environmental changes would have been dynamic as sea level rise resulted in changes to the wetland–dryland interface, especially in areas of subdued topography such as Cardigan Bay. As a consequence of these vegetation changes the hunter-fisher-forager groups that exploited this environment had to adapt not only to a seasonally variable biomass, but to a biomass that was more dispersed, and less easily exploited (especially in the case of the large meat animals such as red and roe deer). As a consequence it is thought that food procurement strategies generally necessitated a degree of mobility on the part of human groups during this period.

Table 2.1: Generalised biostratigraphic sub-division of the Holocene (Flandrian) in England and Wales (after Simmons and Tooley 1981; Goudie 1996; Evans 1975; Roberts 1991). Note: the scheme of Blytt and Sernander is based on vegetation change, as opposed to climate change. (See Appendix for correlation between uncal BP and cal BC ages).

Blytt-Sernander	Godwin pollen zonation	Vegetation development	Inferred climate	Radiocarbon years uncal BP	Archaeological period
Pre-Boreal	IV	Birch-Pine-Juniper-Willow	cool/dry	10,200–9500	Mesolithic
	V	Birch-Pine-Hazel Hazel-Pine-Oak-	warm/dry		
Boreal	VIa	Elm-Lime		9500–7000	
	VIb	Alder			
	VIc	Pine-Hazel-Lime			
Atlantic		Elm			
	VIIa	Oak-Elm-Alder Elm Decline	warm/wet	7000–5000 (3800 cal BC)	Neolithic
Sub-Boreal	VIIb	Oak-Alder	warm/dry	5000–2500	Bronze Age–Iron Age
Sub-Atlantic	VIII	Alder-Grasses	cool/wet	post-2500 to present	Iron Age–present

The vegetation changes were characterised by an initial colonisation of species such as birch, pine, juniper and willow during the Pre-Boreal period (Godwin's 1940b; 1975) pollen zone IV (PZIV)), when the climate was characterised by cool and dry conditions. This re-colonisation resulted in a vegetation mosaic comprising areas of woodland and more open grassland patches in the landscape during the earlier part of the Mesolithic. In the more open areas the grasses were available for browsing ungulates to exploit, and these areas would have provided Mesolithic hunters with environments that were probably more familiar to them than the developing deciduous woodlands. As temperatures continued to rise, hazel colonised during the warm and dry conditions that characterised PZV, in the second half of the Pre-Boreal. The archaeological evidence appears to indicate that this species was of some significance to Mesolithic groups, perhaps helping to off-set the difficulties inherent in hunting endeavours in the developing woodland landscape. Finds from the islands of Islay and Colonsay, in the Hebrides, have suggested that intensive collecting, referred to as harvesting by Steve Mithen (1999a; 2001: 233), was undertaken by some (if not all) of these Mesolithic groups.

During the subsequent Boreal period (Godwin's PZVI), oak, elm and lime are added to the mosaic forest cover throughout the British Isles as the warm dry conditions prevail. As is evident elsewhere in northwest Europe, the continued colonisation of tree species led to the formation of relatively dense mixed oak forest, a consequence of which was the shading-out of understorey species and grasses (e.g. Karsten 2004: 72). By contrast, Jacobi (1980, cited by David 2007: 189) has suggested that as lime would have been less dominant in Wales than in areas further east, understorey species may have been better able to compete, perhaps resulting in a greater density of browsers in Wales. In general, by the Late Mesolithic, there is evidence for the expansion of woodland up to heights of *ca.* 500m AOD throughout Wales.

As we move into the Atlantic period the climate becomes increasingly warm and wet. It is during this stage that the deciduous woodlands reached their maximum extent, presumably making movement through the landscape more difficult for Mesolithic human groups at this time. Alder increases in frequency in many pollen diagrams during this period (see below), but as might be anticipated there is considerable variability in the composition of the woodlands, depending on factors such as location, soil type, altitude and aspect etc. The dense woodlands would perhaps have restricted access to inland locations limiting movement to routes that followed river and stream valleys, or established pathways. As a consequence, coastal areas may have become more attractive to settlement as the woodlands expanded, and restrictions to movement and less predictable returns from hunting endeavours may have also necessitated the exploitation of a wider range of ecological niches (*ibid.*: 72). In light of these observations, it is clearly important that we understand the nature of landscape developments across the Mesolithic period in order to interpret the strategies used by human groups in these changing environments. As such, this chapter will outline the evidence for landscape and vegetation change throughout the Mesolithic period, and it will endeavour to set these changes in the context of human-landscape interactions and the development of Mesolithic society at this time.

Introduction

It is often easy to forget that, throughout much of the Mesolithic period *ca.* 10,200 to 5000 uncal BP (*ca.* 9900–3800 cal BC (Tolan-Smith 2008; Bell 2007)), hunter-fisher-forager groups were effectively able to walk across the North Sea Basin (occasional river crossings excepted), into what is now Britain (Fig. 1.1). This was possible because the basin was in fact a dryland plain wherein the Dogger, Leman and Ower banks would have been raised areas (Sheenan and Andrews 2000). In her speculative survey of what she termed "Doggerland" Bryony Coles (1998) reminds us that finds such as the antler harpoon, dredged up from the sea bed by the fishing trawler "Colinda", between the Leman and Ower banks in 1931, attest to this fact. Furthermore, it should be noted that *ca.* 500 early Mesolithic barbed bone and antler points have been recovered by fishing boats from the Eurogeul-Maasvlakte area of the Netherlands, and earlier, Middle Palaeolithic handaxes have been dredged up off the East Anglian coast at Great Yarmouth (Peeters *et al.* 2009). However, despite the fact that we know that these submerged landscapes preserve peat deposits, often dredged up as "lumps" of material by trawlers, and termed "*moorlog*", very few palynological investigations have been carried out in order to determine Late-glacial and Holocene vegetational changes and successional processes using material cored from the bed of the North Sea, with the focus instead being placed on the use of these peat horizons for dating Holocene sea level changes (Wolders *et al.* 2010: 1707).

This situation persists despite the fact that these deposits can be found at depths as shallow as *ca.* 33m below current sea level, and that they hold the potential to provide important insights into patterns of peat formation and mire development under the influence of rapid sea level rise. They also offer the potential to assess changes in natural resources against the background of sustained land loss, as the peats studied by Wolders *et al.* were shown to date to the Boreal period between *ca.* 10,700 and 9350 cal BP (*ibid.*: 1708, 1710). Furthermore, Wenban-Smith (2002: 13) notes that:

> it has been suggested (e.g. Clark 1954; Coles 1998) that the North Sea Basin was the heartland of the Early Mesolithic way of life [which was] based on the exploitation of rich coastal regions, and a rich archipelagic environment combining littoral marine and terrestrial resources.

These observations are of considerable interest given the consideration of hunter-fisher-forager landscape perceptions and resource use discussed below.

As emphasised in Chapter 1, for much of the past 0.7 million years or so, we have evidence which indicates that the dominant tendency was for sea levels that were much lower than at present, such that Britain should simply be viewed as the northwestern extent (effectively a peninsula) of the European landmass, and not as an island, right up until the end of the Mesolithic period. As discussed in Chapter 1, Tolan-Smith (2003) has suggested that there are three discrete phases of settlement in Britain across the Late-glacial, and into the Holocene period. Of interest in this section is the hypothesised re-colonisation event that occurs *ca.* 9000–7000 uncal BP (*ca.* 8250–5900 cal BC), when the rapid expansion of human groups throughout the British mainland and large areas of Ireland, is attested (*ibid.*). According to Tolan-Smith, the significance of this rapid expansion lies in the "social context in which groups had learned what the newly encountered landscapes had to offer [having] developed a pattern of socio-economic organisation capable of responding to opportunities the landscapes presented" (2003: 125). As this was a time when significant restructuring of both the landscape, environment and concomitantly the available flora and fauna is occurring, the established knowledge may have been in need of continual "relearning" as familiar landscapes were in a constant state of flux in the first few centuries, and even the first millennium, of the Holocene period. We will return to these ideas at the end of this chapter when considering the nature of landscape change and human-landscape interactions in the earlier part of the Holocene period.

In Wales, in the southern and western areas, at locations such as Borth Beach, Ceredigion, Abermawr, Pembrokeshire, Goldcliff in the Severn Estuary and at various other locations around the coast of Britain, the "submerged forests" exposed at low tide attest the different environments and greater land areas that existed in "coastal regions" (see Bell 2007a: figs 1.1 and table CD 1.2). In some of these areas, such as Cardigan Bay and the Bristol Channel, large areas of land were exposed during periods of lowered sea level, and there is little doubt that these landscapes were exploited by hunter-fisher-forager groups in the earlier Holocene (after *ca.* 10,200 years ago). Jones (2002: 9) reports that around the Welsh coast notable locations where submerged peat beds occur include the Severn Estuary (e.g. Goldcliff), Carmarthen Bay, Cardigan and Llandudno. Sea levels were rising quite rapidly at the start of the Holocene period, such that Lynch *et al.* (2000: 26) have suggested that by *ca.* 9100 uncal BP (*ca.* 8300 cal BC), sea level may have been around −35m OD. As such, Figure 1.1 provides an indication of the possible land area that would have been exposed at the start of the Holocene, at *ca.* 10,200 uncal BP (*ca.* 10,000–9900 cal BC), whilst Figure 2.1 would allow us to picture the potential amount of land lost by *ca.* 9100 uncal BP. Bell (2007e: 320) has reported that the Lower Submerged Forest was growing from 6179–5826±19 cal BC (not allowing for missing sapwood), and that the evidence indicates that this was not a single inundation event but a series of events occurring over one or two centuries.

Intercalated marine and peat deposits attest subsequent phases of transgression and regression, with a second regression episode that is dated to *ca.* 5500 cal BC (second peat), indicating significant phases of variability in relative sea level tendencies in the Caldicot Levels area (*ibid.*: 320; Allen 2005). The rapid rates of sea level rise slow down in the later Mesolithic, as attested by peat formation that occurs at *ca.* 5000 cal BC (third peat) and by an Upper peat which is dated to 4600–4000 cal BC (Bell 1999; 2007e; Allen 2005), although periodic positive and negative sea level tendencies (again often referred to as transgressions and regressions) occur across the later Mesolithic period (discussed below). At this point it is worth noting that Weerts (2013: 149) argues that archaeologists and historians are slow to recognise that geologists have abandoned the terms transgression and regression in favour of the terms "retrogradation" and "progradation" respectively, as the interplay between factors such as tidal range, sediment budgets, and accommodation spaces, etc. all influence the process of land "gain" or land loses in the earlier part of the Holocene, and these factors are very specific to the local and regional level around the North Sea Basin. Importantly, it has been estimated that earlier Holocene rates of sea level rise may have been in the region of 16mm/year (from *ca.* 9000 uncal BP), decreasing to *ca.* 8.5 mm/year by *ca.* 6600 uncal BP (Jennings *et al.* 1998: 175; Bell 2000: 19). This inundation has resulted in the accretion of up to 15m of fine-grained minerogenic sediments and peat in estuarine and coastal areas (Bell 2007a: 4).

For clarity it should be noted that the contours used in Figures 1.1 and 2.1 are actually based on current bathymetry for the area around the British landmass, and as such, they do not take into account the finer detail inherent at the local/regional level around the coast, and in the North Sea Basin. Despite this observation, the point is that Britain, far from being an island, has simply been an area at the north-westernmost extent of the European landmass throughout large portions of both the Pleistocene and into the Holocene (particularly for about the first 4000–6000 years of the last 12,000–10,000 years or so). As such, the "view from the hills" portion of the title to this chapter is not only a reference to the uplands of Wales, but also to those of the North Sea plain, where, from the top of the Dogger Bank, the changing landscapes of the earlier Holocene would have been a very visible and at times potentially an awe inspiring phenomenon to witness (Chapman and Lillie 2004). Similarly, in terms of human–landscape interactions and the perception

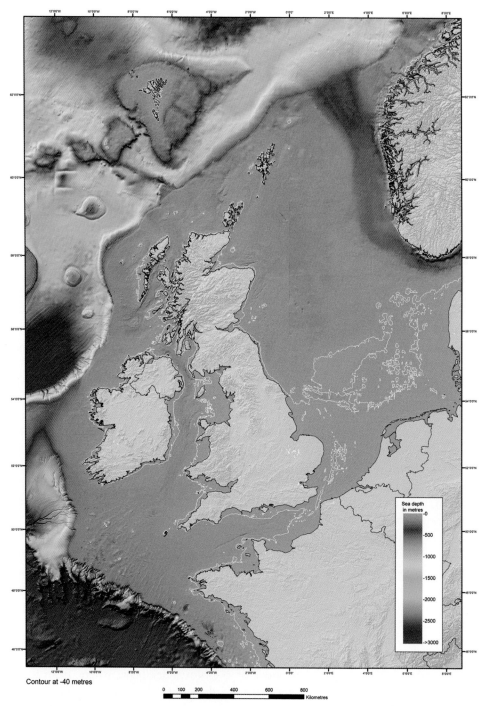

Fig. 2.1: Map showing land exposed in the North Sea Basin and around the Welsh coast when sea levels were at –40m OD (marked by white lines). © Author, WAERC, University of Hull.

of the landscape, as the open landscapes of the earlier Holocene were colonised by the deciduous forest species discussed below, it would only be in certain locations, such as river valley floodplains, coastal and upland areas, or clearings (whether natural or anthropogenic in origin), that Mesolithic people would have been able to experience the more extensive views that we are so used to in our modern arable dominated countryside, and which they themselves would have been used to in the open steppe-tundra landscapes of northwestern and central areas of Europe during the Palaeolithic period.

In witnessing these landscape changes the hunter-fisher-forager populations of the Mesolithic period would most likely also have recognised the fact that significant areas of coastline, to the northern fringes of the North Sea Plain and around the coast of Wales, along with the rich riparian environments, wetland areas and differing topographic and vegetated locations that existed in these areas, were being modified and/or lost as sea levels rose. It is precisely these areas that offered Mesolithic hunter-fisher-foragers access to a diverse range of resources, which in northwest temperate Europe would have been characterised by marked seasonality.

As the coastal and riverine areas provided relatively easy routes by which to travel, the changes outlined above would have the potential to disrupt the natural rhythms of daily life for hunter-fisher-forager groups. Furthermore, these landscape shifts could potentially have had a significant impact on the subsistence activities and landscape perceptions of Mesolithic groups in the initial stages of the Holocene. The transient nature of this landscape may have been particularly marked at the time of the tsunami event that was caused by the Storegga slide off western Norway at *ca.* 6200–6100 cal BC (Bondevik *et al.* 1997; 2005; Weninger *et al.* 2008), for, as these authors note, at *ca.* 6100 cal BC sea levels were potentially between *ca.* 10–15m lower than they are today, and as such, the effective height of this tsunami event, as indicated by the Shetland evidence, would have been in the region of *ca.* 20m (*ibid.*).

When we consider the devastating impacts of tsunami events such as those in Indonesia (2008) and Japan (2011), and the earthquakes that preceded these, we can begin to identify with Mesolithic people in a more intimate fashion, as the stress and trauma we feel at seeing these events today would, no doubt, be mirrored in the past. Of course, due to the lower population densities the effects, in terms of loss of life, "property" and "infrastructure" that would have impacted upon Mesolithic hunter-fisher-forager groups would probably have been significantly less than experienced in the present. However, we must always remember that any loss of life could, and would, have a significant impact on the small close-knit family or extended family groups of perhaps 20–50 hunter-fisher-foragers at a time when a skilled hunter, a knowledgeable elder, a parent or child, all contributed to the success of the clan or group in their own way. One other factor to consider is the fact that in the present, mass media and the internet ensure that information and knowledge are widely available, during the Mesolithic period the cause of a tsunami would have been unknown and probably unknowable, and the attribution of cause may well have been placed in the spiritual realm or the realm of the gods. We can only guess at the impacts that such events would have had on Mesolithic peoples in Britain at the time.

As sea levels rose, the loss of coastal areas would have been marked along the Welsh coast, especially in the west where the Cardigan Bay area would have been an expanse of low plain flanked by the limestone ridge that currently demarcates parts of the modern coastline. In this region, Davies (1989) has noted that many of the caves that are currently inaccessible due to higher sea levels, would have provided excellent vantage points for the hunter-fisher-forager groups that exploited coastal areas of Wales during the Mesolithic period. The presence of these earlier Holocene hunter-fisher-foragers is attested at sites such as Ogof Garreg Hir where human and animal remains, including those from red deer, roe deer, wolf, pig, hare, fox and several species of bird are all attested, along with artefacts such as a narrow backed bladelet and a bone awl (Jacobi 1980) (Fig. 2.2).

As might be anticipated, in some instances the landscape losses could have severely restricted seasonal activities as movement through the landscape would, in certain locations, become more difficult or constrained. Furthermore, as low-lying areas were progressively inundated, the vegetation structure from dryland to wetland and the inter-tidal zone, along with the hunting grounds associated with these environments would change, as would the movement of animals through the landscape. This variation would be associated with changes in the dominant vegetation, which would also impact on foraging zones as these were modified in response to inundation. The myriad changes brought about by rising sea levels are difficult to conceive of given our current perception of sea level as a *relatively* stable phenomenon, although future sea level change may well modify our understanding of such changes and their impacts.

As the above observations indicate, the situation in the North Sea Basin would have been replicated at other locations around the coast. Rising sea levels, across the Mesolithic period, significantly altered the coastal landscape of Wales, whilst also submerging the hunting, fishing and foraging zones exploited by human groups in the northwestern fringes of Europe. As with the issues related to our "visualisation" of the glaciated landscapes of the Pleistocene period, it is difficult for us to picture these transformations or to conceive of the impact that such changes may have had on the landscape perceptions of the hunter-gatherer groups at this time, especially as the nature and rate of change is difficult for us to determine archaeologically (Chapman and Lillie 2004). Also, as we no longer subsist as hunter-fisher-foragers such habitat losses have less meaning in an environment where the majority of the "wild" has been given over to the domesticated. However, archaeologists, conscious of the need to enhance public awareness of the past have, in addition to the earlier work undertaken by Bryony Coles, undertaken more complex studies using new virtual media in an attempt refine our attempts at visualising the changing nature of both Doggerland (Gaffney 2011) and the submerged landscapes of the Bristol Channel and Liverpool Bay (Dyfed Archaeological Trust 2011) across the earlier Holocene. This latter project has demonstrated the existence of both Palaeolithic and Mesolithic features in these areas, and identified Holocene coastlines, channels with infill sequences, areas of raised topography, basin structures, floodplains and peat/organic floodplain deposits. In the Bristol Channel area the project also identified two large lake basin features and long sinuous rivers flowing out towards the contemporary coastline (Fitch and Gaffney 2011).

Fig. 2.2: Map showing location of key cave sites with evidence for Mesolithic material (either human, faunal or material culture) in Wales. 1 – Ogof Garreg Hir, 2 – Potter's Cave , Caldey Island, 3 – Daylight Rock Cave, Small Ord Point, Caldey Island, 4 – Worms Head, South Gower, 5 – Paviland Cave, Gower, 6 – Foxhole Cave, 7 – Pontnewydd Cave, St Asaph (north Wales).

There is little doubt that these locations would have provided rich and varied vegetational environments and a broad range of resources for exploitation by Mesolithic groups during the earlier Holocene period, despite the rapidly rising sea levels at this time.

Recent research into the mapping and characterisation of "Doggerland", under the auspices of the Shotton River Project (Ch'ng *et al.* 2004), has sought to recreate the Mesolithic activity occurring in the area now covered by the North Sea using "Virtual Reality". Using seismic datasets and visualisation technology the project has identified a large river valley *ca.* 600m wide and observed over a *ca.* 27.5km length of the sea bed which is thought to date to *ca.* 10,000–7000 years ago. By using analogies to recent dwellings found in Northumberland and Dundar, Ch'ng *et al.* have attempted to reconstruct the vegetation, dwellings and general environmental setting of Mesolithic activity in the vicinity of the "Shotton" River (2004). Whilst certain aspects of the modelling were clearly problematic in a British Mesolithic context the attempts to animate the campfire with particle smoke and the integration of bird noises and other effects such a fog etc. highlight an important limiting factor in our attempts to reconstruct the past, this being, that whatever our evidence, we need to remember that the past was not a static place, hunter-fisher-foragers would have seen, smelt, tasted, heard and touched their environment, and experienced the myriad changes that occurred as sea levels rose and the vegetation of post-glacial Britain developed across the Mesolithic period. The fact that vegetation changes were asynchronous across the landscape, both between lowland and upland and between north, south, east and west, and even between different catchments within these areas, means that significant vegetational zonation would have occurred, and the plants and animals that were available for exploitation varied spatially and temporally throughout the Mesolithic period due to factors such as climate, altitude, migration rates etc. As is emphasised below, Mesolithic people experienced a very dynamic environment as the current interglacial developed after the removal of the ice sheets.

Furthermore, we must always be aware of the fact that whilst the addition of significant amounts of glacial meltwater to the world's oceans caused increased sea level rise throughout the Mesolithic period (and indeed this sea level rise continued until the later prehistoric period), there are also a number of other waterbodies in evidence in the earlier Holocene landscape. These features are often remnants of the earlier glaciated landscapes, which occurred in the form of pro-glacial lakes, such as Lake Flixton in the Vale of Pickering, Cefn Gwernffrw in Mid Wales (Chambers 1982), Llyn Cororion in North Wales (Watkins *et al.* 2007), or Craig-y-Fro in the Brecon Beacons (Walker 1982a). These remnant waterbodies would have created "micro-environments" where wetland species (faunal and floral) would have offered rich environments for hunter-fisher-foragers to exploit during the Mesolithic.

It should also be noted that, whilst sea levels were rising due to the addition of glacial meltwaters, the removal of the ice sheets results in a concomitant rise in the level of the land (glacio-isostatic rebound) as the weight of the ice diminishes (Bailey and Flemming 2008). These changes result in a complex interplay of sea level rise and isostatic rebound across the Holocene, and also settlement of the landmass to the south of the ice sheets; and to some degree it could be suggested that the modern shape of the British coastline did not even begin to form until the latter part of the Mesolithic period as some degree of slowing occurred in the rates of rebound. One other point of note is that throughout the last *ca.* 10,000 years or so there are periods where sea levels rise and flood low-lying areas (transgressive episodes/positive tendencies), and periods when sea level rise slows, or even effectively retreats (regressive episodes/negative tendencies) (Roberts *et al.* 2011: 147). The changing sea level tendencies result in the varying deposition of minerogenic sediments (in the form of saltmarsh silts or clay-silt alluvium and under higher flow regimes, sands) and the accumulation of peats as the environments shift between marine, brackish, freshwater and terrestrial conditions (Scaife 1994; Waller 1994).

Finally, alongside the rising sea levels, temperatures were also rising during the earlier Holocene (Simmons *et al.* 1981: 90), with a (conservative) mean warming rate calculated at *ca.* 1°C per century being inferred from the marine records (Bell and Walker 2005: 88); although it should be noted that the evidence from the ice core and insect data suggest that very rapid warming occurs at the beginning of the Holocene, and apart from the 8200 uncal BP event (marked by colder conditions), there is only relatively minor variation thereafter (Alley 2000a; van Asch *et al.* 2012; see also Ashworth 1973). As noted above, this changing climate is accompanied by the re-colonisation of the landscape by temperate vegetation and faunal species as the environment becomes more similar to that of today. Again though, we should remember that the rate of spread and composition of the flora is controlled by additional factors such as soil type, slope aspect and altitude, and the specific ecological characteristics of the species that migrate into Britain at this time.

So, when we evaluate the vegetation in evidence during the Mesolithic period, it is also worth considering the nature of the sites that we have available to us for reconstructing the landscape. Site location (i.e. coastal, riverine, wetland, lowland, upland), slope aspect (e.g. north, east, west or south facing), degree of saturation and soil type (i.e. heavy clay [e.g. till], free-draining sandy loam, alluvial, etc.) will all exert an influence on the type of vegetation that is established, and this in turn will influence the continued development of that vegetation and the ease with which humans would have been able to modify the environment. These factors will become important when we consider the nature of the changing vegetation and forest development during the Mesolithic as we assess the palaeoenvironmental evidence for the landscapes of Wales, and human–landscape interactions, during this period.

In turn, a wide range of conditions related to each of the above factors will also influence the nature of the associated fauna in the landscapes of the Mesolithic. As such, some regions will have a high carrying capacity in terms of the biomass available for exploitation by hunter-fisher-forager groups whilst others might be considered less attractive, depending on the range and seasonality of the resources available. We should also consider the fact that the hunter-fisher-forager groups themselves will have a direct impact on the landscape either through their gathering activities, wherein some species may be over-exploited due to seasonal availability and lack of species diversity, or through the deliberate manipulation of the environment. This latter aspect will be considered below in greater detail, but the evidence from sites such as Star Carr in the Vale of Pickering, Yorkshire (Mellars and Dark

1998) and Waun Fignen Felin in the Black Mountains of South Wales (Smith and Cloutman 1988), vividly highlights the *potential* for deliberate human interference in terms of firing (vegetation burning) episodes during the Mesolithic. The purposes of this burning have been suggested as being related to a "promotional strategy to increase productivity of nut and fruit trees and shrubs, wetland plants, and possibly native grasses" (Zvelebil 1994: 35), as elements of hunting strategies, or other land management strategies (Simmons 1996; Walker *et al.* 2006).

Nicholas (2007a: 54–5, citing Ross 1999: 283) has noted that the Spokane of northwestern North America regularly burned tule and cattail patches after harvesting, as this was a practice that improved both the yield and quality of future growth. As discussed below, there is a significant body of evidence to support the use of firing episodes as a management tool by Mesolithic peoples, but in many cases the evidence is circumstantial. However, as will be suggested in Chapter 4, the opening up of the landscape through firing activities may also have had a more profound rationale during this period, and whatever the reason or more likely, reasons, for this activity, we should again remember that it is not only farmers that can manage the landscape in order to enhance the productivity and reliability of the resource base.

Finally, when we evaluate the evidence presented throughout this volume the reader is encouraged to consider the various factors that the people of the Mesolithic would have experienced whilst exploiting the landscapes of Wales; for instance, while a hunting camp, by definition, might have a purely functional use, the person/s using the site could also choose their location for a range of aesthetic considerations, alongside the inherent functionality. For example, if we decide on a fishing spot we will often choose our location for a range of attributes, e.g. sun/shade, views, ease of access, familiarity, peacefulness/ tranquillity and even for the sounds of running water or bird song, in addition to the fact that it is potentially a good fishing spot. Hunter-fisher-foragers in the Mesolithic were probably similar to us in their aesthetic appreciation of their landscape and environmental setting, and this could, no doubt, have influenced their decision making processes; they did not simply react to their environment, for as noted above, they saw it, heard it, smelt it, touched it and even tasted it, it is important that we remember this when we attempt to reconstruct the past.

Sea level rise and post-glacial landscape change

As noted by Lambeck and Chappell (2010: 679), "sea level change during the Quaternary is primarily a consequence of the cyclic growth and decay of ice sheets", although the reality is that most of the available data for sea level change actually relates to the period after the last deglaciation, i.e. the Late-glacial to Holocene periods as opposed to the Quaternary in general. During the earlier Holocene sea levels rose at a relatively rapid rate (e.g. Heyworth and Kidson 1982) as the water that was released from the melting glaciers in the northern hemisphere fed into the oceans, and over the past 7000 years or so there has been a relatively consistent, albeit punctuated, rise in sea level (Lambeck and Chappell

2010). In general the rise in sea levels from the earlier Holocene continued until around 4000 years ago when relative sea level had reached an altitude that was either equal to, or greater than, levels that occur today (Edwards 2006: 576).

However, as mentioned above, it should also be remembered that the removal of the weight of the ice has resulted in a rebound of the landmass, with a hinge line running roughly from the Severn to Humber Estuaries. The rebound effect has resulted in the occurrence of raised beaches in Scotland, which date to the Mesolithic period, and as the northern and western parts of Britain rise up, the southern and eastern areas are slowly being lowered. Sea level rise during the Holocene is offset to some degree by this rebound in northern and western Britain, of course, the opposite effect occurs to the south of the "hinge points", but in effect, there is a complex interplay of variables across both temporal and spatial scales of analysis (Bell and Walker 2005: 116–23; Weerts 2013). Furthermore, as noted by Bryony Coles (1998), and as hinted to above, we should remember that using modern bathymetry when mapping former coastlines fails to account for the influence of such processes, and whilst the contour maps created may well provide a good general impression of the situation in the past, the finer resolution is lost.

Similarly, it is easy to forget that amongst the impacts of the postglacial sea level rise was a dramatic loss of land in areas such as the North Sea Basin, which was not just a lowland area, it was an area characterised by streams, rivers and estuaries and a range of productive vegetation zones from "upland" to lowland in which an equally productive range of animals, fish and birds would have been exploited (Clarke 1978). The vegetation of "Doggerland" would have included mixed birch and pine woodland with willow, alder, hazel and juniper, and as noted by Coles (1998: 63) the distribution and density of woodland areas would have varied depending on the specific landscape attributes of a given location (as outlined above). However, in addition to the observations made by Coles (1988) it should also be noted that in recent times, debate into the density of the early Holocene forest canopy and the nature and extent of animal (and human) impacts has been on-going (Vera 2002; Zvelebil 2003a; Buckland 2005; Fyfe 2006). Vera (2002: 13) has hypothesised that in reality Holocene landscapes would have looked more like "parks" than closed forests, as a number of species, such as oak and hazel, "do not naturally rejuvenate in forest reserves in the lowlands of central and western Europe". Vera has suggested that these light demanding species are better suited to regeneration in more open terrain, grazed by large herbivores such as deer and aurochs, especially where thorny or unappetising species of shrubs form copse that acts as a barrier to grazing ungulates (*ibid.*: 13), and that as such, it is possible that large herbivores were fundamental to phases of forest regeneration and the maintenance of open areas through natural grazing pressures. In this model, open areas are not simply created by minor disturbances such a tree-throws, but in actual fact herbivores are the dominant driving force in maintaining open areas, at least from the later Mesolithic onwards (Buckland 2005: 57). The problem is of course that there are no absolute data in relation to the spatial scales of Vera's hypothesised park-like landscapes (Kirby 2003; Hodder *et al.* 2005), although it is perhaps sufficient here to realise that the closed-woodlands or *Urwald* (Buckland 2002) of the Mesolithic should not simply be viewed as dense and foreboding environments. Bell (2007b: 322) has highlighted two significant weaknesses in Vera's hypothesis in that grazers would have been spatially restricted in their distribution, and that grazers are not the only factor influencing environmental disturbances. In addition to the above, debate also continues in relation to the extent that woodlands provided numerous elements essential to everyday life in the Mesolithic, such as plant and animal food, the natural resources for use in construction and tool production, medicinal herbs and fundamentally, fuel for fires; the difficulties lie in the nature of the evidence that is available for use in interpretations. And, in addition to the fundamentals, as Graeme Warren (2003: 22) has noted, woodlands are an integral part of the natural world, a world that would have been engaged with in both practical and ritualised ways, often with both activities being intertwined so that Mesolithic people could come to terms with and experience the world around them.

It is probable that during the Mesolithic, by *ca.* 6900 cal BC forests may have been more uniform, and comprised of mixed hazel dominated, oak, elm, lime and alder woodland (Coles 1998). As noted above, vivid examples of the inundation of coastal woodlands as sea levels rose during the earlier Holocene occur at locations such as Borth, to the south of the Dyfi Estuary (Fig. 2.3) (dated to 5106±48 uncal BP: GU-715 (Bell 2007: 11)), which calibrates to 4030–3785 cal BC at 2σ. This date has been refined by the work of

Fig. 2.3: View south across the Dyfi Estuary from Aberdovey; Ynyslas and Borth (not visible) are to the right of the picture on the south side of the estuary. © author.

Nigel Nayling, using denrochronology, to 4184–3981 cal BC (Nayling 2002: 28, section on Neolithic). Bell (2007: 3) in his introduction to the Holocene coastal sediments of Wales and adjacent areas, maps a total of 75 locations where intertidal peats and submerged forests are recorded. Interestingly the date obtained by Scaife (1994: 77) from the submerged forest at Caldicot Pill produced an assay of 5760±70 uncal BP (Beta-54827), 4780–4460 cal BC, which is comparable to dates obtained from locations such as Uskmouth and Goldcliff, which have produced ages of 5810±80 uncal BP (OxA-2628), calibrated to 4845–4465 cal BC, and 5850±80 uncal BP (CAR-658), calibrated to 4930–4520 cal BC, respectively (also Bell 2007: 36–47). However, despite the landscape and habitat losses that occurred as sea levels rose, as noted by Clarke (1978: 22–3), the loss of the riparian and coastal habitats may well have been offset by the creation of even more productive coastal shallows, replete with edible molluscs, crustacean and fish species.

Research in the Baltic and North Sea areas (Flemming 2004a; Fisher 2004; Grøn and Skaarup 2004; Bailey and Flemming 2008) has shown that submerged archaeological sites in shallow coastal areas comprise settlements (so far found down to *ca.* 16m below modern sea level), which were located near rivers, lakes and the sea shore, where fish weirs, log boats, midden (food refuse) sites, fire places, flintworking areas and even graves occur (Fisher 2004: 27). At Møllegabet II (southern Denmark), Grøn and Skaarup (2004: 54–6) recorded a Mesolithic dwelling structure along with the burial of a young adult male who was apparently placed inside a dugout canoe. The dwelling at this location was interpreted by the authors as a two-family structure (*ibid.*: 56).

As the above examples demonstrate, the potential of submerged archaeology to considerably enhance our understanding of past hunter-fisher-forager activity, especially given the possibilities for the preservation of organic remains, is considerable. This bias is worth remembering when we consider the nature of burial and ritual during the Mesolithic period (Chapter 5 below). Continued investigations in shallow coastal areas (such as Cardigan Bay) are clearly warranted in light of the exceptional results obtained from underwater sites in Danish coastal waters where >2000 sites have been recorded, and where, as noted by Bailey and Flemming (2008: 2160), their location can be predicted by identifying topographical conditions favourable for fishing camps and communal fish weirs.

In Wales, in general, and in the Severn Estuary and Cardigan Bay areas in particular, a number of palaeoenvironmental studies have been undertaken, and many of these have considered the environmental context of the sedimentary sequences in evidence. These studies use techniques such as pollen, ostracod and diatom analysis, alongside the radiocarbon dating of organic material, in order to produce an absolutely dated framework for the changing phases of marine and saltmarsh conditions, and freshwater and fen environments, and to track the gradual shifts in vegetation that occur between these environments (Scaife 1994; Scaife and Long 1994).

As might be anticipated in an environment as dynamic as the Severn Estuary, the analysis of these intertidal depositional sequences is fraught with difficulties, and a simple dichotomy wherein mineral deposit equals marine transgression and peat equals terrestrialising (regressive) conditions has been shown to ignore the finer detail of the transgressive/regressive tendencies that persisted throughout the Holocene (Bell 2001: 73). Factors influencing the viability of these studies, in both the present and the past, include those associated with the scouring and removal of unconsolidated surfaces (whether mineral sediment or peats), sediment compaction, the mixing of the pollen, diatoms and organics within these sequences, faunal mixing of soil profiles, the drying out and desiccation of exposed surfaces, different pollen sources, and differences in plant pollen productivity and dispersal mechanisms. Indeed, there may be other factors that need to be considered in this context, as the evidence from the human and animal footprints found in the intertidal zone attest (Scales 2007); both humans and animals may have been exploiting the environments in this zone for a variety of reasons (discussed below), and human gathering activities and grazing pressures from animals may impact on the vegetation in various ways. The recent discovery of human and animal footprints and possible evidence for structures in the form of a floor, timber stakes which would have been part of a wall, as well as flints and other utensils, all dated to the Later Mesolithic at *ca.* 5800 cal BC, at Lunt Meadows in Sefton near Merseyside (Liverpool Landscapes 2012) further reinforces the potential of the intertidal zone for significant discoveries and also emphasises the significance of this zone to Mesolithic groups (Cowell and Innes 1994, Leah *et al.* 1997). The possibility is that these remains are indicative of at least three structures, and along with the discovery of chert used in tool production, which is probably imported from sources in northeast Wales, Lund Meadows potentially expands the networks that Mesolithic hunter-fisher-foragers in Wales were engaged within.

One other issue that needs to be considered when undertaking work in the intertidal zone is, of course, the tides; due to the high tidal range in the Severn Estuary there were numerous occasions during field surveys undertaken when working for the Glamorgan-Gwent Archaeological Trust in the 1980s when we found ourselves wading through sticky intertidal muds as the tide lapped at our heels. For the few individuals amongst us who couldn't swim these were very exciting times indeed! As noted by Martin Bell during subsequent work in the Severn Estuary, one of the most frustrating aspects of intertidal archaeology is the ease with which the tide can redeposit sediment that has taken a team of archaeologists numerous hours of painstaking work to clean.

Additional factors to consider when looking at past sea level data relates to the specific context of the data points themselves, the datum point, termed Sea Level Index Points or SLIPs for short, are assumed to equate to a reference tide level of mean high water of spring tides (Scaife and Long 1994). The height of the sample point will only be accurate to *ca.* ±0.50m due to sediment compaction, assumed equivalence of spring tide high water levels, and the levelling in of the point itself (see also Shennan and Horton 2002; Edwards 2006). The optimum sampling points for use in determining past sea level heights are the previously mentioned transgressive and regressive contacts. As noted, there are some additional issues to consider in using these contacts, as erosion and scouring can have an influence on the heights of the contact points. Allen (2001: 18) also notes that sea level is in fact a variable water level "very high in or at the top of the tidal frame", and also that "tidal levels are affected as much by secular and long term changes as by the movement of mean sea level itself". Furthermore, spatial change can be of particular significance in an estuarine context *(ibid.)*.

Despite these limitations, Scaife and Long (1994) have shown that a reduction in marine environments (i.e. a regressive tendency) is occurring at *ca.* 5710–5480 cal BC (6666±80 uncal BP; Beta-79886), at Caldicot Pill in the Severn Estuary, at a time when sea level was at –9.18±0.5m below present sea level. Subsequently a transgressive contact at this location is dated to *ca.* 5475–5215 cal BC (6360±70 uncal BP; Beta-79887), when sea level was at –7.52±0.5m below present sea level. One further note of caution, as highlighted by Mike Reynier in his reconsideration of Thatham III in Berkshire (discussed below in Chapter 3), is the fact that the earlier Holocene radiocarbon timescale is compromised by the occurrence of a number of plateaux or compression events, which effectively result in periods of radiocarbon time where "time stands still" for a range of decades or even centuries, even up to *ca.* 400 calendar years. As a consequence, all radiocarbon determinations that fall within these "time" ranges can produce the same age (2000: 33). These events occur at 10,000 uncal BP (*ca.* 9655–9390 cal BC), 9600 uncal BP (*ca.* 9150–8840 cal BC) and 8700 uncal BP (*ca.* 7740–7610 cal BC) *(ibid.)*.

In addition, the "absolute" ages produced by radiocarbon dating of these deposits only provides a broad period (range) within which the dated event is likely to have occurred (at 2σ this is a 95% confidence interval). However, as the above date ranges demonstrate, these events, which in the case of a transgressive episode could easily have been a rapid phase of inundation, can only be considered over a *ca.* 340 year timescale when using the radiocarbon method. Whilst this is perfectly adequate for the construction of a generalised sea level curve, it is difficult to resolve when we are trying to gauge the nature of landscape changes and the responses of hunter-fisher-forager groups to these changes over a generation or so.

An important contribution to our understanding of sea level changes in the Bristol Channel and Cardigan Bay is the early work of Heyworth and Kidson (1982). These authors used data from 13 locations around the Welsh coast, along with 25 locations from the southwestern peninsula of England (Figure 2.4) to produce a modified sea level curve for southwest England and Wales. The curves for the Bristol Channel, Cardigan Bay and North Wales are presented in Figure 2.5 below. Recent research by Roberts *et al.* (2011) has added much needed resolution to the data from North Wales, and these data provide greater resolution in relation to the glacial isostatic adjustment (GIA) model for correlation to the British-Irish ice sheet data. This work has added a further ten new SLIPs and nine new limiting dates for the Devensian Late-glacial and early Holocene to the 12 existing SLIPs and one limiting point for North Wales. Whilst a number of limitations are highlighted by these authors, the stratigraphic data indicates that these points are derived from a series of conformable transitions between marine intertidal and terrestrial saltmarsh conditions *(ibid.*:147–52). The tidally corrected RSL data indicate initial breaching of the Menai Strait between 8.8 and 8.4ka BP to form a tidal causeway, with final submergence between 5.8 and 4.6ka BP (Roberts *et al.* 2011: 141). Prior to this breaching, there would have been a dry land connection between Anglesey and mainland North Wales (as it is now) *(ibid.*:153). According to Roberts *et al.* *(ibid.*:142) the North Wales data support the notion of a thick

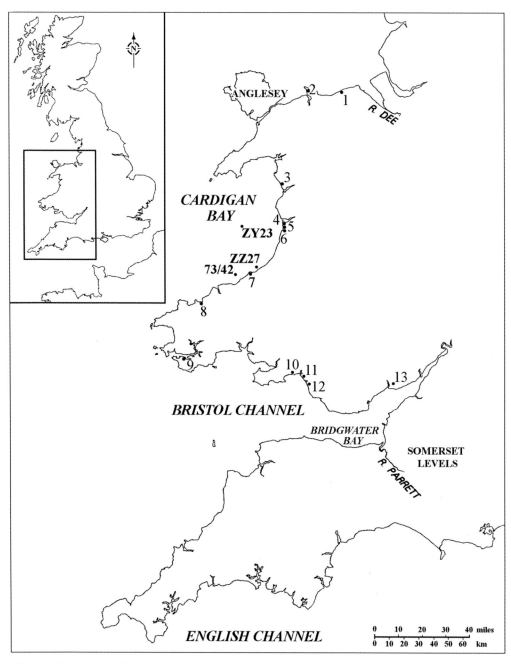

Fig. 2.4: Location map showing Welsh sites used by Heyworth and Kidson (1982) in their construction of sea level curves for southwest England and Wales. 1. Rhyl, 2. Llandudno, 3. Llanaber, 4. Ynyslas, 5. Borth, 6. Clarach, 7. Newquay, 8. Newport, 9. Freshwater West, 10, Swansea Bay, 11. Port Talbot, 12. Margam, 13. Llanwern. (redrawn by author from Heyworth and Kidson 1982: fig. 1). ZY23, ZZ27 and 73/42 are submarine boreholes studied by Haynes et al. (1977: 130), and these are discussed in text.

and extensive ice sheet over north and central Ireland and in the Irish Sea Basin with
rapid deglaciation after the LGM, and in addition, these authors observe that there is no
indication from the RSL curve for a Holocene highstand (*ibid.*: 152).

As is immediately apparent from Figure 2.5 (irrespective of the issues discussed above),
the rate of sea level rise in the earlier Mesolithic is considerable (as outlined above), and
is a factor that must have significantly influenced early Mesolithic human–landscape
interactions and exploitation strategies through to *ca.* 6000 uncal BP (*ca.* 4935–4845 cal BC)
when rates of rise are reducing (e.g. as recorded at Caldicot Pill (Scaife and Long 1994)).
Importantly, Hayworth and Kidson (1982: 102–3) also provide some information of the
context at Borth and Clarach Bay (5 and 6 on Figure 2.4). At Borth the deposits consist of
fen, alder carr and forest beds, which underlie the raised bog complex of Borth Bog (Cors
Fochno) (*ibid.*: 102). These sequences in turn all overlie saltmarsh clays at just below OD,
and the sequences also outcrop on the beach at Borth. The entire sequence was recorded

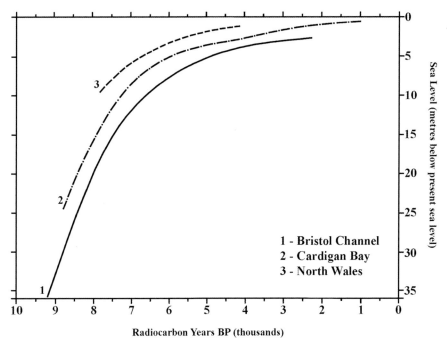

*Fig. 2.5: Sea level curves for the Bristol Channel, Cardigan Bay and north Wales as drawn by Heyworth and Kidson
(1982) on the basis of data from the points indicated in Figure 2.4. These authors noted that with the exception of
the north Wales data the separation between the Bristol Channel and Cardigan Bay curves related to the inherent
uncertainties in the data points and the use of MHWST and the common reference datum (redrawn by author from
Heyworth and Kidson 1982: fig. 5). Note: Allen (2000: 18) suggests that the work of Sheenan et al. (2000a), and
others, indicates that one of these curves (the Bristol Channel curve) may be too low by as much as "a few metres",
due to a lack of consideration of the impacts of sediment compaction on dated peat horizons, and the work of Scaife
and Long (1994: 83) at Caldicot Pill indicates that there is a ca. 1m discrepancy.*

for *ca.* 5km, between Borth and Ynyslas, rising *ca.* 2m in height from north to south (*ibid.*). At the northern end the oldest trees have been dated to *ca.* 5400 uncal BP (approximately 4330–4240 cal BC), i.e. towards the end of the Mesolithic, whilst at the southern end of the sequence the ages are placed towards the end of the Neolithic period at *ca.* 2400 cal BC.

Earlier ages have been obtained from the sequences at Clarach Bay, where a submerged forest bed can be traced from the coast, back up the narrow valley that enters the sea at this location. The infill sequences in this valley as recorded by Heyworth and Kitson are *ca.* 3.3m in thickness, and they have been shown, through diatom analysis, to have a sensitive response to fluctuating marine influence between 6000 and 1100 uncal BP, i.e from *ca.* 4930–4850 cal BC to cal AD 900–980 (Heyworth and Kidson 1982: 103).

Work by Heyworth *et al.* (1985) subsequently demonstrated the existence of Late-glacial to Holocene sequences centred on SN588830, with some suggestion that sedimentation may have been occurring at this location from at least *ca.* 13,600 uncal BP. Within these sequences, a peak in alder pollen is recorded at *ca.* 8875 uncal BP (*ca.* 8200–7960 cal BC), suggesting a local presence and hazel also expands after this time. By 5760 uncal BP (*ca.* 4680–4550 cal BC) alder and hazel are colonising the surface of a freshwater clay that began to form at *ca.* 6000 uncal BP. At *ca.* 6000 uncal BP (*ca.* 4930–4850 cal BC) alder carr became established at this location, and this persisted for the next *ca.* 3500 years. Around *ca.* 5400 uncal BP (*ca.* 4330–4240 cal BC) large oaks are growing at this location, but these are inundated by rising sea levels soon after this date (Heyworth *et al.* 1985: 471). The data recovered from Clarach reflects a complicated series of marine and freshwater influences on the local vegetation, but these authors have suggested that sea level rise is implicated as the underlying cause of peat accumulation at this location (*ibid.*: 479).

Previous work by Haynes *et al.* (1977) focused on three submarine cores from Cardigan Bay (Fig. 2.4); one from *ca.* 5km west of Aberaeron (Hydrocore ZZ27), one located 27km west of Aberystwyth (Vibracore ZY23), and the third was recovered from a location *ca.* 8km north of Aberporth (Borehole 73/42). The results of these analyses, in relation to the Holocene stratigraphy, provide important information in relation to relative sea level as in Hydrocore ZZ27 a thin well-humified brown–black freshwater peat horizon at −20.5m OD produced a radiocarbon date of 8740±110 uncal BP (*ca.* 8200–7590 cal BC). Whilst the accuracy of the absolute heights for the cores is put at ±1.5m, and the large error on the date results in a very broad time frame for this event, this information does generally provide a useful indication of the changes in relative sea level at this location, with relative sea level at this time being at *ca.* −22.6m OD (Haynes *et al.* 1977: 152). The sequences either side of this dated horizon also indicate variability in relation to marine transgressive and regressive tendencies. Foraminiferal faunas obtained from laminated clays and silts above the dated peat horizon in ZZ27 are analogous to modern low marsh (muddy tidal flats) species (i.e. the zone between MHW Neap and MHW Spring tides (*ibid.*: 134). The correlations of foraminiferal species are indicative of low marsh environments in the lower silts, and the correlations reduce as the analyses moves up through the borehole, indicating that between −20.5m OD and −19.00m OD the foraminiferal faunas are reflecting a gradual sea level transgression at this location.

The ostracod faunas from ZZ27 indicate that the sequences below the peat horizon are reflecting brackish water estuarine environments, whilst those above the peat, in the laminated clay-silts reflect initially marine and then brackish conditions, with brackish environments dominating the sequence (Haynes *et al.* 1977: 142). Ostracod species such as *Hirschmannia viridis*, and to some degree *Semicytherura nigrescens* and *Hemicythere villosa*, are indicative of an environment that was rich in plant life, as these phytal species live on both sea grasses and algae at present, and also an environment in which sea temperatures were similar, albeit slightly colder, than those of today (*ibid.*: 142).

Pollen analysis of the peats in ZZ27 indicate that hazel and willow shrub dominate just below the dated horizon, with oak dominated woodland, with elm, pine and birch as significant components occurring away from the sampling site reflecting more closed canopy conditions than those that persisted in the tidal flats area. Shrubs decrease and saltmarsh communities appear to increase in frequency at the level of the dated horizon, with these reflecting more open conditions as tidal inundation progresses (Haynes *et al.* 1977: 144). Above this horizon it is clear that the sequences are again reflecting increasing inundation and the incorporation of the regional forest pollen signal as opposed to local saltmarsh communities (*ibid.*), and the data indicate that the relative composition of the forest flora is consistent throughout the upper stages of sediment deposition at this location (i.e. 6m of sediment accumulation that occurs between *ca.* 8740–8140 uncal BP (7810–7070 cal BC) on the basis of sediment accumulation rates of 1m per century (Haynes *et al.* 1977: 157)). Finally, Shi and Lamb (1991: 234) note that a convenient reference date for studying the stratigraphy of the estuarine coast in Cardigan Bay is *ca.* 6000 uncal BP, when sea level rise begins to slow down (see Fig. 2.5). In this work, these authors also characterise the evolution of the Dyfi Estuary (Fig. 2.3) during the Mesolithic period (*ca.* 10,000–6000 uncal BP) as a deep-water, low energy estuarine environment with the coastline being located at *ca.* −10m OD (*ibid.*: 243). The 6000 uncal BP (*ca.* 4935–4845 cal BC) stage is also significant in being the proposed date for the full inundation of the North Sea Basin (Sheenan *et al.* 2000).

Allen (2001) presents a comprehensive synthesis of the evidence for sea level change in the Severn Estuary across the Ipswichian–Devensian–Holocene periods, and records the areal distribution of Holocene sediments in this region (Fig. 2.6). In this study Allen notes that a peat deposit, cored *ca.* 25km to the south of Swansea, confirmed the location of the 9000 uncal BP (*ca.* 8270–8235 cal BC) shoreline in the Bristol Channel. Evans and Thompson (1979: 12) record a buried peat unit between *ca.* −35 and −35.66m OD in their core 070. This freshwater peat unit (between *ca.* −35.04m OD and −35.32m OD) is bracketed by deposits containing foraminifera and ostracods that are indicative of shallow marine, probably estuarine, environments, with the overlying sediments suggesting that inundation was rapid enough to prevent the formation of saltmarsh floras (*ibid.*: 12). The peat contains a range of tree species such as birch, pine and juniper, with grasses, sedges, aquatics such as Filicales, sphagnum moss, and herb and shrub species such as *Artemisia*, *Rumex* (dock/sorrel family) and Asteraceae (aster/daisy etc.). It is considered to have formed between *ca.* 10,300 and 9800 uncal BP, during PZIV, the earlier part of the Boreal

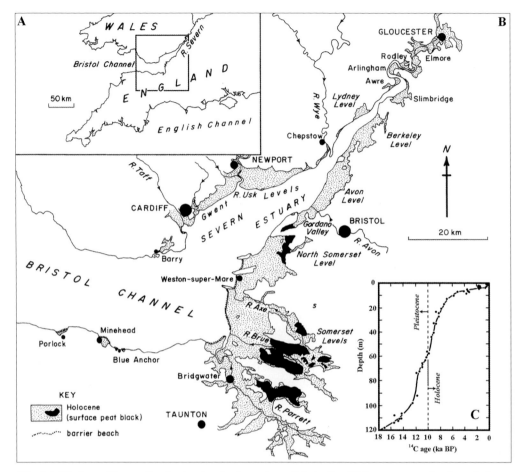

Fig. 2.6: The Severn Estuary Levels: A – location in southwest Britain; B – Holocene outcrops that form the Severn Levels; C – Global sea level rise across the Pleistocene-Holocene boundary based on radiocarbon dating of coral reefs (mainly from Barbados region), modified from Allen (1991 and 2001: figs 1 and 4; used with permission of author). Generically, the Wentlooge Levels are the areas of Holocene sediments mapped to the west of Newport, whilst the areas to the east of Newport are classed as the Caldicot Levels.

period (*ca.* 10,185–9255 cal BC) (Evans and Thompson 1979: 12). To the north and east of Swansea docks, work undertaken by Godwin (1940a: 321) indicated that during the Boreal period (PZVia–VIb) rapid transgression was occurring, but also that there are five intercalated peats between *ca.* –15.25m OD and –3m OD, at around the transition to zone VII (the Boreal–Atlantic transition).

In addition to this evidence, the presence of intertidal peats at locations such as Goldcliff in the outer part of the Severn Estuary, attest to inundation during the later Mesolithic period (Allen 2000b: 17; 2001: 18; 2005; Bell 2000; 2007). Allen (2001; 19) notes that the Holocene sediments of the Severn Estuary are, in general, *ca.* 10–15m thick, and comprise primarily of silts, representing intertidal mudflats and minerogenic saltmarshes. These sequences are intercalated with organic marsh deposits (peats), which as mentioned above record the successive phases of positive and negative sea level tendency as sea levels have fluctuated through the Holocene. The presence of features such as the Mesolithic activity site at Goldcliff and Bronze Age structures and trackways, and human footprints at Redwick all provide vivid insights into human–landscape interactions in the Severn valley during the early-mid Holocene (e.g. Fig. 2.7 after Allen 2001:19).

The occurrence of a number of peat units within the sedimentary sequences used to chart general trends in sea level rise indicates that the "simple" curves presented in Figure 2.5 and 2.6c mask considerable variability in these trends as "higher frequency fluctuations of sea level were superimposed on the underlying upward trend" (Allen 2001: 18). Allen and Bell (1999) were able to record a depositional sequence through four peat units intercalated with intertidal estuarine alluvium down to an early Mesolithic oak forest which lay at the base of the Holocene succession at Redwick in the Gwent levels, and Bell (2001: 75) notes that similar intercalated peat units occur at Goldcliff.

Whilst the focus of Allen and Bell's research was the palaeochannel feature itself these authors also radiocarbon dated the peat horizons and obtained a date on one of the oak trunks (Fig. 2.7). These oaks were probably growing in a "closed-canopy" forest, during the Mesolithic period between 6375–6060 cal BC (7330±70 uncal BP: Beta-134637). This date provides a *terminus post quem* (date after which) for the subsequent marine inundation at this location. The four subsequent phases of peat formation (Fig. 2.7) occurred (from the lowest to highest stratigraphical unit) at 6550±70 uncal BP (Beta-134640), 6030±80 uncal BP (Beta-134641), 5670±90 uncal BP (Beta-128779) and 4910±70 uncal BP (Beta-113004) respectively. These radiocarbon dates calibrate to the Mesolithic period at *ca.* 5630–5370 cal BC, 5210–4720 cal BC, and 4710–4340 cal BC, and the earlier Neolithic at *ca.* 3940–3520 cal BC.

As we have already alluded to, the nature of the sedimentary sequences that occur in riverine, estuarine or coastal environments represent a complex interplay of vertical and lateral accretion, erosion and re-working, channel incision, meander cut-offs, chutes and creeks, oxbow lake formation and infilling, and the influence of the transgressive and regressive sea level tendencies mentioned above, and possibly other factors. Allen (2001: 20) has noted that "the most abundant and widespread facies" (depositional units), formed away from river influences in the Severn Estuary, are alternating sequences of silts and peats

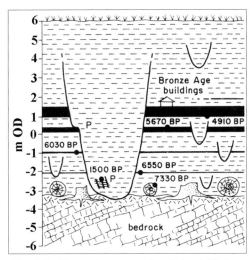

Fig. 2.7: Composite measured and dated Holocene sequences in the Redwick area, Severn Estuary Levels (after Allen 2001: fig. 5; used with permission of author).

as outlined in Figure 2.7. The diverse range of influences on sediment deposition can mean that when we core a transect across a river floodplain or estuarine area, the layers of sediment encountered in one core will not necessarily match those in an adjacent core, even when there is only 10m between them. Similarly, at a larger scale, it is often difficult to resolve the stratigraphies between surveys that are undertaken in different areas, often kilometres apart; although Allen (2001: 20) notes that there are generic similarities in evidence in the sediment units of the Severn Estuary.

Finally, recent research by Edwards (2006) at the Llanrhidian marshes in the Loughor Estuary, West Glamorgan has provided new radiocarbon dated sea level index points that enhance the available record for sea level change around the welsh coast. This data is however of only limited interest to the current consideration of Mesolithic Wales, as it is confined to the past 4500 years, partially due to the fact that in recent studies many researchers have sought to estimate the potential rates of sea level rise into the future in order to allow for the development of mitigation strategies around the coasts of Britain. An interesting aspect of this research is that Edwards (2006: 575) notes that, the Intergovernmental Panel on Climate Change estimated that average sea level rise of *ca.* 88cm is anticipated at a global scale by 2100. However, as the above discussion has hopefully indicated, the nature, extent and impacts of any sea level rise will be influenced by a myriad of factors at the local and regional scales, and modern responses will hopefully benefit from our knowledge of past sea level changes and the ability to predict/anticipate future impacts.

Climate change and changing environments

The period *ca.* 10,200–5200 uncal BP (*ca.* 11,500–6000 years ago) saw significant climatic amelioration when compared to the temperatures in evidence at the end of the Late-glacial period (Loch Lomond Stadial). Whilst mean temperatures have been discussed above, a perhaps more realistic estimate for temperature increases at the start of the current interglacial, based on coleopteran studies, suggests that temperatures may initially have risen by as much as 1.7°–2.8°C per century, so that by *ca.* 9500 uncal BP seasonal temperatures were similar to those of today (Simmons 2001; Bell and Walker 2005), although variability is evident (e.g. Brooks *et al.* 2012). In terms of the designated vegetation zones as developed for the Holocene, the Mesolithic period covers the Pre-Boreal (PZ IV at *ca.* 10,200 uncal BP or 10,000–9000 cal BC to 8000 cal BC), Boreal (PZ V–VI at *ca.* 8000–5880 cal BC) and Atlantic (PZ VIIa at *ca.* 5880–3800 cal BC) periods (Table 2.1 *after* Simmons 2001), i.e. the Mesolithic covers the "mesocratic" phase as defined by Bell and Walker (2005: 130). As can be seen from these dates, the latter part of the Atlantic period spans the transition from the Mesolithic to earlier Neolithic periods.

As noted, in Britain, in general, the Pre-Boreal and Boreal periods represent phases of rapid climatic amelioration, from average July temperatures of *ca.* 9.6°C at 10,000 uncal BP to *ca.* 17°C by 8000 uncal BP (*ca.* 7000 cal BC) (Simmons 2001: 7). A "climatic optimum" occurs *ca.* 8000–4500 uncal BP, which is characterised by temperatures that were *ca.* 1–3°C higher than at present, although this event was both spatially and temporally variable (Bell and Walker 2005: 89). In a relatively rapid sequence the climate amelioration that began at *ca.* 9500 cal BC results in a shift away from the open grassland environments of the late Devensian as more diversified temperate vegetation expanded northwards. The initial stages of colonisation by warmth loving flora in the earlier Holocene sees the expansion of juniper and birch, along with pine and willow (e.g. Birks 1989, see Figs 2.8 and 2.9), and also herbs such as meadowsweet, from their glacial refugia. By *ca.* 8400 cal BC hazel had spread extensively through Wales (Caseldine 1990; Burrow 2003: 3). Subsequently oak and pine expand into south and mid Wales by *ca.* 8200 cal BC. By the start of the later Mesolithic period at *ca.* 7900 cal BC hazel woodland extended throughout Wales, and

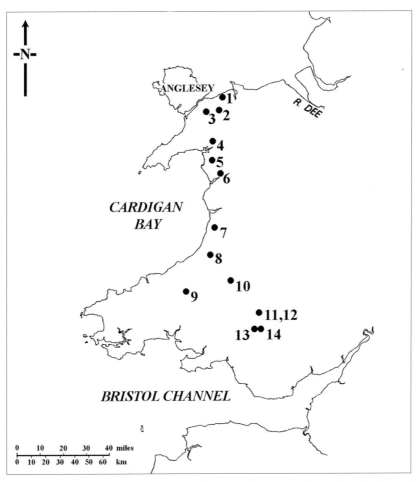

Fig. 2.8: Sites used by Birks (1989) for constructing Holocene isochrone maps of vegetation development in Wales. Sites listed are: 1 – Melynllyn; 2 – Cwm Gywion; 3 – Nant Ffracon; 4 – Cors Dolfroig; 5 – Moel y Gerddi; 6 – Llyn Gwernan; 7 – Clarach Bay; 8 – Cors Tregaron; 9 – Cledlyn Valley Pingo U; 10 – Cefn Gwernffrwd; 11 – Craig-y-Fro; 12 – Craig Cerrig-gleisiad; 13 – Traeth Mawr; 14 – Coed Taf (adapted from original by author).

oak and elm had colonised South and Mid Wales (Burrow 2003: 17). Alder expands from around 5800 cal BC, followed by lime and ash by *ca.* 4800 cal BC (*ibid.*). The timing and areal extent of the colonising tree species is considered in greater detail below, whilst the nature of the associated faunal species is considered in Chapters 4 and 5.

The generalised sequence of Holocene tree colonisation into Wales, as developed by Birks (1989) is presented in Figure 2.9, although juniper is absent from these maps. Bennett (1986: 528) notes that:

> because of the high densities necessary for detection of taxa in the pollen record, we actually know little about the dispersal rates of the various taxa and hence cannot readily discuss this aspect in relation to known dispersal mechanisms.

It should also be noted that, as the following discussion will highlight, there is considerable regional variation in the timing of initial expansions and contractions of tree species throughout Wales (and Britain) during the Mesolithic period (e.g. Moore 1972; Smith and Pilcher 1973), although this should be contrasted with Hibbert and Switsur's (1976) work at Tregaron and Nant Ffrancon. Other indicators of the increased temperature range include mollusca and the European pond tortoise, which are found in southeast England, Denmark and southern Sweden during the climatic optimum; these species are now restricted to the Mediterranean and eastern Europe (Bell and Walker 2005: 90). In Wales, the early Holocene landscape is initially colonised by a range of herbs and grasses, with a short-lived expansion of juniper soon after the climate begins to warm up (Walker 1982a; Caseldine 1990: 33).

Lowe and Lowe (1989) have noted that at Llyn Gwernan, a small freshwater lake on the northern flank of Cader Idris (located at an altitude of 165m OD), the earlier part of the Holocene sequences (their pollen zones GW9–12, for the early Holocene/Flandrian in profile A) record a succession that is "typical" of the early Holocene in Britain, with successive maxima in grasses and docks/sorrels (Poaceae-*Rumex*), juniper (*Juniperus*), birch (*Betula*) and hazel (*Corylus*) (Lowe 1981). Willow (*Salix*), which is not always well represented in early Holocene pollen spectra from Britain, appears to have played an important role at Llyn Gwernan, while crowberry and gorse (*Empetrum*), which seems to have played a key role in other parts of Britain (notably Scotland), is poorly represented at this location (*ibid.*: 401). Interestingly the rise in *Rumex* identified in their Profile A is not mirrored in their Profile B during the earlier Holocene; the dates for these zones are placed at 10,040±80 uncal BP (SRR-1700), *ca.* 10,000–9320 cal BC at the onset of biogenic sedimentation, through to GW12 where there is a marked rise in hazel that is dated to 9070±70 uncal BP (SRR-1698) which calibrates to *ca.* 8540–7990 cal BC, i.e. up to a chronological position just before the transition to the later Mesolithic.

Handa and Moore (1976) recorded high frequencies of willow in their cores from three pingo basins in the valleys of the Cledlyn and Cletwr in west Wales. Willow is recorded at pingo W (in LPAZ Wc) (228m OD), and also at pingo U (in LPAZ Ia onwards), and pingo I (LPAZUa onwards). Radiocarbon dating of the basal detrital muds at each of these sites produced ages of 10,080±320 uncal BP (B-489) and 10,060±380 uncal BP (B-488) from

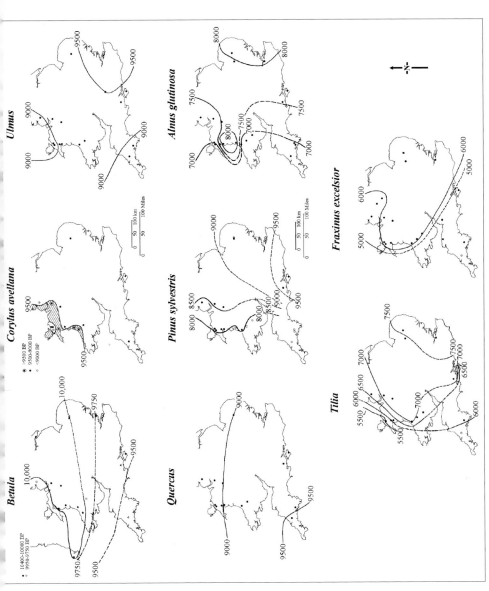

Fig. 2.9: Isochrone map showing the rational limits of birch, hazel, elm, oak, pine, alder, lime and ash, as developed by Birks (1989) on the basis of data from radiocarbon dated pollen diagrams in Wales (see list in Fig. 2.8). Lines denote expansion limits in radiocarbon years uncal BP (modified from Birks 1989). Note: for Hazel (Corylus avellana) the approximate areas where this species was present before 9500 uncal BP are shaded.

pingo U, 9380±340 uncal BP (B-368) from pingo W, and 10,170±220 uncal BP (B-388) from pingo I respectively. The large errors associated with these dates result in calibrated ranges of *ca*. 10,645–8820 cal BC (B-489), *ca*. 10,710–8640 cal BC (B-488), 9800–7730 (B-368) and *ca*. 10,580–9290 cal BC (B-388). At pingo W the sequence opens with high values for dwarf birch (*Betula nana*), with juniper present at <10% of the total pollen sum (TP) (zone *Wa*) and evidence for pine, elm and alder at varying levels throughout the sequence. Grasses dominate at 50%, and Cyperaceae, Ericaceae, *Empetrum*, *Rumex acetosa* and several other herb types are all in evidence at the start of this zone (Handa and Moore 1976: 208). In zone *Wb* juniper rises to over 30% TP and birch is over 10%, whilst grasses and Cyperaceae fall. Willow attains high representations in zone *Wc*, but by zone *Wd* juniper, willow, grasses and meadowsweet/dropwort all exhibit considerable falls, whilst there are slight increases in hazel and alder whilst *Filicales* and *Sphagnum* are frequent (*ibid.*: 213).

There are fluctuations in hazel and juniper through until zone *Wf* when hazel begins to rise steadily, reaching its maximum in zone *Wg*. During this zone oak begins to rise, having been present at low levels since zone *Wc* (*ibid.*). Oak continues to rise in zone *Wh*, wherein alder, which has been erratic up until this point, also begins to climb steadily at the expense of birch and hazel, these trends continue into zone *Wi* (Handa and Moore 1976: 213). The zonation at pingo U (LPAZ *Ua – Uc*) (197m OD) shows some variability in the relative abundances of species, but the trends are similar to those from pingo W. At pingo I in the Cletwr valley (195m OD), despite a shortened sequence of *ca*. 0.5m due to disturbances in the upper part of the profile, the LPAZ Ia–Id follow similar trajectories to the early Holocene sequences at pingoes W and U (*ibid.*: 220). The earlier Holocene sequences obtained from these three pingoes are correlated to Godwin's PZ III/IV and IV, whilst the earliest part of the sequence is placed in Godwin's PZIII by Handa and Moore (1976: 221). The transitional and early Holocene zones comprise birch, juniper and meadowsweet/dropwort (PLAZ *Wb*, *Ub*, and *Ib*) and what has been termed the birch assemblage zone (Godwin's zone IV) which includes LPAZ *Wc/Wd*, *Uc* and *Ic/Id* respectively; these illustrate the early occurrence and rise of juniper at the start of the Holocene in this part of west Wales.

Similar sequences to those at Llyn Gwernan were recorded by Ince (1983: 161) from two upland cwms in Gwynedd, North Wales, Cwm (Llyn) Llydaw located to the east of Snowdon at 440m OD, and Cwm Cywion, which lies between the peaks of Y Garn and Foel-Goch at a height of 600m OD. At these locations early herbaceous communities were invaded by birch and juniper, then birch-hazel-Myrica woodland at Llyn Llydaw and pine-hazel-Myrica woodland at Cwm Cywion. The juniper rise is placed at *ca*. 9900 uncal BP (*ca*. 9370–9300 cal BC) at these sites on the basis of the available radiocarbon dates obtained, and Ince suggests that juniper is established in the uplands by this date (Ince 1983: 167–9). Subsequently birch, pine, oak and alder increase in significance as the environment develops (*ibid.*: 163).

Tipping's (1993) study of the (undated) sequences at Cwm/Llyn Idwal, located *ca*. 3.5km to the south of Nant Ffrancon at a height of 375m OD demonstrated the presence of grasses, herbs and mosses in the earlier Holocene, and these communities are colonised by juniper shrub in LPAZ IDWAL C, when juniper rises to dominance in the grassland communities (1993: 184–5). Subsequently, as birch becomes established at Llyn Idwal juniper declines, possibly due to the "shading out" effect of closed birch woodland, a possibility that is supported by the concomitant reductions in grass and herb communities as birch woodland is established (*ibid*.: 185). Continued woodland developments at Llyn Idwal see the colonisation of hazel, *Myrica*, elm and towards the end of the sequence oak may have also become established at this location. In general, by the Late Mesolithic, there is evidence for the expansion of woodland up to heights of *ca*. 500m OD at the start of the Late Mesolithic period (Burrow 2003: 17).

Contrasting a lowland location for north Wales against the upland sites discussed above, Watkins *et al*. (2007) have studied the site of Llyn Cororion which is located at a height of 82.5m ASL (above sea level) on the Arfon Platform, *ca*. 1km northwest of Tregarth village (SH 597688). At this location 11 radiocarbon dates were used to construct a chronology for the 9.49m sequence of deposits that were recovered from this kettlehole. Whilst the Llyn Cororion sequence does not have the transitional Loch Lomond Stadial (Younger Dryas) – Holocene herbaceous communities in evidence, as organic sedimentation did not begin until 9680±65 uncal BP (SRR3477) (*ca*. 9280–8835 cal BC), the earlier part of the record does contain juniper (which dominates), with willow and increasing levels of birch (Watkins *et al*. 2007: 173).

At Bryn y Castell, Snowdonia, located at *ca*. 364m OD (Gwynedd, North Wales), Mighall and Chambers (1995), whilst recording similarities in the earlier Holocene sequences of tall herb and meadow-type communities giving way to birch, hazel and to a lesser extent pine and willow, as noted at other welsh sites, do not record any presence of juniper in their 10m (BYC 2) sequence from the valley mire at this location. However, it should be noted that Mighall and Chambers (1995: 313) were unable to date the earliest part of their deep sequence, and as such it is possible that the lower sediments represent vegetation development after *ca*. 9700 uncal BP (*ca*. 9200 cal BC), as juniper appears to decline in mid and north Wales between *ca*. 9700–9500 uncal BP.

Throughout Wales, considerable regional variability is in evidence, and David (2007) has noted that there is no linear expansion of deciduous tree species in western Dyfed due to the fact that an apparent climatic deterioration delays the colonisation of birch until around *ca*. 9400 uncal BP (*ca*. 8730–8630 cal BC). Variations in the values for juniper appear to indicate lower values at lowland sites such as Glanllynnau, Aberaeron and Hendre Fach, whilst sites at higher altitudes (with the apparent exceptions of Bryn y Castell, above, and Waun Fignen Felin, discussed below) exhibit higher frequencies for this species. As can be seen from the discussion of Llyn Cororion (Watkins *et al*. 2007: 173), this site contrasts with Glanllynnau, Tre'r Gof and Llyn Hendref due to the high values for juniper, and as noted above, whilst the Bryn y Castell sequence does not have evidence for juniper, this might be accounted for by the problems with dating and consequent uncertainties in the onset of organic sedimentation at this location (Mighall and Chambers 1995: 313).

An undated sequence obtained by Hyde (1940) from Ffos Ton Cenglau near Craig-y-Llyn, Glamorgan, South Wales, located at an altitude of 488m OD (on the road between

Hirwaun and Treorchy), has produced in excess of 6m of bog deposits, with evidence to suggest a pre-Boreal age for the lowest part of the sequence (Hyde 1940: 230). At this location the pre-Boreal stage deposits are dominated by birch, with some pine and hazel, and minimal elm, in evidence. The PZV spectra indicate a rapid reversal in the relative abundance of pine and birch, and elm increases during this zone. The Boreal period (PZVI) has birch and pine well represented throughout, but the zone is subdivided into zones VIa-c due to variations in tree species representation though the Boreal period (see Table 2.1 above). At Ffos Ton Cenglau in PZVIa elm is relatively abundant and hazel is increasing rapidly, whilst in PZVIb oak increases in significance along with hazel, and elm declines to just over 10%. In PZVIc pine increases in significance to fall away rapidly at the end of the zone into PZVIIa (the Atlantic period), lime and alder also appear during PZVIc, and hazel declines. Concomitant with the decline of pine at the Boreal–Atlantic transition (PZVIc–VIIA) is the continued increase in significance in alder across the transition and throughout PZVIIa (Hyde 1940: 230–1).

Whilst slightly later in date, the sequence identified by Thomas (1965) at Llanllwch, near Carmarthen in southwest Wales also exhibits elevated frequencies of alder at the expense of birch at the PZVI/VII boundary (Thomas's PZA/B boundary). At this location however oak represents the secondary tree species after birch in the Pre-Boreal, with elm and pine next in terms of frequency. At the very start of this zone willow is well represented, along with ferns, suggesting that these initial colonisers are rapidly shaded out as a closed birch canopy develops (Thomas 1965: 110). Alder is only present in low counts of *ca.* <5% throughout Thomas's PZA, but it rises rapidly to frequencies of between 60–70% at the beginning of PZB (PZVIIa, the Atlantic period). Elm, pine and birch all decline across PZB (Godwin's PZVIIa), whilst alder remains dominant, and oak is still the secondary species in terms of dominance. In PZC (PZVIIb, the Subboreal (equivalent to the start of the Neolithic period)) oak increases in frequency at the expense of alder, and hazel increases steadily throughout this zone, suggesting drier climatic conditions at the site in the earlier Neolithic period. Birch, elm and pine also continue to be represented at low frequencies across this zone. One final point of note is that Thomas reports that hazel frequencies are low during PZA, and suggests that as similar low frequencies occur at Tregaron and Craig-y-Llyn, a similar situation to that identified in the non-calcareous regions of Ireland during the Boreal period is occurring in similar regions in Wales during this period (1965: 112). The variability that is in evidence in the pollen diagrams from Wales cannot be accounted for in a straightforward manner as:

> local distribution may have been determined as much by local site factors such as aspect, exposure, soil moisture variability, ground surface wetness and variations in atmospheric moisture levels, as by macroscale climatic amelioration. (Walker 1982a: 160)

As noted at Llyn Cororion, local factors produced a well established juniper population on the Arfon Platform, and vegetation that is more in line with the evidence from the uplands than sites at lower altitudes (Watkins *et al.* 2007: 173). However, the dominance of juniper is short-lived at Llyn Cororion such that by *ca.* 9600 uncal BP birch replaces juniper in the vegetation record, this again contrasts with other areas in that juniper co-exists with birch at uplands sites (Watkins *et al.* 2007: 173). Irrespective of regional variability Simmons (2001: 28) suggests that by 9000 uncal BP, all of Britain "was in a deciduous forest province", with oak forests dominating by 8000 uncal BP; albeit with significant regional variations in evidence. Above the tree line the mountains were characterised by rich cold-tolerant herbs of "arctic-alpine" type (*ibid.*).

The discussions below further highlight the fact that local conditions will influence the ability of certain species to become established in a given area, and as such we need to pay attention to the local environment (e.g. Smith and Cloutman 1988) when assessing the nature of postglacial vegetation change. However, the rise in species such a birch, hazel, pine, alder and willow is the general pattern in many areas during the earlier Holocene, as evidenced at sites like Tregaron, Clarach and Gwarllyn (David 2007: 59; Hibbert and Switsur 1976; Heyworth *et al.* 1985), although as noted above juniper is also evidenced at a number of welsh sites at the beginning of the Holocene, e.g. at Tregaron (Dyfedd) and Nant Ffrancon (Gwynedd) (Hibbert and Switsur 1976) and Llyn Cororion (Watkins *et al.* 2007). Moore (1972) has noted that at Gwarllyn, a small bog on Mynydd Bach in Cardiganshire, located at an altitude of 312m OD and *ca.* 7km west of Tregaron Bog and *ca.* 15km east of Aberaeron, the earliest zone of Moore's pollen diagram PZ-Ga, is characterised by low percentages of arboreal pollen (*ca.* 10–15% of total pollen), comprising birch and pine, with open habitat herbs being abundant, especially Poaceae and Cyperaceae, as well as *Artemisia* and *Rumex acetosa* type (1972: 951), equivalent to Godwin's PZIII. Towards the end of PZ-Ga juniper reaches a peak and hazel is present at *ca.* 10% of the arboreal pollen sum. Unlike the situation at other sites (e.g. in the Elan Valley, Llyn Mire in the Wye Valley (Moore 1978), Clogwyngarreg in Snowdonia (Ince 1996) and at Nant Ffrancon), hazel is rising before Juniper has reached its maximum. This situation is atypical for a PZIII–IV pollen assemblage as hazel generally appears to increase after juniper had reached its maximum and declined, and as such is interpreted as indicating that hazel was present locally at this time and also that its temperature threshold for flowering was crossed before juniper had reached its maximum (*ibid.*: 955).

As plant colonisation continues, increasing species diversity occurs in the expanding deciduous woodlands, reflecting the increasing suitability of the landscape as the environment and soils continue to develop and climate continues to warm through the Mesolithic period. Additional species that characterise the deciduous woodlands include elm and oak, which have colonised much of Wales by *ca.* 9000 uncal BP (8200 cal BC: the PZ V–VI boundary), along with lime and ash, which had a limited distribution in western parts of Wales. These latter species were present within the catchment at Llyn Cororion in north Wales from *ca.* 5700 uncal BP (*ca.* 4550–4500 cal BC) (Watkins *et al.* 2007: 178). In addition, a range of plants such as bog myrtle and other herbs, ferns and aquatic species are in evidence at this time.

David (2007) has noted that the main expansion of hazel in Wales occurs at around 9000 uncal BP, and in south-western regions of Britain and Ireland birch also expands at around this time. Smith and Cloutman (1988) have reported that at Waun Fignen Felin birch characterises the earliest Holocene woodlands, often dominating woodland assemblages at over 90%, and they also record that this species declines across the period *ca.* 10,100–9800 uncal BP, in addition, at this location hazel appears to expand around *ca.* 8100–8000 uncal BP at the expense of birch, and hazel generally tends to decline before *ca.* 6000 uncal BP. At Llyn Cororion, Watkins *et al.* (2007: 174) record an age of 9365±65uncal BP (SRR3476), calibrated to *ca.* 8810–8350 cal BC, for the rise in hazel (its empirical limit), which is late when compared to sites in low-lying west coast areas, and sites in the uplands of Snowdonia. These authors also note that the point at which the continuous curve for hazel begins to rise to high levels in pollen diagrams (the rational limit: *cf.* Smith and Pilcher 1973; Bennett 1986) occurs at *ca.* 9215±65 uncal BP (SRR3475), which calibrates to *ca.* 8610–8290 cal BC, again being earlier in the lowlands, but elsewhere the timing of its establishment is variable throughout the uplands, "suggesting that expansion was delayed until critical environmental requirements were satisfied" (Watkins *et al.* 2007: 174). These data refine the generalised outline proposed by David (2007), but again, as noted, the evidence from sites like Waun Fignen Felin and Llyn Cororion indicates localised vegetation signatures, and numerous factors are influencing the vegetation distributions at the regional level. At Llyn Cororion elm is established at *ca.* 8800 uncal BP, and it remains unchanged in abundance through until 4985±65 uncal BP (SRR3469), *ca.* 3940–3650 cal BC, when the elm decline is recorded at this location (*ibid.*). Oak was important at this location from *ca.* 8600 uncal BP, and pine is relatively well represented after *ca.* 8300 uncal BP (Watkins *et al.* 2007: 174–7).

Mike Walker (1982a) has suggested that by the Mid-Holocene period, the upland woodlands of Wales were characterised by oak, birch and pine, with the latter being locally dominant, and that at this time mixed deciduous woodland had reached *ca.* 450m OD, and possibly even reached altitudes of 610m OD in some areas (*ibid.*: 33–4). Research at Craig-y-Fro (located at *ca.* 365m OD) and Craig Cerrig-gleisiad (at a slightly higher elevation in excess of 400m OD), both located in the Brecon Beacons, have produced palaeoenvironmental material dated to the earlier to Mid-Holocene (Walker 1982a: 149). At both sites seven local pollen assemblage zones (PAZs) were defined, with these being characterised by sufficiently similar plant species to allow the designation of a regional pollen assemblage scheme. The sequences have dates of 10,030±100 uncal BP (calibrated to 10,021–9298 cal BC) and 10,860±70 uncal BP (*ca.* 10,970–10,650 cal BC) respectively at their bases (lab numbers not given) although Walker (1982a: 159) argues that the date from Craig Cerrig-gleisiad is too early and must be considered erroneous.

At both locations the initial stages of vegetation development are characterised by high juniper (shrub or dwarf) frequencies (>45% of the total land pollen sum) and grasses, with lower levels of birch and willow. The expansion of juniper, grass and birch across this pollen zone reflects the expansion of shrub heath across the northern slopes of the Brecon Beacons during the earlier Holocene as temperatures are increasing. In addition, the presence of indicators of open ground occurring alongside the thermophilous indicator species reflects the fact that this is a very early, pioneer, stage of colonisation (Walker 1982a: 151). A similar, early Holocene, shift from open habitats to a rise in juniper also occurs at Traeth Mawr (Walker 1982b), where pine, willow and birch are also recorded as secondary components in the developing woodlands. At this location birch values increase across the local PAZs (TM-9–TM-10), reaching a maximum in LPAZ TM-11, at which point juniper "virtually disappears from the record" to be replaced by hazel (Walker 1982b: 181). The onset of Early Holocene (organic) sedimentation at Traeth Mawr is placed at 10,013–9256 cal BC (9970±115 uncal BP: SRR-1560), and is associated with a shift from the alpine and montane communities of the Loch Lomond Stadial, to the more stable grassland, with dwarf shrub, and heathland communities that characterise the Early Holocene period in this region.

In the regional PAZ-2 birch, willow and grasses continue to expand in frequency at the expense of juniper, reflecting the rapid immigration of tree birch, which dominates the woodland component in the Brecon Beacons by PAZ-3. In this zone birch comprises *ca.* 70% of the woodland taxa, with species such as pine, oak and hazel as secondary components of the developing woodlands. The latter species, hazel, colonises the lower site of Craig-y-Fro first as its altitudinal range extends beyond the valley floors and up onto the upper slopes in the Beacons, and an early date for the arrival of this species has been recovered from Tregaron, where a calibrated age of 10,023–8571 cal BC was obtained (9747±222 uncal BP).

In PAZ-4 hazel expands into the region to reach frequencies of *ca.* 60% of the total dryland pollen sum, at the expense of birch which falls to levels of *ca.* 20% regionally. Juniper is eliminated from the regional woodlands, whilst oak and elm gain in importance. Pine is consistently seen as a background species across PAZs 1–4 in the Brecon Beacons. Some variation in the nature of the mixed woodlands occurs between Craig-y-Fro and Craig Cerrig-gleisiad after PAZ-4 as at Craig-y-Fro PAZ5–6 comprises mixed hazel-oak-birch-elm woodland, whilst at Craig Cerrig-gleisiad this phase is only attested in PAZ5. Willow is locally dominant in PAZ6 at Craig-y-Fro. At both sites alder appears in the pollen record at the start of PAZ6, but during this zone at Craig-y-Fro there is evidence for disturbance in the catchment and the drying-out of the area, with some indicators of woodland clearance and colonisation by non-arboreal species (herbs, ferns and grasses).

Mighall and Chambers (1995: 315) report that the major rise of alder at Bryn y Castell in north Wales occurs by 6680±45 uncal BP (GrN-17585), calibrated to 5592–5524 cal BC, an age that is similar to the date of 6880±100 uncal BP (Q-900), which calibrates to *ca.* 5980–5625 cal BC, as obtained by Hibbert and Switsur (1976) at Nant Ffrancon. Once alder is established at Bryn y Castell "its rate of increase appears to have been quite rapid, suggesting that habitat conditions were well suited for alder" at this location as alder carr was established around the lake margins (Mighall and Chambers 1995: 315). At Llyn Cororion, Watkins *et al.* (2007: 177) record an age of 7745±65 uncal BP (SRR3471), *ca.* 6690–6450 cal BC, for a rapid expansion of alder, seen as alder carr at the lake margins. The rise in alder coincides with a decline in pine in the catchment, but it appears that the remainder of the mixed deciduous woodland continues relatively unchanged at this time.

At Craig Cerrig-gleisiad a longer record of Mid-Holocene vegetation changes is recorded, and here oak increases in frequency across PAZ6, whilst pine decreases in abundance. At both sites there are peaks in the abundance of birch during PAZ6, albeit asynchronous in nature, which probably reflect re-colonisation by this species into the "gaps" that are left by elm and pine. The decline of the latter of these species may be an indicator of increasing wetness in the region, as also suggested by increasing frequencies of alder (Walker 1982a: 156). The alder rise is only represented at Craig Cerrig-gleisiad in PAZ7, where it is accompanied by high levels of oak and hazel/sweet gale, and by reductions in the frequencies of birch, pine and willow and a slight increase in the representation of elm (*ibid.*). As noted by Walker (*ibid.*: 157) the changing vegetation during PAZ7 is indicative of a major climatic shift to increasingly maritime conditions, away from the more continental conditions that had occurred previously. Whilst the alder rise has often been attributed to increasingly wet climatic conditions in Britain, Bell and Walker have suggested that local site conditions may have been the principal determinants, and that the pedological evidence suggests that a climatic wet shift occurs at *ca.* 7800–7000 uncal BP (2005: 130).

Pollen analysis of an upland lake basin (at *ca.* 395m OD), at Cefn Gwernffrwd, near Rhandirmwyn in mid-Wales, undertaken by Chambers (1982a), produced a *ca.* 5m profile (named GWC) covering some 9500 years of sedimentation. This core had four distinct charcoal bands in evidence (suggestive of burning episodes during the Neolithic period), which were located between the depths of 2.4–2.0m from the surface, and also within a wood peat horizon in this sequence. Chambers (1982a: 611) noted that whilst the overall vegetation sequence in evidence at Cefn Gwernffrwd conformed to Godwin's (1975) Holocene sequence for Britain, there were significant differences in evidence. In particular, birch woodland persists through the Mesolithic period at this location, and it was growing around the small lake at the end of the Pre-Boreal (PZIV, *sensu* Godwin 1975: 51–3). It subsequently invaded the developing reedswamp environment of the lake, forming birch carr conditions. Interestingly, as noted by Godwin (*ibid.*: 53), the later stages of the Boreal period appear to correspond to increasing evidence for dryer conditions and the terrestrialisation of many lakes, bogs and fens in Britain. The increasing encroachment of birch onto lake sites such as Cefn Gwernffrwd, as mentioned above, reinforces the fact that this element of landscape development is in evidence in Wales, as well as other areas of the British Isles.

Throughout the Boreal period (PZV–VI) at Cefn Gwernffrwd pine and elm remain low in frequency, whilst oak rises slightly, suggesting to Chambers (1982a: 612) that pine was being outcompeted by oak; although these three species are not significant Boreal forest components at this location. In actual fact, the high frequencies of hazel indicate that this species was dominant during the Boreal period at this site, although during the subsequent Atlantic period (after *ca.* 5880 cal BC) oak and alder appear to out-compete hazel. Chambers suggests that hazel may have been a significant upland forest component in Wales during the Boreal period, and that factors such as the presence of glacial refugia, and Mesolithic influences on vegetation, through periodic burning activities (see Bell and Walker 2005: 195), could have contributed to the ability of this species to maintain dominance into the later Mesolithic period. The elm decline, often considered to represent a pollen "marker horizon" for the transition from the later Mesolithic into the Neolithic period, occurs at 3950–3530 cal BC (4930±85 uncal BP: CAR-45) at Cefn Gwernffrwd.

Analysis of three palaeoenvironmental sequences from an area of upland moorland at *ca*. 400m OD, in Mid-Glamorgan, South Wales, located at SN 988 108 (Chambers 1983), produced one sequence, designated Coed Taf C, which encompassed the Mesolithic period between *ca*. 6900–4865 uncal BP, the late Boreal to Atlantic (PZVIIa) periods. At this site, the earlier (Late Boreal) woodland development is characterised by oak and hazel, with some local willow, and a significant regional presence of pine and elm. As at Llyn Cororion alder is seen to rise in frequency at Coed Taf C concomitant with a fall in pine frequency, from about 6000–5610 cal BC (CAR-88; 6885±110 uncal BP). Chambers notes that this date is considerably later than the date obtained from Tregaron Bog, and at sites in northwest Wales, where dates in excess of 7000 uncal BP have been obtained (1983: 482). At Coed Taf the rise in alder is protracted as it takes *ca*. 2000 years before this species achieves a representation of around 10% of the total land pollen sum. In northwest Wales, analysis of a valley mire located near Moel y Gerddi, Ardudwy, by Chambers and Price (1985), has shown that at this location alder was already well established in the environment before peat developed in the valley. As a result, these authors indicate an empirical limit for alder (the point where the pollen curve for this species is continuous) in northwest Wales that pre-dates their estimated basal date of 8700 uncal BP (*ca*. 7750–7600 cal BC) for this location (*ibid*.: 337). This age was reported as representing the (then) earliest available age for the empirical limit for alder in Wales, as it predated the age obtained by Hibbert and Switsur (1976) from valley fill lacustrine sediments at Nant Ffrancon (at 8450±150 uncal BP: Q-898; *ca*. 7935–7070 cal BC). The prolonged expansion of alder at Coed Taf C, and the different ages for Nant Ffrancon, Cefn Gwernffrwd (*ca*. 7035 uncal BP) and Tregaron Bog (7130±180 uncal BP: Q-936; *ca*. 6385–5675 cal BC) (Chambers and Price 1985: 337) are perhaps not as unusual as they might first appear, as Bennett and Birks (1990: 124–7) have noted that the spread of alder is patchy and erratic during the earlier Holocene due to a lack of suitable habitats, and as noted by Chambers in 1983, site type and topographical position also influence the rates of alder expansion.

During the Atlantic period (Godwin's PZVIIa (e.g. Godwin 1940b)) there is evidence to support the dominance of tree pollen in the palynological record, indicating a maximum stage of woodland development. The birch-pine woodland of the pre-Boreal has been superseded by mixed deciduous woodlands, with local conditions influencing the relative frequency and/or dominance of certain species over others. For instance, hazel, elm and oak might be anticipated in dryer areas of the landscape, although damp oak/hazel fen carr woodland is reported at Caldicot Pill during this period by Scaife (1994), whilst alder and willow (carr woodland) would exhibit a preference for wetter areas in and around the rivers, lakes and wetlands of Britain.

The analysis of two sequences obtained from blanket peats at Cefn Ffordd and Brecon Beacons (at altitudes of 600m OD and 715m OD respectively) (Chambers 1982b) produced material of undated Mesolithic age from Cefn Ffordd (the Brecon Beacons site produced material from the Neolithic and later periods). At Cefn Ffordd, Chambers recorded oak-hazel woodland as a regional signal, with open hazel woodland as the local flora. Birch, pine, hazel and grasses with Ericaceae and Filicales as significant components of the landscape characterise the earliest phase of the pollen diagram (zone FFa) at this location. Hazel rises to a peak in zone FFb, and alder enters the sequence during this zone, whilst birch levels fall throughout the zone. Alder shows a low and steady increase into zone FFc, whilst hazel falls to very low levels and hazel also drops off during this zone (Chambers 1982b: 450). Whilst these changes are of probable Mesolithic age they remain undated, although they probably encompass the late Boreal to Atlantic periods at Cefn Ffordd.

Early work by Smith and Morgan (1989) in the vicinity of Goldcliff, in the intertidal zone to the east of Hill Farm, analysed a peat bed sandwiched between units of estuarine clays. The main peat unit comprised 1.68m of sediments, with the base of the peat being located at OD. The sequence comprises, in general, *Phragmites* peat at the base (reedswamp), which gives way to alder fen carr peats. There is a thin unit of "buttery" clay between 1.23m and 1.38m depth in the sequence which is estuarine in origin, and this is overlain by *Phragmites* reedswamp peat, *Cladium*-dominated fen peats and a further reedswamp/ fen peat phase to 0.95m depth. These peats give way to *sphagnum-calluna* dominated peats indicative of raised bog development, through to 0.14m depth, and these are overlain by a thin (*ca.* 40mm) horizon of *Phragmites* reedswamp peats. A 0.10m unit of estuarine clays overlies the entire sequence, indicating a return to estuarine conditions that remove the reedswamp from the immediate area (Smith and Morgan 1989: 148).

Radiocarbon dating of the sequences indicates that peat formation began before *ca.* 4920 cal BC (and possibly at 5150 cal BC). In the local PAZ GC1–1a, which ends at 4860 cal BC (after 5950±80 uncal BP: CAR-659), Chenopodiaceae (goosefoot family), and pine are common along with alder, oak and willow. In general though, the pollen assemblage in the zone is dominated by grasses. The subsequent Zone GC1–1b is a short lived unit which ends at 5850±80 uncal BP: CAR-658) and is characterised by a peak in fern followed by a peak in willow and a decline in grasses, suggesting drying out of the reedswamp and the establishment of carr woodland. GC1–2 is dated to 4800–4075 cal BC (end date 5440±80 uncal BP: CAR-655) and indicates that there is a rapid rise in alder to *ca.* 70% of the pollen sum over a period of only *ca.* 20 years. Marine influences occur 4520–4180 cal BC within this zone. The removal of marine influences at the end of this zone coincides with a decline in alder and a rise in birch and *Potamogeton*. The subsequent zone GC1–3 is dated to between 4075–3780 cal BC, i.e. the end of the Mesolithic into the earlier Neolithic period. Smith and Morgan note that the sequence at Goldcliff is retrogressive, following a succession from fen-carr to reedswamp to tussock sedge and back to fen (1989: 160). The shift from fen to raised bog is interpreted as being a consequence of nutrient depletion in the area. In general the sequence identified between GC1–1b to GC1–3 reflects increasing sea levels at the end of the Mesolithic period *ca.* 4500–4000 cal BC and the establishment of alder carr woodlands, with the alder apparently being tolerant of saline conditions.

At Caldicot Pill, Scaife (1994) has analysed two peat sequences (Oscar 3, zoned CP1, and context 333–340, zoned CP2), the former sequence being 1m thick, and the latter 0.5m. The sequence in Oscar 3 indicated changing environments from marine, saltmarsh conditions through to freshwater and fen, with a subsequent return to marine conditions at the top of the sequence (*ibid.*: 76). Scaife reports that the organic peats in 333–340 and the freshwater muds in Oscar 3 date to the Mid-Holocene (Late Boreal to Atlantic period, PZVIc–VIIa) at 6660±80 uncal BP (Beta-79886), *ca.* 5710–5480 cal BC, and 6360±70 uncal BP (Beta-79887), *ca.* 5475–5215 cal BC, respectively (Scaife 1994: 77). The younger date marks the transition to brackish/marine environments from the earlier fresh/brackish environments, and this contact is placed at –0.82m OD, whilst the older date marks the removal of marine conditions, and the onset of freshwater-dominated environments, and is placed at –2.48m OD. The pollen in this sequence commences with mixed deciduous woodlands with oak and elm dominated woodland with lime and ash as secondary components, and hazel as an understorey species. There is also evidence for alder carr woodland, possibly either growing in river valleys discharging into the estuary, along the wetter foreshore, or in lagoonal areas (*ibid.*: 77–8). Pine is recorded as a component of the woodland in pollen assemblage zones CP1:1–3 and CP2:1, and lime is also present from the start of CP1:1, confirming its presence from the Atlantic period at this location.

As the freshwater fen develops variation in the local wetland ecology indicate changes from wet to dryer conditions and dryer reedswamp in which oak and hazel woodland may have been either very local, or growing on-site (Scaife 1994: 79). The pollen in context 333–340 shows a progression from marine saltmarsh through reed swamp to sedge fen and eventually oak woodland across zones CP2:1–3. This variability is interpreted as representing spatial and temporal variability in wetland development as the dynamic and colonising species create asynchroneity in the fossil record (*ibid.*: 79). Given that the analyses at Caldicot Pill were undertaken in a relatively discrete area of foreshore (*ca.* 1 × 1km in area), we should perhaps be less surprised at the fact that there is considerable variability in the relative proportions of deciduous woodland between lowland and upland and in different regions of Wales throughout the Mesolithic period.

At the Mesolithic occupation/activity sites at Goldcliff, in the Severn Estuary, concentrations of activity around hearth features have produced a range of lithic, faunal and environmental material since initial survey work was originally carried out at this location by GGAT staff with funding from Newport Museum and Art Gallery in the late 1980s (Bell *et al.* 2000: 6 and 33). Subsequent research in this area, between Goldcliff island and areas up to *ca.* 1.5km to the west, to a point *ca.* 420m west of Goldcliff Pill (Bell 2000: fig. 3.2), undertaken by Bell and colleagues since 1991 has provided an extremely detailed record of human activity and landscape development throughout the prehistoric period (Bell 1995; 1999; Bell *et al.* 2003). A more detailed consideration of the finds from the Mesolithic horizons containing charcoal at Goldcliff is presented in Chapters 3–5.

Bell *et al.* (2003: 5) note that the earlier Holocene landsurface at Goldcliff dips eastwards from the former bedrock island, such that archaeological sites occur at decreasing heights in relation to OD. In addition, burial of the old land surface is diachronous (i.e. time transgressive), and depending on the location studied, it is overlain by either peats or laminated minerogenic sediments. Recent dating of the intercalated peats (Bell *et al.* 2004), has shown that the horizon containing the later Mesolithic activity at Site J is dated to between 5749±23 uncal BP (OxA-12356) and 5061±21 uncal BP (OxA-12355), which calibrate to 4690–4500 and 3950–3790 cal BC respectively. At site D a thin reed peat developed on a sandy silt (basal Holocene unit), and this peat has been dated to 6790±38 uncal BP (OxA-12359) at its base, which calibrates to 5740–5620 cal BC, with the top dated to 6726±33 uncal BP (OxA-12358), which in turn calibrates to 5720–5560 cal BC (Bell *et al.* 2004: 14). An oak from this unit produced a date of 6770±70 uncal BP (Beta-60761), which when calibrated again fully overlaps with the dates from the base and top of the peat at 5800–5530 cal BC (*ibid.*: 14–15). The significant overlaps between these calibrations reflect the fact that the peat unit is only 6cm in thickness, and as such represents a relatively short sequence of development. Furthermore, the evidence from this location (Goldcliff west) indicates that Mesolithic activity was seasonal in nature, with hunting, fishing and the procurement of raw materials being undertaken during the autumn/winter months (Bell *et al.* 2003; Bell and Walker 2005: 164).

Caseldine (2000) has noted that the Mesolithic environment at the time of the earliest occupation at Goldcliff is not directly attested, due to the fact that pollen did not survive in the sediments of the land surface on which the activity occurred. This situation is apparently related to the fact that inundation of this deposit occurred after the Mesolithic occupation of the site. Basically, this horizon was dry during the human occupation of the site and waterlogging only occurred when sea levels rose and saturated the soil. Pollen does not preserve well in dry, aerated soil horizons. However, Caseldine (2000: 214) also notes that some indication of the contemporary environment may be forthcoming from a relatively thin band of charcoal-rich clay at the estuarine/Mesolithic soil boundary. This horizon produced Chenopodiaceae (goosefoots) indicative of local saltmarsh conditions, with pine in association. Initially grasses (Poaceae) are well represented, suggesting the development of reedswamp as sea levels were rising (*ibid.*). The vegetation on Goldcliff island and dryer areas comprised oak woodland with some elm, lime and ash, with hazel as an understorey component, and there is an indication that alder carr was present in the region (from the pollen analysis). Caseldine notes that herbaceous pollen that can be attributed to human activity is lacking, but high bracken (*Pteridium*) values may be a reflection of the burning activities in the area, as could the growth of hazel (2000: 214). The charcoal is dominated by hazel with substantial amounts of hawthorne type (Pomoideae), oak and elm (*ibid.*). Whilst the dry conditions that prevailed at the time the site was occupied limits the pollen, beetle and plant macrofossil evidence, some resistant species are represented by their seeds, with elder (*Sambucus nigra*) and nettles (*Urtica dioica*) being indicative of disturbance and as such probably the human activity at this site (Caseldine 2000: 214). A range of species indicative of woodland (three-nerved sandwort – *Moehringia trinervia*; hedge woundwort – *Stachys sylvatica*), disturbed ground or saltmarsh communities (oraches – *Atriplex* spp.; knotgrass – *Polygonum aviculare*) and swamp/fen environments (gypsywort – *Lycopus europaeus*; sedges – *Carex* spp.) are also in evidence in the palaeoenvironmental record for this location (*ibid.*). For a more detailed account of the environmental evidence from Goldcliff the reader is directed to Caseldine (*ibid.*: 208–44).

The research by Bell and co-workers (1999: 17) at Goldcliff has shown that the peats at this location record a sequence of succession from reed peat, to fen woodland and raised bog (also Bell 2000: 25; Caseldine 2000), and that the occupation occurs during a marine regressive stage when oak woodland was expanding out from the island edge between *ca.* 5600–5300 cal BC (Barton and Bell 2000: 60). At Goldcliff East (Trench D) pollen analysis has shown that the local vegetation initially comprised a mixture of sedges (Cyperaceae) and reeds, with a rise in Poaceae reflecting reedswamp development that progressively gives way to saltmarsh as inundation of the site progresses (Bell *et al.* 2003: 22). The initial woodland was dominated by hazel, with some oak, but oak soon expands in frequency whilst hazel decreases. There are two distinct peaks in charcoal abundance in this sequence, both of which appear to have had a marked impact on the composition of the vegetation, and one of the peaks appears to reflect burning of the reedswamp vegetation whilst the other, later, event impacted on the oak woodland itself (*ibid.*). Marine inundation occurs between *ca.* 5200–4900 cal BC, when the onset of bog formation occurs (Barton and Bell 2000: 60).

Peat forming from around *ca.* 5000 cal BC in the Wentlooge Formation (middle peat) contains the main concentration of archaeology in the levels. These peats are underlain by finely laminated marine sands, silts and clays of the lower Wentlooge Formation (transgressive silts largely saltmarsh), and overlain by marine clays of the Upper Wentlooge Formation (Allen and Rae 1987), the latter accumulating rapidly during the Iron Age (Bell 1999: 17–18). The mid-Holocene sequences have been traced by Allen and Haslett (2006: 1420) for *ca.* 15km on the Welsh side of the Severn Estuary, and with only one exception (between Cold Harbour Pill and Sea Street Lane where the upper peat unit [Bed 6, called the Cockle Bed peat] has a sharp to mildly uneven, eroded top) the peats succeed the silts gradationally (i.e. exhibit a conformable as opposed to erosive contact).

Allen and Haslett also record an erosional/sharp contact which is assumed to occur between their Beds 4 (peat) and 7 (silts) in the exposure between Porton House, towards Goldcliff Island (2006: 1421). The intercalated horizons of peat that occur at Goldcliff (Fig. 2.7) attest to the fact that periodic regressive and transgressive tendencies occur in the Severn Estuary across the Mesolithic and later periods. The analyses undertaken by Allen and Haslett on Bed 3 in this sequence (silts of saltmarsh derivation) have indicated that when these silts were being deposited (resolvable bands formed over intervals of a few decades during the periods *ca.* 5660–4610 cal BC and 5380–4721 cal BC), i.e. during the late Mesolithic, the data from their sites G, R and also M, may suggest a climate that is generally milder than today (2006: 1442). At this time average summer temperatures were *ca.* 0.5°C warmer and winters were 0.5–0.75°C colder than at present (*ibid.*, quoting Davies *et al.* 2003).

Moving away from the coast and into the upland zone, the detailed studies undertaken by Smith and Cloutman (1988) at Waun Fignen Felin bog, Powys (SS825179), have not only produced a *ca.* 5m deep sequence from deposits that were developing in a Devensian Late-glacial basin, but also from a number of additional sequences in and around the basin. The sequences cover the period *ca.* 10,200–2650 uncal BP (based on interpolated ages). The oldest and youngest radiocarbon dates from this location are 10,180±110 uncal BP (CAR-692) and 3520±70 uncal BP (CAR-624), *ca.* 10,430–9400 cal BC and *ca.* 2035–1670 cal BC respectively. The analyses undertaken by Smith and Cloutman have produced a considerable amount of data, including a detailed pollen zonation for the development of the vegetation and landscape at this location, indicators of asynchroneity in the timing of wetland developments and changes in the local flora, and some evidence to suggest that Mesolithic people were influential in the maintenance of open areas in the landscape and also that the firing episodes that were undertaken also exerted an influence on the types of vegetation that developed at this site. The depositional sequences comprise muds and reedswamp deposits which underlie blanket peat in some areas. Smith and Cloutman (1988: 159–60) suggest that the outlet of the basin was probably blocked by the development of ombrogenous peat around *ca.* 6500 uncal BP. Despite the variations that are outlined below (Table 2.2) in relation to the dating of the zone boundaries, Smith and Cloutman consider the zone boundaries to be synchronous given the limitations inherent in the methods used to calculate the boundary dates.

The general sequence of development at Waun Fignen Felin comprises birch woodland from the start of the depositional sequences at *ca.* 10,100 uncal BP, with declines in values occurring across the period *ca.* 10,100–9800 uncal BP (Smith and Cloutman 1988: 180–1). High grass values indicate the persistence of open conditions near the site at *ca.* 8400–8200 uncal BP. Hazel expands in the catchment around 8100–8000 uncal BP, and hazel continues in the catchment through to *ca.* 6000 uncal BP, although values for hazel away from the main blanket peat area are low at this location. Heather rises to *ca.* 20% of the pollen spectrum at *ca.* 7900 uncal BP in two locations, suggesting local presence. Heather is initially present at basin margin locations, and organic sedimentation begins at *ca.* 6700–6400 uncal BP, but peat development is asynchronous across the site (*ibid.*: 183). Alder is evident in the landscape from before *ca.* 7000 uncal BP and there are marked rises in the alder curves after *ca.* 6500 uncal BP, and the data indicate that alder first became established in the basin area, spreading out as conditions suitable for its establishment developed (*ibid.*: 181). Smith and Cloutman (1988: 169) link the rise in alder to continued burning of the local environment, being able to take advantage of forest damage to establish itself in new habitats.

There is a marked decline in hazel after *ca.* 6000 uncal BP at a number of the sites analysed, although localised hazel stands persist until *ca.* 5000 uncal BP. Alder shows a general rise throughout the study area at *ca.* 6000 uncal BP. Most of the sites with high heather representations show a decline in frequencies at *ca.* 6200–6000 uncal BP, and heath dominance appears to come to an end at the same time when there is a transition from mor to ombrogenous peat (Smith and Cloutman 1988: 183–6).

The "classic" elm decline is recorded across the zone 3–4 boundary at *ca.* 5500–4850 uncal BP. By *ca.* 5000 uncal BP all of the sites considered by Smith and Cloutman have evidence for the accumulation of blanket peat (1988: 186). After 5000 uncal BP hazel declines, but values begin to rise again at *ca.* 4000 uncal BP and local variations in hazel through until *ca.* 3700 uncal BP suggest that some of the mineral soils in the basin remained peat free until this time. Coincident with the decline in hazel, grass values rise after *ca.* 5000 uncal BP at two locations in the area, and there is a general rise in heather after *ca.* 4500–4300 uncal BP (Smith and Cloutman 1988: 183 and 186).

Table 2.2: General sequence of landscape developments at Waun Fignen Felin, with interpolated dates for zone boundaries based on radiocarbon dates outlined in Smith and Cloutman (1988).

Local pollen zone	Interpolated radiocarbon dates (uncal BP)	Vegetation	Environment
6		Birch-Ash-bog asphodels	Minimum of trees, maximum of grasses. Zones 6a–6b boundary has a marked elm decline. Frequent evidence for disturbance and single cereal grain – LBA agriculture.
5–6 Boundary	3150–2950–2800–2650	Rise of Ash and Bog Asphodels – minimum Elm	After 3000 BP there is a decline in tree pollen, possibly related to climatic changes and increased surface wetness and clearance activities.
5		Oak – Alder – Ribwort Plantain	Area is substantially peat covered, although high values for heather suggest a dry surface. Heather rises at *ca.* 3500 BP following declines in oak and hazel from 4000 BP. Bronze Age clearance and agricultural activities.
4–5 Boundary	4050–3950–3900–3850–3800–3750	Rise of Ribwort Plantain	Woodland persists in the central blanket-bog area until 3600 BP.
4		Oak – Alder	Woodland nearby with birch and willow. Elm decline recorded at 4600 BP, the zone 4a–4b boundary. Increase in possible agricultural indicators. By 4200 bog surface dominated by heather – heath.
3–4 Boundary	5500–5350–5200–5100–4950–4900–4850	Decline of Elm	5000 BP blanket peat accumulating across site. At 5200–4800 BP there is a decline in woodland in some areas of the site – fen and carr conditions with possible Neolithic farming away from the site.
3		Oak – Elm – Alder	5700 BP blanket peats develop, alder rises to the middle of this zone, after which bracken rises in frequency and there is a change from heather to grass dominance towards the end of the zone. Open water is in evidence.
2–3 Boundary	7500–7300–6600–6500–6200	Rise of Alder	Organic deposition at 7500 BP under acidic conditions. Alder is established by 7000 BP and Hazel woodland is replaced by heath and blanket bog by 6000 BP. Carr environments. Chenopodiaceae indicative of disturbed ground.
2		Hazel – Heather – Elm – Pine	Birch is present, oak rises in the zone along with elm, and willow is re-established. Rushes are evidenced across zones 1–2a.
1–2 Boundary	9300 and 8000	Rise of Hazel and fall of Birch	8000 BP first Mor deposit forms, possibly due to anthropogenic impacts. Mixed woodland with pine, oak and elm. Sedges and carr environments – open habitats.
1		Birch – Grasses – Willow	Early Holocene birch woodland, mainly closed forests. Open water and marsh or fen and reedswamp conditions in evidence at the site.

In general, there are a number of locations at Waun Fignen Felin where disturbances by people or animals are thought to exert an influence on the timing of vegetation developments (Smith and Cloutman 1988: 190); the influence of people is discussed in greater detail below. Interestingly, one of the key changes in the vegetation at Waun Fignen Felin is also a key marker for the transition from the Mesolithic to the Neolithic in Britain, the Elm Decline. At Waun Fignen Felin Smith and Cloutman (1988) have recorded consistency in the timing of the elm decline across the Atlantic to Sub-Boreal transition at *ca.* 5500–4950 uncal BP, equivalent to the local pollen zone 3–4 boundary. However, these authors also note that there are three declines or minimum levels in the elm curve at the zone 3–4, 4–5 and 5–6 boundaries; the latter boundaries are dated to 4050–3750 uncal BP and 3150–2650 uncal BP respectively. Smith and Cloutman (1988) suggest that the elm decline may be asynchronous in Wales, and that high resolution studies such as theirs are required to ensure that an accurate picture of vegetation development is produced.

The elm decline at Coed Taf C is dated to 3650–3100 cal BC (CAR-91; 4615±95 uncal BP), again reflecting the asynchronous nature of this "marker horizon" in Wales in the earlier part of the Neolithic period. In his discussion of the evidence at this site Chambers (1982a: 484) suggests tentative links between human landscape interactions and the onset of bog development, and also the regression of forest carr in phase C of his.pollen diagram, i.e. during the Mesolithic period and before *ca.* 3650–3100 cal BC. Tenuous links to Mesolithic archaeological material at Pant Sychbant (which is of possible later Mesolithic date), and to the assertion by Roger Jacobi (1980) that Mesolithic people would probably have exploited these uplands, fail to demonstrate that there is any secure evidence for anthropogenic influences in the catchment at this location during the Mesolithic period.

Elsewhere, palaeoenvironmental analysis in the vicinity of Thatcham in Berkshire has suggested that even within a river valley system, a mosaic of environments would have existed during the Mesolithic period (Scaife in Healy *et al.* 1992a: 66–70). It is worth remembering that even relatively slight local variations in climate, or even slope aspect, will influence what plants are available in a given landscape context, and when they are available, and of course we have already considered the probable impacts that grazing would have had on woodland composition (Vera 2002; Kirby 2003; Hodder *et al.* 2005). The site investigated by Healy *et al.* was located in a fairly open woodland with pine and hazel, and areas of oak and elm woodland (1992). In the floodplain areas fen vegetation and meandering streams are attested, whilst dry grassland habitats are also in evidence at this location, and there is some suggestion for anthropogenic modification of the vegetation in the period that the sites were occupied (i.e. post *ca.* 8600–8000 cal BC).

Scaife (1992a: 67) reports that there are increasing levels of herbs through the environmental sequence at Thatcham, suggesting that the hunter-fisher-forager groups are responsible for some opening up of the woodland canopy, which consequently promotes the expansion of ruderals that are characteristic of disturbed ground. Of course, it is also possible that tree-throws, natural fires and grazing by ruminants (Smith and Cloutman 1988) could all contribute to the expansion of the herbs in this area (especially in light of the finds of aurochs and red deer in the earlier excavations by Wymer (in Healy *et al.* 1992: 72)), although continual grazing would usually suppress herb populations.

The above examples demonstrate that, whilst there is considerable circumstantial evidence for human induced landscape modifications, to date the evidence from Star Carr remains the most compelling in suggesting Mesolithic firing and manipulation of the environment. By implication however, it seems unlikely that this knowledge was restricted to the people who were exploiting the environment around Lake Flixton during the Mesolithic period.

Mesolithic vegetation change, faunal variation and the impact of humans

A number of recent surveys, alongside finds from archaeological excavations, combine to provide us with a broad range of evidence that is perhaps suggestive of the manipulation of the contemporary vegetation, and its modification, in relation to the exploitation of the associated fauna that was available to hunter-fisher-forager groups during the Mesolithic period. In addition, for the later Mesolithic period at least, there is some suggestion that grazing herbivores may have been influential in the maintenance of open areas within the landscape, and even that these animals were of fundamental importance to woodland regeneration at this time (e.g. Vera 2002; Zvelebil 2003a; Buckland 2002; 2005; Hodder *et al.* 2005; Fyfe 2006).

In North Wales, work associated with the Upland Archaeology Initiative, and funded by RCAHMW, has been undertaken by Fiona Grant in the Clwydian Hills at Moel Llys y Coed (Grant 2008; 2009). Analysis of a core from a small basin mire located to the south west of Moel Llys y Coed (SJ 1471 6493), at an altitude of *ca.* 445m OD has shown that the organic sediments began to develop at this location before 7060–6700 cal BC (Beta-234073; 7990±50 uncal BP), and that towards the later part of the Mesolithic period the mire surface was colonised by alder at 4690–4410 cal BC (Beta-253802; 5700±50 uncal BP). By extrapolating the dates to the base of the core Grant (2008: 8) infers an onset date of 8600 uncal BP (around 7600 cal BC) for her local pollen assemblage zone (LPAZ) MLC-1, at which time the landscape is largely wooded, with hazel as a canopy tree and birch and pine as significant components in the woodland, and with willow and juniper present as secondary elements. The presence of juniper confirms the fact that local environmental factors are influencing the late survival of this species in Wales (see also Watkins *et al.* 2007). Towards the end of this zone at *ca.* 6200–6100 cal BC (placed at 7300 uncal BP; again by extrapolation of the dates) the vegetation is characterised by oak, elm, ash and lime, all of which are key elements in the woodland, which is generally characterised by a closed-canopy, except perhaps in upland areas around the site. A marginal fen community around an open water body, comprised alder and horsetail, with *Phragmites* at the water's edge at this location (*ibid.*: 8). Hazel dominates towards the end of this zone at *ca.* 7400 uncal BP (interpolated age), which calibrates to *ca.* 6350–6220 cal BC. This hazel dominance is associated with a burning event that also coincides with a fall in the frequency of birch and pine (Grant 2008: 8).

The burning in evidence at Moel Llys y Coed, has been linked to a number of Mesolithic activity sites in the region, and Grant (2008) suggests that the promotion of hazel, and as a consequence the promotion/production of nut availability, alongside management of herd movements implies that Mesolithic hunter-fisher-foragers were actively managing the landscape during the middle Mesolithic period. However, the evidence for a decline in hazel and the expansion of species such as birch, pine and ultimately, alder, in Grant's LPAZ MLC2, indicates that these activities did not continue into the later Mesolithic period, and in addition, there is little evidence for a human presence during this phase. There is however a subsequent burning phase at 6000 uncal BP (interpolated), and associated declines in birch and pine are considered to support the view that the uplands are again being actively managed at *ca.* 4940–4840 cal BC.

Grant's work may provide us with some important insights into the nature of Mesolithic human–landscape interactions in the upland zone, as the discrete burning episodes that are recorded may suggest that the periodic firing activity undertaken by Mesolithic people was both a regular event, and one that ultimately contributed to changes in the nature of the vegetation in this zone as the regeneration after burning resulted in increased grazing pressures (*ibid.*: 10, also Russell-Smith *et al.* 1997: 174–6 for ethnographic insights into fire management practices in Western Arnhem Land, Northern Australia). However, whilst there is a general acceptance of the use of fire by human groups as a "management tool" during the Mesolithic period, the discussions below will demonstrate that, whilst compelling, much of the evidence remains circumstantial in nature, and proof of an anthropogenic cause for the firing episodes is seldom conclusive.

In this context, Watkins *et al.* (2007: 178) have suggested that whilst there is little evidence to suggest human modifications of the landscape before the end of the Mesolithic period at Llyn Cororion, the palynological evidence does support the notion that people were potentially maintaining "small-scale, temporary, unselective clearances within the forest" at *ca.* 6350 uncal BP. The evidence for clearances includes high levels of charcoal and herbaceous taxa such as such as *Artemisia, Cirsium, Achillea* type, *Plantago lanceolata, Rumex* undiff., *Urtica* and *Pteridium*, suggestive of anthropogenic influences (*ibid.*: 178), but again, proving that this activity was deliberate is difficult. An interesting observation from this work is that there is no evidence for firing episodes between 6250–5800 uncal BP, i.e. spanning the Mesolithic–Neolithic transition. Mighall and Chambers (1995: 315) have discussed the fact that there has been considerable debate into the nature of the spread and establishment of alder during the Early Holocene, with factors such as Mesolithic human activity, natural fires, beavers, or the creation of suitable habitats through hydroseral successions and floodplain developments all being proffered. As noted by these authors, and as the discussion of Waun Fignen Felin (presented below) suggests, whilst peaks in Poaceae, *Artemisia* and Chenopodiaceae, charcoal and the rise in alder often coincide, the evidence from locations such as Bryn y Castell and Waun Fignen Felin is not unequivocal when trying to determine whether human or natural vectors are responsible for the firing episodes that have occurred. Similarly, Ince (1983: 170) has linked climatic influences to the decline in pine and rise of alder at Llyn Llydaw and Cwm Cywion at *ca.* 6900 uncal BP (inferred on the basis of dates from Nant Ffrancon), as there are no indicators of anthropogenic impacts, and lithostratigraphic changes (a distinct silt layer) at Llydaw appear to suggest local flooding of the mire surface.

The above evidence clearly suggests that inferring anthropogenic, as opposed to natural, causes for changes in the abundance of certain species can become a somewhat circular debate due to the paucity of direct evidence for human interference, irrespective of the evidence for burning episodes. Perhaps more robust support for the suggested anthropogenic vector in vegetation change is forthcoming from the work of Bell (2001; Bell *et al.* 2002), who has outlined the results from sites such as Redwick and Goldcliff in the Severn Estuary. Bell (2001: 75) notes that peats that are dated to 6380–6050 cal BC (7330±70 uncal BP: Beta-134637) on the basis of a sample of oak, have produced evidence for a burning episode (from a charcoal horizon in the peat). However, whilst in this case the burning episode is not associated with any evidence for a human presence, at a slightly later Mesolithic date there is a charcoal spread on an old landsurface at Goldcliff that is associated with Mesolithic artefacts and faunal remains, including red deer, which is dated to 5540–5210 cal BC (6420±80 uncal BP: Swan-28). It is entirely possible that both episodes were anthropogenic in origin, but caution must always be taken when interpreting this type of evidence.

Bell also reports that there is evidence for burning on the fringes of Goldcliff Island at *ca.* 4800–4540 cal BC (5820±50 uncal BP: GrN-24143), and suggests that it is improbable that the evidence for burning, on the scale apparent at Goldcliff and Redwick, are purely the product of campfires, or wildfire (*ibid.*: 75). This, alongside other evidence from locations such as Star Carr, is taken to suggest that Mesolithic people were using fire as a deliberate form of environmental management/manipulation, in both upland and lowland contexts.

As noted, the high-resolution palaeoenvironmental studies carried out in the vicinity of Star Carr in the Vale of Pickering, northeastern Yorkshire, have suggested that hunter-gatherer groups deliberately fired the vegetation around Lake Flixton, presumably in order to promote new growth and encourage browsing by ungulates such as red and roe deer (Day 1993; Mellars and Dark 1998). Browsing activity at the wetlands edge, or within woodland, will have an effect on openness, the maintenance of clearings, the establishment of pathways and woodland regeneration, such that the notion of impenetrable closed woodland may need to be modified in order to facilitate a more nuanced approach to the evidence (e.g. Fig. 2.10 and discussion above).

Cummins (2000) has noted that the impact of firing episodes, or at least the increased "visibility" of the use of fire for the manipulation of the vegetation around Lake Flixton, appears to be far more extensive in the later Mesolithic when compared to the small scale impacts observed during the earlier Mesolithic period at this location. It is of course conceivable that as the deciduous woodlands reached their climax state during the Mesolithic period the use of fire as a management tool became more of a necessity than in earlier periods. Elsewhere in the Star Carr area Cummings (2000) notes that research at sites such as No Name Hill, located *ca.* 1.25km to the northeast of Star Carr, or Flixton School on the south side of the lake, has indicated that the charcoal deposition in evidence can be

Fig. 2.10: Differing aspects of deciduous woodlands in August; Note that even where relatively dense canopy occurs clearings are in evidence and arise from factors such as tree-throws, grazing pressure, the establishment of animal/ human pathways and both natural and anthropogenic firing episodes. © Author.

correlated to a domestic origin, i.e. small camp fires for cooking, warmth and light, as there is no discernible corresponding impact on the vegetation in these areas.

In the upland areas of South Wales, at Waun Fignen Felin, Smith and Cloutman (1988: 163) recorded high concentrations of charcoal at the base of the blanket peats and in the underlying mor deposit, the former of which is described as being "greasy and amorphous". The mor deposit is dated to pre-8000 uncal BP (although its inception dates vary across the site) suggesting that human impacts on the landscape pre-date this age. A decline in birch is linked to the burning episodes at Waun Fignen Felin.

The rise of hazel and heather into zone 2 at Waun Fignen Felin is thought to be contingent on the suppression of birch through burning and the resistance of hazel and heather to firing episodes (*ibid*.: 169). The asynchronous nature of mor soil formation and the frequent presence of charcoal suggest that climatic conditions are not the cause of mor development.

Smith and Cloutman (1988: 198) propose that the burning episodes were carried out on heath, woodland and/or scrub, and that whilst direct evidence for human manipulation of the environment by firing is not forthcoming, the presence of cultural material of Mesolithic age alongside the fact that young heather can withstand grazing by red deer more readily than old heather, suggests that heath-burning, whether natural or anthropogenic in origin, would have been very beneficial to Mesolithic people in this area. In addition further support for the association of human/animal activity to the maintenance of open areas at Waun Fignen Felin, and its links to ombrogenous peat development, is provided by Smith and Cloutman's (1988: 200; also Moore 1973; 1975) observation that their evidence suggests that woodland regeneration on the heathland, especially colonisation by birch and even oak, is suppressed, possibly by a combination of burning and grazing.

Recent research at Esgair Ffraith, near Lampeter (Walker *et al*. 2006) has further reinforced the growing acceptance of the fact that Mesolithic people used burning/firing episodes either as an aid to hunting, to promote the growth of a new range of plant species, or as a means of controlling vegetation. The fact that this form of deliberate manipulation is effectively a form of land management, more often attributed to later farming populations, is an important observation in this context. It should always be remembered however that whilst the intimate association of human activity with firing episodes in the landscape is suggestive of deliberate modification, the impact of natural phenomena such as lightning strikes can also be implicated in the firing episodes that are recorded (e.g. Brown 1997).

Re-evaluation of the potential significance/meaning of firing episodes by Davies *et al*. (2005) has sought to consider these landscape "features" from the perspective of the social aspects of Mesolithic lifeways. These authors argue that the focus on optimal foraging and resource procurement strategies as reasons for the firing and maintenance of openings in the woodland canopy during the Mesolithic fails to account for social activities such as play and dance (*ibid*.: 282), or story-telling near a fire in a clearing, enjoying the warming sunlight after moving through the forest understorey, or even entering a clearing where, at night, a lost hunter can gauge their location by the stars.

There are many potential threats and challenges when moving through the earlier Holocene landscapes of Britain, not least from the chance encounter with a wild boar or wolf, or the difficulties inherent in finding one's way through an unfamiliar forested landscape. Davies *et al.* remind us that the earlier Holocene landscape was not necessarily a safe, sterile, Garden of Eden, but a dynamic, changing and at times dangerous environment that had, in the view of these authors, the potential to be "malevolent" (2005: 283). It should not be forgotten however that deciduous woodlands can also be dynamic in terms of their perception as dangerous places, as during the summer even in bright sunlight the woodland can be a dark and foreboding place, albeit one with openings in the canopy, whilst conversely in winter, when devoid of foliage the trees allow differing levels of light to filter through and offer the potential to navigate, to some degree, using the sun or even the night sky (Fig. 2.11).

Further afield, at Schwarzenberg Lake, South Bohemia, Czech Republic, Pokorny *et al.* (2010) have recorded evidence for anthropogenic impacts in the landscape, such as controlled burning, potentially identifiable by patterns of carbonised remains identified at the site, charcoal inputs into the lake sediments, and the pollen of species expanding in areas affected by fires and de-vegetation events (such as *Pteridium aquilinum* [Bracken] and *Calluna vulgaris* [Heather]), and also the subsequent appearance of pollen species with a preference for open grassy areas such as *Thalictrum, Rumex acestosella, Melampyrum, Plantago*

Fig 2.11: Deciduous woodlands in January; In addition to open areas, differing light conditions and visibility would influence the perception of the woodlands on a seasonal basis. © Author.

lanceolata, Gramineae). Furthermore, Mesolithic activity is also suggested by the presence of hazel nuts, raspberries and strawberries within the lake itself; elements that are not easily explained by natural events alone (Pokorny *et al.* 2007; 2010).

There is a considerable corpus of evidence to support the use of fire as a means to control the environment, manage resources (both plant and animal) and to provide foci for the everyday activities of people during the Mesolithic throughout Europe. As will be readily apparent from this outline, the nature of the woodlands that are attested by the above descriptions are such that the composition of the animal communities in the Mesolithic environment would differ markedly when compared to those that were exploiting the steppe grasslands that characterised Britain throughout much of the Palaeolithic period. Unfortunately, faunal remains from Mesolithic Wales are relatively sparse, although a characteristic woodland species, pig, has been identified at Lydstep, and red deer have been recovered from Goldcliff in the Severn Estuary. The Lydstep pig was associated with a pair of microliths, and was dated to the later Mesolithic at 4350–3940 cal BC (5300±100 uncal BP: OxA-1412) (Caseldine 1990: 40) (see Chapter 5). Other Mesolithic faunal remains have been recovered from Freshwater west, Borth, Amroth and Whitesands Bay, with the species represented including aurochs, red deer, pig, roe deer and brown bear (*ibid.*). Cave sites with apparent associations of Mesolithic artefacts and faunal remains include Potters cave on Caldey and Ogof Garreg Hir, South Pembrokeshire. At these locations additions to the faunal inventory for Mesolithic Wales include fox, wolf, hare and dog.

Discussion

The changing landscapes, environments and vegetation of the earlier Holocene, and more specifically the Mesolithic period itself, would undoubtedly have necessitated the constant re-orientation of human–landscape interactions and people's perceptions of their environment. There are numerous interlinking factors influencing the nature of the environment during the Mesolithic period, and whilst the influence of Mesolithic groups may perhaps have been significant at a local level, it is unlikely to have been significant at the landscape level. Consistent background factors during the earlier Holocene, across the entire Mesolithic period, include the continuous expansion of woodland and changes in the relative frequency of the various tree species, rising sea levels (or phases of progradation and retrogradation *cf.* Weerts 2013), changes in the composition of the flora and fauna, and differing levels of human impact on the environment as population size increases (or fluctuates). As mentioned above, there were also significant and very "visible" changes occurring in the landscape of the North Sea Basin as the tsunami event that was caused by the Storegga slide off western Norway at *ca.* 6200–6100 cal BC would have had an effective wave height of *ca.* 20m (*ibid.*). One final, and perhaps influential aspect that must be considered here, is the potential that browsing animals had on the maintenance of open areas and also on the regeneration of woodland (e.g. Vera 2002).

Throughout this period hazelnuts are recorded as an almost ubiquitous element of the diet, although as noted by Edwards (1999: 535), there is little evidence to support high fire frequency as a factor in the earlier Holocene hazel rise. Edwards preferred instead to suggest that natural succession is a simple explanation for the rise of this species during the earlier Mesolithic (*ibid.*). Whatever the mechanisms for the rise in hazel during the Mesolithic period, there is little doubt that this species provided an important food resource, and Mithen's work has shown that some forms of management were in place during the Mesolithic period (Mithen *et al.* 2001). In addition, the branches of hazel have a proven use in the construction of dwellings, trackways, drying racks and fish traps etc. The exploitation of hazel is attested at a number of sites in Ireland during the Mesolithic, e.g. Mount Sandal, on the River Bann in Co. Londonderry and Lough Boora in Co. Offaly, and at the former site the charred hazelnut remains found in several pits may indicate the storage of this resource, perhaps for use as a winter food supplement (McComb and Simpson 1999: 8; citing Woodman 1985; 1986). At Lough Boora "both carbonised hazel shell fragments and a significant amount of preserved, uncarbonised, whole and fragmented hazelnuts were recovered" from an early Mesolithic habitation site, again suggesting that this species was an important dietary staple (McComb and Simpson 1999: 10). As has been highlighted throughout this chapter, a significant issue in Mesolithic studies is the variable visibility of the archaeological and environmental record of human–landscape interactions imposed as a consequence of rising sea levels, degradation and destruction of the wetlands resource and a failure to identify locations where wetland/dryland resources are preserved (as evidenced at Star Carr) and from where greater insights into Mesolithic groups will be forthcoming. This situation is still in need of redress, but despite the inherent limitations in our datasets, the information presented above has shown that significant insights are forthcoming from the environmental record of vegetation changes across the Mesolithic period.

As might be anticipated, in some instances the landscape losses that resulted from changes in relative sea levels could have severely restricted seasonal activities as movement through the landscape would, in certain locations, become more difficult or constrained. The progressive inundation of low-lying areas such as Cardigan Bay and the Severn Estuary would have been accompanied by shifts in the structure of the vegetation from dryland to wetland, and also with altitude as tree species expanded to their viable limits. These shifts would influence animal movements through the landscape, necessitating a constant reorientation of engagement with the available biomass on the part of the human groups that were exploiting this environment. As resources varied spatially and temporally across the Mesolithic period, there is little doubt that the sensory experiences of people at this time would also have changed significantly, even at the level of the single generation. During the earlier Holocene period it is likely that the entire landscape perception of human groups, and their engagement with the world, would have been in need of constant negotiation and re-negotiation.

We have noted above that the past was not a static place; hunter-fisher-foragers would have seen, smelt, tasted, heard and touched their environment. Whilst we cannot know the aesthetic considerations of the choices made by the men, women and children that lived during the Mesolithic period it is very unlikely that all choices were made for purely functional reasons, as certain locations would have specific attributes, such as a good view, a south facing aspect or spiritual/ritual significance (amongst other factors). In attempting to paint a picture or write a social narrative of Mesolithic lifeways it is the viewer or reader that imbues the narrative with their own lived experience. With this in mind the reader is encouraged to reflect on their own memories of the upland and lowland zones (of Wales, Europe or elsewhere) and the variations in environments within these zones, and those of coastal, riverine and lacustrine environments, in order to give meaning to this narrative. Whilst our modern landscape is predominantly a construct of farming and industrial developments there are many locations where a semblance of the "wild" (or what we might imagine to be a wild and untamed landscape) still exists and excites our imagination, with these images in mind we can perhaps begin to develop more meaningful reflections on the past as experienced by Mesolithic groups in the pages that follow.

3

Tools of the trade: post-glacial tool-kits, their use and their significance

... the Eskimo say that only a fool comes home empty handed ... (Binford 1979: 259)

Introduction

A visit to the four Historic Environment Records (HERs) for Dyfed, Gwynedd, Clwyd-Powys and Glamorgan and Gwent, leaves the researcher under no illusions as to the complexities inherent in curating the archaeological record for Wales; and it also reveals a seemingly extensive record of Mesolithic finds spots for Wales. There are some limitations with the records however; as is fully acknowledged by the various curators of the HERs. This is due, in no small part, to the fact that the collectors of the archaeological resource have varied in their approaches, with this being evident in terms of the different levels of rigour in relation to finds recording and the accurate location of their finds (Silvester and Owen 2002). The fact is that some collections represent the conflation of numerous visits to a number of finds spots in the same area, and it is often difficult to confirm the provenance of the finds, a factor that is embedded in the different approaches adopted over time as amateur and professional archaeologists alike have developed, and generally improved, their methodologies for site identification and recording.

In illustrating this point, research by Locock (2000), assessing 673 stone finds spots from the then Sites and Monuments Record in southeast Wales, reported that "a significant number of records had been erroneously described as "single find", and that many records lacked any quantification" (2000: 7). Indeed, after the initial assessment of the available data for Glamorgan and Gwent, Locock determined that 70 of the recorded stone finds for the prehistoric period were not significant, and as such were excluded from his survey, whilst of the 603 find spots remaining, only 48 were attributed to the Mesolithic period. Similarly, research by Cambria Archaeology undertaken in 2003–4 (Page 2004) noted that a) some collectors in southwest Wales often grouped together large amounts of material gathered from a number of locations as a single record, thereby creating a totally unsatisfactory inventory and negating accurate identification of findspots; b) that the SMR (Sites and

Monuments Record) itself contained numerous inconsistencies, with many records only containing a six figure grid reference, thereby making accurate identification of finds location improbable (if not impossible); and c) additional collection biases appear to occur as 73% of the recorded total of lithic scatters are located in Pembrokeshire and all but two of the sites with 8-figure grid references are in this region of southwest Wales. Other areas with Mesolithic activity include the Towy Valley and the Cardigan Bay coastline, and the two sites outside of Pembrokeshire that have 8-figure grid references are the Isolation Hospital site, Aberystwyth and Coygan Camp in Carmarthenshire (Page 2004: 6). Some degree of collection bias is also alluded to by Silvester and Owen (2002: 15) who note that the overall distribution of the *ca.* 900 flint and chert collections recorded in the CPAT database highlights concentrations in The Walton Basin, the Black Mountains, the central Brecon Beacons and the Vale of Clwyd. When we consider these issues against the fact that archaeological assemblages are, in general, the final result of multiple factors of deposition, preservation and recovery (Midgley 1992: 369), the inherent problems of what is already a fragmentary and biased record are readily apparent.

These observations add weight to other limitations highlighted by earlier researchers who have suggested that "the conventional archaeological site is a poor unit of analysis in considering regional settlement patterns" (Smith 1992b: 37), as defining the site itself appears to be problematic given the available records. David (1989: 241) however, had also noted that due to the paucity of contemporary environmental evidence and lack of faunal collections to which a human presence could be associated, a consideration of the distribution, composition and potential function of lithic assemblages was undertaken "out of necessity". In this context it is perhaps worth noting that the lithic scatters themselves are probably all that remains of the settlement/activity site after the less durable organic components have degraded, and as such, they offer the potential to function as "markers" for the identification of buried features such as hearths, pits and post-holes in areas where little in the way of discernible structures or upstanding archaeology is forthcoming. An additional aspect of the lithic inventories for Mesolithic activity lies in the suggestion that these sites may represent evidence for a long-term commitment to particular locations in the landscape (Pollard 1999: 82), and as suggested by Cummings (2000: 90), the coastal sites of Pembrokeshire "show that Mesolithic sites were not randomly positioned in the landscape, but meaningfully situated". These observations will be explored more fully in Chapter 4.

Following on from the above, it should also be borne in mind that we need to distinguish that it is people and not their stone tools that inhabited the Mesolithic landscape, and that failing to embed stone tools in their social and economic context, and to recognise that they represent the people who made them, is tantamount to a failure to understand the archaeological record of the Mesolithic (Zvelebil 2003a: 1). Furthermore, Nyree Finlay (2003a) has attempted to delve deeper into our understanding of microlith production processes by exploring the notion of multiple authorship and the social significance of artefact production itself. The fact is that, at a fundamental level, people produced stone tools as functional items for use in subsistence activities, and aspects such as age, gender and the social relations of production are all embedded in the production process. The artefacts themselves may well be integrated into interlinking processes of production, or *chaîne-opératoire* (Finlay 2000a: 24, see also Conneller 2000a). In Britain, the concept of *chaîne-opératoire* is equivalent to the concept of the reduction sequence, with the former incorporating "an additional element in that technology is conceived as a socially transmitted body of knowledge, and as a socialised suite of gestures on matter" (Conneller 2008: 163). This concept has resonance to the theories put forward by Zvelebil (2005: 89) who has suggested that knowledge and material culture are forms of cultural inheritance that are socially embedded structurally, modified by routine practice, agency and historical constraint, and are passed on through learning, either intergenerationally or between individuals and communities, and which are modified by innovation. Ultimately, these processes generate material culture signatures and patterns that can be "read" and understood, to some degree, as a consequence of processes of learning and the implementation of knowledge (*ibid.*: 89). It must be borne in mind that "identities and culture are not imagined once and for all, but must constantly be recreated", such that identities are often articulated through "subtle social relations, in ways which could, and did, change and develop over time" (Macdonald 1997: xvi–xix).

As a consequence of the above discussion, we can assume that lithic technologies will not only reflect function, but they also have the potential to reflect individual identities and cultural trends as these are articulated over time. We should always remember the identities that can be articulated through the product of knapping also have the potential to allow for the identification of the *incipient specialists* whose knapping skills are developed during an apprenticeship that may start in young childhood or adolescence, however these are defined culturally (e.g. Sternke and Sørensen 2009: 722; Högberg 2008). Furthermore, it is now recognised that multiple ownerships of the component parts of the tool that is produced may also occur (Finlay 2003a: 174–5). These "ownerships" may well have conferred rights of access to the "product" e.g. the animal that is killed or the grasses that are harvested, when using a composite tool that is produced by a number of people, or they may have engendered an obligation, or reinforced relationships between individuals in the group (Finlay 2000a: 30). To quote Finlay (2003a: 175) further, "because of its reliance and emphasis on multiple components, microlithic technology can be seen as a forum for group participation and expression rather than individual action". So, whilst it is the people who occupied the Mesolithic landscape, their stone tools may well offer much greater insights into their socio-economic and ritual activities than might be suggested by the simple occurrence of a lithic scatter in that landscape. A good example of this, in terms of ritualised activity, is the observation that analysis of a wide variety of Danish Mesolithic sites has shown that up to 88% of the arrowheads found at certain locations were hardly ever used in hunting activities (Price 2009: 686, *citing* Fischer 1985). Price suggests that unused points may have been produced for a specific hunting trip, or for the hunting of a specific animal, and that their reuse may not have been considered appropriate, either in terms of the object itself or the animal that was being hunted (*ibid.*: 686).

Unfortunately, in terms of our understanding of context, the fact is that many of the finds records that are listed in the regional HER inventories for Wales do not provide any indication of the numbers or types of artefacts that were recovered. This is compounded by descriptions such as multiple findspot, findspot, find scatter and/or finds, which are less informative than descriptions such as cave occupation, occupation site, flintworking floor/site, multiple findspot (81 objects), or more importantly, where individual finds are described as microlith, burin or core, and where the identification of broad or narrow blade microlith is offered. The use of generic designations limits the degree to which we can interrogate the data with a view to determining the likely date and function of a site, and without a detailed knowledge of flintworking technology our ability to further refine certain finds records is limited. Additional limitations also exist in that "multiple" findspot designations can be followed by "2 artefacts" in the description, and whilst it might be legitimate to argue that two finds are "multiple", the significance of two lithic finds is perhaps somewhat less than a multiple findspot of say 3466 objects, especially if those objects are described in detail. However, despite the difficulties that are clearly inherent in attempting to provide some sort of indication of the nature of the sites that are recorded by the finds records, mapping of the overall distribution of finds for the Mesolithic will be undertaken throughout this chapter (see Fig. 3.1).

In addition, where possible, and where the records are of sufficient resolution to do so, those sites that can be classed as potential occupation sites, flintworking sites, or activity sites will be highlighted in the discussion below. By contrast, whilst individual find spots or sites with a very low number of probable Mesolithic finds should (at the very least) be considered as providing some indication of the potential distribution of human activity and range of landscape contexts that were being exploited by our Mesolithic ancestors, these are included, but should only be considered as possible or potential findspots until their provenance can be investigated further, i.e. through a detailed study of the existing collections. Records that were too limited in terms of the information provided have been excluded from the distribution maps in order to try to reduce the background "noise" in relation to Mesolithic findspots.

The caveats highlighted by Silvester and Owen (2002: 11), in relation to the fact that defining a function to an assemblage is a speculative activity, and that realistically for surface material this is nearly impossible, are noted, but some degree of interpretation is clearly warranted when trying to understand the past. An additional caveat to this discussion must be made in relation to collection bias; the uplands of Wales are remote and sometimes inaccessible, meaning that large-scale systematic surveys are often few in number, with the exceptions noted above, and of course, as we have also already discussed, the coastal areas of Wales were once more extensive (e.g. Wainwright 1963). As a consequence, the "dots on the map" can seldom represent anything more than a partial picture of Mesolithic human activity in the landscape, but as prehistoric archaeologists are amongst the most optimistic of people, we always hope that the distributions maps we create are "representative" samples of the "reality" that existed in terms of Mesolithic human–landscape interactions. The task, as highlighted for the Neolithic period by Josh Pollard (1999), is not to simply look at the dots, but to join the dots in such a way that we can build a picture of (in this case) the Mesolithic period that allows us to understand time, space and place in relation

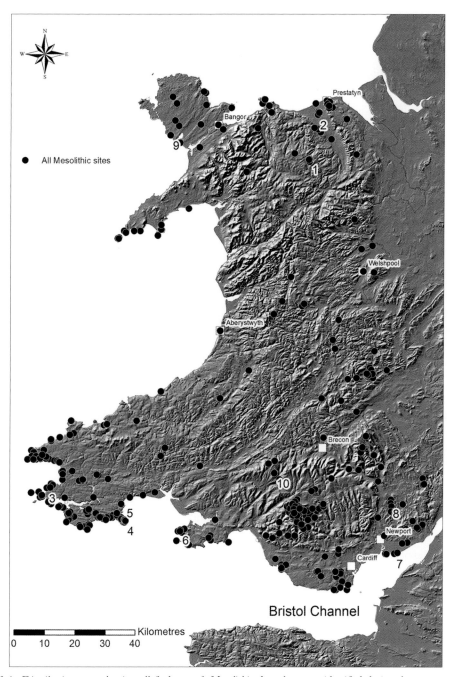

Fig. 3.1: Distribution map showing all findspots of Mesolithic date that were identified during the current study. Only sites with secure attributions to the Mesolithic period are included. Whilst 484 locations form the basis for this distribution map, inevitably, this will require updating as new finds have been made during the writing of this volume: 1 – Brenig 53, 2 – Rhuddlan, 3 – the Nab Head, 4 – Daylight Rock, 5 – Nanna's Cave, 6 – Burry Holmes, Llangenydd, 7 – Goldcliff, 8 – Trostrey Castle, 9 – Trwyn Du, 10 – Waun Fignen Felin.

to socially embedded and constructed practices. Finally, it is worth noting that there is currently no general consensus on key lithic categories for Britain, resulting in "competing and largely incompatible definitions", which consequently results in inherent limitations when comparing lithic assemblages (Ballin 2000: 9).

Ultimately, this chapter will therefore aim to provide some insights into the nature of post-glacial tool-kits, their use and usefulness in relation to the changing environments of this period, elaborate on the nature of the raw materials exploited, and discuss the nature of the HER records in relation to human–landscape interactions, subsistence strategies and settlement patterning. This preliminary assessment links directly in to Chapters 4 and 5, where settlement and subsistence economies are considered in greater detail, as without the right tools, hunting-fishing and foraging in the changing environments of the earlier Holocene would undoubtedly have been a much less effective and less successful endeavour than the evidence appears to indicate.

Post-glacial Britain – The Lithic Evidence

It is now some time since Roger Jacobi (1976: 67) suggested that, despite an extended nomenclature, the British Mesolithic lithic inventories showed sufficient similarities to allow them to be considered to be closely linked at the techno-complex level, such that the Mesolithic could be divided into an Early, Later and latest stage. In simple terms, the lithic industries characterising each of these stages comprised microliths (considered to be the type artefact for the Mesolithic) of broad-blade (with a width that is usually greater than 8mm) and narrow-blade type (consequently less than 8mm in width) respectively (Switzur and Jacobi 1979), with the latest stage having broad blades trimmed by a double truncation into a trapezoidal to rhomboidal outline (Jacobi 1976: 75). The generic date for the shift from the "early" broad-blade to "late" narrow-blade stages of the Mesolithic in Wales is placed at *ca.* 8700 uncal BP, which calibrates broadly to 7740–7610 BC. The Madawg rock shelter in the Wye Valley (English side), has produced one of the earliest radiocarbon dates for a Late Mesolithic flint assemblage, where a date of 8710±70 uncal BP (OxA-6081) was obtained on a charred sloe stone (Lynch *et al.* 2000: 23); this date calibrates to 8165–7586 cal BC, and as will be readily discernible when considering the calibrated dates from the earlier Mesolithic assemblages at Trwyn Du, Anglesey and Rhuddlan, Clwyd (Table 3.1), the Madawg "Late" assemblage date fully overlaps with those of "earlier" lithic assemblages. Similarly, the dates of 8730±90 uncal BP (OxA-2269) and 8700±100 uncal BP obtained at Prestatyn both span the range 8200–7550 cal BC (Burrow 2003: 17). As such a generic date for the shift from broad blade to narrow blade technologies in Wales is given as 7900 cal BC by David and Walker (2004).

Kozłowski (2003: xvii–xviii) has questioned the simplistic and unidirectional sequence of broad triangles→narrow triangles→trapezes as a generalisation for the evolution of Mesolithic flint industries across Europe, highlighting the fact that firstly, these forms were used by Palaeolithic populations (a point noted by Jacobi in 1987), and secondly that the stylistic, typological and technological differences in stone tool assemblages relate to

Table 3.1: Dates for a number of early Mesolithic sites in Wales (after David 2007; Quinnell and Blockley 1994: 57 and 75; Lynch et al. 2000; Schulting and Richards 2002a; Tolan-Smith 2008; Meiklejohn et al. 2011).

Site	Location	Lab. no.	Date uncal BP	Calibrated age BC (1σ)	Calibrated age BC (2σ)
West Wales					
Daylight Rock, Caldey Island	SS 1495 9663				
Daylight Rock, Human (M)		OxA-7686	8655±60	7580–7500	7940–7580
(nutshell)		OxA-2245	9040±90	8346–7993	8540–7960
(nutshell)		OxA-2246	9030±80	8320–7998	8450–7960
(nutshell)		OzA-2247	8850±80	8203–7832	8250–7720
Ogof-yr-Ychen YY114 (M)	SS 1465 9691	OxA-7690	*8280±55	7180–6990	7490–7140
Ogof-yr-Ychen YY115 (F)		OxA-7691	8210±55	7040–6820	7450–7070
Ogof-yr-Ychen 'A' (M?)		OxA-22987	8476±38	7350–7170	7583–7490
Ogof-yr-Ychen 'B' (F?)		OxA-2574	7020±100	5790–5590	6070–5720
Ogof-yr-Ychen 'B'* (M)		OxA-7742	7880±55	6600–6480	7030–6610
Ogof-yr-Ychen 'C' (M?)		OxA-7741	8415±65	7420–7170	7580–7340
Potter's Cave (PC1)	SS 436 9707	OxA-7687	7880±55	6670–6530	7030–6610
Potter's Cave		OxA-7688	8580±60	7580–7490	7730–7530
Worm's Head Human	SS 3836 8770	OxA-4042	8800±80	7950–7660	8210–7615
		OxA-19844	9255 ± 45	8480–8330	8612–8329
		OxA-16607	9294 ± 49	8570–8350	8701–8343
		OxA-11129	9360 ± 50	8620–8480	8764–8478
		OxA-11083	9420 ± 55	8710–8570	9109–8556
		OxA-11128	9450 ± 50	8720–8590	9118–8609
		OxA-13131	9920 ± 160	9750–9210	10,096–8,861
The Nab Head (Site I)	SM 7906 1108	OxA-1495	9210±80	8540–8315	8620–8280
		OxA-1496	9110±80	8440–8250	8570–8020
North Wales					
Upper Kendrick's cave	SH 7800 8283	OxA-5862	9945±75	9650–9300	9760–9270
Rhuddlan Site E	SJ 0256 7788	BM-691	8739±86	7940–7615	8200–7590
Rhuddlan Site M	SJ 0261 7777	BM-822	8528±73	7600–7520	7730–7460
Trwyn Du, Anglesey	SH 3523 6787	Q-1385	8640±150	7940–7545	8230–7460
		HAR-1194	8590±90	7715–7540	7940–7490
(date thought to be too young)		HAR-1193	7980±140	7060–6690	7320–6530
South Wales					
Trostrey Castle, Usk	SO 3595 0435	Beta-098452	9510±60	9120–8740	8945–8420

Note: It appears that CPAT PRN-81666 erroneously lists BM-691 as 8639±86 uncal BP and *Tolan-Smith (2008) lists OxA-7690 as 8290±55 uncal BP. Sites in italics are those sites with earlier Mesolithic industries and human remains, the latter dated by Schulting and Richards (2002a) for which marine offsets have been calculated; (M) = Male, (F) = Female (Dates on human remains. *: Schulting and Richards note that the Ogo-yr-Ychen B samples are from 2 separate individuals, as alluded to by David (1990). The three dated samples on nutshell from Daylight Rock are from David and Walker (2004). Eleven dates are listed for Worm's Head in Meiklejohn *et al.* (2011: 33), these include dates originally reported as Mewslad Bay, but which Schulting feels are probably also Worm's Head.

both technology and morphology, as influenced by factors such as differing environments, raw materials, exploitation strategies, function, inter-regional differentiation and zonation. We should perhaps take from this observation that, even in Britain, we might anticipate some variation in lithic assemblages at the regional level (McCartan 2003) as the nature of subsistence and other every-day activities undertaken by a specific group will determine the nature and character of the tool-kit being used.

Following on from the above observations, Mithen (1999a: 49–50; using Pitts 1979, Jacobi 1981, Mellars 1976 and Barton 1992) has shown that at certain sites the proportions of stone tools can provide an indication of the activities that were being undertaken (see also Binford 1979). At Star Carr, the proportions of end scrapers to burins was used to infer antler working; at other locations a predominance of microliths would probably suggest a specialist hunting location; whilst at Oakhanger VII in Hampshire the predominance of scrapers, serrated blades and truncated pieces is suggestive of processing activities such as hide cleaning. Of course, we should always be aware of the fact that there will potentially be considerable diversity in the lithic assemblages that we study, and that these classifications fail to account for the multiple socio-political, economic and ritual factors that were articulated in and around the location where the lithic scatter was produced. For instance, an individual or group may stop for a short break whilst out on a hunting or gathering trip and use the time to produce some of the tools that will be required in their subsistence endeavours. In addition, the locations identified need not relate *per se* to the structured subsistence activities of the group, for, as blanks and tools can be prepared, made and modified as the individual knapper sees fit, it is logical that an aesthetically pleasing location with good views is as good a place as any to relax and prepare the equipment that is needed in hunting, fishing and foraging activities. At some locations the lithic assemblages may also represent a palimpsest of activity over time at a preferred location in the landscape, but it does not necessarily follow that all of the assemblages produced will relate to the same activity, or that the location has direct relevance in relation to hunting or gathering endeavours.

In the context of palimpsest sites, Craig-y-Llyn, Rhondda has a microlith and flint dominated assemblage (371 pieces) with chert (75 pieces) and one piece recorded as debitage from rock crystal. The flint assemblage comprises ten microburins, one Early Mesolithic broad blade microlith and six Late Mesolithic microliths along with a further 63 microliths (including a crescent shaped piece), one burin, four retouched flakes, 250 pieces of knapping debitage, 23 cores including a bipolar core, nodular core and four single platform cores, six blades, six scrapers (three of which are convex) and one flint knife. The chert assemblage comprises 11 microliths (one of which is Late Mesolithic), 21 cores (two of which are single platform blade cores), 41 pieces of debitage, one blade and one flake. One of the flint microliths is recorded as being burnt, with its tip missing, one is recorded as an oblique piece, and one is recorded as a mis-hit. The debitage makes up over 65% of the assemblage, indicating a flintworking site, and microliths comprise over 18% of the remainder of the entire assemblage. In terms of tool types microliths dominate the assemblage, suggesting that a key activity undertaken using the material that was processed at this location was hunting, although scrapers and blades would suggest processing activities. As both early and late material is attested at Craig-y-Llyn the "events" that occurred represent a minimum of two visits, and could easily represent a number of repeated visits to this site.

The microliths that characterise the tool-kits of Mesolithic groups in Europe are, simply defined, small stone artefacts that are usually made from sections of small blades (Whittaker 1994: 37). These small stone objects were insufficient in themselves to function as discrete tools, such as the handaxes and blades that were discussed in Chapter 1, or the axe/adzes that are in use during the Mesolithic period itself, and as such the microliths were usually incorporated into what are termed "composite" tool forms (Finlay 2000a; 2003a). These composite objects could take the form of an arrow or harpoon point (Figs 3.2 and 3.3), a knife, or a sickle for harvesting wild grasses etc. The final product will represent the culmination of numerous activities in the collection, modification and production of the composite parts (e.g. David 2009; Lord 2009). In addition, and as indicated above, we

Fig. 3.2: Find of an arrow with four triangles attached by resin from the Rönneholms mosse bog, southern Sweden in 2009. The arrow, made from a 1-year-old branch of hazel was 10.2cm in length when reconstructed. A V-shaped furrow was cut into the wood, and was filled with resin, into which the microliths were inserted. The arrow has now been dated to 7905±60 uncal BP (LuS 8992) based on resin and 7855±60 uncal BP (LuS 8993) based on the wood (from Larsson and Sjöström 2010: fig. 6; used with permission).

should also always be aware of the potential for all stone tools to be assigned a number of values and meanings beyond their pure utilitarian purpose, with the possibility that significance and authority could be embedded in the transformation of a flint pebble into a hunting weapon or harvesting tool (Finlay 2000a).

A detailed description of the qualities that are required of the raw materials used in making stone tools, the nature of the raw material itself, e.g. flint, chert and obsidian amongst other materials, and techniques of manufacture, can be found in Whittaker 1994 (who also lists a range of other reference sources if the reader wants to delve deeper into this subject area). In addition, Warren (2005: 27–31) has produced a number of schematic diagrams showing the stages involved in stone tool manufacture across the late-glacial and Mesolithic periods, and Lord (1998) provides a detailed account of the methods used to produce a harpoon. The literature is replete with images of Mesolithic artefacts, for instance Roger Jacobi (2005) provides illustrations of the lithic assemblage from Aveline's Hole in North Somerset, and whilst discussed in greater detail below, Jacobi's text is also a useful point of departure for understanding the nature of the late-glacial and earlier Holocene stone tool forms that were used by hunter-fisher-forager groups in Britain. Elsewhere in Europe, distinctive preservation conditions at sites such as Vis I, located in a peat bog near Lake Sindor in the Vychegda Basin, northeast Europe (Burov 1998: 53) have also suggested that finds of objects such as unfinished bows and drill-bows for making fire are indicative of the manufacture and storage of wooden blanks, from which the finished objects were produced. Whilst we are generally able to identify the activities relating to stone tool procurement and use to some acceptable degree, it is only with the detailed evidence afforded by the exceptional preservation at sites such as Vis I that we can begin to understand the processes involved in the manufacture of the organic component of these composite tools.

Some important insight into the nature of stone tool production is presented by Finlay (2000: 25–6) who notes that in reality the processes and routines of microlith manufacture involve a number of discrete stages, including the provision of a suitable blank, which necessitates blade or blade-like flake production, and modification of the blank by retouch. This is a stage that can be undertaken using a stone retoucher or an antler, bone or wooden point supported on an anvil stone (*ibid.*). Other aspects of microlith production highlighted by Finlay (2000: 26) include "the execution of retouch, sequences of modification, the criteria for blank selection, the influence of blank form and breakage rates during manufacture", and the microburin technique. For the non-specialist stone tool manufacture is a complex and skilled craft that was fundamental to Mesolithic subsistence activities, but beyond this, factors such as handedness, design, production process and concealment (Finlay 2000a: 28) all need to be considered. This latter aspect, the notion of concealment, may imbue microlith production with a deeper significance than might first be expected for a process that is, to all intents and purposes, a utilitarian activity. We will explore this aspect of stone tool production in greater detail when constructing a social narrative of lithic production and use at the end of this chapter.

One final observation in relation to handedness is warranted here, recent work by Warren and Conneller at the Scottish site of Sands of Forvie in Aberdeenshire has identified patterning in cortical location and microburin lateralisation, with the suggestion that blades that retain their cortex on the right side indicate knapping by a left-handed person, and with microburins that have a left-sided notch suggesting that they were made by a right-handed person (Conneller 2006: 166). At this location the evidence suggests that at least two people were involved in the production process; assuming of course that there was not one ambidextrous person who favoured their left hand for rough-outs and the right hand for finer work!

Returning to the discussion of Mesolithic stone tool use, throughout Britain, numerous locations provide important insights into the procurement, transportation and utilisation of raw materials by hunter-fisher-forager groups. Mithen's work on Colonsay as part of the Southern Hebrides Mesolithic Project has suggested that the raw materials used for tool production, in this case beach pebbles (which has resonance to the situation in Wales), were probably brought to the island of Colonsay in the form of pre-prepared blade cores (Mithen and Finlayson 1991: 5). At other locations in Britain, such as Lundy Island, the local beach pebbles were utilised by the hunter-fisher-forager groups during their intermittent visits to this elevated plateau, which was located at the edge of the emerging Bristol Channel in the earlier Holocene (Schofield 1994).

As the locations where raw materials for use in tool production are limited in their distribution in Wales (Smith 2005: 39), we might anticipate that there would be occasions when Mesolithic people would have carried the raw materials with them during hunting and gathering expeditions, as is evidenced on Colonsay (Mithen and Finlayson 1991). These raw materials would perhaps be transported as rough-outs or blanks that could be worked into the desired form when needed, or, it is also possible that small caches of material (see discussion below in relation to Burry Holms) would have been placed at specific locations in the landscape in anticipation of future need. The fact that raw materials such as flint and chert were of limited availability, generally

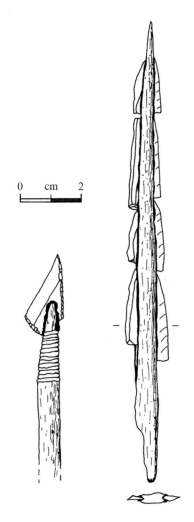

0   cm   2

Fig. 3.3: Hafted microliths: arrow point and reconstructed Mesolithic projectile point from a Scandinavian bog (after Whittaker 1994: 37, fig. 3.10, based on images in Montelius 1888: 25, fig. 25 and Tringham 1971: 39, fig. 4).

being found in secondary contexts in glacial tills or beach deposits, might actually be an additional factor in the distribution biases alluded to above, as a skilled knapper would no doubt have been able to curate the tools that they were using, re-working and modifying an artefact from its original form as need demanded. This element, i.e. curation, might also be necessitated if the observations made by Binford (1979: 259) in relation to the Nunamuit have resonance. In his work Binford notes that the raw materials used in the manufacture of implements are "normally obtained incidentally to the execution of subsistence tasks", and it was only when something had gone wrong that people actually went out in search of the raw materials used in tool production (*ibid*.: 259).

At this point it is perhaps important to note that Jacobi (1987: 164) has suggested that patterns of raw material procurement might also be useful in identifying a reduction in the scale of annual territories in the later Mesolithic period, after *ca*. 6000 uncal BC, when compared to the earlier Mesolithic evidence. This point will be revisited later in this consideration of hunter-fisher-foragers in Wales, but it does imply that these groups may have been becoming more "restricted" in their movements towards the latter part of the Mesolithic period. As greater sedentism is often considered to be a fundamental aspect of (or precursor to) the farming way of life, observations such as these might be providing us with tantalising insights into the mechanisms through which hunter-fisher-foragers eventually become farmers, or how they ultimately decide that the "leap" from a dependence on biologically wild to domesticated resources is viable or even attractive.

Throughout Wales there are only a limited number of locations where primary flint sources are available for exploitation, such as the exposures at Ogmore, Vale of Glamorgan and Llanmelin (Locock 2000), and as the evidence from sites such as the Nab Head indicates, beach pebbles were a very important source of material for lithic production. The exploitation of these resources would necessitate two alternating strategies as in the case of the former, procurement would be part of an organised strategy, whilst in the case of the latter, the collection of beach pebbles could have been integrated within coastal food resource collecting strategies, i.e. embedded procurement (Woodman 1987: 142). Locock (2000: 5) and Smith (2005: 39) note that the restricted availability of flint resources in Wales, which usually only occur in the previously mentioned secondary contexts in glacial gravel exposures in the lowlands, means that the presence of flint at any location away from an identified source can be taken as a direct indicator of human activity; meaning that with the exception of a limited number of locations flint is not usually found in the landscape unless it has been moved there by people. Lynch *et al.* (2000: 367) note that locally sourced material is common on sites throughout Wales during both the earlier and later Mesolithic periods, such that, in northeast Wales black Gronant chert from the limestone on the east side of the Vale of Clwyd dominates in stone tool assemblages, forming 84% of the stone tool assemblage at Rhuddlan (discussed in detail below), a location where Sites E and M produced some 11,045 flint and chert artefacts from a total of 13,330 pieces (Berridge 1994a: 95–114), whilst at Tandderwen in the Vale of Clwyd, Brassil *et al.* (1991: 77) note that only 13% of the lithic assemblage recovered from this location was made from flint, with the remainder being made on chert that was sourced from locations such a Gronant, Gwaunysgor and the Halkyn Mountains.

As noted above, the composition of Mesolithic tool-kits differs between the earlier and later Mesolithic periods, and between regions of Britain and Ireland, with the general shift being between broad-blade and narrow-blade industries, with much smaller microliths occurring after *ca*. 8,000 uncal BP (Mithen 1999a; Switzur and Jacobi 1979; Tolan-Smith 2008: 140). In general terms David (2007: 97), notes that the broad blade microliths of the earlier Mesolithic are characterised by minimal modification to the outline of the original blade blank, whilst smaller, later microlith forms are usually defined by elaborate retouch.

The Early Mesolithic

David (1989: 242) has suggested that the earliest (although undated in absolute terms) Mesolithic flint assemblage in south Wales may come from the surface collections recovered at Burry Holms, West Glamorgan (Walker 2000: 88–9). There are three National Museum of Wales (NMW) records for Burry Holms, which list 1387, 196, and 68 objects respectively (Fig. 3.4). The collections from Burry Holms include obliquely and partially backed artefacts, short end-scrapers, blade-cores, blades, micro-denticulates and knapping debitage (David 1989: 242; Walker 2000: 88). The details of the three finds collection records for Burry Holms include, 196 objects in the first record, where all of the finds are of flint, and they include: 113 spalls (flint chips), 26 blades, one core rejuvenation flake, 30 flakes, 11 records of knapping debitage, one microburin, two microliths, one scraper, one end scraper, one silicified mudstone core and a number of natural stones.

A second finds record for this location includes 68 finds that have: a bone tool, perforated Boar's tusk and a sawn antler tine found in association with chert objects that include three blades, two core trimming blades, four core rejuvenation flakes a burin and flake, and flint material that includes 12 cores, 19 microliths, one blade (debitage), two serrated blades, four scrapers and two end scrapers, one notched blade, 11 blades, and one microburin. Walker (2003: 12) notes that the blade cores that are common to this period include both single platform and opposing platform types, usually produced on pebble flint or other local raw materials, derived from beaches or glacial drift deposits.

The final, and largest finds record for Burry Holms, has some 1387 finds (1391 listed) and is recorded as a flintworking site. The finds include a number that are listed as natural objects, such as fire cracked stones (4), flint nodules (9), a piece of haematite and a piece of ironstone, and two objects recorded as Mesolithic bone (but secondarily recorded as flint). Of the entire 1391 objects only 13 chert pieces are recorded in association, these include two spalls (chips), five flakes, five blades and a microlith. Overall the material in this assemblage is similar in composition to the first two records, comprising predominantly flint, although the assemblage is, as might be expected, more diverse. There are some 672 flint spalls (chips), 257 flakes and 316 blades dominating the assemblage. Secondary finds include 27 microliths, 13 blade cores and 11 cores, five core rejuvenation blades and four core rejuvenation flakes, seven hammerstones, seven scrapers, six crested blades and one crested blade that has been used as a denticulate, eight microdenticulates, two retouched blades and two retouched flakes, single instances of a microburin and a burin, and 19 finds

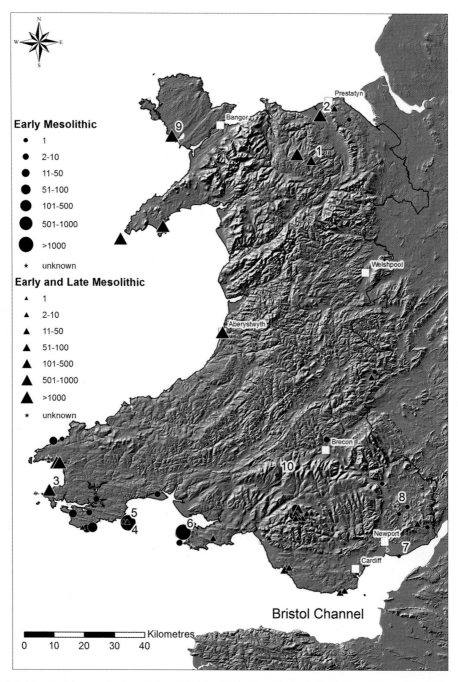

Fig. 3.4: Distribution map showing all sites with either Early Mesolithic or both Early and Later Mesolithic artefact associations. Sites Numbered: 1 – Brenig 53, 2 – Rhuddlan, 3 – the Nab Head, 4 – Daylight Rock, 5 – Nanna's Cave, 6 – Burry Holmes, Llangenydd, 7 – Goldcliff, 8 – Trostrey Castle, 9 – Trwyn Du, 10 – Waun Fignen Felin.

recorded as knapping debitage. Jacobi (2005: 275) has noted that microdenticulates are also reported from other earlier Mesolithic sites in Britain, such as Marsh Benham near Newbury, Berkshire, and Oakhanger sites 5 and 7 in east Hampshire. The final, non-lithic item in this assemblage is a limestone bead.

Finally, Walker (2001: 126) has reported that during the last season of excavation at Burry Holms, the blade-cores and hammerstones were found in an horizon underlying later prehistoric pits in Trench 3 of the excavations, and some of the knapping debitage was also found in this horizon. This material is recorded as contrasting with material from the same layer, but found in Trench 1 of the excavations, where there were a high proportion of finished tools to debitage (*ibid.*). These descriptions would appear to suggest discrete areas within the spatial patterning of the site, possibly where initial tool production and subsequent finishing activities were being carried out. Burry Holms represents one of 11 early or probable early Mesolithic sites mapped by Jacobi (1980: 138–9), with other locations including Rhuddlan (sites E and M), Trwyn Du, Daylight Rock (Fig. 3.5), Pencilan Head on the Lleyn Peninsula, the Nab Head (discussed below), Freshwater East, Valley Field on Caldey, Palmerston Farm near Haverford West, and Aberystwyth. The presence of organic finds from Burry Holms would suggest that this site has the potential to be dated, as these finds, which include a bone tool, perforated Boar's tusk and a sawn antler tine would all be suitable for radiometric dating assuming their survival and curation, along with the good preservation of organic (collagen) content.

The general composition of earlier Mesolithic flint collections from sites elsewhere in Britain, such as Thatcham in Berkshire is similar to that from Burry Holms, and includes; primary flakes, blade-like flakes, cores, core-rejuvenation flakes, microburins and axe-adze sharpening flakes, which at Thatcham, make up 96.5% of the assemblage, and which Wymer viewed as waste material (Wymer 1962: 339). The remainder of the

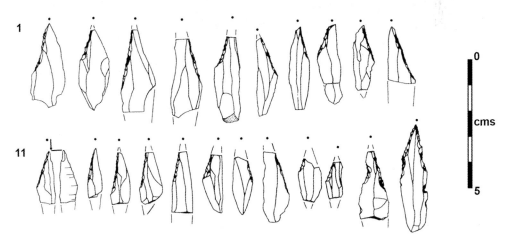

Fig. 3.5: Early Mesolithic obliquely blunted points from Daylight Rock, Caldey (redrawn by author from Jacobi 1980: 148, fig. 4.14).

collection from Thatcham comprised finished tool forms, including; microliths, axe-adzes, segmented blades, gravers, scrapers, awls, saws, ground-edge blades, punches, fabricators? hammerstones and flakes that were variously backed and trimmed (*ibid.*). Recent re-evaluation of the Thatcham III assemblage by Mike Reynier (2000) has suggested that, as opposed to the material from this site representing a single homogeneous Early Mesolithic assemblage, there are in actual fact two discrete sub-assemblages, one that is characterised by a blue patination and the second being comprised of unpatinated pieces. The inference is that the blue patinated material is similar in character to the material from Star Carr, dated to *ca.* >9500 uncal BP, whilst the unpatinated material is more similar, typologically, to the later material from Deepcar, and dated to *ca.* 9200 uncal BP. The significance of this observation, according to Reynier (2000: 33), is that there are compelling arguments to suggest that each early Mesolithic techno-complex, Star Carr (at 9700 uncal BP), Deepcar (at 9400 uncal BP) and Horsham type (shortly after 9000 uncal BP), represents distinct archaeological entities, and not the seasonal or task-specific variations of a single social complex as alluded to by Jacobi (1976) and Kozłowski (2003).

Reynier (1998: 174–5) characterises the earliest Mesolithic assemblage as "Star Carr" type, which is dominated by broad, obliquely truncated points, with isosceles triangles and trapezes as the secondary components; the subsequent "Deepcar" assemblage type is characterised by long slender partially backed points that can occasionally equal the obliquely blunted points in terms of frequency. This assemblage has a new addition with the occasional backed point and some basally modified points, whilst isosceles triangles and trapezoids are rare. The final assemblage in the sequence, the "Horsham" type, has a broad range of forms, in which short, squat obliquely blunted points dominate. The characteristic microlith in this assemblage is the hollow-based point, which can, in some assemblages, outnumber the obliquely blunted points. In addition, geometric forms such as small isosceles triangles and rhomboids occur (Reynier 1998). Whilst these assemblages follow a general chronological sequence, the earlier assemblages are not replaced by later assemblage types, such that by the end of the earlier Mesolithic period all three assemblages overlap (*ibid.*: 175).

Reynier (2000: 35–6) distinguishes the earlier (Star Carr type) blue patinated assemblage from the unpatinated (Deepcar type) assemblage at Thatcham on the following grounds: the patinated assemblage of 820 pieces is characterised by a restricted range of microliths, of a reduced length (*ca.* 22mm average), dominated by simple obliquely truncated points, and there are no partially-backed, fully-backed points or rhomboids in the assemblage. The only other microlith form consists of two isosceles triangles and a single trapezoid, and none of the microliths has additional retouch to the leading edge. Other tools include short end scrapers, well-made burins and blade cores, but axes and microdenticulates are absent. The later unpatinated "Deepcar" type assemblage comprises 13,080 pieces, including microliths, with oblique points, with partially-backed variants, trapezoids, isosceles triangles, backed points and rhomboids. The microliths are long and slender with a mean length of 33.2±9mm, and 15 of these points have additional retouch applied to their leading edges. The remainder of the assemblage has a wide range of typical forms including short end-scrapers, burins, piercers, microdenticulates, truncated pieces, core axe/adzes and blade cores. This later, unpatinated assemblage is associated with a date of 9200±90 uncal BP (OxA-2848) on resin, which calibrates to 8640–8260 cal BC, and according to Reynier's analysis, this is the only reliable date currently available for Thatcham III (2000: 43).

Whilst Reynier (2000) should be consulted for a more detailed consideration of the Thatcham III material, the implications of the identification of two discrete Early Mesolithic assemblages at Thatcham, in terms of chronology, distribution and typology, could suggest that the Early Mesolithic lithic inventories for Wales may warrant re-examination in order to determine their precise temporal position in relation to the "compression chronology" outlined by Reynier (2000: 33). This compression chronology occurs as a result of three plateaus in the radiocarbon record, the maximum duration of which is 400 years (Reynier 1998: 175). Whilst such a study is beyond the scope of the current volume, the problems in dating that Reynier discusses for Thatcham may resonate with those alluded to by David (2007) in relation to the seemingly late dates for the "Early" assemblages at Trwyn Du and Rhuddlan (see below), and of course, a reassessment of these assemblages may enable their correlation to one of the three typo-chronological phases – Star Carr → Deepcar → Horsham, as proposed by Reynier (2000). One final note in relation to the work undertaken by Reynier is his identification of two "Star Carr" type assemblages for Wales; Daylight Rock and Waun Fignen Felin; Reynier notes that this earliest Mesolithic assemblage type exhibits a mixed distribution with sites located below 100m AOD and above *ca.* 300–500m AOD. The later assemblage types of "Deepcar" and "Horsham" type exhibit a primarily low altitudinal distribution, below 200m AOD, although the "Deepcar" assemblages do have occasional occurrences up to 500m AOD (Reynier 1998: 177).

In Wales, early Mesolithic stone tool assemblages are generically typified by Lynch *et al.* (2000: 33) as comprising a combination of broad blade microliths shaped into obliquely blunted points, scalene and isosceles triangle forms, tranchet axes, awls, a drill bit called *mèches de foret*, convex end scrapers, burins and micro-denticulates (or saws), the latter being found at Burry Holms. In addition, Jacobi (1980: 146) has also suggested that stray finds of transversely sharpened core-adzes appear to be associated with an Early Mesolithic technology. Given the discussion so far, we should now be aware of the fact that no two assemblages will be identical. The activities undertaken at each location will influence the nature of the assemblage produced, and that ultimately, the material recovered will only represent a partial picture of activity at a given location. Furthermore, due to differing patterns of use, re-use, discard and loss, the patterns will vary over time and space.

Thus far, the earliest absolute dates for Mesolithic flint assemblages in Wales have been recovered from sites such as Daylight Rock, Caldey Island, dated to 8550–7900 cal BC (OxA-2245; 9,040±90 uncal BP) and the Nab Head near St. Brides, at 8630–8260 cal BC (OxA-1495; 9210±80 uncal BP), with the sites of Trwyn Du, Anglesey, Rhuddlan and Prestatyn, Clwyd being slightly later in the sequence (David 2007) (Table 3.1). According to David (also Jacobi 1980: 146), the "late" dating of the latter sites has proven problematic given the timing of the earliest dates for the Mesolithic elsewhere in Britain, and Quinnell and Blockley (1994: 57 and 75) have also noted that the dating obtained on combined

samples of hazelnut shells appeared inconsistent with the lithic assemblage from site M
at Rhuddlan. To some degree David's work at Daylight Rock has enhanced the resolution
of the data, but it is apparent that currently, the key excavated site in Wales, with an Early
Mesolithic assemblage is the Nab Head (David 2007), which is discussed in greater detail
below. This site, which has both early and late Mesolithic material in evidence, improves
our understanding of Mesolithic lifeways considerably, due in no small part to the presence
of a range of material culture not normally found on Welsh Mesolithic sites, to date.

Returning briefly to the sites of Trwyn Du and Rhuddlan; at Trwyn Du on Anglesey, a
"chipping floor" was identified beneath a Bronze Age barrow during excavations undertaken
in 1956 (Gwynedd HER PRN-3003), and further excavation was undertaken due to erosion
at this location in 1972. Subsequently, excavations in 1974 produced 7000 flints, whilst
sieving of the eroded material in 1972 had produced 563 pieces. There does not appear
to be any quantification of the number of flints recovered during the 1956 work in the
HER, but amongst the finds listed are worked flint and the waste from knapping, tools
such as microliths, including obliquely blunted points, a microlithic rod (backed bladelet),
microburin, scrapers, cores, and two fine "tranchet" axes. David and Walker (2004: 310)
report that 127 of the 5320 artefacts from Trwyn Du are made from local chert, and they
also note that primary sources of chert are actually more widespread in Wales than has been
suggested to date. One of the radiocarbon dates presented in Table 3.1 was obtained on
charcoal from a "camp fire", whilst two were obtained on a bulk sample of burnt hazelnut
shells (Q-1385 and HAR-1194). The viability/validity of these dates are questionable due
to the bulking of the sample and the young age of the remaining date (Quinnell *et al*. 1994:
127). As only *ca.* 60% of the barrow was excavated it is possible that further evidence for
Mesolithic activity exists here. The excavations in 1974 also identified "flint packed pits"
at this location. This reference to "flint packed pits" is intriguing, as these could represent
caches for use on subsequent visits to this area, or even the ritual structuring of deposits,
but the lack of detail in relation to these pits frustrates further inferences in relation to
function; they could of course simply be rubbish pits!

The excavations undertaken at Rhuddlan represent the accumulation of evidence from
a number of excavations in and around the southern areas of the town, initially undertaken
from 1969-1973 by Henrietta Quinnell (Quinnell and Blockley 1994). At present, "Rhuddlan
is situated on the right, east bank of the River Clwyd, *ca.* 4km south of its present estuary
at the lowest fording point and at the highest point reached by the tides", and it is located
on a bluff at *ca.* 15m AOD (*ibid.*: 1). A considerable amount of prehistoric activity is
attested at this location (Quinnell and Blockley 1994: 1), with Mesolithic activity recorded
at sites T (SJ02637788), V (SJ02607787), K (SJ02557792), S (SJ02567809), D (SJ02277827),
E (SJ02567788), M (SJ02617777), the Abbey Nurseries (Site A: SJ0267577832) and Hendre
(SJ02807810), amongst others (CPAT PRN-57767). Many of these locations produced
significant quantities of flint and chert artefacts, along with decorated (incised) pebbles
at sites E, T and S (Berridge 1994b), a possible Mesolithic soil at site V, and two working
sites (with 976 flint and chert artefacts), hazelnuts, charcoal and seeds at Hendre etc. Site
T produced 1351 pieces of chert and flint, while site V had a scatter of pebbles, some of

which were fragmentary and burnt, along with 11 pieces of struck chert and flint and 257 residual pieces of worked flint (Quinnell and Blockley 1994). A number of these locations are undated in absolute terms.

Sites E and M at Rhuddlan have both produced radiocarbon dates (Table 3.1), and at site E (CPAT PRN-81666) 8408 flint and chert finds including microliths (Fig. 3.6), scrapers, awls, notched pieces, ground pieces, axe sharpening flakes, microdenticulates and utilised/retouched pieces were recovered. Site M (CPAT PRN-81667) produced 2637 pieces which included the same range of material as Site E (Fig. 3.7). Amongst the tools recorded at other sites in Rhuddlan are microliths, scrapers, awls, microdenticulates and utilised/retouched pieces from Site S (CPAT PRN-57739), cores, a chert microlith, chert scrapers and two (possible) decorated pebbles from Abbey Nurseries (CPAT PRN-58050), and at Hendre (CPAT PRN-102571) 976 flint and chert finds, including flint and chert cores, a chert knife, microburins and microliths, blades, awls and scrapers are recorded.

Whilst two of the HER records for Rhuddlan do not provide any indication of the number of flint and chert finds recovered, the remaining 11 records indicate that a minimum of *ca.* 14,318 flint and chert finds have been recovered from features such as working floors, pits and soil horizons of Mesolithic age at this location. Of note in relation to the composition of the lithic assemblages at both Trwyn Du and Rhuddlan is the absence of burins, which Jacobi (1980) suggested might imply that certain "craft" activities were not undertaken at these locations (also David 2007: 86). Rhuddlan clearly represents a significant location in relation to Mesolithic activity in Wales, and the location itself was undoubtedly important to Mesolithic people, a point that will be discussed in greater detail in Chapter 4.

In West Wales, the Mesolithic site at Daylight Rock, Caldey Island, Dyfed (Dyfed HER PRN-3445) was originally excavated by Brother James van Nédervelde of the Cistercian Community on Caldey in 1951–2 (David 2007: 63). The results of these excavations, which were undertaken in an area measuring 19 × 9m, with a total area calculated at just over 110 m² (Jacobi 1980: 149), were the recovery of some 7454 flint and flaked stone artefacts, apparently found in two discrete concentrations at the foot of a small inland cliff, and alongside material culture evidence that included charcoal and other domestic refuse (David 2007). During the earlier Mesolithic period Caldey Island would have been an inland location, with the contemporary coastline some *ca.* 10km away (see Fig. 2.1). David notes that only identifiable tools were kept by the original excavator, with the surviving assemblage comprising eight microlith forms, end scrapers, burins, truncated pieces, nosed pieces, notched pieces, *mèches de forêt*, an ?axe/adze, retouched and utilised pieces and axe/adze-sharpening flakes, a total of only 175 artefacts currently remain from the 7454 that were originally excavated.

Microliths make up 29% of the Daylight Rock assemblage, and these comprise large, simple obliquely-backed points (59% of the microlithic component), large scalene triangles (22%), and convex, trapezoidal and rhombic forms (15%), but end scrapers dominate the assemblage at 31% and the *mèches de forêt*, interpreted as awls or drill bits, are the next in significance at 10% of the assemblage (David 1989; 2007: 64). The only English site with

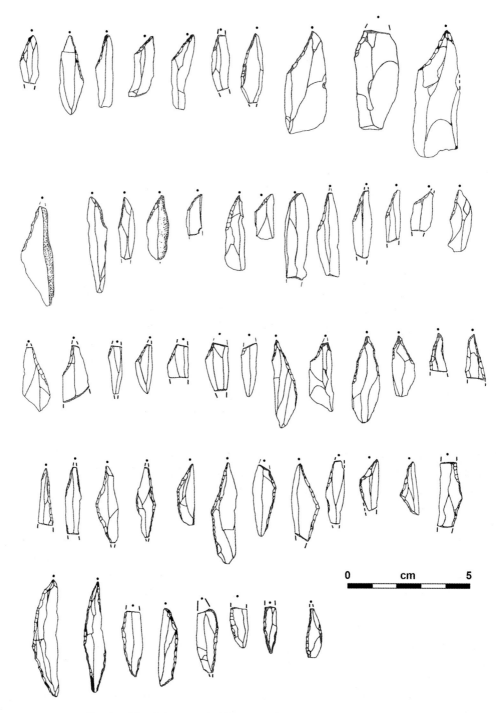

Fig. 3.6: Microliths from Rhuddlan Site E (after Jacobi 1980: 141, fig. 4.5).

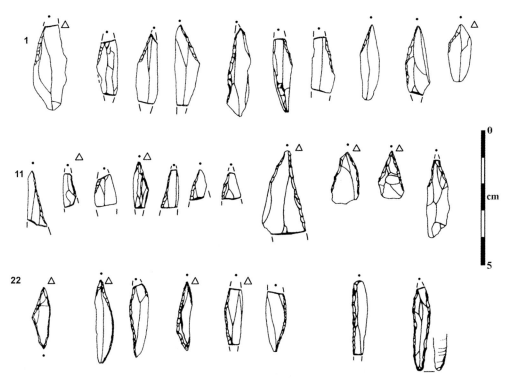

Fig. 3.7: Microliths from Rhuddlan Site M (redrawn by author from Jacobi 1980: 145). Δ denotes finds that are associated with radiocarbon dated material (7741–7481 cal BC; BM-822, 6598±73 uncal BP).

equivalent numbers of *mèches de forêt* is Star Carr, where these objects make up 12% of the assemblage (Jacobi 1980: 154). New excavations, undertaken by David in 1988 produced an additional 84 lithics from Daylight Rock, with the only artefact not represented in the earlier lithic assemblage from this location being a serrated flake. The 1988 excavations also extended up onto the top of the small cliff above the site, where 1515 additional flint artefacts were recovered, along with fragments of charred hazelnuts and charcoal. The lithic assemblage comprised primarily flint material (97%), with 51 pieces being of an igneous stone that resembled rhyolite (David 2007: 68). The dates obtained from this site (Table 3.1) are consistent with, although slightly later than, the dates from sites in England, such as Star Carr, Flixton I and Seamer Carr in Yorkshire, and Thatcham II and Broxbourne further south (Switsur and Jacobi 1979).

It has been suggested that the Daylight Rock assemblage differs from the Star Carr, Seamer Carr and Thatcham assemblages due to the differing proportions of microlith shapes that are represented, with convex-backed points being proportionately well represented at the expense of obliquely-backed points, and with scalene triangles being almost absent from this assemblage (David 2007: 69). However, Jacobi (1980: 149), in noting these differences also states that "13 of the microliths from this site are triangles, with five being isosceles triangles and eight being large scalene forms". As such, the re-assessment of Thatcham III (Reynier 2000) may allow Daylight Rock to be re-evaluated, as whilst the dating would not be inconsistent with the date of 9000 uncal BP that is cited for the Horsham-type assemblage, the calibrated dates from Daylight Rock fully overlap with the date of 9200±90 uncal BP (OxA-2848) for the unpatinated assemblage at Thatcham III, which is classed as Deep Carr assemblage type by Reynier. In addition, the microliths from Daylight Rock are generally >25mm in length, even with the damage that is apparent in Figure 3.8 of David (2007: 69), and this would fit well with the mean of *ca.* 33mm that Reynier gives for the "Deepcar-type" assemblage at Thatcham. The above discussion may also provide further context to the site of Valley Field, where the presence of broad blade microliths, convex scrapers, mèches de forêt and burins amongst the 703 pieces of debitage analysed by David (2007: 76) led him to suggest that the Valley Field assemblage was almost identical in composition to Daylight Rock, whilst other sites such as Palmerston Farm and Penpant, Solva also have components that are clearly of earlier Mesolithic date (*ibid.*: 81).

David (2007: 60) provides a map showing the distribution of all known early Mesolithic findspots in Wales, with only six sites being located outside of southwest Wales (although see Burrow 2003: fig. 1); the sites outside of southwest Wales include Waun Fignen Felen and Gwernvale in the south and Prestatyn and Rhuddlan in the north, along with Trwyn Du on Anglesey. There are *ca.* 25 sites located to the west of a line from Burry Holms in the south to Aberystwyth further north. Thirteen findspots of isolated broad blade microliths also occur in this region.

Jacobi (1980: 160) has noted that the 523 shale beads that had been found at the Nab Head during excavations by Gordon Williams in 1925 (this figure had risen to 692 after the excavations undertaken by Andrew David in 1979–80), were identical to 27 from Star Carr, and single specimens from Freshwater East and Linney Burrows; and that the evidence of an unfinished piece and unworked discs at the Nab Head supported the suggestion that at least some of these beads were made at the site. The presence of drill bits (*mèches de forêt*) would certainly fit with the idea that bead production was being undertaken at the Nab Head, and David (2007: 105) notes that the rounded tips of the drill bits fit neatly into the bead perforations (Figs 3.8 and 3.9). According to David and Walker (2004: 309) the mèches de forêt are an unusual, distinctive artefact on early Mesolithic sites in Scandinavia, as well as in Britain. Beads are also recorded from sites such as Waun Fignen Felin, Palmerston Farm, Dyfed, the Nab Head, Linney Burrows, Dyfed and Freshwater East.

An additional location in Wales, where shale beads are recorded, is that of Cwm Selsig, Rhondda. At this location three complete, centrally perforated shale beads, one find recorded simply as a shale bead, and three halves of centrally perforated beads are found in association with a utilised flint blade, three oblique microliths and a scalene triangle microlith; along with a Late Mesolithic micro-scalene type microlith and Late Mesolithic microlith with its tip missing.

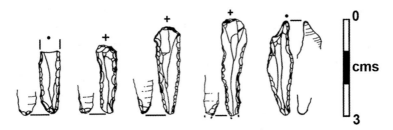

Fig. 3.8: Mèches de forêt *from the Nab Head (redrawn by author, after Jacobi 1980).*

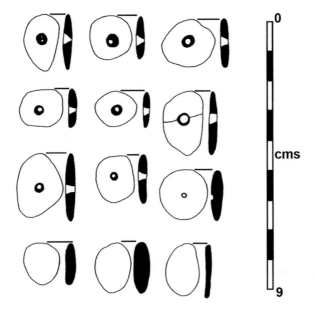

Fig. 3.9: Stone beads from the Nab Head (redrawn by author, after Jacobi 1980: 158; fig. 4.18).

Simpson (2003: 45–7) has referred to the use of beads in her discussion of body adornment in the Palaeolithic and Mesolithic of Britain, arguing that body ornamentation can convey an array of unspoken messages that could be related to age, sex, tribal identity, war or peace status, cosmological beliefs and territoriality, and that importance is attached both to the location that ornaments are placed on the body and the materials used in their manufacture. An interesting observation, in relation to the increased use of beads at sites like Star Carr, the Nab Head and Waun Fignen Felin (amongst others) is the suggestion that there is a shift across the Palaeolithic to Mesolithic periods that may represent an ideological change in emphasis, away from animals and their totemic status towards a more specific, deep rooted relationship with the landscape, and perhaps an expression of individual and group identity in relation to space and place in the Mesolithic world (Simpson 2003: 47).

Other locations where early Mesolithic artefacts have been recovered include the cave sites of Ogof-yr-Ychen, Nanna's Cave, Eel Point and Potter's cave on Caldey Island. At Ogof-yr-Ychen the finds from Chamber 3 comprise microliths, including a convex-backed point, two obliquely-backed points and a large isosceles triangle, three flakes, and a bladelet that may have been previously used as an awl or piercer. All of these finds occur "in association" with human material from two individuals and faunal remains from species such as wild boar (David 2007: 70–1). Chamber 4 at this location also produced "broad blade" microliths (*ibid.*: 71). Direct associations between the human and artefactual inventory at this location cannot be demonstrated.

Schulting and Richards (2002a) have provided a series of AMS dates on the human remains from Ogof-yr-Ychen and other sites on Caldey Island (2002: 1014, and Table 3.1), with four male/probable male and two female/probable female individuals producing ages of between 7865–5640 cal BC, i.e. the earlier to later Mesolithic. Whilst the artefactual evidence from this location cannot be directly linked to the fragmentary human remains that have been recovered, the AMS dating is, in part, consistent with the earlier Mesolithic age of the artefacts. Unfortunately, whilst Nanna's Cave and Eel Point have both produced earlier Mesolithic artefacts, in the form of microliths and a broken blade, the dating of the human remains from these caves is inconsistent with the age of these artefacts; the humans being later in date (Schulting and Richards 2002a: 1014). Jacobi (1980: 149) adds the sites of Burry Holms and Freshwater East to the sites with an early Mesolithic lithic component in this region. The latter site has been mentioned above in relation to the perforated shale bead that was recovered there, whilst the lithic assemblage at this location also includes obliquely blunted points, microburins, an awl, a burin and a pair of end scrapers (*ibid.*).

At Potter's Cave, two human individuals have produced age ranges of 7790–7170 cal BC and 6805–6455 cal BC respectively (Schulting and Richard 2002a), suggesting an Early to mid-Mesolithic age for at least two of the "interments" at this location. The associated artefacts include an un-diagnostic microlith fragment, and there is also a post-glacial fauna that includes dog, but in reality, the association of the burials to the lithics and "post-glacial fauna" are unproven.

At the Nab Head, Dyfed (Fig. 3.10), excavations by the Reverend J. P. Gordon Williams in 1925, and subsequent collecting visits made by him, produced the 523 shale beads mentioned above, along with two objects that have tentatively been identified as either Venus figurines, or a phallus and a representation of a vulva (Jacobi 1980). The lithic assemblage excavated in 1925 has, according to Jacobi, been lost or is largely unrecognisable, and there are issues relating to the fact that Williams may well have conflated material that he had collected from other sites in Pembrokeshire, such as Stackpole, Castlemartin and Brownslade Burrows (*ibid.*: 160). The material that Jacobi determined could be securely provenanced to the Nab Head includes obliquely blunted points, a broad isosceles triangle, large scalene triangles, a pair of bi-truncated points, convex backed microliths, *Mèches de forêt*, denticulated scrapers and cores adzes (*ibid.*: 161). A very detailed overview of the history of research at the Nab Head can be found in David (2007), and this work is summarised below.

Fig. 3.10: The Nab Head viewed from the east (© author). White arrow shows location of site 1 excavated by DAT and Andrew David in 1979–80, Site II is located upslope (left) of this.

Excavations were undertaken at the Nab Head by Andrew David, along with Don Benson and Dyfed Archaeological Trust during field seasons in 1979 and 1980, when over 12,000 flints were recovered from disturbed contexts at Site 1 (called "the neck") and high densities of finds were recovered from the undisturbed horizons, where "as many as 866 chipped artefacts were found per grid square" (David 2007: 92–7). As has been noted by Lynch *et al.* (2000: 28), unlike the present day setting of The Nab Head as shown in Figure 3.10, at the time of the Mesolithic occupation this site would have been on a hill with gently sloping sides, with easy access to the wide, contemporary, coastal plain.

Charcoal from oak, alder, willow/poplar, *Pomoideae*, *Prunus*, *Leguminosea* and hazel was found during the excavations, being abundant in grid square omega. Analysis of the flint and flaked stone artefacts indicated that they were probably sourced from local beach erratics, with 98.8% of the lithic assemblage being made from pebble flint, with the majority of the remaining 488 non-flint artefacts from Site 1 being of fine-textured extrusive igneous rock types such as tuffs and rhyolites, and a small quantity of Cretaceous Greenstone chert objects (*ibid.*: 97).

The excavations at Site 1 produced 39,863 flaked flint and stone objects, although 98% of the assemblage was waste flakes (debitage), whilst there were 155 blade and bladelet cores, both broad and narrow blade microliths, end scrapers, burins, *mèches de forêt*, denticulates, and a single core axe/adze, and by-products including axe/adze sharpening and thinning flakes, burins spalls and microburins (David 2007: 98). The majority of these lithic forms will now, no doubt, be identifiable as being of Earlier Mesolithic type, whilst the later Mesolithic forms, the narrow blades and denticulates, indicate some subsequent activity at this location (*ibid.*). The overall composition of the lithic assemblage would be consistent with the working of the lithics and their subsequent use in activities such as the processing of foodstuffs and the production of the shale beads (discussed above).

In a similar situation to that at the Nab Head, the investigations at Waun Fignen Felen have produced evidence for both earlier and later Mesolithic activity, although in this case the activity occurs around a small lake basin located at 485m AOD in the Black Mountains. The lake was an open water body in the Late-glacial period, and was terrestrialising during the Holocene (see Chapter 2). The location of the Mesolithic activity areas, consisting of 12 distinct scatters and 54 other findspots, is focused primarily on the northeastern shores of the lake, and recovered from the mineral sediments beneath the blanket bog or around the edge of it. The available dating evidence indicates that all of this activity pre-dates *ca.* 5330–4940 cal BC (CAR-689: 6240±90 uncal BP) (Barton *et al.* 1995: 84).

At this site seven discrete earlier (or probable early) Mesolithic activity areas are located in the same vicinity as four subsequent later Mesolithic areas of activity (*ibid.*). The material used in stone tool production comprises Cretaceous flint, the dominant material at this location, a fine-grained Greensand chert, and a Carboniferous chert. The flint was probably derived from beach gravels at the contemporary coast at least 60km to the south of Waun Fignen Felen, the Greensand chert is probably from some 80km away on the south side of the Bristol Channel, the Carboniferous chert appears to be associated with the later Mesolithic activity at this location, and is of probable local derivation (*ibid.*: 89).

The evidence for the earlier Mesolithic activity indicates that the material for use in lithic production was imported to the site in the form of whole nodules, as attested by the presence of cortical flakes and evidence for all stages in the core reduction sequence (Barton *et al.* 1995: 106). Interestingly, Barton *et al.* also note that at their sites WWF/6 and WWF/8, despite the presence of other earlier Mesolithic flint scatters in the area, there is no evidence to suggest scavenging of residual material and no refits were found between scatters (*ibid.*). Given the upland and remote location of the activity at Waun Fignen Felin, the discrete areas of knapping activity and lack of evidence for palimpsests of activity, suggest that any earlier activity was either simply ignored, or was deliberately avoided for social reasons or reasons relating to hunting taboos. In the latter case taboos might revolve around the avoidance of "contamination" of hunting activities by the reuse of earlier material, as the success or failure of previous endeavours would not necessarily be known to subsequent hunters in this area.

The analysis of the lithic assemblages indicates that knapping was undertaken at Waun Fignen Felen, with the Early Mesolithic flint material including broad blade microliths, oblique points, end scrapers, microburins and only two cores. The Early Mesolithic material occurs at sites WWF/2, 6, 7, 8, 12, 14 and 15. At site WFF/6 a number of perforated beads were also recovered; these were possibly manufactured at this location, and they have a similar petrology to those from Palmerston Farm, Linney and Freshwater West, where associated Early Mesolithic flint forms are also in evidence (Barton 1995: 92). Also at this location, the finds distribution, in a sub-circular scatter, suggests the presence of a relatively undisturbed chipping floor (Barton *et al.* 1995: 94–5).

Barton *et al.* (1995: 92) report that WWF/6 contained 200 flint artefacts that are mostly >5mm in size. Interestingly Barton *et al.* note that there is a high proportion of breakages in the blade and flake debitage, and that the presence of all of the major stages in core reduction are attested at this location indicates that on-the-spot knapping took place here (1995: 93). The tools include five microliths (one of which is an oblique point, one is a scalene triangle, and three of which are represented by tips), 18 blades, one end scraper and a proximal microburin. This assemblage is smaller and less diverse than that found at WWF/8, the site that is located at the furthest distance from the lake edge, where six end scrapers, 18 microliths and two microburins, one piercer, two retouched flakes and 17 micoburins are in evidence, along with two possible hammerstones (*ibid.*: 94). The material at this location is made from flint and Greenstone chert, and whilst there are some microliths, the majority of the material is reported as being bladelet debitage by these authors.

An important observation in relation to the assemblages from Waun Fignen Felin is the fact that the assemblages at this upland location differ in composition to those from coastal sites in south Wales in that objects used for processing activities, such as burins, adzes, axes and bevelled pebbles, are all absent (Barton *et al.* 1995: 99). We should remember of course that this may simply be a reflection of the differences embedded in the activities undertaken at Waun Fignen Felin, where a very specific task, that of hunting is being undertaken and where the activity is confined to brief episodes of tool production and use in the earlier Mesolithic period.

By contrast, at the "coastal" sites in Wales we are in fact looking at locations that could have been up to *ca.* 10km from the coast in the earlier Mesolithic period, e.g. the Nab Head, and even where less distance was involved this would not necessarily mean that the coast was immediately accessible. As such, the sites that are currently coastal in their distribution were in fact transitional locations between the coast and the uplands during the earlier Mesolithic. The fact that we see evidence for a range of production activities at these locations is perhaps unsurprising as these sites would be logical foci for more "permanent" and durable events in relation to hunter-fisher-forager landscape interactions. One significant limiting factor in our efforts at "visualising" these locations in their earlier Holocene landscape setting is the fact that we need high resolution topographical studies of the seabed in order to "situate" the sites in their Mesolithic context. In suggesting this approach it is recognised that simply mapping site locations is only one aspect of landscape studies, and that numerous other factors, alluded to throughout this text, need to be considered.

The later Mesolithic

David (1989; 2007) indicates that a late, or later, Mesolithic site in Britain is characterised by a more varied geometric, narrow-blade lithic inventory, with backed bladelets that are usually smaller than those in evidence prior to *ca.* 7950 cal BC (*ca.* 8800 uncal BP). Unfortunately, there are few transitional sites that have well-stratified and dated assemblages (Burrow 2003: 17). Mithen (1999a) however, has suggested that the reasons for the shift from the broad-blade lithic forms of the earlier Mesolithic (which have parallels with the Maglemosian traditions on the continent), to the narrow-blade, more geometric forms of the later Mesolithic (which appear to represent an insular cultural development), is poorly understood, although the rising sea levels discussed in Chapter 2 may be implicated in reduced continental influences in the later Mesolithic (David 1989; Darvill 1987). The dating of the shift in lithic technology is securely placed at *ca.* 8000–7700 cal BC, at a time when significant changes in bone and antler technology are also occurring (Tolan-Smith 2008: 134). Tolan-Smith also notes that the earliest dates for narrow blade industries come from northeast England and Ireland at *ca.* 8000 cal BC (*ibid.*: 147), although as noted above the welsh evidence supports a similar chronological boundary.

Another factor influencing the shift in lithic, bone and antler technology is the fact that by the start of the Late Mesolithic period, oak-hazel-lime woodland was replacing the more open landscapes of the earlier Mesolithic period, with this colonisation extending up to *ca.* 500m AOD (Burrow 2003). It is interesting to note here that the Irish later Mesolithic also contrasts with the British later Mesolithic due to the occurrence of a macrolithic lithic technology, characterised by Bann Flakes and a reliance on butt-trimmed forms, which dominate the retouched component in lithic assemblages (Finlay 2003b: 87). The contrasts between Ireland, Britain and the continent effectively give us three later Mesolithic's, which, as Nyree Finlay notes, provide us with an opportunity to consider differing types of "Mesolithic", with the potential to engage with different expressions of Mesolithic identity, and to contrast and compare the accepted narratives and discourses of the British Mesolithic (*ibid.*: 87).

In recognising the variability between earlier and later Mesolithic lifeways, we must consider factors such as sea level rise, which have clearly biased against the identification of earlier Mesolithic activity. However, as the rates of sea level rise lessen by the later Mesolithic the evidence from both cave and open air sites is much more prolific, with cave sites such as Cathole, Friar's Point, Goat's Hole, Gop Cave, Daylight Rock, Eel Point, Nanna's Cave, Ogof-yr-Ychen, Pontnewydd and Potter's Cave all producing later Mesolithic material (Fig. 3.11). "Coastal" sites include Aberystwyth, Burry Holms, Freshwater West, The Nab Head and Ogmore-by-Sea, whilst inland and upland sites include Brenig, Capel Eithin, Craig-y-Llyn, Pant Sychbant, Gwernvale, Hendre, Llyn Aled Isaf, Rough Close and Waun Fignen Felin (Burrow 2003: 387). Additional sites of interest dating to this period include the shell middens at Nant Hall Road, Prestatyn and the human and animal footprints that have been found in the intertidal zone of the Severn Estuary at locations such as Uskmouth, Nash, Redwick, Magor and Goldcliff.

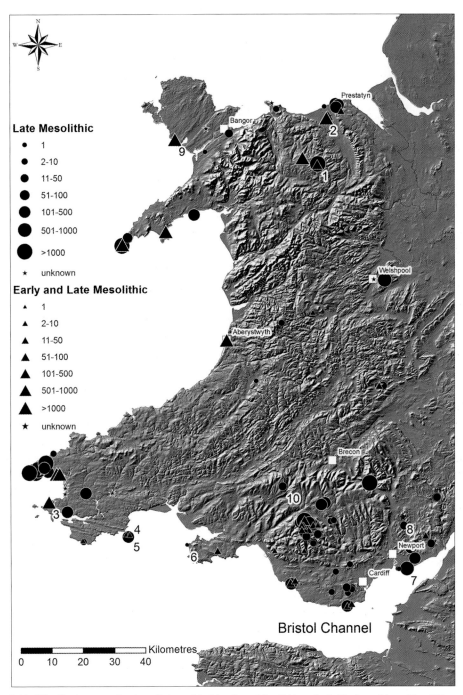

Fig. 3.11: Distribution map showing all sites with either Late Mesolithic or both Early and later Mesolithic artefact associations: 1 – Brenig 53, 2 – Rhuddlan, 3 – the Nab Head, 4 – Daylight Rock, 5 – Nanna's Cave, 6 – Burry Holmes, Llangenydd, 7 – Goldcliff, 8 – Trostrey Castle, 9 – Trwyn Du, 10 – Waun Fignen Felin.

Jacobi (1980: 169) notes that scalene micro-triangles and narrow straight rods are characteristic artefacts on later Mesolithic sites in Wales, and that assemblages are best represented by the excavated sites of Prestatyn and Rhuddlan, Clwyd, Pen-y-Bond, Glamorgan, and Brenig site 53 in Denbighshire, although surface collections from St. David's peninsula and the Glamorgan uplands around Craig-y-Llyn (Fig. 3.12) and Pant Sychbant are also important for this period. At the time Jacobi was writing, these sites were only <2% of the known Late Mesolithic findspots in Wales (including Anglesey and the Marches), where a total of 66 sites were recorded. In addition to the scalene micro-triangles and narrow straight rods discussed by Jacobi, David (2007: 115) reports that other artefacts that characterise the Late Mesolithic stone tool assemblages in Wales are "convex-backed bladelets, lanceolate points, burins and less commonly four-sided and 'micro-*petit-tranchet*' forms, amongst others".

Jacobi (1980: 169) has suggested that the later Mesolithic narrow-blade microlith assemblages in Wales resemble those from the "micro-triangle" assemblages in southern Britain, with associated finds including scrapers, truncated pieces, burins and awls, but he also observes that core adzes appear to be absent. David and Walker (2004: 314) note that burins and microdenticulates are also known to occur in these later Mesolithic assemblages, and that, in general these artefacts can be difficult to distinguish from those occurring in

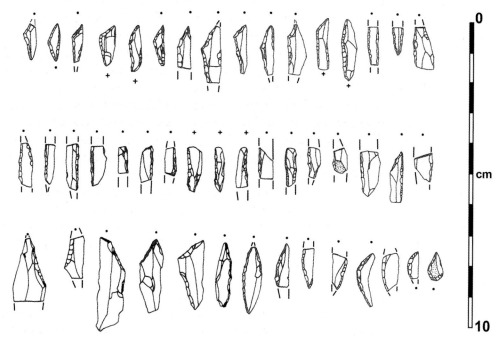

Fig. 3.12: Microliths from a group of sites around Craig-y-Llyn in the Glamorgan uplands (ca. 457m OD). Note: the first five microliths in the bottom line are "archaic" forms of earlier Mesolithic date and do not belong with the rods and microtriangles in the upper two rows (redrawn by author, after Jacobi 1980: 169).

earlier Mesolithic assemblages. In addition, *Mèches de forêt* appear to be absent from micro-triangle assemblages in Wales during the later Mesolithic (*ibid.*: 314).

The main sites for this period include Craig-y-Llyn and Pant Sychbant in the Glamorgan uplands, other sites such as Goldcliff and Uskmouth in the southeast, the numerous sites around the Pembrokeshire coast (especially the Nab Head site II), and locations in the north such as Llyn Aled Isaf, Brenig and Rhyl (Jacobi 1980, David 1989, 1990) (Table 3.2), all of which have produced material that provides further insights into this period. Goldcliff (discussed below) is important in this context as the lithic assemblages occur in a context that provides associated settlement, subsistence and environmental evidence (Bell 2007a). At another important location, Bryn Newydd, Prestatyn (SJ 0724 8270), material recovered by Gilbert Smith from small raised islands in a shallow basin in the boulder clay at the Bryn Newydd Building Estate have been interpreted as a "microlithic chipping floor" (Clarke 1938: 330). At this location a mixed sand and clay horizon was found overlying a deposit of angular stones, and formed a low plateau in the basin (Clarke 1938: 332). David (2007: 116) notes that overlying this 'plateau' is a black soil *ca.* 0.05m thick, which contains the archaeological material discussed below. This soil horizon was, in turn, buried beneath a clean white tufa deposit (0.56m thick) and topsoil (0.33m thick). The lithic material was found in the buried soil layer in association with artefacts of bone, antler and seashell, including a perforated oyster shell disc, pointed bone object and an un-worked antler tine; all contained in a secure depositional context (Clarke 1938: 330; 1939: 201; David 2007: 116).

Clarke (1938: 330) has shown that the raw material utilised for the Bryn Newydd assemblage was mainly locally obtainable dark chert (sometimes banded), with grey chert and flint (both pebble flint and chalk flint) in small quantities. Jacobi (1980: 169) reported that the assemblage had scrapers that are generally small and convex, along with steeply retouched flakes. David (2007: 116) lists the composition of the lithic assemblage at this site as comprising 141 items which include microliths (dominated by narrow scalene triangles, and including small obliquely-backed bladelets, straight-backed bladelets and an isosceles micro-triangle) (Fig. 3.13), scrapers, retouched flakes, cores and core rejuvenation flakes, with a low occurrence of other forms such as notched flakes, microburins, mis-hits and an obliquely truncated flake (*ibid.*: 207; Jacobi 2005; Clark 1938: 330).

The well-stratified nature of this location is unusual for Wales, and as such David (2007: 116) sought to date some of the additional organic material from this site; this material included large numbers of broken hazelnut shells, two fragments of which produced AMS dates of 8700±100 uncal BP (OxA-2268) and 8730±90 uncal BP (OxA-2269) respectively (Table 3.2). As noted by David (2007: 117) these dates represent a very early chronological position for a narrow blade industry in Britain and adjacent areas, suggesting that whilst the spatial and temporal resolution of the transition from "Early" to "Late" Mesolithic lithic industries requires more work, the "northern bias" in early dates for the later Mesolithic narrow blade industries must now be extended into north Wales. In light of the considerable range of Mesolithic material from the area of Rhuddlan, Rhyl and Prestatyn, Healey (2007: 302) has suggested that the evidence is indicative of prolonged activity exploiting the lithic sources in the area in prehistory.

Table 3.2: Radiocarbon dates for Late Mesolithic sites in Wales, after David (2007); in which comprehensive detail of the dated material and its context can be found, see also Schulting (2005); Thomas (1993). Jacobi (1980: 169) lists the dates from Brenig 53 as 5240±100 uncal BC and 5350±100 uncal BC. A more detailed list of dates is provided in David and Walker (2004: table 17.12).

Site	Location	Lab. no.	Date uncal BP	Calibrated age BC (1σ)	Calibrated age BC (2σ)
West Wales					
The Nab Head II	SM 7906 1108	OxA-860	7360±90	6355–6100	6420–6050
		OxA-861	6210±90	5295–5055	5370–4930
		OxA-1497	8070±80	7170–6830	7310–6700
		OxA-1498	4950±80	3895–3650	3953–3545
Abermawr, Dyfed	SM 881 345	OxA-1411	7640±150	6650–6270	7030–6215
Freshwater West, Dyfed	SM 886 000	Q-530	5960±120	5005–4705	5210–4555
Foxhole Cave (FX41)	SS 438 860	OxA-8316	6785±50	5720–5650	5730–5560
Paviland Cave	SS 4372 8588	OxA-681	7190±80	6060–5910	6230–5900
Lydstep, Dyfed	SS 094 985	OxA-1412	5300±100	4245–3995	4350–3950
North Wales					
Pontnewydd Cave	SJ 015 710	OxA-5819	7420±90	6390–6110	6440–6089
Bryn Newydd, Prestatyn	SJ 0724 8270	OxA-2268	8700±100	7940–7595	8200–7540
		OxA-2269	8730±90	7940–7610	8200–7580
Splash Point, Rhyl, Clwyd	SJ 0200 8250	OxA-1009	6560±80	5615–5470	5340–5370
Brennig 53, Clwyd	SH 9830 5726	HAR-1167	7190±100	6210–5990	6330–5845
		HAR-1135	7300±100	6250–6050	6390–6005
Aled Isaf Reservoir, Clwyd	SJ 2915 3595	No Lab Ref	5810±150	4840–4495	5030–4350
Nant Hall Road, Prestatyn	SJ 3070 3832	CAR-1424	5470±80	4445–4240	4470–4050
		CAR-1423	5270±80	4230–3990	4330–3950
		CAR-1420	5530±80	4460–4275	4550–4230
		CAR-1422	5110±80	3980–3790	4250–3700
South Wales					
Goldcliff, Gwent		CAR-656	5360±80	4325–4065	4350–3990
		CAR-659	5950±80	4940–4730	5050–4610
		CAR-658	5850±80	4825–4605	4910–4500
		Beta-60761	6770±70	5725–5625	5740–5490
		CAR-1502	6480±70	5505–5370	5490–5330
		OxA-13927	7002±35	5975–5845	5990–5790
		OxA-12359	6871±33	5785–5720	5840–5670
		OxA-13928	6629±38	5615–5535	5630–5480

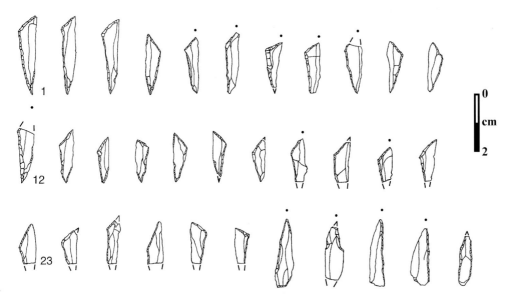

Fig. 3.13: Microlithic artefacts from Prestatyn (after David 2007: 117, fig. 5.2).

As has been discussed above, the fact that the Prestatyn dates on a narrow-blade industry appear to pre-date broad-blade material at Trwyn Du and Rhuddlan site M (Fig. 3.7 above), and fully overlap with Rhuddlan site E, warrants the suggestion that the Prestatyn dates might indicate a technological development that is sequential with earlier forms, as the Prestatyn "narrow" triangles are of a simpler and larger form than "true" narrow-blade forms (David and Walker 2004: 317). However, as these authors also note, it is entirely possible that the variations in evidence relate to changing hunting strategies and changes in the nature of the available raw material for use in lithic tool production (*ibid.*).

One further site of note is the relatively recent recovery of a significant flint assemblage from Bardsey Island, Gwynedd between 2002 and 2003 (Edmonds *et al.* 2002; 2003). The material recovered from this location includes a range of lithic sources such as till flint, pebble flint, chert, quartz and rock crystal. Some of the pieces recovered were cracked from light burning. Material from the preliminary survey included 49 punch struck flakes or fragments, several of which were thin and blade-like; a thick core trimming piece, a pebble fragment, and two retouched pieces were also recovered. The two retouched pieces comprised a narrow blade, scalene triangle microlith which is 9mm × 5mm, and retains its bulb. The second retouched piece was a denticulate scraper. Edmonds *et al.* (2003) reported on the fieldwork undertaken in May of 2002 when 6500 pieces were recovered from an area *ca.* 85 × 100m. The assemblage comprised tool and tool components, including scrapers, microliths and simple blades, along with cores and waste material (*ibid.*: 100). All of the material in the assemblage is dated typologically to the period *ca.* 7500–4000 cal BC. The range of lithic sources used suggests that some of the material was probably imported to the island and was processed at an occupation site (settlement or working area) once there. Further work at this location, comprising the excavation of 65, 1 × 0.5m test pits, in June–July 2004 produced "several thousand pieces of worked stone overall and some individual pits yielded more than 200 pieces" (Edmonds *et al.* 2004: 145). A similar range of material to previous years was recovered, with the addition of a few pieces of igneous rock, possibly derived from the Mynydd Rhiw source (*ibid.*: 146). These authors note that there appears to be an earlier Mesolithic component to the assemblage, thus dating to a time before rising sea levels made Bardsey an island, but that this requires confirmation.

Elsewhere, in southwest Wales, during excavations of Site 1 at the Nab Head a number of flints were located during test pitting to the landward side of the cliff, designated site 2 (David 2007). The finds comprised small bladelet cores and narrow scalene triangles in an apparently homogeneous later Mesolithic assemblage (*ibid.*: 131). As such, this site (site 2) provides important information in relation to the narrow blade industries of Wales. This assemblage comprised over 31,000 pieces of flaked flint and stone, and included a range of cores, denticulates and convex end scrapers (David 1989: 248). Jacobi (1980: 161) noted that a small number of the microliths that he analysed included a narrow rod-like piece, the forepart of a scalene micro-triangle and "four-sided" forms that were characteristic of later Mesolithic assemblages. In addition to these observations Jacobi also notes that the denticulated scrapers found on later Mesolithic sites in South Wales are similar to those found on sites in Devon and Cornwall, whilst in North Wales the scrapers are generally small and convex in form (1980: 169). Whilst a detailed description of the excavations undertaken at the Nab Head site 2 is presented in David (2007: 131–59) a short summary of the finds from this location is presented below.

The excavation of more than 195 m^2 of the Nab Head Site 2 produced 31,797 artefacts, with 603 recognisable tools, and with bevelled pebbles, three ground stone axe- or adze heads and a perforated "macehead" (David 2007: 135). In assessing the distribution of flint across the excavation area David identified three concentrations of activity, with an area of low flint density in the centre of these flintworking areas. There appeared to be a concentration of burnt flint producing an "edge" between the scatters and the central area, and in general the lithics also respect this patterning. Whilst it is generally concluded that the broad span of dates from the Nab Head, covering some 3000 years, represent a palimpsest of activity, it should be noted that even with this palimpsest of activity at the Nab Head, the discrete clustering of activity foci and the avoidance of earlier areas of activity might suggest that subsequent visitors to this location are respecting or avoiding the earlier foci of activity, a factor that suggests that these activity areas remained visible (were marked, or were remembered) over time (David and Walker 2004).

A small scoop, *ca.* 40 × 30cm and 15cm deep, delineated by tightly packed stones and filled with burnt soil and charcoal was interpreted as a possible hearth feature at this location, and the charcoal from this feature produced an AMS date of 7360±90 uncal BP (OxA-860) (Table 3.2). Another concentration of charcoal and burnt soil was located in a northwestern scatter of flint, perhaps again indicating a hearth feature (David 2007: 135). Dating of this material produced a radiocarbon age of 6210±90 uncal BP (OxA-861), and a location 4.5m to the south west produced a third date of 8070±80 uncal BP (OxA-1497).

The flint at the Nab Head site 2 was derived from local beach pebbles, and there are rare flakes of Cretaceous greensand chert and two cores made from igneous material (David 2007: 137). All stages of the core reduction process are in evidence at the site; there are 20 un-worked cobbles, 88 preliminary primary removals and 337 cores, the latter dominated by single platform types, although with double- and multiple-platformed examples also in evidence; 95% of the assemblage comprises flakes, bladelets and fragments (*ibid.*: 137). There are 313 microliths, including obliquely-backed points, other "broad-blade" forms, narrow scalene triangles, convex-backed pieces, straight-backed pieces, lanceolate pieces and four-sided forms. "Points" and points with concave basal retouch dominate the assemblage and there are a further 324 unclassified microliths and microlith fragments in this assemblage (*ibid.*: 138).

David reports that an important element of the artefact assemblage from the Nab Head II site are the pebble tools, which comprise 55 bevelled forms, 16 unmodified elongated pebbles and 20 fragments of these, 3 ground stone axes, 3 ?hammerstones and a ground and perforated disc (*ibid.*: 141). It is now generally accepted that the earlier designation of bevelled tools (stone, bone and antler forms) as "limpet scoops" or "limpet hammers", is a limiting and possibly erroneous classification in certain contexts. Furthermore, David suggests that the wide range of forms and sizes of these objects might suggest that they served a number of different functions; with treatment of seal pelts, the use of the stone objects in woodworking activities, or even the possibility that they were actually used for shellfish gathering in some form, all being suggested; and also that they might well have had multiple, as opposed to specific functions (*ibid.*: 150). A similar set of suggestions is proffered by Warren (2006: 18–20) in relation to Mesolithic technology and the use of bevelled tools in the Mesolithic. In endeavouring to move beyond simple definitions of these objects and their uses, Warren reminds us that irrespective of their use, these objects are embedded in the rhythms of daily life, being sourced, imported from the coast, modified and used within a set of socially defined relations and actions. The aesthetics and tactile nature of these objects may also have been influential in their adaptation and use, for whatever purpose, during the Mesolithic.

In addition to the bevelled pebble tools, the finds of three pecked and ground stone axe/ adzes at the Nab Head, with no known parallels in British prehistoric contexts, is significant as these types of object are identified at other Welsh sites including Scalby Moor, near Dale, Caron-uwch-clawdd, near Strata Florida, Dyfed, Stackpole Warren, Dyfed and Brunt Farm near Dale, Dyfed (David 2007: 150 and 152). Perhaps of even more interest is the suggestion that David's axe number 1 from the Nab Head site 2 excavations "was found in contact with, and underlying, two bevelled pebbles" which he suggests indicates contemporaneous use and possible caching of these objects (*ibid.*: 150). An alternative to the suggestion of caching is of course that these objects were deposited as a structured deposit aimed at highlighting their interlinked significance and meaning to the late Mesolithic population that exploited this region. A more detailed consideration of British axes is given in David (*ibid.*: 150–4).

One final point to add in relation to the recording of bevelled pebble finds is the recent suggestion (David 2011: 76) that an unworked flint lithic from layer 604 in trench 4 of the excavations undertaken by Crane and Murphy between 1995–8 at the promontory fort of Porth y Rhaw could also be a fragment from a bevelled pebble. This find adds to those listed from Pembrokeshire coastal locations.

A later Mesolithic flintworking site is recorded at Cwm Bach, Pembrokeshire (Dyfed PRN-9835). The lithic assemblage reported in the HER included some 250 cores, 28 scrapers, 26 gravers, 40 microliths, a microburin, 103 flints and many flakes and waste material. However, David (2007: 174) lists some 26,916 lithic finds from this location; which has a mainly flint component, but with 67 objects (0.2%) of Cretaceous chert and 47 objects (0.17%) of igneous rock. It is likely that this location represents the conflation of a number of knapping episodes, i.e. it is a palimpsest of activity. The microlithic component of this assemblage is dominated by scalene micro-triangles (46%), with obliquely-backed points, lanceolates, straight-backed pieces, convex-backed pieces, micro-*petit-tranchets*, one four-sided piece, ten other narrow-blade forms and 75 unclassified microlith fragments (David 2007: 182). The composition of the Cwm Bach I assemblage is similar to those from Prestatyn and The Nab Head II, and the micro-*petit-tranchets*, "points" and the four-sided piece are rare pieces which may be indicative of a very late Mesolithic date (as mentioned by Jacobi 1980; David 2007: 182). There are also 227 denticulates and 31 large scrapers in this assemblage. David and Walker (2004: 329) note that this site contained significant numbers of burins (12% of the retouched component – 82 pieces), truncated pieces (70), and 16 "becs" (or piercers) as well as unusual pebble tools such as "countersunk pebbles". David (2007: 182) notes that burins are not a frequent find in Welsh narrow-blade assemblages. This variation in the stone tool assemblage is thought to be linked to varying, perhaps "specialised" subsistence activities, but unfortunately, the lack of associated organic material culture finds limits any realistic inferences in relation to the actual activities that are suggested by such assemblages. Cwm Back I also has 21 bevelled pebbles recorded amongst the finds list (*ibid.*: 174), and according to David the number of burins (82) also marks Cwm Bach out as an interesting site amongst locations with a "narrow blade" component in Wales (*ibid.*: 182).

At Goldcliff in the Severn Estuary the 2002 and 2003 excavations at site B produced lithics from the minerogenic soil and the overlying peat, but with the exception of one microlith from the overlying peat all of the tools were recovered from the minerogenic soil (Bell 2007d). Bell records that 46 pieces of flint were recovered from this area, with the 2003 work producing a slight concentration of flakes and a core, probably reflecting knapping activity (Bell 2007c: 42). Two microliths and a notched piece were the only other artefacts from the 2003 excavations, but the 2002 work produced flakes and a wide range of artefacts including tools such as a scraper, one retouched and one utilised piece, a core and a hammerstone (*ibid.*). Nine flint flakes were recovered from the peat and eighteen flakes were recovered from the underlying minerogenic soil, and in addition the excavators recovered the majority of the sieved micro-debitage from the minerogenic soil (*ibid.*: 42). The structure of the material culture remains, including a hearth, and both burnt and un-burnt bone from the minerogenic soil and overlying peat, and the lack of evidence for flintworking, led the excavators to conclude that during the formation of the peat unit, this area was used for the processing of animals; specifically the butchery and cooking of red deer (*ibid.*). The nature of the finds from area B are suggestive of small-scale, probably short-term activity (Bell 2007c: 45). Fortunately, the presence of organic material has allowed this activity to be bracketed by a date obtained on a charred hazelnut in the minerogenic soil, and dating of the surface of the peat from a pollen monolith. These dates are calibrated to 5990–5790 cal BC from the hazelnut shell (OxA-13927; 7002±35 uncal BP) and 5840–5670 cal BC for the surface of the peat (OxA-12359; 6871±33 uncal BP) (Bell 2007c: 45).

One hundred and twenty metres to the west of site B at Goldcliff excavations at site A revealed a charcoal-rich horizon containing worked lithics and bone (Bell 2007d: 57). A concentration of artefacts was identified in an area of *ca.* 20m in diameter, on the Holocene soil surface, which coincidentally also had an imprint of an ungulate footprint in it, probably from a deer (*ibid.*: 58). Dating of a hazelnut shell from the 2003 excavations of the occupation surface at site A indicates that occupation occurred between one and three centuries later than at site B, at *ca.* 5630–5480 cal BC (OxA-13928; 6629±38 uncal BP). The lithics from the main concentration in this activity area comprises mainly struck flints, several cores and a number of retouched pieces, whilst material from two areas investigated in 2002 produced a lower concentration of material including flint/chert flakes, two tuff flakes and scrapers from area 7/2, and a cluster of flakes, two microliths and two scrapers from area 10/2 (Bell 2007d: 60). The densest concentration of microliths occurs in the main cluster of lithics from site A, which Bell (*ibid.*: 61) interprets as a flint knapping area (also area 7/2), whilst area 10/2 is interpreted as an area where tools were being used as opposed to knapped.

At the edge of Goldcliff Island site J, the wetland/dryland interface, also produced archaeological and palaeoenvironmental material (Bell 2007e: 63). This site is located *ca.* 120m west of site A. As in the other excavations at Goldcliff the Holocene landsurface, comprising a sandy soil horizon, contained charcoal, worked flints, heat-fractured stones, bone, and in addition, worked wooden artefacts. The lithics from these excavations comprised struck flakes, tools and cores. In the excavation area artefacts were recorded in three clusters (A–C), with cluster A on the west edge of the trench comprising flakes with 14 tools, 22 cores and core fragments and a hammerstone (*ibid.*: 75). Cluster B, located near the centre of the excavations, comprised flakes, with 28 cores and core fragments, one hammerstone, a microlith and 19 other tools, whilst Cluster C, on the east side of the trench, is simply described as a less dense scatter of lithic material (*ibid.*: 75). As the discussion in Chapters 4 and 5 will highlight, the significance of these locations lies more in the overall context of the lithic finds as opposed to the finds themselves. The material from Goldcliff is recorded in exceptional detail for finds from a series of Mesolithic sites, with the spatial distribution of associated material such as hearths, bone, charcoal, worked wood, and even human and animal footprints and defecation areas all being recorded alongside palaeoenvironmental material and detailed stratigraphy (Bell 2007a; Bell *et al.* 2000).

Earlier excavations at Goldcliff, undertaken between 1992–4, produced a large collection of both worked and un-worked (flaked) pieces along with un-flaked objects. Of the 633 lithics recovered from the 1992–4 excavations, all bar eight are from the charcoal horizon (Context 1202), with six finds from the overlying clays (Context 1201) and two from the peats above the clays (Context 1200) (Barton 2000: 40). These finds include flakes (409/633), which dominate the assemblage, and are defined as waste pieces whose length is less than twice their width, and which are produced primarily from flint, but also from tuff (27 pieces) and chert (18 pieces). The nature of these pieces, many of which have corticated surfaces, indicates that primary flaking was undertaken on-site (*ibid.*: 40). Eleven blades/bladelets were recorded by Barton, the blades are conventionally classified as have a length/width ratio of 2:1, whilst the bladelets have a narrower width of 12mm or under (Barton 2000: 40). Small flakes (<10mm in length), which are described as chips or micro-debitage, only comprise *ca.* <4% of the excavated assemblage (25 pieces), whilst cores make up less than 6% of the assemblage (36 pieces). These cores are mainly single platform (16) and multiple platform (11) types. Twenty of the remaining artefacts in this assemblage are classified as core rejuvenation flakes, whilst 66 irregular fragments of struck flint are classified by Barton as unidentifiable waste pieces (2000: 43). Of the six non-flaked stone artefacts in this assemblage Barton was able to re-fit two pieces which appear to be a sandstone rubber (interpreted as arrowshaft smoothers or skin stretchers in Mesolithic contexts), and two other objects appear to have been utilised as hammerstones (*ibid.*). The retouched component of this collection comprises 15 pieces, with three microlithis (including a scalene form, a bilaterally "backed" piece and a tip), two end-scrapers and ten retouched flakes (Barton 2000: 43–5).

Other objects found at the Goldcliff site include pieces interpreted as scrapers, piercers or borers, and a small bi-facial piece similar to objects known as *feuilles de gui* in late Mesolithic contexts in the Netherlands (Barton 2000: 46). The two axe/adzes that were recovered in the surface assemblage at Goldcliff (both found by Derek Upton) cannot be directly associated to the occupation horizon, but these objects are of interest as one is in an unused condition suggesting that it was abandoned as a rough-out as opposed to a finished piece. The second axe/adze was found *ca.* 1.2km to the east of the main site, and in contrast to the first object this piece was clearly finished and used, with evidence to suggest not only primary flaking, but also secondary trimming and attempts at re-sharpening (*ibid.*: 46). This assemblage is securely attributed to the Late Mesolithic on the basis of the assemblage as a whole, but also due to the presence of narrow blade geometric forms and the preponderance of flakes, as laminar flake production is a consistent feature of the later Mesolithic period (Barton 2000: 48).

Interesting "inland" locations, although in this case only 2km from the present coast, include sites such as Treito (SM1722) and Priory Farm (SM1921), and these are discussed by David (2007: 185). Treito is intriguing as the site covers some 5000m², and later elements are included in the material collected. The late Mesolithic component includes four denticulates, three unclassified microlith fragments and 165 platform bladelet cores, with the latter being identical to other late Mesolithic cores. In combination, the assemblage is indicative of a microlith manufacturing site, but there are no complete microliths or microburins in the assemblage. David (2007: 185) suggests that it is possible that this scatter is representative of a bladelet manufacturing (or provisioning) site which produced blanks for hunting equipment, which was trimmed and finished elsewhere, or that it is also possible that the bladelets were manufactured and hafted without any retouched modification. The only truly "inland" location (given above discussion of the contemporary coastline) however is Priory Farm, which is *ca.* 9km from the sea. At this location a late Mesolithic component in an assemblage of 381 artefacts is suggested by the presence of three narrow-blade microliths (a small isosceles triangle, a convex-backed piece, and an oblique micro-*petit-tranchet*), and by three microlith fragments. It is possible that a denticulate, three burins and a flake are also of late Mesolithic age, as well as 25 small bladelet cores with an average height of 28mm (David 2007: 185).

Other Late Mesolithic findspots include Hendre, Rhuddlan and Llyn Aled Isaf Reservoir in Clwyd, and the Craig-y-Llyn area in the Glamorgan uplands of South Wales, where sites are usually located at heights above *ca.* 500m OD (David 2007: 124). At Hendre, Rhuddlan, Clwyd (SJ 027 781) a group of *ca.* 1182 artefacts of a similar assemblage composition to Prestatyn has been identified (*ibid.*). At this location the finds include objects of chert, including 3 microburins, 25 cores, 13 microliths, 20 core rejuvenation flakes (core trimming flakes), 52 pieces of debitage, 10 chips, 6 flakes, 7 blades, 2 retouched flakes, four serrated denticulates, 1 scraper, 3 awls and a knife. The flint elements include 30 pieces of debitage, 6 blades, 11 chips, 14 microliths, 10 cores (including a burnt core), 6 core rejuvenation flakes, 9 flakes, 4 microburins, 1 serrated denticulated blade, 4 scrapers, 2 awls and 3 retouched flakes. There is also one natural quartz crystal recorded in the NMR records for this location. The material from the Llyn Aled Isaf reservoir is reported as comprising 3380 objects (CPAT PRN's 17458 and 81486, NMW-102). There is evidence for an earlier Mesolithic component in the lithics from this site, although it has a substantial later Mesolithic component made on flints and local chert (David and Walker 2004: 331). This site is listed in the CPAT HER as comprising an extensive flintworking area revealed on the foreshore of Llyn Aled Isaf reservoir and multiple findspot (HER PRNs 101313 and 97.17H/10), with a record of soil and pollen sampling, and radiocarbon dates associated with charcoal in the soil horizons (Table 3.2), but no further detail on the composition of the lithic assemblage is available at present (Burrow 2003).

At Brenig 53, North Wales, the only location in Wales with dates that can be directly linked to the later Mesolithic micro-triangle industry discussed by Jacobi (1980), worked flint recovered from a pit feature (pit 19) below a barrow included waste flakes and blades, and a single scalene micro-triangle. The pit is one of a number of intercutting features in which successive fires had been lit, and which were subsequently covered by a soil horizon (Burrow 2003: 146). The dates obtained on charcoal from these features are presented in Table 3.2 above. Unfortunately, whilst a larger assemblage of lithic material was recovered from beneath the barrow, with this assemblage including narrow-blade microliths, scalene micro-triangles, rods blunted down one or both sides, and some 1467 pieces of debitage, Roger Jacobi notes (1980: 174) that there is no way that the dates from the pit feature can be reliably linked to the larger lithic assemblage at this location.

Recent research on Ynys Enlli, an island located *ca.* 3km west of the most westerly tip of Pen Llŷn (the Lleyn Peninsula), separated from the mainland by Swnt Enlli (Bardsley

Sound) which Edmonds *et al.* (2009: 385) report are characterised by "fierce tidal patterns (which) make it one of the most difficult stretches of water in the British Isles", has added to our evidence for Mesolithic activity in Wales. The island itself has a number of later Mesolithic sites, and fieldwork undertaken by Edmonds *et al.* (2009) at Bae y Rhigol on the northern end of the island has produced in excess of 5000 artefacts, making this assemblage the largest in northwest Wales. The material in this assemblage is primarily dated, typologically, to the period 8000–4000 cal BC, and it includes scrapers, microliths, simple blades, cores, bevel ended tools, hammerstones and waste material, with raw materials in the form of till flint, pebble flint, chert, quartz, rock crystal and other materials all being utilised (2009: 386). It is suggested that at least a proportion of the raw materials used in lithic production at Bae y Rhigol would have been imported to this location, and the authors also note that numerous "landmarks" are visible from Ynys Enlli, including Snowdonia, the coast of Anglesey and much of Pembrokeshire, but also to the west the setting sun occasionally picks out landmarks on the east Irish coast, such as the Wicklow Mountains (*ibid.*: 386). The wider regional interactions and landscape perceptions that would have been embedded in the memory of the people who exploited Ynys Enlli are considered in greater detail in Chapter 4.

As noted above, at Waun Fignen Felin, Powys, in the Black Mountains, a number of activity sites are located around the northeastern side of a small lake. Whilst some detail in relation to the activity at this location is given above in the discussion of the earlier Mesolithic material, Barton *et al.* (1995: 107) note that the use of the lake marsh edge during the later Mesolithic differs to that of the earlier period. In contrast to the earlier activity, the later activity does not represent single knapping episodes, and the scatters cannot unequivocally be shown to be undisturbed. At sites WWF/1 and WWF/9 two instances of small groups of scalene micro-triangles may represent the loss of composite projectile points, and the nature of the activities undertaken at the site in the Later Mesolithic would indicate that pre-prepared and hafted flint implements are being used (Fig. 3.14). Another important observation is that there appears to be a lack of Greensand chert as a raw material, perhaps reflecting a combination of reduced availability due to rising sea levels along with a concomitant reduction in the hunting territories exploited by later Mesolithic peoples (Barton *et al.* 1995: 107).

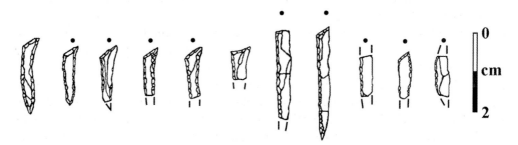

Fig. 3.14: Selection of narrow blade microliths from Waun Fignen Felin (redrawn by author from David 2007: 122, fig. 5.5).

There are numerous locations in Wales, with a small lithic assemblage, that are dated to the later Mesolithic period. In particularly a number of these "sites" are located in upland areas, and in many instances these locations probably represent short-term/overnight campsites, temporary processing sites, hunting areas or stone tool preparation areas. At Cwm Selsig, Rhondda, Glamorgan (SS9499) an assemblage comprising two flint cores and a chert core, a retouched flint flake, obliquely blunted flint blade and eight narrow blade microliths is located in the Brecon Beacons to the southeast of Waun Fignen Felin. This site is one of a large number of sites in this region, with some fifty-two sites mapped in a relatively discrete area by Burrow (2003: 18, fig. 6). These small assemblages are clearly limited in relation to the information that they provide in terms of human activity, but sites like Cwm Selsig may reflect the preparation of hunting equipment, while sites like Cwm Bach I have been suggested as having a lithic component that would have been used for piercing or grooving of different materials (David 2007), and as mentioned above there is evidence for bead manufacture at sites like Star Carr in the Vale of Pickering and Daylight Rock, Caldey, where *mèches de forêt* make up a small, but significant proportion of the lithic assemblage.

A number of small activity sites have been reported by Clarke *et al.* (2012: 114–17) in Monmouth. The finds were made during a watching brief on the renewal of a gas main, and the lithics were recovered from stratified contexts in floodplain sands (*ibid.*: 114). Analysis of the flint assemblages by Dr Elizabeth Walker (NMW) has shown that the finds from each of the sites are consistent with a late Mesolithic date for these sites, which are interpreted as either small task sites or temporary camps located adjacent to the river, where a range of plants, fish and fauna could be exploited. The larger assemblage (comprising 75 worked flints and eleven natural stones) was recovered from St. James' Street, and included a number of diagnostic late Mesolithic pieces such as narrow blade microliths (scalene triangles), an end-scraper, a single platform blade core, knapping debitage and a number of blades and bladelets. Scalene triangles are characteristic of the later Mesolithic, and have been recovered from locations such as Goldcliff, Usk, Trostrey and Llanmelin (Clarke *et al.* 2012: 116). The second, smaller assemblage (found at Wyebridge Street) comprises some 34 objects, and whilst there were no diagnostic pieces in this assemblage, Elizabeth Walker also attributes these finds to a later Mesolithic date (*ibid.*: 116).

Other locations with a limited, but potentially important, late Mesolithic component include Mynydd Ystradffernol, Blaenrhondda, Glamorgan, where a mixed flint and chert assemblage of some 46 pieces, includes four flint and four chert microliths with all but one of the flint microliths described as being of narrow blade form has been recovered. Other finds at this location include a combination of flint and chert blades and cores, along with knapping debitage. At Llanmelin wood, use of the flint source at this location has been suggested to relate primarily to Neolithic activities (over 900 flints), although McFarlane (1995: 46; also Locock 2000: 11) has noted that three late Mesolithic microliths have been recovered from this location, perhaps suggesting its use as a source of flint during this period.

Lithics, whilst clearly a key element in Mesolithic tool production, are just one part of the story. Whilst a wide range of processing activities, of wood, bone, antler, hides etc. would have been undertaken using the stone tools that are in evidence, we should remember that the stone tools themselves were components of more complex tool forms. We should also probably remember that certain tools could have multiple functions/uses, they are very flexible, being used as knives, spears etc., and it may be that we are being "too reductive in attributing a single function to a particular tool class" (Finlay 2003b: 90). As such, it would be prudent to realise that whilst we attribute a function to a particular tool class, it is very likely that some of the uses that these items may have been put to may be difficult for us to recognise/interpret in the present.

The lithic material that is recovered from discrete locations in the landscape may represent activities that are specific to their locations, e.g. the processing of marine resources, the collection and processing of plants of the saltmarsh zone, riparian resource exploitation in river valleys and fishing and gathering of freshwater resources, and hunting activities in the uplands. However, as the stone tools are components of utilitarian items, the preparation of lithics for use at different localities could easily occur anywhere in the landscape, as people planned ahead during their tool producing activities. As we have seen from the above discussion, many locations have lithic assemblages with evidence to suggest repeated visits over the *longue dureé*, and we should consider the probability that variations in tool types at discrete locations in the landscape need not necessarily reflect the activities that were undertaken in the immediate vicinity of any given site, as curation and caching could produce some parts of the assemblage, especially when the fine detail of the original deposition is difficult to disentangle from the post depositional context of the finds location. The record is fragmentary and complex and the tool-kits in evidence are equally diverse and may represent a number of functions or activities that were being undertaken throughout the landscape as it was exploited as part of the seasonal round. We must always be aware of the inherent limitations in the data given factors such as collection bias, which includes the likelihood that larger lithics will be identified over smaller forms, that lithic inventories can be culturally mediated, and that individual stylistic expression can also influence tool form (David 2007: 187).

In the later Mesolithic, pebble tools, some used as hammers or anvils, become important (Lynch *et al.* 2000: 35), but the reasons for this are not readily apparent. For example there are two pebble finds described as either hammerstones/rubber stones with wear at both ends, recorded from Merthyr Mawr Warren, in Mid Glamorgan. This area incorporates a NNR, SSSI and partial SAM (Gm 432) (GGAT HLCA 013), and is located primarily on the north side of the Afon Ogwr (Ogmore River) where it enters the sea immediately north of Ogmore-by-Sea. At this location a total of 76 additional finds including a flint assemblage comprising 21 microliths, 2 broad blade microliths (one with secondary working along back of blade – patinated creamy white) and 2 narrow blade microliths, 5 blades and 2 retouched blades, 11 scrapers, 7 retouched flakes, 7 cores, 2 pieces of debitage/flakes, 2 pieces of knapping debitage, 2 arrowhead tips, 1 bifacially worked tool, 1 notched flake (probably EM), 1 awl (possibly EM), 1 retouched point, 2 retouched blades, 1 retouched core, 1 debitage/retouched flake, 1 core rejuvenation flake, 1 debitage/point, 1 debitage/ flake and 1 flake have been recovered to date. The problem with this assemblage is that it incorporates elements of both earlier and later Mesolithic date, from a broad area, and as with many similar locations in Wales, there is insufficient stratigraphic integrity to allow for the separation of the various phases of activity. As a consequence, the significance and meaning that may have been attributed to this location in the Mesolithic period is severely "blurred", despite the fact that there is a clear suggestion that this area was revisited during this time.

Elsewhere, excavations on Lundy Island, in the approaches to the Bristol Channel (Schofield 1994) have shown that Mesolithic people exploited this plateau during the earlier Holocene. At present the granite island rises to *ca.* 100m above sea level, being 5km north–south and 1km east–west (*ibid.*). During the earlier Mesolithic period the granite plateau would have commanded an even higher topographic position as sea levels were *ca.* 20m or so lower than they are today. At the start of the Mesolithic Lundy would have formed a promontory jutting out into the emerging Bristol Channel, becoming an island towards the end of the Mesolithic period at around 5500 cal BC, as sea levels continued to rise (Dyfed Archaeological Trust 2011: 33–5). Lithic artefacts (stone tools) characteristic of the later Mesolithic period include bi-polar and micro-blade cores, blade segments, backed blades, microliths (both non-geometric forms and a trapezoidal microlith), and a microburin (Schofield 1994: 428–9). The significant point to be drawn from these excavations is that the visits that Mesolithic people made to the plateau were intermittent in nature, and occurred during the later Mesolithic period after Lundy had become an island. This would suggest that Lundy was accessed by boat, and that the resources that were available on Lundy, or around its rocky shoreline, were of sufficient value to warrant the investment in time and energy to get to the island in order to exploit these resources.

An important additional to the inventory of Late Mesolithic sites in the coastal zone is the site of Llandevenny, located *ca.* 5km east of Newport and 7km northeast of Goldcliff, where work in 2002 produced 96 worked lithic artefacts, including a Late Mesolithic microlith and tuff flakes similar to those found at Goldcliff. This site has produced a *ca.* 5.5m peat sequence along with charcoal from two occupation layers sealed by peat and silts (Brown 2004). Excavations in 2003 produced an additional 244 finds included flakes, flake shatter, cores, blade-flakes, a thumbnail scraper and an edge retouched flake (projectile point), heat fractured stones and a probable hammerstone. The assemblage comprises flint pebbles and cobbles (95.08%) and chert (1.64%: Greensand and Carboniferous chert types), and tuff artefacts (3.28%). This is the only Late Mesolithic site other than Goldcliff to produce tuff, and the assemblage is very similar to Goldcliff (Brown 2004: 52). The lithic assemblage indicates *in situ* knapping activities at this location.

In addition to this find a very interesting inland site has been identified at Langstone, near Newport (Couper 2011). Initial fieldwork at this location in 2004 identified a number of later Mesolithic blades (found during fieldwalking). The flint finds were concentrated on a south facing slope next to a small brook, and were interpreted as a task site probably for tool manufacture (Couper 2011: 82). At the bottom of the field a deposit of natural flint, with many small nodules, some of which may well have provided raw material for knapping at this site, was identified (*ibid.*). Between 2008 and 2011 Rod Couper returned to this location and undertook a solo fieldwalking strategy, during which some 1096 worked flints were recovered. Of these, 174 objects of later Mesolithic date, including 22 microliths (one with a microdenticulate edge), 3 microburins, 7 single platform cores, 132 blades/blade fragments, 5 core rejuvenation blades, 1 awl and 2 utilised blades, were recovered. This particular location provides some intriguing elements for our interpretations of Mesolithic activity, with the south facing aspect of the field, the presence of a water source, and a flint source, all combining to illustrate the sort of location that we might use to predict potential locations for Mesolithic activity during future studies.

Towards the end of the Mesolithic period, there are only a few locations in Wales that have produced micro-triangle finds that appear to post-date *ca.* 7000 uncal BP (Jacobi 1980: 176–7). Two of these locations are Frainslake and Lydstep Haven, on the south Pembrokeshire coast, and both occur in inter-tidal peat deposits. Both sites are considered in more detail in Chapters 4 and 5, but the main point in highlighting these sites here is the fact that Jacobi (1980: 175) suggests that a number of the microlith shapes in evidence do not occur in lithic assemblages before *ca.* 7000 uncal BP. These lithic forms include micro-rhomboids and micro-tranchet forms, and whilst the precise dating of these forms has been questioned by Jacobi, it is clear that a more considered approach to the dating of the context of these finds is still required. An additional location with a latest Mesolithic date on a hazelnut shell is Goldcliff in the Severn Estuary (Bell *et al.* 2000).

Discussion

The consideration of "tools of the trade" outlined in this chapter has sought to expand beyond the simple consideration of technology as a means to enable subsistence and routine activity and endeavoured to incorporate aspects of culture and landscape interactions within the social, ritual and economic elements of Mesolithic lifeways. These interlinking elements are fundamental to the construction of a social narrative of lithic production and use, as well as bone, antler and woodworking production and use. These initial steps are aimed at re-orienting our thought processes towards the Mesolithic and to help us to begin to think about the "hidden" meanings behind tool production and use, alongside the ways in which context is constructed and mediated through social and reflexive practice. When considering these factors we need to think about our own lives; whilst there is no way that we can "know" what the lived experience of a man, woman or child was in the Mesolithic period, the ways in which we live, our knowledge, or lack of it, our practical abilities and those of others, our experiences and the ways in which our lived experience informs our own decision making and ability to negotiate complex situations or unforeseen problems, all have resonance to life in the past. In the same ways that we use the social and practical skills that we acquire as we move through each stage of our lives, and the ways in which we understand what is and is not socially acceptable, and how we understand our place in society, so to would people in the past.

As noted by Price (2009: 684), when considering the Mesolithic period it is apparent that:

> everyone is not equal in skill and knowledge ... not everyone can do everything ... actions are performed in relation to the social acceptability of their performance, or they can challenge what is acceptable ... *and* ... there are diverse relationships and interactions between people and different aspects of the world. (*my emphasis*)

The point is that in the present, as in the past, each individual has a distinct lived experience and skills/knowledge base, irrespective of the socio-economic and ritual conditions that they exist within. We should also not forget however, that *deviant* behaviour would undoubtedly have occurred in the past, as it does in the present, e.g. inter-personal violence or theft, or the "simple" decision to not follow prescribed rules etc., and also that carefully considered and constructed activity could be used to change people's understanding of *normal* social conventions. People in the past undoubtedly experienced a different world to the one we now experience, but they would still have felt pain, embarrassment, love, hate and the myriad emotions, problems and experiences that we all encounter today; we need to realise that the Mesolithic past is not really as far removed from the present as the "simple" dimension of time might imply!

As we move through the following chapters a range of approaches to the data will be introduced in order to expand the potential for developing a more holistic overview of the Mesolithic experience and world views, and as such a move towards a social narrative of the past. Within this, some relatively recent perspectives, such as those of Warren (2006), Finlay (2000; 2003a), Conneller (2000a) and others, will be woven into the discussion. In addition, concepts such as the temporal nature of landscape interactions, the ecology and visualisation of landscape context, and the nature of the activities undertaken at specific locations within the landscape will all be integrated as the discussion develops. The latter element, relating to the activities undertaken at specific locations within the landscape, includes the idea that lithic assemblages relate to a range of processes and other aspects of landscape interaction, as has been alluded to in the discussion so far, and that there can be multiple authors of the record. We need to consider the probability that the elements of procurement, processing and concealment (Finlay 2000a: 28) may all be imbued with differing levels of significance and meaning. However, whilst multiple authorships may have pertained in relation to composite tools, the fact is that individuals may well have also specialised in hunting, i.e. from the levels of initial procurement to the production of the final implement/s and the execution of the hunting activity (i.e. a Jack, or Jill, of all trades!). Another point of note is the need to embed individuals into the Mesolithic itself, as men, women and children all existed in, and were integral to, the day-to-day aspects of life during this period.

Children in particular have been shown to have multiple roles in society, and of course, they were fundamental to group continuity and the reception/transmission of knowledge. In terms of lithic inventories, the fact is that learners develop their skills through a combination of mimicry and ultimately, guidance, with this extending to activities that are fundamental to socio-economic life, such as the gathering of flint pebbles, tending animals (where necessary) and gathering firewood, collecting fruits and berries, fishing, helping with the preparation of foodstuffs, the cleaning of hides and many other possible "chores" (Högberg 2008: 115–6). Fundamentally, it appears that the identification of children in relation to lithic material culture lies in their inexperience, and as a consequence the stone objects that are produced are likely to be less "refined" than those produced by more skilled individuals, or as Högberg (2008: 117) suggests, "more simple and unstructured" when compared to the products of a skilled flint worker; although in this context the skilled individual need not be an adult *per se*. Karsten (2004: 102) has alluded to the possibility that the occurrence of unused flakes on Kongemose period sites in Scania, alongside "the tentative direct technology, the large number of hammerstones, and some of the simpler tools" are in fact "visible traces of the hunters' children". The intriguing element of Karsten's work is the observation that the children were producing flakes that were unlike the adults' blades and blade tools, and that the technique used was completely different to that of the adults. The implication is that the children were developing an "understanding of how flint can be worked and how it breaks" using simpler techniques than they would ultimately use when their training was considered to have been effective enough to enable progression (*ibid*.: 104).

Whilst the stages of production begin with the selection of the correct wood for the shaft and the bow, the right flint for the arrow tip, feathers for the flights etc., along with the shaping of the bow, straightening of the arrow shaft, stringing of the bow, the fletching of the arrow and the attachment and design of the arrow point, we should consider the possibility that all of these stages do not necessarily require multiple inputs. This is clearly an involved process, and only one element of the daily round, but the point is that the skills necessary to ensure that the bow and arrows serve their purpose are not beyond the abilities of a single individual. Fundamentally, concealment is more meaningful when it is limited to a discrete group (or even individual) within society. Knowledge is power after all! Furthermore, the idea that Mesolithic tool-kits were multi-functional can be extended to the basic tenet that the multiple components of the hunting kit can be carried in their separate/component parts (sinew, resin, microliths, feathers and shafts) and constructed "on-site", as such these elements could also function as repair kits when needed. Given that we know that Mesolithic people were able to plan ahead and leave caches of equipment for future use at strategic points in the landscape (e.g. Burov 1998), the idea that individuals could have also carried such kits should be considered likely. At Vis I, Burov (*ibid*.: 53) has noted that, judging by the frequent finds of split logs, boards, runners and skis, laths for baskets, and oars, the inhabitants of this site were familiar with woodworking techniques. Furthermore, a number of lithic tools were used for working wood, including flint blades, microscrapers, points and borers, with the microscraper perhaps being used to cut slots and the blades being used to carve decorative ends and perhaps shaving small surfaces (*ibid*.). The point here is that, whilst the stone tools were elements of composite objects, they were also tools in their own right, and each may have served multiple purposes in the production process of the myriad organic objects that were used in the Mesolithic period, and that elements of composite objects could be prepared in advance/anticipation of future needs.

As discussed above, and as noted by McFayden (2008: 126, *citing* Edmonds 1997) different components of a stone tool assemblages relate to different tasks such as hunting and butchering of animals, the processing of plants and fish, the cutting of wood, and a myriad of other activities (e.g. those indicated by Burov 1998). In this context hunting entails the use of lithics as components of arrows and knives, as scrapers, burins, awls, and flakes for processing activities. Axes and scrapers could be used in the cutting and smoothing of wood for bows and arrow shafts, handles and other items, and microliths, serrated blades and flakes would be used in the gathering and processing of plants as inserts for sickles, knives etc. (McFayden 2008: 126), in addition, notched pieces could be used in the smoothing of the arrow shafts and of course borers could have been used in the perforation of holes through which sinews or straps could have been passed for bindings (Burov 1998: 54). Finally, in relation to fishing activities, the use of twisted leaves and roots from sedges (*Carex* sp.) and willow, as cord in the production of nets is attested at a number of locations in northern Europe, including Vis I (Russia), Antrea-Koilahti (Karelia) and Siivertsi (Estonia) (*ibid.*: 61), and similar twisted fibres have been used in the production of traps and mats.

This is another aspect of human-landscape interaction that needs to be considered when attempting to reconstruct Mesolithic lifeways, as it is often easy to neglect the fact that the composite tool-kits that we find are a tangible representation of the complex ways in which hunter-fisher-forager groups interacted with their environment, modified elements of it to ensure that their socio-economic and ritual activities continued to function, and negotiated and renegotiated these socio-economic and ritual aspects of life in the arena of the everyday processes of learning and knowledge transfer (*sensu* Zvelebil 2005). Fundamentally, beyond the basics of hunting, fishing and foraging, technology is essential for, and integrated into, multiple aspects of the socio-political and ritual actions of life in the Mesolithic period. Hopefully, the above discussion has outlined some of the more tangible aspects of Mesolithic tool-kits and their possible meaning in terms of the negotiation and renegotiation of identities and culture during the Mesolithic period.

We should also evaluate the locational aspects of sites in the landscape and consider the fact that different classes of site may be specific to certain contexts (Jochim 2006). Jochim's research in southwestern Germany has suggested that the largest sites in the study area (possibly interpreted as residential/base camps or persistent places?) were located closest to water sources, whilst distance from water varied at the medium and smaller sites (task sites or hunting locations?) with a trend of increased distance from water as the size of site diminished (e.g. large – median distance of 25m from water; medium – median of 75m from a water source and small sites have a median of 150m from a water source) (*ibid.*: 206). This would clearly suggest that the resources at each location differ in importance, as the large sites are primarily located near lakes with a broad resource base, whilst the medium to small sites are located near large or small lakes, rivers, streams or springs, where fish could have been caught and the presence of fresh water may have proven attractive to game (*ibid.*). The greater proportions of microliths at the medium-small sites are thought to reflect the fact that these sites functioned as hunting locations, alongside other activities, and as such were locations where the repair and maintenance of hunting gear was being undertaken on a more regular basis than at the larger sites (*ibid.*). At the large sites the high percentages of scrapers, burins, borers and notched tools (at *ca.* 35% amongst the retouched tools) suggest that "maintenance activities" such as the working of skin, wood, bone and antler were being undertaken (Joakim 2006: 210), alongside a range of other subsistence, social and ritual activities.

It is, perhaps, apparent from the above discussion that the shifts in lithic, bone and antler technology that occur as oak-hazel-lime woodland expands in the middle Mesolithic, and as sea levels continue to rise across this period, should not simply be seen in functional terms. However, we cannot neglect the fact that the shift from the more open landscapes of the earlier Mesolithic period, with woodland expanding to altitudes of *ca.* 500m AOD (Burrow 2003), would have resulted in a very different set of environmental constraints (and potentials) for hunter-gatherer groups. It could even be suggested that the, potentially, less predictable nature of animal–landscape interactions in a woodland setting, with a shift towards smaller group size and also solitary animals, could have resulted in some severe seasonal shortages in the meat portion of the diets of Mesolithic groups. Ultimately, whilst meat is not the "be all and end all" of Mesolithic subsistence strategies, as will be discussed in Chapter 5, the allocation, or control of allocation, of an important resource (whether important in real or symbolic terms), can be a significant tool in the mediation of social relations within society (Stig Sørensen 2000; Zvelebil 2003a). Ultimately it is this mediation of the social, i.e. the management and negotiation of cultural norms and the perpetuation or modification of embedded socio-political and ritual aspects of society, which ensures group continuity. Food is fundamental to all aspects of existence, and the ways in which subsistence activities influence human-landscape interactions, and socio-political and ritual interactions, are explored in greater detail in Chapters 4–6.

4

COMING HOME TO A REAL FIRE: LANDSCAPE UTILISATION AND SETTLEMENT PATTERNING

> When faced with the dilemma of securing a continuous food supply from resources that are unevenly distributed in space and time people ... can either move around ... from one source of food to another (group or residential mobility) or they can develop technological, social, and economic means of coping with periodic scarcity of resources (residential permanence and logistical mobility) ... (Zvelebil 2003a: 2)

> Mesolithic sites in Pembrokeshire were not simply placed at random in the landscape ... they were meaningfully situated for a variety of reasons relating to the myths, metaphors and memories that were associated with the lived-in and active landscape. (Cummings 2000: 93)

> A misplaced reliance upon ethnographically known groups has precluded an appreciation of the diversity of hunting-gathering adaptations. (Price and Brown 1985: 4)

Introduction

As might be anticipated, the generally peripatetic nature of the hunter-fisher-forager lifestyle means that settlement patterning is occasionally difficult to assess due to the diverse range of environments that would have been exploited by these groups as they moved between terrestrial, marine and freshwater environments, and between lowland and upland areas; both in relation to seasonal animal migrations and seasonality in the availability of different fish, plants and other animal resources. In addition, alongside the biases outlined in Chapters 2 and 3, the nature of the available resources, and the activity being undertaken at any point in the landscape will influence whether a more or less permanent occupation/activity site is required or preferred (Binford 1980; Kelly 1995; Grasis 2010), and as the quote from Cummings (above) indicates, ritual, alongside a range of social, economic and environmental factors will also influence the settlement patterning of a given group of hunter-fisher-foragers (David and Kramer 2001: 237). The limitations of classifying groups as either mobile (nomadic) or sedentary, or variations of these categories, and relating this to subsistence strategies (e.g. foragers, horticulturalists or farmers) is acknowledged (Kelly 1992).

Milner *et al.* (2004: 13) have suggested that, based on a population density of 0.1 individuals per km² in a land area of *ca.* 150,000km² (this estimate is at the low end for ethnographically known hunter-gatherers), a conservative population estimate would put the hunter-fisher-forager population of Britain at *ca.* 15,000 individuals at any point in time. As Zvelebil (2003a: 2) has noted, globally coastal/lowland environments appear to have enabled hunter-fisher-forager groups to be more stable in terms of residence permanence and group size when contrasted to groups that exploited interfluve and upland areas of the landscape. As such, we might anticipate concentrations of population in coastal regions (or locations with a stable resource base) and more dispersed settlement patterning elsewhere in the landscape. Wetlands in general offer ecologically-rich and diverse environments with a varied and reliable range of resources that could influence population densities and settlement patterning in certain regions and at certain times of the year (Nicholas 2007a; 2007b). By their very nature coastal wetlands (and riparian wetlands) are relatively easy to access, and would have provided familiar environments for colonising groups as they expanded into Britain at the start of the Holocene; we should remember that the environment of the earlier Holocene was constantly remodelling as climate improved and sea levels continued to rise, and as such early colonists would have needed to develop their cognitive maps of the landscape accordingly (Kelly 2003), and to some degree these maps would have been in a constant state of flux. Population density then, in addition to landscape characteristics and food procurement strategies, will clearly influence site visibility during the Mesolithic period.

In attempting to determine the territories of past hunter-gatherer groups, archaeologists have used factors such as distance from lithic sources as a proxy for prehistoric mobility strategies. However, suggestions that stone transport distances can be used to understand prehistoric mobility are in all probability too simplistic, and fail to account for the decision making processes; including those of procurement, transport and discard (e.g. Brantingham 2006). Furthermore, as noted by Binford (1979), the sites studied are often context specific (situational), and as such will generally retain the signatures of the activities that are undertaken at them, and as a consequence lithic source itself may not be too informative in relation to site distributions. However, when analysing the lithic residues found at hunter-fisher-forager sites, the techniques that are used to study the tools, such as use-wear and residue analysis, can provide significant insights into the activities that were undertaken at a particular location in the landscape. It is this activity that needs to be determined if we are to begin to attribute "significance" to the sites that we identify in the landscape, especially when endeavouring to define territories and groups size/dynamics.

When using lithic sources in this way, we need to be aware of the fact that once procured, the raw material itself will be task specific in terms of its production, and it will be influenced by differing responses to tool manufacture and use, thus influencing its spatial distribution to some significant degree. However, a further complicating variable is in fact the availability of the raw material, and its type; beach pebbles tend to dominate at many sites in Mesolithic Wales, and as this material occurs discontinuously throughout the landscape, it is conceivable that caching of raw materials (i.e. passive gear) could result in a significant degree of movement from source over time (Binford 1979: 258).

An important observation at this point is the fact that large areas of south west Wales, the southern coastal strip, and Anglesey are below the 444m (800ft) contour (Silvester 2003: 9), and as such given Zvelebil's observations above (2003a: 2), these areas could be anticipated as regions where greater stability in residence permanence and group size might be anticipated, and are areas where the lithic sources are already in place. Unfortunately, significant parts of the lowland zone, where earlier Mesolithic activity sites would be anticipated, are now submerged due to earlier Holocene sea level rise. Consequently, we should anticipate that the evidence that is available to us is never going to allow us to identify the full range and potential variety of lithic sources used in the earlier part of the Mesolithic. Elsewhere, e.g. northeast Wales, a number of locations have produced lithic inventories that are either dominated by, or have a significant proportion of stone tools that are produced from chert (see Chapter 3 and discussion below). As such, the distribution of sites in this part of Wales will potentially be influenced by the proximity of this resource, to some degree, alongside the resources available from flint sources, although again, the spatial distribution of chert finds does suggest that distances from source can be considerable.

Beyond Wales, albeit of relevance given the recorded activity at cave locations in Wales, recent work by Hardy and Svoboda (2009) at the Robečský Brook canyon in northern Bohemia, Czech Republic, has shown that between *ca.* 9400 and 7400 cal BC it is in fact the duration of occupation at rockshelter sites in this region that influences the nature of the lithic assemblage, along with the specific activities that are undertaken at these sites. For instance, long term occupation at the site of Pod zubem has produced evidence for multiple activities, including hearths, pits, abundant artefacts of stone and bone, faunal remains, and a multi-layered stratigraphy (2009: 163), whilst a short term occupation at the Pod křídlem site (which is possibly a specialised activity, satellite site, of the main occupation site) produced only limited evidence; however, the application of use-wear analysis indicates the use of lithics in the processing of plant resources (including starchy plants) at this location. At the long term occupation site of Pod zubem, residue and use-wear analysis produced residues that included plant and wood tissue (Fig. 4.1), and single instances of hair and feathers, suggesting tool use on a wide range of materials. In addition, nearly half of the blades studied showed evidence for hafting (*ibid.*: 165).

As is readily apparent from this example, the sort of analyses undertaken by Hardy and Svoboda (2009) could significantly enhance our efforts at interpreting the activities that are undertaken at sites in the hunter-fisher-forager landscapes of Wales and adjacent regions, irrespective of whether the activity is of long- or short-term duration.

These forms of analysis also offer an opportunity to gain a greater understanding of the range of uses that specific lithic artefacts were designed for during the Mesolithic period. An important observation from the above example is that the residue and use-wear analysis at both sites produced evidence for the processing of plant tissues, an element of subsistence activity that considerably less "visible" archaeologically than hunting or coastal resource gathering activities (e.g. shellfish collecting), or hazelnut gathering. Unfortunately, whilst gender-differentiated activities are also difficult to "see" archaeologically (David

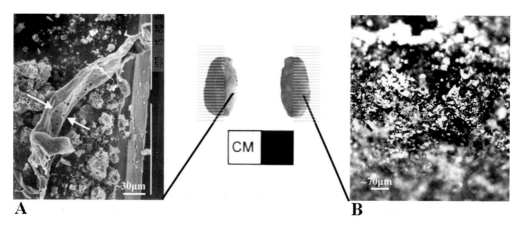

Fig. 4.1: Pod Zubem: bladelet (PZ 503) with evidence for hafting and woodworking, a) SEM of softwood tracheid with paired bordered pits indicated by arrows, b) resin. Shading indicates areas under the haft (after Hardy and Zvoboda 2009: 167, fig. 5; used with permission).

and Kramer 2001: 255–6), these techniques are unlikely to enhance our understanding of such activity. An important (further) limitation in this respect is the lack of a burial record for the Mesolithic in Britain as a whole (see Chapter 6), as the associations of artefacts in burials, if found in sufficient numbers, would potentially allow us to begin to tease out gendered patterning in lithic use. Regrettably, given the current state of the archaeological record, this suggestion is perhaps moving the potential of the record for Britain into the realms of nirvana at this point in time.

The above observation leads us to realise that, as has been noted throughout this volume, the difficulties inherent in the interpretation of hunter-gatherer sites are further compounded by the numerous biases that are introduced into the archaeological record by the diversity in hunter-fisher-forager activity, especially where those activities go beyond the purely subsistence oriented aspects of daily life. Factors such as seasonality, external threat (e.g. from predators), duration of occupation, the specific activities undertaken at a given location, divisions based on age/sex and/or division of labour, and social context, all contribute to the formation of the record (David and Kramer 2001: 265–6), and many of these are difficult to tease out from the available datasets for the Mesolithic period in Britain. In addition, as mentioned above, biases are also introduced by issues such as rising sea levels, which have obscured a significant amount of low-lying land; land that would have been of considerable significance to hunter-fisher-forager groups during the Mesolithic period (as the example from Goldcliff in the Severn Estuary, discussed below, highlight). Similarly, kill/butchery sites, lithic sources, preferred gathering locations, base camps, fishing spots, watering holes, meeting places, spiritually or symbolically significant places, or any number of locations within a territory, all have the potential to produce evidence of human activity, but only if that activity results in the deposition (and subsequent survival) of durable material culture remains.

Unfortunately, the fact is that, in many cases, these locations do not produce a "visible" Mesolithic presence into the present (Schulting 2008), and as such whilst there is little doubt that such locations will have been integral to past socio-economic and ritual articulations in human-landscape interactions, we are often left with the need to introduce a more nuanced anthropological/ethnographic context to our reading (interpretations) of the archaeological record (sensu Binford 1962). Recently, it has been suggested that a further biasing factor must be considered when studying the archaeological record of past hunter-gatherers in Europe, as our own preconceptions of the nature of earlier Mesolithic hunter-fisher-forager activity (i.e. that it is often small-scale and ephemeral) has led to only limited excavations at key locations (Conneller *et al.* 2012: 1017); a point made by Larsson in 1988 during his research at Skateholm (1988: 12–13). Basically, on the basis of the recent work undertaken at Star Carr, Conneller and co-workers have suggested that assumptions about the degree of mobility, and consequently the duration of occupation and size of site of earlier Holocene hunter-fisher-forager groups, have led to an inadequate approach to their study. As a consequence limited excavations have produced limited evidence; in effect archaeological approaches have resulted in self-fulfilling research agendas.

As the above discussion highlights, a group's resource procurement activities can result in the formation of numerous activity/task sites of different duration and intensity in a given landscape, this, and many other factors, can therefore combine to make the assessment of settlement patterning difficult (Kelly 1995). In the earlier Holocene period colonising foragers may well (in fact) have been more mobile, in residence terms, than subsequent, more established groups (Kelly 2003: 52). In addition, we should also try to remember that the act of settlement and dwelling is, in itself, a conceptually complex activity (Pollard 1999: 76). Pollard has suggested that, to date, our studies of settlement patterning function well at a basic level, in allowing us to examine the data from the perspective of regional patterns or structural and economic factors, but that this functionalist approach fails to allow insights into the past lived experiences of the groups being studied (*ibid.*: 76–7).

Pollard's observation resonates with the early work of Thomson (1939: 211) who noted that whilst seasonal factors influenced landscape exploitation and settlement strategies for the Wik Monkan tribe in Queensland, Australia, and clan membership conferred hunting rights over the groups territory, other factors such as kinship ties, influenced who was permitted to hunt in the groups territory and also who was permitted to hunt and forage between differing territories. These scalar variations (and differing levels of contact) may reflect a combination of the local and the extra-local in terms of intra- versus inter-personal relationships, and the need to ensure exogamy, the procurement of raw materials, dispersal of innovations, and trade in exotic items etc. through long-distance trade and exchange networks (Kelly 2003: 51). We might, therefore, anticipate that archaeological assemblages will reflect a combination of social and spatial scales of contact during the Mesolithic (e.g. Zvelebil 2006: 180). Zvelebil has also noted that settlement and resource use varied over time and between regions (*ibid.*), but in addition, we should also consider the likelihood that the nature of intra- and inter-personal relationships (social affiliation) will have tended towards fluidity as regional interactions and social relations are negotiated and re-negotiated over time (e.g. Jochim 2006: 211).

Put simply, whilst Smith (1992b: 37), has suggested that it is possible that "all sites within a 100km² area, and within an appropriate temporal span, could be attributed to the activities of a single group", the basic act of mapping of the distribution of sites fails to tease out the social practice that is embedded in settlement (and subsistence) activity as interactions and social affiliations shift throughout the Mesolithic. This observation is reinforced by the work of Lovis *et al.* (2006: 271) who have observed that it is apparent that prehistoric hunter-fisher-forager groups would have operated at multiple spatial scales, but, in moving their narrative towards that advocated by Pollard, these authors also note that the social, economic and ritual interactions that these groups engaged in would have differed depending on the spatial scale that these interactions were articulated through and within (*ibid.*; also Zvelebil 2003b).

An additional point to add to this introductory section is the fact that the landscape itself differs at many levels, and, as noted by Cummings (2000, after Thomas 1993), the landscape is an active part of the world as experienced, engaged with, and appropriated by individuals. That is to say that people not only experience the landscape that they are in, but they obviously interact in/with it, modify it, exercise rights of access over it, and even engage in the demarcation of territorial boundaries (however these are articulated); this is perhaps more evident in the present than it was in the Mesolithic, but to people in the Mesolithic period even a relatively subtle modification of the landscape, whether practical or symbolic in expression, could serve to de-mystify, domesticate or even sanitise the landscape to some degree (e.g. Jordan 2003a; Zvelebil 2003b). For instance, in discussing northern Sweden, Mulk and Bayliss-Smith (1999: 365) note that human influences include changes in the frequency of forest fires, changes in grazing pressure (a factor that would be enhanced by firing of the vegetation at sites such as Star Carr), and slash and burn cultivation. Elsewhere in Europe, the location of cemeteries at significant locations in the landscape, e.g. at the Dnieper Rapids in Ukraine (see Chapter 6), could symbolise ancestral rights of access or "ownership" to the rich fish resources at this location, in addition to the "basic" act of memorialisation of the dead. We need to be aware of the fact that even subtle articulations of group identity can symbolise important socio-economic, political and ritual significance in the Mesolithic landscape; these articulations may be difficult to identify, but, given ethnographic parallels, there is little reason to doubt their resonance to Mesolithic lifeways.

Interestingly, in relation to the suggestion (Chapter 2) that the opening up of the vegetation through firing activities would have created "familiar" landscapes for earlier Holocene hunter-forager groups, the distribution of the earlier Mesolithic sites discussed by Reynier (1998: 181) suggests that activity is focused on the lightly wooded lowland river valleys and upland hill tops, where a more open aspect would pertain. This information can be added to the evidence for upland exploitation in Wales, at sites like Waun Fignen Felin, in indicating that more open landscapes and the deliberate maintenance of "open" areas in the landscape, were potentially important to Mesolithic peoples (this is explored further in Chapter 6). The mental maps of the places that were fundamental to subsistence strategies were integral to the socialisation of hunter-fisher-forager landscapes. They were constructed and maintained by Mesolithic groups, who potentially not only created "sanitised" environments, but also created landscapes that functioned to "domesticate the wild and to link people" (Cooney 1999: 50). In effect these "managed" open areas in the landscape may well have formed important focal points within the territory or the region exploited, and as noted by Darvill (1999: 106), these territories or regions had "integrity, structure and symbolic meaning"; all elements that allowed for the identification of patterning and the "management" of the landscape by Mesolithic groups.

"Visualising" Mesolithic landscapes

In a seminal (albeit functionalist) paper on hunter-gatherer settlement systems Lewis Binford (1980) considered settlement and subsistence strategies from the perspective of differing organisational components of the cultural system, alongside the patterning and nature of the evidence that is produced by this behaviour. In this work Binford used the ethnoarchaeological study of Nunamiut Eskimos (Inuit) of north-central Alaska, along with a consideration of documented ethnographic studies of other groups, in order to consider the settlement systems of hunter-fisher-foragers in differing environments, and to assess the nature of settlement/subsistence activities in relation to their by-products. This research was undertaken in an attempt to identify patterning that would allow meaningful insights into the archaeological evidence of past hunter-fisher-forager activities (i.e. the archaeological record). Whilst this approach has been modified in recent years, there is no doubting the value of studies that seek to understand how the archaeological record may have formed, as long as we also seek to understand the social and spiritual influences that might have pertained at the time of formation (e.g. Zvelebil 2003a), alongside the fundamental practical aspects of site function/formation.

Furthermore, the use of ethnographic studies of modern "hunter-fisher-foragers" (to whatever degree each activity contributes to subsistence strategies) provides important insights into the *potential* use of archaeological artefacts in the past and their *potential* role in settlement and subsistence activities, as well as providing insights into the *possible range* of site types, exploitation strategies, and social and ritual/symbolic activity etc. of past groups (Clark 1968). As noted by Mitchell (2005: 150), archaeological artefacts of both inorganic and organic origin, that are similar to those in use by extant populations, can be more easily understood in this way because ethnography can provide insights into the use/ function of items such as ornamental objects, items of personal decoration, specialised hunting and gathering equipment such as bows and arrows, digging sticks, collecting bags, fish traps, nets, hooks and line and net sinkers etc. Obviously, many of these objects will be recognisable in the present, if conditions of preservation permit, but as the discussion of microlith production in Chapter 3 has highlighted, the "meaning" embedded in the transformation of the raw materials into the finished object, and the meaning of the object itself, can also have significance.

Whilst finds of organic Mesolithic artefacts are relatively limited in Britain, with the obvious exception of the material at Star Carr, which is discussed below, we do have

numerous examples from Europe that illustrate the potential range of items that would
have been used by hunter-fisher-forager groups at this time. For instance, Mikhail Zhilin's
work in the Volga Basin (2007a; 2007b; Zhilin and Matiskainen 2003), has highlighted a
wide range of preservation at a number of locations where the excellent *in situ* conditions
of sites sealed beneath gyttja and peat, that were located on the edges of former lakes
(in a similar context to Star Carr), has led to the recovery of Mesolithic material culture
remains. These remains include bone (including elk scapula knives), antler (including antler
scrapers), wood, bark, seeds, plant fibres, resin, coprolites, insects and other organic remains.

In the Volga Basin, at sites located in the Ozerki, Dubna, Ivanovskoye (Fig. 4.2),
Podozerskoye and Sahtysh peat bogs, a wide range of hunting and fishing equipment is in
evidence, with wooden arrowheads that preserved their microblade insets still in the slots,
fish hooks, nets and fish traps, along with leisters all being represented. This material clearly
supports the observation that the lakes in the Volga Basin were resource rich environments
where hunter-fisher-foragers were exploiting a range of stable and reliable foods, and also
where some degree of stability in relation to residence was afforded by the reliable resources.
We should anticipate that similar locations in Wales will have had the potential to provide
resource rich environments for exploitation by Mesolithic hunter-fisher-forager groups.

In addition to the evidence for food procurement activities at the Volga Basin sites, a
wide range of ornamental objects (including elk and beaver incisor pendants), and probably
ritual artefacts are all found (see Fig. 4.2). All of these artefacts were recovered alongside
faunal remains from elk, beaver, roe deer and very occasionally reindeer, and a range of fur
bearing animals, waterfowl, and fish remains. As might be anticipated, the faunal, avian and
fish remains all provide significant insights into the range of species being exploited by the
hunter-fisher-forager groups in the Volga Basin during the Mesolithic period. Importantly,
all of these finds are preserved in association with waterlogged deposits, which in turn
provide an organic matrix from which palynology (pollen analysis) and other environmental
studies can be undertaken in order to provide a "window" into the nature of the landscape
and environment at the time the sites were exploited (see Zhilin 2007a).

These, and other studies, are considered in more detail elsewhere in this volume in
order to enhance our understanding of the nature of Mesolithic societies in general, but it
should be noted that the "embarrassment of riches" that occurs through much of northern
Europe, in terms of organic finds from waterlogged contexts is, unfortunately, yet to be
mirrored to any great degree in the Mesolithic finds from wetland/waterlogged locations
in Britain. This observation may well suggest that alongside the limitations imposed in
mapping hunter-fisher-forager interactions at the landscape level, as discussed above (and
in Chapters 2 and 3), more research is required in relation to the identification of potential
wetland locations that might produce evidence for Mesolithic activity, as the information
potential of such contexts is considerable when the possible range of organic preservation
is considered (Fig. 4.3) (Lillie and Ellis 2007).

In this context, it has been noted that wetlands (throughout the human past) have
been exploited for obvious resources such as food, but also for medicines, textiles and
building materials (Nicholas 1998: 722). Species such as cattail (*Typha* sp.) provide edible

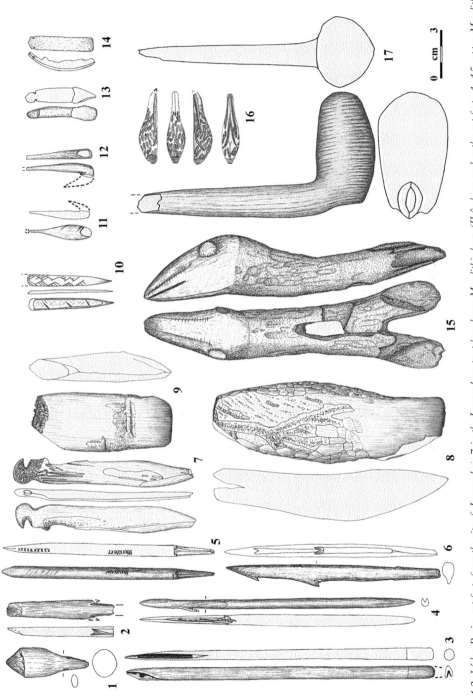

Fig. 4.2: Volga Basin, artefacts from the site of Ivanovskoje 7 in the Ivanovskoje peat bog: lower Mesolithic layer (IV); bone and antler artefacts. 1–15: upper Mesolithic layer (IIa), bone and antler artefacts; 1–5: arrowheads; 6: barbed point; 7: knife; 8–9: antler adze blades; 10: awl; 11–12: fishing hooks; 13–14: tooth pendants; 15: antler figurine (staff top?); 16–17: middle Mesolithic layer; 16: bone merganser bead; 17: wooden swimming swan figurine? (from Zhilin 2007a: 70; used with permission).

154 Malcolm Lillie

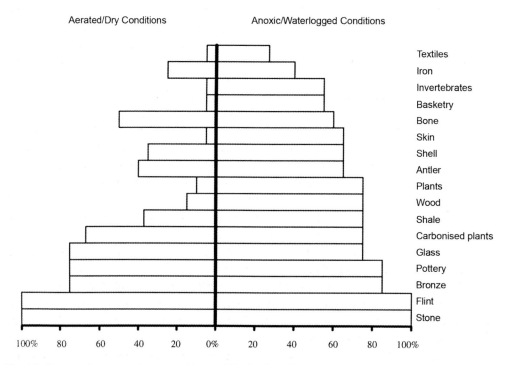

Fig. 4.3: Comparative preservation potential between "Dryland" and "Wetland" locations (redrawn from Coles 1988). Note: dry sites can, and do, preserve waterlogged contexts such as in ditches, wells and pits, which all have the potential to produce material in the preservation ranges to the right of the diagram, and as such enhance the information that is recovered. Equally, and as noted throughout the text, wetlands are a threatened resource and numerous factors are causing these fragile systems to be degraded at an often alarming rate (globally).

parts of the plant throughout the year, and in addition the pollen can be processed into storable flour. Furthermore, both cattail and reeds (*Phragmites* sp.) provided the material for bags, baskets, decoys, mats, buildings and clothing, amongst other items (*ibid.*: 722). The archaeological and ethnographic records demonstrate a wide range of additional "pull" factors to wetland environments; these include a broad range of fish and fowl, and both large and small mammals, alongside the resources discussed above (Nicholas 1998). It is these attributes, amongst others, that make wetland environments so attractive to hunter-fisher-forager groups.

Furthermore, the evidence for greater degrees of residence permanence in and around wetland/riparian areas, as attested throughout the world by sites in the Danubian Iron Gates (Bonsall *et al.* 1997; Radovanović 1996), Star Carr (Clarke 1954), Shanshan in the Lower Yangzi River, China (Jiang and Liu 2006), numerous sites in western Japan, such as Sobata, Saragawa and Tsukuda (Miyaji 1999), Robbins Swamp in Connecticut (Nicholas 1988), or Key Marco on the Gulf Coast of Florida (Cushing 2000), suggest that these locations were not only significant in the past, in relation to settlement and subsistence, but also formed a foci for ritual activities (e.g. Oleneostrovski Mogilnik, a cemetery located on an island in Lake Onega, Karelia: Jacobs 1995; O'Shea and Zvelebil 1984). It has also been observed that within resource-rich areas, such as the wetlands that were occupied by hunter-fisher-foragers, territory size is often smaller than it is elsewhere (Nicholas 2007b: 250), due to the diverse and reliable resources that are available for exploitation.

Obviously, when attempting to interpret settlement/activity sites, ethnographic analogy must be utilised with some caution, especially when we are not contrasting like for like in terms of location and environment (e.g. Binford 2009; Thomson 1939). However, there is little doubt that Binford's (1980) research, which contrasted the Nunamiut with forager groups in equatorial and subequatorial environments, emphasising the considerable variability among foragers in relation to the duration of stay at different sites, and showing that greater mobility results in lower archaeological "visibility", has provided an important enhancement to our attempts at understanding past hunter-fisher-forager groups (Table 4.1, after Binford 1980: 7 and references therein). This observation has particular resonance when we consider the fact that, since the advent of agriculture and the shift from the procurement of wild food resources to the integration of domesticated resources across the prehistoric period in Europe, few of us currently have the capability or knowledge of hunting and gathering activities to enable knowledgeable interpretations of the evidence, at least not without the integration of ethnographic/anthropological studies to aid/enhance our understanding and interpretation of the past.

Interestingly in this context, according to Binford, groups such as the Punam and Guayaki, who are characterised as highly mobile foragers, do not necessarily re-locate to locations of previous activities; a factor that would influence our interpretations of past hunter-gatherer activity in a given landscape. However, by contrast Tilley (1994) has noted that certain localities are revisited by Mesolithic groups in Britain over significant timescales. These contrasting observations lend weight to the hypothesis that "persistent places" (*sensu* Barton *et al.* 1995) have significance beyond purely utilitarian considerations, and we could

Table 4.1: Summary of group sizes and annual mobility for a number of Equatorial and Subequatorial groups of hunter-gatherers.

Group Name	Modal group size	No. annual residential moves	Mean distance between sites (miles/km)	Total circuit distance covered annually
Penum	65	45	4.2/6.8	195
Semang	18	21	7.1/11.4	150
Mbuti	120	12	8.3/13.4	100
Siriono	75	26	14.2/22.9	370
Guayaki	20–50	50	3.7/6.0	220
Aeta	45	22	8.0/12.9	178
Hadza	–	31	8.2/13.2	256
Dobe !kung	25	5	14.8/23.8	75
G/wi	18–55	11–12	16.8/27.0	193

anticipate that other "pull" factors such as ritual activities or social gathering/meeting places might influence "persistence" in a landscape. In archaeological terms (as noted above), whilst the evidence may be ephemeral, it is clear that hunter-fisher-forager activity could result in multiple site locations over a given landscape. This could, in turn, create a biased picture of the density and duration of hunter-fisher-forager landscape interactions, especially where we lack high resolution dating. In addition, the archaeological signatures at certain, perhaps ephemeral, locations have the potential to contrast markedly with the evidence occurring at more permanent, or to use the term above, more "persistent places" in the landscape (e.g. Jochim 2006).

As the above discussion has indicated, amongst the key problems that occur when attempting to elucidate the nature of settlement patterning and the specifics of hunter-fisher-forager subsistence, economic and ritual activities, beyond the rudimentary facts that people need shelter, warmth and sustenance, is the paucity of the available evidence. It has been suggested (Schulting 2000, and as noted above) that a significant, confounding aspect of the data lies in the fact that the populations exploiting inland areas of Britain during the Mesolithic do not appear to have been undertaking activities that resulted in the formation of *stratified* deposits relating to their occupation, subsistence, economic or ritual activities in the landscape. An alternative explanation can be proffered, in that it is entirely possible that we have not yet been able to identify/recognise the signatures of these activities, and as a consequence, we cannot predict/determine the locations where these deposits might survive in the landscape, at least not beyond the factors alluded to by Jochim (2006) wherein distance from water source may have been influential in the size of the site and the range of activities undertaken. Another complicating factor also lies in the likelihood that whilst considerations such as those outlined above will result in a certain degree of structuring of hunter-fisher-forager landscapes, these practical landscapes can, at the same time, be ritual landscapes (Zvelebil 2003b: 66). As such, we need to consider an additional range of possible activities within the landscape; activities that may be wholly embedded in ritual practice.

Despite these observations in relation to visibility and the inherent limitations embedded in studies of hunter-fisher-foragers landscapes, we do have instances where more durable locations occur in Britain; such as the Oronsay middens (Mellars 1987), Staosnaig, Colonsay (Mithen *et al.* 2001), Mount Sandal, Co. Antrim, Ireland (Bayliss and Woodman 2009), Thatcham in Berkshire (Healy *et al.* 1992), Deepcar in Yorkshire (Radley and Mellars 1964), the Nab Head (David 2007), Goldcliff (Bell 2007a–d; Bell *et al.* 2000), and Prestatyn and Rhyl (Armour-Chelu *et al.* 2007; Clark 1938); and see examples below. However, due to the myriad complicating factors discussed throughout this volume, the precise nature of the activities that were undertaken at many of these locations, the duration of this activity, and the reasons for the repeated use of certain sites still remains a matter of debate and sometimes speculation.

We can, of course, use the evidence from slightly later time periods to provide insights into the potential range of activities in the landscape during the later Mesolithic period. The evidence from the Thames Valley, at Eton, offers evidence to suggest long-term midden use across the earlier Neolithic period at *ca.* 3800–3500 cal BC (i.e. for *ca.* 2–300 years), with some suggestion that the middens may have been in use for up to 600 years (Hey and Barclay 2007: 410). As is often the case with Neolithic activity, the material that was deposited at the middens is not considered to represent casual discard. Similarly the pre-tomb construction midden material found at Wychwood and Hazelton North in the Cotswolds is interpreted as representing the re-deposition of rubbish accumulated elsewhere (*ibid.*). In a comparable fashion to Mesolithic activity, the Neolithic midden deposition in the Thames valley is considered to represent repeated visits (perhaps including social meetings) to a significant place, with the middens providing a mnemonic of these events (Hey and Barclay 2007: 410–11). The act of adding material to the middens ("construction" events?) may have functioned to reassert the significance of these locations, emphasise group belonging and provide a mechanism through which dispersed groups were regularly able to interact socially, economically and probably ritually (*ibid.*). Alternatively, they may have been municipal rubbish tips used to ensure that the main settlement sites were not rendered uninhabitable due to the accumulation of too much refuse, although "mundane rubbish disposal" (*ibid.*: 413) is not generally considered to be synonymous with Neolithic activity. The early Neolithic dating of these sites could be used to suggest that there is some degree of continuity across the Mesolithic to Neolithic periods, and that the modification of activity, towards ritual depositions, could have served to re-orientate Mesolithic mindsets towards those of the newly acquired "Neolithic".

One further point for consideration is the lack of thought paid to the "social actors" that were responsible for the deposition of material at the midden sites. If these activities were indeed significant then, presumably, the individuals involved in constructing these locales could be significant people within the earlier Neolithic society; in a similar way we might anticipate enhanced significance at the individual level during the Mesolithic period, especially when the activities involved engagement with the spirit world, the enactment of taboos or the mediation of pollution events. Surely it would be naive in the extreme to assume that only Neolithic people saw meaning and significance in ritual articulations, especially when there is a significance corpus of data to indicate that there is continuity across the Mesolithic to Neolithic periods in relation to such activities (e.g. Karsten 2004: 130, and see Chapter 6).

Returning briefly to the importance of sites in lowland wetland locations, both in terms of the evidence for subsistence activities, and the fact that enhanced preservation often leads to an enhanced archaeo-environmental record, the site of Dudka in the Masurian Lakeland in Poland (Gumiński 1998) has provided significant insights into changing subsistence strategies across the Mesolithic period in this part of Europe. Excavations at this location have shown that hunter-fisher-forager groups occupied a small island (*ca.* 15ha in area) in a shallow lake (*ca.* 9m maximum depth) which covered *ca.* 25sq. km in area. Infilling and terrestrialisation of the lake led to the formation of extensive peat bog deposits, known locally as the Staświńskie Łąki (Staświny Meadows; *ibid.*: 103). The excavations at Dudka have produced nearly 62,000 animal bones and 24,500 fish bones, and the nature of the finds appears to indicate increased subsistence activity across the Mesolithic period, with fishing comprising a significant part of the economy, and with fish bones being in excess of 50% of all bones in the Late Mesolithic (a similar emphasis on fishing has been noted at Tågerup by Karsten (2004: 116)). It is this level of information and insight into past subsistence strategies that is considerably lacking in the Mesolithic record for Wales (and elsewhere in Britain).

Throughout the whole of the Mesolithic and Neolithic periods at Dudka 70–80% of the fish bones were from predatory species such as pike, eels and perch, with non-predatory species such as roach and bream (Cyprinids) also in evidence. Big game animals comprised 65–85% of the hunted component from the earlier Mesolithic to Late Neolithic at Dudka (primarily red deer with elk of secondary importance), and interestingly, during the later Mesolithic tortoise make up 35% of the hunted component. Bird bones comprised about 10% of the hunted portion of the diet. The excavators at Dudka have noted that the importance of tortoise in the later Mesolithic reflects increased population size during the Atlantic period, alongside cooking traditions, the use of their shells as containers, over-exploitation and the habitation season of the sites.

This example highlights the fact that the changing environments of the Pre-Boreal, Boreal, Atlantic and Sub-Boreal periods in Poland clearly influenced species abundance (including fluctuating frequencies of wild pig/boar, roe deer, horse, bison/aurochs) across the Mesolithic and into the Neolithic periods. It is also across these periods that settlement activity shifted from seasonal camps to permanent settlements, and some form of incipient domestication of species such as pig and cattle occurs; it is argued that the process of indigenous domestication is interrupted by the first appearance of new Neolithic groups in the region (Gumiński 1998: 108–9). Unfortunately, Gumiński's work does not include any consideration of the palaeoenvironmental record from this area, and there is no consideration of the potential range of plant species that would have been exploited in this zone. However, what this site does do is further highlight the considerable potential of wetland locations for enhancing our understanding of the Mesolithic in northern Europe. Additionally, the evidence for shifts in economic activity with changes in the environmental composition of the region is also important as similar changing environments characterised the entire Mesolithic period in Wales, and Britain in general, and these changes continued into the subsequent Neolithic period.

In light of the above discussion, we also need to remember that as certain animals/resources will occupy/be available in different parts of the landscape at different times, e.g. deer move to upland areas during the summer months; and also that a site in the upland zone will be exposed to the elements (and physical weathering) and in all probably only be exploited for a short period of time, i.e. in order to hunt and also process the kill, the likelihood is that many sites are unlikely to preserve a great deal of evidence for the presence of human activity beyond the more durable, inorganic components of that activity. Similarly, the food gathering activities of a group of people during the Mesolithic would be all but invisible to us in the present, unless those activities are represented in the organic remains at a processing site (see Mithen *et al.* 2001), camp site or base camp, and are preserved through mechanisms such as charring or waterlogging (e.g. Star Carr, Dudka and the Volga Basin sites).

Furthermore, some of the activities undertaken by Mesolithic groups, such as the management of woodland resources, may never be visible to us in the archaeological record, unless perhaps (exceptionally) preserved in the palynological (palaeoenvironmental) record of a region. An example of the potential management activities that were undertaken by Mesolithic groups is alluded to by the work of Karsten (2004: 117) who informs us that some of the evidence from Danish excavations indicates that hazel and lime, in particular, were being coppiced in woodland glades in order to provide the raw materials for use in the production/construction of the fish traps that were used at Late Mesolithic "fish catching stations". A number of these factors combine to help explain the paucity of the archaeological record, and highlight the fact that ethnographic (and obviously palaeoenvironmental) data can help us "flesh-out" the record by allowing us to recognise the potential range of activities relating to hunter-fisher-forager settlement and subsistence patterning, and landscape utilisation strategies, in a given landscape setting.

However, whilst overnight or short term camp sites may be difficult to detect archaeologically, there are occasional finds of important locations, such as Thatcham in Berkshire (Wymer 1962; Healy *et al.* 1992), the Kennett Valley (Ellis *et al.* 2003), Iping Common, Sussex (Keef *et al.* 1965), Star Carr, in Yorkshire (Clarke 1954; 1972), and of course the Welsh sites such as the Nab Head, Rhuddlan, Prestatyn and Goldcliff (amongst others), that all combine to allow us to develop our understanding of hunter-fisher-forager activity in the British landscape. The find of a possible hut structure during excavations at Star Carr in the 2008 field season, demarcated by a ring of post-holes (Taylor *et al.* 2010: 16) further enhances the importance of this site to Mesolithic studies, as do the finds of 24 discrete areas of human activity in and around Lake Flixton that have been identified during fieldwork undertaken since 1975 (Taylor and Jones 2009). The possible hut structure, dubbed the "Little House by the Shore" by Taylor *et al.* (2010), was located in trench SC23 (see Fig. 4.7 below), on the dryland edge just above the lake shore, and was close to the location where the timber "platform" had been discovered in the 1980s.

Milner *et al.* (2012: 18) report that they had already found areas of carcass processing and tool production and use in the previous season of excavation at Star Carr. An extension to their earlier dryland margins trench produced a ring of holes (which would originally have held posts) arranged around a shallow hollow almost 3m wide (Taylor *et al.* 2010). The deposits within the hollow were highly organic and it is likely that it had been lined with plant material, possibly reeds; in addition, finds of burnt stones suggest that it had contained a small hearth (*ibid.*). The arrangement of the post-holes points to occasional repair or rebuilding. The team recorded several more hearths outside the post-hole ring, along with the evidence of flintworking and animal processing, as mentioned above (Milner *et al.* 2012). In a similar fashion, the research undertaken by Healy *et al.* (1992) at Thatcham, in advance of the construction of the Newbury Sewage Treatment Works, reinforces the fact that this location, and the Kennet Valley in general, is/are potentially of (at least) equal significance to Mesolithic studies as Star Carr and its environs are proving to be.

Another useful example in the context of understanding hunter-fisher-forager activity in the landscape, albeit at a different scale, is that of an upland hunting camp that was identified by Roger Jacobi at Pule Bents in the central Pennines in 1983 (Stonehouse 1997). This site is located at 366m AOD and has extensive views out onto the Colne Valley. Erosion and an acid soil would have compromised the preservation of any bone at this location, but the excavations produced 93 microliths and microlith fragments (with only ten un-worked pieces). This location did not produce evidence for knapping activities. The unusual distribution of the artefacts, absence of flint-knapping debris and dominance of microliths, along with the topographic situation at Pule Bents, which is located near a narrow route through the Pennines at this point, led Stonehouse to suggest that this would be an ideal location for the ambushing and killing of migratory animals (1997: 6). An important observation in relation to the microliths, identified as "rods", is that one of these objects had evidence for impact fracture, i.e. it may have been used as a projectile point (see also the work of Nuzhnyi 1989; 1990; 1993, on projectile point damage and the use of the bow and arrow in Ukraine, discussed in Chapter 1, above). This location presents a tantalising glimpse into the nature of upland hunting activity, but we still lack the resolution necessary to "see" who was doing the hunting, what symbolic activities were undertaken before, during and after the hunt, how the carcass was processed and, obviously, how the kill was divided up between members of the group.

In addition to the above observations, and the biasing factors inherent in the ephemeral nature of such sites, which include the consequent lack of stratified deposits, we must always be aware of the fact that natural impacts upon the archaeological resource (e.g. erosion, mixing and re-burial) are more acute when we study earlier Holocene (and obviously even earlier, Pleistocene) evidence for human activity in the landscape (Lillie 2003a). Similarly, more recent impacts, such as quarrying or the erosion caused by footpaths, both of which impacted upon the site of Deepcar in Yorkshire (Radley and Mellars 1964), can result in the mixing and disturbance of sites with thinly stratified depositional sequences. Furthermore, whilst it might be anticipated that cave sites would afford a greater degree of preservation of the archaeological record, potentially offering a relatively "closed" depositional context, problems still exist. The fact is that sites such as Cathole, Nanna's Cave, Ogof yr Ychen, Potter's Cave, Priory Farm, and Ogof Garrog Hir, amongst others have all produced Mesolithic material (Jacobi 1980), but it is often impossible for archaeologists to make sense of this material. As discussed in Chapter 3, the dating, association of the lithics to the contemporary human and faunal remains, and the lack of integrity of the cave deposits, have all frustrated attempts to produce meaningful narratives of the activity at these locations during the Mesolithic period.

Leaving aside issues relating to social and ritual influences in the articulation of material culture remains, there is considerable evidence, as outlined above, to indicate that the material remains of past activity may also be biased by the variation inherent in people's efforts to obtain and process the diverse elements necessary for shelter, warmth and sustenance (Binford 1980; 1983; Hodgetts and Rahemtulla 2001). Furthermore, these biases have, in the past, led to a reliance on faunal studies in dietary reconstructions (e.g. discussion of Dudka above), so much so that perceptions of socio-economic articulations within hunter-fisher-forager societies remain orientated around the role of hunting, and consequently, males, within such societies. This situation has persisted despite considerable ethnographic evidence to suggest that hunting often provides only a limited proportion of daily calorific intakes for hunter-fisher-forager groups when compared to foraging/gathering activities (Marlowe 2002), and that in actual fact females often participate in hunting activities (see Estioko-Griffin and Griffin 1981; Berndt 1981); and this biased perspective persists despite the efforts of recent researchers to introduce females (and children) into the debate (e.g. Moore and Scott 1997; Stig Sørensen 2000).

We have already alluded to the biasing issues introduced by sea level change, but as Jacobi (1980: 161–3) has noted, when considering the economic activities that were undertaken at sites like Rhuddlan and Trwyn Du, these locations actually take on a more terrestrial focus during the Mesolithic, as lowered sea levels mean that Rhuddlan would lose its areas of fen and coast (being *ca.* 10km from the contemporary coast at *ca.* 7600 cal BC, but within 3km of estuarine environments (Bell 2007f: 308)), and Trwyn Du, whilst still being within reach of a coastal area for use in subsistence endeavours, would not have been a cliff top site as it is today, and in actual fact Anglesey was not even an island in the earlier Mesolithic period (see Chapter 2). These are all clearly important considerations, not just in terms of Mesolithic subsistence, but also in terms of our own perceptions and of course, Mesolithic landscape perceptions and the rationale behind the choice of these locations as occupation/activity areas. Drawing analogies to Star Carr, Jacobi (1980: 163) noted that the sites of Burry Holms, Daylight Rock, the Nab Head and Aberystwyth would have all had sufficient dryland ungulate resources to ensure year-round availability, even with coastal resources at the very edges of their respective territories. Expanding on this observation, and following on from Marlowe's (2002) work, it is apparent that these inland areas would also provide a wide array of plant and freshwater resources (see also Zvelebil 1994; Mithen *et al.* 2001; and discussion in Chapter 5 below).

As a consequence of the myriad biases outlined above, we should always try to move beyond the consideration of hunting simply in terms of subsistence, especially as the work of Jordan (2003a; 2003b), Zvelebil (2003b) and others, has shown that hunting activities (along with many other aspects of hunter-fisher-forager activity) can be imbued with numerous ritual and symbolic meanings that transcend the "fundamental" function of hunting as a food procurement activity. Our attempts at "visualising" hunter-fisher-forager landscape interactions clearly need to transcend the basics by assessing (and accepting) the myriad biasing factors inherent in the archaeological record.

Finally, as discussed, we should always be aware of the fact that whilst the subsistence activities of hunter-fisher-forager groups will influence the nature of settlement patterning within a given landscape, certain locations will have had other levels of meaning. The significance attached to a given location will differ depending on the individual who is experiencing the location, and over time the nature of the meaning attached to any given location can be changed, mediated or abandoned as personal biographies, social and power relations are played out (Cummings 2000: 88). Recent research in northern England (Donahue and Lovis 2006) has sought to use ethnographic data from studies of North American hunter-gatherers in order to develop models of forager land-use that facilitate a more nuanced approach to our understanding of the mobility and subsistence activities of foragers in the northern hemisphere. This work is intriguing, and whilst North American hunter-gatherers may not be directly comparable to northwest European groups in prehistory, the ideas embedded in this study will be integrated within the next section of the current discussion, alongside a range of archaeological, ethnographic and more recent studies aimed at determining the nature of hunter-fisher-forager settlement and subsistence activities, in an effort to tease out pertinent observations in relation to the activities of Mesolithic groups in Wales.

Home is where the hearth is: hunter-gatherer settlements and settlement patterning

Mesolithic settlement sites are poorly represented, or not easily recognised, in Wales, and generally in Britain as a whole, although in recent years the picture is certainly improving (e.g. Waddington 2007; Conneller *et al.* 2012; and of course the discovery at Echline, near Edinburgh in late 2012). Despite these discoveries though the evidence remains relatively sparse for many reasons, not least that the many small-scale occupations representing temporary (for instance overnight) camp-sites are unlikely to leave an easily recognisable archaeological signature (David and Kramer 2001; Binford 1980), and optimal group size for foragers appears to be *ca.* 25 individuals, with 7–8 active foragers in each group (Kelly 2003: 51). As such, a recognisable archaeological presence remains elusive in many locations. Indeed, as has been noted in Chapter 3, Locock (2000: 7) has suggested that the lack of quantification and problems in the recording of lithic finds has also led to significant difficulties when attempting to determine whether the find spots of Mesolithic activity can be defined as being representative of settlement or domestic activity, or indeed whether the location being studied represents a camp, a temporary lithic or food resource processing site, or is representative of other socio-economic or ritual activities.

There are, however, a number of significant locations in Wales where it could be argued that the lithic inventories and associated material culture support the designation of certain locations as potentially being either settlement or occupation areas, or "persistent places" in the landscape (see Figs 3.3 and 3.4). With this in mind it is worth noting that Binford (1990: 121) has reported that there are no known examples of modern hunter-gatherers where shelters are not made at residential sites, irrespective of the anticipated duration of stay. As such, (and as suggested above) we might anticipate that the lack of evidence for shelters at many locations may reflect a lack of targeted excavation and/or issues related to the sites stratigraphy, or a failure on the part of researchers to address these (and related) issues of visibility. In addition to this observation, as noted by Nicholas (2007a) the resources used in the construction of shelters may actually result in a visible environmental impact, as the plants used in construction may have a range of functions/uses in hunter-fisher-forager economies, but the fact that we rarely have associated organic sequences in association with activity sites limits the potential to identify such impacts. In the case of tule and cattail Nicholas (2007a: 56) notes that these wetland plants were intensively harvested for use in lodge coverings (Fig. 4.4), and that a single lodge constructed by Interior Plateau hunter-gatherers could require as many as 1000 tule or cattail stems for just one structure. Again, these observations argue for a considered multi-disciplinary approach to the study of Mesolithic sites in Britain.

This observation further suggests that we should anticipate that, in the absence of excavation, the collection of surface lithic scatters does relatively little to enhance our understanding of the nature of settlement activity during the Mesolithic period. By contrast however, recent studies by Sergant *et al.* (2006) have suggested that the frequent occurrence of burnt ecofacts (hazelnut shells and bone) and artefacts (flint, quartzite) indicate the presence of surface hearths at nearly every campsite in the cover sands area of the northwest European Plain. A corollary of this suggestion is that despite the paucity of structured stone-built hearths, as found at the Nab Head II, and poor "visibility" in general, we can potentially determine the existence of these features if we adopt a considered approach to our analysis of the spatial patterning of burnt/charred material at "activity" sites.

Amongst the sites that were discussed in Chapter 3, the early Mesolithic sites of Burry Holmes, Daylight Rock, the Nab Head I, Rhuddlan and Trwyn Du, amongst others, will be discussed in greater detail below; both in terms of their landscape setting and the likely subsistence economies that their inhabitants were engaged in. For the later Mesolithic period sites such as Prestatyn, Pen-y-Bont, Brenig site 53, the Nab Head II, Goldcliff and Waun Fignen Felin, again amongst others, all provide insights into the activities of human groups after *ca.* 7740–7610 cal BC. Jacobi (1980: 169) has noted that, of the locations with flint assemblages that are characterised by scalene micro-triangles and narrow straight rods, i.e. elements of the "narrow-blade" assemblages that indicate a later Mesolithic age, some 66 findspots could be mapped for Wales, including Anglesey and the Marches. However, Jacobi (1980) only mapped 11 of the more important sites on his figure 4.22 at the time of writing. Jacobi has also noted that sites such as Craig-y-Llyn, Rhondda, provide a location with a multiple findspot of some 178 objects and 466 pieces of debitage, and an assemblage dominated by microliths, along with a significant proportion of both flint and chert cores; suggesting hunting activities and on-site processing of stone

Fig. 4.4: Modern example of a traditional Interior Plateau tule mat lodge at Secwepemc Heritage Park, Camloops, British Columbia (photo © George Nicholas, used with permission).

tools. The distribution maps provided in Chapter 3, are developed on the basis of over 480 locations that combine both single and multiple findspots (which were considered to represent relatively robust records of Mesolithic material), that were identified in the regional HERs, the NMW catalogue and Archwilio. By far the most prolific site, in terms of lithic finds, is the Nab Head where both early and late Mesolithic activity has been identified (see below).

As indicated in Chapter 3, the location itself, wherever studied, may represent more than one phase of activity e.g. at Craig-y-Llyn the blade technology in evidence contains both "archaic" and late Mesolithic forms, perhaps suggesting more than one phase of activity at this location (Jacobi 1980: 169). As the ethnographic evidence for hunter-fisher-foragers generally supports the notion that the nature of subsistence activities is (logically) influenced by the available resources in a given region, which in turn influences site type and distribution in the landscape (Marlowe 2005; Mithen and Finlayson 1991), repeated visits to sites such as Craig-y-Llyn and Waun Fignen Felin, or Rhuddlan, are perhaps unsurprising, and potentially even to be anticipated given the results obtained from "small scale" (or targeted) landscape surveys in areas like the Walton Basin, Powys. At this location 16 flint scatters and finds are located within the lower part of the basin, and a single findspot is recorded at a (slightly) elevated position towards the western side of the area, with all of this evidence probably reflecting repeated hunting activities (Gibson 1999). Again though, these interpretations are purely functionalist in scope and fail to attempt to expand on our understating of hunter-gatherer landscape interactions from the social and ritual perspectives. Another factor that may have made the uplands attractive to Mesolithic hunter-gatherers is the fact that woodland cover is less "intrusive" in hunting terms, resulting in more "familiar" open landscapes in which to engage in hunting activities. The discussion in Chapter 2 outlined the changes in vegetation across the Mesolithic period, and as discussed throughout the text so far, the nature of hunting and foraging activities, alongside the economic activities, and the socio-political and ritual activities of Mesolithic groups, also appears to have been renegotiated over time. Given these observations, repeated visits to certain locations may well have been influenced by ritual and social memory, alongside more practical considerations.

In terms of landscape exploitation strategies, Marlowe (2005) notes that the more that hunting contributes to the diet, the larger the area a group exploits and the more frequently camps are moved (see Table 4.1 for a comparison of forager movement and annual distances travelled). An additional aspect of forager activity is the general lack of storage, as foragers usually gather their food on a daily basis (Binford 1980: 5). By contrast, it is often accepted that populations who subsistence base is focussed on the exploitation of marine or freshwater resources such as fish or shellfish, are more stationary in the landscape than hunter-forager groups due to the reliability and predictability of such resources (e.g. Skateholm and Tågerup in Sweden; Andersson *et al.* 2004; also Nicholas 2007b for wetlands in general). Furthermore, the presence of stable resources often results in a reduction in mobility and greater archaeological "visibility". For example, in the Baltic region, a high degree of settlement permanence is correlated to the exploitation of lacustrine resources, especially freshwater fish (Bērziņš 2010: 37; Zvelebil 2008). In addition, ownership and/or rights of access to preferred fishing grounds may also have been marked by the establishment of permanent cemeteries at key locations, with the dead establishing (conferring) ancestral rights of access for the living (Larsson and Zagorska 2006; Zvelebil 2008: 35; also Lillie 1998; 2004). In the Iron Gates region of the Danube the site of Lepenski Vir stands out due to the combination of domestic, ritual and funerary activity being enacted at a single location (e.g. Bonsall *et al.* 2008). Clearly then, the actual subsistence strategy itself and the availability of stable resources will influence the degree to which settlements are more or less "permanent" in the landscape, and locations such as Waun Fignen Felin may have been considered to be "resource rich" due to the repeated (seasonal) presence of grazing ungulates during the Mesolithic period.

Furthermore, the activities that are in evidence around Lake Flixton in the Vale of Pickering, e.g. at Star Carr and associated sites, are clearly influenced by the presence of a large water body, which provided both a stable source of water and a wide range of freshwater resources. Both of which would have acted as "pull" factors for both humans and animals in the region. Referring back to the suggestion that the more open aspect of the uplands may have proven attractive to hunters who were used to exploiting these environments during the Late-glacial period, we might perhaps consider an additional reason for the burning of the reeds at Star Carr, which has primarily been suggested to have acted as a mechanism to promote new growth which would attract browsing animals. The removal of vegetation would also create openings in the landscape, which, once established would have resulted in concomitant increases in grazing pressure, which would have had the effect of maintaining these cleared spaces. For early Holocene hunter-gatherers this factor may have produced a "value added" element in that more "recognisable" environments are created for their hunting (and associated) activities. An additional point to consider here is the fact that elsewhere in Europe the greater degrees of residence "persistence" that occur at coastal, lacustrine or riparian sites, are often accompanied by evidence for burial, occasionally expressed as cemetery sites. The evidence from Star Carr must surely highlight this area as a potential location for the recovery of this sort of burial evidence if the soil conditions prove favourable.

When defining a focus of hunter-fisher-forager activity Locock (2000) suggests that evidence for increased intensity, duration or frequency of activity at any given location may be supported by the quantity and diversity of waste material in evidence; this is certainly the case at Burry Holms where in excess of 1600 finds have been recovered to date. However, as debitage often makes up a significant proportion of such assemblages it is apparent that the inherent difficulties embedded in determining the meaning of this activity are compounded when the available dataset (derived from the regional HERs) is often made up of multiple single finds from a given location. Similarly, where the records lack any overview of the nature of the assemblages and their potential function (Chapter 3), the combination of biases renders Locock's assertion moot. As noted above, disentangling the reporting of single finds spots from what may have actually been small scatters of lithics somewhat weakens the validity of any distribution maps that are created using the available databases, even where a concerted effort has been made to establish provenance and significance (Locock 2000). The reader should not consider this observation as a criticism of the databases however, for as noted in Chapter 3, this observation is in fact a criticism of a failure on the part of collectors, in general, to adequately record the location of finds in relation to earlier collecting activities, which can effectively result in a "snowball" effect of multiple individual records for a given finds location. Basically, casual or unsystematic collecting activities over the years have weakened the resolution of the data that has been generated, and as a result it is difficult to quantify how biased the available dataset actually is.

Returning to the landscape context of Mesolithic sites, it is obvious that to a large degree the availability of predictable and reliable food sources, such as freshwater, estuarine and marine resources, would have contributed to the viability of residence "permanence" in a given region. As such, resource availability should result in a more durable archaeological record, and will probably have resulted in evidence for more permanent and/or substantial residence structures, such as the huts and pits at Mount Sandal, Northern Ireland (Woodman 1985), Howick, Northumberland (Waddington 2007a–c; Fig. 4.5), or the recently discovered hut structure at Star Carr.

At Mount Sandal a number of hut structures, stake-holes, hearths and pits were excavated in an activity area that was located on a bluff, *ca.* 30m above the River Bann. The site is located adjacent to a series of narrow rapids that were ideal for the emplacement of fishing traps (Jacobi 1987: 166). Whilst purely speculative in nature, one might hypothesise that the "pits" could have functioned as storage areas where the gathered resources were kept for later consumption (we can also envisage a scenario wherein hides could have been used to provide watertight storage for keeping fish fresh, or more obviously, for storage of water itself). The artefacts recovered from these excavations included narrow blade geometric microliths, core and flake tools, axes and other tools, along with carbonised plant material, i.e. hazelnuts (Woodman 1985). This site has been considered to be representative of the earlier Mesolithic in Ireland.

Recent re-dating of the site and its associated features (Bayliss and Woodman 2009: 115) has shown that Mesolithic activity at Mount Sandal started at 7790–7635 cal BC and continued through until 7570–7480 cal BC – i.e. over a period of *ca.* 80–290 years. The first hut was constructed 7755–7615 cal BC, and continued in use until *ca.* 7700–7595 cal BC, with the structures associated with the hearths being used for 1–120 years (*ibid.*). The smaller pits at Mount Sandal were dug between *ca.* 7720 and 7597 cal BC, with the last of these pits excavated around 7630–7535 cal BC, suggesting that the pits were dug over a period of 1–160 years. This study reinforced concerns about the early dating of Mount Sandal, which Woodman had considered to be problematic, and highlighted the fact that Mount Sandal had a number of local artefact types with no parallels in Britain (Bayliss and Woodman 2009, fig. 14, 24). This dating is significant as it pushes the dating of narrow blade lithic industries back towards the earlier stages of the Mesolithic, suggesting that the generic partitioning of lithic industries into broad blade = earlier Mesolithic and narrow blade = later Mesolithic is in need of revision (a point noted by Jacobi in 1987).

One important observation in relation to Mount Sandal is the fact that it is located on the River Bann, and rivers, by their very nature, offer a relatively easy to follow, predictable and resource-rich route inland from coastal locations. The rivers also offer transport routes, via the use of watercraft, and offer a more open aspect, allowing for longer distance views than would normally occur in a wooded environment.

In a similar fashion to the evidence from Mount Sandal, the site of Deepcar in Yorkshire (Radley and Mellars 1964) was located on a small spur *ca.* 13m above a confluence of the rivers Porter and Don. The site was ideally located to look out over the low-lying wetlands around these rivers and would have afforded the inhabitants a relatively easy access to the valley for hunting purposes. The site had a southerly aspect with good views in all directions (*ibid.*: 2), and in addition to the obvious hunting aspects, the location would have provided a range of freshwater resources including fish and the plants of the riparian zone, whilst also being located with ease of access to the higher upland zones above the *ca.* 170m contour line that the site sits on.

The work of Mithen and Finlayson (1991) at the shell midden site of Cnog Coig on Oronsay, in the southern Hebrides, provides a tangible link to the debate in relation to hunting, shellfish exploitation, manufacturing sites and settlement patterns. At Cnoc Coig it appears that red deer skeletal elements (including antler and metapodials [equivalent to the bones of the hand (metacarpals) and feet (metatarsals) in humans]) were related to manufacturing activities, whilst the presence of meat-bearing bones suggests that some food resources were also transported to the site. Mithen and Finlayson (1991) also report the identification of Mesolithic encampments on Colonsay at Loch Staosnaig, in a small sheltered bay, behind a raised beach. These encampments were located in a situation that is similar to other locations on Jura, at Lealt Bay and Lussa River, and on Rhum, at Kinloch (1991: 3). The general conclusions that were drawn in relation to this study were that the sites on Colonsay probably represent a palimpsest of activity that is characterised by small intermittent visits to Oronsay/Colonsay, as opposed to any prolonged settlement activity (*ibid.*: 7).

Two sites in Britain, Howick in Northumberland, northeast England (Waddington 2007a), and East Barnes in Scotland (Gooder 2007), have produced earlier dates than those from Mount Sandal. At Howick, the site is located on a modern cliff edge overlooking a small estuary, and the excavations indicate that three successive hut structures, representing continuous occupations, occur here (see Fig. 4.5 for a reconstruction of one of these huts). The dating of the site indicates initial construction at 7970–7760 cal BC and abandonment around 7740–7560 cal BC (Bayliss *et al.* 2007a: 71). The phases of activity at the site extend beyond the occupation of the hut, with phases of 20–230 years (Phase 1), 1–110 years (Phase 2), 1–100 years (Phase 3) and a final phase of activity (Phase 4) lasting from *ca.* 7560 to 7330 cal BC, in evidence. Bayliss *et al.* suggest that the site appears to have been abandoned between phases 3 and 4 for a period of *ca.* 50–360 years (*ibid.*: 71). The finds from Howick include concentrations of lithics, indicative of activity areas beyond the confines of the huts, along with other areas marked by pits that support the notion that processing activities were undertaken in the immediate vicinity of the huts. The lithic

Fig. 4.5: Reconstruction of the Mesolithic hut at Howick © Clive Waddington (used with permission).

assemblage contains all stages of the reduction sequence, with primary waste, cores, blade blanks, flake debitage and finished tools all being represented (Waddington 2007b: 32).

The excavation of the hut structures at Howick produced evidence for post-holes, post-sockets, stake-holes, and pits and hearths, along with 13,000 flints, 32 bevel-ended tools and tool blanks, several hundred thousand charred hazelnut shells, burnt bone, occasional mollusc shell fragments and ochre (*ibid.*: 36). Howick is one of the key sites in Britain that serves to place the narrow blade industries of the later Mesolithic near the 8000 cal BC age, and furthermore the successive phases of activity would suggest that this location is a "persistent place" during the Mesolithic period in northeast England. Waddington has noted that it appears the dating of the narrow blade industries on the northeast coast of England occurs from *ca.* 8400 cal BC (Clive Waddington pers. comm. August 2014 and in press). One final point of note for Howick concerns the 19 bevelled pebbles found at this location. These finds are similar in form to the examples from the Nab Head, and as with the suggestion of David (2007: 153), i.e. that the objects could have been used in hide processing, Waddington *et al.* (2007c: 194) also suggest that a realistic interpretation of the function of these objects would be their use as skin softeners, as their recovery from within the confines of the hut structures suggests that they were used "indoors and close to a fire". Referring back to Chapter 3 and the observations of Warren (2006), we should be aware of the fact that whilst the observations for Howick provide us with a neat and "visible" categorisation for the use of bevelled tools at this location, these objects also functioned within a much broader network of landscape-settings and socially-mediated settings/interactions, meaning that we should not preclude other functions for these objects.

At the site of Thatcham, located on a gravel terrace in the Kennet valley, Berkshire, Healy *et al.* (1992) identified two concentrations of worked flint in close proximity to the earlier excavations undertaken by Wymer in 1958–61 (Wymer 1962). Wymer's excavations produced in excess of 16,000 worked flint artefacts along with hearths, one of which was surrounded and lined with large flints and pieces of sarcen stone (*ibid.*: 333), and a range of bone and antler implements. Wymer also noted that the numerous spreads of charcoal, calcined bone and flint, along with burnt pebbles and hazelnuts all indicate Mesolithic fires, and that the distribution of these finds suggests multiple phases of activity at Thatcham (*ibid.*: 335), although the temporal separation of these events was not determined. Environmental studies at this location indicate that the Mesolithic activity occurred at the edge of a floodplain that supported open fen vegetation, with several infilled channel features (Healy *et al.* 1992: 43). A wide range of flint material, including waste flakes, cores, core rejuvenation flakes, chips, flakes, blades, microburins, retouched and burnt and broken pieces were recovered during the 1989 excavations (Healy in Healy *et al.* 1992: 47–53), and Healy (*ibid.*: 51–2) reports that the 1989 assemblage exhibited many similarities with the material recovered in 1958–61, and also exhibited similarities to material from earlier excavations undertaken in 1921.

A radiocarbon date obtained from charred hazelnut shells in the southern part of this site produced a determination of 9100±80 uncal BP (BM-2744), which when calibrated (to 2σ using OxCal v.4.2) produces an age of 8564–8011 cal BC (with a 93.9% probability that this range occurs between 8564 and 8201 cal BC). As the flint assemblage in the northern area of the site has diagnostically later material, it would appear that there are at least two distinct periods of activity at this location (see discussion in Chapter 3, and Reynier 2000). Use-wear analysis of the flint artefacts has indicated that a wide range of activities were undertaken at this location, suggesting that it was used as a "home base" with an emphasis being placed on the gathering of plant (vegetal) food as opposed to hunting (Grace in Healy *et al.* 1992: 53–63). It is also suggested that the southern, earlier activity area, may represent a specialised location where antler and bone was being processed. Furthermore, Carter (2001: 1056) has noted that whilst no structures have been identified at Thatcham, the clustering of flint scatters close to hearths, and an area with limited numbers of flints may reflect the presence of a shelter. Of considerable interest, in relation to the flint knapping activities at Thatcham, is the identification (at Wymer's site II) of "a complete pair of red deer antlers and part of the skull cup" which "was found inverted on the ancient surface, so that part of the interior of the skull stood proud of it by about a foot [*ca.* 30.5cm]" (Wymer 1962: 338). The beam of another antler, with the tines broken off, was found lying against this frontal bone (Fig. 4.6), and one end of this beam showed signs of impact damage, suggestive of its use as a hammer. Wymer interpreted these objects as representing an anvil, i.e. the inverted antlers, used for the removal of flakes, with the hammer (the beam) being used in the removal of these flakes (*ibid.*: 338).

The activities undertaken at each of the sites discussed above begin to provide considerable insights into the nature of Mesolithic socio-economic and ritual activities. In general though the site of Star Carr in the Vale of Pickering remains the "type site" for

Fig. 4.6: Antlers and skull "cup" found in situ at Thatcham, Berkshire (after Wymer 1962).

the Mesolithic in Britain, or for the earlier Mesolithic period at least. This designation is primarily due to the broad range of organic material culture in evidence, and the important work that was originally undertaken at the site by Grahame Clark between 1949 and 1951; but in reality other sites have also produced significant material culture remains for the Mesolithic period in Britain. The significance of Star Carr is probably embedded, in no small part, in the prolonged emphasis on the use of the material culture remains from this site in the development of Mesolithic studies,

and methodological studies in general (Mellars 1998: 9), which has continued for more than six decades of research. This site has, in many respects, transcended its significance as a location (formerly) with excellent *in situ* preservation of organic remains, to become an iconic symbol of the Mesolithic in Britain. Due to this elevated status the next section will provide a brief overview of Star Carr and outline some of the key attributes of the site and its environs in relation to Mesolithic studies in general.

Star Carr: unique and perfectly typical

It has been argued that the work of Grahame Clark in the 1940s–1950s, and in particular his influential work at the site of Star Carr in the Vale of Pickering (Clark 1954), laid the foundations for subsequent, holistic studies of Mesolithic subsistence (Milner 2006). Unfortunately, relatively few British sites have matched the diversity of the material culture (in particular organic artefacts and faunal material) and duration of research activity occurring at Star Carr, and in its environs (Fig. 4.7). Many aspects of the work at Star Carr have provided important insights into the activities of hunter-fisher-forager groups in Mesolithic Britain, and the research agenda, whilst producing an extensive literature, has reached a point where debate in relation to the long term sustainability of Star Carr and its environs has come to the fore (Boreham *et al.* 2011). After more than six decades of intermittent research at Star Carr, with synthesis volumes produced by Clark (1954) and Mellars and Dark (1998a), excavations undertaken between 2004 and 2008 produced evidence for severely demineralised antler and bone, and also wood degradation at this location (Fig. 4.8; Milner 2007; Milner *et al.* 2011; cited in Boreham *et al.* 2011: 2833).

These authors have also noted that the sediments at Star Carr had changed from circum-neutral pH values to highly acidic conditions, and that de-watering and deep ploughing had resulted in compromised burial environments (Boreham *et al.* 2011). This situation is typical of many lowland wetland areas throughout Britain, where over-abstraction of the

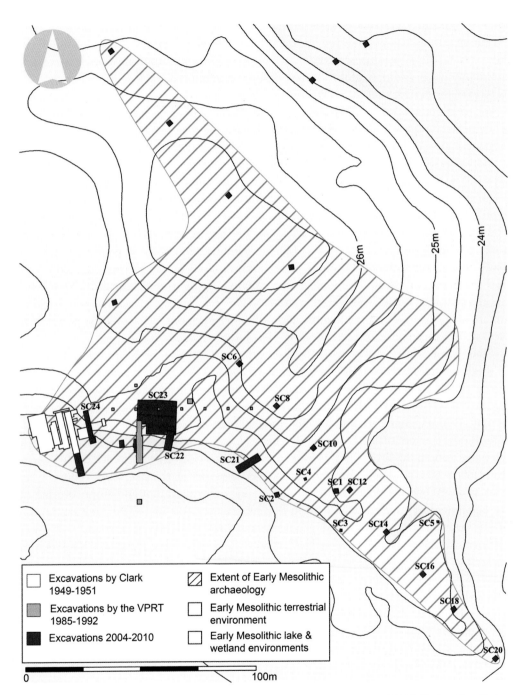

Fig. 4.7: Location map showing excavations undertaken at Star Carr between 1949 and 2010 (© Star Carr Project, used with permission).

aquifer, aggregates extraction, de-watering through drainage, the introduction of agro-chemicals through agricultural activities, and where development for a range of industrial, domestic and pleasure purposes, continue to impact upon and compromise lowland wetland environments. In addition, global climate change, with unpredictable weather patterns and more extreme events, such as the 2007 floods that occurred in Britain, is already beginning to impact negatively on lowland wetlands, to the point where sustainability and long term *in situ* preservation in waterlogged burial environments is in need of re-evaluation and a measured approach to management (Lillie *et al.* 2008; 2012).

With this in mind, the lack of comparable sites to Star Carr necessitates a considered approach to the study of Mesolithic landscapes, especially if we hope to identify sites with a similar (or analogous) range of material culture evidence. However, we also need to be aware of the fact that these sites are finite, even after 10,000 years of preservation *in situ*. The changes that are occurring in lowland wetlands have been recognised for some time now, e.g. Macklin and Needham (1992), Lillie and Smith (2007), and others, and it is apparent that as these environments continue to be compromised by the factors outlined above, sites like Star Carr are all the more significant when trying to understand the Mesolithic, and the past in general. However, this situation also reinforces the fact that we should be undertaking research into the identification of other locations/sites with the potential to produce enhanced *in situ* preservation of Mesolithic organic remains.

The site of Star Carr was originally discovered in 1949 by John Moore, who had been fieldwalking and excavating in the carr lands of Flixton and Seamer, near the eastern end of the Vale of Pickering; Moore carried out excavations at Flixton I after discovering a flint blade exposed in a field ditch. He also identified a number of archaeological locations in the vicinity, including Star Carr, and he undertook a borehole survey in the area in an effort to determine the extent of the Late-glacial to early Holocene lake, Lake Flixton, that occupied the valley floor in this area (Clark 1954: xvii and 1). After opening up a trench that extended from a "low glacial hillock" into the waterlogged deposits of the lake, Clark reported that "this single trench multiplied tenfold the material, other than flint and stone, bearing on the equipment of Maglemosian man in Britain; securing our first substantial assemblage of narrowly dated post-glacial fauna; and revealed the existence of a rough birch-wood platform (which was dated to 10,000–7700 cal BC), on which the Mesolithic hunters were enabled to camp on the reedswamp close to the very waters of the lake" (*ibid.*: 1). Whilst recent work has questioned Clark's interpretation of this brushwood platform (Conneller *et al.* 2012: 1010), split aspen and willow timbers were identified in one of Clark's trenches (cutting II), below the brushwood horizon. This research has shown that the split timbers that flank the wetland edge represent parts of at least one or more substantial structures that span at least 30m of the lake edge at this location (2012: 1012; Fig. 4.8).

After undertaking excavations at Star Carr in 1949–51 Clark concluded that the site was a location, on the northern shore of the western end of Lake Flixton, where Mesolithic people made the tools and equipment that they needed in their everyday life, and where they undertook the dismembering of animals and the preparation of food. Flint-knapping and the working of bone and antler were the main "handicrafts" undertaken at this site, and the preparation of hides for use in clothing and shelters is attested by the presence of scrapers (Clark 1954: 21). The evidence included the "brushwood platform" and a flint industry that incorporated a significant proportion of burins in the assemblage. Clark felt that a wide range of activities, including the preparation of birch bark resin, probably for use in fixing microliths to arrow shafts or handles (see Chapter 3); the manufacture of thread and line for use as harpoon lines and weapon bindings; wood and antler working; and the drilling of beads and pendants, were all undertaken at the site (*ibid.*: 22). Elliot and Milner (2010: 76) note that in addition to the platform, large quantities of animal bone, a total of 193 barbed points (including the two examples from recent work at the site), 102 red deer antlers, deposits of ochre, 21 sets of worked stag frontlets and three pieces of amber have also been recovered from this site.

Frazer and King (in Clarke 1954: 70–95) when assessing the seasonality of the site on the basis of the faunal species that were represented, concluded that in order to obtain the un-shed antlers used in harpoon point production the hunters at Star Carr must have occupied the site in the winter–spring months, October to April. Walker and Godwin (1954: 25–69) provide an overview of the lake stratigraphy and vegetation history of the site which they place in the earlier Holocene during the latter part of PZIV, when birch woodland dominated the landscape. In addition to the activities outlined above, the specialised production of barbed harpoon points made from red deer antler splinters, produced using the groove-and-splinter technique, resulted in the recovery of the original 191 harpoon points; although Clark notes (1954: 123) that only 54 of these objects were found in a complete, or near-complete state. As noted by Mellars (1998: 7) these finds increased the total number of these objects previously found in Britain by over 20-fold, and they represent *ca.* 97% of all Early Mesolithic barbed points known in Britain (Elliott and Milner 2010: 75). The 21 antler frontlets, which have been interpreted as either possible hunting gear or ceremonial head dresses, are intriguing, and are perhaps put into a more realistic context by the work of Jordan in his studies of the Khanty of western Siberia (2003a; 2003b).

In the period between Clark's original research and the work undertaken by Mellars and Dark (1998a), discussed below, a number of reassessments and reinterpretations of the data from Star Carr had been undertaken. In addition, Tim Schadla-Hall undertook palaeoenvironmental and archaeological mitigation work in the Seamer area during the 1970s in response to the threats imposed by a proposed waste disposal plant (Conneller and Schadla-Hall 2003: 85). Clark himself re-evaluated his 1954 conclusions on the basis of advances in method and theory in his 1972 work, whilst in 1978 Seamus Caulfield was the first of a number of researchers to present a re-assessment of Frazer and King's work on the faunal remains from the site. Additional studies were undertaken by Jacobi (1978), Pitts (1979), Andresen *et al.* (1981) and Legge and Rowley-Conwy (1988), all of whom sought to refine the data in relation to the nature and duration of occupation at the site, while studies undertaken by Tim Schadla Hall and co-workers (1987; 1989; Conneller and Schadla-Hall 2003) sought to place the site in its wider landscape context by identifying activity in and around the former Lake Flixton. Mellars (1998: 12–17) provides a summary

Fig. 4.8: "Brushwood" overlying the platform at Star Carr (©Star Carr Project, used with permission).

of the research in the Vale of Pickering between 1975 and 1997, and the reader is directed to this work for a more detailed overview of the distribution of the sites that had been investigated up to this date.

The investigations undertaken by Paul Mellars and Petra Dark, and their colleagues, in 1985 and 1989 have shown that prior to the first phase of human activity at this location, the lake edge was fringed with reedswamp, which was itself fringed with willow/aspen carr and had open birch woodland in the dryland areas (Dark 1988: 153). The arrival of hunter-fisher-forager groups led to the cutting down of trees and the firing of the reedswamp vegetation that flanked the lake margins. Petra Dark also notes that overhanging aspen and probably willow also appear to have been charred during these firing episodes. Ultimately, the intensity of the firing episodes results in a significant reduction in the representation of reed; probably due to regular, seasonal firing activities (Dark 1988: 154–6), but also potentially due to its use in buildings, mat and basket making etc. Mellars and Dark (1998b: 209–14) concluded that the activities at Star Carr were undertaken in a much larger area than originally suggested by Clark, with activity attested for *ca.* 120–150m along the lake edge.

Perhaps one of the more interesting aspects of this research, in terms of providing insights into the activities of Mesolithic people in the landscape, is the identification of the charcoal horizons in the lake sediments, which as mentioned above, have been interpreted as evidence for the manipulation of the environment by fire during the Mesolithic; an activity that is attested at other sites in Europe (Chapter 2). Whilst this is a significant observation in its own right, it should be remembered that fire also provides heat, light and a medium through which food can be modified in many ways through cooking, and it is possible that some of these activities could have contributed to the material that was incorporated into the lake sediments. Obviously, fire would also provide a measure of protection from wild animals, especially during the earliest periods of its use, e.g. in the Middle Pleistocene period (Canti and Linford 2000), at a time when the threat from predators was ever present, although in this context the identification of domesticated dog remains from Star Carr might also indicate that these animals were used as guard dogs, and they were also probably used in hunting activities and as companions, again with an element of protection being embedded in such companionship.

Mellars and Dark (1998b: 210) refined the chronological resolution of the activity at Star Carr using data from their Trench A, although this was not directly related to Clark's excavations, and these authors concluded that activity occurred *ca.* 8800–8400 cal BC, with an initial phase of activity of *ca.* 80 years which commenced at *ca.* 8770 cal BC, followed by an hiatus of *ca.* 100 years, and a second phase of activity of *ca.* 130 years duration which commenced at *ca.* 8590 cal BC. Refining this data, Dark *et al.* (2006), used Bayesian statistics to bracket the phases of activity at Clark's Star Carr excavations to 8800–8380 cal BC, with the second phase of activity occurring between 8710 and 8290 cal BC.

The sequences in Clark's trench, and those in trench A, appear to indicate slight discrepancies in the duration and timing of activity at Star Carr (*ibid.*: 191). Dark *et al.* also report that "comparison of the pollen sequences and associated radiocarbon dates suggests that the first burning phase at Clark's site corresponds broadly with the first phase in Trench A (but probably continued to a later date), while the second would seem to post-date the second major (and third minor) burning phase in Trench A. New dating of four faunal samples, including a red deer antler crown, tine and barbed point, and a red deer antler splinter, probably representing a "blank", all of which were recovered from the unexcavated sediments at the edge of Clark's trenches by Tot Lord, produced dates that were consistent with the first phase of burning at Clark's trench (*ibid.*: 198).

The more recent debate has also included a consideration of stable isotopic evidence, following a general trend in archaeological research towards the application of stable isotope studies of diet (e.g. Day 1996; Schulting and Richards 2002b; Dark 2003); this aspect of the research will be considered below in the discussion of stable isotope studies and diet during the Mesolithic period. The research agenda at Star Carr has been continued by the activities of Nicky Milner and colleagues in recent years (as some of the above references demonstrate). This more recent work has extended the investigations into the dryland areas on the north side of the lake sequences and has shown that worked flint occurs over an area up to 200m to the southeast of Clark's original excavations and at least 80m to the north (Conneller *et al.* 2012: 1007). Furthermore the work undertaken in 2007–8 produced nearly 8000 lithic artefacts and 210 pieces of animal bone, and a "structure" (*ibid.*: 1012). The structure is a hollow *ca.* 3m in diameter and 0.2m deep, with a dark infill, and with 18 post-holes that created a curvilinear zone about 4m across, flanking it (Conneller *et al.* 2012: 1012 and their figs 6 and 7).

Whilst this find is of considerable significance, highlighting the potential for the recovery of similar structures in the future, and potentially even the recovery of a small cemetery at this location, the assertions that this evidence is sufficient to "rewrite the character of early Mesolithic settlement in Europe" (Conneller *et al.* 2012: 1004) must be treated with caution, as whilst there is no doubting the significance of the evidence for relatively "sophisticated" woodworking at this site, the structure is not unique in this context and in no way allows for an interpretation that suggests a sedentary community at this location. These authors recognise this fact and acknowledge that the archaeological record at Star Carr is likely to have been generated through differing modes of occupation (*ibid.*: 1017), although as the combined dataset indicates, there is little doubt that Star

Carr represented a "persistent place" (*sensu* Barton *et al.* 1995) in the earlier Holocene landscape in Britain.

The Welsh evidence

In Wales, despite the apparent paucity of secure settlement sites, there are a number of important locations in the archaeological record for hunter-fisher-forager activity that do illustrate the nature of settlement and subsistence across the Mesolithic period, with these locations including the Nab Head (David 1989; 2007), Goldcliff (Bell 2007a), Waun Fignen Felen (Barton *et al.* 1995), and Rhuddlan (Quinnell and Blockley 1994), amongst others (see Figs 3.3 and 3.4). The addition of finds spots that can realistically be shown to conform to the premise that increased evidence for human presence may support the identification of a location representing more than a brief stopping off point in the daily hunter-fisher-forager subsistence round should further enhance the current discussion of settlements and settlement patterning.

As noted in Chapter 3, whilst Burry Holms, West Glamorgan remains undated in absolute terms, the number of finds from this location (*ca.* 1650 artefacts), which include fire cracked pebbles, suggests that this location included hearth settings along with activities such as lithic processing. Furthermore, Walker (2001: 126) has indicated that the nature of the distribution of the finds between excavated areas suggest discrete foci of activity in the spatial patterning of the site, possibly where initial tool production and subsequent finishing activities were being carried out. Elsewhere, the site of Daylight Rock, on Caldey Island, is classed as an occupation site on the basis of the 7454 flint and flaked stone artefacts that have been recovered, alongside material culture evidence that included charcoal, charred hazelnuts and other domestic refuse, all indicative of the use of fires and general everyday activities (David 1989: 242). Daylight Rock has been dated to 8540–7720 cal BC on the basis of three charred hazelnut shells, whilst a fragment of human bone from this site has been dated to 7940–7580 cal BC (Table 3.1). Both of these sites have been compared to Star Carr and Flixton site 1 in North Yorkshire in terms of their material culture inventories (*ibid.*: 242).

The sites of Rhuddlan (site E and site M) and Trwyn Du, all of which have produced "late" dates for earlier Mesolithic sites, represent significant foci for Early Mesolithic activity. The lithic inventories from Rhuddlan in North Wales have been summarised in some detail in Chapter 3. This material was recovered from a number of excavations at Rhuddlan, with the identified Mesolithic features including working floors, pits and soil horizons. Rhuddlan site E comprises 8408 flint and chert finds recovered during the excavation of a 600m² area in the grounds of the Edwardian Castle (Ysgol-Y-Castell) in Lôn Hylas (Quinnell *et al.* 1994: 57). Much of the excavated area preserved a soil horizon (H39) that contained flint and chert and some charred hazelnut shell, and in addition, a number of features, including a hollow (J104) and two pits (J92 and J86), all of earlier Mesolithic date, were also excavated (*ibid.*: 57). Again charring and pit features point to general domestic activities alongside the processing of lithic material at this location.

Rhuddlan site M, located in the playing field of Ysgol-Y-Castell, produced 2637 pieces of chert and flint, with 786 pieces of worked chert and flint being recovered from the Mesolithic soil horizon (M26). A number of features were identified below this soil horizon, with two post-holes (M52 and M46), a hollow or pit (M50), a second pit (M60) with three possible post-sockets in its base, and two additional pits (M122 and M132) excavated, and a larger "complex" (M90) with six small pits or hollows at its base also being identified. This latter feature is of interest as the description of the smaller "pits" is suggestive of posts having been burnt *in situ*, as the excavators describe fills that are black in the centre, appearing to contain flecks of charcoal (Quinnell *et al.* 1994: 75). The fill of the hollow (M90) contained a large quantity of worked chert and flint, an incised pebble, and some carbonised hazelnuts.

Sites E and M at Rhuddlan form part of a complex of locations that preserve evidence for what is primarily earlier Mesolithic activity, and a lithic assemblage comprising some 13,330 artefacts, the majority of which (84%: 11,175 pieces) were produced using Carboniferous (Gronant) chert (Berridge 1994: 95). Berridge also notes that the percentages of chert to flint and other lithic forms identified at Rhuddlan are very similar to those at Hendre, and that chert also predominated at the later Mesolithic site at Prestatyn (*ibid.*). The flint was probably derived from pebble flint, perhaps from beaches to the north of Rhuddlan, or from local drift deposits (Berridge 1994: 95). The features at Rhuddlan may be a combination of natural tree throws and man-made features such as postholes, but as Berridge (*ibid.*: 128) notes, there are numerous sites in Europe where tree-throws have been utilised by Mesolithic groups. The post-holes at Rhuddlan could have been part of a hut structure or a wind break, although their contemporaneity has not been established (*ibid.*, 128–9). The possible post-holes in feature M50 (from the second phase of activity at this location) may also have been part of a structure within this hollow.

Rhuddlan is ideally located in terms of hunter-fisher-forager activity sites for numerous reasons; being elevated and overlooking low lying areas where animals may have been moving through, and being within 3km of estuarine environments, and within easy access to the diverse resources of these environments and the riparian zone, such as fish, birds, molluscan resources and a diverse mosaic of plant communities, along with a range of grazing animals such as red and roe deer, wild boar and aurochs (Berridge 1994: 129; Quinnell *et al.* 1994: fig. 1.2). Finally, in terms of the activities that were undertaken at Rhuddlan, Berridge has noted that the sparse representation of micrburins indicates that specialist hunting and butchery sites must have formed part of the ancillary sites around Rhuddlan, and that stone tool procurement and burial locations would obviously have also been located in the vicinity of the main activity areas (1994: 130). Clearly then, Rhuddlan is potentially one of the more significant locations in Britain for developing our understanding of Mesolithic activity, and a location that might provide burial evidence for this period. The effort expended at sites like Star Carr could prove fundamental to studies of Mesolithic sites like Rhuddlan if funding were available for exploratory research-led investigations at such locations.

Trwyn Du on Anglesey is located on a rocky headland overlooking the mouth of the River Ffraw (David 2007: 86). As noted in Chapter 3, over 7000 artefacts were recovered from this location, and the general character of this assemblage is earlier Mesolithic. Flint-packed pits were described by the excavators at this location, and radiocarbon dates were obtained on charred hazelnut shells from a "camp fire", and from material in the pits. David (*ibid.*: 86) has questioned the validity of these dates as they are very late for an earlier Mesolithic stone tool assemblages (a similar situation to the dates from Rhuddlan), overlapping with later narrow blade dates. The samples were collected from bulked material which could, of course, have incorporated later material. It should be noted that Berridge (1994: 127–8) convincingly argued that a number of British later Mesolithic sites were dated using questionable samples, many of which were produced by the "bulking" of material such as charcoal from a range of generalised contexts, e.g. as at Filpoke Beacon, Broomhead V and Stump Cross (Berridge 1994: 128). In general the discussion of the flint packed pits at Trwyn Du might bring to mind caches of material, or the collection of waste material so that working areas were not cluttered and difficult to walk on (or of course a combination of these two suggestions). The setting of a fire has been described as a standard activity for hunter-gatherers when making stops of even relatively short duration, and these may have functioned as markers of "place" in areas that were perhaps unfamiliar to these groups, and in all locations the hearths would provide the usual attributes of warmth, light and protection, and a medium for cooking, in addition to the sense of place that they may have imbued.

Further south, whilst there is relatively little evidence for the subsistence activities of the groups that occupied the Nab Head in Pembrokeshire (site I), it is suggested that the lithic inventory attests to the fact that the people using this location, during the earlier Mesolithic, would have made regular trips to the coast, which at that time would have been up to *ca.* 10km away, in order to obtain beach pebbles. An alternative to the suggestion that regular trips were made to the coast to collect flint pebbles is simply that beach pebbles and other raw materials were collected during regular visits to the coast for gathering and fishing activities, as opposed to targeted lithic resource procurement visits (David 2007: 113), although it is recognised that this is a circular argument. This site is currently located on a small eroded promontory on the southern edge of St Brides Bay in Dyfed, but in the earlier Mesolithic, lowered sea levels would have meant that this location was in fact an inland location (David 1989: 243). Interestingly, the focus of activity at the Nab Head is such that the occupants of this site, during both the earlier and later Mesolithic phases of occupation, would have been positioned to look out towards the coastal lowlands (to the northwest), northwards across the current bay to Solva and St David's, on the St David's peninsula, and Ynys Dewi (Ramsey Island), and around St Brides bay to the east of the site, as opposed to being able to look inland. This situation occurs because, when looking inland (to the south-southeast at *ca.* 160° compass bearing), the land surface rises quickly to *ca.* 60+m AOD behind the activity site, thus effectively obscuring an inland vista as the site itself sits at *ca.* 8m AOD.

The main finds from Nab Head site 1 include end-scrapers, broad blade microliths and *mèches de forêt*, the latter artefact type has already been interpreted as the drill bits that were being used in the production of beads at this location. In addition, charcoal from oak, alder, willow/poplar, Pomoideae, *Prunus*, Leguminosea and hazel was also found during the excavations. These species were clearly used as kindling and firewood, but species such as hazel, and others e.g. *Prunus* may also be indicative of a gathered resource. The broad range of finds from this location indicates that stone tool production, processing of foodstuffs and the production of shale beads were amongst the activities undertaken at the Nab Head.

In addition, David (2007: 113–4) notes that the scrapers, and possibly some of the burins, would potentially have been used for processing hides, bone and antler, although the direct evidence for this sort of activity is lacking at this and many other earlier Mesolithic sites throughout Wales, and England. As earlier Mesolithic groups were hunter-fisher-foragers, the exploitation of the diverse range of plant and animal species that occurred in the developing post-glacial deciduous woodland around the site would undoubtedly have also been undertaken. There is a general assumption that the microliths functioned as inserts for arrows or other hunting weapons, and as the discussion below (Chapter 5) will outline, the returns from a single kill of red deer would provide significant daily calorific inputs to the diet of these groups.

David has indicated that there is little evidence for the seasonality of site occupation at the Nab Head, but increasingly there is evidence to suggest that occupation of a site could have occurred at almost any time of year, as it is not simply the seasonal availability of subsistence resources that would make a site attractive to hunter-fisher-forager groups. This latter observation may well be of particular relevance for the Nab Head as the recovery of nearly 700 shale beads would indicate that this site was potentially a significant "production site" for these objects in the Mesolithic period.

Given the hypothesised "significance" of the production of shale beads at the Nab Head, and the identification of an amulet of shale that is unique for the British Mesolithic, this location could well have functioned as a base camp, production site, site of ritual importance, or a persistent place in the territory exploited by these groups in the earlier part of the Mesolithic period, or of course, a combination of some or all of these elements. The beads themselves have been considered from the perspective of body adornment, and their association with both burials and everyday life during the Mesolithic is seen as being embedded in a system of procurement at the local level, perhaps symbolising a deep rooted relationship to the landscape (Simpson 2003: 47).

Elsewhere in Wales we have sites that clearly indicate Early Mesolithic activity and the repeated use of certain locations in a landscape. At Trostrey Castle, Trostrey, Monmouthshire, the Trostrey Excavation group dated a number of Mesolithic features that appear to indicate the presence of a short-term hunting camp, with evidence for flintworking activity in three discrete locations, and there is even evidence for "structures" in the form of a possible windbreak. This latter feature comprised a number of stakeholes forming a straight line of undefined length, with the point from one of the stakes used in the construction producing a radiocarbon date of 9510±60 uncal BP (Beta-098452), which when calibrated at 2σ produced a range of 8945–8420 cal BC (Mein 1996: 64) (NOTE: the earliest part of this range is equivalent to the earliest occupation at Star Carr in the Vale of Pickering, Yorkshire). As noted above, there are a number of discrete flintworking areas in the vicinity of the Mesolithic site, one of which has been interpreted as a temporary camp which has charcoal and a setting of stake-holes that may have been associated with a fire (Mein 1992: 11). The evidence from Trostrey might suggest that even a temporary camp could have had a series of structures associated with it, and whilst fortuitous, the finds at Trostrey may well reflect the potential range of features that we could anticipate finding at similar locations in Britain if our approach to these locations is more structured and extensive (in terms of the areas excavated). Finally, the Early Mesolithic age of the "windbreak" makes this an exceptional find location in Britain.

Later Mesolithic activity at Prestatyn, in north Wales (Armour-Chelu *et al.* 2007) has produced evidence for mussel middens, with charcoal, lithics and fragments of animal bone in association. The environmental studies undertaken at this location have led Bell (2007a: 311) to conclude that the small scale of the middens that were identified, the limited environmental impact and the low occurrence of artefacts, all combine to suggest that the middens are indicative of limited, short-term activity, and that it is possible that each of the middens could be interpreted as the debris from a single collecting episode. Bell (2007e: 312–3) also suggests that the Nant Hall Road middens can be interpreted as short-term extraction/activity sites. Rhuddlan is the only location in this area that has sufficient evidence to support the identification of a longer-term activity site, possibly related to a periodically occupied base camp or aggregation camp.

Elsewhere in northwest Wales, on the island of Ynys Enlli, Edmonds *et al.* (2009) have identified four sites with diagnostic Mesolithic artefacts, one of which, Bae y Rhigol on the north side of the island, has produced in excess of 5000 lithic artefacts (see discussion in Chapter 3). Of interest in this context is the potential landscape setting of the site and the possible importation of lithic material to the island. These authors note that the Bae y Rhigol assemblage is larger than other sites in the region, including Trwyn Du and Bryn Refail, and that the evidence may be indicative of a location that is repeatedly visited during the Mesolithic period (*ibid.*, 387). This suggestion is based on the densities of finds from test pitting and field-walking at Bae y Rhigol, all of which indicated the existence of several concentrations within high-density "backgrounds" (*ibid.*: 387). Moving beyond "basic" interpretations of the lithic assemblages from Ynys Enlli Edmonds *et al.* (2009: 388) go further to suggest that not only were the communities of the time undertaking relatively difficult sea crossings, they were also engaged in a wide range of contacts and interactions, and were exercising similar choices in lithic working; choices that "evoked connections between scattered communities". In addition, the working of stone from both local and more distant sources would have provided a way for these communities to "recognise and think about the broader social landscapes of the time" (*ibid.*, 388). This approach to the interpretation of Ynys Enlli in its wider context is clearly important in highlighting alternative ways of exploring the socio-cultural landscapes of the Mesolithic period, and it would certainly offer possible routeways into the generation of more nuanced narratives of Mesolithic lifeways.

Further south, at Nanna's Cave on Caldey Island over 193 lithic objects, including blade cores and over 80 blades, four scrapers, an awl and two perforated mollusc shells from flat-topped winkle (*Littorina obtusata*) and netted dog whelk (*Hinia reticulata*), along with the debris from flintworking, indicate that during the later Mesolithic this location was not only used for the preparation of stone tools but also probably for the processing of foodstuffs. The burning in evidence on some of these objects would also suggest that a hearth feature was associated with this activity. The finds of three human bones (including two patellas and a phalange) are also of significance in this context. Finds of perforated shells are not uncommon on Mesolithic sites, and a perforated oyster shell from Bryn Newydd, Prestatyn may lend weight to the idea that personal decoration/ornaments were worn during this period (Simpson 2003), although perforated shells may have had other uses, for example in the preparation of foodstuffs (Mears and Hillman 2008).

David (2007: 131) has noted that there is circumstantial evidence to suggest that the lithic residues recorded at Site I at the Nab Head (discussed above), included a later Mesolithic component. This observation and the presence of later Mesolithic flint scatters elsewhere in the vicinity of the site suggest that there was widespread Mesolithic activity in the surrounding area (*ibid.*: 131). As noted in Chapter 3, at the Nab Head (site II) the later Mesolithic activity included finds of some 31,797 pieces of chipped flint and stone along with bevelled pebbles, three ground stone axe- or adze-heads and a perforated "macehead" (David 2007: 135). The assemblage is overwhelmingly dominated by flint, much of which would have been derived from beach pebbles. Trenches that were excavated at site 2 failed to produce any indications of features, but variations in the density of the finds appeared to suggest that there were discrete concentrations of activity around a central area where less "noise", in terms of artefacts, occurred. It is intriguing to note these distributions are not dissimilar to the communal areas identified at !Kung San camp sites, where activities such as dancing and meat distribution take place in the centre of activity areas (David and Kramer 2001). Alternatively, Lynch *et al.* (2000: 31) note that the "empty space" at the Nab Head II is around 5m in diameter, and as such is comparable to the diameters of the hut structures at Mount Sandal in Ireland, and slightly larger than the recent hut find at Star Carr (Conneller *et al.* 2012).

The presence of a small, shallow pit (or scoop), suggestive of a small hearth feature or the remnants from one, at the Nab Head site II produced an AMS radiocarbon date that calibrated to 6420–6050 cal BC (see Table 3.2). A number of locations produced evidence for burning, and the northwestern of the three activity scatters produced charcoal which included species of oak, *Prunus* spp., hazel, apple family and legumes; again, whilst these species could have simply been used as kindling for the fire, the fact that hazelnuts are found at many Mesolithic sites may be suggestive of the gathering and utilisation of a portion of these species for consumption or other purposes. It is clear from the lithic inventory that flintworking occurred at site II, and all stages of the core reduction sequence are in evidence (David 2007: 137). Microliths are the best represented tool type at site II, with narrow scalene triangles dominating within the narrow blade assemblage (*ibid.*: 138). The other "key" artefact types at this location are the bevelled pebbles (considered in detail in

Chapter 3), the combination of tool types, which also includes scrapers, denticulates, and a range of truncated pieces, retouched and utilised flakes (*ibid.*: 156) coalesce to indicate that a range of activities, including lithic production from initial preparation to the production of finished tool forms, the making of beads, the preparing of hides and probably the shaping of arrowshafts, and ultimately the daily activities of food procurement and consumption, hunting, fishing and gathering, sleeping and waking, making and tending fires and any number of social and ritual interactions would probably have been undertaken at sites like the Nab Head.

Away from west Wales, Barton *et al.* (1995) discuss the evidence for early postglacial exploitation in the southern welsh uplands at the site of Waun Fignen Felin, Powys, in the Black Mountains. At this location, discrete lithic scatters of both earlier and later Mesolithic date were identified on the edge of a shallow lake basin at 485m AOD (see discussion in Chapter 3). The evidence does not support anything more than short-term, "highly transitory events" that are probably related to individual hunting forays at this location. There is no suggestion of a more permanent hunting camp i.e. there is no evidence for hearths, pits or post holes, associated with the earlier Mesolithic activity, and by the later Mesolithic period the evidence indicates that time was not even spent in the preparation of hunting equipment as this was brought to the site in a pre-prepared form (Barton *et al.* 1995).

Whilst Waun Fignen Felin is a place marked out by the repeated visits of hunting groups across the Mesolithic period, i.e. is a "persistent place", and the location itself is a very attractive hunting location (*ibid.*: 122), in terms of settlement activities, this location cannot perhaps be considered as a significant element in the mapping of the distribution of settlements or camps during the Mesolithic period in Wales. However, a caveat to this observation must be the fact that archaeological studies of heat fractured rock has led to the suggestion that in areas where archaeological visibility is reduced due to factors such as the exposure and erosion of hearth features, the actual "signature" of the hearth may not be immediately visible (Backhouse and Johnson 2007). As such, the lack of evidence for more "permanent" features such as hearths and shelters need not negate the possibility of short-term camps at this location, i.e. overnight or one or two night's duration.

In the Severn Estuary, Bell *et al.* (2000: 33–63) outline the evidence from the Late Mesolithic activity site at Goldcliff (Fig. 4.9), which is dated to 5400–4000 cal BC. This site was first located by Derek Upton and Bob Trett in 1987, being identified by a layer of charcoal with flint flakes on the western edge of Goldcliff Island. The site was subsequently surveyed and gridded by Malcolm Lillie and Nigel Page during the April of 1990, and the grid was subsequently used by Bell and co-workers during their research at this location in 2000 (Bell *et al.* 2000: 33). Charcoal from this location was dated to 6430±80 uncal BP (GU-2759), calibrated to 5535–5226 cal BC (at 2σ using OxCal 4.2 [on-line]). The excavation work undertaken by Bell and co-workers has indicated that the Mesolithic activity is concentrated in a thin charcoal horizon, containing lithic artefacts and bone, which is stratified between the underlying head deposits and overlying estuarine clays and peat unit

Fig. 4.9: Artists impression of the Mesolithic activity site at Goldcliff in the Severn Estuary (reproduced by Permission © Victor Ambrus and the Council for British Archaeology).

in the lowest part of the site (detailed descriptions of the stratigraphic units are provided in Bell *et al.* 2000: 34). The earliest stages of peat formation are dated to 5920±80 uncal BP (CAR-1501), still within the Mesolithic period (*ibid.*: 36).

A number of features were recorded on the Mesolithic surface, including a probable hearth and possible post-cast, as well as another charcoal concentration. 1650 artefacts were recorded during the excavations at this location (1992–4), with these comprising primarily charcoal, flint and the fragments of unidentifiable bone mentioned above (Bell *et al.* 2000: 36). This material was concentrated in distinct "patches of increased density" which are thought to equate to foci of human activity (*ibid.*: 36). These activity areas are considered to relate to activities such as food processing and cooking (indicated by burnt bone and charcoal). The lithic sources utilised at Goldcliff included pebbles and small cobbles (flint, chert, tuff and quartzite), with artefacts such as two axe/adzes and large cores being recovered prior to the excavations.

As noted in Chapter 3, of the 633 lithic recovered from the 1992–4 excavations, all bar eight are from the charcoal horizon that relates to the occupation at this location. The nature of the assemblage indicates on-site flintworking activities, and associated activities, as discussed above, whilst other artefacts, such as the non-flaked items, indicate that the preparation of hunting equipment and animal hides (sandstone rubbers used as arrowshaft smoothers or skin-stretchers) was also occurring at this site. All of these activities are precisely those that we might anticipate encountering at a residence/activity site.

The Goldcliff faunal assemblage has been studied from the perspective of seasonality, due to the rarity of sites like this in terms of the stratigraphy and contained assemblage, and also because of its location in the inter-tidal zone (Coard 2000: 51–2). The evidence from the red deer and pig bones suggests that, on the basis of the non-eruption of the 4th premolars in pigs, the site would have been occupied during the winter–spring (*ibid.*: 52). Unfortunately, the faunal remains from Goldcliff have not proven suitable for use in refining the season of occupation beyond the winter–spring periods. The faunal assemblage is however suggestive of short occupation for a range of activities including the processing and consumption of animals at the site (the red deer), and it appears that the pig was also processed at the site, but that the major meat-bearing parts were taken off-site (*ibid.*: 53). Fortunately, the evidence from the fish remains, particularly eel, at Goldcliff lends further weight to the seasonality data obtained from the fauna, in that the eel data is indicative of winter catches (Ingrem 2000: 54). The finds of smelt reinforce this observation, with a slight modification for seasonality, as the data indicate autumn-winter activity for the catching of this particular species of fish (*ibid.*). Overall, the evidence from Goldcliff suggests repeated visits by Mesolithic groups across the later Mesolithic period, with an emphasis on procurement activities across the Autumn to Spring months. This information may suggest that the resources of the coastal/inter-tidal zone were of particular importance during the seasons when the available flora was either at, or nearing, its lowest in terms of productivity.

In Gwynedd, small scale Mesolithic activity has been recorded at Llandygai (Parc Bryn Cegin) by Lynch and Musson (2001) and Kenney (2008). The earlier work recorded a microlith, small blade core, two retouched flakes (one with burin blow on the tip), and three other small fragments, all of late Mesolithic form, from a shallow feature in the area of Henge B (Lynch 2001: 24). This hollow is recorded as being no more than 50mm in depth, and probably representing the remnants of a pit or hollow/scoop? in the Mesolithic landsurface (*ibid.*). The more recent evidence for Mesolithic activity at Llanygai comprises a complete narrow-blade scalene triangle, two fragments of narrow-blade microliths, a small scalene triangle, serrated blade, and two blade cores (Kenney 2008: 14). In combination the material is indicative of lithic working, probably as part of the daily subsistence activities of the individuals using this location during the later Mesolithic, but the evidence would suggest that any settlements or more permanent activity sites would have been located elsewhere in the landscape.

At Frainslake, on the south Pembrokeshire coast, Jacobi (1980: 174–5) notes that when writing in 1926, Gordon Williams reported seeing a "windscreen of gorse, birch, hazel and alder ... set in the peat ... (with) ... on the north side of this shelter which ran is a gentle curve for (*ca.* 4m) ... an area bearing much charcoal, flint chip, a large rabattu point, etc.". The majority of the 56 worked pieces that survive from the two discrete flint scatters at Frainslake were made on beach pebble flint, with two being made on cretaceous chert and a greenish stone (*ibid.*: 175). Within this assemblage Jacobi reports that two flakes show signs of utilisation, and one flake has a shallow notch, and that there are seven cores, a pair of core fragments and a broken scraper (*ibid.*). In addition to the flint finds there are six bevelled pebbles and a bone object, the latter object has been suggested as a "limpet scoop", but given the rolled condition of this object, which is a proximal fragment of the radius from a juvenile *Bos*, Roger Jacobi suggested that this object may well be derived from the modern beach shingle as opposed to the peat at this location (*ibid.*). Whilst this site may be limited to the designation of a temporary processing site, the identification of a wind break and large quantities of charcoal, along with two discrete concentrations of flint, might suggest that the hunter-fisher-foragers that used this location lit fires whilst undertaking their processing activities. This sort of evidence is invaluable in providing insights into short term foci of activity as it is conceivable that the establishment of a fire and the erection of a wind break have resonance to the evidence from the earlier Mesolithic activity site at Trostrey Castle in Monmouthshire.

More recent research in the vicinity of the Severn Estuary, as part of the Mesolithic to Neolithic Coastal Environmental Change Project, has produced evidence for a later Mesolithic to earlier Neolithic activity site at Llandevenny, Monmouthshire (Brown 2007: 250–6). The analysis at this location was designed to assess the nature of the wetland-dryland interface, and included a combination of excavation and off-site environmental analysis, with analytical techniques including pollen, plant macrofossil and quantified micro-/macro-charcoal analysis (*ibid.*: 249). At Llandevenny a stratified Mesolithic–Neolithic occupation site located at the wetland edge produced a dense concentration of lithics and charcoal in two occupation layers sealed by a metre of peat (Brown 2007: 250). Radiocarbon dating failed to produce an absolute age for the lower occupation horizon, but the upper horizon produced a calibrated age of 3770–3640 cal BC (OxA-13527; 4912±31 uncal BP).

The excavations (in 2002 and 2003) produced 345 worked lithic artefacts, which included a late Mesolithic microlith, tuff flakes similar to Goldcliff, and charcoal from two occupation layers sealed by peat (Brown 2004). The 2003 excavations produced the majority of the finds, 244 in total, included flakes, flake shatter, five flint cores, blade-flakes, a proto-thumbnail scraper, an edge retouched flake (projectile point), a microlith (obliquely blunted point), and heat fractured stones, a probable hammerstone, and pebbles and cobbles. Of the lithic assemblage, 95% was produced on flint, whilst the remainder comprised chert, including greensand and Carboniferous chert types, and tuff artefacts. According to Brown, all the lithic material at Llandevenny could potentially have been acquired from either a localised source amongst the Pleistocene terrace deposits of the major river valleys and/or marine gravel deposits along the intertidal zone (2007: 250).

This location is the only Late Mesolithic site other than Goldcliff to produce tuff, and the general character of the assemblage is very similar to Goldcliff. Brown (2007) interprets the activity at this location as representing *in situ* knapping activities undertaken in an environment that was characterised by lime woodland with oak as an important secondary species, and with alder-carr woodland on the encroaching wetland (*ibid.*: 252–3). Lime declined in the upper occupation horizon at this location, and the species identified in this zone also suggest an increasingly marshy component to the vegetation. The wood charcoal component within these samples is considered to represent woodland clearance, as the arboreal pollen levels decrease in tandem with the four significant peaks in charcoal in these sequences (*ibid.*: 253). Along with a total of 193 charred seeds, calcined bone and anthropogenic indicator species such as *Plantago lanceolata*, Poaceae undiff. and *Rumex* (*cf. acetosa*), the species in evidence all support the suggestion of anthropogenic burning at this location, particularly in the upper occupation layers.

The activities indicated by the lithic assemblage at Llandevenny suggest a combination of hunting, fowling, and cutting or piercing, and the burnt bone indicates the cooking and consumption of the caught component of the wild fauna. Furthermore, the charred and uncharred plant material indicates a reliance on the gathering of soft fruits and also the *in situ* burning of berry patches following collection (Brown 2007: 255). It is clear from this study that modern multi-disciplinary studies are enhancing the potential range and significance of the data that we can generate from studies of Mesolithic activity sites.

As noted in Chapter 2, according to Ross (1999: 283) the regular burning of tule and cattail patches after harvesting, by the Spokane of northwestern North America, improved both the yield and quality of future growth (cited by Nicholas 2007a: 54–5). Interestingly, the plants indicate activity at this location during the summer and early autumn (June to October), with a minimum period of occupation during August and/or September (*ibid.*). In a similar manner, the evidence for burning at Llandevenny may also indicate seasonality in burning activities, with summer–autumn burning at the woodland edge, and possible winter-spring burning of reedbeds (Brown 2007: 255). This suggested pattern of burning could perhaps indicate that there is evidence for seasonal mobility, delayed return strategies, advanced planning in exploitation strategies, and the management of the environment in order to promote re-growth during the later Mesolithic period. Brown (2007: 256) also suggests that the levels of mobility indicated by the activities at Llandevenny appear to reduce into the earlier Neolithic period. As is apparent from this work, the excellent level of analysis undertaken at Llandevenny makes this a particularly significant location for our understanding of human-landscape interactions across the later Mesolithic to Neolithic periods in Wales.

Towards a social narrative of Mesolithic hunter-fisher-forager settlement and subsistence

From the above discussion we can begin to reconstruct the social aspects of hunter-fisher-forager settlement and subsistence activities in the Mesolithic period in Wales; as the two activities are clearly inter-linked to some significant degree. We have touched on a number of important considerations in relation to the ways in which "landscape" itself it classified. In this context, the discussion has considered aspects such as the "lived experience" of people in the landscape (Layton and Ucko 1999: 12), and the fact that "the term 'landscape' itself is a generic term for particular ways of seeing the world" (Darvill 1999: 104). An important consideration, and one that has considerable resonance for us in the present, is that *seeing the landscape* is just one aspect of a person's experience of the world, as "stimuli from other senses, and the feelings that they generate, are also significant in experiencing landscape: smells, sounds, textures, tastes, atmosphere", and these all contribute to the mental images and constructs of landscape (*ibid.*: 109; see Finlay 2004 for alternative ways to consider "scapes"). An additional dimension to the study of landscape is generated by the study of Mesolithic activity on Ynys Enlli by Edmonds *et al.* (2009: 388), an island located off the most westerly tip of the Lleyn Peninsula, as these authors see structuring in the procurement of raw material, and the working of this material, which is occurring at a variety of scales. Intervisibility, between Ynys Enlli and distant locations, beyond those of the sources for the raw materials, may have, in the view of these authors, invited "reference (to) and the memory of more extended connections".

To some degree these observations have resonance to locations further south, for as noted by Cummings (2000: 93) in the Mesolithic in Pembrokeshire one element of the attraction to the coast would obviously have been ease of resource procurement, but, other factors such as myths and spirits may have influenced people's choice of settlement location. Persistent locations, such as the Nab Head, Waun Fignen Felin, and the Walton Basin may have gained significance through enduring memory or through their "link(s) to past generations of ancestors" (*ibid.*: 93), but they could also have been significant as places that were "good to experience" for a range of aesthetic reasons that extended beyond the economic or ritual aspects of daily life. We experience socially constructed landscapes in the present, and in fact there are few "real" wilderness's left in mainland Europe and Britain, as the landscape has been subtly (sometimes dramatically) modified over time. As noted by Mulk and Bayliss-Smith (1999: 362), the landscape is an aspect of the "shared meanings (of 'culture') that ... (are a) ... construct ... (whilst simultaneously) a real world of hills, forests and *buildings* ..."; for the Mesolithic "buildings" would be just one aspect of the social space, as the huts and camp sites formed a part of the medium through which people articulated their social, political and ritual engagement with each other, and these locations formed the basis for their shared experience(s) of the world.

We know that hunter-fisher-foragers experienced a world that was very unlike our own, and they also engaged with the world differently due to their varying requirements and perceptions of the landscape and their relationships to the spirits of the ancestors, and even the animals, fish and plants that they exploited. As noted by the work of Lewis Binford (1980) the nature of forager–landscape interactions influences the resultant archaeological record, and these interactions also have the potential to create significant biases in the evidence that is left for the archaeologist to find. As such, different elements of hunter-fisher-forager subsistence and resource procurement strategies would result in differing "signatures", and factors such as the seasonal availability of resources and the socially mediated aspects of engagement with the environment would all influence the archaeological record that is produced. Clearly then, some activities will be all but invisible to us in the present, e.g. a temporary camp with a hearth used to embody a specific location with a "sense of place"; this is because a surface hearth with only a limited range of material remains is often unlikely to survive into the present due to a range of taphonomic factors (amongst others) that will have influenced these locations over time, consequently this type of location is liable to be "lost" to archaeology. Similarly, sites that are located near the water's edge in riparian (and coastal) zones during the Mesolithic period will have the potential to be inundated, eroded, and also buried under alluvium and/or peat (often to considerable depths), and as such they can effectively become "invisible" archaeologically. With this in mind, more durable locations such as the Nab Head are important, but upland locations such as Waun Fignen Felin, and perhaps to a lesser extent the Walton Basin, i.e. the "persistent places" as defined by Barton *et al.* (1995), provide us with tantalising glimpses of the sort of evidence that we might actually anticipate finding throughout the landscape, were it not for all of the biasing factors discussed above.

Obviously, amongst the other complicating factors that we have considered throughout the previous chapters is the nature of sea level and vegetation changes across the earlier Holocene. Sea level change in particular can obscure significant areas of the landscape that would have been exploited by these groups; as a consequence we cannot realistically reconstruct human-landscape interactions at certain coastal locations until after the middle part of the Mesolithic, i.e. after *ca.* 7500 cal BC, simply because much of the evidence is below modern sea level. This bias results in an additional limitation to our studies of space and place, in that we cannot easily evaluate changes in landscape perception across the Mesolithic, and in addition, we also lack the potential to recover sites that would allow us to assess the nature of "place" in a sufficiently nuanced way, particularly for the earlier part of the Mesolithic period. It is recognised that progressive changes in vegetation and coastline may not necessarily have been perceptible at a generational level during the Mesolithic, but the cumulative effects would obviously result in significant changes across the period itself (Cooney and Grogan 1999: 9).

Further resolution can be added to the topic of human perceptions of sea level and landscape change by modelling macro-scale processes in a GIS digital terrain model using available sea level data points (or index points; e.g. Chapman and Lillie 2004: 66–7). Whilst the resolution of the model developed by Chapman and Lillie is obviously dependent upon the available data (which has a number of inherent limitations), when modelled at 10 year intervals across the earlier Holocene the model that was produced demonstrated that after 100 years wherein relatively little change occurred, there was a subsequent phase of extremely rapid inundation, followed by periods where significantly greater inundation (flooding of large areas of low-lying land) occurred in a very short period of time (2004: 67). The landscape block used by these authors was the Holderness region, which was applied as an analogy to "Doggerland". Irrespective of the limitations however, the point of this example is that at certain times the impacts of fluctuations in relative sea level could have been considerable, and intriguingly in the model used by these authors the period during which the more significant impacts were observed was the later Mesolithic, a time when the rates of sea level rise were already reduced when compared to the earlier Mesolithic period. We can envisage a scenario wherein the general trends of progressive inundation that may not have been noticeable at the generational levels (*cf.* Cooney and Grogan 1999) are punctuated by episodes of extremely rapid inundation, perhaps even over a seasonal timescale, that would have altered the landscape considerably, and perhaps irreversibly (Chapman and Lillie 2004: 68). These major inundation events would, no doubt, have significantly altered the frames of reference through which Mesolithic people produced their "mental maps" of the landscape, and the routes or pathways that were used to connect the various parts of the landscape (the cultural locales (*cf.* Tilley 1994)) could also be in need of renegotiation as a result of such events (Chapman and Lillie 2004: 69).

However, despite the caveats outlined above, it is clear that certain aspects of hunter-fisher-forager landscape interactions can be teased out through a combination of archaeology, ethnography and a nuanced reading of landscape context and perception. Bell (2007e: 313) has suggested that the evidence from Prestatyn indicates that during the later Mesolithic "a settlement pattern of logistical mobility, i.e. with seasonal base camps and short-term activity areas" was followed. In addition, Bell also notes that this settlement pattern extends into the subsequent Neolithic period and continues until *ca.* 3400 cal BC (*ibid.*). This latter observation might suggest that the rigid division between Mesolithic and Neolithic periods, which is placed at *ca.* 4000–3800 cal BC is unwarranted, as people do not simply "become" Neolithic overnight, and the data would appear to indicate continuity across the traditional transition between these two periods. Group mobility is reducing across the 7th–5th millennia cal BP as the above evidence indicates, and whilst seasonal movements were still clearly occurring, it has been suggested that the size of the territories being exploited is reducing towards the end of the Mesolithic period, e.g. Darvill (1987: 49).

In discussing the evidence from north Wales, Martin Bell (2007e) notes that there are a number of "pull" factors in the Prestatyn area that would have made this location attractive for settlement. Lithic sources are clearly a useful element in relation to the attractiveness of an area, as the existence of the raw materials for stone tool production adds to the viability of this location for settlement and subsistence activities. The beach pebble flint, and the chert which outcrops near Gronant, which Smith (1923: 170) records as overlying the Carboniferous Limestone and underlying black limestones and shales near Gronant, and which also outcrops on the hillside to the south of Prestatyn, along with the landscape context, would all combine to make this a very attractive location for hunter-fisher-forager groups. Locations such as Craig-y-Llyn, Rhondda, where Lynch *et al.* (2000: 367) report that *ca.* 84% of the stone tool assemblage is made on black Gronant chert from the limestone on the east side of the Vale of Clwyd, and also finds at Burry Holms, West Glamorgan, all reinforce the fact that chert was an important resource during the Mesolithic. Many locations have evidence for the use of chert in stone tool production, and the evidence does also indicate that chert is exploited across the earlier to later Mesolithic periods (see Chapter 3). At some locations (e.g. Trwyn Du, the Nab Head, and Prestatyn) the low numbers of chert objects could be an indication of trade and/or exchange items and curated pieces, or, as noted by Bell (2007e: 314) they may indicate that the local chert is not of sufficient significance to act as an attractor to settlement at locations such as Prestatyn, particularly in the later Mesolithic and earlier Neolithic periods. Alternatively, chert itself may have been seen as a very distinctive raw material for use in stone tool production, and its significance may have been imbued with meaning beyond its functional attributes.

Returning to the evidence for settlement, this, and the recognition of "persistent places" in the landscape can be linked to the ethnographic literature in suggesting that hunter-fisher-foragers of the Mesolithic would have operated at a number of spatial scales (discussed below), with a range of settlement activities, from base to temporary camp, occurring within a groups territory. Similarly, the ethnographic literature offers potential insights into the ways in which a place can have significance beyond a location for resource procurement activities and settlement. However, problems still exist in that we do not always have sufficient archaeological evidence to facilitate a realistic reconstruction of hunter-fisher-forager settlement and subsistence patterning in Britain as a whole, and as noted by Bell (2007e: 314) this is again due in part to the loss of the earlier Mesolithic landscape as sea levels rose during this part of the Holocene. Furthermore, Locock (2003: 59) has suggested that the available archaeological evidence is also limited when trying to determine whether transhumance and winter exploitation of marine resources were integral aspects of Mesolithic subsistence strategies. Although it is noted that the assumption that Mesolithic hunter-fisher-foragers were wholly peripatetic in their engagement with the landscape is a somewhat myopic perspective from which to base our interpretations upon.

In a landscape context however, it is also acknowledged that hunter-fisher-forager base camps do not necessarily suggest any degree of annual permanence, as they could also be linked to aggregate seasonal resources, e.g. plant exploitation; such as the hazelnut harvesting in evidence on Stoasnaig on Colonsay (Mithen 1999a), where intensive resource exploitation is indicated (*cf.* Zvelebil 1999). Similarly, Locock (2003: 59) has suggested that the available evidence from locations such as Caldey Island do not suggest that a winter coastal marine base was being exploited, but that these locations were part of a range of sites that were being utilised; although there is some circularity in these arguments. When considering variability in terms of landscape context, and the resources that were being exploited throughout the Mesolithic period, Bell (2007e: 314–5) notes that salmon usually run from April to early Autumn, making these a rich seasonal resource which could act as a pull factor to the rivers that the salmon migrate up to spawn, whilst upland areas would generally have been attractive during the summer months due to the presence of grazing ungulates. Such seasonality in resource availability would, no doubt, produce a dispersed pattern of hunter-fisher-forager activity sites of differing degrees of duration and visibility throughout the landscape, but activity sites do not preclude the existence of more permanent, tied, base camps.

Any number of seasonal resources would have been available throughout Britain during the Mesolithic period, and it is likely that the hunter-fisher-forager groups in Wales would have followed a logistical strategy in their food procurement activities. Coastal, estuarine, lake and riparian environments, lowland and upland locations, all provide a range of seasonal resources, and the evidence for the possible deliberate burning of the vegetation at locations such as Waun Fignen Felin in the Black Mountains of south Wales (Smith and Cloutman 1988), may reflect deliberate human interference in terms of firing (vegetation burning) episodes during the Mesolithic. As noted above (Chapter 2), this burning may have been related to a "promotional strategy to increase productivity of nut and fruit trees and shrubs, wetland plants, and possibly native grasses" (Zvelebil 1994: 35), although more open "familiar" environments would also be a product of such activities.

The Welsh evidence continues to expand as more sites are investigated in the modern context (e.g. Brown 2007). Larger scale excavations and surveys are providing greater insights into the nature of human–landscape interactions and Mesolithic lifeways, and also the potential range of activities that were undertaken at settlement/activity sites. Locations such as the Nab Head and Goldcliff allow greater resolution of the data and they are beginning to put "meat on the bones" of the Mesolithic archaeological record. Sites such as Trostrey Castle in Monmouthshire (Gwent) provide us with some tantalising insights into the evidence that might be anticipated at well-preserved/stratified sites, with short-term activity at this location including a number of flintworking areas (recorded in three discrete locations) and a possible "windbreak", all of which has been dated to the earlier Mesolithic period. Given the relatively limited evidence forthcoming from many of the Mesolithic sites in Wales, Locock (2003) has suggested that Mesolithic groups at this time may well have functioned at a smaller scale, with a very mobile pattern of land use, and with aggregations of population occurring at known flint resources, such as those at Ogmore and Llanmelin (2003: 59–60).

However, despite Locock's suggestions, there are locations where we have evidence to suggest that some greater level of activity, whether related to longer stays, regular/repeated visits, important production sites, or special/ritual locations in the landscape (or a combination of these and other factors), is occurring; e.g. at sites such as Burry Holms, West Glamorgan, Bardsey Island, Gwynedd, Trwyn Du on Anglesey, Rhuddlan, Clwyd, Bryn Newydd and Prestatyn in northeast Wales, or the Nab Head near St Brides in Pembrokeshire; but in general the picture is still biased by a lack of excavation and the relatively limited nature of archaeological survey in general.

When considering the diverse range of evidence that has been recovered from locations such as Rhuddlan, we begin to build a picture of human activity through the identification of "working floors", soil horizons and a range of pits and hollows that may be linked to a range of structures and the day-to-day activities undertaken at settlement/activity sites. Significant concentrations of worked flint and chert have been found in association with the pits and hollows at Rhuddlan, suggesting that hut structures and windbreaks, along with hearth features and processing/production areas are all in evidence. As noted above, the Rhuddlan sites are located in an area overlooking a range of environments where resources such as freshwater, estuarine and even marine fish and molluscs, birds (including migratory species) and grazing ungulates, and a wide range of plant resources were all within a *ca.* 3–10km range in the earlier Mesolithic. In addition, Berridge (1994), on the basis of the lack of microburins recovered, has suggested that specialist hunting and butchery locations must have formed ancillary sites around this location, perhaps marking Rhuddlan out as a location where more "persistent" foci of activity were occurring, and where more research might produce holistic insights into Mesolithic human-landscape interactions. This evidence would mark Rhuddlan out as a location where residence could occur for a substantial part of the year, or even year-round, and as noted by Cooney and Grogan (1999: 21) locations where "resource clustering" occurs are precisely those locations where base camps might be anticipated.

At Trwyn Du on Anglesey, in a location overlooking the mouth of the River Ffraw, the "ubiquitous" Mesolithic finds of hazelnut shells, suggestive of gathering activities, are associated with a camp fire and a number of flint packed pits (David 2007: 86). As noted above, these pits may represent a range of activities, such as the caching of material for later use, the "cleaning-up" of the waste material (debitage) from tool production activities, or even some ritual element intertwined with phases of activity being undertaken in the process of tool production (i.e. the *chaîne-opératoire*; see Chapter 3), and their separation, that is no longer "visible" to us in the present. Similarly, possible hearth settings are identified at Burry Holms in West Glamorgan, where the spatial distribution of the finds was suggestive of discrete areas of activity, again possibly linked to phases of tool production at this location. Evidence for a range of similar activities is repeatedly identified at a number of locations in Wales, irrespective of differing temporal- and landscape-scale spatial patterning. As such, there are clearly a number of activities that can be seen to be indicated by a range of archaeological "signatures" during the Mesolithic period in Wales, and it is these signatures that we need to be mindful of when researching hunter-fisher-forager sites of this period.

When considering aspects such as the re-use of preferred locations, or persistent places, the combination of both Early and Late Mesolithic activity at the Nab Head provides us with an additional suite of information in relation to the range of hunter-fisher-forager activities in the landscape of Wales during the Mesolithic. At this location in the earlier Mesolithic the coast would have been *ca.* 10km away from the site, and procurement activities at the coast may have combined gathering forays with the collection of the raw materials (beach pebbles) used in lithic production. One of the tool forms found at the Nab Head, the *mèche de forêt*, was used as a drill bit during the production of shale beads at the site, and as noted in Chapter 3, there are numerous locations in west Wales where these objects have been found, and similar beads have also been found at Star Carr. Whilst there is no direct evidence for the foods that were consumed by the people occupying the Nab Head, the charcoal found in hearths at this location includes evidence for hazel, oak and *Prunus*, species which might provide an indication of the range of fruit and nuts available to these groups (see Chapter 5 for a more detailed discussion of the resources exploited by Mesolithic groups in Britain).

The archaeological evidence from the Nab Head I site thus combines to suggest that a range of activities including bead production, lithic production, the processing of hides, bone- and/or antler-working, hunting activities, food gathering and processing, and obviously the cooking and eating of food, and in all probability sitting around the fire enjoying each other's company, arguing, laughing, crying, occasionally defecating, lovemaking, and engaging in the undertaking of rituals and obviously sleeping, to name but a few possibilities, were all taking place at the Nab Head during the phases of occupation at this location during the earlier Mesolithic period.

During the later Mesolithic period, whilst all of the above activities were presumably undertaken in the vicinity, the lithic material at the Nab Head II includes three pecked and ground stone tools, which include two axes or adzes (Fig. 4.10), and a perforated stone disc which had been bilaterally ground to an edge around its perimeter (David 1989: 248). As noted in Chapter 3, whilst these objects have no known parallels in British prehistoric contexts, it is perhaps of even more interest that axe number 1 "was found in contact with, and underlying, two bevelled pebbles" which David suggests indicates contemporaneous use and possible caching of these objects (David 2007: 150). An alternative to the suggestion of caching is of course that these objects were placed as a structured deposit aimed at

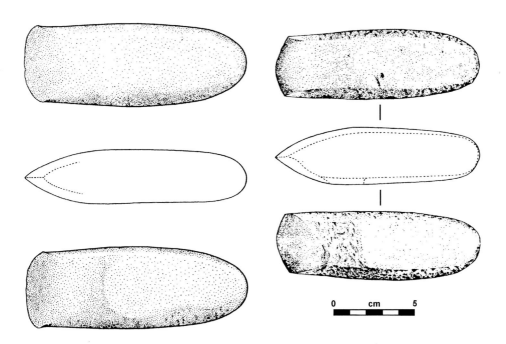

Fig. 4.10: Pecked and ground stone axes from the Nab Head II (after David 1989: 248).

highlighting their interlinked significance and meaning to the late Mesolithic population that exploited this region. Importantly, Cummings (2009: 19) notes that later Mesolithic pits with deliberate deposits of flint, bone and other organic material may prove to be important contexts for future study (see also Finlay 2003 for northeastern Ireland), and the Nab Head II deposit is clearly significant in this context.

Whilst a similar range of activities to those suggested for the earlier Mesolithic at the Nab Head I can be anticipated for the later Mesolithic occupations at the Nab Head II, there are a number of added elements that enhance our interpretations of this location. In addition to the significance of the possible ritual articulation and deposition linked to axe number 1, the association with bevelled pebbles may add resonance to the meaning behind these articulations. There are 55 bevelled pebble forms, along with 16 unmodified elongated pebbles and 20 fragments of these at site II, and whilst their function has been linked to shellfish gathering or processing, as "limpet scoops" or "limpet hammers", David (2007) suggests that the wide range of forms and sizes of these objects might suggest that they served a number of different functions (see Chapter 3). Finally, there is clearly some form of spatial patterning in the areas of activity foci at site II, which potentially suggests that the people who visited the site over time avoided earlier areas of activity; perhaps because they acted as markers of place or memory. As noted by Cummings (2009: 19) "Late Mesolithic people were involved in a range of practices, some of which may have overlapped considerably with everyday activities, but which indicate a careful and considered treatment of all forms of material culture". However, we should of course also be aware of the possibility that whilst the earlier lithic scatters did mark this location out as being linked to the past or even the ancestors, and that whilst this recognition may have been important, it is equally likely that avoiding scatters of sharp debitage (waste) material also has a practical aspect.

In north Wales, the later Mesolithic activity at Nant Hall Road, Prestatyn is associated with middens, again interpreted as indicating small scale, short-term activity sites, and given the available evidence it does appear that there is an increasing dataset to support a relatively mobile population, or sub-groups, utilising a range of locations for food extraction activities. This observation is further supported by the evidence from Nanna's Cave on Caldey Island, Dyfed where it is suggested that this location was used for tool production and food preparation, perhaps again associated with a hearth. The short term activity sites identified above also link into the evidence from locations such as Waun Fignen Felin in the Black Mountains where a number of discrete lithic scatters and associated finds suggest short-term activity foci, in this case in the form of the discard relating to hunting forays (Barton *et al.* 1995).

We currently appear to have a number of locations that are representing varying levels of hunter-fisher-forager activity across the Mesolithic period. If Rhuddlan is a more permanent site, then Nant Hall Road may be a coastal collecting site and Caldey could be a tool production site, and many locations have evidence to suggest the setting of a fire (perhaps to imbue each location with a sense of place), and in addition at many sites food preparation activities are evidenced. As the new research at Star Carr is suggesting that human groups during the earlier part of the Mesolithic had the potential to produce "a large site with evidence for substantial constructions - including a large timber platform and post-built structure" (Conneller *et al.* 2012: 1017) we should perhaps consider the possibility that larger scale excavations at locations like Rhuddlan or the Nab Head might produce a more robust picture of the activity that occurred at these and similar locations (although it is recognised that the Nab Head does not have the potential to produce extensive organic deposits). The numerous "task" sites that have been identified in Wales suggest that the dataset is becoming increasingly robust in terms of the distribution of small to medium sized foci of activity, and the locations with significant numbers of finds, such as Brenig 53, Prestatyn, Rhuddlan, Porthllisky Bay, the Nab Head, Freshwater West, Craig y Llyn and Trywyn Du, may well prove to be of considerable significance if reinvestigated along the lines of the research that is being undertaken at Star Carr; as noted by Conneller *et al.* (2012: 1017) it is "unlikely to be a coincidence that Star Carr, the most thoroughly investigated Preboreal Mesolithic site in Europe, has also yielded the most abundant evidence for intensive settlement"!

Furthermore, the evidence for human activity that has been recovered from the Severn Estuary significantly enhances our database for Mesolithic settlement and subsistence activities in Wales, and Britain in general. At Goldcliff, features such as a probable hearth, possible post cast, finds of charcoal, flint (1650 artefacts) and fragmentary bone, that appear to be concentrated in areas of increased density have been identified, and these are thought to relate to food processing and cooking activities (Bell *et al.* 2000: 36). A range of lithic sources were exploited at this location (see above), and in addition to processing and cooking of food it is clear that people were working lithics, preparing their hunting equipment, possibly repairing and maintaining this equipment, and also undertaking the processing of animal products such as hides. The data from the faunal and fish remains suggests that activities at Goldcliff may have occurred during the autumn to spring months, with this activity representing a series of stays of varying duration. As Goldcliff has been dated to the period up to 4000 cal BC, it is apparent that there is evidence to suggest that Mesolithic groups were continuing their hunter-fisher-forager activities up to (and probably beyond) the hypothesised transition to the Neolithic period. As with the Nab Head, it is clear that the people who exploited the estuarine environment of the Severn undertook the full range of occupation activities, and unlike other sites in Britain, Goldcliff has evidence for a "toilet area" (Bell *et al.* 2003: 15), which is attested by the presence of human intestinal parasites (see Chapter 5). The above examples clearly indicate that the picture of life in the Mesolithic in Wales is expanding, even to the point where we potentially have evidence for people using the toilet in a designated area of the occupation/activity sites being exploited. The dating of locations such as Goldcliff is also significant in indicating that the classification of activity as either Mesolithic or Neolithic, primarily on the basis of the dating evidence, is perhaps an unsatisfactory approach to the study of hunter-fisher-foragers at around 4000 cal BC.

In addition, as outlined in Chapter 2, and in the above discussion, we have evidence to suggest that throughout the Mesolithic period in Wales a number of locations appear to indicate that Mesolithic groups were maintaining open areas in the landscape, through the use of firing of the vegetation. At Goldcliff, Caseldine (2000) cites circumstantial evidence to suggest firing of the vegetation in the vicinity of the activity areas during the later Mesolithic period. This is apparently indicated by high bracken values and the growth of hazel in the immediate vicinity. Other locations such as Cefn Gwernffrwd, near Rhandirmwyn in mid-Wales (Chambers 1982a), Moel Llys y Coed in the Clwydian Hills of North Wales (Grant 2008; 2009), and Waun Fignen Felin in the Black Mountains of south Wales (Smith and Cloutman 1988), all have similar, albeit circumstantial, evidence which appears to imply that Mesolithic groups were perhaps regularly engaged in the firing of the vegetation. Again, new, targeted investigations along the lines of the palaeoenvironmental work that has been undertaken at Star Carr (e.g. Mellars and Dark 1998) may well enable researchers to generate more robust data in relation to this area of Mesolithic activity.

Of some significance in this context is the activity from Llandevenny, Monmouthshire where Brown (2004: 253) has identified evidence for woodland clearance that is associated with a date of 3770–3640 cal BC, i.e. in an "earlier Neolithic" context. The lithic inventories from this location may also suggest that Later Mesolithic groups are burning vegetation patches to enhance productivity, i.e. hunter-fisher-forager groups are managing their resources across the Mesolithic-Neolithic periods. The activities at Llandevenny have been interpreted by Brown (2004) as including a range of food extraction activities, along with food processing and preparation. Unfortunately, as discussed previously (Chapter 2) the evidence for the deliberate burning of vegetation and maintenance of open areas in the Mesolithic landscape is not unequivocal and when trying to determine whether human or natural vectors are responsible for the firing episodes that have occurred, the arguments presented to date have tended to take on a certain degree of circularity. In Wales, at least, there are very few locations that produce any evidence that is as compelling as that recovered from Star Carr in the Vale of Pickering (Day 1993; Mellars and Dark 1998), although Llandevenny comes close.

After the end of the Mesolithic period it appears that there is good evidence to support the notion that some "Neolithic" groups followed similar patterns of mobility and subsistence strategies to those of later Mesolithic groups; potentially for some *ca.* 600 years or so after the "transition" to the Neolithic period in Britain (Bell 2007f: 316). Finally, Bell also notes that sites such as Gwenvale and Llandygai may indicate that some foraging communities were becoming increasingly sedentary soon after 4000 cal BC (2007e: 317). Unfortunately, despite instances where there may be data to support the continuation of Mesolithic economic activity into the Neolithic period, the data is seldom robust or reliable and as such it is often open to criticism. The debate around the continuation of hunter-fisher-forager subsistence strategies across the artificial boundary that marks the Mesolithic–Neolithic transition at *ca.* 4000–3800 cal BC is protracted, and often revolves around hypothesised stability in gathered resources or the occurrence of markers of "sedentism", such as cemeteries. For Britain there are few sites that can provide direct and reliable insights into this period, and whilst the continental evidence often appears more reliable, many gaps remain, and as such this element of the debate is considered in more detail in Chapter 7.

As the above discussion has outlined, and as is the case throughout Europe, the transition from hunter-fisher-forager lifeways varies depending on the context of the groups being studied; the available evidence would therefore suggest that the Mesolithic groups that occupied Wales were no different from their counterparts across the European landmass in this respect, despite some 3000 years or so of presumed "isolation" across the later Mesolithic period. The patterns of landscape exploitation and the activities associated with hunter-fisher-forager lifeways are undoubtedly being made clearer by more recent multi-disciplinary targeted studies of significant foci of activity and their associated environments.

In conclusion, if the above discussion has done nothing more than to emphasise the need for a more considered approach to studies of the Mesolithic period, then it will have served its purpose. As outlined at the start of this chapter, settlement and subsistence activities are interlinked, and it is with this in mind that the following chapter considers the nature of the resources that were available to human groups across the Mesolithic period.

5

FOOD FOR THOUGHT: SUBSISTENCE STRATEGIES
AND ECONOMIC ACTIVITY

Economic diversification consisted of encounter foraging practices by logistical task groups on a wide range of resources. This practice was reflected in faunal evidence by the "broad spectrum" of food remains characteristic of the Mesolithic since the Maglemosian period (*ca.* 7500–6000bc). (Zvelebil 1996: 42)

... it is now clear that hunter-gatherer societies exhibit considerable variation in terms of their settlement systems, hunting strategies, subsistence logistics, patterns of mobility, use of space, butchery practices and responses to fluctuations in the seasonal availability of resources. (Lane *et al.* 2004: 146)

Introduction

We are social animals; we need food, shelter, clothing, warmth and social interactions, and these activities are by their very nature, socially bounded and mediated. As noted by Price (2009: 683) the social context of action is enacted through lived experience of the world, and as the social context of each of the above activities is integral to life in the Mesolithic period, as archaeologists we need to incorporate a broad range of interpretative approaches in order to generate meaningful narratives of the past when considering food and its uses.

In the Mesolithic period people often lived and worked together in relatively small groups (although see discussion in Chapter 4), allocating different subsistence tasks to different members in the group, and by extension, exercising influence, authority and even some degree of leadership (Spikins 2008: 176); albeit within the socially bounded and mediated dynamic of the group. Task allocations were probably influenced by simple factors such as age and ability, or more complex factors such as social relations, ritual and the taboos imposed during a person's life, or even the specific landscape context and experiential knowledge of an individual, to name a few. As has been recorded for Australian Aborigines (Rouja *et al.* 2003: 400), and other aboriginal groups (e.g. Thomson 1939), and also for groups in temperate northern latitudes during the Mesolithic period (e.g. Zvelebil 1994; 1996), we know that the resources that were exploited by hunter-fisher-foragers would have be characterised by strong seasonality in relation to availability, with the material culture inventories varying depending on the resource exploited and/or the season/environment within which the group functioned (Thomson 1939: 209). By extension, we can assume that the activities that are undertaken may also vary seasonally. Indeed, ethnographic studies of the Hadza in Tanzania have shown that activities that are characteristic of the wet season tend to be avoided during the dry season, and *vice versa* (Woodburn 2009: 52). Yellen's (1976) study of the !Kung indicated that they tended to aggregate in the dry season and disperse in the wet season, whilst other groups followed differing settlement patterns (Barnard 1983: 200); it is therefore conceivable that a similar range of variability may well have occurred during the Mesolithic period as seasonal trends, environment and social factors all influence a groups mobility and food procurement strategies.

Obviously, to some degree the carrying capacity of the environment will have exerted an influence on group size in the absence of strategies to increase resource productivity, and as noted by Smith (1992a: 14) the net primary productivity of the earlier Holocene boreal forests and deciduous woodlands would vary in terms of ungulate biomass, and also be limited by the critical carrying capacity of these environments. Basically, this would suggest that there is therefore a notional upper limit to the numbers of animals that can be hunted before the population of a region is potentially over exploited, and as such, the density of people in the environment cannot exceed its carrying capacity without resulting in food (especially meat) shortages. Obviously, human groups do not live on meat alone (Speth and Spielman 1983; Speth 1990), and as will be discussed below, where available a broad range of terrestrial and marine/freshwater resources will be exploited (Smith 1992a: 15). In addition, individuals within a group may consume differing diets depending on factors such as age and/or sex, culturally imposed taboos, or obviously, personal preferences. Ultimately though the return rate of the resources being exploited is one factor which will influence the degree of mobility of a group as there may be a point in time when the returns from foraging are insufficient for group survival, or return rates diminish to the point where the effort expended in procurement outweighs the value of the resource (Kelly 1992: 47), thus necessitating relocation.

Lee and Devore (2009a) noted that Sahlins' characterisation of hunters as the "original affluent society" was clearly not applicable in all ethnographic examples. However, they did note that it is clear that a "routine and reliable food base appears to be a common feature among modern hunter-gatherers" and as such Lee and Devore hypothesised that "ancient hunter gatherers living in much better environments would have enjoyed an even more substantial food supply" (*ibid.*: 6). Furthermore, these authors noted that modern hunters rarely depend solely on meat resources, generally exploiting vegetable foods, fish and shellfish, with hunting appearing to provide "only 20–40% of the diet" (*ibid.*: 7).

As noted by Zihlman (1981: 91), studies of the !Kung San of the Kalahari in Tanzania, undertaken in the 1960s, demonstrated the fundamental role of women in food procurement through gathering activities. In this context, Lee's (2009) observations are of considerable interest. He observed that vegetable foodstuffs comprised 60–80% of the total diet by weight (2009: 33). Whist !Kung men do collect plants and small animals, women usually spend 2 or 3 days a week collecting gathered foodstuffs, with their contribution to the diet constituting 2–3 times as much food by weight as the men. A similar situation, albeit more complex in terms of who collects the plant foods and how these are consumed, exists with the Hadza, who are a small group of hunters and gatherers living in the vicinity of Lake Eyasi in Tanzania (Woodman 2009: 49). Both the men and the women in this population gather plant foods and, in addition, children are integrated into the gathering activities of the Hadza women, who generally gather on an almost daily basis. Given these examples, it is clear that we need to be aware of the fact that food gathering/collecting is not simply an activity that was undertaken by adult individuals, and that this activity can be undertaken by both males and females.

It is, of course, entirely realistic to assume that relatively young children could undertake food procurement activities, especially if working with their mothers, or slightly older siblings or grandparents. An alternative approach would be that rather than treating these activities as "work", the gathering/collecting activity could have been "disguised", such that it is treated as a game wherein younger children would learn where the optimum foraging areas were in a landscape whilst also negotiating and practicing aspects of gender identity and ritual observance (Keith 2006: 30). Indeed, Blurton Jones (1976) has suggested that play is probably a way in which children make a start on learning many things, including social and emotional self-regulation. As might be anticipated, there are some potential problems in relation to this aspect of gathering activity as a generalised way for children to learn, as the ethnographic record does have examples wherein children are actively discouraged from engaging in foraging activities due to either "perceived" or real dangers (Lamb and Hewlett 2007: 409); e.g. the !Kung do not allow children to forage due to the distances travelled and the lack of water available while foraging (Keith 2006: 35). Furthermore, whilst experiential learning may begin in childhood, many studies show that knowledge and experience can continue to accrue into adulthood, such that older Ache hunter-forager males had significantly enhanced prey encounter rates due to their accrued experience in locating potential prey (Bock 2007: 112, citing Walker *et al.* 2002). Learning is complex, situational and effectively a long term endeavour, as new experiences are integrated with established knowledge. We should anticipate the possibility that this may have been a particularly marked aspect of Mesolithic lifeways as individuals and groups negotiated the changing perceptions and meanings embedded in changing environments and landscape contexts when constructing their world views.

A fundamental problem in Mesolithic studies is that, as archaeologists, we do not have direct access to the communities that we study, and as such the ways in which landscape was socially constructed, conceptualised, manipulated and transformed in the past, is effectively "invisible" to us, such that our interpretations are not "authorised" (Layton and Ucko 1999: 13–16). As a consequence, all interpretation is a subjective, as opposed to an objective, reflection of cultural reality (Layton and Ucko 1999: 16, quoting from an ESSO exhibition in the National Gallery of Australia).

Despite our limitations, it is clear that ethnographic analogies offer the potential to inform our interpretations of past social action. Returning to aspects of learning, Bock (2007: 111–12) has suggested that the effectiveness of experiential learning in childhood can be constrained by factors such as body size, and the "costs" of the production of the technology used, especially where the use of technology is integral to food procurement strategies, e.g. as in the case of lithic production. Interestingly, Bock notes that the ability to accurately shoot a bow is only one element of hunting endeavours as the entire process entails the technology production, locating and tracking of prey, hunting prowess in terms of tracking or waiting for the prey, and hitting a moving target (2007: 112; also discussion in Chapter 3 of this volume). In addition to these observations the initial procurement of the raw materials, the selection and subsequent production of the projectile points and the arrows and bow, knowledge of animal behaviour, and activities after the kill such as the skinning, butchering, selection of body parts for consumption and further processing of the carcass (and of course the cooking and consumption of the animal: see e.g. Milner 2006: 76–8) are all embedded in hunting activities, and all probably have an integral range of rituals and taboos that need to be considered. Finally, at a basic level, the ability to adequately fire a bow with sufficient strength to ensure a penetrating wound, or kill, may require a level of strength that a younger child could have difficulty in producing/achieving, and it is probable that the required practical knowledge of the landscape may be insufficiently developed in younger individuals to ensure success in the hunt, unless these activities are undertaken with a more experienced member of the group.

When considering hunting activities, despite past assertions that hunting was a male preserve, this activity could, in reality, be undertaken by individuals of a broad age range and of either sex. This observation is perhaps reinforced when we consider the role of dogs in hunter-fisher-forager societies, as these animals had been domesticated during the Upper Palaeolithic (Germonpré *et al.* 2009), and their association with Mesolithic groups throughout Europe as companions (in both life and death), protectors and hunting companions, and as a food resource in their own right, is well established (e.g. Benecke 1987; Larsson 1990a; Clutton-Brock and Noe-Nygaard 1990; Garcia-Moncó 2009; Detry and Cardoso 2010). However, despite this observation, in the case of hunting it is possible that in certain circumstances "who" undertook this activity would also be dependent on the animals being hunted, and obviously, the methods used to catch them. For instance, it might be unwise for a young person to try to kill an aurochs (wild cattle) or an adult red deer, but perfectly acceptable/viable for even a youngster to trap small game, again perhaps, under the supervision of older siblings (e.g. Bird and Bliege Bird 2007). Adult females and males could, of course, easily engage in the hunting of all available animals if their strength and skill levels permitted, with the caveat that some older individuals may experience limitations when hunting large animals; and taboos (e.g. relating to menstruation) may result in an individual being excluded from hunting activities at certain times.

In the case of the Hadza, hunting is a purely male preserve, whether adults or boys, and it is only undertaken using a bow and arrow. Interestingly, according to Woodburn (2009: 51) in a similar fashion to the Hadza women, who satisfy their hunger before returning to camp with any remaining gathered foodstuffs, Hadza males normally satisfy their hunger at the place where the kill is made, lighting a fire, cooking and eating on the spot any small animal that is killed, and only after this initial consumption event is any leftover meat taken back to camp. These scenarios, wherein the females, males and children sate their hunger away from the main camp could lead to a significant bias in our interpretations of the archaeological record, as these locations, even if a fire is lit, would leave very little evidence for the consumption of a small animal, or the majority or the vegetal foodstuffs, consumed. This scenario would significantly compound the biases inherent in the representation of the foodstuffs consumed by Mesolithic hunter-fisher-foragers, and as a consequence introduce further biases in relation to the mapping of their activities in the landscape.

As with foraging activities, fishing can be undertaken by a broad range of people in the group, from the very young to the very old, again depending on factors such as the species being exploited. The methods used will also be influenced by strength, age, ability and the available technology, with taboos and exclusions potentially being imposed on the basis of factors such as age and sex and the rites of passage that a person is undertaking during their transition through life (Rouja *et al.* 2003). Similarly, the collection of shellfish and other coastal resources could be undertaken by the majority of the individuals in the group. In general, foraging activities will only be limited by factors such as size, strength and knowledge, and (again) ritual and taboos, although the latter three elements can be informed and mediated by social factors.

Bird and Bliege Bird (2007: 131) have shown that, as in the case of Hadza children who forage, their studies of the Meriam of Australia's Torres Straits Islands show that a child's ability to forage is mainly constrained by height (and walking speed) and not the complexities of learning to forage like an adult. Also, if size allows, Meriam children can even learn the most complex of fishing skills very quickly (*ibid.*). We should, of course, always remember that the nature of the environmental context of the hunter-fisher-foragers will influence the foraging activities of children, as in some environments children can easily dig their own tubers and pick their own fruit (Tucker and Young 2007: 148), but a range of other considerations (e.g. social, ritual, economic), which are perhaps less apparent in the present, would influence who hunted, fished and gathered and at what time in their lives this was permitted, or avoided.

Furthermore, beyond hunting, fishing and foraging activities, all individuals, and particularly children can engage in activities such as the collection of fuel for use in fires, an activity that younger individuals could easily have contributed to if the risks were considered to be low/acceptable or if they were supervised, and even the gathering of raw materials such as flint pebbles could conceivably have been undertaken by individuals of all ages and of either sex if they were shown how to identify those pebbles that were potential good to use. Similarly, the gathering of herbs for use in flavouring would be a low impact/low risk activity, in most cases, and once the herbs were recognisable to the individual who had been allocated the task of gathering them, this activity could be undertaken by a broad range of individuals within the group. The point here is that all individuals in a group, even very young children, could be integrated into the subsistence (and other) activities of Mesolithic hunter-fisher-forager groups from an early age, if socially embedded practice allowed; thereby potentially making them important contributors to group success and continuity, and as a consequence, important social actors. This latter observation may well have resonance in relation to the burial of the dead, as in many cases we see children and adults (and even dogs), being afforded identical burial rites, suggesting that individuals of all ages could be considered "significant" enough to warrant the expenditure of effort in terms of a structured burial (e.g. Lillie 1998; 2008).

In general, issues of food procurement activities aside, the quantification and even identification of the less robust elements of forager diets has, to date, been one of the more elusive, and perhaps generalised, aspects of studies relating to the subsistence activities of earlier Holocene populations. The fact that a bias exists and that plant and other food sources were fundamental to earlier dietary pathways, is obvious, and fully acknowledged in the literature (e.g. Holliman 1991; Lillie 2003a; 2003b; O'Connell *et al.* 2001; Willoughby 1991, etc.). In addition, there is an extensive literature on the exploitation of marine and freshwater resources by hunter-fisher-forager communities in the Mesolithic period. Similarly, as noted in Chapter 3, the fact that food is central to existence and that its allocation, or control of that allocation, can be a significant tool in the mediation of social relations within a society is an obvious, but under-emphasised aspect of studies into diet (Stig Sørensen 2000). These, and other factors related to the subsistence activities of hunter-fisher-forager groups in the Mesolithic period, will be explored in greater detail below.

Subsistence strategies and exploitation patterns

> … the facts of archaeological preservation have tended to preserve tools associated with hunting, an activity which has been presumed to be primarily, if not exclusively, a male preserve; it would not, perhaps, be too whimsical to suggest that the first Plains females appear with the advent of ceramics. (Duke 1991: 280)

> … emphasis on males and hunting by males was used to interpret socio-economic aspects, "such as the sexual division of labour, food sharing, co-operation amongst males, and planning and technical skills, a perspective that was diametrically opposite to the views of ethnographers who emphasised the role of gathering in such societies" (Willoughby 1991: 285)

Historically, as the above quotes suggest, there has been a bias towards the role of meat as a resource, and by extension the hunting activities of males, when archaeologists have considered Mesolithic socio-economic and even ritual activities, e.g. interpretations of antler frontlets from Star Carr as either possible hunting gear or ceremonial head dresses. As noted by Nyree Finlay (2003b: 88) in Britain, "imagining a Mesolithic without red deer is in itself a challenge", as "… the legacy of Star Carr has had a powerful influence in defining the parameters of our Mesolithic imaginations". However, for Wales these observations, in terms of the role of meat as a resource, are difficult to assess, for as discussed in Chapter 3, when writing in 1989 Andrew David noted that there was, in fact, a dearth of faunal collections associated with human activity in Wales. Unfortunately, to date, the situation has not really changed to any great degree. David (1989: 232) has reported that in general there are isolated animal bones, sometimes associated with flint débitage (the waste from flintworking), found in partially submerged deposits around the southern and western coasts of Wales. However, again, we cannot avoid the issues of bias and taphonomy when considering the paucity of faunal evidence for Wales. As is always the case, the biases inherent in the British evidence can be counteracted by considerations of the evidence from northwest Europe in general, as a "broad brush" approach to the data will have the potential to provide a more rounded understanding of Mesolithic groups and their subsistence activities.

In terms of the actually species exploited in Wales, artefacts such as the mattocks made from red deer antler that were found at Splash Point, Rhyl and Uskmouth have produced ages of 5640–5360 and 5320–4850 cal BC respectively (David and Walker 2004: 327), thereby confirming the exploitation (and presumably consumption) of this species during the later Mesolithic. Reading beyond the identification of the species exploited to produce the mattocks, these objects could also be an indication that the digging of roots and tubers was being undertaken with these tools (e.g. Zvelebil 1994), or that they were used for soil preparation in general. Alternatively we should consider the possibility that they could even have been used as weapons, if needed. There are a number of other finds spots that provide insights into the faunal species exploited during the Mesolithic (David 1989; 1990), and we should not be limited in our discussions of Mesolithic subsistence strategies by the limitations of the evidence in Wales, as it is not a great leap in inference to consider the wider evidence for Mesolithic fauna (and fish and flora) from elsewhere in Britain and northwestern Europe, in constructing a social narrative of hunter-fisher-forager socio-economic activity during this period. In addition, as noted by Reynier (1998), there is in fact limited evidence for earlier Mesolithic settlement in England in general, with a restricted distribution of sites in northern and western England occurring after *ca.* 9700 uncal BP; so the limitations for Wales apply elsewhere in Britain as a whole.

In this context we can perhaps see a more tangible insight in hunting practices during the Mesolithic in Wales when we consider the find of a pig (boar) skeleton, with two backed bladelets in association that was discovered by Leach at Lydstep Haven in 1918; the backed bladelets were found in the peat deposits immediately above the neck vertebrae of this animal (Jacobi 1980: 171–2; David 1989: 242). The pig has been dated to 4350–3940 cal BC by Lewis (1992; cited by Bell 2007: 12), i.e. at the cusp of the "Neolithic" period. Interestingly, there is a general assumption that once an animal has been shot by a flint-tipped arrow, if the wound is not fatal the wound will not close (cauterise), and as a result the hunter can simply track the trail of blood that is left by the animal as it bleeds out. It would appear that in the case of the pig from Lydstep, the desire not to become part of the hunter's meal was sufficient to ensure that this animal avoided capture, although death would probably have come as a result of its wounds, if as has been suggested, a tree had not fallen on the animal and crushed it! Chatterton (2006: 105) however, has suggested an alternative explanation in which the animal had been killed and deliberately weighted down beneath the water by the tree as part of a ritual act.

If the pig had escaped, the irony painted in this scene provides a bizarre insight into the Mesolithic period, wherein the animal was hit; presumably by a skilled archer, but for some reason the kill was not made, only for nature to finish the job. Of course, whilst evocative, there is no way to know whether the tree actually fell on the animal and caused its demise, or whether the animal simply expired beneath the tree and the tree subsequently fell onto the animal when the tree itself died. Irrespective of the chain of events, this pig does appear to be the one that got away, unless of course Chatterton is correct in seeing this as a ritual act.

What is also important in this context is the fact that the microliths that were embedded in the neck of the pig were both narrow "rod" like pieces that were blunted along one edge (Fig. 5.1, after Jacobi 1980: 171–3). The absolute dating of this animal pushes the use of narrow blade technology to the cusp of the Neolithic period. We should again remember that it is entirely possible that the hunter in this example could have been either male or female, especially given the fact that the women of Agta Negritos of northeastern Luzon in the Philippines hunted forest game, with a focus on wild pig and deer, using bow and arrow technology (Estioko-Griffin and Griffin 1981: 122).

The dearth of finds of faunal remains, as highlighted above, is perhaps further exacerbated, for the Mesolithic in Britain as a whole, by the notable absence of significant evidence for human burial; a situation that contrasts markedly with that of continental northwest Europe. As a consequence, in combination, we have only limited *direct* evidence for Mesolithic subsistence, via stable isotope studies of human bone, from which to reconstruct past diet (discussed below). Unfortunately, we are reliant on the generally limited evidence from environmental archaeology when trying to reconstruct the diets of the humans that lived in Wales (and Britain as a whole) during this period. However, syntheses of the potential range of foodstuffs available to prehistoric groups have been produced by Clarke (1978) and Zvelebil (1994), and in addition, a broad range of publications on this topic do in fact allow us to gain important insights into food procurement strategies in the Mesolithic period in general.

In order to fully understand hunter-fisher-forager subsistence activities we must acknowledge the fact that variability in exploitation strategies occurs, and that both males and females, and in a range of circumstances, children, would have engaged in food procurement, its processing and obviously, consumption (as discussed above). The point is that despite the biased perspective embedded in the portrayal of man as the hunter, successful food procurement strategies would often result in males gathering and women hunting, and children being integrated into subsistence

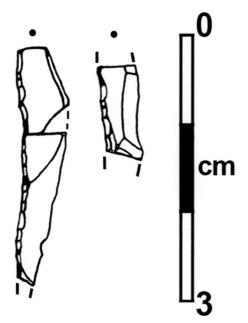

Fig. 5.1: Microliths found in association with pig skeleton at Lydstep Haven (redrawn from Jacobi 1980: fig. 4.25).

strategies where this was deemed viable, as is both apparent in the ethnographic literature (e.g. Estioko-Griffin and Griffin 1981; Hudecek-Cuffe 1996), and as logic dictates. In addition, the nature of temperate faunal species available to Mesolithic peoples in the expanding deciduous woodlands also differs somewhat to those in evidence in earlier periods due to the fact that the woodlands themselves limit group size in animals, and whilst species diversity is still broad, the predictability of species movement is perhaps less reliable/predictable than in earlier periods. This factor must have influenced who hunted and how subsistence activities were undertaken by members of the group.

It is apparent that the range of foodstuffs in evidence in the Mesolithic period varies depending on the nature of the environment being exploited by hunter-fisher-forager groups. Furthermore, whilst variation occurs between coastal and riverine/riparian environments and between lowland and upland contexts, we must always remember that resource availability also varies seasonally during the Holocene. Wetlands, whether coastal or inland, can offer a broad range of resources to hunter-fisher-forager groups, and the nature of exploitation strategies will differ depending on the resources being utilised (Rippon 2000), but unfortunately, as mentioned in Chapter 2, the evidence that we have for coastal exploitation in the earlier Mesolithic is limited due to sea level rise (although this is not necessarily the case in Scotland where isostatic rebound results in raised beaches, etc.). However, despite this bias, it should also be remembered that beyond the opportunities for fishing, fowling, reed and plant gathering and hunting (Nicholas 1998), wetlands offer the opportunity for relatively rapid movement through the landscape via water-borne transport (Rippon 2000). The lack of evidence for exploitation does not negate the fact that these environments would obviously/logically have been exploited for a range of reasons, and resources.

As mentioned above, a consideration of the ethnographic literature provides potential insights into the nature of food procurement strategies, in that individual choice often plays a considerable part in consumption patterns, and despite suggestions that hunter-fisher-foragers are generally egalitarian in their sharing of food, consumption patterns differ depending on factors such as the region, season and ultimately individual choice, as well as due to social, symbolic and ritual factors, and taboos. Of considerable interest in this context is the recent work of Price (2009: 685), who, in evaluating the relationships between people, raw materials, objects and animals, has noted that the Scandinavian evidence indicates that certain animals were dealt with in different ways depending on factors such as the life stage of the animals (i.e. young or old), and the yearly cycle or place of interaction, and that as such, the symbolic interactions were contextually dependent. In addition, Price also hypothesised that, depending on the context of interaction, certain animals had different relationships with people and were treated accordingly.

Furthermore, Milner (2006: 63; and as outlined above) has noted that food is central to life; it lies at the heart of social relations and is related to gender, power and cultural identity. In addition to this, the distribution of food can create ties between members of the group, and in certain groups, such as the Hadza of Tanzania, access to meat resources is expected if a member of the group asks for it, and pregnant women in particular have the right of access to meat irrespective of who "owns" it (Woodburn 2009: 53). This latter observation is of considerable significance in relation to our understanding of the various taboos and requirements of food sharing as in many examples the social "requirements" act in favour of certain individuals in the group. In the case of pregnant women in Hadza society access to good quality foodstuffs enhances the likelihood that a healthy mother will give birth to a healthy child.

In terms of subsistence activities, the environment and season will also influence the way in which the group moves around the landscape. In the case of the Hadza, camps are normally located near water sources in the dry season, often within a mile of the water source (Woodburn 2009: 50), and whilst Hadza women took the children with them on the gathering expeditions, they usually collected within an hour's walk of the camp site. Similarly, the !Kung are often "tethered" to a waterhole, and generally source their animal and plant resources from within a six mile radius of the camp, as this is considered to be a comfortable distance to walk (Lee 2009: 31). Interestingly, in the case of the !Kung, Lee notes that there is a strong emphasis on sharing, such that at the end of the day the members of the group return to the camp to pool the collected foods "in such a way that every person present receives an equitable share" (2009: 31). However, it should be remembered that returning with food does not negate the fact that, as with the Hadza, individuals will undoubtedly have consumed gathered resources during the day, bringing foodstuffs back to the camp in order to ensure that they benefit from the variable resources that have been gathered by other members of the group during their foraging endeavours. One final point to remember at this juncture is that plants and animals have other uses, beyond being a foodstuff, as a wide range of by-products are obtained from both resources, and processing activities will extend beyond the fundamentals of processing for consumption.

Meat as a resource

> ... it is a culturally induced assumption that hunted mammals were the main source of *Mesolithic* food supply and meat quantitatively the most important food-stuff. (Clarke 1978: 6)

> ... the hunt is the interface between culture and nature, a ritual defining humanity and epitomising masculinity ... it has always been about more than simply the acquisition of adequate supplies of protein. (Finlay 2000b: 70)

Clarke did much to dispel the myth of "meat fixation" by outlining the biases inherent in our understanding and quantification of the relative contribution of plants, alongside animals and fish, to prehistoric subsistence strategies (1976; 1978: 5–37). Whilst the Welsh evidence is relatively limited for the Mesolithic period the available evidence supports the observation that species such as red and roe deer, wild pig and boar, aurochs (wild cattle), brown bear, fox and wolf were available for exploitation, as were a broad range of marine and freshwater resources and an increasing range of bird and plant resources (David and Walker 2004, and discussion below).

The faunal species available in Britain as a whole, as evidenced by the material from sites such as Star Carr and Thatcham, also includes horse, pine marten, hedgehog, hare, badger, beaver and domesticated dog, with elk persisting into the earlier Holocene period, in addition to red deer (Evans 1975: 88). At Thatcham the full faunal inventory indicates that red and roe deer, pig, beaver, pine marten, badger, fox, hare, wild cat and possibly elk, were all exploited for their meat, fur, fat, bone or antler, and the dog was probably kept to help in hunting activities. In addition, aurochs and horse were also occasionally caught (Wymer 1982: 337). As noted by Wymer, the pollen and radiocarbon dating for Thatcham puts this site in the earlier Mesolithic, and it is apparent from the above descriptions that this site exhibits many of the conditions of preservation inherent at Star Carr in the Vale of Pickering, Yorkshire. In addition, the percentages of flint waste, and finished tools, also have similarities to the material from Star Carr (*ibid.*: 339).

Additional faunal species listed by Roberts for the Mesolithic period in Britain (1991: table 4.1) include reindeer, lynx, otter, stoat, shrew, wood mouse, wild cat, mole, red squirrel, weasel, voles and rabbit. Although it should be noted that the relative contribution of the smaller mammals in terms of meat yield may be minimal as in a number of cases the "secondary products" such as fur, sinew and bones, the latter for use in making awls and needles etc. may have been of greater economic importance to society at this time.

Bell (2001: 79–80) notes that the animal tracks in the lower Wentlooge formation in the Severn Estuary attest the presence of deer and aurochsen, although the absence of the bones of the latter species from Goldcliff is of interest as Bell suggests that aurochs was absent from the wetlands during the winter, and this is the time of year when the site was being exploited by human groups; a seemingly small but nonetheless significant observation in terms of our understanding of this location. The Oronsay (and other Scottish) middens have produced evidence for red deer, wild boar, otter, badger, fox, marten and Felidae (cat family) (Pickard and Bonsall 2012: 83), although these authors have suggested that the faunal bones were brought (imported) to the Obanian midden sites for use in tool production (Pickard and Bonsall 2012: 84–5, citing Anderson 1895; 1898; Grigson and Mellars 1987).

It is realistic to assume that the perceived significance of meat may well lie in the substantive contribution that a deer produced, in terms of calorific intakes, for, as noted by Milner (2006: 71; quoting from Bailey 1978: 39), it would take "... either 52,267 oysters, 156,800 cockles or 31,360 limpets to match the calorific value of a single red deer carcass". This would, on first reading, suggest that the obvious subsistence strategy would be hunting of red deer (Fig. 5.2). However, the collection of oysters, cockles and limpets probably entailed significantly less expenditure of effort and a greater degree of predictability than the tracking and killing of a red deer in the forested environments of earlier Holocene Britain; unless of course the strategy of reed burning at Star Carr proved to be a very efficient method for encouraging animals to browse and thereby facilitate a kill with relatively low energy investment.

As might be anticipated, the successful hunting and killing of larger animals would have provided human groups with a substantial supply of meat, and it also provided the group with numerous other (again "secondary") products such as antler for use in harpoon point production (as identified at Star Carr) or antler mattocks, hides for use in shelters and clothing, bone for manufacturing tools such as bone points, needles or bevelled

Fig. 5.2: "The Skeleton Hunt" (modified and enhanced from Cornwall 1956).

tools, marrow, and sinew and gut for use in the production of composite tools. Given the secondary products that would have been available from the hunting of large ungulates during the Mesolithic period, it is conceivable that the returns from a hunting expedition may have been considered sufficient to counteract the expenditure of time and energy that was necessary for their procurement.

The key faunal species that were exploited during the Mesolithic period exhibit a range of characteristics, a number of which are listed below:

Red deer (*Cervus elaphus*): at present this species occupies a wide range of habitats from open moorland and mountain, to forest, mixed forest, and agricultural land. In general red deer exhibit a preference for woodland habitats and are characterised by small core group size, although they can form large herds and can live up to 15 years of age. The rutting season occurs from autumn through into the earlier winter months (end of September through to November) and after an 8-month gestation period the calves are born between mid-May and mid-July. The possibility of summer migrations to the uplands, and aggregation of animals in the lowlands during the winter months (David 2007: 189) would have occasionally made this species a somewhat seasonally available resource, perhaps even influencing the distribution of later Mesolithic activity/occupation sites (as discussed in Chapter 3). However, Berridge (1994: 30) has pointed out the fact that at locations like Rhuddlan the subsistence potential would facilitate year round occupation that would offer a broad range of resources for exploitation. As such, even if a single resource like red deer was not readily available this would not necessarily result in a significant disruption to a group's resource procurement activities. Obviously, by implication upland locations such as Waun Fignen Felin, which has a shallow lake with fringing vegetation and opportunities for fowling and hunting of grazing/browsing ungulates, and lithic evidence to support hunting activities during the late Mesolithic, may be providing us with important insights into at least one element of later Mesolithic subsistence activity, in this instance probably during the summer months.

Red deer are a component of many archaeological assemblages, especially at sites such as Star Carr, and whilst Legge and Rowley-Conwy (1988) have shown that seasonal migrations are not necessarily correlated to forested landscapes, as would have characterised the later Mesolithic period, it appears that the situation in Wales is perhaps somewhat different to that pertaining in the Vale of Pickering (David 2007: 189).

At Thatcham (Carter 2001: 1055) notes that red deer, roe deer and wild pig appear in the faunal assemblage, and that the high number of red deer limb bones is indicative of the off-site procurement and processing of the carcass and the transportation of prime joints back to the camp. Using radiographs of six red deer mandibles Carter (*ibid.*: 1059) has inferred seasonal use of Thatcham, during the cooler autumn/winter months of the year, suggesting that river valley locations would have proven attractive due to their sheltered conditions and wide range of terrestrial and aquatic resources.

At Goldcliff, the research undertaken by Bell and co-workers has shown that, at their site B, short term processing activities, specifically the butchery and cooking of red deer can be identified from a careful analysis of the spatial distribution of the material culture remains at this location (Bell 2007c: 42–5). It is worth noting that this level of resolution of the archaeological record is seldom achieved beyond wetland contexts due to the limitations inherent in relation to the preservation of the organic part of the record and other biases linked to taphonomic processes.

One final point to note is that the antlers that were used in the production of harpoon points at sites like Star Carr (see Chapters 3 and 4) are obtained from the male animals, as females do not grow antlers (the same situation occurs for roe deer). The antlers begin their growth cycle in the spring, and are generally shed during the winter months, in an annual cycle. As a consequence, the use of unshed antlers in the production of barbed harpoon points can be used as an indicator of the seasonal range, within which a site may have been exploited.

Roe deer (*Capreolus capreolus*): are smaller, and more woodland adapted than red deer, though modern studies have shown an ability to adapt to open areas. Group size is small, with the maximum present-day recorded agglomeration being 14 individuals. In general the maximum life span of roe deer in the wild is *ca.* 10 years. Roe deer have been identified at sites such as Star Carr and Goldcliff, and whilst their smaller size would not necessarily produce "significant" meat yields, they would obviously have proven important as a food source, and again, their secondary products would have been of some importance to Mesolithic groups. The breeding season for roe deer occurs between mid-July and mid-August, although once fertilised the egg does not implant until after the winter period.

Wild boar/pig (*Sus scrofa*): is a very adaptable animal which has a generalised omnivorous diet, and exhibits considerable environmental variability. This animal is widely distributed in Europe, with its preferred habitats including forest and marsh areas where it favours a diet that comprises primarily herbaceous food sources. David (2007: 191) has argued that wild boar would have been very much at home in the Late Mesolithic woodlands of Wales, occupying territories of 20–200 hectares per animal, and that reduced mobility and territory size during the winter months would have made these animals vulnerable to exploitation at this time. Wild boar have been identified at sites in England, such as Star Carr, Faraday Road near Thatcham and Marsh Bentham (Milner 2006: 73–4), and Burry Holms (Walker 2003) and Goldcliff (Bell 2007c: see discussion in Chapter 4) in Wales. Interestingly, wild boar have an average weight of *ca.* 50–90kg, which may make these animals more significant in relation to meat yields when compared to roe deer, which are usually only *ca.* 15–35kg in weight (obviously meat yield will be dependent on the butchery skills of the processor but assuming a (conservative) 40% yield, roe deer will produce 6–14kg whilst, at a *ca.* 40% meat yield, a wild boar will potentially produce between 20–36kg). Again, as with deer, the secondary products from wild boar may have some value, and an example of possible secondary products is forthcoming from Mesolithic and Neolithic sites in Ukraine, where boar tusk plates were sewn onto the clothing of individuals that were found interred in cemeteries such as Yasinovatka in the Dnieper Rapids region (Fig. 5.3), whilst at Strøby Egede in eastern Zealand "various combinations of animal bones were sewn onto the clothes" of the eight individuals that were buried at this location (Larsson 1990b: 284).

The final large species considered here, the **aurochs** (*Bos primigenius*), or wild cattle, became extinct in the 17th century. The aurochs was a very large animal, with males being a maximum of *ca.* 180cm (nearly 5 ft 10 in) at the shoulder. Aurochsen appear to have occupied similar ecological niches to red deer, being adapted to both open and forested areas. While unavailable for modern comparative study it appears, on analogy, that the aurochs would likely have had low group size in forested areas and larger group size in open areas, possibly with seasonal aggregations. Finds of aurochs around the coastlines of Wales may suggest that this species exhibited a seasonal preference for these environmental zones during the Mesolithic period (changes in sea level noted), and this species has also been identified at Star Carr, indicating their presence in a lacustrine setting. These finds could of course simply reflect the fact that such locations were also frequently exploited by Mesolithic groups, and that chance encounters were more likely in these more open environments than in areas of closed woodland, especially if this species did exhibit a tendency towards large aggregations in the more open environments.

0   cm   3

Fig. 5.3: Boar's tusk plate from the cemetery of Yasinovatka in the Dnieper Rapids region of Ukraine (© author).

In 2003 Bell *et al.* reported that there was evidence for a hearth with probable evidence for the butchering of an aurochs at Goldcliff East in the Severn Estuary (2003: 8); four of the bones recovered from this location exhibited cut marks, and as noted above, animal footprints (both deer and aurochs) were also recorded within the proximity of the Mesolithic activity areas.

In terms of the importance of herbivores, from a subsistence perspective, Bērziņš (2010), reports that these animals accrue their maximum fat reserves and grow new winter coats in the autumn. This factor would not have been ignored by Mesolithic hunters, and the work of Speth (1989; 1990) and Speth and Spielman (1983) has demonstrated that the amount of fat in food is of considerable importance to foragers, as it is fat that makes the food taste good and is a critical source of fat-soluble vitamins and essential fatty acids (1990: 152). Of crucial importance in relation to meat consumption is the fact that there appears to be an upper limit to the amount of dietary proteins that can be safely consumed, with this limit being *ca.* 300g or about 50% of total energy. On the basis of these observations it would appear that an individual consuming high levels of dietary protein could quite literally be having too much of a good thing. In this context it is worth pointing out that protein intakes vary between populations of hunter-gatherers, with the !Kung Bushmen or Basarwa obtaining at least 10% of their daily protein from mongongo nuts (Speth 1990, *cf.* Blurton Jones *et al.* 1994). One other point to note is that hunting expeditions might take a few days and result in the hunters being away from the base camps during this time, as such, when the kill is made the animal will be processed away from the main site, and certain parts of the animal, e.g. the liver and blood, will be consumed at the kill site. Consequently, the consumption of different parts of the animal will be regulated to some degree by differential access to the carcass, with the processed body parts being removed and transported back to the base camp. This activity will also produce a potentially biased and fragmentary archaeological record, with two sites having evidence for kill/butchery activity and differing body part representations, even though these activities could relate to the killing and processing of a single animal.

As the above observations might suggest, we should always be aware of variability both at the inter- and intra-population levels when considering the nature of the diets being consumed by hunter-fisher-forager groups. It is highly unlikely that food sharing will result in a totally equal distribution of food across all sectors of society, and indeed, the ethnographic evidence does indicate that ritual and taboos will also influence the allocation and consumption of foodstuffs. In addition, different areas of the globe have varying environmental constraints and potentials; different times of the year can result in a glut of foodstuffs, or a dearth of certain resources, and at different times in a person's life cycle certain resources may produce negative as well as positive systemic responses to consumption, and as indicated above, society itself can impose cultural restrictions on the nature of the foods that an individual can consume (see below).

Beyond the broad range of variables inherent in dietary strategies, as implied by the above examples, we often neglect to consider the most obvious of all human actions – personal choice. Indeed, according to the Bardi of One Arm Point, Western Australia, resources that do not possess any particular taste or fatness are labelled as "rubbish", i.e. as being too dry or tasteless to be enjoyed (Rouja *et al.* 2003: 400). One alternative perspective in relation to "taste" is given by the recent work of Saul *et al.* (2013), who have noted that phytoliths, which were preserved in carbonised food deposits on prehistoric pottery from the western Baltic region, indicate that garlic mustard seeds were used in the flavouring of both terrestrial and marine animal foods. These seeds have a strong flavour and would undoubtedly enhance the "taste" of the foodstuffs being consumed by both hunter-fisher-foragers and later farming groups (*ibid.*: 1). Taste therefore can of course be modified, and there is little doubting the fact that Mesolithic people would have been well aware of the potential of a range of herbs and plants to add to the flavours of the foodstuffs that they consumed.

As we all know, individual choice can result in very different subsistence strategies being followed in modern society; for instance an individual can chose to be vegan, vegetarian, an omnivore or even predominantly carnivore; there is no reason to discount the idea that even in the past, certain individuals may have made a conscious decision to avoid certain species due to a dislike of the taste, texture, smell or even the look of a particular plant, fish or animal. We do see differences in the stable isotope signatures of individuals in certain hunter-fisher-forager groups, to the extent that marked differences in the consumption of terrestrial (plant and animal) or freshwater/marine resources have been reported in the literature (e.g. Lillie and Richards 2000).

In terms of the meat portion of the diet, until recently there were only a limited number of locations with faunal remains in Wales, from which to infer the range of species that were exploited by Mesolithic groups (David 1989). Despite this paucity of sites Jacobi (1980: 163) calculated the daily kill potential for red deer, and the yields that these might produce, using the parameters that Clark had applied to Star Carr. David (2007: 113) provides a summary table of Jacobi's calculations, which indicated that the possible meat component from a number of the earlier Mesolithic sites in Wales could have been comparable to, or even have exceeded, Star Carr in terms of the meat yields from hunting (Table 5.1). The yields at Star Carr are considered to have been sufficient to feed four families of about six persons each.

Milner (2006: 72) provides a summary list of the faunal species in evidence at Star Carr, within which additional species to those discussed above include, elk, hare, beaver, bear, fox, dog, pine marten, badger and hedgehog, and in addition, otter has been recorded at Goldcliff (Coard 2000: 49). The Welsh Mesolithic evidence from sites like Goldcliff includes faunal remains from red deer, wild pig, wolf and roe deer, along with fish from both estuarine and coastal waters

Table 5.1: Potential meat yields of red deer expressed as meat weight (60% of deadweight) that could be obtained within a 10km radius of key earlier Mesolithic sites in Wales located below 61m AOD; with Star Carr for comparison (after David 2007: 113, table 4.2).

Site	Meat weight (kg)
The Nab Head	21.5
Daylight Rock	21.0
Rhuddlan	26.0
Trwyn Du	26.0
Burry Holms	31.0
Aberystwyth	22.7
Star Carr	21.7

(Nayling 2002: 27). Bell (2003: 12) also reports that in the densest areas of burnt fish bone at Goldcliff Site A, the presence of lithic micro-debitage indicates that knapping occurred in the same areas, and the recovery of charred hazelnut shells from this location combines to suggest that this area was a location where the drying and processing of fish was undertaken alongside other consumption activities. The Oronsay middens also provide evidence for the exploitation of a wide range of avian fauna, including razorbill, cormorant and great auk, with the majority of reported species being seabirds that nest on cliffs or inhabit inshore waters (Pickard and Bonsall 2012: 83).

The fruit and nut case

> ... successful farmers have social relations with one another, while hunter-gatherers have ecological relations with hazelnuts. (Bradley 1984: 11)

> ... little is known about the importance of plant foods, shellfish, fish, or marine mammals in *Mesolithic* subsistence. (Price 1989: 48)

Throughout Europe the remains of hazelnuts, water-chestnut, pear, *Prunus* spp. and raspberries found on archaeological sites provide an indication of some of the plant species that were potentially available for exploitation by Mesolithic human groups. Clarke (1976; 1978: 20) suggested that between *ca.* 250–450 edible plants could have been exploited from temperate deciduous forests in Europe, and *ca.* 200–350 species would have been available from Mediterranean mixed woodlands. However, it would be unrealistic to assume that all available species would have been exploited, and it should be remembered that many plant resources, though perhaps present year-round, frequently become edible or produce significant edible quantities of fruit and nuts only at specific times, e.g. hazelnuts and acorns would be available in August and September (David 2007: 191). As such, their exploitation often follows patterns that are predicated on seasonal changes (Rouja *et al.* 2003: 400).

Clarke has also noted that it is probable that in the temperate latitudes (35–55°N) gathered vegetable foods would have provided 60–80% of the consumed diet by weight, while meat from all sources – hunted mammals, and gathered land, sea and riverine molluscs, crustacea, insects, fish, amphibians and small reptiles – would only constitute 30–40% (*sic*) by weight *in toto* (1978: 6–7). As many of the wild plant species that were available to Mesolithic communities would have been concentrated in wetland habitats, along coastal, lacustrine and riparian (river) shores (Zvelebil 1994: 101), the integration of shellfish and fish species could have been a fundamental element that was added to the diet during foraging activities.

Zvelebil (*ibid.*: 35) used macrobotanical remains, palynological data, artefactual evidence and the human biological record to provide an outline of the evidence for Mesolithic plant use in northwest Europe, and also to argue for wild plant food husbandry as opposed to the incidental and opportunistic use of plants as a food resource, and furthermore, for the intensive use of plant resources during the Mesolithic period. Obviously, significant difficulties exist in our efforts at assessing the nature of plant exploitation in the Mesolithic as we cannot necessarily see the (management) activities that hunter-gatherers may have undertaken in order to ensure that plant resources were available for continued exploitation (e.g. see Mithen *et al.* 2001 and discussion below). Simple activities such as the removal of competition through weeding or ensuring that over exploitation is avoided during food collecting activities would not be visible in the archaeological record. Similarly, whilst the burning of vegetation, as evidenced at Star Carr, is visible to us, the precise reasons for these activities can only be hypothesised in relation to plant exploitation and management, and the promotion of new growth to attract browsers (see discussion in Chapter 2). Furthermore, any deliberate selection, planting, habitat creation, removal of browsing ungulates or other forms of "management" that may have been undertaken by Mesolithic groups is often difficult to identify and even more problematic in terms of quantification.

Mithen's (1999b: 481) work in the Hebrides, especially on the islands of Islay and Colonsay, has resulted in the recovery of large quantities of charred hazelnut shell fragments; as are found at sites elsewhere in Britain such as Broom Hill in Hampshire, the Oronsay middens and Culverwell. At Stoasnaig on Colonsay, located off the western coast of Scotland, a 4.5m diameter pit, 0.3m deep, which is dated to 7022–6381 cal BC (7720±110 uncal BP: Q-3278; calibrated using IntCal13), is estimated to have contained several hundreds of thousands of charred hazelnut shell fragments (*ibid.*: 481). Reinforcing Zvelebil's (1999: 64) assertion of intensive plant use strategies in the Mesolithic, analyses by Mithen *et al.* (2001) at Staosnaig have identified a number of features containing plant remains, and in the case of the pit (Mithen 1999b), there is a chipped stone assemblage which contained high frequencies of blade cores and microliths typical of the narrow blade industry of the Scottish Mesolithic (2001: 225). The pit (F-24) produced an estimated weight of 15,848g of charred hazelnut shell fragments which, on the basis of experimental charring, is indicative of a total original whole nut sample of some 37,733 hazelnuts, suggesting that a figure of *ca.* 30–40,000 nuts would be a realistic estimate (*ibid.*: 227). Hazelnuts are high energy foodstuffs that are rich in Vitamin E, fibre and other vitamins and minerals, and they also have a high fat content.

Consideration of the micromorphology of the soil within the pit feature at Staosnaig suggests that the charred remains may represent only *ca.* 12–25% of the original fill of the pit as *ca.* 75–88% of the material may have been un-charred and, as a consequence, decayed over time. This would result in a total original pit content of some 0.12–0.33 million nuts in this feature alone, and in all probability this figure represents only a proportion of the original number of shells at this site (Mithen *et al.* 2001: 229).

A second plant species that was identified at this site is lesser celandine (*Ranunculus ficaria* L.), the tubers, roots and leaves of which are known, from ethnographic studies and historical sources, to have been used as a foodstuff and for medicinal purposes (*ibid.*: 231). Other plant remains from the site may well provide an indication of additional species that were being exploited, such as crab apple, vetch, dock and ribwort plantain. The formation of the pit deposits appears to have primarily occurred between 6590 and 6470 cal BC (1σ) and between 6600 and 6460 cal BC (at 2σ), with minor depositional episodes occurring 7050–6650 cal BC, and at later dates between 6420–6160 and 6020–5780 cal BC (Mithen *et al.* 2001: 232). The activity attested at Staosnaig is clearly suggestive of intensive hazelnut harvesting, possibly from as many as 5000 trees. This is a strategy that would most likely have had a "substantial impact on the local vegetation", and it is likely that these impacts may be attested in the palynological record from this area (*ibid.*: 233).

In addition to the "ubiquitous" hazelnut, amongst the other species exploited in Britain, as outlined by Zvelebil (1994: 43), are vetches, goosegrass, wild pear/apple, white water lily, yellow water lily, raspberry, acorn, barren strawberry, chickweed, bog myrtle, bog bean, Iron root, fat hen, knotgrass, annual knawel and corn spurrey. Other species evidenced in the European record include water-chestnut from the Netherlands, Sweden, Finland and the East Baltic, pear from Téviec, Brittany and Mount Sandel in Ireland, *Prunus* in the Netherlands and Belgium, and raspberries at Muldbjerg and Argus Bank in Denmark (*ibid.*: 41). Numerous sites have evidence for *Chenopodium* or a range of wetland plants such as water lily, reed and bog bean, and at Sarnate in Latvia the contextual data indicates intensive exploitation of water-chestnut (Zvelebil 1994: 41; 1998: 15). This latter species is not attested in a British context before *ca.* 5400–5000 uncal BP, during a phase of climatic warming, when summer temperatures were *ca.* 2°C higher than the present (Flenley *et al.* 1975: 39), and as such would not have been available to Mesolithic groups for exploitation.

The wide range of fruit and nut trees, and small seeded grasses that are found in the Mediterranean region have led to an increased visibility of plant remains at sites such as Franchthi cave, Greece; Uzzo, Italy; Aberadou, Montclus and Fontbregua in France; Balma Margineda and Cingle Vermell, Spain, and along the Atlantic coast of Portugal (Zvelebil 1994: 41–3), where nuts such as walnut, almond, pistachio, pine nut, hazel and acorn are all in evidence, additionally grains and pulses, fruits such a cherry, plum, strawberry, hawthorne, blackthorn, blackberry, wild grape, olive and pear are also all recorded.

A key problem in prehistoric research is the fact that the exploitation/consumption of plants in the Mesolithic diet is difficult to assess with any degree of certainty due to the fact that it is only in exceptional circumstances that this (generally) less robust portion of the dietary spectrum preserves. One frustrating exception to this general observation is, as previously mentioned, the "ubiquitous" hazelnut; this food resource is found on a number of sites in Britain (e.g. Howick, Thatcham, Star Carr and Flixton, in England, and in Wales at the Nab Head site I, Trwyn Du, Prestatyn and Brenig 53; David 2007: 191), and as Scaife notes "it seems inconceivable that hazel-nut kernels were not used as a source of nutrition along with other natural plant resources – seeds, bulbs, roots, berries, grasses and mushrooms" (Scaife 1992b:66). However, as noted by Bonsall (1981: 461), it is not so much a case of showing that plants were utilised by Mesolithic groups, but more a case of assessing how much emphasis was placed upon them as a source of food (see also Zvelebil 1994). Bonsall (1981: 462) actually notes that "most of the edible plants found in temperate deciduous forests are in fact extremely poor sources of food energy, especially the fungi, green vegetables and the majority of berries". However, such a reductionist stance negates the fact that humans do not simply chose the food they consume from the perspective of the energy it provides, many fungi, vegetal foodstuffs and berries would have provided sources of flavouring, seasoning and colour to a meal. We should always remember that as we like flavour or the aesthetic of a well presented meal in the present so to would/could our ancestors, no doubt.

Irrespective of this observation, it is likely that the emphasis placed on the exploitation of vegetal foodstuffs that are considerably lower in protein content than meat or fish, with carbohydrates being in a form that is indigestible to humans (Bonsall 1981), may be considered to be lower than the 60–80% estimate provided by Clarke (1978). A more realistic estimate of the contribution of plant foods to the overall resource spectrum is that plants probably comprised *ca.* 30–40% of Mesolithic dietary requirements (at least), even when considered against Speth's (1989; 1990) evaluation of human intolerance to lean meat-based diets (*cf.* Zvelebil 1994: 118).

It is unfortunate that, in archaeological terms, the quantification and even identification of the less robust elements of forager diets has, to date, been one of the more difficult, elusive, and generalised, aspects of studies relating to earlier Holocene populations (Lillie 2003a). In the absence of targeted sampling strategies aimed at recovering plant (and small mammal and fish remains), the recovery of plant remains is often piecemeal, limited and fortuitous. Furthermore, as plant resources are usually only available for exploitation at certain times of the year, with exploitation strategies being determined on the basis of seasonal availability, the identification of plant gathering/processing sites within a Mesolithic landscape setting is difficult, at best. In addition, it is worth emphasising that, in general, our modern perceptions of landscape fail to consider the inherent variability occurring in different zones. For instance, the riparian zone has been shown to be an ecosystem of high net primary productivity with a diverse range of plant communities occurring along a transect from dryland to riverine ecological units (Mitsch and Gosselink 1993). As such, whilst it is difficult to move away from our modern river equals fish perspective, during the Mesolithic period the riparian/coastal zones would have offered an environment rich in plant species and the animals that browsed upon them along with fish and shellfish resources; a combination of factors that clearly contributed to the value of these wetland zones (Lillie 2003b).

In addition to preservation in exceptional conditions such as frozen, dry or waterlogged contexts, it is the charring of plant remains, especially the now ubiquitous hazelnut, that provides us with one of the key indicators of past plant exploitation. As might be obvious in a northwestern European context, preservation in arid and frozen environments is seldom encountered, but waterlogging is. In the latter context waterlogged environments, such as peat bogs or lake margins, are the more likely locations for the recovery of organic remains from the Mesolithic period. In addition to the physical preservation of macrofossil remains in waterlogged contexts, it is important to note that microfossils, such as pollen grains, are also preserved in such contexts, and, when used with caution, these remains can provide important insights into local and regional vegetation, changes or modifications that might have an anthropogenic origin, and also changes in species availability over time. More recently, the analysis of food residues in pottery is proving informative for those Mesolithic groups that utilised ceramic vessels for cooking and storage purposes (e.g. Saul *et al.* 2013), but unfortunately for British Mesolithic contexts this technique is of little value.

Research by Pallarés and Mora (1999) on Mesolithic sites from the eastern Pyrenees has shown, from the analysis of carbonised plant remains, that the gathering activities of hunter-forager populations in this region included the exploitation of a number of wild fruit species. The species identified included *Corylus avellana* (hazel), *Quercus* sp. (oak) *Prunus spinosa* (blackthorn, sloe), *Malus sylvestris* (crab apple) and *Pyrus pyraster* (wild pear). Fish and land snails were also exploited and the presence of numerous grinding stones attests to the processing of plant resources, as does the evidence from lithic microwear analysis (*ibid.*: 67). In this context an additional functional use for the bevelled pebbles found at the Nab Head in west Wales could be their use in plant processing activities such as the pounding and grinding of plant fibres and roots. Furthermore, the application of modern analytical techniques for the identification of charred plant remains (Perry 1999) has provided additional insights into at least a part of the range of plants exploited in the Mesolithic of northwestern Europe (Lillie 2003a).

Research in the northern Netherlands, where early Holocene foragers exploited numerous seasonal lakes situated in a dune system, has shown that the range of plant species that may have been exploited also included tubers of *Typha* sp (cattail). Two aquatic or semi-aquatic species of this genus were probably present in the Mesolithic of the study region, *T. latifolia* L. and *T. angustifolia* L., both of which have edible rhizomes (Perry 1999: 234). Ethnographic uses of this species, as outlined by Perry, include the treatment of burns, the construction of houses, mats and cloth, medicinal uses and its use as a food resource (*ibid.* and references). In addition, as noted by Nicholas (1991: 32), the roots and pollen of cattail can be processed into storable flour, and in the Pacific Northwest Coast region, resources such as water lilies (*Nymphaea* sp.), wapato (*Sagittaria latifolia*), the tuber of which was an important carbohydrate source, and cattail (*Typha latifolia*) were widely and intensively utilised as staple foods, as well as for more utilitarian uses such as making mats, baskets and sandals (Nicholas 2007a: 52). Similarly, water lilies (Fig. 5.4) have edible stalks and roots, and members of the Kotandji tribe expressed such a close relationship between themselves and water lilies that not only were both men and women involved in their collection, but they also buried the remains of their dead in the banks of the lagoon to keep them cool and to assist in the growth of the lilies (Mulvaney 1987: 108, cited in Nicholas 2007a: 52).

Fig. 5.4: Water lilies on the edges of a small waterbody at Barlockhart, southwest Scotland (© author).

Other edible species identified from charred remains in hearth-pit features in the Netherlands include *Scirpus* sp. (club rush), *Dryopteris felix-mas* (L.) Schott (the buckler fern) and *Beta vulgaris* ssp *maritima* (L.) Arcangeli (wild beet) (Perry 1999). Whilst some measure of incidental inclusion within the contexts analysed must be an aspect of their formation, it is unlikely that such contexts are made up solely of non-utilitarian plant foods. In general, wetland environments are very productive and have a range of attractors that include the type, diversity, productivity, reliability and seasonal availability of the flora and fauna sought. Of considerable significance in relation to the study of Mesolithic populations, in areas where wetlands have a rich and productive resource base, Nicholas (2007a: 51 and 53–4) has observed that population densities appear to have been relatively high. As such, current research in Britain may benefit from concerted efforts to identify areas where productive wetland environments existed in the earlier Holocene, as these regions may well prove important in enhancing both the burial inventory and biogenic record for the Mesolithic period.

In this context, recent research by Brown (2007: 253) at Llandevenny, Monmouthshire, has provided evidence for the charring of a range of plant species such as *Rubus fruticosus/idaeus* (blackberry/raspberry), along with *Plantago lanceolata* (ribwort plantain), Poaceae undiff., *Stachys palustris* (marsh woundwort), *Sambucus nigra* (elder) and *Urtica dioica* (nettle). Brown notes that much of the charred and uncharred plant material at Llandevenny can be regarded as being from species that were integral to the subsistence economy. In particular, *Rubus fruticosus/idaeus*, which is not a common find on Mesolithic/Neolithic sites in Britain suggests a reliance on the gathering of soft fruits, whilst the charcoal evidence from this site also suggests that *in situ* burning of berry patches was undertaken after gathering in order to increase the productivity of the locally growing edible wild plants (*ibid*.: 255).

Whilst the above observations might suggest that there is generally relatively little evidence for plant exploitation in the Mesolithic, there are a number of contexts that do in fact provide evidence for the range of plants that may have been exploited by Mesolithic hunter-fisher-forager groups (Zvelebil 1994). Zvelebil (1994; 1995) has provided an in-depth evaluation of the range of plant foods available during the Mesolithic period in Europe. Expanding upon Clarke's (1976; 1978) research, Zvelebil's synthesis has shown that much of the evidence from northern European sites revolves around remains of hazelnuts, with secondary evidence for water-chestnuts, goosefoot, sorrel, water lily, raspberry, apple, meadowsweet, and acorns, amongst others (1994: 39–40).

It is also worth noting that, despite the relative paucity of the available evidence for plant use by prehistoric hunter-fisher-foragers in general, even in sub-arctic contexts, such as those exploited by the Athapaskan group, the role of gathered plant foods is significant, with *ca*. 80% of the diet being derived from this resource (Reed 1991: 292). In this context plant food consumption is the direct result of the activities of women in food procurement. Interestingly, despite the significant contribution of plant foods to Athapaskan diets, Reed notes that researchers have commonly described Athapaskan dietary patterns by focusing on hunting, trapping and fishing, and either neglecting or minimising gathering activities (*ibid*.). On the face of it this would appear to be an unreasonable observation, but we must always be aware of the biases that are inherent in anthropological research, as the "Man the Hunter" misconception has persisted until relatively recently.

One final note is required at this point, in none of the above discussion has any mention been made of the methods by which Mesolithic people processed and cooked their food, despite the discussion of charred plant remains (Pallarés and Mora 1999; Brown 2007). Some theoretical discourse has been entered into in the literature (e.g. Milner 2006), but as noted by researchers such as Jordan (2003a; 2003b) and Rouja *et al.* (2003, discussed below), the consumption and discard of certain animal and fish, and presumably also plant species, can be complicated due to the observance of various symbolic activities and taboos. The presence of hearths and cooking pits, that have been found in association with middens, are all effectively the remains of food preparation and consumption activities that could have been anything from a small scale event such as a snack whilst out on a hunt, a family meal, or a stay of limited duration, through to a feasting event linked to a significant social or ritual occasion e.g. a birth, a rite of passage, "marriage" (or whatever was the equivalent during the Mesolithic), or even death.

The inclusion of food in burials, often interpreted as food for the afterlife (see Chapter 6), reinforces the suggestion that food preparation, consumption, and distribution were imbued with meanings beyond the mundane function of subsistence. As Milner (2006: 82) has suggested, "food is material culture ... people consume and process food in different ways and in different settings and groups, all of which maintain and reconstitute social relations". These observations are clearly important, and fundamental to any consideration of subsistence in prehistory, and as such they will be considered further in the discussion at the end of this chapter.

Fishing for clues

> ... to the Kets of the central Yenisei basin in Siberia, both meat and fish are denoted by the single term "food". (Zaliznyak 1998: 45)

> ... only occasionally do we get stories of sea-faring, fishing, shell collecting, or indeed, hazelnut pickers ... we rarely get to see the women and children in such accounts. (Finlay 2000: 67)

During the Mesolithic period the resources available in freshwater, estuarine and marine contexts would have provided an important and predictable food source for exploitation by human groups. In the case of the boreal forest zone in Europe, Zaliznyak (1998: 45) notes that during the warm months of the year, when hunting was "ineffective", fish would have been an effective substitute for hunting of large ungulates, and conversely when freezing weather made fishing ineffective, hunting was relied upon. Unfortunately, again, the fact that rising sea levels during the earlier part of the Mesolithic have obscured many of the sites that would have formed part of the hunter-fisher-forager landscapes (or task-scapes), means that whilst it is likely that the sites in the coastal zone (or lacustrine and riverine areas) would have been imbued with varying levels of significance (Pollard 2011), there is little direct evidence for the exploitation of marine and/or freshwater resources from Wales for a large part of this period (although; see Schulting *et al.* 2013 and discussion of the isotopic evidence for diet presented below). Exceptions to this lack of evidence are provided by the Obanian shell middens, in western Scotland, which are found in a number of locations including coastal caves/rockshelters and open-air sites (Bonsall 1996). In this particular context the isostatic rebound that occurred with the removal of the ice sheets over Scotland has resulted in the formation of raised beaches and sites/locations of Mesolithic activity that are generally lacking in coastal areas further south.

Irrespective of the lack of direct evidence for the exploitation of freshwater through to marine resources in Wales, fish would undoubtedly have been an important resource during the Mesolithic period (e.g. Bartosiewicz *et al.* 2008; Bell 2001; Coles 1971; Gumiński 1998; Lillie 2003b; Rowley-Conwy 1998; Schulting 2009). At the early Mesolithic site at Morton, Fife, Scotland (Coles 1971: 346–9), material from the middens associated with occupation at this site produced evidence for the exploitation of a range of fish and birds, including cod, haddock, turbot, sturgeon and salmon or sea trout, along with shag, gannet, guillemot and cormorant, and red deer, aurochs and pig, and shellfish (including limpet, periwinckle, pelican's foot, necklace shell, common mussel, prickly cockle, venus shell, and a number of other species). Coles (1971: 353) suggests that the evidence for large cod suggests that they may have been caught in deep water, presumably from boats, although near shore deep water sites could explain the presence of at least some of these species.

Throughout Europe the evidence for the exploitation of fish as a resource is well established, and the work of Grasis (2010) on a middle Mesolithic site in western Latvia has shown that a dwelling (hut or tent) with associated hearths, flint knapping (of local poor quality material) and other activity areas were located on dune sands on the western edge of a freshwater lake. In this example the site may have been occupied on a temporary basis, in the warmer part of the year. Analogies to a fishing hut are tempting given the topographic setting of this site, and Grasis (2010: 67) suggests that craft activities may also have been undertaken at this location. It is likely that similar situations occurred throughout Britain during the Mesolithic period, and whilst the evidence is patchy, the location of sites like Nant Hall Road, Prestatyn, Goldcliff and Redwick in the Severn Estuary, and probably even Star Carr, with its relative ease of access to coastal resources, must surely reinforce the evidence from the skeletal record in suggesting coastal, estuarine and riverine resource procurement activities (i.e. fishing). To date, a lack of targeted sampling strategies, in addition to the ubiquitous issues of poor preservation and the limited area of excavations, has clearly hindered attempts to enhance the archaeological evidence for this area of Mesolithic subsistence.

In Scania, the site of Tågerup has produced middle to later Mesolithic activity (from the Kongemose and Ertebølle cultures respectively), that spans 1500 years and that provides insights into hunter-fisher-forager economic strategies, art, dwellings, settlement structures, and death and burial, in an environment that clearly allowed for some degree of residence permanence (Karsten 2004). The age of the individuals that were buried in the cemetery that is associated with Tågerup further suggests that this location was of considerable importance in subsistence terms, as there is a female aged around 50 at the time of death, a double grave of a (possible) man and a woman, both of whom were around 45 at the time of death, and some evidence for cremation as part of the burial rituals at this location (*ibid.*: 109–11). Over the time that Tågerup was being exploited there is evidence to suggest an intensification of the subsistence economy, possibly even "primitive woodland gardening", and increases in the range of fish species that were exploited, alongside fishing in deep waters, with cod, saithe, pollack, mackerel, herring and flatfish all being exploited (Karsten 2004: 127). The intensification of the fishing economy is such that the excavators of this location refer to the structures in evidence as representing fish-catching stations, with wicker traps, possibly nets, and leisters all used in the procurement of this resource (*ibid.*).

In addition to the significant potential at coastal or estuarine locations Nicholas (1991: 31) has noted that wetlands, and temperate-zone swamps and marshes in particular, are among the most biologically productive ecological zones anywhere in the world, and as such these locations would have been very attractive to hunter-fisher-forager groups in the past. The attractiveness of the riparian zone itself also appears to have proven sufficiently robust to have produced activity foci for the earlier Holocene communities of Europe (Lillie 2003b), and the late Mesolithic fish traps that have been discovered in the Liffey Estuary, Dublin (McQuade and O'Donnell 2007), underpin the potential of such environments. It should also be borne in mind that these finds reinforce the fact that whilst organic preservation is relatively scarce in our region of northwest Europe, there are still sites waiting to be found. The significance of these finds is highlighted by Zaliznyak (1998: 45), who has noted that ethnographers have yet to find hunting communities in the forest zone of northern and Eastern Europe that never turned to fishing, and that no real division can be detected between settled fishers and mobile hunters.

Furthermore, the exploitation of marine resources attested in the later Mesolithic period in Brittany has suggested that exploitation strategies that place an emphasis on these resources can lead to reduced mobility and limit the size of the territory that is exploited by Mesolithic groups (Dupont *et al.* 2009). In this example however the inferred limited mobility is based on the differences in $\delta^{13}C$ values between the two sites of Téviec and Hoëdic, which are *ca.* 30km apart. The slight, but according to Schulting and Richards (2001) statistically significant difference in $\delta^{13}C$ values is recorded as −15‰ at Téviec and −14‰ at Hoëdic, with the more depleted value from Téviec being used to infer a (slightly) greater emphasis on terrestrial resources at this site. By extension, the fact that these sites are only 30km apart is used to further hypothesise that these differences suggest that the territories exploited by these groups is restricted when considered against the general perception of fisher-hunter-foragers populations as being relatively mobile (Dupont *et al.* 2009: 97). It is immediately apparent that, in this particular example, the inferences that are made on the basis of the stable isotope values are extremely speculative and somewhat tenuous, and that in reality they are not supported by the data, as the values are averaged. To some degree the above discussions, and the literature on fisher-hunter-foragers, also bring these observations into question as these groups are generally characterised by a considerable degree of heterogeneity in subsistence strategies and there is no reason to suppose that two groups *ca.* 30km apart would not have differing levels of logistical mobility, settlement patterns and food procurement and consumption activities.

In addition, as has been discussed above, numerous social, political, ritual and taboo based conditions will influence the nature of subsistence strategies between groups, and even between individuals within the group. As noted by Schulting and Richards (2001: 326–7), in order to reinforce their observations, the exploitation of resources with values that are intermediate between marine and terrestrial sources would need to be assessed by stable isotope analysis of the available resources, and given the range of values in evidence at these sites, this is clearly warranted. Finally, the sample size for each site, whilst limited by the individuals available for analysis, necessitates a considerable degree of caution when attempting to tease out the subtle levels of difference between the activities undertaken by the occupants of the sites of Téviec and Hoëdic.

Despite the above observations it is clear that the French Mesolithic shell middens of Beg-an-Dorchenn in Finistère, and Beg-er-Vil, Téviec and Hoëdic in Morbihan are useful sites when considering the possible nature of marine exploitation strategies as the first two sites have been shown to have been located within *ca.* 500m of the contemporary shore in the later Mesolithic (Dupont *et al.* 2009: 96). Téviec would have been a coastal site and Hoëdic would have been an island during the later Mesolithic, with the maximum distance to the sea being *ca.* 1km at this time. Both of these sites also differ from the first two examples in that they were both used as burial locations, with ten graves at Téviec containing 23 individuals, nine graves at Hoëdic containing 14 individuals, and both sites also contain dwelling areas. The marine-based portion of the diet, as attested from recent study of these locations has shown that, as may perhaps be expected, shellfish make up a large portion of the middens, but other species, such as crabs and fish (obtained from the shore), bird (at Téviec these included razorbills, guillemots, and great auks), and sea birds are also represented at Beg-er-Vil, and grey seal and crustaceans are in evidence at a number of sites (Dupont *et al.* 2009: 98).

At these sites, terrestrial resources include red deer and wild boar, with some evidence for roe deer, aurochs, beaver, marten, wild cat, hedgehog and dog, and also hazelnuts and wild pear, but these are considered to represent relatively minor components of the diet (*ibid.*: 98). A broad spectrum of resources are attested by these sites, and at Beg-er-Vil and Beg-an-Dorchenn the shellfish remains indicate that 33 and 23 different species were exploited respectively, although only four or five species dominate the assemblages. The dominant species include limpets and cockles, which are common to both sites, with mussels, flat oysters and periwinkles being common at Beg-er-Vil, and peppery furrow shells and carpet shell being common at Beg-an-Dorchenn (Dupont *et al.* 2009: 98). An important observation from the wide range of resources that have been identified at all of these sites is that in combination, whilst strong seasonality is attested, the evidence indicates year-round foraging activities along this coastline; albeit not necessarily year-on-year or continuous occupations by the entire group (*ibid.*: 103–5).

The above examples are of considerable importance in highlighting the potential value of the coastal zone to hunter-fisher-forager groups, and in highlighting just how much evidence could have been lost around the British coastline as sea levels rose throughout the Mesolithic period. One other aspect that is lost is the fact that groups occupying the coastal zone may well have had a totally different perception of landscape, or potentially seascape, than contemporary inland foragers, and also that the degree of marine/coastal resource exploitation in the earlier Mesolithic cannot be reliably assessed at present.

However, despite this issue there is no doubting that the potential nutritional returns from collecting activities in coastal locations are high, and whilst, when compared to the returns from hunting of large ungulates, these returns seldom appear to warrant the time investing in collecting activities, the expenditure of effort and the guaranteed returns appear to balance out. The coastal zone has a wide range of resources available for collection, located in marine, intertidal, littoral and inland habitats along the coastal strip, and as attested by the Ertebølle culture of Western Denmark, the exploitation of stable resources such as fish and shellfish can lead to high population densities. In the case of the Ertebølle these densities may have been as high as about one individual per 2km^2; i.e. "similar to that of recent sedentary groups in California and the Northwest Coast, and much greater than typical densities elsewhere" (Rowley Conwy 2011: S440). In Britain, shell middens attest to repeated collecting activity at certain locations, e.g. Oronsay, or Nant Hall Road, Prestatyn (discussed below), and when considering the potential returns from gathering activities in the coastal zone Rowley Conwy (1984: 303) has noted that:

> at Llanrhidian Sands in South Wales, Hancock and Urquhart (1966) reported that the cockle beds were uncovered about 2½ hours after high water, indicating a collection time of about 7 hours. In this time, 100–150kg may be collected. This is about 14–21kg/hour. Meat is 20% of the total weight, so the hourly rate is about 2.9–4.3kg meat. This represents about 1750–2600 kcal/hour.

So, if the conditions are right, when combined with the diverse range of environments that could be exploited at the coast, the returns could be significant.

Research into the seasonality of shellfish exploitation (cockles) at Morton, Fife, by Deith (1983: 434) has suggested that whilst the main collecting season was the winter, there is evidence for a second, summer, collecting period from context 1387 at this location. A second context studied from the midden at Morton produced evidence for an addition collecting episode during August, in addition to the winter and summer activities (*ibid.*: 436–7). Deith (1983) has argued that whilst the evidence indicates that there was a heavier seasonal presence in the winter months, the phases of activity argue against any significant degree of residence permanence at the midden. This assertion is supported by the range of species in evidence, which includes "red deer, pig, wild cattle, several species of fish and seabird and many species of mollusc, that are all found in the midden, along with evidence of plant food" this data combines to suggest that this location could be characterised as a small-scale camp (*ibid.*: 438). As this location also appears to have been a preferred collection point for flint resources, we might envisage a scenario in which a small task group is repeatedly visiting Morton to obtain the raw materials for stone tool manufacture, and whilst undertaking this task the individuals are (unsurprisingly) procuring the necessary subsistence resources to ensure that they do not go hungry during their collection activities (although all of the attributes make this location the sort of "permanent" place that may well be characteristic of a groups regional foraging round). We might anticipate that there would have been a number of locations within the hunter-fisher-forager landscapes of the later Mesolithic where similar activities were undertaken.

At Prestatyn investigations (1991–3) in advance of a planned housing development at Nant Hall Road (Armour-Chelu *et al.* 2007) reinforce the above observation, and expand upon the data from sites such as Rhyl (Splash Point perforated antler mattock which is dated to 5640–5360 cal BC (OxA-1009; 6560±80 uncal BP)), and Rhuddlan. Midden D at Prestatyn is dated to 4400–4000 cal BC at the base, whilst a human skeleton from the base of a peat unit has been dated to 3980–3780 cal BC (*ibid.*: 266). Midden D is located on the margins of the wetland area, as mapped by Armour-Chelu *et al.* (2007: fig. 20.4). A thin palaeosol overlay the Pleistocene drift deposit at this location, and the palaeosol contained fragments of charcoal, and occasional flint (102 pieces) and chert (10) pieces, knapped from small flint pebbles and chert (*ibid.*: 272). The overlying shell midden deposits were comprised of highly fragmented mussel shells with occasional shells of other marine and non-marine Molluscs, including the mussel *Mytilus edulis*, with small numbers of common periwinkle (*Littorina littorina*), cockles (*Cerastoderma edule*) and oyster (*Ostrea edulis*) in evidence (Johnson and Bell 2007: 277).

Midden D at Prestatyn appeared to have been formed through the conflation of a series of shallow heaps of material, which included occasional lithics, charcoal and fragments of animal bone (including a red deer femur with cut mark evidence for the filleting of the meat from the bone (Armour-Chelu 2007: 296)) in its matrix (Armour-Chelu *et al.* 2007: 272). A small midden (E) of later Mesolithic to earlier Neolithic date (4550–3700 cal BC) was identified through auguring, and this was shown to contain charcoal, animal bone and stone fragments, with the lower horizon (Context 105) being dated to 4550–4230 cal BC (CAR-1420; 5530±80 uncal BP). The finds in this midden included mussels, with small numbers of cockles, periwinkles and whelks (Johnson and Bell 2007: 277). Other fauna attested by the material from middens D and E at this location include material from larger animals such as aurochs or elk and smaller ungulates, one of which has been tentatively identified as sheep or goat (Amour-Chelu 2007: 296).

Pollen analysis of the depositional sequence at site D at Nant Hall Road (Brayshay and Caseldine 2007: 294) has suggested that the midden was "deposited" in woodland at the dryland edge, with alder carr fringing the dryland edge just beyond the tidal limits, and with saltmarsh deposits accumulating to the north of this location. This scenario is also attested by the sequences at site A, located some 100m north-northwest of site D. The pollen analysis from site A indicated that the woodland composition in the local and regional landscape included oak, pine, lime and hazel, with reedswamp and alder carr in the adjacent wetland and wetland marginal areas (*ibid.*: 294). Some very limited episodes of anthropogenic disturbance of the vegetation are reported as occurring at this location, with one episode being correlated to the formation stages of Midden D, during the later Mesolithic period.

The evidence from middens D and E has been used to calculate the relative contribution of the species exploited to the diet of the later Mesolithic groups at Prestatyn. For instance, midden E produced 15,300 shells which are equivalent to 40,847 kilocalories (Bell

2007e: 312). As this is the only midden at Prestatyn that was fully excavated, these data are considered to be the more robust, and the values would indicate that a single person could have subsisted for 18 days on this resource, assuming an average daily calorific intake of 2550 kilocalories (*ibid.*). Obviously, it is unlikely that the site was only exploited by a single individual, or that they subsisted entirely on the mussels that were collected. As such, the duration of stay will have been dictated by the number of persons engaging in the collecting activities at this location and the nature of the plant and animal resources that were exploited, in addition to the molluscan species in the midden (*ibid.*: 312); and of course, the subsistence strategy of the group as it moved through the later Mesolithic landscapes of North Wales. Similarly, Pickard and Bonsall (2012: 82) have noted that:

> the faunal and floral remains recovered from Mesolithic shell middens on both the east and west coasts of Scotland suggest significant dietary diversity which must, in part, reflect the resources available in distinctive micro-environments as well as individual or group preferences in resource selection.

Given the above observations, it is perhaps unsurprising that the exceptional preservation conditions in the Severn Estuary have produced vivid and unique insights into human (and animal) interactions in coastal environments, with the preservation of human, animal and bird prints in the intertidal zone (Bell 2004). The animals that are attested by these tracks include deer, aurochs and wolf, and also birds such as crane, alongside human footprints from adults and children as young as four or five years of age. The evidence suggests that both summer and winter visits were made to the estuary (*ibid.*), and it is likely that the resources that were being exploited on a seasonal basis in the Severn Estuary were an important element of subsistence strategies across the earlier Holocene, as the analysis of human bones from Caldey Island (dated to *ca.* 7500–6500 cal BC) have indicated (Schulting and Richards 2002b; Schulting 2008).

At Goldcliff (at *ca.* 5300 cal BC) the large assemblage of fish bones, comprising 1519 bones, included eel (59%), goby (29%), smelt (8%), stickleback (6%) and flatfish (1%) (Ingrem 2000). Bell (2001: 85) has suggested that, despite the small size of many of these fish, the fact that *ca.* 7% of the bones have evidence for burning indicates that they were the debris from meals or fish drying. Of course, given the extensive evidence for hearths and firing episodes at this location it is entirely possible that a proportion of the assemblage, say 7% or so of the smaller fish, could have been discarded and burnt accidentally.

Similarly, the Scottish middens have produced evidence for a broad range of fish exploitation, although as noted by Pickard and Bonsall (2012: 82) the actual reporting of the species in evidence, with only a few exceptions, is of limited value. Key species reported include cod and saithe, and sea mammals such as "the very large rorqual (*Balaenoptera* spp.), and several smaller species – seals (Phocidae), and dolphin or porpoise (*Delphinus delphis/ Phocaena phocaena*)" are all in evidence, as were crustaceans (*ibid.*). The middens at Ulva Cave, on the island of Ulva, near Mull, Inner Hebrides, on the western coast of Scotland, have produced evidence for the exploitation of limpets, periwinkles and dog-whelks, along with the bones of large mammals, fish bones and otoliths, fragments of crabs' claws, and rare carbonised fragments of hazelnut shells and seeds (Russell *et al.* 1995). As with the other Scottish midden sites, the evidence suggests that a broad range of marine and terrestrial species were being exploited by these groups during the Mesolithic period.

At Culverwell, Isle of Portland, south coast of England, Mannino and Thomas (2011: 1101 and 1105) have reported that rocky-shore intertidal molluscs (such as limpets, thick top shell, purple top shell, edible and flat periwinkle, dog whelk, common edible cockle, carpet shell) and common edible crab, were exploited intensively and frequently (possibly annually) at the site in the Mesolithic (*ca.* 6000–5200 cal BC), with collection episodes occurring during the late Autumn and Winter months. Despite this, the range of resources available for exploitation would suggest that year-round exploitation would have been feasible at this location. Mannino and Thomas have also shown that "changes in the abundance of the three main species during the later phases of occupation of the Culverwell midden reflect the impact of increased levels of human predation on nearby shores", i.e. intensive shellfish collection led to over exploitation, with younger aged shellfish being exploited, and consequently, compromised and reduced population numbers (Mannino and Thomas 2011: 1112).

The evidence for both marine and freshwater resource exploitation is abundant throughout the Mesolithic period in Northwest Europe. However, there has been some debate in relation to the nature of marine resource exploitation, especially in terms of offshore or deep-sea fishing activities. Pickard and Bonsall (2004: 273–4) have not only provided definitive oceanographic definitions of marine habitats, wherein three zones are identified on the basis of water depth, e.g.:

- Littoral Zone – shallow waters from the shore to 30m depth
- Offshore (or Neretic) Zone – at least 30m depth (over the continental shelf)
- Deep-sea regions – are defined as waters on or beyond the continental slope, with a depth greater than 180–200m

... but they move beyond the above categories in an attempt to make the classifications more applicable to an archaeological context. The categories they present include land-based fishing activities, those relating to inshore fishing using a water-craft up to 5km away from shore, offshore fishing over 5km away from land, open-sea fishing out of sight of land, and deep-sea fishing (which can include offshore or open-water fishing; *ibid.*: 274). In their discussion Pickard and Bonsall argue that despite suggestions that deep-sea fishing was a regular activity during the Mesolithic period, only six of the 80+ species of fish attested at in excess of 230 sites in Europe during the Mesolithic would have necessitated deep-sea fishing, and the sites that these occur on are restricted to the coasts of Norway, Sweden and the Aegean Sea (2004: 279–80). Furthermore, in the Scandinavian examples, the sites are located on coasts where deep water occurs near the shore, again suggesting that the evidence for deep-sea fishing during the Mesolithic period is relatively weak.

In the context of freshwater fishing there are a number of locations where fishing from the shore, or from a water-craft could have occurred throughout Britain, and it should also be remembered that there are locations where large freshwater lakes could have necessitated a considerable degree of boat handling skill in deep waters, especially in inclement weather conditions. Similarly, whilst freshwater fish might be regarded as a resource that could have been utilised practically all year round in certain regions (Bērziņš 2010: 37), a considerable degree of knowledge would be required in relation to seasonal patterns of fish availability, growth patterns and fatness, and also the techniques of capture and processing (Rouja *et al.* 2003). As many species of freshwater fish spawn in the spring and early summer, e.g. pike, perch, roach, bream, grayling, chub and dace, whilst species such as tench, pike-perch, wels and crucian carp spawn at higher, i.e. summer, water temperatures (Bērziņš 2010: 38), exploitation strategies would need to be structured in order to limit impacts from over-exploitation at the wrong time in the life cycle of the fish, and also in order to ensure that fish are caught when they are at their most productive in terms of meat yields and fatness.

The archaeological record for fishing activities is well-represented in Europe, with finds of fish hooks (Telegin and Potekhina 1987), net-sinkers (weights) and even fragments of the nets themselves (Zhilin 2007a), harpoon points and fish traps (McQuade and O'Donnell 2007; Zhilin 2007a) all in evidence. Zaliznyak (1998: 49) indicates that there were four main modes of fishing in the Boreal taiga, comprising spearing (using harpoons as found at Star Carr), stream dams with traps, stationary nets, and fish hooks and tackle, and in addition, the finds of paddles from the sites of Ulkestrup and Holmesgaard in Denmark, in direct association with harpoons, would indicate that pike were caught by spearing from boats.

At the Ozerki peat bog in the Volga Basin, Russia, Zhilin (2007a: 66) has excavated a number of sites which contained a range of stone and organic finds, including items such as a pine bark float, pebble sinkers, and a limestone sinker from Ozerki 17, which had a fragment of twisted rope, 5mm in diameter, still preserved in it. In addition, finds such as bone and antler arrowheads, including needle-shaped and uniserial arrowheads, barbed points and harpoons, intact fishing hooks, a wooden paddle suited to use with a dugout canoe, fish scaling knives made from split ribs, and scrapers made from Beaver mandibles have all be found at the wetland sites in the Volga and Oka basins (*ibid.*). The finds of arrowheads embedded in the former lake bed at the sites of Ivanovsko 3 and 7 probably indicate the use of a bow and arrow in fishing activities, and the floats, net weights and fishing hooks all reinforce Zaliznyak's (1998) observations in relation to fishing techniques in the forest zone. Added to these finds are the finds of traps, along with net sinkers and bark floats at Tågerup, and the traps from the Liffey Estuary, Dublin, all of which reinforce the considerable significance afforded to fish resources in the later Mesolithic in northwest Europe.

Obviously, drawing on the observations of Pickard and Bonsall (2004), it is likely that in some instances the finds identified as net-sinkers could have functioned as line weights for use in long-line fishing, depending on the location being exploited. The perforated stone discs from the Nab Head could conceivably be used in such an endeavour as the shape in section would function well in this context, and whilst David (2007: 154–5) discounts this function, it is perhaps premature to limit the potential range of uses for such objects. Furthermore, whilst the finds from the Nab Head might not exhibit the sort of use wear that would occur during line fishing, the likelihood that such objects were a regular loss during fishing expeditions might limit the identification of utilised objects at locations such as the Nab Head, instead perhaps, we might anticipate finding pre-prepared objects that were intended for use in long-line fishing endeavours.

At Goldcliff, Bell *et al.* (2003: 12) have reported on the identification of a probable fish drying and processing site at site A. As noted above, an additional observation from this work is that the fish were small in size, and as such it is likely that they would have been caught with either a trap or net. These authors interpret the concentrations of microliths in this area as representing the implements, e.g. knives, that were used in the processing of the fish, "or some other activities" (*ibid.*: 12). Whilst there is a measure of speculation in this observation, there is clearly a need for us to move beyond basic interpretations of the material culture remains that we find during archaeological excavations.

It should also be noted that the evidence for fishing activities can be biased by ritual activities that influence the nature of exploitation patterns, as indicated by Rouja (1998) and Rouja *et al.* (2003) who have studied the Bardi of One Arm Point, Dampier Peninsula, Western Australia. The Bardi, or their ancestors, are known to have inhabited the northern tip of the Dampier peninsula for over 27,000 years (Rouja 1998). Rouja's research has added significant insights into the role of fish as a resource, and also its management and redistribution amongst the Bardi population. Basically, fish are taken when they are considered to be at their fattest stage, during specific seasons, and at specific physiological life stages, or through on-site evaluation, i.e. if they look fat (Rouja *et al.* 2003: 399). It is precisely this sort of ethnographic study that highlights the fact that when trying to develop a nuanced understanding of hunter-fisher-forager subsistence strategies in the Mesolithic, irrespective of the inherent differences between modern and past social groups, we can use ethnography to both inform and provide a balance to our interpretations of the past.

Importantly, Rouja's research has shown that numerous factors affect which fish species are eaten and exactly who is allowed to eat them. In fact, the system of ritual and social organisation used to manage these resources is considerably complex (1998: 3). One of the most significant determining factors in this resource exploitation strategy is the fact that the Bardi (and their southern neighbours the Yawuru) deliberately avoid species during spawning (*ibid.*), for obvious resource-management reasons. This also means that seasonally, procurement and fatness coincide, and, as such, there is an inverse relationship between fatness and spawning. Consequently, despite the fact that we can, to some degree, determine the seasonality, resource procurement methods and consumption patterns of past populations in their hunter-fisher-forager activities, it is only through comparison with ethnographic and anthropological studies that we can develop inferences relating to the potential cultural biases inherent in the subsistence activities of past populations.

Interestingly, whilst sea-fishing may not be well attested for the Mesolithic period, according to Pickard and Bonsall (2004: 276; and references therein), the evidence for travel across the sea is attested by the presence of Mesolithic sites on islands in the Inner and Outer Hebrides of Scotland, and other areas of Europe, and none of these locations are beyond the sight of land or other islands. Similarly, as noted by Edmonds *et al.* (2009) the Mesolithic groups that exploited Ynys Enlli, an island located *ca.* 3km west of the most westerly tip of the Lleyn Peninsula, had wide ranging vistas, including across to the east coast of Ireland, thereby suggesting that advanced navigational skills were not necessarily needed for sea faring during the Mesolithic. However, conversely, the presence of later Mesolithic groups on islands such as Ynys Enlli (Edmonds *et al.* 2009), a location which entails a very hazardous sea crossing, suggest that we should be aware of the possibility that the skills needed to reach Ynys Enlli itself make it conceivable that voyages of relatively long distances would have been possible given the right weather conditions. As a consequence, the potential for the trade and exchange of artefacts and ideas would clearly have been a realistic proposition during this period, and voyages of exchange that involved long-distance sea-faring could conceivable have been imbued with a considerable degree of prestige on the part of the seafarers (see for example Malinowski 1922). Furthermore, as we develop our understanding of the potential social dimensions of the period, it is clear that seafaring activities, whether following coastal routes, or involving extended voyages from locations such as Ynys Enlli to the east coast of Ireland, the Pembrokeshire coast or areas to the north of the British Isles, would have proven beneficial in terms of trade and exchange relations, whether these were for prestige items, knowledge, marriage partners, status, or any combination of these and potentially, other reasons.

One final point of note is that David (2007: 192) has indicated that historically Welsh rivers were very productive environments, and also that salmon is a food resource that has an equivalent food value to deer, with less waste. The reliability and economic value of salmon as a resource is vividly highlighted by the excavated sites of the northwest coast American Indian tribes, as the sites of Namu on the central Northwest Coast, and the Five Mile Rapids site on the Columbia River in Oregon attest (Ames 1994: 216; Cannon and Yang 2006). Similarly, in the case of the Makah located around Neah Bay, Washington, excavation of the Ozette village, which was buried by a mud slide in *ca.* AD 1750, provides important insights into cultural complexity and subsistence strategies that integrated a range of marine and coastal resources (Ames 1994: 220). The exceptional preservation afforded by the waterlogged anoxic deposits at Ozette produced evidence for plank built houses and a rich material culture inventory linked to whaling activities, and the exploitation of fish such as salmon and halibut. The remains that were excavated indicated that this society had social stratification and material wealth that was comparable to contemporary farming population's (Ames 1994: 212–3; 2003). The importance of reliable resources such as salmon-rich rivers and estuaries in relation to group size, degree of sedentism and cultural complexity are obvious, and perhaps in need of further investigation in Wales, and northwest Europe in general.

David (2007: 192) argues that runs of salmon and sea trout would have occurred throughout the summer months, after an initial congregation at river estuaries. It would seem likely that as these fish migrated upstream to spawn any number of the methods used by northwest European Mesolithic groups to procure fish resources (as outlined above), could have been used in the procurement of this resource in Wales (*ibid.*). We should be aware of the fact that there would potentially be a considerable degree of variability in the productivity, diversity, and duration of fish runs (Moss and Erlandson 1995: 8), but of course, there are many other species of fish available for exploitation in the streams, rivers and estuaries, and along the coastal margins of Wales during the Mesolithic period (David 2007: 192). Whilst we have yet to locate the many sites where such exploitation unquestionably took place, there is no reason to doubt the potential and probable significance of this resource to Mesolithic groups.

This potential has recently been highlighted by the work of David Jacques, who, with colleagues and students from the Open University has been excavating at Blick Mead Springs, between 2005 and 2012 (Jacques 2013). This site, which is located about a mile from Stonehenge in Wiltshire, is, as might be anticipated given the name, the site of a natural spring, which may also have been linked to a seasonal lake at this location. Whilst this site appears to have been a focus of ritual activity across the Neolithic through to Roman periods, it is the Mesolithic activity that is of considerable interest here. This site has produced large amounts of worked lithics, over 9000 pieces of both burnt and un-burnt flint (some reports state 12,000 pieces), along with over 300 pieces of animal bone. The exceptional waterlogged conditions at the site offer considerable potential in terms of environmental reconstruction, and the organic preservation has already shown that aurochs made up over 60% of the faunal assemblage at the site, along with wild boar and red deer, and there is some evidence for cooking on the bones discovered (*ibid.*).

Initial analysis of the stone tool assemblage at Blick Mead Springs has led to suggestions that this may be a base camp, and the dating places the activities at this location between 6250–4700 cal BC, although the stone tools also appear to indicate even earlier activity at this site. When reported in the Society of Antiquaries Newsletter (*Salon* 307, October 2013), it was noted that analysis of the food remains from the site, by Simon Parfitt of the Natural History Museum, indicates that not only were salmon, trout, blackberries and hazelnuts a standard part of the diet, but frogs' legs were also consumed at this location. This site clearly has considerable potential, not only in terms of enhancing our understanding of later Mesolithic diet, but also, given the waterlogged nature of the burial environment, in terms of expanding our knowledge in terms of the organic part of the material culture inventories used by later Mesolithic hunter-fisher-foragers in Britain.

Stable isotope studies of diet

> …trying to work out the relative importance of plant and animal foods in the ancient diet on the basis of floral and faunal remains is probably impossible. (O'Connell *et al.* 2000: 303)

Lillie (2003a: 2) has noted that:

> the analysis of diet through isotopic and palaeopathological studies of human skeletal remains facilitates an empirical understanding of an individual's diet that can be used to compare patterns of consumption and identify variability in access to dietary resources between males and females. (see also Bridges 1989; Jackes *et al.* 1997; Lillie and Budd 2011; McGovern-Wilson and Quinn 1996; Richards and Hedges 1999; Schulting and Richards 2002b).

The technique of stable isotope analysis works because by analysing the $\delta^{13}C$ and $\delta^{15}N$ ratios in human bone collagen we can generate direct insights into the protein portion of the diet of the person being studied, as the carbon and nitrogen values of the plants and animals that are consumed are stored in the bodily tissues. In general, the foods that are consumed by humans have relatively well known stable isotope ratios, and as we move up the food chain, there are slight variations (enrichments) in $\delta^{15}N$ relative to $\delta^{14}N$, termed trophic level shifts, between the plants, herbivores, omnivores and carnivores in the system (whether marine or terrestrial). In terms of the carbon ratios in human bone collagen Richards *et al.* (2003: 366) note that the consumption of cereal crops that use the C_3 photosynthetic pathway, and also the consumption of "managed" animals, should produce a "terrestrial" bone-collagen carbon isotope signature ($\delta^{13}C = -20\pm1‰$, where $\delta^{13}C$ represents the $^{13}C/^{12}C$ ratio), whereas marine foods give a much higher ^{13}C content ($\delta^{13}C = -12\pm1‰$).

This allows researchers to determine what animals, marine or freshwater resources, and plants (C_3 and C_4 species) were being consumed by the human individuals being studied. As bone collagen is often used in the analysis (carbonate and dentine have also been used), this method allows insights into (mainly) the protein component of the diet in the last 10 years or so of an individual's life (due to turnover rates) (Richards *et al.* 2003; Müldner and Richards 2005). Certain plant species, such as C_4 plants, and certain animals, such as marine species, have quite distinct carbon isotope ratios which can be determined through isotope analysis. Overall the carbon isotope value, $\delta^{13}C$, provides an indication of how much marine protein there was in the diet, as compared to terrestrial protein (Schwarcz and Schoeninger 1991), whilst the nitrogen values ($\delta^{15}N$) tell us about the trophic level of an organism in an ecosystem, as consumers have bone collagen $\delta^{15}N$ values that are *ca.* 2–4‰ higher than the protein of the species they consume (Schoeninger and DeNiro 1984).

It should be emphasised that, as noted by Schulting and Richards (2000: 55), as collagen is a protein, and is built by the animal or human body using proteins ingested in the diet, the other main components of diet such as carbohydrates and lipids are not represented in stable isotope studies that use bone collagen, even though some plant species, such as nuts (hazelnuts being ubiquitous finds on Mesolithic sites), are relatively high in protein. One other point to note is that the technique, when applied to bone, offers insights into the adult diet, but when applied to the dentine of teeth the analysis of tooth collagen gives insights into the diet during tooth formation, i.e. during childhood (Lidén *et al.* 2004: 24).

As noted above, overall, humans with a diet where all of the protein is from marine sources will generally have bone collagen $\delta^{13}C$ values of approximately $-12\pm1‰$ (Chisholm *et al.* 1982; Richards and Hedges 1999; Schoeninger *et al.* 1983), whilst $\delta^{13}C$ values of *ca.* $-20‰$ are indicative of terrestrial C_3 pathway plants, and the meat or milk of animals consuming these, or the exploitation of freshwater resources (Richards *et al.* 2003: 69). If the collagen yield falls within a certain range, determined by DeNiro (1985) as a C:N ratio of between 2.9–3.6, the assumption is that the $\delta^{13}C$ and $\delta^{15}N$ ratios can provide a reliable indicator of past protein consumption, as this range indicates that organic preservation is sufficient to allow for reliable results to be generated.

In general, it has been assumed that freshwater resources such as fish have similar $\delta^{13}C$ values to terrestrial resources, at *ca.* $-20‰$, but as noted by Lillie *et al.* (2011) the analysis of fish remains from Neolithic hunter-fisher-forager contexts in the Dnieper Rapids region of Ukraine have demonstrated considerable variability, with ranges of −26‰ to −16.75‰ for δ^{13}C and ranges of 10‰ to 14.27‰ for δ^{15}N. Unpublished ratios obtained on modern fish samples from the Dnieper region (central Ukraine) and Chernovtsky Rivers (western Ukraine), obtained by these authors, reinforce this considerable degree of variation in isotope values, with δ^{13}C ratios ranging between −24.85‰ and −17.65‰ and δ^{15}N ratios of 5.1‰ to 17.15‰ being recorded. This considerable degree of heterogeneity in freshwater fish isotope ratios is clearly a complicating factor when studying human groups that exploited a broad resource spectrum during the Mesolithic period.

As the above discussion will hopefully have indicated, humans consuming a range of terrestrial, marine, and freshwater resources will exhibit stable isotope ratios that can be used to determine the degree to which each of these food resources contributed to the diet. One useful aspect of marine and freshwater resource consumption is that, in general, the δ^{15}N ratios of these resources are usually considerably higher than in terrestrial systems (although note the low end range obtained for the freshwater fish in Ukraine), whilst for marine resources the less depleted δ^{13}C ratios can be used to calculate the degree to which marine resources contributed to the diet. As such the trophic off-set for humans consuming fish resources can be elevated to >14‰ for δ^{15}N (Schulting and Richards 2000c: 56). These elevated ratios from freshwater resource consumption have been recorded for Mesolithic and Neolithic populations in the Dnieper Rapids region of Ukraine (Lillie and Richards 2000; Lillie *et al.* 2011; Lillie and Budd 2011), and in the Danubian Iron Gates (the 230km long section of the Danube Valley where the river forms the border between Romania and Serbia) by Bonsall and co-workers (2007; Bonsall *et al.* 1997; 2000; 2002; 2004). This final observation is important as, depending on the region of Europe being studied, it is now standard practice to analyse the stable isotope ratios of terrestrial herbivores, carnivores and if possible the marine and freshwater resources that would have been exploited in a given region, in order to provide an isotopic baseline for comparison; so that we can calculate the most likely contributors to the diet of these groups and identify the potential for freshwater reservoir effects in dating (e.g. Lillie *et al.* 2009).

In their on-going research into the evidence for British Mesolithic and Neolithic subsistence, Schulting and Richards (2000) have investigated the human remains from Thatcham, in the Kennet valley, Berkshire (Wymer 1982) and Aveline's Hole, Somerset (also Schulting and Wysocki 2002). Thatcham is a Mesolithic site sealed beneath peat on the floodplain of the River Kennet. There are, in fact, a number of concentrations of activity in this area, with earlier surface collecting and excavation work producing a number of microliths, gravers, scrapers, blades, cores and waste material, including a few conjoined flakes, and also hearths, and "scraps" of bone (Wymer 1982: 331). Site III at Thatcham produced a considerable quantity of flint per square yard (0.914m²), with the maximum quantity in one square being 764 flints (*ibid.*: 335). The material from site III was heavily patinated, suggesting that this area might represent an earlier phase of activity when contrasted against the other concentrations at Thatcham. The flint material that was being worked at Thatcham may have been sourced from the chalk uplands of the Hampshire Downs, *ca.* 6 miles (*ca.* 9.6km) away from the site. Organic preservation was excellent, with red deer antlers being found around the site, suggesting processing activities, and charcoal, burnt bone and flint, burnt pebbles and hazelnuts indicating hearth areas from successive phases of occupation. Interestingly, despite Wymer's interpretation of a shallow artificial channel in site III as a possible run for trapping fish (1982: 336), Schulting and Richards (2000: 57) report that the stable isotope analysis of a human from Thatcham produced stable isotope ratios that are wholly consistent with a terrestrial diet in which fish were relatively unimportant, and in which plant foods were exploited alongside terrestrial herbivores.

The analysis of a human humerus from Thatcham, alongside the analysis of a dog bone from the same site produced results that sit comfortably within the range of values from Aveline's Hole (Fig. 5.5), with the human producing a $\delta^{13}C$ value of −21.9‰ and a $\delta^{15}N$ of 8.4‰, and the dog producing a $\delta^{13}C$ of −19.5‰ and a $\delta^{15}N$ of 7.5‰. The C: N ratio of the human bone is outside the accepted range for well-preserved collagen as outlined by DeNiro (1985), but Schulting and Richards (2000: 57) have argued that, on the basis of the similarities with the dog values, the human stable isotopes values from Thatcham can be considered to be acceptable. A note of caution is now warranted in relation to the Thatcham humerus, as Meiklejohn *et al.* (2011: 47) have suggested that the palynological work on sediment from the inside of the shaft only produced *ca.* 60 pollen grains, and whilst the inferred age may be adequate for the sedimentary context it is hardly sufficient to infer an accurate chronological age for the bone as the bone appears to be redeposited. Furthermore, the bone itself is not in fact dated by absolute dating techniques, and the radiocarbon date that has apparently been associated with the Thatcham humerus comes from site V, and not site III, which is the site that the bone was recovered from. These authors note that "a direct date is needed", and as such the terrestrial signature from Thatcham could equate to a later period altogether, and not to the Mesolithic period at all.

The isotope data from Aveline's Hole are consistent with a fully terrestrial diet within which there is little evidence to suggest any consumption of marine or freshwater resources (although the discussion of the Ukrainian freshwater fish isotope ratios could complicate this). The British data is presented in Figure 5.5 (also Table 5.2), and in addition to the suggested terrestrial diet, the data indicate that plant resources clearly contributed to the diet of these populations. Schulting and Richards (2000: 58) note that the absence of a marine signature is not unsurprising given that during the earlier Mesolithic period Aveline's Hole would have been *ca.* 100km from the contemporary coast.

As might be anticipated, sites that were closer to the coast have the potential to provide contrasting evidence for diet in the Mesolithic. The data from the Oronsay middens, particularly Cnoc Coig and Caisteal nan Gillean II are a case in point (Fig. 5.5; Table 5.2). Analysis by Richards and Mellars (1998) has demonstrated a heavy reliance on marine resources for the individuals from Cnoc Coig. In fact the evidence indicates that the majority of the foodstuffs consumed by the individuals represented by fragmentary skeletal material at this location are of marine shellfish and fish origin, although the five samples from Cnoc Coig may well actually only represent two individuals (Schulting and Richards 2000c: 59).

By contrast, the Caisteal nan Gillean II sample exhibits a range that is intermediate between terrestrial and marine resource exploitation values. This may reflect intra-group dietary variation or a range of alternative options such as movement between inland and coastal locations, or dietary differences between the sexes etc. (*ibid.*: 60). These results emphasise the fact that we have few later Mesolithic sites for study, in part no doubt due to the rising sea levels that obscure the coastline around England and Wales. However, as noted by Schulting and Richards, the lack of coastal locations during the Atlantic period does not help explain the lack of human remains from inland locations.

The Welsh data includes material from Worm's Head and Caldey Island (Schulting 2009; Table 5.2). The results presented by Schulting and Richards (2000) and (Schulting 2009) have suggested that some degree of variation in diet occurs across the Mesolithic period in Britain, and that inter- and intra-site differences are in evidence; with a broad range of terrestrial through to marine-oriented diets attested (Fig. 5.5). The data presented by Schulting and Richards (2000: fig. 6.3) separated out into three discrete clusters, with three of the Ogof-yr-Ychen samples (representing at least two individuals) exhibiting a strong marine signal ($\delta^{13}C$ at -14.8 ± 0.4‰) (*ibid.*: 62). The recent analysis of the Late Mesolithic "Tilbury Man", from Tilbury in Essex (Schulting 2013: 27) add to the above data in that this individual has a $\delta^{13}C$ value of -19.3‰ and a $\delta^{15}N$ value of 11.7‰. Thus, whilst the $\delta^{13}C$ value is slightly elevated Schulting does not consider this value to represent a significant contribution of marine foodstuffs to the diet, but the $\delta^{15}N$ is clearly sufficiently elevated to indicate that freshwater resources "such as fish and/or waterfowl" may have contributed to the diet of this particular individual.

Samples with $\delta^{13}C$ values in the region of -20.0‰ are suggestive of no (or very little) use of marine resources, and it appears that there is clear variability between the individuals studied (i.e. a simple linear reading of the values would imply that a $\delta^{13}C$ of -18.0‰ would indicate *ca.* 25% contribution of marine resources; $\delta^{13}C$ of -16.0‰ would equate to *ca.* 50% marine contribution and a $\delta^{13}C$ of -14.0‰ would equate to *ca.* 75% marine contribution). As such, the values from Ogof-yr-Ychen would suggest that marine resources contributed between *ca.* 30–75% of dietary proteins, with clear evidence for variability in consumption between the samples analysed (however, if three of these samples only represent two individuals, the data may be indicative of variation in the turnover rates of the individual bones sampled i.e. ribs have been shown to remodel the fastest, and as such should provide the most accurate evidence for the diet immediately prior to death). Due to the complexities involved in the recovery of material from caves (as discussed above), Schulting and Richards (2000: 62–3) have suggested that a number of the individuals with terrestrial isotope values from the Welsh caves sites may well be later in date (i.e. not of Mesolithic age), and preliminary AMS dating has supported this suggestion (see discussion of new data below).

At present the Aveline's Hole (and perhaps Thatcham) data would seem to suggest that earlier Mesolithic groups in England were not exploiting either marine or freshwater fish resources to any significant degree, and it is clear that the data suggest that a combination of mainly terrestrial proteins (i.e. animal and plant resources) would have contributed to the diets of these groups. However, it should also be considered possible that earlier Mesolithic coastal foragers may well be "invisible" to us due to the fact that rising sea

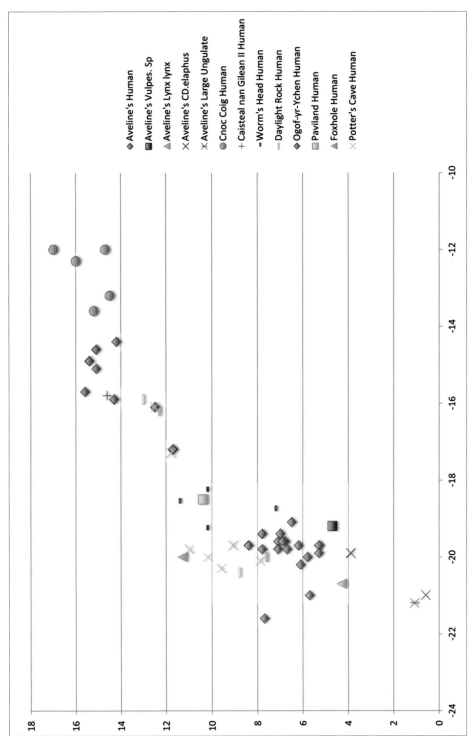

Fig. 5.5: Stable isotope data from Mesolithic contexts in Britain (based on data in Schulting and Richards 2000; 2002b, and Schulting 2009).

Table 5.2: Stable isotope ratios for material (human and faunal) from British Mesolithic contexts (after Schulting 2005; 2009; 2013; Schulting and Richards 2000c).

Site	Period	Sample no.	Species	Skeletal element	δ¹³C	δ¹⁵N	C: N
Aveline's Hole	EM	M1.11/307	human	cranium	−19.4	7.0	3.1
(England)		M1.13/38	human	left ulna	−19.7	5.3	2.9
		M1.13/118	human	left ulna	−19.7	5.3	2.9
		M1.13/114	human	left ulna	−21.0	5.7	3.5
		M1.13/152	human	left ulna	−19.6	6.8	2.9
		M1.13/154	human	left ulna	−19.6	7.1	3.1
		M1.13/159	human	left ulna	−19.9	5.3	3.0
		M1.13/160	human	left ulna	−19.8	7.1	3.2
		M1.13/161	human	left ulna	−19.4	7.8	2.9
		M1.13/163	human	left ulna	−19.8	6.7	3.2
		M1.13/164	human	left ulna	−19.1	6.5	3.2
		M1.13/166	human	left ulna	−21.6	7.7	**3.8**
		M1.13/172	human	left ulna	−20.0	5.8	2.9
		M1.13/300	human	left ulna	−20.2	6.1	3.0
		M1.13/301	human	left ulna	−19.8	7.8	3.2
		M1.13/302	human	left ulna	−19.7	6.2	3.3
		M1.13/329	human	left ulna	−19.7	8.4	3.1
		M1.14/99	human	left ulna	−19.6	6.9	3.4
		Temp V-1	*Vulpes* sp.	n/a	−19.2	4.7	N/A
		Temp L-1	*Lynx lynx*	n/a	−20.7	4.3	N/A
		Temp C-1	*Cervus elaphus*	n/a	−19.9	3.9	N/A
		Temp C-2	*C. elaphus*	n/a	−21.0	0.6	N/A
		Temp U-1	large ungulate	n/a	−21.2	1.1	N/A
Thatcham, Berkshire	EM	N/A	human	humerus	−21.9	8.4	3.7
		N/A	dog	n/a	−19.5	7.5	3.4
'Tilbury Man', Essex	LM	N/A	human	right tibia	−19.3	11.7	3.2
Cnoc Coig	LM	18104	human	clavicle	−13.2	14.5	3.1
(Oronsay)		17157	human	clavicle	−12.3	16.0	3.1
		17203	human	metacarpal	−12.0	14.7	2.9
		18284	human	metacarpal	−12.0	17.0	3.1
		18089	human	frontal	−13.6	15.2	3.1
Oronsay	Indet.	N/A	grey seal	n/a	−11.9	19.1	3.5
Carding Mill Bay, Oban	Indet.	C VI: 21	sea otter	mandible	−12.0	16.0	3.2
Caisteal nan Gillean II (Oronsay)		1281	human	metatarsal	−15.8	14.6	3.1
Worm's Head	EM	2001.4H/4	human	left scapula	−19.3	10.2	N/A
(Wales)		WH 1	human	ulna	−18.3	10.2	N/A
		1924.6.35	human	femur	−18.8	7.2	N/A
		WH 2	human	cranium	−18.6	11.4	N/A
Daylight Rock	EM	63.336/84.1a	human	mandible	−15.9	13.0	N/A
		63.336/84.1b	human	mandible	−16.2	12.3	3.2
		63.336/84.2	human	mandible	−20.4	8.8	3.1

Site	Period	Sample no.	Species	Skeletal element	δ¹³C	δ¹⁵N	C: N
		63.336/84.3	human	mandible	−20.0	7.6	3.1
Ogof-yr-Ychen	E/LM	98.2H/36	human	cranium	−17.2	11.7	3.3
		98.2H/1	human	tibia	−14.6	15.1	**2.8**
		98.2H/179	human	mandible	−15.9	14.3	3.2
		98.2H/142	human	innominate	−15.1	15.1	3.2
		98.2H/145	human	innominate	−14.4	14.2	3.0
		98.2H/54	human	cranium	−15.7	15.6	N/A
		63.337/20	human	metacarpal	−16.1	12.5	N/A
		98.2H/14	human	mandible	−14.9	15.4	3.3
Paviland	LM	2	human	humerus	−18.5	10.4	N/A
Foxhole	LM	FX41	human	tooth	−20.0	11.3	N/A
Potter's Cave	LM	91.7H/308	human	ulna	−17.3	11.8	3.1
		63.337/20	human	metacarpal	−16.1	12.5	3.3
		91.7H/260	human	radius	−20.3	9.6	3.2
		91.7H/271	human	rib	−20.0	10.2	3.0
		91.7H/274	human	rib	−19.7	9.1	3.1
		91.7H/283	human	rib	−20.1	7.9	3.0
		91.7H/284	human	rib	−19.8	11.0	3.1
marine	Indet.	1983: 2521	angler-fish	vertebra	−12.6	7.6	3.0
terrestrial omnivore	Indet.	1983: 2527.A	dog?	mandible	−19.8	8.0	3.4
	Indet.	1983: 2527.A	dog?	mandible	−20.4	8.1	3.4
Nanna's Cave	Indet.	63.335/61.1(NC1)	human	phalanx	−20.5	9.3	3.2
		63.335/61.1(NC2)	human	patella	−21.7	9.4	3.4
		63.335/61.1(NC3)	human	patella	−21.1	9.7	3.2
		91.9H/4	human	femur	−21.3	9.0	3.1
		91.9H/7	human	rib	−21.0	8.1	3.1
		91.9H/10	human	rib	−21.4	9.6	3.1
		91.9H/15	human	rib	−21.1	9.0	3.1
		91.9H/16	human	rib	−21.4	9.5	3.1
terrestrial herbivore		1983: 2589.A	cattle	humerus	−21.2	7.3	3.2
Ogof-yr-Benlog	Indet.	88.71H/2	human	vertebra	−20.1	7.2	2.9
Little Hoyle Cave terrestrial omnivore	Indet	1983: 2381.4	dog?	ulna	−21.6	7.7	3.3
	Indet	1983: 2437.1	dom.? pig	long bone	−21.2	7.2	3.4
terrestrial herbivore	Indet	1983: 2439.2	sheep/goat	femur	−20.9	5.0	3.3
		1983: 2384.6	sheep/goat	metapodial	−20.8	5.1	3.2
		1983: 2441.3	cattle	long bone	−22.2	5.6	3.2
		1983: 2441.1	cattle	mandible	−22.2	6.3	3.4
Eel Point terrestrial Omnivore	Indet	1983: 2577.A	wild boar	mandible	−18.5	8.6	3.3
terrestrial herbivore	Indet	1983: 2613	red deer	antler base	−20.5	4.4	3.3
		1983: 2580	red deer	hoof	−21.8	5.4	3.3

Note: Sample 1 from Daylight Rock is listed as a and b because different values appear in Schulting and Richards (2000; 2002b), and Schulting (2009). Numbers in bold indicate samples with collagen yields outside of the range recommended by DeNiro (1985).

levels have covered these areas and effectively "removed" any burial areas from easy access. The later Mesolithic Oronsay middens indicate that marine resources (probably shellfish and fish) were being exploited (contributing *ca.* 50–100% of dietary intakes), although the five isotope values may in fact only represent two individuals. The archaeological evidence from the Scottish middens suggests "harvesting of the seashores" following a "least-effort" strategy wherein the species exploited were "readily collected at low tide with little or no equipment" (Pickard and Bonsall 2012: 84).

The Welsh evidence indicates that a combination of marine-, intermediate- and terrestrial-economies are evidenced across the Mesolithic period, but the dating resolution remains patchy despite the fact that 25 human bone samples have been recovered from the Caldey sites (Schulting and Richards 2000c: 62). In general, the Ogof-yr-Ychen samples have a marine signature, and other sites (e.g. Potter's Cave) have values that indicate reduced marine consumption (at *ca.* 40% marine contribution to diet), whilst those samples with values of *ca.* –20‰ are indicative of terrestrial diets, that are (in some cases) equated to the Neolithic period. At present the intermediate dietary groups often remain undated in absolute terms (as do a number of the samples from the terrestrial-oriented diet part of the sample), and as such the significance of these samples in relation to Mesolithic subsistence strategies in Wales remains uncertain, as the dietary pathways in evidence could fit with either an earlier, or later Mesolithic chronological positioning on the basis of the evidence to date.

Schulting (2009: 356–7) has argued that there is a marked difference between the Worm's head and other Gower sites when compared to the isotope values from Caldey Island, with the latter exhibiting between two and seven times more marine protein in the diet. Intriguingly, on the basis of the statistical analysis of this small sample size, Schulting argues that the consistent differences between these two locations is such that a possible explanation may be found in the relative distance that each location is in relation to the contemporary coast. Basically at *ca.* 8500 cal BC Worm's Head would have been *ca.* 20km from the coast whilst at 7500 cal BC Caldey would have been within 5km of the coast. Two other possibilities are postulated; the first being that the temporal differences could mean that earlier groups were not exploiting marine resources to any significant degree, and the second being that cultural factors were influencing subsistence strategies.

Recently published research (Schulting *et al.* 2013) has enhanced the resolution of the data with the inclusion of material excavated during two limited excavation seasons in 2008 and 2010 at Foxhole Cave, Gower (Fig. 5.6). The excavations produced fragmentary remains from at least six individuals, three of which were dated by Schulting *et al.* (2013: 12) to the Mesolithic period at 6096–5921 cal BC (OxA-20835; 7355±40 uncal BP), 5615–5486 cal BC (OxA-26273; 6772±38 uncal BP), and 5522–5375 cal BC (OxA-20838; 6681±36 uncal BP), respectively.

The skeletal elements used in this study comprised a right mandibular first molar from a child aged about 6 years at death, a vertebra fragment and a lumbar vertebra from an adult. These human bones exhibited elevated $\delta^{13}C$ ratios of between –16.8‰ and –15.4‰, suggesting that marine proteins contributed 45–60% of the diet of these individuals; correction of the calibrated ages was undertaken by these authors to allow

Fig. 5.6: Foxhole Cave viewed from the southwest, Goat's Hole is located on the headland a short distance to the west of this location to the left of the image (© author).

for the marine inputs in evidence (*ibid.*: 11). The stable isotope values for the Mesolithic individuals, from oldest to youngest, are $-15.4‰$ ($\delta^{13}C$) and $12.2‰$ ($\delta^{15}N$) for the child, and $-16.8‰$ ($\delta^{13}C$) and $11.7‰$ ($\delta^{15}N$), and $-16.3‰$ ($\delta^{13}C$) and $11.4‰$ ($\delta^{15}N$) for the adults from this location (averages of triplicate measurements; Schulting *et al.* 2013: 12: table 3).

Schulting *et al.* (2013: 15) suggest that the material from Foxhole represents at least two individuals, an adult and a child. The $\delta^{15}N$ values are relatively high, but given the marine inputs into the diet of these individuals, Schulting *et al.* suggest that the nitrogen levels are low enough to suggest that the marine species that contributed to the diet were shellfish and relatively low trophic-level fish.

The results of this new analysis are of some significance in that the evidence for a marine isotopic signature of *ca.* 45–60% aligns Foxhole and Gower with the material that has been studied from Caldey Island (*ibid.*: 16). The variations between Paviland and the find from Foxhole in 1997, when contrasted with the strong marine oriented diets attested by Caldey and the new Foxhole data, are all discussed in some detail by Schulting *et al.* (2013) and the reader is directed to this article for further consideration of both Mesolithic and Neolithic dietary data from this region.

The dietary information that has been forthcoming from the isotopic analysis of the fragmentary human remains in Wales is clearly of fundamental importance given the paucity of faunal remains from stratified archaeological sites in the country. Similarly, whilst the human remains are seldom found in association with faunal material, and whilst it has seldom proven possible to link the human remains to the artefact inventories from these excavations, the absolute dating of all human skeletal material is clearly significant in providing a chronological context for these human remains, and for enabling the integration of the stable isotope studies into the wider context of the Mesolithic–Neolithic transition in Britain. The aims of future research, as has been suggested elsewhere in this volume, must now be focussed towards the prediction of those locations where cemeteries/burials are more complete, and/or where stratified sites might be preserved for study. The data does still appear to support a shift away from marine resources in the Neolithic period, but a caveat to this observation remains in that the period after 5000 cal BC, and across the Mesolithic-Neolithic transition at 4000–3800 cal BC, is still lacking in human skeletal material for use in studies of diet and subsistence strategies.

Taboos and culturally imposed restrictions on food procurement and consumption

In the discussion of meat consumption, it was noted that there was an upper limit to the amount of protein that could be consumed by hunter-fisher-foragers (*cf.* Speth 1990). It has been reported that of critical importance in this context is the fact that there appears to be an upper limit to the amount of dietary proteins that can be safely consumed, and it would appear that, in terms of dietary taboos, certain foraging populations impose restrictions on protein consumption, not necessarily for punitive reasons, but for positive demographic purposes (*ibid.*: 154–5). The hypothesised upper limit to protein intake is considerably lowered in the case of pregnant women, being given an upper limit of *ca.* 100–150g of protein or about 20% of total calories. Levels above this can lead to declines in infant birth weights and possibly lead to increases in perinatal morbidity and mortality, as well as cognitive impairment (Speth 1990: 156). The evidence presented by Speth's research would suggest that the imposition of taboos can be used to make sure that group continuity is enhanced by ensuring that negative impacts are mitigated against in the weeks immediately before and after birth.

Similarly, Rouja (1998) and Rouja *et al.* (2003) who studied the Bardi in western Australia, have noted that in relation to fish consumption patterns there are a number of socio-political, and seemingly tradition-based, concepts that, whilst apparently relating to the texture of the fish being consumed, reinforce the complexities of cultural and individual choices that affect the group, and consequently our understanding of the issues relating to "egalitarianism". Certain of the >80 fish species available for exploitation are subject to restricted access to specific groups in the community during rites of passage (*cf.* van Gennep 1960). In addition, women actively "self-impose" their own restrictions on consumption.

These restrictions act against what are perceived as "culturally loaded" species (Rouja 1998: 232). In this context it is the fish that remain fat all year that have restrictions imposed upon them, and as such these impositions regulate these species against over-exploitation.

These self-imposed restrictions actually occur throughout Bardi society, with pre-initiate sub-adults and women often expressing a, "distaste", for the culturally loaded species. An additional and important cultural taboo revolves around the provision of fish for older individuals within the group. In this example, a wide range of fish, pieces of turtle, dugong and stingray, are only consumed by mature adults. The selected fish and body parts are those elements that preserve longer, thereby ensuring the provision of fresh meat to individuals that may not be able to be present at the kill/capture site. In essence, it is increasingly obvious that these particular groups are significantly altruistic in terms of resource sharing practices (Rouja 1998), and that the "selection" in evidence is a positive aspect of sharing for these people.

Clearly then, in light of the above discussion, it is wholly unacceptable to assume that restricted access to resources is enforced on any individual for simple age/sex, socio-cultural or political reasons or that any such taboos necessarily serve to reinforce inequality (Lillie 2003b). However, it would also be unwise to impose a "unidimensional definition of egalitarianism", whatever the subsistence context of the societies we study (Borgerhoff Mulder 1999), and as such, we can probably accept the fact that there will have been situations in the past where inequality and even punitive restrictions in access to resources will have been occurring. We should also consider the possibility that the identification of individuals who exploited diets dominated by fish, meat, or vegetal foodstuffs need not suggest anything more that an individual's choice, however defined, in their own diet. The fact that women choose to avoid culturally loaded species in Bardi society may well reflect the fact that such avoidance measures also serve to assist the young individuals who are following prescribed taboos during their rites of passage. After all, it is a lot easier to give up a resource, whether fish, as in this context, or cigarettes or alcohol, as is often the case in western contexts, when those around you all follow the same restrictions.

Towards a social narrative of Mesolithic hunter-fisher-forager subsistence

In a recent assessment of 229 hunter-gatherer societies listed in the *Ethnographic Atlas*, Cordain *et al.* (2000: 687–8) noted that "no hunter-gatherer population is entirely or largely dependent (86-100% subsistence) on gathered plant foods, whereas 20% (*n* = 46) are highly or solely dependent (86-100%) on fished and hunted animal foods". These figures are obviously influenced by location, although whilst hunting remained relatively constant regardless of latitude, unsurprisingly plant food use markedly decreased with increasing latitude, with a threshold of >40°N or S.

Whilst an important aspect of the hunting of animals, fishing and the gathering of plants is obviously the subsistence value of these resources, it should always be remembered that, unlike today, these resources also provided hunter-fisher-foragers with some of the main materials used in their settlement, ritual and subsistence activities, thus making them important elements of economic lifeways (Binford 1980). In addition, the pull factors to areas such as the coast in Wales would also include exploitation of resources other than food, i.e. lithic resources. The procurement of food during the Mesolithic period was undertaken in a landscape that would have been imbued and encoded with many layers of meaning, which would have been both culturally and socially constructed, and which would have had varying levels of significance related to factors such as human lifeways, the seasonality of resources, and even the engendering of social space and cultural landscape (Mulk and Bayliss-Smith 1999: 372). Furthermore, it is unlikely that Mesolithic people evaluated their foodstuffs from the perspectives of protein content and calorific intakes, as assessed in many recent studies, but that they chose the food they consumed for similar reasons to today, i.e. it looks good to eat, tastes good to eat and makes you feel good to have eaten it!

There remain innumerable gaps in our conceptualisation of subsistence in the Mesolithic; obviously individual choice, resource availability, engendered partitioning of food allocation, taboos and other factors come in to play, but even at the fundamental level of the gathering, processing, preparing and cooking of foodstuffs (before any allocation takes place), we remain relatively ignorant of these aspects of human culture. We are also biased in our interpretations of the past due to perceptions of male and female roles in food procurement and processing; such that the stereotypical male = hunter, woman = gatherer partitioning persists despite considerable efforts to redress the balance. Similarly, whilst we began this chapter with a consideration of the possible roles that younger children and adolescents could have had in relation to food procurement strategies, the problems of identifying the roles of children in the past still persist.

Whilst we can use ethnographic analogy to illustrate the potential range of activities, and variability, that would have characterised male, female and non-adult activity in the past, and we can even begin to discuss the possible structuring of camp sites, we must remember that identifying or relating ethnographic examples as relevant to past activity is fraught with uncertainties. For instance, whilst an activity radius of 6 miles in relation to a water source, as defined by a convenient walking distance, has been discussed in the literature as a reasonable gathering distance (Lee and DeVore 2009b: 31), we have no way of knowing if this was considered a realistic distance to cover in the past, as terrain, resource "value", and the ability of the gatherer (to name a few), will all influence the viability of the distance covered in gathering activities. The fact that for some societies males do actually undertake some gathering has been discussed above, but in reality women can be shown to provide more food by weight than men (*ibid.*: 33). Whilst these are all important observations, they still fail to allow us to actually interpret the material culture remains that we find at Mesolithic sites, simply because the record is rarely robust enough for us to differentiate between activities that were age or gender specific. The question is perhaps, do we actually need to do this, or alternatively is it simply sufficient that we know that this situation existed and that males, females and non-adult individuals could all have engaged in all (many of, or the majority of) aspects of daily life if the social and cultural rules of the group permitted this engagement?

As already discussed, beyond the difficulties in determining whether men enjoyed cooking and women enjoyed hunting, and whether children experimented with both activities irrespective of gender, we rarely see the other aspects that relate to food procurement, preparation, consumption and the various taboos and rituals that may have been linked to these activities. A glaringly obvious "gap" in our narrative of the past is the fact that whilst we discuss the roles of children and adolescents, and whilst we have examples from the archaeological record that suggest that women died in childbirth (e.g. Larsson 1985: 371), rarely do we ever consider the act of procreation, or "how babies are made"! and nor do we have easy insights into marriage alliances or the nature of relationships etc. Our relatively sanitised past even avoids discussions of defecation, as we rarely find evidence for this in the archaeological record. However, as noted above exceptions do exist, and in discussing the evidence from site D at Goldcliff in the Severn Estuary Bell *et al.* (2003: 15) noted that "Petra Dark's evidence for human intestinal parasites suggests a toilet area, the earliest evidence perhaps, at least in Britain, of ... *a very* ... particular dimension of the social use of space". In trying to engender a reflective and nuanced approach to Mesolithic lifeways throughout this volume, the reader has been constantly encouraged to realise that people in the Mesolithic were essentially the same as us in their everyday needs and activities, albeit without the "benefits" (or curse) of mobile phones, computers, tablets and music storage devices.

The identification of a toilet area related to the activities at the Goldcliff Mesolithic site adds an entirely new dimension to the discussions so far, in that we talk about the procurement of food and the range of foods that were consumed by people in the past, but we seldom consider the fact that consumption, whilst a socially mediated activity, is also an activity that can lead to sickness, increased parasite loads, food poisoning, diarrhoea, vomiting etc., especially if food is not properly prepared and cooked, or if the wrong berries or fungi are consumed, or for myriad other reasons. In fact, when studying human remains from the past we are often left without the direct evidence for cause of death as many insults to the system do not necessarily cause a reaction on the skeleton, and as such they remain invisible to us in the present. Faecal matter is a direct means to identify the foodstuffs that were consumed in the past, and even the parasites present in the gut, but unfortunately (Goldcliff aside) amongst the only really useful evidence that has been recovered for the prehistoric period in northwestern Europe is the evidence from bog bodies of Iron Age date, such as Lindow Man, Cheshire, England and Tollund Man, Denmark; in general, for earlier periods the record is lacking.

Returning to the foods consumed, the perception of meat as a significant resource in the past cannot be avoided, indeed in some considerations of hunter-fisher-foragers plant foods are seen purely as a means to provide energy for the hunt. In an effort to offer an alternative perspective on subsistence during the Mesolithic, the discussion throughout this volume has introduced examples that have deliberately been directed at offering alternative perspectives on the value of gathered foodstuffs and marine/freshwater resources. This approach is designed to offer the reader a perspective on these resources as being integral to a broad spectrum approach to subsistence in the Mesolithic, and not a simply subsidiary to meat as a resource. Additionally, as the examples used throughout this chapter have hopefully highlighted, the consumption of coastal resources such as shellfish, and coastal, lacustrine and riverine fish has been shown to be an essential element of Mesolithic subsistence strategies.

As has been discussed above, there is limited evidence to suggest that some of the species exploited in coastal waters would have come from deep water environments, and that their procurement could have necessitated fishing from a boat (e.g. Pickard and Bonsall 2007; Coles 1971). In this context, the ability to traverse difficult seascapes, such as those indicated by Edmonds *et al.* (2009) when discussing the Mesolithic groups that exploited Ynys Enlli, would indicate that deep water fishing was entirely viable during the Mesolithic.

In addition, Bonsall (1996: 190) has noted that whilst some of the evidence from the Obanian middens indicated the exploitation of a range of land mammals, birds and marine mammals (e.g. otter and seal), the primary function of these sites was the processing of shellfish and fish, such that the sites represented "special-purpose processing camps associated with the exploitation of sea food resources … and that food prepared at the sites was carried back to residential camps located some distance away".

Unfortunately, as noted throughout this chapter, the fact is that it is difficult to assess the proportional contribution that plants would have contributed to the diet (see below). The specific nature of stable isotope studies, that use bone collagen, which assesses the protein part of the diet, means that this technique is biased against the identification of plant resources. Similarly, the fact is that the more robust organic parts of the archaeological record are usually the human and animal bones as these elements are less likely to degrade than plant materials. Although, as noted throughout the text so far, different contexts will influence precisely what is preserved into the present. Perhaps, to some degree we have to accept that we simply do not currently have the ability to assess the relative contribution that plants made to Mesolithic diets in Britain with the resources currently at our disposal. Again though, this observation surely points to the need for targeted studies aimed at redressing this imbalance.

This chapter has also highlighted the numerous limitations inherent in our studies of food consumption patterns, in that the range of plants that were exploited in the past is relatively unknown, and the evidence that we do have is usually biased by factors such as preservation context and sampling issues (see e.g. Zvelebil 1994). For instance, whilst the larvae and pupae of wood ants are an edible resource, we have now way of knowing if Mesolithic groups exploited this resource, or even if they knew of the potential of this resource in relation to subsistence. Similarly, whilst cowberries can be used as a preservative for meat, we have no evidence to suggest that Mesolithic groups utilised similar resources in this way. Equally though, we have no evidence to suggest that they did not! As such, whilst there is considerable evidence to suggest that between *ca.* 250–450 edible plants could have been exploited from temperate deciduous forests in Europe (Clarke 1976, 1978: 20), we seldom consider the fact that many plants species have a variety of uses, including those of construction elements, use for making baskets or woven mats, medicinal purposes, as dyes, as flavourings, or potentially a myriad other uses (e.g. Nicholas 1991; 2007a; Perry 1999), or alternatively, that exclusions, taboos or perceived negative attributes, could mean that certain resources were only exploited occasionally, if at all. It is clearly unrealistic to assume that all available species would have been exploited for food, and it should be remembered that many plant resources, though perhaps present year-round, frequently become edible or produce significant edible quantities of fruit and nuts only at specific times of the year, although this does not negate the exploitation of a resource for any of the additional uses outlined above. In terms of our studies of landscape exploitation and settlement patterning (Chapter 4), we must, of course consider the probability that the presence of certain plant species would certainly be one pull factor that helps us to account for repeated visits to specific locations in the landscape during the Mesolithic, and consequently for the establishment of "persistent places" within these landscapes.

Finally, whilst the above observations have sought to move towards a social narrative approach to the Mesolithic period, we should acknowledge that, as Layton and Ucko (1999: 12–13) have noted "the performers of the past cannot correct our misreading of the meaning that they imbued in the construction of their world", and as a consequence our interpretations are "not authorised". However, we need to recognise the fact that whilst our biographies may not be authorised, they can be made more accurate/realistic, especially when we endeavour to integrate a full reading of the archaeological record in an attempt to gain insights into the meanings that were imbued in socio-political, ritual and subsistence activities in the past.

The fact that greater resolution is afforded by certain locations/contexts, for example wetlands/waterlogged contexts, is hopefully readily apparent given the examples that have been used throughout the text. This is because the information that can be generated from the wetlands archive is often more extensive that we find on "dry" sites. However, bone, antler etc. seldom preserves well in the acidic environments of peat bogs, and as such it must always be recognised that burials and stratified sites in "dryland" contexts can be equally informative, especially when we use the ethnographic and anthropological records to enhance our understanding of hunter-fisher-forager societies and the potential levels of complexity imbued in "everyday" activities (see Chapter 6). It is also worth pointing out that a "dryland" site can have archaeological horizons that are deeply stratified, and that as a consequence can be located below the watertable, e.g. ditches, wells and pits, and that as such enhanced organic preservation might/can be anticipated in such contexts.

Furthermore, if we are able to move beyond the "keyhole" approach that has characterised excavations of Mesolithic sites in Britain to date (see e.g. Conneller *et al.* 2012), we may perhaps begin to discover the more elusive elements of Mesolithic subsistence, settlement and ritual activity (even at dryland locations) and as a consequence enhance our narration of the past.

6

THE LIVING AND THE DEAD: RITUAL ASPECTS
OF MESOLITHIC LIFE

... skeletal remains offer not only corporal evidence of human existence, but also a biological material that has been crafted and shaped through the cultural experiences of life and death. (Agarwel and Glencross 2011: 1)

... prehistoric communities acted within and made sense of *the* material and social world through their own set of understandings rich in subjective meaning and symbolism. (Jordan 2003a: 129)

Introduction

As the discussion in previous chapters has highlighted, we clearly need to be aware of the limitations inherent in studying Mesolithic groups in Britain, as a number (probably the majority) of the locations/foci of activity, or sites, in a hunter-fisher-forager landscape will not necessarily have survived into the present, whilst others will be buried beneath later alluvial sequences, or the sea itself, and effectively lost to us. This situation is particularly marked when we consider the nature of the burial evidence, as it would not be inaccurate to say that the burial record for the Mesolithic period in Britain is considerably impoverished when contrasted with the evidence from some parts of the European mainland.

When reflecting on the work of Parker Pearson (1993), it could be suggested that the lack of cemeteries or discrete burials in the Mesolithic record inhibits, to some significant degree, our ability to interpret social organisation and social change during this period, as we cannot see how people articulate their relationships between themselves and the dead, or assess how "powerful" the dead are perceived to be by the living. Indeed, some researchers have suggested that cemeteries "are in fact our most important source of information on the lifeways of prehistoric people" (Jelsma 2000: 1). From an ethnographic perspective Evans-Pritchard (1976: 222) noted that when coping with death, the Zande (or Azande) believed in witchcraft, oracles and magic which link together as procedures and ideologies at death, suggesting that coping with death would also necessitate a series of ritual actions aimed at mediating what is, in fact, a complex situation. Given these observations, the lack of a skeletal inventory for the Mesolithic in Britain is clearly limiting.

However, the recent identification of human remains of earlier Mesolithic age from Greylake in the Somerset Levels, which is dated to *ca.* 8300 cal BC (Brunning 2013), and located only *ca.* 15 miles/*ca.* 24km to the south of Aveline's Hole, may be extremely important in this context, as combined these two sites make up a significant proportion of Mesolithic burials in Britain, and they also appear to represent two discrete cemetery sites from this period. In contrast to Aveline's Hole, the remains at Greylake, near Othery were found in 1928 in an open air location; a small island in the floodplain of the Somerset Levels (Brunning and Firth 2012: 19), as opposed to the "usual" cave finds for the Mesolithic period. It is suggested that the open air context of these finds may indicate that this was a small cemetery where at least *ca.* five individuals were interred. Brunning and Firth (2012: 21) argue that the association of a cemetery, dated to *ca.* 8500–8300 cal BC, with an earlier Mesolithic flint assemblage, may offer up a unique perspective in highlighting that, where cave sites were not available, the use of open air sites was "the norm". To some degree the more recent analysis of "Tilbury Man", Essex (Schulting 2013: 33) also begins to redress the imbalance, as it is suggested that this "deeply stratified" find (*ca.* 10m below the contemporary ground surface at the time of discovery) represents burial activities in a river valley setting. As such, the nature of this find may also offer some insights into the reasons behind the dearth of Mesolithic burials in Britain. As discussed below the finds from middens may require separate consideration in relation to ritual articulations at this time.

Chantal Conneller has recently listed the British sites containing skeletal remains from the Mesolithic in Britain (2009: 692). This list contained four sites from Somerset (Aveline's Hole, Badger Hole, Gough's Cave and Totty Pot), two caves from Devon (Kent's Cavern and Oreston), Thatcham in Berkshire and Staythorpe in Nottinghamshire. The Welsh sites listed by Conneller include Ogof-yr-Ychen, Daylight Rock and Potter's Cave on Caldey, Paviland and Worm's Head, Gower, and Pontnewydd in Clwyd. The Oronsay middens of Cnoc Coig, Caisteal nan Gillean II and Priory midden are also included in this list. With the exception of Aveline's Hole, which apparently had both articulated and disarticulated material in evidence (of 50–100 individuals according to Conneller 2009; although see discussion below), and the Gough's Cave individual which was articulated (Fig. 6.1), the total number of individuals indicated by the disarticulated remains from the remaining sites represents only 26 discrete individuals. In addition to these, the fragmentary remains excavated by Schulting *et al.* (2013) increases this number by two, to 28. This is not a significant figure by any stretch of the imagination.

Recent reconsideration of the radiocarbon evidence for Mesolithic burials in Britain, undertaken by Meiklejohn *et al.* (2011), has identified six regional groupings of sites with Mesolithic skeletal material, comprising northwest Scotland, the Midlands, the Thames Valley, the Mendips and southwest England, and both south and north Wales. There are 17 sites with directly dated Mesolithic remains in Britain, and whilst a number of these are mentioned above (and in Tables 3.1, 3.2 and 5.2), additional directly dated sites listed by Meiklejohn *et al.* (2011) include Bower Farm Cave in Staffordshire (one adult individual of Mesolithic date) and Foxhole Cave in Derbyshire where the fragmentary remains of three adult individuals along with an adolescent (aged 11–14) and child (aged 8–11) were

Fig. 6.1: Reconstruction of the burial of a Mesolithic individual (dated to ca. *8700–7790 cal BC; Oxa-814 and BM-525) at Gough's Cave (© author).*

recovered. The latter site has two dates that potentially place it at the end of the Mesolithic and into the earliest Neolithic period, although Meiklejohn *et al.* (2011: 38–9) suggest that an earliest Neolithic age is perhaps more likely for this location.

It is apparent that, when discussing burial activity during the Mesolithic period in Britain, irrespective of the biases that occur due to acidic soils or sea level rise, we should consider the probability that the lack of burials for this period is potentially more of an artefact of our inability to identify those locations in the landscape where Mesolithic people buried their dead than a real lacuna; perhaps the finds from Greylake and Tilbury will reinvigorate our search for these "cemeteries" or burial places. It is also fully acknowledged that, as noted by Conneller (2009: 691), disarticulation and/or the deliberate removal of skeletal elements are both significant biasing factors, and these practices are also, unfortunately, a ubiquitous aspect of Mesolithic burial rituals in Britain.

Ritual landscapes and embedded meaning

In addition to the current lack of skeletal remains, further biases are inherent in our understanding of the Mesolithic period due to the fact that we may never know the specific details of the non-material aspects of past human activity. Whilst burials afford us a glimpse of some of the mortuary rituals that were undertaken they cannot allow us to "see" other ritual elements, that may have included song and dance, prayer or music, or ritual observance of taboos relating to the cadaver etc. (Jelsma 2000: 2). Similarly, we will never know just how important a particular location in the Mesolithic landscape, marked for instance by an unusual rock formation (Bradley 2000: 6), the presence of mythical entities, or embedded memories, actually was to the hunter-fisher-forager groups of the time; simply because we can never know this level of landscape perception and enculturation by Mesolithic people in Britain (even with ethnographic analogies to offer insights into the possible ways that landscapes were perceived in the past).

As in the present day, Mesolithic individuals were treated differently at different times in their life, e.g. at birth or while pregnant, during puberty, marriage and death (Van Gennep 1960; David and Kramer 2001: 280), or at other socially/ritually determined times, and these "transitions", or rites of passage, may be marked by special ceremonies and/or undertaken in segregated/defined locations in the landscape. Of course, the more visible of these transitions (for archaeologists) is *usually* the transition from being alive to being dead, but other transitions are equally significant and may be defined by criteria such as gender or age, amongst other factors.

Despite the limitations inherent in trying to make sense of the past lived experience (and we have discussed many limitations in preceding chapters), we can hopefully gain some appreciation of the possibilities and the potential levels of meaning that are imbued in prehistoric social-, task- and land-scapes through a considered approach to the archaeological, ethnographic and anthropological data relating to hunters-fisher-foragers (e.g. Lane 2008: 240–1; Zvelebil 2003; Jordan 2003a; 2003b). To some degree this approach is quite "traditional" in terms of studying the Mesolithic in Britain (and indeed the Mesolithic in general), but *contra* Cummings (2009: 7–10), the rationale behind the current volume is that it is embedded in the perspective that our studies of the past can only be contextualised by the use of analogy, whether this is "authorised" with ethnography, with the archaeological evidence from Scandinavia, or by comparison with other sites and regions in Europe; as long as we endeavour to exercise a degree of caution in our use of the available evidence.

Whilst many elements of Mesolithic activity are difficult to determine from the archaeological record, we can consider specific aspects from a theoretical perspective, e.g. the nature of boundaries (McCarthy 2008), particularly those between the living and the dead. We can also consider the mediation of the landscape of the living with that of the dead through the placement of burial locations and the associated burial rituals in evidence throughout Europe during the Mesolithic period. Obviously, given the nature of the British evidence outlined above, out of necessity we are forced to consider the "bigger picture" of Europe in order to generate meaningful narratives of the Mesolithic past in relation to aspects of ritual and socially bounded activity. Importantly, some insights into the potential significance of the dead is highlighted by the fact that cemeteries, defined as discrete areas that are set aside purely for burial, are in evidence from the earliest part of the Mesolithic in Britain (i.e. Aveline's Hole, Burrington Combe, in Somerset: Schulting 2005), and even earlier in the rest of Europe, and that these locations can offer insights into the ritual treatment of the dead, and greater insights into palaeopathology, body processing and differential treatment related to age and gender etc. It is fully acknowledged that ritual and symbolic activity are not necessarily all pervasive (*cf.* Fahlander 2008), but the diversity that is evident in cultural actions reflects the fact that humans mediate their existence in myriad ways. Consequently, whilst "the dead body has no intentional powers" (*ibid.*: 30), different individuals and groups may imbue the deceased with varying levels of meaning, threat or power etc.; beyond the simple fact that the individual is dead. Fundamentally, as Fahlander (2008: 31) notes, there is no single approach to these myriad variations in ritual expression, and each study needs to be approached from a context specific perspective.

Whilst the British burial evidence is sparse there are a number of important locations elsewhere in Europe, including Skateholm I and II in southern Sweden, Zvejnieki, Latvia, Olenii Ostrov in Karelia, Vasilyevka I and III, Voloshkoe and Vasilyevka II in the Dnieper Rapids region of Ukraine, amongst others (Alexandersen 1988; Jacobs 1995; Larsson and Zagorska 2006; Telegin and Potekhina 1987) where substantial cemeteries have been studied. In some cases the location of these sites, such as the positioning of Olenii Ostrov on an island, or the location of the Dnieper Rapids cemeteries in places that may have been intended to demarcate ancestral rights of ownership to the rich fish resources at this location, suggest that these sites probably had significance beyond the "simple" functional aspect of burial (Bradley 2000; Lillie 2004).

We should also consider the probability that other landscape features, whilst ephemeral in nature, e.g. paths through the Mesolithic landscape, a sacred rock or a "spiritual" location, could conceivably have been important, or imbued with significance, due to associations with "cult" or ritualised activities. As a consequence, pathways could have been layered with meaning beyond their utilitarian function of getting from A to B (Bradley 2000: 6; Jordan 2003a), and similarly a rock outcrop or "spiritual" place could have been significant despite a total lack of obvious "utilitarian" function. There are even instances in the European Mesolithic where carved anthropomorphic figures suggest that "totem poles" (for want of a better descriptor) may have been used as route way or territorial markers, or alternatively these objects may even represent the ancestors or guardians of special places. The Shigir (or Shigirsky) Idol from the Trans-Urals region near Yekaterinburg (Fig. 6.2), which is dated to 7886–7498 cal BC, i.e. securely within the Early–Middle Mesolithic period, and which has been housed in the Sverdlovsk museum since its discovery in 1890, is an excellent example of such an object. This idol is *ca.* 5.3m in height when reconstructed, and it was carved from a single plank of larch; this fact alone attests an advanced woodworking capability for Mesolithic hunter-fisher-forager peoples at this early date (see also Conneller *et al.* 2012: 1009–10).

As noted by Lillie *et al.* (2005), the anthropomorphic elements that are carved into the Shigirsky idol comprise images of human faces, on both the obverse and reverse surfaces of the plank, with geometric ornament throughout (Fig. 6.2). Only the carved head of the idol has the characteristic oval shape and facial features of human form, with the remaining four representations of faces being formed using raised profiles for the nose and relief for

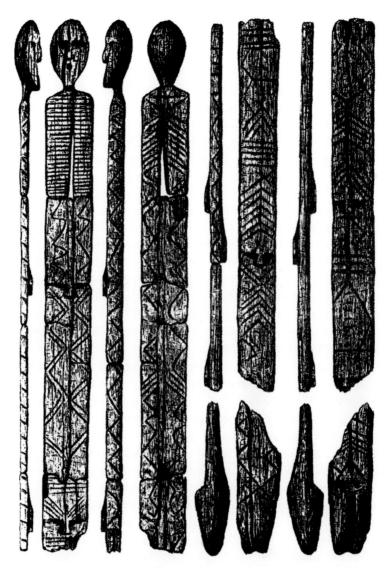

Fig. 6.2: The Shigirsky Idol, central Russia (after Lillie et al. 2005).

the eyebrows. The idol was associated with over 3000 organic finds, all recovered from a peat bog located to the immediate south of the Severnaya Shuraly River, in central Russia, with the Urals to the west (Lillie *et al.* 2005). This idol and the associated finds; which include oars, sculptures of birds and snake figurines, wooden skis, arrow heads and fishing hooks, to name a few examples (for similar examples see Fig. 4.2 above), all further attest the potentially rich, and seldom preserved, nature of the organic part of the archaeological record for the Mesolithic period.

As this example demonstrates, and as has been mentioned elsewhere in this volume, the scarcity of waterlogged burial environments containing Mesolithic cultural remains in Britain severely limits our understanding of this part of the archaeological record for hunter-fisher-foragers in this period. Recently, the discovery of a carved wooden post dating to 6270 years ago, i.e. the later Mesolithic period, has been announced. This post was found during development for a wind farm at Maerdy, Rhondda Cynon Taf; it was discovered in a waterlogged peat deposit, and measured 1.7m in length. It is suggested that this find may have marked a tribal boundary, hunting ground or sacred site. If proven to be anthropogenically modified this would certainly qualify as an exceptional discovery for Wales, and given the constant reference to the need for targeted research into locations with precisely this sort of potential for the preservation of organic remains, this discovery clearly further reinforces the assertions made throughout the text so far.

Whilst the general lack of waterlogged preservation is limiting in relation to similar objects, the investigation of a total of five pits during the development of a car park at Stonehenge (1966 and 1988 work), and the analysis and dating of charcoal deposits from the pits, has led to the suggestion that posts were erected in four of these pits during the Mesolithic period. The environmental evidence indicated that they were located in an area of open, or recently cleared, pine and hazel woodland that was typical of earlier Holocene (Boreal) environments. Furthermore, it has been suggested that these pine posts were *ca.* 3m high, and could possibly have been "totem poles" or some other form of symbolic/ceremonial markers (Allen and Gardiner 2002: 143); it is not inconceivable to suggest that they were perhaps similar in "function" to the Shigirsky idol. Recalibration of the radiocarbon determinations presented in Allen and Gardiner (using IntCal09) produces a range of 8800–6650 cal BC (at 2σ) for the erection of these posts (with the majority of the dates calibrating to before 7000 cal BC), i.e. the earlier part of the Mesolithic period.

Intriguingly, Allen and Gardiner (2002) outline a number of locations in southern England, e.g. Strawberry Hill, Thickthorn Down, Boscombe and Hambledon Hill, where similar evidence of Mesolithic activity can be shown to exist, and where Neolithic monuments subsequently become established. Allen and Gardiner (*ibid.*: 148–9) go so far as to suggest that Mesolithic clearances around such sites may have resulted in long term, or even permanent, impacts on the local vegetation, such that these locations retained a level of difference that marked them out as sites that, in later periods, became imbued with ritual or sacred meaning.

For Wales, the identification and analysis of a series of between five and eight post-holes outside the entrance to the Bryn Celli Du passage tomb on Anglesey is of some significance as this research has produced radiocarbon dates from two of the post-holes that indicate that they are Mesolithic in age (Burrow 2010: 255). The samples used to obtain these dates were from pine, pine bark and charcoal, and they calibrate to 5990–5730 cal BC (UB-68322; 6982±48 uncal BP and UB-6823; 6968±47 uncal BP). As noted by Burrow, these dates pre-date the construction of the Neolithic monument by some 3000 years, and they have no parallels in Wales (2010: 255). However, as the above discussion has hopefully shown, there are a number of sites in England that have similar activity, and these are locations where subsequently "permanent" monuments are constructed. The interpretation of the posts that were placed in these holes is fraught with difficulty, but again, as noted above the possibility that they were "totem poles", or symbolic carvings like the Shigir Idol, cannot be discounted. Similarly, as suggested by Chatterton (2003: 75–6), when using analogies to the evidence from Stellmoor in Germany in order to interpret the material from Star Carr, it is entirely possible that deer skulls were placed on top of stakes driven into the deposits at the edge of the lake at sites like Star Carr. As such, the nature of the totems in use need not simply be carved poles, but they could conceivably relate to rituals and hunting magic. For instance, the Itenm'i of the Kamchatka Peninsula, northeastern Russia, followed each bear kill by venerating the skull, and "venerable wooden figures were placed at important subsistence locales" (Shnirelman 2002: 150). We might even suggest that the posts themselves could have functioned as symbolic trees, and that their placement in cleared habitation areas enabled the continuation of the ritual articulations that would normally be engaged in within the forest setting, thereby linking the wild to the "domesticated" to some degree. Veneration of the spirits of the animals that are processed at the kill- or settlement site may still have been necessary in order to ensure appeasement of the spirits of the forest; thereby guaranteeing continued success in hunting endeavours (see for example the discussion of the Evenki of eastern Eurasia by Anderson (2002); also see Jordan (2003a: 133) for similar observations regarding the Khanty). Beyond the embedded meaning in these features and activities, the fact that certain locations are often the focus of subsequent Neolithic activity suggests that, even if their original significance has been lost over time, these locations may still retain some of the attributes that originally made them important in the Mesolithic period.

Whilst the above examples all offer potential insights into the nature of Mesolithic "mindscapes" (*cf.* Allen and Gardiner 2002), it is perhaps easier, by contrast to explore the identification of more permanent, socially constructed landscape features, such as settlements, dwelling spaces and cemeteries, in order to offer alternative insights into group identity and memory (Zendeño 2008; Bonsall 2008). As might be anticipated, settlements, dwelling spaces and activity foci may be of particular significance in areas where the burial record is lacking. Consequently, as activity areas/features are often more visible for the Mesolithic in Britain, when compared to burial sites, they may (in future research) allow some assessment of the potential landscape routes that were travelled through and experienced (e.g. when modelled in a GIS package), along with providing insights into the construction and maintenance of social and ritual space.

We might anticipate that the identification of settlements, routeways and "persistent places" in the Mesolithic landscape could eventually lead to the recognition of those areas where burial sites could be "anticipated". Furthermore, they may also offer inroads into the nature of the socio-political and ritual aspects of daily life in the Mesolithic. In reality, divorcing (dichotomising) social and ritual spaces is not necessarily a realistic way to approach the past as it is evident that ritual and symbolic behaviour was intertwined in everyday activity, to the point where it may well have been engaged with both consciously and subconsciously at a number of levels. This potential is particularly visible at sites such as Skateholm on the southern Swedish (Baltic) coast and Vedbæk on the Danish Øresund coast (Larsson 1988; Albrethsen and Brinch Petersen 1977), where, at both locations, settlement activity occurred alongside burial activity in the day-to-day articulation of socio-economic and ritual aspects of life for the Mesolithic inhabitants (these are discussed in more detail below). Of course, in this context for Britain we do have some indications of structured/ritualised deposition at sites like Star Carr in England (Pollard 2000), and the Nab Head in Dyfed, southwest Wales (David 1990; 2007; David and Walker 2004) that are not (obviously) linked to any form of burial activity. However, given the extensive evidence at Star Carr for structures such as the substantial "platform" "spanning at least 30m of the lake-edge wetlands" (Conneller *et al.* 2012: 1012), and the dryland structure identified in 2007 and 2008, it seems unlikely that such communal "monumental-scale" structures (*ibid.*: 1016), ritualised activity and the sense of place that these features must have imbued, did not result in the construction of a space for the dead, i.e. a cemetery.

Landscapes and landscape perception

Referring back to the work of Davies *et al.* (2005; discussed in Chapter 2), and considering the nature of the archaeological evidence for humans in the landscape (Chapters 3–5), we can perhaps begin to think about the ways in which Mesolithic people were "static" within, engaged with, and moved through the landscape; with the notion that movement would not necessarily have been random, but prescribed to some degree. Tilley (1994: 202) has suggested that "ancestral connections between living populations and the past were embodied in the 'Being' of the landscape and an emotional attachment to place", with paths being seen as foci for repeated activities linked to a "series of known, named and significant places". However, it is potentially more difficult to determine whether, as suggested by Davies *et al.* (2005: 284), the establishment of paths was dictated by a fear of the unknown, of wild animals or spiritual entities, or whether paths simply functioned purely to avoid getting lost (Mears 2010: 29), or to avoid a range of potential hazards (Fig. 6.3). Again the secular and spiritual are not always easily separated.

Pathways may well have allowed for "safe" movement through a landscape that was populated by various spirits (of the forest or coast, or even the ancestors), gods, or other entities, but paths, once established, also functioned as attractors to people in their daily activities, effectively constraining (or channelling) movement and acting as a focal point against the "wilderness" and "unknown" areas in the landscape. Undoubtedly, a number of these considerations could interlink to make a routeway more (or less) permanent in the Mesolithic landscape/mindscape, and the path/routeways would/could link a range of places with a variety of meanings, from the secular to spiritual or social, economic and political (e.g. Cummings 2000: 88).

Tilley (1994: 203) has asserted that Neolithic monuments "'anchored' place such that the landscape was understood in relation to the setting of monuments", as opposed to the scenario during the Mesolithic, wherein place was understood in relation to the landscape. However, this suggestion might overstress the importance of artificial constructions over

Fig. 6.3: A pathway to the water's edge at Lake Svarzenberk in the Czech Republic; the path was established by the author during fieldwork with Marek Zvelebil in 2010. Broken branches and trampled grasses mark a safe path to the water's edge, avoiding deeper pools in the peaty, terrestrialising lake margin deposits; in this instance the broken branches also avoid an earlier, deep archaeological excavation which is hidden from view by the grasses to the left of the trees on the right side of the picture. This image highlights the ephemeral nature of a pathway that affords safe passage and leads to a freshwater lake margin where a number of resources could be obtained (© author).

landscape features, as "permanence" and "place" cannot (surely) have a more fundamental time depth than in the natural setting of a mountain, a rock outcrop or other landscape feature, e.g. the bare porphyritic cliff of Treskavec which sits opposite the Mesolithic site of Lepenski Vir, on the left bank of the Danube. At Lepenski Vir this landscape feature may well have influenced perceptions of "place" and in the case of settlement architecture it also clearly influenced hut design (these were trapezoidal like the cliff face) at this location during both the Mesolithic and Neolithic, albeit in a context where subsistence strategies remain orientated around fishing and hunting across the two periods (Srejović 1972; Borić 2002: 1037).

Monuments are by definition artificial and constructed, and articulated in the landscape through their positioning in relation to more permanent landscape features (e.g. Tilley 1994). Neolithic monuments only gain "permanence" over time, and through association with place, and to some degree it could even be suggested that chambered tombs are simply substituting for caves in areas where caves are not present? Whilst these structures can obviously become integral landscape features, to suggest that anthropogenic structures have greater resonance in relation to human understanding of landscape than the features of the landscape itself negates the fact that they are additional to, as opposed to replacements of, embedded landscape elements. Whilst there might be some circularity in this argument, this viewpoint perhaps reflects the differences in research perspectives between individuals whose focus is on "farmers" as opposed to those who study hunter-fisher-forager groups, and we could even argue that we might also be seeing elements of the modern urban city-scapes versus rural landscapes dichotomy being applied to the past (i.e. Neolithic = civilised and Mesolithic = wild).

There are of course limitations in our conception of all aspects of Mesolithic (even prehistoric) cosmology and belief systems, let alone something that is as seemingly intangible as paths/routeways through the Mesolithic landscape (Warren 2005: 73). However, as Tilley (1994) has eloquently argued, site location may well have been entwined with both resources and landscape features, with the latter being imbued with symbolic significance through the naming of special places; thereby moving settlement locations beyond purely functional considerations, and by extension, the ways through the landscape may well have been important beyond the simple fact that they facilitated movement. In support of this observation, Cummings (2000: 90) has suggested that people's choice in relation to settlement was "also heavily influenced by ideology and ritual practice", and we can envisage a situation wherein certain routes may have had significant ritual/spiritual significance, whilst others were perhaps more "mundane" in their meaning. Again though it is important to realise that seasonal changes would potentially influence an individual's perception of the routeways that they used, and any path through the landscape could be imbued with meaning due to the "history", memory or meaning that was related to it (Warren 2005), and equally the meanings would not necessarily be universal, or universally acknowledged.

Whilst any number of the above considerations could overtly influence the establishment and continued use of paths between "sites" (i.e. settlements, activity areas, collecting or hunting grounds, ritual or symbolic locations etc.), new paths could be followed or established purely out of curiosity, because of ease of access, a sense of adventure, or simply while tracking an animal through the forest along an established animal migration/foraging route, or even whilst foraging for gathered resources. In the present, we constantly seek "short-cuts" across areas of designated/structured spaces; humans have a tendency towards taking the most expedient path (in most things), and there is nothing more tempting than a "Keep Off The Grass" sign!

In this context a natural clearing (perhaps created by a wind throw) could become a focus of activity as a result of various aesthetical attributes (i.e. an opening in the forest canopy allowing a light airy space to relax in the warmth of the sun and prepare or repair hunting gear, and have a snack or a chat about the plan for the rest of the day's hunting and gathering activities) as opposed to more structured/practical considerations. Ultimately this space may gain currency during later hunting and gathering activities, and subsequently become a focal point along a pathway through a wooded area.

By contrast, the deliberate manipulation of embedded cosmological and/or belief systems by an astute individual or group could serve to disrupt the common ideological code of the group, such that the diversion of a path/routeway away from one particularly significant location towards a setting of divergent symbolic meaning or significance, could serve to re-orientate the group consciousness. Referring back to the present, the "short cuts" that people follow away from designated routeways are often imbued with a "rebellious streak" or a reaction against societies rules, in effect, a disruption of the common ideological, socially constrained, code of the group. If pathways are imbued with symbolic power or meaning, a seemingly "rebellious" or "daring" divergence might initially be seen to be of only limited significance, even amusing, but the shift in the balance of power that is potentially put in place by such actions could conceivably lead to a significant reorientation of the "natural" (socially prescribed) order of the group, if left unchecked.

The possibilities are numerous in all respects; paths, clearings, preferred and constructed social spaces/places, symbolic locations etc. are all embedded in Mesolithic land-use, landscapes and mindscapes. The rationale behind their establishment, continued use/ maintenance and/or abandonment will be dependent upon perceived value in socio-economic, political, ritual, symbolic, practical and even aesthetic terms, and/or even by individual choice. These elements will be considered as we move through the evidence for ritual and its role in everyday life during the Mesolithic period in the pages that follow, but we must again return to the situation that persisted across the Mesolithic, wherein sea levels were rising throughout the earlier part of this period, and many earlier sites could potentially have been located in differing environments or settings to those of the later Mesolithic. This is entirely possible as the hinterland between the coast and the inland/ upland zone would have been of much greater extent in some regions in earlier periods, and subsistence strategies may have differed in their composition across the earlier to later Mesolithic periods as the environmental zones shifted. In this context, we once more need to recall that numerous earlier Mesolithic sites will now be located below modern sea level. Again, our understanding of earlier Mesolithic lifeways is severely limited due to the lack of contemporary lowland/coastal landscapes and the associated settlement, cemetery, activity and ritual/spiritual contexts that would have characterised these environments around the coasts of Wales. It is even possible that the rhythms of daily life were disrupted by changing sea levels and changes in vegetation, as the discussion in Chapter 4 has suggested, perhaps to the extent that movement through the landscape could have been curtailed by significant periods of both marine and freshwater transgressions.

As noted by Cummings (2000: 91) many sites were clearly located in relation to available resources, e.g. at the coast, whilst also most likely having a range of other "meanings", but, the specific meaning and the rationale for repeated visits to certain locations is difficult to assess, even with reference to the ethnographic record. These difficulties are clearly compounded by the fact that certain "coastal" locations in the present will potentially have been some distance from the coast in the earlier part of the Mesolithic period, and vistas would have changed as we moved through the Mesolithic, with a "dense" forest canopy influencing landscape perception into the later Mesolithic, especially as the forest canopy expanded to higher altitudes as the climate ameliorated. The meaning imbued in space and place during the Mesolithic will undoubtedly have changed over time, both as landscapes changed, but also as group ideology changed.

The fact is that locations "similar" to those embedded in the Khanty spiritual world (Jordan 2003a; 2003b) would most likely have existed within Mesolithic landscapes in Britain. Whilst in many cases their precise identification may be difficult to determine in the present, the acknowledgment that such special places existed should allow modern researchers the opportunity to recognise the potential for such locations and perhaps even allow us to begin to predict where they would/could have occurred in the past. This is made more viable when the mapping of site locations provides insights into significant and possibly ritually meaningful landscape characteristics; for instance as the colourful rock outcrops of the west Welsh coast at locations such as Cwm Bach, the Nab Head, Porth y Rhaw and Swanlake, (as discussed by Cummings 2000: 92), might imply.

This suggestion has considerable resonance to the situation pertaining at Lepenski Vir in the Danube region, as mentioned above, where Srejovi (1972: 33–4) notes that "the spot chosen for building the settlement was clearly the most suitable in the area; on the southern and northern sides it was bordered by low crests of dark red porphyry", and "above Lepenski Vir itself, sediments formed during the Jurassic and Calcareous period are exposed: grey-green sandstone, reddish limestone and bluish-grey marl" and a little further on "the waters have laid bare Palaeozoic schists, granite, serpentine and gabbro, as well as Permian formations of porphyrite and red sandstone". Finally, Srejović states that "when the water level is low, the Danube leaves behind on the bank a brilliant polychromatic mosaic of ores and minerals brought down by the swift flowing tributaries from the mountainous hinterland" (*ibid*.: 34). The descriptions of the landscape setting of one of the most iconic Mesolithic hunter-fisher-forager settlements in Europe has clear resonance to the hypothesised significance of rock outcrops as alluded to by the work of Cummings (2000). These observations may well help to further facilitate a more nuanced approach to landscape setting and settlement context in the British Mesolithic.

Furthermore the use of ethnography, and examples such as Jordan's insights into the Khanty's complex landscape interactions in relation to the spirit world (outlined above), allows us the potential to be more "open" to the recognition of locations that could have been sacred in the past, i.e. beyond the sites that we currently recognise through the archaeological record. This example from Jordan's research touches on only one or two aspects of Khanty ritual life, but in doing so it highlights the myriad possibilities that may be inherent in Mesolithic cosmology and ideological structuring principles. A word of caution is probably warranted at this point (although this has been raised previously); we must always remain mindful of the fact that, when discussing the archaeological use of ethnographic data at the "Man the Hunter" conference in 1968, Lewis Binford emphasised the limitations of *both* disciplines, and in particular the lack of time depth afforded by ethnography, and also the fact that the use of ethnographic examples by archaeologists to develop explanatory postulates "must be undertaken with caution" (Binford 2009: 268).

Landscapes of the living – landscapes of the dead

It is particularly unfortunate that, at present, we have relatively little evidence for the treatment of the dead in Britain during the Mesolithic, as one other interesting aspect of Jordan's research is his treatment of Khanty belief systems in relation to the dead. The Khanty believe that in addition to sacred settlements, cemeteries themselves represent settlements of the dead as the souls of the deceased are believed to live on after death (Jordan 2003b: 32; see also Parker Pearson 1993: 204). Interestingly, pathways are important in relation to remembrance feasts that are held at the cemeteries, as after honouring the dead the Khanty symbolically close the path that was used to access the cemetery with felled saplings, in order to ensure that any unsettled souls do not wander into the community of the living at night (Jordan 2003b). As saplings would represent new life and the living world, presumably their placement across the pathway would act as a barrier to the movement of spirits and entities from the land of the dead into the land of the living, thus the liminal zone is symbolically "closed off".

The above example suggests that during the Mesolithic period it is entirely feasible to suppose that the movement of the living between cemetery areas or primary burial contexts could have incorporated a range of taboos and/or rituals. Similar meaning may have been enacted in relation to the appeasement of the ancestors, with the placement of the dead in cemeteries engendering a sense of belonging, stability and identity for the living (and possibly the dead), whilst also potentially allowing avoidance of conflict between the world of the living and that of the dead.

Ethnography clearly indicates that our perception of Mesolithic human–landscape interactions, especially the ritualised articulations that were most likely enacted during the daily round, needs to be approached from the perspective that, as our own choices in the present have multiple influences, so too did those of people in the Mesolithic. In the present day many "superstitions" have a practical element, e.g. walking under ladders can result in an individual being injured if a workman drops his tin of paint or tools, and as such the idea that it is unlucky to walk under a ladder has an obvious practical connotation; admittedly other superstitions are less easy to resolve but in general it appears that taboos (or superstitions) will often have practical as well as ritual undertones.

We obviously need to acknowledge that the formation of landscape is potentially (or very likely) a complex process, or set of processes, which intertwine with natural and socially structured principles (see for example Zendeño 2008). These processes have a beginning, a history of use, whether as a single event (of varying duration) or as multiple/repeat episodic activity, and an end; the processes are cumulative, varied and often socially mediated. Whilst this may be more tangible in subsequent periods of prehistory, there is little doubt that it applies to the Mesolithic period, as is evident at sites such as Thatcham in Berkshire, Star Carr in Yorkshire and the Nab Head in Pembrokeshire. All we need to do is to identify the factors that would have served to create Mesolithic landscapes and/or mindscapes in the archaeological record of hunter-fisher-foragers (Zvelebil 2003; 2008). Unfortunately, "All we need to do" is an ambitious task, for as noted by Jordan (2003b: 27), there has been relatively little research into the ways in which hunter-fisher-foragers either venerated or transformed their landscape.

Given the inherent difficulties outlined above, it is perhaps prudent for archaeologists who study the Mesolithic to continue to make use of ethnographic analogy when attempting to illustrate the arenas of past ideology, cosmology and symbolic constructs, irrespective of the inherent limitations that exist. This is especially pertinent as Zvelebil (2008: 42) suggests that ideology "must have been fundamental in specifying the nature of social relations ... and in encoding subsistence strategies with social meaning".

In relation to the socially structured aspects of Mesolithic landscape interactions, as early as 1990 Lars Larsson highlighted both the exceptional preservation conditions that occur in southern Scandinavia and the potential that this preservation had in informing our understanding of social practice and landscape interactions in this period (Larsson 1990b). This preservation is particularly important due to the wealth of sites and finds in evidence, and also due to the frequency of lakes in the post-glacial period in Scandinavia, which produced an environment that was particularly attractive to hunter-fisher-foragers. As has been noted above in the discussion of the Volga Basin sites excavated by Mikhail Zhilin, the combination of locations and resources that were attractive for settlement, and the specific environmental context of sites that were located on the margins of infilling lakes, riparian, estuarine or coastal zones, produces a situation wherein preservation of organic remains is particularly rich and where this preservation enhances and compliments the information that is generated from "dryland" locations. Finds of sites in these "watery" or waterlogged contexts are currently lacking for Wales in general, and elsewhere in Britain the general paucity of sites with an organic component clearly highlights a need for targeted and well thought out research agendas.

This is emphasised by the fact that at earlier Mesolithic sites like Ulkestrup and Duvensee 13 in Scandinavia, both located inland from the coast, the enhanced organic preservation afforded by waterlogged burial conditions has produced material culture evidence that includes the wall posts and the bark floors of hut structures, along with preservation of bone, antler and wooden artefacts (Larsson 1990b: 276). The distribution of hearths and clusters of artefacts also provide an indication of the spatial structuring of social (and ritual?) spaces within these dwellings. However, despite this wealth of evidence at inland locations, it is perhaps the later Mesolithic coastal sites that provide the most important insights into the ritual aspects of Mesolithic lifeways in southern Scandinavia (Larsson 2004).

At a number of Scandinavian coastal sites we have evidence for the waste material (middens) that was dumped along the shore, we also have dugout canoes (up to 10m in length) that were grounded on the beach, fish traps that were constructed near settlements, and pits, houses and hearths that are found on the contemporary beach, with graves being located above these (Larsson 1990b: 279–80). At Tågerup the evidence indicates that burials were located close to the dwelling areas and in some cases these were even placed inside the houses (Karsten 2004: 108). Along with the cemeteries (discussed below), Larsson has reported that structures used for ritual purposes, and assemblages of material for "special" activities, are in evidence (1990b: 280; 2000: 91). Since 1975 cemeteries such as Bøgebakken on the eastern coast of Zealand, and the three adjacent cemeteries at Skateholm in southern Scania, have all confirmed the association of cemeteries to settlement sites during the Ertebølle period. In this context cemeteries are defined as discrete areas that are set aside purely for the interment of the dead in defined grave contexts (see Meiklejohn *et al.* 2009; Meiklejohn and Babb 2009). The evidence indicates that a considerable degree of heterogeneity occurs in relation to burial and the orientation of the dead during the Mesolithic period in Scandinavia, with cremations also occurring at this time.

During this period numerous artefact associations occur in burials throughout Europe, with deer and fish tooth necklaces, bracelets and decorations on clothing and other items, such as amber and shell objects, lithics and other stone and bone objects all attested in the rich artefact inventories that accompanied burials (e.g. Larsson 1990b; 2004; Zagorska and Larsson 1994; Lillie 1998; Midgley 2005). The inclusion of ochre (possibly representative of fire for the afterlife, or rebirth), reinforces the suggestion that hunter-fisher-foragers did not see death as the final stage in an individual's "existence". In addition, dog burials have been found with associated grave goods in Scandinavian cemeteries (Larsson 1990b: 284–5), perhaps reflecting the perceived social significance of these animals during the Mesolithic period; this probably relates to the fact that dogs would have acted as guardians of the camp, hunting assistants, companions, and in lean times they would have been an easy to procure food resource (and source for furs and bone for tool production etc.).

At Skateholm the interment of eight dogs (Larsson 2000: 90–2) appears to allow insights into "stratification" in relation to the significance of the animals that were interred, as an individually interred dog at Skateholm II had grave goods that included a red deer antler laid along the spine and three flint blades in the hip region. These artefacts were placed with the same structuring principles as are found in male burials, and a decorated antler hammer was also placed at the chest of the dog; this latter object is unique in terms of grave goods at Skateholm (*ibid.*: 91). Dogs also had red ochre in their burials in the same way that humans did. The structuring principles in evidence would certainly appear to suggest some form of significance, however, Fahlander (2008) has questioned the suggested meanings, and the observations (by a number of researchers) that dog burials may represent substitutions for human bodies lost at sea, symbolic representations of shape-shifters or shamans, or symbolic watchdogs. Instead, Fahlander has suggested that dogs were potentially simply "dear members of the household" and were buried as low status individuals (2008: 36), although the Stakeholm II example would not appear to represent a low status interment. Whatever the meanings embedded in these burials, it is clear that a substantial investment is made in recognising the loss of these animals.

Of considerable interest in burial ritual during the Mesolithic period is the occurrence of human body parts that appear to have been kept in dwellings following the deliberate dismemberment of the individual, as indicated by the burials at Skateholm (*ibid.*: 285), and Ageröd I: HC (Larsson *et al.* 1981). A similar situation occurs in southern Belgium, where Cauwe (2001) has assessed the nature of collective burial in the caves of Grotte Margaux and Abri des Autours in the Meuse Valley. At these sites secondary burial appear to have been practiced, and skeletal elements are missing from the interments. Interestingly, it is suggested that only adult females, *ca.* ten or 11 individuals, were interred at Grotte Margaux, whilst at the Abri des Autours a single inhumation of a woman and a collective burial of at least five adults (both males and females) and six children (aged between 2 and >15 years) are reported. The suggested removal of body parts and differential treatment of the dead indicates that the funerary rituals that were being employed were both "systematic and complex" (Cauwe 2001: 157).

The structured deposition and removal of skeletal elements occurring in the Mesolithic throughout Europe has resonance with Neolithic activity in both Scandinavia and Britain (Whittle 2009: 91), and may reflect a long tradition of ritual structuring related to the ancestors, that evidently has its origins in the Mesolithic period. The identification of secondary burial and the discrete emplacement of skeletal elements have also been suggested as being a characteristic of British Mesolithic mortuary practices (Conneller 2009: 690). The rationale behind the movement of skeletal elements between primary and secondary sites of interment may relate to factors such as a desire to keep the ancestors included in the daily lives of the inhabitants at a particular site, furthermore, the ancestors may also instil a sense of "place" or "belonging", and their integration may also have served to prevent the angering of the ancestors. Fahlander (2008: 38) hypothesises that other interpretations can be suggested e.g. "an act of aggression towards the previously dead" or an act intended to ensure that the "dead individual is refused serenity in the afterlife because the grave has been destroyed or the bodily remains have been disturbed".

This observation resonates with earlier research into the nature and evidence for interpersonal violence in the Dnieper Rapids region of Ukraine (Lillie 2004), where a number of interments in the earlier Mesolithic (or Epipalaeolithic) cemeteries of Voloshkoe and Vasilyevka I and III have evidence for the removal of body parts prior to interment. At Voloshkoe, individual 5 appears to have had his hands cut off prior to interment, whilst individual 16 at this cemetery appeared to be disarticulated, and to have had the right hand and adjoining long bones cut off prior to burial. A third individual (number 15) had the hands and both legs below the knee missing (Lillie 2004: 91, *citing* Danilenko 1955). Balakin and Nuzhinyi (1995) have suggested that this sort of "ritual" dismemberment may be interpreted as an attempt to inhibit the passage of the deceased into the afterlife, although an obvious additional possibility is that this sort of "aggression" may also serve to prevent the interred individuals from hunting in the afterlife, thereby effectively "killing" them twice.

In Sweden, 87 of the graves dating to the Mesolithic period have been recovered from Skateholm I (65 graves) and II, which are dated to the early part of the Ertebølle culture at *ca.* 5600–4800 cal BC (Karsten 2004: 130); by contrast only two graves have been securely dated to the earlier Kongemose culture (*ibid.*: 108). Within these cemeteries both cremation and inhumation burials are in evidence, and there are also the dog burials mentioned above. In some examples there is evidence to suggest that the graves were reopened, after an indeterminate period of time, and that body parts or skeletal elements were being removed, and/or that new bodies were being buried (*ibid.*: 130; see also Nilsson Stutz 2010: 38 and discussion below). It has been suggested that in order for the graves to have been accessible in this way, some sort of grave marker, made of stone or earth, a wooden platform or even a "totem" pole (see discussions above), may have been used (Karsten 2004), and that these markers were probably used in both the Kongemose (Early Mesolithic) and Ertebølle (later Mesolithic) periods.

Recent studies undertaken by Liv Nilsson Stutz, using the anthropologie "de terrain" approach (Duday 2006) to understand burial context (combining knowledge of decomposition processes with detailed field observations based on physical, anthropological and archaeological knowledge), have significantly enhanced our interpretations of Mesolithic burial practices (e.g. Nilsson 1998; Nilsson Stutz 2003; 2009; 2010), particularly in terms of the ways in which the dead individual can inform us about fundamental cultural and social concerns, the control of which is imposed on the cadaver by the survivors (Nilsson Stutz 2010: 33 and 35). An important set of observations made by Nilsson Stutz are that: "the ritual redefinition of the dead body, which often involves an idea of separation between the physical remains and the spirit, soul, or memory of the dead, allows the mourners to separate from the dead, and at the same time, structure an acceptance of death" (2010: 35); to paraphrase Nilsson Stutz further, the rituals surrounding death and burial are effectively a way for the living to *cope with cadavers* (2009: 657).

Nilsson Stutz's research at Skateholm (Southern Sweden), Vedbæk/Bøgebakken (Eastern Denmark) and Zvejnieki (Northern Latvia) has approached the burials from the perspective of the ritualised practices that relate to the treatment of the corpse. In these treatments Nilsson Stutz sees mortuary ritual as a means of "renegotiation" of the corpse through the liminal phase between "being alive" and "being dead" or "the redefinition of the cadaver from abject into an object of death" (2009: 658). In her analysis of the burial practices at Skateholm and Vedbæk/Bøgebakken Nilsson Stutz has noted that individual primary burial, placed on the back and with limbs extended, dominated (although greater variability in positioning occurred at both Skateholm I and II), and burial goods and/or ochre were often included in the grave. In addition to this Nilsson Stutz was also able to establish that, in a couple of instances, the individual was placed on a wooden platform, or wrapped in a softer material (possibly hide or bark) (*ibid.*: 659; 2003), and that the graves were immediately filled.

Similarities also occur between Stateholm and Zvejnieki in that primary burials with similar positioning of the dead are in evidence (Nilsson Stutz 2010: 37–8). The repetition in burial practices, or lack of variation thus facilitated the creation of "a normative conception of death and image of the dead" (Nilsson Stutz 2009: 659). Contradictions to the norm are seen in the cremation that occurs at Skateholm; individuals at Skateholm II being interred in a seated position (individuals II, VIII, Xb, XV and XXII) (Nilsson 1998: 11); the processing of the cadaver in Grave 13 at Skateholm I; or the removal of a fresh cadaver from grave 11 at Vedbæk/Bøgebakken (Nilsson Stutz 2009: 661; 2010: 37). Interestingly, it appears that whilst the cadaver is treated with considerable care, once skeletonised the integrity of the remains is not considered significant in relation to the negotiated rituals that pertained at the time of interment (Nilsson Stutz 2010: 37).

The deliberate removal of human skeletal elements at Skateholm is interpreted by Lars Larsson as indicating that the deceased had a symbolic function, even if only in partial form, in the land of the living (Larsson 2000: 87), and Nilsson Stutz (2010: 38) suggests that "perhaps we see a precursor here of the extensive manipulation of human remains that we have come to expect during the practices of periods to follow in the region, including the Neolithic Funnel Beaker culture". This latter observation links back to earlier discussions about the meaning of the skeletal elements found at midden sites in British contexts, where the inclusion of smaller elements or fragmentary skeletal material may represent a symbolic act of inclusion (of the spirits of the ancestors) in daily life, and wherein the ancestors may also be granting similar rights of access at such locations to those that were conferred at the more permanent cemetery sites. If this is a realistic interpretation of the evidence we can probably extend the data from the British middens to suggest that cemeteries, or formal disposal areas, which may well have been marked in a similar manner to the Scandinavian burials, must have existed in order for Mesolithic people to obtain the skeletal elements of their ancestors for inclusion in these (e.g. midden) contexts.

Further insights into the ritual treatment of the dead and the processing of the body are highlighted by the work of Toussaint (2011) who has analysing the material for the Margaux Cave in Belgium (discussed above). This site has produced the remains of 7–10 adult females, with one skull (CR3) having evidence for cutmarks. These marks were recorded on both zygomatic processes, the frontal squama, along the two coronal sutures and on the left part of the posterior cranium (Toussaint 2011: 100). The cutmarks have been interpreted as representing the removal of the mandible and the scalp as part of the mortuary ritual, i.e. processing of the dead. The patterning of the cutmarks on the cranial vault suggest that the scalp was divided into three segments for removal peri-mortem (occurring at a point after death), whilst the marks on the zygomatic processes and the inferior edge of the mandibular fossa relate to the removal of the mandible (*ibid.*: 103). Toussant notes that this evidence is unique in a European Mesolithic context, and that the evidence indicates that these activities were related to some form of funerary practice (*ibid.*: 106).

As the above discussion has suggested, ritual articulations, ritual space and the construction of the landscape can be complex and mediated to a considerable degree by the "social and symbolic dimensions of the material culture and inhabited space", such that "a complex hierarchical network of sacred sites" may occur in a groups territory (Jordan 2003b: 28). The evidence from Britain will be considered below, and whilst the evidence from Wales forms the backdrop to the discussion, the paucity of skeletal material from Wales necessitates a wider reading of the literature in order to illustrate the potential of human skeletal remains to inform us about Mesolithic lifeways and the treatment of the dead. The wider context is considered out of necessity, for as noted by Conneller (2009: 690), there are only 18 locations in Britain that have produced human remains for the

Mesolithic period, and in Wales only Daylight Rock, Potter's Cave and Ogof-yr-Ychen on Caldey, Paviland (Goat's Hole) and Worm's Head, Gower, and Pontnewydd, Clwyd, have produced evidence for human remains of Mesolithic date. In addition to these sites, Foxhole Cave, Paviland, also has material that has been dated to the Mesolithic period (Meiklejohn *et al.* 2011), whilst Nanna's Cave and Ogof-yr-Benlog remain to be dated in absolute terms (Schulting and Richards 2000, Schutling 2009) (see Table 5.2).

Life, death and burial

Approaches to burial in the Mesolithic throughout Europe vary considerably, and include both multiple and single inhumations and cremations, burials in caves, rock shelters and open air cemeteries, ossuaries and skull nests, variability in terms of the completeness of the burials, the placement of skeletal elements in middens and on settlement sites, and in addition, variations in the age range of the individuals interred at these sites (Ahlström 2003; Brinch Petersen and Meiklejohn 2003; Larsson *et al.* 1981; Lillie 1998; 2008; Meiklejohn 2009; Meiklejohn and Babb 2009; Meiklejohn *et al.* 2009; 2011; Nilsson Stutz 2003; Schulting 2003; Toussaint 2011). It is clear from the literature that varying approaches to, and the manipulation of, human remains is a recurrent aspect of mortuary rituals throughout Mesolithic Europe, and these traditions clearly continue into the subsequent Neolithic period (Whittle 2009).

Unlike the extensive record that exists in parts of Europe, both for Mesolithic cemeteries and individual burials, the examples of "burials" in Britain are rare, fragmentary and difficult to interpret (*cf.* Conneller 2009). Indeed, Meiklejohn *et al.* (2009: 646–9) listed only four British sites; Aveline's Hole, Gough's (new) Cave and Totty Pot, Somerset and Ogof-yr-Ychen in Wales, out of 118 European burial sites, in their assessment of chronology in Mesolithic burial practices (stray finds were excluded from this study). Further issues exist, as noted by Warren (2007), in that even contexts that were thought to provide relatively secure associations, i.e. the Scottish midden (rubbish tip) sites, are now in need of reconsideration in light of new dating and the lack of other burial locations with which to contextualise the material in the middens. However, as noted by Pollard (2011: 389), there are examples of single bones or groups of bone apparently deliberately placed in Mesolithic midden environments at Ferriter's Cove, Rockmarshall, and Killuragh Cave in Ireland, that mirror the practices seen in Scotland. As such, there may be some potential for a comparative study of these locations i.e. between the sites in Scotland and Ireland.

In general, with the inclusion of Greylake, we currently have evidence for cave burials, cemeteries, and middens in the British record, along with fragmentary remains, and it can surely only be a matter of time before we locate further burial contexts, including cremations and individual burials, as well as more cemeteries, that are dated to the Mesolithic period, as the Tilbury and Staythorpe examples (discussed above) might suggest.

Whilst we will return to the midden sites at the end of this section it is perhaps more fruitful to first consider the other lines of evidence that we have for burial in British contexts during the Mesolithic. Returning directly to Wales, there is limited evidence for human remains available from the cave sites that we discussed in Chapters 1 and 2. In this context Richards (2000: 75), reporting on the isotope analysis of human remains from Paviland and Foxhole Caves, has shown that the evidence from Foxhole Cave, which is dated to 5730–5560 cal BC, is only represented by a single dated human tooth, which has isotope values that do not indicate any significant contribution of marine protein to the diet ($\delta^{13}C$ of –20‰ and $\delta^{15}N$ of 11.3‰). This is important as variation in diet suggests (perhaps unsurprisingly given the evidence from elsewhere in Europe) that both inland and coastal locations were exploited during the Mesolithic period in Wales, and as such we should anticipate the potential for the recovery of burials in contexts at inland locations. Some caution is warranted with the results from Foxhole though as Richards (2000) notes that this analysis was undertaken on an adult canine, a tooth that forms during childhood, and as such the evidence for diet could conceivably be a "false" or residual childhood dietary signature as opposed to the actual diet consumed in adulthood.

Irrespective of this observation, the fact that terrestrial as opposed to marine diets are indicated still suggests that there is the potential for residence sites, and associated burial locations, in contexts away from the coast. The problem highlighted by this example is that even where we have "some" (admittedly extremely limited) human skeletal remains to study, the elements available are not always "fit for purpose", and even where direct dating and stable isotope analysis is undertaken, the degree of completeness and the skeletal element represented, all influence the level of information that can be generated. As noted in Chapter 5, stable isotope analysis of human bone collagen is only significant in relation to the protein component of the diet in the last *ca.* 10 years of an individual's life, and it does not indicate the nature of the carbohydrates and lipids that were consumed (Schulting and Richards 2000). So, ultimately, it is apparent that we need to develop a research agenda for Britain that is designed to identify optimum locations for settlement and burial, and perhaps consider the fact that previous excavation strategies have resulted in only the partial analysis of sites such as the Nab Head and Thatcham, and that a number of sites warrant reinvestigation, particularly where such an approach is viable (as is the case at Star Carr).

For Mesolithic Britain in general, Jacobi (1987: 165–6) noted that the only "formal disposal area" for human remains occurs at Aveline's Hole, Burrington Combe, on the north side of Mendip, where in 1805, nearly 50 "perfectly preserved" skeletons were reported as lying parallel to each other (the site was originally discovered in 1797); this observation has obviously been modified with the recent work at Greylake (discussed above). The dates for the Aveline's Hole burials match those for "Cheddar Man", an isolated inhumation of a male in the vestibule of Gough's Cave (*ibid.*: 166; Fig. 6.1 above). Recent re-analysis of the surviving human remains from Aveline's Hole (Schulting and Wysocki 2002; Schulting 2005), has shown that the partial remains of at least 21 individuals survived a bombing raid on Bristol in World War II, making this the only surviving material from this location. The preserved skeletal remains comprise material from adult males and females along with the remains of a number of children and infants. AMS and conventional radiocarbon dating of five individuals from Aveline's Hole have shown this site to be early Mesolithic in age. The dates cluster around 9000 uncal BP, calibrated to 8460–8140 cal BC, and Schulting

(2005: 171) suggests that activity at this site may have been concentrated within a period of only 70–180 years (i.e. 2–3 or up to 7 or 8 generations). Schulting and Wysocki (2002: 258) report that at least 15, and probably 16, adults of both sexes are currently attested, although in the subsequent (2005) paper (p. 192) Schulting adds "or adolescents" after adults, i.e. individuals that are not yet classed as adult in terms of their skeletal development; the estimate is based on proximal left ulnae. The probable number of males and females as calculated by Schulting (*ibid.*: 196) is five males and six or seven females. In addition, three children aged *ca.* 2.5–4.5, 3.5–6.5 and 5.7 years respectively, an infant aged 6–18 months and an at or near term (i.e. neonatal or perinatal) infant are represented (*ibid.*: 193).

Whilst the evidence for pathology on this population is limited, due to the extremely fragmented nature of the remains, Schulting and Wysocki (2002) report the presence of *cribra orbitalia*, an indicator of iron deficiency anaemia, and a non-specific indicator of disease or nutritional stress (Angel 1966; Mensforth 1991), on two individuals. *Cribra orbitalia* was originally thought to reflect iron deficiency caused by reduced nutritional status, although Stuart-Macadam (1992) hypothesised that hypoferremia is in fact an adaptation to disease and micro-organism invasion (elevated pathogen load), and that diet plays a relatively minor role in the development of this pathology. Other indicators of *stress* in this population include the presence of linear enamel hypoplasias, which are developmental defects of the enamel, in evidence on a number of anterior teeth. Hypoplasias are "non-specific indicators of metabolic and nutritional disruption" that occur during childhood (Goodman *et al.* 1987: 8), and they are often associated with a wide variety of childhood diseases including, but by no means limited to, hypoparathyroidism, vitamin A and vitamin D deficiency, fever, maternal diabetes, neonatal asphyxia and jaundice, nephrotic syndrome, and gastro-enteritis (Goodman *et al.* 1984: 259). Hypoplasias are a relatively common dental pathology throughout prehistory and there is a recurring theme suggested, in that the shift from breast feeding to the "adult" diet as the child is weaned is considered to be implicated in hypoplasia development due to the nutrient deficiencies that occur in the new diet. The data from Aveline's Hole appears to suggest that recurrent stress episodes are occurring at less than a yearly interval between the ages of 3–4 and 6 years (Schulting 2005: 205). The consistent evidence for stressors might relate to weaning, but could also relate to seasonal variability in the availability of resources as the accuracy in relation to timing of the insult is such that the less than yearly interval suggested could possibly be indicating a seasonal disorder (*ibid.*: 205). As such, despite the inherent problems associated with such a fragmentary assemblage, the information that has been generated does provide some significant insights into earlier Mesolithic populations in Britain. One final point of note in relation to the analysis of the dentitions at Aveline's Hole relates to the analysis of dental microwear, undertaken by McLaughlin (2005: 218), who suggests that this analysis indicates wear caused by plant phytoliths, and therefore (perhaps unsurprisingly) plant consumption.

In general, palaeopathological evidence for inter-personal violence occurs in the burial record throughout Europe, and there is an increasing corpus of evidence for violent interactions/conflict during the Mesolithic. However, Thorpe (2003: 153) has noted that there is a lack of direct (skeletal) evidence for violence in the archaeological record from the Near East and the Mediterranean, although sample size may be an issue for central and eastern Mediterranean areas. By contrast, despite some 400 burials from the western Mediterranean region, only two secure examples of violence are in evidence (it should be noted that an arrow in the foot at Moita de Sebastião could conceivably be an embarrassing hunting accident! thus leaving only one example?). In the Danube region Thorpe (*ibid.*: 155) reports that about one third of the burials at the site of Schela Cladovei had either projectile injuries or unhealed cranial trauma, and at Vlasac, injuries from projectile points also occur, but the numbers are in fact quite small in reality as *ca.* 400 individuals are in evidence, but only eight have injuries from projectiles, and ten have cranial trauma in evidence (Chapman 1999: 105).

Earlier evidence for inter-personal violence, including injuries caused by projectile points (arrowheads) has been recorded from three of the main cemeteries in the Dnieper Rapids region of Ukraine (Konduktorova 1974; Nuzhnyi 1989; 1990; Lillie 2004). The sites of Voloshkoe (19 interments), Vasilyevka III (a minimum of 44 interments as the central part of the cemetery was cut by a later ravine) and Vasilyevka I (26 burials including three double burials and one burial of the lower half of a skeleton), all located on the rapids, have produced 12 individuals with evidence for inter-personal violence. This evidence includes three individuals at Voloshkoe with projectile points embedded in the skeleton (Lillie 2004: 90–1), five at Vasilyevka III with arrowheads (and spearpoints) embedded in the skeleton and one individual with arrowheads in association (*ibid.*: 92-4). The fact that an arrowhead could produce a fatal injury without actually embedding itself into the skeleton, as suggested by the slotted bone points in association with a female aged 20–25 at Vasilyevka III, should not be overlooked as arrowheads may well be included with the interment (in the soft tissue) and become dislodged during the decomposition of the cadaver, with the result that the arrowhead/projectile point could be misinterpreted as a grave good.

At Vasilyevka I only two individuals have evidence for violence, but in the case of individual 17, an adult male, this evidence comprises four projectile weapon injuries, i.e. this adult male was shot four times by arrows. There can little doubt that this was a deliberate act of violence, as opposed to a hunting accident, but even with this level of insult, we cannot rule out the possibility that such "overkill" is evidence for ritualised killing as opposed to conflict. Of considerable significance in relation to the violence to the person that occurs at these three cemeteries is the fact that many of these individuals were shot using bow and arrows, these cemeteries date to *ca.* 10,400–9200 cal BC on the basis of the dates from Vasilyevka III, and whilst sex determinations are not available for the burials at Voloshkoe and Vasilyevka I (Dolukhanov reports that Vasilyevka I comprised only mature males (1999: 79–80)), at Vasilyekka III, three of the five individuals with impact damage from arrows are females aged 18–25, and two of these are actually at the lower end of this range at 18–22 years of age at death (Lillie 1998; 2004).

The fact that females are included in violent interactions is perhaps unsurprising given the composition of hunter-fisher-forager groups during the Mesolithic, but at the Dnieper Rapids cemeteries the suggested competition for the rich fish resources at the Rapids is

Fig. 6.4: Gøngehusvej 7, Vedbæk, burial of 40-year-old female and 3-year-old child. As can be seen from the image, the burial included ochre, and there are two bone pins on the left side of the adult's chest, resting on the ribs and with the points beneath the distal end of the left humerus (© Lennart Larsen, Nationalmuseet Arbejdsmark, Denmark, used with permission).

clearly leading to all portions of society being subjected to violent interactions at this early date. This may reflect inter-group competition for access to the resources at this particular location.

Similarly, as noted above, in Scandinavia, Larsson (2000: 86) has discussed the excavations from Skateholm, in Scania, and Bøgebakken in eastern Denmark, suggesting that in part the cemeteries must be considered as territorial markers (as suggested for the Dnieper Rapids cemeteries above), wherein the ancestors facilitated a claim to "ownership" and "rights of access" to the regions resources. Whilst a considerable range of ritual activity is involved in the burials at Skateholm, including patterning in the grave goods and the positioning of the dead, there is also possible evidence for a last meal as indicated by fish bones in the area of the stomach of one individual, and the inclusion of skeletal parts from animals such as marten, red deer and roe deer, perhaps as food for the journey into the afterlife (*ibid.*: 87). Again, the lack of similar sites in Britain severely limits our attempts at developing nuanced perspectives in relation to social and ritual practice in the Mesolithic period, but we should not ignore the possibility that faunal remains, that are proven to be of Mesolithic date, could well have been food for the dead, and not just rubbish.

At Gøngehusvej 7, Vedbæk, a cemetery was excavated which again included a combination of cremation and inhumation burial. The burials included graves for children with evidence to indicate that they had been interred laid on a wooden "tray" perhaps similar to the interments at Skateholm, as discussed by Nilsson Stutz

(2009). In addition, a well preserved inhumation burial of a 40-year-old woman and a 3-year-old child is in evidence (Larsson 2000; Figs 6.4 and 6.5). Red ochre was spread over the woman and child, and they had a number of amulets in association, comprising beads made from the teeth of red and roe deer, wild boar, elk, bear and aurochs. The child had two flint knives in association; one (of light grey flint) can be clearly seen resting in the area of the right hip (Fig. 6.4), whilst a second, black coloured knife is visible near the head (Fig. 6.5).

The female had two bone netting needles placed on her chest, and foot bones from roe deer hooves in association. These are interpreted as coming from an animal skin that

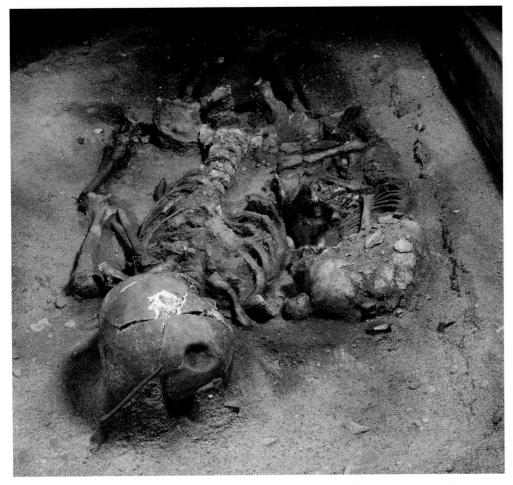

Fig. 6.5: Gøngehusvej 7, Vedbæk, view of the head of the adult female showing blunt impact injury on the rear of the vault, on the parietal. The bone hairpin is clearly visible to the left of the vault, and red ochre staining occurs at the head of the child as well as the adult (© Lennart Larsen, Nationalmuseet Arbejdsmark, Denmark; used with permission).

had been wrapped around her body for the burial (again highlighting the sort of organic information that is lost in "dryland" contexts when compared to the preservation potential from wet/waterlogged sites). A bone hairpin and a grebe bill were found near her head, and it has consequently been suggested that she may have worn a cap of bird skin, and that the bill is again the only element preserved. As can be seen from Figure 6.5, the wearing of a cap would have served to conceal the cranial trauma that this individual had clearly experienced during her life (Thorpe 2003: 156). This blunt instrument trauma could have resulted from interpersonal violence linked to conflict, but it could equally be the result of inter-personal violence between partners or even siblings.

In addition to Gøngehusvej 7, Vedbæk, there are a number of other instances of violent interactions recorded throughout Europe, e.g. at Téviec in Brittany, Stellmoor in Germany, Tybrind Vig on Fyn and Møllegabet II on Ærø (Thorpe 2003, and references therein). Of course the scale of the interpersonal violence that is attested by these examples is low when contrasted to sites like Ofnet cave in Bavaria (Frayer 1997), where two pits containing the skulls of thirty-eight individuals have been excavated. The composition of the population at Ofnet is five males, three females and ten unsexed subadults, with the males having 2–7 impact wounds (on average), while females and unsexed individuals generally have fewer injuries (*ibid*.: 192). The composition of the burials at Ofnet has led to suggestions that a group of "mainly" women (which appears to contradict the sexing information) and children may have been attacked, possibly in an effort to undermine the viability of the community at this location (Thorpe 2003: 157).

There is little doubt that some significant instances of inter-personal violence occurred during the Mesolithic period throughout Europe, and whilst the evidence from the Dnieper Rapids might fit the suggested conflict over access to the rich fish resources available at this location (Lillie 2001; 2004), Dolukhavov (1999) sees these sites as reflecting a "deep ecological and social crisis" during the Mesolithic period. As no major settlements occur in the Pontic steppe during the earlier Mesolithic Dolukhanov suggests that the "impoverished" natural resources (Bison being extinct by the Late Palaeolithic) led to a "growing scarcity of food resources (such that) ... the local groups resorted to warfare" (*ibid*.: 78–9). However, in reality it is probable that in actuality the fact that the resources at the rapids were most likely seasonally rich might indicate that these dietary stressors were not endemic to the Mesolithic *per se*, but that they were concentrated at certain times of the year, when access to such resources was considered important for the groups exploiting this region. In reality though Lillie (2004, and as discussed above) has noted that the incidence of *direct* evidence for pathology at Vasilyevka I and Voloshkoe is in fact limited to only a single individual at Vasilyevka I and three at Voloshkoe, and in both cases the injuries are multiple impact damage from arrows, perhaps suggesting ritualised killings as opposed to warfare. Of course, we cannot discount soft tissue injuries, poisoning or other insults that are not visible after skeletonisation. One further point of note, to support the suggestions of seasonal resource fluctuations, is the fact that indicators of nutritional stress in these populations are very low throughout the Epipalaeolithic to Eneolithic periods in Ukraine (Lillie 1998).

These examples highlight yet another significant bias that occurs due to the lack of evidence for formal burial areas in the British Mesolithic record, as we lack an important resource for understanding the social and ritual aspects of burial, and we also do not have direct insights into the health status of Mesolithic individuals, furthermore, there is currently relatively little potential for the identification of inter-personal violence during this period. As such, a number of important insights into Mesolithic lifeways are lost when the burial record is lacking.

Other examples of interpersonal violence that have been identified during the Mesolithic period suggest that a range of causes, such as skirmishes, theft, muggings? wife/husband beating, family feuds etc., can be invoked as causes for the pathologies in evidence (Wilkinson 1997; Walker 1997; Thorpe 2003: 160). The level of violence is generally low, and whilst there are instances where a number of individuals are killed, e.g. at Ofnet in Bavaria, and where "warfare" might be invoked as a cause, in most cases it is possible that causes other than "warfare" can be suggested. This observation is not made with the intention of pacifying the past (*cf.* Kelley 1996: 17, *quoted by* Chapman 1999: 102), but more to ensure that the reader does not confuse interpersonal violence as ubiquitously meaning warfare, as the evidence is clearly not robust, or extensive, enough to allow for such an assertion. In addition, it should also be considered probable that the evocative terminology used to imbue significance, i.e. *warfare*, may not realistically be applicable to the Mesolithic period.

The dead in Wales

There is clearly a considerable degree of variation in the ways that people engaged with the dead, coped with taboos and "placated" the spirit world. Unfortunately, the Welsh burial evidence is limited, to say the least, and as noted by Conneller (2009) and Meiklejohn *et al.* (2011), the sites that contain human remains in Britain as a whole are dominated by locations that incorporate fragmentary, disarticulated remains in contexts such as caves and middens. Whilst the only sites where articulated inhumations have been recorded to date are Aveline's Hole (discussed above), Greylake, Gough's Cave and Tilbury (Schulting 2013), Conneller (2009: 691) does suggest that we should consider the possibility that other locations may originally have contained articulated burials that were disturbed by subsequent taphonomic processes (both natural and anthropogenic in origin); as indicated by the evidence from Scandinavia (e.g. Larsson 2000). Interestingly, as noted above, there is considerable evidence to suggest that inhumation burials may have been only one element of Mesolithic burial practice and ritual activity in Europe. In this respect British researchers have perhaps failed to approach the archaeological record from a balanced perspective, due in no small part to the considerable bias that is introduced by continued research at Star Carr in the Vale of Pickering, Yorkshire, as the focus on a limited number of "key" sites has perhaps diverted attention away from the search for "new" stratified settlements, activity sites, and burial locations.

As outlined in Chapter 5, Schulting and Richards (2000a) have analysed material from Welsh sites such as Nanna's Cave, Potter's Cave, Daylight Rock, Ogof-yr-Ychen and Ogof-yr-Benlog. Calibrated absolute dates for Potter's Cave, Daylight Rock and Ogof-yr-Ychen are presented in Table 3.1 (above). On the basis of the admittedly limited dataset for Wales, and England, Conneller (2006: 147) has suggested that there is no evidence for the association of caves with human bone deposits during the 7th, and the first half of the 6th millennium BC, but that this association occurs up to *ca.* 6000–5700 cal BC (based on the latest date from Ogof-yr-Ychen), and that association with caves recommences at the start of the Neolithic (see also Burrow 2003: 21, *citing* Chamberlain 1996). The reasons for this hiatus are yet to be established, although Schulting's (2013) suggestion that riverside contexts may be significant is an important observation in this regard.

The human material that has been studied from the welsh sites is very limited, with eight finds from Nanna's Cave (comprising a phalanx, two patella's, a femur and four rib fragments), and six from Potter's Cave (including a radius, four rib fragments, a metacarpal and an ulna fragment) (*ibid.*: 60). At Daylight Rock the three samples analysed were all from mandibles, and there is also a vertebra from Ogof-yr-Benlog. The final site studied was Ogof-yr-Ychen where a cranial fragment, two innominates, a mandible and tibia fragment were analysed. Significant issues have been highlighted with these assemblages due to the unstratified nature of many of these sites. As noted by Schulting and Richards (2000: 62), the Caldey Island sites are such that "no associations between the scattered human remains and diagnostic artefacts and/or fauna from the period of interest ... can be considered as secure". At Ogof-yr-Ychen, the human remains appear to have been dropped, or fallen, down the chimney/blowhole (David 1990; Davies 1989), resulting in mixing of the sediments and finds at this location.

At the Worm's Head, Gower excavations undertaken in 1923–4 produced human bones, which were separated by a sterile stony horizon from the underlying Pleistocene bone layer (Davies 1989: 86). The material recovered included a human scapula, ulna, femur and cranial fragment, and a date of 8210–7610 cal BC has been generated from the analysis of this material. In addition, the remains of one or two individuals from Paviland Cave are placed at 6230–5905 cal BC, i.e. the later Mesolithic, although this latter site lacks associated material culture remains (Lynch *et al.* 2000: 37).

There are clearly significant problems with our analysis of burial contexts for the Mesolithic period in Britain as a whole, and the data is somewhat limiting. The considered and detailed analyses undertaken by Schutling and co-workers have sought to provide a dated burial inventory, but this has, out of necessity, focussed on individual finds from unstratified contexts, both in the case of Wales, and elsewhere, and it has relied on the re-examination of previously excavated materials such as Aveline's Hole, Greylake and Tilbury. Further resolution is provided by the material from the Scottish middens, which also offer another depositional context for human skeletal material in Britain, and these sites are discussed below.

Finally, we need to consider the possibility that the deposition of the material at sites like Ogof-yr-Ychen may be incorrectly interpreted, or that it represents just one element of burial ritual in Wales, with the likelihood that caves are seen as "other wordly" locations, possibly where the ancestors and the spirits of the underworld resided. The fragmentary remains that are found at some of these sites are likely to have been secondary deposits, perhaps representing a similar ancestral engagement with place as we see elsewhere in the European record. As such we should seriously consider the possibility that burial sites or cemeteries will have existed elsewhere in the Mesolithic landscape, and that these locations remain to be identified; as alluded to throughout the text so far.

Structured deposition in middens

Returning to Oronsay, the human bone material recovered by Paul Mellars from these late Mesolithic shell middens (dated to 4400–3800 cal BC), and in particular Cnoc Coig (Meiklejohn *et al.* 2005: 85) resonates with the evidence from Scandinavia and Belgium that was discussed earlier in this chapter. Two types of human bone deposit have been identified at this location, with this material, which occurs in secondary deposits, comprising one group of "loose bone" and one containing material from the hands and feet of Mesolithic individuals. The midden deposits at Cnoc Coig appear to have developed around a hearth and hut like structure in the earlier phases of the sites occupation, when subsistence activities were focussed on the exploitation of marine resources such as limpets, crustaceans, saithe (just one of 12 species of fish identified, although saithe makes up 95% of the total), seals and marine birds, with these activities taking place between September and November (*ibid.*: 88, Mellars and Wilkinson 1980: 19).

The seasonality data are open to alternative interpretations though as Mellars and Wilkinson (*ibid*: 34–5) note that growth rates could conceivably be commensurate with all samples from Cnoc Sligeach, Priory Midden and Cnoc Coig, indicating activity spanning the late Autumn to early Winter months, and even spanning up to the earlier Spring months. However, Cnoc Sligeach and three of the four otoliths from Caisteal nan Gillean II would appear to suggest fishing (at least for fish in their second year) during the mid-Summer months (*ibid.*: 36), although the Caisteal nan Gillean data also indicate a longer duration of fishing activity at this location, including fishing into the colder winter months. This latter site is placed in the later Mesolithic at 4220–4050 cal BC (OxA-8005: 5480±55 uncal BP at 1σ; Meiklejohn *et al.* 2011: 36).

As noted, the human bone assemblages at Cnoc Coig (with dates spanning the later part of the Mesolithic between 4370–3920 cal BC; *ibid.*) comprise a combination of loose material, and what are described as discrete clusters, with teeth making up 8% of the total bone assemblage and the bones of the hands and feet representing 61% of the sample, with the remaining material comprising cranial, clavicle, rib, vertebral and innominate fragments (Meiklejohn *et al.* 2005: 89). These authors identify two groups (2 and 3) with a minimum of three individuals represented in each, and whilst they suggest that the sample as a whole differs from other European examples the loose bone finds are in fact similar to the European data, and especially the Scandinavian material (*ibid.*: 95). When contrasting the evidence from Cnoc Coig (Groups 2 and 3) with that from the other Oronsay sites of Caisteal nan Gillean (*ca.* 4200–3970 cal BC) and Priory Midden, Meiklejohn *et al.* see similarities between all of these sites (2005: 96).

A total of only *ca.* seven individuals are represented by the dated fragmentary material in the Oronsay middens of Cnoc Coig and Caisteal nan Gillean II, and Milner *et al.* (2004: 12) have noted that when considered alongside the data from Wales (which consists of perhaps ten individuals), there are in fact only seven individuals dated to the later Mesolithic period (6th–4th millennium cal BC) for Britain as a whole. In addition, the find of a femur from Staythorpe, Nottinghamshire (Meiklejohn *et al.* 2011: 35) can be added to the list of later Mesolithic material, and these authors have also suggested that the find of a hand phalanx from the Priory Midden, whilst undated, comes from a secure Late Mesolithic context, and as such can be included in the list of human material for this period (*ibid.*: 37). The specific contexts of the human bone finds, from middens and coastal caves in general, clearly do not represent an unbiased and representative sample for use in the study of Mesolithic groups and their ritual and symbolic activities, as the finds from Greylake (open site) and locations such as Staythorpe and Tilbury which may reflect burial near rivers (see Schulting 2013) indicate.

Meiklejohn *et al.* (2005: 97) have suggested that whilst a possible explanation for the spatial patterning of groups 2 and 3 at Cnoc Coig may lie in the articulation of a "culturally specific and overt act of placing bone on a site prior to leaving or deserting it", the latter part of this supposition is perhaps unsustainable on stratigraphic grounds, as this activity relates to the earlier phases of the sites use. However, Meiklejohn *et al.* note that whilst repeated visits are in evidence, this does not negate the idea that in leaving the site, the placing of the hands and feet of the ancestors marked a symbolic reference to "ownership and belonging" for the people exploiting the resources on Oronsay, despite the fact that the site was being "left" for some indeterminate period of time (*ibid.*: 103).

As Meiklejohn *et al.* (2005: 102) see some significance in the association of the human remains in group 2 with those of seal flipper bones, with this being "a structured symbolic act that has no known parallels in Mesolithic Europe", there is clear evidence for the intermingling of socio-economic and ritual activities at Cnoc Coig, in a way that is reminiscent of the activities alluded to by Zvelebil (2008: 42) in the quote at the start of this chapter, wherein it was proposed that ideology "must have been fundamental in specifying the nature of social relations ... and in encoding subsistence strategies with social meaning". It is precisely these structured articulations of ritual/symbolic activity with socio-cultural activity that reinforce ethnographic evidence for the complex interplay of these variables in the daily lives of hunter-fisher-forager groups (e.g. Jordan 2003a; 2003b).

In north Wales, a recent overview of Prestatyn (Armour-Chelu *et al.* 2007) has shown that a total of six middens are preserved at this location, four being located at the wetland edge and two within peat (Bell 2007e: 309). The middens of Mesolithic age consist of predominantly mussel shells, with charcoal, lithics and fragments of animal bone. Unfortunately, whilst Prestatyn, Rhyl and Bryn Newydd may all have evidence for middens, and there are possibilities that middens also occur at Daylight Rock, Nanna's Cave and Freshwater West (*ibid.*: 309), the evidence from these sites has yet to produce stratified evidence for the incorporation of human skeletal material. However, Bell (*ibid.*: 311) has suggested that evidence for a ritual component in the structuring of these sites may be forthcoming from the knapping debris, which includes flakes from polished axes. Bell sees the inclusion of these lithics within the midden context as representing a deliberate act of votive deposition.

Ritual deposition and ritual objects

Throughout Europe we have considerable evidence for structured depositions during the Mesolithic period, and as with the removal and secondary interment of human skeletal remains, structured depositions are a Mesolithic phenomenon that continues into the Neolithic period. In discussing the structured deposition of stone and amber beads and the bone harpoon points at Star Carr, Pollard (2000: 126) has noted that "deposition can occasionally operate as a more overtly conscious action; drawing upon the range of meanings embodied in material elements and associated practice". Pollard also notes that beads have been shown to have associations to burials at Vedbæk in Denmark. The structured deposition of these objects at sites like Star Carr may well link through to funerary contexts. On the basis of this link, Pollard suggests that at The Nab Head site I, the association of a group of beads with an "anthropomorphic" shale "amulet" may have ritual meaning beyond purely functionalist interpretations (2000: 126). Jacobi (1980: 159) has discussed the shale object as possibly representing a Venus figurine or phallus. In addition to the figurine, there is also a flattened ovoid pebble which has an incision just over 7mm long at its base. Jacobi was tempted to interpret this as a simplified representation of a Venus, and Pollard sees the composition of such structured deposits as potentially representing "acts surrounding the creation of social identities, principally as part of rites of passage" (2000: 127).

At the Nab Head, the beads that were recovered have clear evidence for on-site production, but beyond the hypothesised creation of social identities linked to rites of passage, we can also link these finds to more overt expressions of social identity, via body ornamentation. In this context the use of beads for decoration can convey an array of unspoken messages that could be related to age, sex, tribal identity, war or peace status, cosmological beliefs and territoriality, and perhaps an expression of individual and group identity in relation to space and place in the Mesolithic world (Simpson 2003: 47). This observation is of some interest as the deposition of such objects could have considerable resonance in relation to the sense of place and community identity for the occupants of this location (or other sites like Star Carr and Waun Fignen Felin). The beads at the Nab Head were not uniform in shape, and Jacobi (1980: 160) notes that they ranged from circular to oval in outline, through celtiform to triangular or even rectangular. Given Simpson's (2003) suggestions, it is conceivable that the range of forms of the beads that were produced have a specific range of meanings imbued within their form, and that these meanings were recognisable to individuals within the group, and that they also potentially conveyed meaning to individuals beyond the group.

Additional structuring in the deposition of artefacts at the Nab Head revolves around the three pecked and ground stone axe/adzes, which both Jacobi (1980) and David (2007) report have no known parallels in British prehistoric contexts. As noted in Chapter 3, this deposit may well have considerable significance when considering structured deposition, and the interlinking of the more commonly occurring bevelled pebbles with a "unique" artefact type may well (following Pollard 2000: 126–7) draw upon meanings embodied in these objects that transcend their utilitarian function, and reflect embedded symbolic action and belief that pervaded the routines of daily life. Jacobi (1980) was inclined to suggest that the figurine and the beads at the Nab Head, which in combination might make up a necklace of some 42 in (*ca.* 107 cm) length, could well have been associated with structured deposition in a burial context, and that the weathering and erosion at this location had obscured their original depositional context. This suggested linking of artefacts types to a structured burial context may well prove informative if we are able to identify actual cemetery sites in Wales, as the hypothesised structured articulations will be testable when we identify Mesolithic burials in Britain in general.

One other notable find in terms of objects with possible ritual significance are the engraved pebbles from Rhuddlan (Berridge 1994: 115–9; Roberts 1994: 119–24). These six objects are decorated with incised lines interpreted as a "tree" motif on SF1 (Small Find 1), SF2 from the Mesolithic hollow has two separate designs which Berridge (*ibid.*) does not offer an interpretation of, whilst SF3 is decorated with "criss-cross" lines. Both SF4 and 5 have a number of incised lines of no discernible patterning, but SF6 does appear more complex, exhibiting a pattern that on first viewing could be described as not unlike a hut structure (see fig. 11.2, p. 118 in Quinnell and Blockley 1994), although Berridge mentions that Roger Jacobi saw this as a fish trap on the basis of similarities to early post-glacial wheals from sites like Lille Knapstrup and Nidlose in the Holbæk district of Zealand (1994: 126). Roberts' (1994: 119–24) scanning electron microscope analysis of the engraved lines on SF1 indicates that the decoration was undertaken using chert engraving tools. However, this was the only pebble that this could be determined for as the post-depositional damage to the other pebbles meant that whilst the engraved lines were probably produced using either the unretouched edges of flint or chert bladelets, the precise tool used could not be determined (*ibid.*: 124). Perhaps most significantly Roberts notes that there are a series of heavily worn engraved lines underlying the more visible motifs, suggesting that the pebbles had more than one phase of decoration and use. This observation would indicate that, whatever the meaning of the designs was, the message that these motifs conveyed was used on more than one occasion. Linear incisions occur on a range of Mesolithic artefact forms throughout Europe, for instance on the bone knives and other implements from Nizhneye Veretye I near Lake Onega (Oshibkina 1990a), the antler tools at Korsør Nor in the Danish Storebælt (Schilling 1997: 96–7), the engraved bone artefacts from Stanovoje 4 in the Upper Volga (Zhilin 2007: 74), antler carvings from Tyrvala in Estonia and Østerbjerg in Denmark (Timofeev 1998), and a decorated elk antler "pointed weapon" from the Maglemose site of Ugerløse in the Åmose of Zealand (Price and Gebauer 2005: 21).

One final point of note relates to the production of the stone tools used in the Mesolithic period. Warren (2006) has discussed the inverted antlers identified by Wymer at Thatcham II (1962; discussed in Chapter 4 above) from the perspective of the hunters' negotiation of their relationship to the animals that they exploited. In this context the technology that is produced is considered to be "intimately associated with the social reproduction of world views" (Warren 2006: 24). The use of the Thatcham deer antlers and skull cap is seen by Warren as a means to "enchant the technology" through the production of tools in intimate association with the red deer. This "enchantment of technology" is extended by Warren (*citing* Woodman 1978 and Finlay 2003b) to include caches or hoards of material at a number of sites in Britain and Ireland, where the structuring principles give "form to people's relationship with stone" (2006: 26). The structured deposits at the Nab Head II include David's axe number 1 which "was found in contact with, and underlying, two bevelled pebbles" which he suggests indicates contemporaneous use and possible caching of these objects (David 2007: 150). Given the multiple of three in evidence at this location, and Finlay's (2003b: 91) concept of a "Mesolithic trinity", the Nab Head clearly links into a wider British and Irish tradition of structured deposition that was part of a wider set of "social strategies and negotiations of the relationships between people" (Warren 2006: 27).

Discussion

This chapter has attempted to develop a considered approach to the potential range of ritual activity that was pertinent to everyday life in the Mesolithic. It commenced with an outline of some of the theoretical aspects of ritual that have not been covered to any significant degree in the volume so far, but which could all be relevant to the Mesolithic period in Wales. It has been argued throughout the text that analogies to modern hunter-fisher-foragers can be used with caution to help us begin to tease out those aspects of Mesolithic life that are all but invisible to us in the present, but which could conceivably have been embedded in the everyday lived experience of human groups in the Mesolithic. Whilst it is important to note that modern forager groups are not going to be identical to, or an absolute example of, Mesolithic populations, as noted by Warren (2005: 71–2) analogy offers us possible options through which we can begin to make sense of the archaeological record of past hunter-fisher-foragers. In the context of material culture, Finlay (2003a: 167) has noted that "recent anthropological studies have demonstrated the potential for ... biographical approaches" which acknowledge "the critical role of objects in the creation of personal and social identities".

The discussion has also outlined the nature of the skeletal inventories for Britain as a whole, and explored some of the ways in which a theoretically informed reading of the Mesolithic could potentially enable us to delve into the past lived experience of hunter-fisher-foragers. Within this theoretical framework we considered the nature of boundaries (*cf.* McCarthy 2008), pathways and the mediation of possible areas of conflict between the living and the dead. This set the scene for the consideration of cemeteries, burial rituals and the mediation of the landscape of the living with that of the dead through the burial rituals in evidence throughout Europe during the Mesolithic period. This has highlighted the fact that, perhaps, the most significant limitation for Britain as a whole is that we lack the stratified settlement sites and cemeteries that are needed in order to generate meaningful narratives of Mesolithic lifeways. The lack of skeletal inventories from which to evaluate ritual treatment of the dead, gain insights into palaeopathology, body processing and differential treatment related to age and gender, and also the ways in which the living cope with death, is clearly very limiting for our interpretations of the Mesolithic period in Britain.

In addition, we have touched on the fact that inter-personal violence, including that between partners, clearly occurred, and there is little doubt that murders were carried out, but equally that the evidence could indicate ritual killings, or reflect a number of other situations. Whilst it is clear that determining cause of death might possibly be considered as straightforward where an arrow in the back is attested, the sociological context of the killing still remains obscure, and of course accidental death cannot be ruled out. The social context of death in the Mesolithic remains ambiguous, even where we have cemeteries and skeletal remains to study.

Fundamentally, we are effectively ignorant of what people actually did on a day-to-day basis, e.g. how the social, economic, political and ritual activities that were clearly embedded in everyday life were articulated. Following on from the consideration of possible areas of Mesolithic ritual activity the discussion has also considered the nature of paths and boundaries and how pathways could have been layered with meaning beyond the utilitarian function of getting from A to B (Bradley 2000: 6; Jordan 2003a), and also that "totem poles" may have been used as route way or territorial markers during the Mesolithic. Alongside Stonehenge and the Bryn Celli Du passage tomb on Anglesey, the recent discovery at Maerdy, Rhondda Cynon Taf may provide examples of these objects in a British context.

Unfortunately, as this chapter has shown, we do not yet have sufficient evidence for Mesolithic burial in Britain to allow for a nuanced reading of past social and ritual articulations through individual burials, cemeteries and the burial rituals that were enacted, and similarly, many other aspects of ritual and symbolic practice are lacking.

The paucity of burial evidence is an unfortunate situation, as at locations elsewhere in Europe e.g. Olenii Ostrov in Karelia, there is significant structuring in the interments, and Bradley (2000: 35) has suggested that the close proximity of rock carvings to this site, that depict the items that are included in the graves of the people buried at this cemetery, indicates that natural places are important in the minds of people in the past. The embellishment of these natural surfaces could have any number of connotations for the living at Olenii Ostrov, and their association with the dead is evident. The permanence of the memories imbued by such locations would have ensured that the inherent tensions between the living and the dead were constantly articulated and negotiated, or renegotiated. Whilst we lack similar articulations between burial sites and landscape features in Britain, the evidence throughout Europe clearly suggests that these links occurred and that Mesolithic people were conscious of the symbolism that was imbued in the rituals undertaken at certain locations.

During the Mesolithic period the living and the dead "interacted" in ways that are often difficult for us to interpret in the present. Many ritual articulations and symbolic actions would have multiple meanings, and even with ethnographic analogy, we can do little more that acknowledge that these meanings existed, and that everyday life in the Mesolithic was understood through the myriad symbols and rituals that were embedded in it. The limitations of the data, for Britain as a whole, necessitate a "broad brush" approach to the consideration of ritual and symbolism, as has been attempted above. To some degree this has allowed us to consider the wider European context, and in doing so it has highlighted the need for more targeted investigations of the Mesolithic period in Wales, and Britain. We have perhaps been too myopic when studying the Mesolithic period, partly due to the apparent "richness" of what went before and what comes after this period, but also because certain locations have proven too tempting to "risk" ignoring.

Sites like Star Carr and Mount Sandal retain their importance due to their proven potential. However, it is hoped that this chapter, in emphasising the limitations of the archaeological record for Mesolithic burial and ritual, has by extension emphasised the need for a reinvigoration of targeted research agendas that are designed to redress the imbalance between Britain and Europe. Despite the fact that Meiklejohn *et al.* (2011: 21) discuss 20 sites with evidence for human remains in Britain, which they note is a four-fold increase on the situation reported by Newell *et al.* in 1979, we still lack sites with primary interments. There may well be many others areas in Europe where a similar lack of data exists, but we now need to put the Mesolithic back on the agenda, especially as many of the "typical" Neolithic traits, such as the removal and secondary deposition of skeletal elements in differing site/landscape settings, are now shown to have occurred in the Mesolithic period. Instead of looking enviously at the Neolithic it is time to recognise that the Mesolithic is not a prelude to the Neolithic, but that the Mesolithic itself is resonant with complex social and ritual articulations that shape and influence what was to follow.

7

THE END IS IN SIGHT: THE ADOPTION OF NEW RESOURCES AND THE SHIFT FROM HUNTING AND GATHERING TOWARDS THE INTEGRATION AND EXPLOITATION OF DOMESTICATED ANIMALS AND PLANTS IN SUBSISTENCE STRATEGIES

... hunter-gatherers have social relations with hazelnuts, whilst farmers have social relations. (Bradley 1984: 11)

... the last hunters were the first farmers; exceptions to this rule occur primarily in areas with small indigenous populations. (Price and Gebauer 1995: 8)

... with the exception of monument construction, the Neolithic is beginning to appear as an exceptionally uneventful period. (Mithen 1999: 478)

Introduction

The shift away from the exploitation of wild resources towards the integration of domesticated plant and animal species into subsistence strategies has been the subject of considerable discourse in the archaeological literature. Within this debate, both exogenous (e.g. climate/environment/population pressure) and endogenous (e.g. social change) factors (Price and Gebauer 1995: 4) are influential, with the latter being linked to the range of technological and ideological aspects that are embedded in the shift towards agriculture (Whittle 2007a; Cummings 2007). As the above quotes indicate, the advent of the Neolithic (usually perceived as being synonymous with the transition to agriculture in western Europe) is viewed by many researchers as the catalyst to sedentism, monumentality, complex society and more fundamentally perhaps, the point at which human groups begin to move towards society as we view it today (e.g. Lukes *et al.* 2008). To some degree it could be suggested that the debate that revolves around the "shift" itself detracts us somewhat from serious consideration of the developments occurring across the Mesolithic period; especially as the evidence presented in Chapter 4 has already alluded to the fact that later Mesolithic groups were possibly becoming less mobile than in earlier periods, and that there is continuity in material culture inventories and hunter-fisher-forager activities across the "traditional" marker horizon of 4000 cal BC in Britain. Lynch *et al.* (2000: 40) have suggested that the reduced mobility may link to such forcing mechanisms as sea level rise, which removed expanses of coastal plain, and which subsequently leads to increased population densities.

We might consider the possibility that reduced mobility, increasing population density and a focus on the procurement of resources from a geographically "limited" area would perhaps make the shift towards the exploitation of domesticated plants and animals less significant in terms of the perceptions of the individual, or society in general. It is worth noting however that mobility would have varied depending on location. The evidence from Goldcliff suggests that residential mobility with transitory encampments are in evidence into the Neolithic period, despite the fact that Lynch *et al.* (2000: 40) have argued for greater degrees of sedentism. As such, we may well be seeing (at least) two differing patterns of landscape utilisation at the end of the Mesolithic period and into the Neolithic, and consequently, the patterns of adoption of agriculture may well be more complex in such a context. Indeed, Milner (2010: 48–9) notes that the available evidence for the introduction of domesticates prior to 3700 cal BC is both varied, and biased towards sites in southern England, and that there are a number of locations that have a "Mesolithic" material culture inventory that continues into the earlier Neolithic period.

We should also be aware of the different processes that are involved in the transition to agriculture as the act of domestication itself is different to the adoption of an existing "package" of resources (e.g. Price and Gebauer 1995; Vanderwarker 2006), and despite the fact that agriculture requires cultivation, cultivation as a process does not necessitate agriculture (*ibid.*: 7). Depending on location (in Europe) it has been shown that there is little doubting the fact that Mesolithic groups were not always simply the passive recipients of the farming "package" (however constituted), and whilst arguments that suggest that transitional economies are virtually absent in Europe are occasionally couched in a persuasive rhetoric (e.g. Rowley-Conwy 2011), they do (of course) need to be contextualised. For instance, a contrasting perspective to the "sharp-shift" to farming (*cf.* Richards *et al.* 2003) has been postulated by Whittle (2007a), who has suggested that the evidence is indicative of a gradualist model for the development of the Neolithic in southern Britain, and despite the appearance of long barrows just after *ca.* 3800 cal BC (with one or two notable exceptions, such as Ascott-under-Wychwood and Hazelton in the Cotswolds, that are placed in the period 3900–3800 cal BC), the evidence does appear to support a combination of integration (acculturation) and colonisation; especially given the fact that domesticated cereals and sheep were not native to Britain (Whittle 2009: 78 and 81; Darvill 1987: 49). Similarly, Meiklejohn *et al.* (2011: 35–6, *citing* Bartosiewicz *et al.* 2010) note that the latest Obanian dates show that on the coast there is continuity of foraging to some degree at a time when Neolithic chambered tombs are present in the interior of Scotland and elsewhere. There would, as a consequence, appear to be at least two processes in the course of Neolithisation in Britain, with the exploitation of either "traditional" or "new" resources occurring at different speeds, and to differing degrees, depending upon the environments exploited and the nature of the exiting and immigrant population base in a given region. Fundamentally, we may well be placing too much emphasis on the identification of difference between these periods, and not accepting the fact that both lifeways do not necessarily represent mutually exclusive subsistence strategies at the onset of the Neolithic period.

The problems associated with the elucidation of the transition from the Mesolithic, in a British context, occur, in part, due to the uneven distribution of the evidence, marked by a paucity of absolutely dated sites at either side of the transition from the Mesolithic and into the earlier Neolithic period (Edmonds 1999: 5; Whittle 2007a), and the fact that the new evidence that has been obtained appears to indicate that, as might be expected, the "transitions" are complex processes, which are situationally specific, and in need of an holistic approach to their study and interpretation (as suggested above). As indicated by Cummings (2007: 507) it is possible that the Neolithic may have been different in different areas, and as such we should consider the possibility of "Neolithics" as opposed to a single entity that is "the Neolithic", or perhaps in this context, "the regional Neolithics and their Transitions" would be more apt; although these do again take the emphasis away from the Mesolithic period and the ways in which Mesolithic people were integral to the processes in evidence.

When discussing the transition to the "Neolithic" period, Thomas (2008: 63) notes that "there are no closed assemblages in Britain that contain both pottery and microliths", and that "the Neolithic presence is not appreciably earlier or later in any part of the country" (*citing* Schulting 2000: 32). By implication this might be taken to suggest that Mesolithic groups are not involved in the process of the developments that lead to farming, and that once introduced this subsistence strategy is rapidly adopted across Britain? We cannot, however, (as alluded to above) easily "see" the transition to agriculture in archaeological terms across the period *ca.* 4200–3800 cal BC (Lynch *et al.* 2000), and to some degree the large monuments of the "established" Neolithic also detract from the fact that there are (in reality) relatively few physical remains to suggest that the population was increasingly sedentary and following arable farming lifeways across the period 4200–3800 cal BC.

Indeed, as noted by Rowley-Conwy (2011: S442) the "dominant model argues that for much of the Neolithic, Britain and Ireland remained effectively 'Mesolithic', based on nomadic hunting and gathering", and Whittle (2007a: 391) has argued for a combination of "small-scale, filtered colonisation from the adjacent continent, and change among the indigenous people in southern and other parts of Britain". Unfortunately, for Wales in general, David (2007: 196) has noted that little interpretative endeavour has been directed specifically to the understanding of the nature of the transition to agriculture, and for Britain as a whole there appears to be some difficulty in determining whether Neolithic equals monumentality or the shift from wild to domesticated resource exploitation strategies. In addition, Lynch *et al.* (2000: 42) have previously noted that there are no enclosures or village groups of any size in the earlier Neolithic period in Wales, and that in some regions, such as central and north east Wales, the lack of communal monuments (e.g. the tombs of the Cotswold-Severn group, portal dolmens and passage graves) is either indicative of a lack of population, or a very dispersed population base.

There is of course one archaeological site in Britain, the Sweet Track, that "stands out from the crowd" in being absolutely dated through dendrochronology to the earlier part of the Neolithic period. Additionally, the absolute dating to 3807/6 BC, of the Sweet Track in the Somerset levels, also provides an absolute date to the associated material culture inventory (Coles and Coles 1986); a level of resolution that is seldom mirrored at dryland sites. As noted by Whittle though, there is evidence to suggest that woodland disturbance or management was in place in the region for potentially over a century before the date of the Sweet Track, and Coles and Coles (*ibid.*: 63) suggest "*they* had been in the area for a generation at least"; as such we perhaps need to consider who may have actually been responsible for this woodland management? i.e. who were *they*? (Whittle 2007a: 397).

By implication, this woodland management could be associated with indigenous peoples, as opposed to incoming farming groups, as the practice is well established by the earliest stage of "Neolithic" activity in southern Britain, and support for the idea that these individuals were farmers is, to quote Coles and Coles (1986: 63) "slight". Interestingly, despite the fact that the Sweet Track may have extended for some 2km from a point near the foot of the Polden Hills, in a northeasterly direction to Westhay Island, being a planned and constructed path between places (Edmonds 1999: 24), Coles and Coles (1986: 64) suggest that once "the arduous work of felling, preparing and transporting the wood to site" was completed, construction could actually have only taken a single day if undertaken by two groups of people with at least half a dozen adults in each group being involved in the work. Given the evidence for wooden structures at Star Carr in an earlier Mesolithic context, it is not unrealistic to propose that by the later Mesolithic the construction of the Sweet Track would be well within the capabilities of indigenous hunter-fisher-forager groups exploiting a stable local resource base, who were also *sedentary* to some degree in such a landscape context.

The finds of smashed pottery vessels along the route of the trackway (Coles and Coles 1986: 59) could easily indicate that hunter-fisher-foragers were either trading with incoming farmers, were adopting elements of the farming "package", or that both hunter-fisher-foragers and farmers co-existed in this region. This material included one vessel that had a wooden stirrer or spurtle beside it, and another vessel that was originally full of hazelnuts when it was dropped (Coles 1989; Coles and Coles 1986: 60).

The available evidence does also suggest that these early "farming" groups practiced a mixed subsistence strategy (Thomas 1999), with gathering of wild fruits and nuts, and the continued exploitation of wild animal resources and coastal resources, as attested by finds around the Welsh coast during the earlier part of the Neolithic period. The evidence from locations such as Prestatyn (e.g. Bell 2007e) support this observation, but we should not discount a combination of adoption by indigenous groups (or acculturation) and immigration/integration of incoming people with the knowledge of farming. The material culture that is associated with the builders of the Sweet Track includes finds that link both hunter-fisher-forager and farming lifeways; again suggesting that a more nuanced reading of the evidence is necessitated at this "transitional" period.

Despite this particular example, it is, as a consequence of the general lack of evidence, difficult for us to generate meaningful narratives of British society across the centuries at the end of the fifth and at the earlier part of the 4th millennia BC, i.e. at the end of the Mesolithic and into the stage when the hypothesised shift to agro-pastoralism and a focus on terrestrial diets is thought to be "rapidly" occurring (e.g. Richards *et al.* 2003). Bonsall *et al.* (2002: 1) noted that there has been a theoretical and conceptual divide between studies of the Mesolithic and Neolithic periods, and whilst the intervening years have seen concerted efforts to redress the imbalance, for regions like Wales and Scotland, this means that we have only really been considering the implications of the transition for a decade or so, and the lack of evidence at either side of this "transition" still leaves more questions than answers. Irrespective of the limitations, we are left with the impression that more work is needed to characterise the nature of society across the 5th–4th millennia cal BC if we are to begin to understand the mechanisms of/for change. In effect there are a number of theoretical and methodological problems that limit the efficacy of our attempts to model the shift from hunter-fisher forager to farming lifeways in Britain, with a significant limiting factor potentially being the perception that these are mutually exclusive categories of subsistence (or lifeways), and that as a consequence the dichotomy of Mesolithic = hunter-gatherers and Neolithic = farmers remains valid to some degree.

The lack of consideration of the functioning of a Mesolithic society that potentially incorporates two subsistence strategies, i.e. immediate and delayed return strategies, is limiting, as the study of this period could prove illustrative in terms of our understanding of the reasons for, or the mechanisms behind, the ultimate transition to agriculture in Britain, and also throughout Europe. As "one of the major characteristics of immediate-return systems is their egalitarianism, which is lost in delayed-return systems" (Barnard 1983: 205–6, *citing* Woodburn 1982), it is clear that these two subsistence strategies have inherent contradictions. As such, the negotiation and re-negotiation of the internal tensions in transitional societies, as appear to be occurring towards the end of the Mesolithic period in Britain, should potentially be "visible" archaeologically. Consequently, generating meaningful narratives of the evidence for hunter-fisher-forager groups that exploit either delayed- or immediate-return strategies could prove to be of potential significance to studies of the subsequent shifts in subsistence strategies that occur across the period *ca.* 4200–38/600 cal BC and beyond in a British context.

We also need to be investigating "bigger" questions about individual and group identities, and assessing the possible reasons for variation in the speed of uptake of Neolithic material culture, domesticates and Neolithic "world views". Whittle (2007b: 620) has touched on the importance of situational context, as discussed in this chapter, by suggesting that in contrast to the evidence for the use of cereals in the earlier LBK (Linearbandkeramik) in Europe, in Britain this use was "muted". As might be expected, this would certainly appear to be the case in other regions where the adoption of domesticates appears to be oriented towards animal as opposed to plant remains. The resolution of the data continues to confound our attempts at developing a subtler reading of the evidence and a more precise discourse in relation to the changes occurring during the later Mesolithic and the transition from the Mesolithic to Neolithic periods in certain regions (although see Bogaard and Jones 2007 for contrasting arguments). It is realistic to assume that there are numerous factors influencing phases of contact and colonisation (e.g. Whittle 2009: 85), and that the adoption of the various elements of the new economic and material culture "package", synonymous with the developed Neolithic, is bound to be different depending on the region, cultural perceptions and individual choice. Given the variability that exists in all societies, is it really any surprise that there is no single viable explanation for the adoption of the "Neolithic"?

Furthermore, it may well prove fruitful to try to assess the reasons for the lack of evidence for human groups during this "transitional" period in Britain, as the lack of easily recognisable sites may well prove fundamental to our understanding of what follows. Of interest here is the observation by Thomas (2008: 66), who has suggested that during the later Mesolithic hunting strategies shifted from "planned interception ... toward opportunistic encounter strategies" as a consequence of the continued expansion of deciduous woodland; which as noted in Chapter 2, occurred to heights of *ca.* 500m OD in the Welsh uplands. Similarly, Hey and Barclay (2007: 404) note that in the Thames valley "later hunter-gatherer sites are smaller in size, suggesting that people moved in smaller groups or stayed in one place for shorter lengths of time". There is clear diversity in the data, and some conflicting evidence, and there are reasons to suspect that targeted research agendas aimed at refining the archaeological record across the later Mesolithic and earlier Neolithic periods are warranted.

The available data appear to suggest that in the later Mesolithic, food procurement strategies were increasingly focussed on resources that were more readily available or easier to procure, e.g. the terrestrial plants and animal in the more open coastal and riparian zones. The evidence is relatively sparse for the period around 4000 cal BC, and whilst some caution is required, as the discussion below will aim the highlight, we should not avoid drawing the conclusion that later Mesolithic groups were in fact experiencing some difficulties due to the lack of predictability of certain resources, and that despite increasing population densities (in terms of the concentration of groups in more limited areas) caused by sea level rise, in reality the population of Britain was still relatively sparse (or unevenly distributed) at this time. As noted by Carter (2001: 1055) the environmental evidence from Thatcham in Berkshire indicates a reduction in human activity in the later Mesolithic period, which resulted in the establishment of alder carr woodland in areas that had previously been kept open through firing activities in the floodplain. Although the difficulties inherent with the assumed "firing activities" as a measure of activity itself needs qualifying at this location, the evidence does again appear to suggest that Mesolithic groups were having to re-orientate their subsistence procurement strategies towards the end of the Mesolithic period in Britain.

A scenario wherein the population base of later Mesolithic Britain was less dispersed when compared to earlier periods, and where there is an assumed focus on terrestrial fauna and flora, could account for the apparent "abrupt shift" in diet in the earlier Neolithic that is "seen" through stable isotope studies (Richards *et al.* 2003), as incoming farmers would not differ markedly in their isotopic composition when compared to hunter-fisher-foragers if no significant marine resources were being exploited. In addition, any gathered wild component in the farmers' diet would potentially be isotopically indistinguishable from a terrestrial domesticated plant signature (see Chapter 5). In reality, even in areas where there appears to be strong evidence for continuity across the Mesolithic-Neolithic transition, i.e. at sites like Ulva Cave near Mull, and the An Corran rockshelter on Skye, as noted by

Bonsall *et al.* (2002: 4), demonstrating continuity of use is not possible, and the "Obanian" middens seldom have evidence for Late Mesolithic and Early Neolithic activity.

The evidence discussed by Hey and Barclay (2007: 407) from sites throughout the Thames Valley, at locations such as Eton and Runnymede, has suggested that later Mesolithic and earlier Neolithic activity sites overlap in floodplain areas, perhaps again reflecting the continuity of hunter-fisher-forager groups across this chronological boundary. At these locations, despite the suggested lack of dietary overlap between these periods, the available evidence could be used to suggest continuity. It does not appear that Mesolithic groups occupied ecological niches that were unattractive to farmers, as the fact is that the lowlands and coastal fringes provided ideal areas for grazing and cultivation. In addition, we should accept the fact that incoming groups of farmers would have exploited other resources as part of a risk buffering strategy in a new environment. In this context, Jones (2000: 79) has stated that "there can be little doubt that both cultivated cereals and collected wild foods contributed to the diet of *Neolithic* people in Britain", and hazelnuts are ubiquitous finds on Neolithic sites, as well as Mesolithic sites. In general terms, as has been noted above, these two food "categories", i.e. domesticated and wild, could either suggest hunter-fisher-foragers transitioning towards the integration of agriculture, or farmers utilising a gathered resource (with the former scenario perhaps being more viable given the admittedly limited evidence), or perhaps a combination of both scenarios is more realistic?

It would appear that any interactions or overlaps between these groups have either failed to result in a visible archaeological "signature", or at least failed to produce a signature that we are able to identify (or read) across the transition. As David (2007: 198) has suggested, there is a bias towards lowland margins in the earlier Neolithic, and this perhaps suggests that indigenous groups were in fact influential in, or at least engaged with, the uptake of domesticated species at the start of this period. It is likely that we may not be seeing the wood for the trees, as in this scenario the trees (humans) blend into one, or significantly overlap, in terms of their subsistence strategies.

Of interest in relation to the above observations is the suggestion that "transitional" economies indicative of the gradual adoption and development of agriculture by hunter-gatherers are virtually absent in Europe (Rowley Conwy 2011: S431). It is obvious that this is a very generic and sweeping statement that fails to account for regional variation, or the finer detail of the evidence throughout Europe. It can also be suggested that this statement obscures our own inabilities to identify these transitional economies as the circumstantial evidence does appear to suggest that we are failing to recognise the patterning in the data, in part at least, due to the lack of resolution alluded to above. For Britain, Thomas (2008: 74) has stated that *contra* Rowley Conwy (2004: 91), the case for the universal adoption of a way of life that is based exclusively on the exploitation of domesticated plants and animals remains to be proven; it would appear that this is still the case, although Bogaard and Jones (2000: 370) suggest that "in terms of the scale of cereal production and the permanence of cultivation plots, farming practices in Neolithic Britain and central Europe appear rather similar". Of course this evidence could also be used to offer up questions about the "purity" of the LBK as an intrusive farming culture into central Europe.

The fact that domesticated cereals and sheep/goat would have to have been brought in to Britain, as there are no wild progenitors, must suggest the probability that individuals from the continent were involved in this process, but the nature of this involvement is still debated. As noted by Darvill (2010: 77), in addition to the archaeological evidence, it is likely that there were fundamental shifts in ideology and the adoption of new world views on the part of the indigenous population in order to manipulate nature and establish a new approach to their food procurement strategies. The hybridisation of both hunter-fisher-forager and farmer lifeways (and ritualised practices) would appear to offer the best fit for the development of farming across the Mesolithic-Neolithic transition, and for much of the earlier part of the Neolithic period in Britain.

It should also be remembered that, despite assertions of a "sharp shift in diet" at *ca*. 4000–3800 cal BC (Richards *et al.* 2003), the reality is that the (archaeological) evidence indicates continuation in the exploitation of wild resources throughout prehistory, and in actual fact, the *ca*. 19 Mesolithic individuals studied by Richards *et al.* (2003) can in no way be considered to be representative of the potentially broad range of subsistence strategies employed by Mesolithic groups, irrespective of persuasive arguments to the contrary. The evidence for mixed subsistence strategies from sites such as Potter's Cave, Daylight Rock and Ogof-yr-Ychen on Caldey, Foxhole, Gower and Pontnewydd in north Wales, which are indicative of both marine and terrestrial subsistence economies, argues against a sharp shift from marine to terrestrial dietary pathways, as hunter-fisher-forager groups could alternate their subsistence activities as needs dictated. Equally, whilst 164 Neolithic individuals with terrestrial isotope signatures are relatively compelling, there is a "gap" of some 400 years (or some *ca*. 16 generations) across the "transitional" period. Similarly, the absence of $\delta^{15}N$ ratios in the study by Richards *et al.* (2003) limits the resolution of the data, and also limits consideration of trophic level shifts between the periods studied, such that the exploitation of freshwater resources is not visible, at present. Nor is there compelling evidence for a wholesale transition to agro-pastoralism.

A further limitation is the lack of faunal remains for use is assessing the dietary shifts and any variations between trophic levels, and finally, a significant, and to some extent unresolved issue, lies in the observation that marine resource exploitation appears to be curtailed, or significantly diminished, after *ca*. 4000 cal BC in Britain and northwest Europe in general. The reasons behind this hypothesised shift away from marine resources are yet to be adequately explained, and the work of Fischer *et al.* (2007: 2137), studying the Danish Mesolithic evidence, also highlights further complications in that variations in climate, forest cover, lake water chemistry etc. may cause isotopic variations among individuals of the same animal species, and the isotope signatures of certain species of fish were also shown to exhibit values of $\delta^{15}N$ that would make them indistinguishable from terrestrial fauna (*ibid.*: 2137–9). In the absence of contemporary fauna and fish for the later Mesolithic and earlier Neolithic periods in Britain, we cannot discount the possibility that certain fish species could be isotopically indistinguishable from terrestrial fauna.

Obviously, as the above discussion suggests, the isotopic evidence for a sharp shift in diet at the "onset" of the Neolithic needs to be contextualised in relation to the precise character of the "terrestrial" signature, and evaluated in terms of what this actually means in relation to either the integration of elements of a farming economy into a subsistence strategy that is primarily based on hunting and the gathering of wild terrestrial resources, or the immigration of farmers and the exploitation of a new suite of domesticated terrestrial resources, along with a limited gathered input. As noted above, Milner *et al.* (2004: 10) have questioned the veracity of the hypothesised sharp shift in diet at the Mesolithic–Neolithic transition in northwest Europe. Their discussion highlights the fact that the archaeological evidence often indicates continuity in the exploitation of marine resources, and it reiterates the sample biases alluded to above. It also suggests that a more cautious reading of the isotope data is warranted. In fact, Milner *et al.* go so far as to suggest that the hypothesised "sharp shift in diet" is either an oversimplification or over-exaggeration of the available evidence (*ibid.*: 12). This contradictory perspective has not gone un-criticised however as Hedges (2004: 34–7) has suggested that the data is, "reliable as standardly interpreted". Hedges also suggests that we cannot "on current understanding, rule out that the level of marine resource consumption which is indistinguishable from terrestrial values from a bulk collagen measurement may, under some conceivable circumstances, be as high as 30 percent" (*ibid.*: 37). The reasons for these inconsistencies are explained, to some degree, in relation to the Ertebølle of western Denmark (Fischer *et al.* 2007, and discussed below), but this situation is clearly in need of further work in Britain. One final point of note here is that Milner (2010; and Hellewell and Milner 2011) has recently pointed out that when considered from the perspective of the human experience, and change over generations, the transition to farming is actually of a similar duration to the entire Roman period in Britain! (*ibid.*: 65); food for thought perhaps?

The fact is that it could actually be argued that in many parts of Europe the Neolithic period itself is merely a prelude to the eventual adoption of full-scale farming, or even an interlude between the period when hunting, fishing and foraging was practiced successfully (to varying degrees) and the period (in a number of regions in Europe, after the Neolithic) when farming is a sufficiently developed food provisioning strategy to allow human groups to place an emphasis on agro-pastoral activities (with the concomitant marginalisation of hunting, fishing and foraging). In Britain there is a considerable amount of archaeological evidence to support the continued exploitation of wild resources throughout prehistory, a fact which, superficially, would appear to be at odds with the situation alluded to by Richards and Hedges (1999; 2003).

In general, researchers have recently begun to suggest that far from there being an abrupt dietary shift across the Mesolithic to Neolithic periods in Europe, the Mesolithic and Neolithic periods are characterised by a (sometimes very) gradual shift in emphasis from a purely hunter-fisher-forager way of life towards subsistence economies that integrate elements of "farming" economies in terms of domesticated plants and animals (Lidén *et al.* 2004). The "pigeon-holing" of groups of people as being either hunter-fisher-foragers or farmers serves to obfuscate this transitional stage in subsistence strategies, and obviously negates the potential for a considerable degree of overlap between "Mesolithic" and "Neolithic" groups. It also potentially obscures the variations that are attested by the archaeological record.

As noted by Borić (2000: 1036), "categories of foragers and farmers ... simplify and dichotomise the construction of past identities", and in essence the suggestion that the Neolithic is characterised by the adoption of agro-pastoral farming clearly underestimates the potential overlaps between these two periods. We need to consider the fact that our delineation of "Neolithic" is flawed, for as suggested by Czerniak (1998: 29) "all definitions of the Neolithic are imperfect and there is no true (universal) definition of this concept". As such, implying that transitional economies are virtually absent is clearly erroneous as transitional economies span the Mesolithic and much of the "Neolithic" throughout Europe; although it is apparent that looking for transitional economies effectively perpetuates the inherent limitations embedded in much of the current discourse relating to earlier Holocene societies (Borić 2000). As noted by Lidén *et al.* (2004: 23) "the transition from the Mesolithic to the Neolithic in Europe is an enigmatic event", and in Britain the shift from foraging to farming could conceivably be argued to span the period *ca.* 4200–2600 cal BC, i.e. the prelude to the adoption of "large-scale" farming in Britain, as it is during the Bronze Age and subsequent Iron Age periods in Britain that we really begin to see a shift to sedentary farming communities, albeit again with continued evidence for the exploitation of wild resources.

One is left with the impression that Czerniak's (1998) suggestion (above) is an understatement, and that in reality we are currently no nearer to understanding the nature (i.e. socio-economic and ritual aspects) of the shift towards food producing economies in Britain after *ca.* 4000 cal BC, than we were in the 1990s, or perhaps even earlier (e.g. Mithen 1999: 479). Despite this, the arguments put forward by Thomas (2008: 70), in support of the hypothesis that the British evidence could lend weight to a scenario in which Mesolithic groups in Britain were less sedentary than Irish groups at *ca.* 4000–3800 cal BC, and that the lack of Neolithic field systems, evidence for a degree of structuring in pits from this period, and the seasonality in use attested by causewayed enclosures, could all be used to argue against sedentary societies, are compelling. But, this does not negate the fact that by the later Mesolithic the population was probably concentrated into a more restricted "landscape context" than in earlier periods, or that the lack of evidence for settlements cannot provide *a priori* proof of a lack of sedentism in the Earlier Neolithic (e.g. Bonsall *et al.* 2002: 3).

We are perhaps at a point where we need to decouple the Neolithic and "sedentary farmers" and recognise that in Britain (and other areas of Europe) the evidence does not support this scenario, and that in actual fact a relatively mobile population utilising a range of resources could potentially characterise the earlier part of this period, and even up to *ca.* 3000 cal BC (or slightly later), and that the introduction of farming is the result of a number of relatively small-scale colonisation events (Whittle 2007a; 2009) coupled with a combination of indigenous adoption and acculturation. The idea that the transition to agriculture in Europe is characterised by "repeated episodes of very rapid spread, followed by long periods of stability", which "provide a more detailed picture that brings the information closer to the social history of particular populations" (Price and Bar-Yosef 2011: S166) contrasts with the evidence from Britain, and reinforces the suggestion that we need to know the specific context of the hunter-fisher-forager groups that we study in order to facilitate a realistic reading of the archaeological record for the period after *ca.* 4000 cal BC.

In exceptional circumstances it has been possible, elsewhere in Europe, to use the environmental evidence to offer an hypothesis for the rapid uptake of domesticates by hunter-fisher-foragers. For example, using evidence from the Ertebølle Mesolithic culture of western Denmark, Rowley Conwy (1984) has previously argued that a decrease in marine salinity caused a decline in oyster availability, which stimulated a rapid adoption of agriculture. However, again, this observation negates the "bigger picture" as the Ertebølle groups exploited both inland and coastal zones, and as a consequence, these groups utilised a broad range of resources, including wild pig, red deer, roe deer, and (in Jutland) aurochs and elk, with plants such as hazelnut being common finds on Mesolithic sites. In reality many other plant foods must also have been utilised (Rowley Conwy 1984: 302). The marine resources exploited by the Ertebølle groups included shellfish (principally oysters as mentioned above), many fish and bird species, and in addition, marine mammals were also exploited (*ibid.*: 302). The complex interplay of social and even ritual factors, alongside subsistence concerns, no doubt influenced the process of transition in this context. Irrespective of any hypothesised "crisis" in the marine-based part of the subsistence economy, the reality is that the data indicate a more complex interplay of socio-economic factors and a wider range of risk-buffering options for Ertebølle groups. Furthermore, the evidence from southern Sweden (Lidén *et al.* 2004: 30) has shown that a considerable degree of heterogeneity and a high degree of dietary diversity occurs across the Mesolithic and Neolithic periods.

The suggestion that the adoption of agriculture is abrupt and indicative of the migration of immigrant farmers in many parts of Europe (*cf.* Rowley-Conwy 2011) has numerous implications both for the Mesolithic period and for hunter-fisher-forager studies in general. If this perspective is correct (or even partly so) then the biggest question that this raises, must be; why did a subsistence strategy that had apparently worked well through previous glacial-interglacial cycles effectively "fail" throughout Europe within only 4000 years or so of the start of the current interglacial, simply because the wild progenitors of certain fauna and flora species were available? We may have to consider the possible range of alternative scenarios in attempting to explain the shift away from hunting, fishing and foraging to farming and accept that the transitions that occurred vary between individual groups and are often specific to discrete regions.

Numerous factors may have influenced the shift towards the domestication of a limited range of resources. Hunter-fisher-forager strategies had persisted across the Pleistocene, yet as Holocene landscapes and vegetation types developed after *ca.* 10,000 years ago, and as a broad range of resources became available in the developing deciduous woodlands of Europe, the wild fauna became less visible and more unpredictable as group size diminished and solitary animals are evidenced. Shifts in climate and environments were integral to these changes across the Pleistocene-Holocene transition through into the mid-Holocene period. On first viewing it appears that the tool-kits used by hunter-fisher-forager groups were adapted accordingly as new resources and environments were being exploited. The bow and arrow are introduced throughout Europe, and as noted in Chapter 4, we have evidence to suggest that there may have been competition amongst hunter-fisher-forager groups for access to stable resources, such as the fish that traversed the rapids along the Dnieper River in Ukraine or in the Danubian Iron Gates region. This competition may well imply seasonal resource shortages or resource scarcity occurring as a result of the expansion of deciduous forests during the earlier part of the Holocene.

The current interglacial period has evidenced the longest period of climatic stability to date, current suggestions of climate warming and hypothesised impacts aside, and it would seem inconceivable that this situation is not implicated in the developments that occur in the shift from food procurement to food production societies. It should also be noted that within this generally improving climatic situation, that there are periods, such as the Boreal/Atlantic transition (Godwin's pollen zones VI–VII – see Chapter 2), where the climate shifts from warm/dry conditions to warm/wet environments, and during pollen zone VII we see a shift back to warm/dry conditions at the zone VIIa to VIIb boundary, i.e. across the Atlantic to sub-Boreal transition. As this latter transition marks the end of the Mesolithic and the onset of the Neolithic periods in Britain, it would seem reasonable to suggest that the underlying trends in climate may link into other socio-economic factors across this period (e.g. Darvill 2010).

It is also conceivable, as implied in the above discussion, that despite the apparent richness of the early Holocene deciduous woodlands, in terms of the plant and animal resources that were available to Mesolithic groups, in reality the exploitation and reliance upon marine and freshwater resources is in fact reflecting a necessary shift in exploitation strategies that is caused by the unpredictability of the wild fauna due to the restructuring of the vegetation across the Mesolithic period. It is also conceivable that despite the "Swiss army knife" approach to tool-kits, these shifts in the focus of resource exploitation and the wide range of tool types in evidence are not, in fact, indicative of successful adaptation to the new environments, but are actually a reflection of the inability of hunter-fisher-forager groups to adequately adapt, or more likely a reflection of the difficulties experienced in trying to adjust to these new environments.

The vegetation firing/burning episodes that have been discussed throughout this volume have often been interpreted as reflecting some degree of "management" by Mesolithic groups, but if the preponderance of sites in open environments is taken further, the burning may have also functioned in creating more familiar landscape settings for Mesolithic groups to exploit. These openings may well have helped Mesolithic groups in developing a sense of "place" in what was an altogether unfamiliar woodland environment (although again it is recognised that divorcing anthropogenic from natural firing episodes is fraught with difficulty). As noted by Lynch *et al.* (2000: 26) woodland had expanded to cover most of Britain to heights in excess of 300m AOD in the earlier part of the Mesolithic, and between 9000–7000 uncal BP as much as 80% of the south welsh landscape was tree covered. In our efforts at attributing volition to Mesolithic groups in relation to the transition to agriculture, we may have failed to consider the alternative perspective, in that Mesolithic subsistence strategies may have already been unsustainable, or difficult to sustain, for all groups in all areas. The possible evidence for incipient agriculture and domestication at some locations in Europe could be used to argue for a scenario wherein Mesolithic groups were already exploring alternative food provisioning strategies. The appearance/immigration of agro-pastoralists at varying times in varying locations across Europe may well have been fortuitous in offering indigenous groups new ways to cope with the developing Holocene landscapes.

Perhaps a useful perspective would be to consider the evidence in terms of why regions such as the Baltic, where hunter-fisher-forager economies persist for longer, appear to be better suited to continuity and resistance to change? The Ertebølle are important in this context, but equally, successful foragers such as those in evidence in the Danubian Iron Gates region or in those regions to the east of the Dnieper in Ukraine, and further east in Russia appear to contradict the assertions made by Rowley-Conwy (2011). These regions may provide the exception that proves the rule, in that successful Holocene hunter-fisher-foragers are those groups that are usually in very specific ecological contexts in Europe, and by contrast Wales and perhaps Britain in general, may never have offered the same opportunities as the Baltic, Danube or eastern European areas in terms of landscape and environmental diversity, and consequently sustainability in hunter-fisher-forager lifeways, as the landscapes of Britain were not extensive or varied enough to sustain stable subsistence bases.

Transitions

As the above discussion has hopefully indicated, in general, there is actually relatively little in the way of archaeological evidence for the people or their settlements at the "start" of the Neolithic period in Britain, and indeed the evidence for large scale sedentary farming communities is also relatively weak (Thomas 2008: 69). Again however, by contrast, Hey and Barclay (2007: 400) have suggested that in the Thames Valley there are "occupation sites and middens with pottery, domesticates, polished stone tools and buildings", that appear in the archaeological record between 4000–3800 cal BC, which could perhaps suggest that in the southeast of Britain there is an "incipient" or transitional phase which may represent the beginnings of the shift towards the use of domesticates in subsistence strategies, concomitant with the migration of people and ideas from the continent.

It is clear however that this period is still in need of more targeted investigation as the resolution of the data remains poor (*ibid*.: 404). This suggestion is reinforced by Rowley-Conwy (2011: S443) who has shown that the largest Neolithic faunal assemblage in Britain has been recovered from Hambledon Hill, and that whilst this assemblage is dominated by domestic animals, the site itself is in fact dated to *ca*. 3650 cal BC, or perhaps slightly earlier (Whittle 2007a: 380, *citing* Healy 2004), i.e. some three centuries or so after the postulated onset of the "Neolithic". In general the evidence from sites like Hambledon Hill would seem to support a broad-spectrum subsistence economy in which domesticated animals such as cattle, sheep and pigs are the focus of the economy, and cereals such as wheats and barleys were integrated within a strategy that incorporated some degree of residential mobility, or a lack of any obvious signs of residence permanence.

There are a number of sites that do indicate a more "settled" way of life for some groups during the earlier part of the Neolithic period. For instance, at Llandegai, near Bangor in North Wales a rectangular house structure (house B1) measuring some 13 × 3.5m has been excavated (Lynch and Musson 2001: 27–32). Charcoal from the post-holes associated with this structure indicates that oak was used for the posts in this building, and that the house itself was comparable to an example from Ballyglass, Co. Mayo, being a tripartite structure (*ibid.*: 30). Similar earlier Neolithic house structures have been identified at Clegyr Boia, near St David's in Pembrokeshire (Lynch *et al.* 2001), and possibly among the features at the Iron Age hillfort of Moel y Gaer, Rhosesmor (Lynch and Musson 2001: 32; Lynch *et al.* 2001: 49). The dates obtained from charcoal in the post-holes from House B1 at Llandygai indicate that occupation occurred between *ca.* 4000–3600 cal BC (Lynch *et al.* 2001: appendix 1; although there are limitations in using charcoal as the wood may already have been of some antiquity prior to its use in the construction of the building). An interesting point of note in relation to these earlier houses is that they are usually found to stand alone, with little in the way of evidence for associated structures (Lynch and Musson 2001: 32), and in addition, they are rarely associated with significant accumulations of rubbish (Whittle 2009: 86). At Llandygai it appears that there was a period of some 300 years between the abandonment of the house and the subsequent phases of ritual activity at this location.

Importantly, there are very few absolute dates for domestic structures during the earlier part of the Neolithic period, and of course, the reliance on charcoal for dating at sites like Llandygai has been criticised due to the potential for an older, or potentially unrepresentative, date to be produced if the exact nature of the original wood used in construction is not identified. In general though, this lack of resolution cannot easily be avoided as there are very few sites, outside of waterlogged/wetland contexts, that contain organic material and well stratified sequences that are suitable for fine resolution dating of the associated deposits.

However, the evidence from Neolithic monuments in Britain, dating to the earlier part of the 4th millennium BC is increasing as new dating projects are undertaken (e.g. Bayliss *et al.* 2007a; 2007b). For Wales perhaps one of the more significant sites in this context is Gwernvale, where a Mesolithic lithic assemblage was recovered from beneath the Cotswold-Severn tomb. This lithic assemblage includes material from the Late Upper Palaeolithic, Early and later Mesolithic and Neolithic periods (Walker 2003: 19; Burrow 2003). A pit cut into the land surface that the lithic assemblages was recovered from produced a date (on charcoal) of 6895±80 uncal BP (CAR-118), which calibrates to 5980–5630 cal BC. Jones (2012: 1) has noted that the group of 12 tombs located in Breconshire, which includes Gwernvale, exhibit distinctive features that suggest they can be classified as a discrete group within the Cotswold-Severn grouping (which includes sites in the region of the Severn Estuary, in southeast Wales, the Cotwolds, and parts of Somerset, Wiltshire and Berkshire). We might perhaps consider this variability in relation to the entire Cotswold-Severn grouping as reflecting a measure of individual group identity at each of these locations, and the early dating of sites like Gwernvale could indicate a measure of continuity from the preceding Mesolithic period.

The fact is that we see precursors of Neolithic "traits" in the Mesolithic period, as attested by the ground stone axes at the Nab Head site II (David 2007), or the perpetuation of activity at significant locations in the landscape, as suggested at sites like Stonehenge or Bryn Celli Du on Anglesey, or the locations in southern England that are discussed by Allen and Gardiner (2002), and which have Mesolithic activity prior to the establishment of Neolithic monuments (e.g. Strawberry Hill, Thickthorn Down, Boscombe and Hambledon Hill). We also see structured depositions and the use of secondary burial contexts during the Mesolithic period, and this again occurs during the subsequent Neolithic period as the dead are moved between monuments. The suggestion that, after an hiatus in the later Mesolithic period, caves are again re-used during the earlier Neolithic may also be significant in that chambered tombs are effectively "caves" (Hellewell and Milner 2011: 66, *citing* Barnatt and Edmonds 2002); it might be interesting to plot the constructed burial sites against the natural locations to see whether they are mutually exclusive, or whether there are regional distinctions in evidence.

As has been indicated throughout the text up to this point, we could view the overlapping of Mesolithic and Neolithic material culture at locations such as Llandygai as indicative of a sense of place, or recognition of the significance of this (and other) locations by both Mesolithic and Neolithic groups (Allen and Gardiner 2002). In combination, the evidence for Mesolithic activity at a number of sites in Britain, alongside some early dates for monument construction, could be indicating that there is some sense of commonality between groups at either side of the "transition", and that there is in reality no great social divide between Mesolithic and Neolithic populations in the earlier part of the Neolithic period itself. The inconsistencies that occur between different regions may be a reflection of a range of variables, including the suitability of the landscape in terms of either pastoralism or cereal agriculture, or a combination of both subsistence strategies. The availability of a broad range of wild resources and therefore greater stability in hunter-fisher-forager subsistence strategies may delay the uptake of new resources, or in areas where resources are less predictable indigenous groups may have seen the new options as attractive in offering risk buffering alternatives, with pottery facilitating more viable storage options. Contacts between western Britain and Ireland, and the Atlantic facade on the continent may have occurred before Neolithic material culture was introduced, and it is not inconceivable to consider the possibility of allegiances forged through marriage, and the consequent dissemination of the knowledge of domestication through such contacts.

At Ferriter's Cove in southwestern Ireland there is evidence to suggest that domesticates occur in a later Mesolithic context at *ca.* 4300 cal BC (Woodman *et al.* 1999), and recent research by Hellewell and Milner (2011) has also shown that there are a number of finds that push the evidence for the integration of domesticates and other "farming package" elements back towards *ca.* 4000 cal BC. Included in this list are the sheep teeth from Ascott-under-Wychwood which are dated to 3990–3780 cal BC (GrA-27093: 5100±45 uncal BP; GrA-27094: 5095±45 uncal BP and GrA-27096: 5095±45 uncal BP) (Bayliss *et al.* 2007b: 34). In general it would appear that the period *ca.* 4000–3800 cal BC brackets the uptake of Neolithic material culture and in particular, the introduction of key domesticates, perhaps with the exception of pig, and that these introductions clearly have continental origins (Bradley 2007: 34).

If we accept that the beginning of the integration of elements of the "farming package" overlaps with Mesolithic activity in Britain, and that there is continuity of Mesolithic subsistence and ritual activity across the "4000 cal BC boundary", then the fact that the evidence across the transition is difficult to "read" is perhaps unsurprising, but in all likelihood it is highlighting continuity and the adoption of elements of the farming "package" by indigenous groups, along with some, perhaps relatively small-scale, immigration into Britain and Ireland.

Hunter-gatherer to farmer in Wales: developing a social narrative

On first viewing it appears that the shift from the Mesolithic to the "Neolithic" occurs at *ca.* 4000/3800 cal BC, although again, dates and finds that securely demonstrate the point of transition are lacking, and this shift is not necessarily one of a ubiquitous uptake of the farming economy over hunting and foraging. Jones (2000: 83) has suggested that cereals may well have formed a staple part of diets during the Neolithic period, and as such this implies that some degree of "sedentism" by at least a part of the population of Britain would probably have occurred. Irrespective of this observation, the fact remains that the wholesale adoption of a subsistence economy based on the exploitation of domesticates remains to be demonstrated for the earlier part of the Neolithic period in Britain.

Interestingly, there is some evidence for the integration of both food extraction and food production subsistence strategies in the earlier Neolithic, as attested by the finds from the Lambourn long barrow in Berkshire, dated to *ca.* 3800–3600 cal BC, where cattle, sheep, red deer and roe deer were represented in the finds from the ditches. At Prestatyn, Bell (2007e: 315) notes that the earliest reliable evidence for cereal cultivation occurs at Nant Hall Road. Here the evidence is indicative of continuity in activity, and the exploitation of molluscan resources extending across the period 4600–3400 cal BC. This evidence is mirrored at other welsh sites such as Bryn Newydd, Melyd Avenue, Bryn Rossa, the other Prestatyn sites, Splash Point, Rhyl and Rhuddlan (*ibid.*: 315).

Jacobi (1976) originally suggested that there is no artefactual evidence (based on the total absence of trapezoids [rhomboids] in British flint assemblages) for social connections between Britain and a *ca.* 1000 mile north–south area of mainland western Europe by 5750 uncal BC, and probably as early as *ca.* 6000 uncal BC. However, the reader is directed to the discussion presented by Thomas (2008), who provides an alternative perspective on the significance of this hypothesised "isolation" in terms of the maintenance of group identities and the likelihood that Mesolithic people were capable of crossing the channel.

It has been argued that throughout Europe most claims for agriculture being practiced by Mesolithic groups are unsubstantiated, and that in actual fact in most places full sedentary agriculture was introduced very rapidly at the start of the Neolithic (e.g. Rowley Conwy 2011).

This assertion is clearly not justified on the basis of the evidence for the Mesolithic and Neolithic periods in large areas of Europe, especially in southern Scandinavia, where Lidén *et al.* (2004) have argued convincingly for a mixed dietary situation in both periods, with both marine and terrestrial subsistence strategies being followed. These authors have stated that "there is no 'simple' general solution regarding the Mesolithic–Neolithic transition, and that there is a need to look more specifically at each region and each site and to examine its particular conditions in order to understand when, why and how the transition took place" (*ibid.*: 31). There is little doubting this perspective as throughout Europe the adoption of domesticates is both regionally and context specific, and no doubt linked to the nature of the environment, society and the cultural group being considered. The British evidence for the period across the later part of the 5th millennium and the earlier part of the 4th millennium BC is lacking and in need of targeted research, and a more careful reading of the available evidence. There are numerous limitations in the archaeological record and there is little doubt that this situation is unsatisfactory.

The above discussion has offered a range of traditional perspectives on the transition from hunter-fisher-forager lifeways towards those that were focussed on the exploitation of domesticated resources. It is an established fact that aspects of the "Neolithic package", such as pottery and polished stone axes, appear at around, or soon after *ca.* 3800 cal BC, but the degree to which the farming economy itself is adopted remains to be determined with any degree of certainty.

Finally, Rowley-Conwy (2011: S443), in discussing the evidence for the transition to agriculture in Britain and Ireland has stated that "we must face the surprising possibility that Ireland 'went agricultural' before Britain, (and) if true, it would be the biggest leapfrog migration in Europe". However, we should also consider the fact that in reality the transmission of agriculture from northwestern France to Ireland is perhaps not such a great leap given the evidence for maritime resource exploitation from the Mesolithic period onwards. As with all other areas of the transition from food-extracting to food producing societies, the data needs to be analysed at the local and regional level in order to ensure that realistic narratives of the processes of change are generated. This observation is pertinent for Europe as a whole, and is not exclusive to research in the British and Irish context.

Epilogue

Archaeologists have long known that the archaeological record is fragmentary, biased and as such difficult to use in isolation, especially when trying to interpret prehistoric human behaviour. For this reason the use of anthropology/ethnographic analogy, as employed throughout this volume, has proven fundamental in offering a range of insights into the numerous alternative interpretations of past cultural behaviour at all levels of analysis. The fact that material culture is the product of a culturally mediated set of socially bounded inter-relationships tied within myriad personal and group signifiers necessitates a cautious use of ethnography when trying to understand the archaeological record for hunter-fisher-forager groups, irrespective of the protracted debate surrounding the origins and use of these terms (see Pluciennik 2004 for a detailed overview). Whilst this "cautious" approach has been attempted in this volume, the reader should be aware that as a researcher and a culturally and socially bounded human being, my own cultural biases and inherent preferences will have influenced the examples that have been used. Similarly, whilst every effort has been made to engage with a broad range of ethnographic literature, there are bound to be "better" or "more appropriate" examples that could have been applied, but this is a matter of opinion and opinions will always differ.

The fact that the archaeological record of hunter-fisher-foragers (a term that I have employed because I like the "fit" for describing these groups in the past; Myers 1988; Marlowe 2005) is impoverished, again due to myriad factors, has necessitated a "broad brush" approach to the Welsh evidence in order to situate the Mesolithic of Wales in its wider context. In addition, in trying to provide a broad overview Chapter 6 has sought to tease out some of the less obvious aspects of Mesolithic life in Wales, and as Jordan (2011: 13) has noted that "recent years have witnessed a growing archaeological interest in cultural landscapes and the symbolic dimensions to social life", but that this has often been done in ignorance of the ways in which belief systems and cosmology might "generate material signatures in northern landscapes", the use of ethnographic analogies has proven fundamental to this narrative. As a landscape archaeologist I have always sought to understand human-landscape interactions, and throughout this volume the fact that ritual, cosmology and belief systems can influence the record of past hunter-fisher-foragers has been considered wherever possible, often with a reliance on the work of individuals like Marek Zvelebil and Peter Jordan. Unfortunately, the lack of direct physical evidence for these elements of the daily lives of Mesolithic peoples in Wales (and many parts of Europe) necessitates levels of inference that can be criticised as being "speculative" at best. This observation is made with the caveat that the work of Jordan (and others) has sought to identify, from the recent ethnographic record, those aspects of the ritualised behaviour of living groups that have the potential to leave an archaeological "signature" (Jordan 2011:

17 and references therein), and through this approach it is hoped that we can generate more meaningful narratives of the past.

However, as also noted by Jordan during his study of the Khanty of western Siberia, whilst there are activities, such as production, processing and storage, that result in the generation of a "modest architectural landscape of cabins, fish weirs, storage huts, clay ovens, cooking and roasting sites" (Jordan 2011: 17) the archaeological signatures that such sites will leave are difficult to identify as many post-depositional factors will come in to play before such locations are eventually excavated by archaeologists. This has been highlighted throughout this volume as we have considered the changing landscapes of the earlier Holocene, the implications of sea level rise and vegetation (and as a consequence faunal biomass) changes, limitations imposed by the lack of sites that occur in wetland/waterlogged locations (or the lack of visibility of such sites), the nature of hunter-fisher-forager landscape interactions in general, and issues relating to our own studies of hunter-fisher-foragers in Britain. All of these biases impact upon our studies of Mesolithic peoples, and as noted above, after all this we still need to try to interpret the past and understand the implications of the symbolic aspects of hunter-fisher-forager lifeways and the way that these influenced the everyday articulations of cultural landscapes and the material signatures of this activity (*ibid*.: 18).

In endeavouring to place a realistic and meaningful emphasis on the myriad facets of daily life in the Mesolithic, this volume has sought to touch upon a broad range of topics and ways of generating "authorised" interpretations of the evidence. The reader will, hopefully, see the rationale for this approach and choose to engage with the text in ways that have resonance and meaning to their own lived experience and culturally embedded perceptions of landscape. Perhaps, by extension, this engagement may help us to begin to understand what it might have meant to be a hunter-fisher-forager in the Mesolithic period. The ethnographic and archaeological examples that have been used throughout this volume have been integrated in an effort to provide a range of possibilities, or options, for use in interpreting Mesolithic lifeways, both in Wales and further afield.

When commencing this project I had hoped to bring a wide range of academic knowledge to the table in an effort to make the welsh evidence more accessible. Unfortunately, what started out as a project aimed at creating an easily accessible summary of the evidence turned into a pretty dense treatise of the myriad aspects of the Mesolithic in general, and whilst I have endeavoured to keep a focus on the welsh evidence wherever practicable, the data does not easily lend itself to this aim. As such, this volume is quite "broad brush" in terms of the examples that are used to illustrate specific elements of the Mesolithic and the ways in which Mesolithic people lived and died during this period. All in all, this volume became a labour of love and a body of work that I hope, if nothing else, provides students of the discipline with a suitably detailed overview of the range of research that has been used in studying the Mesolithic. It is hoped that this detail becomes valued as a strength in relation to this volume, and that once read the text proves sufficiently informative to allow the reader to develop their own opinions on life in the Mesolithic period.

And finally ....

I hope that in some small way this volume excites the imagination and prompts the reader to explore the rich and diverse literature that surrounds hunter-fisher-forager studies and Mesolithic studies in general. At the very least I hope that the reader is encouraged to visit Wales and experience the landscape for themselves, as even today 6000 years after the Mesolithic ended, the more remote parts of the Welsh uplands are still an awe inspiring and beautiful place to visit and experience.

Ac yn olaf...

Yr wyf yn gobeithio bod mewn rhyw ffordd fach gyfrol hon cyffroi'r dychymyg ac yn annog y darllenydd i edrych ar y llenyddiaeth cyfoethog ac amrywiol sy'n amgylchynu'r astudiaethau helwyr-bysgotwr-forager ac astudiaethau Mesolithig yn gyffredinol. Ar y lleiaf yr wyf yn gobeithio y bydd y darllenydd yn cael ei annog i ymweld â Chymru a phrofi'r tirwedd ar gyfer eu hunain, gan fod hyd yn oed heddiw 6000 o flynyddoedd ar ôl y cyfnod Mesolithig a ddaeth i ben, y rhannau mwy anghysbell o'r ucheldir Cymreig yn dal i fod yn arswyd ysbrydoledig a hardd lle i ymweld ag ef a profiad.

REFERENCES

Adovasio, J. M., Soffer, O. and Page, J. 2007. *The Invisible Sex: Uncovering the roles of Women in Prehistory*. New York: Smithsonian Press.

Ahlström, T. 2003. Mesolithic human remains from Tågerup, Scania, Sweden, in Larsson *et al.* (eds) 2003: 478–84.

Aldhouse-Green, S. 1996. Hoyle's Mouth and Little Hoyle Caves (SN 112 003). *Archaeology in Wales* 36: 70–1.

Aldhouse-Green, S. 1998. The archaeology of distance: perspectives from the Welsh Palaeolithic, in Ashton *et al.* (eds) 1998: 137–45. Aldhouse-Green, S. 2000a. Palaeolithic and Mesolithic Wales: Part I: the Palaeolithic period, in Lynch *et al.* (eds) 2000: 1–22.

Aldhouse-Green, S. 2000b. *Paviland Cave and the Red Lady: A definitive report*. Bristol: Western Academic & Specialist Press.

Aldhouse-Green, S. 2000c. Palaeolithic and Mesolithic Wales: Part II: the Mesolithic period, in Lynch *et al.* (eds) 2000: 23–41. Stroud: Sutton.

Aldhouse-Green, S. and Pettitt, P. B. 1998. Paviland Cave: contextualizing the 'Red Lady'. *Antiquity* 72(278): 756–72.

Aldhouse-Green, S., Peterson, R. and Walker, E. A. 2011. *Neanderthals in Wales: Pontnewydd and the Elwy Valley*. Oxford: Oxbow Books/National Museum Wales.

Aldhouse-Green, S., Scott, K., Schwarcz, H., Grün, R., Houseley, R., Rae, A., Bevins, R. and Redknap, M. 1995. Coygan Cave, Laugharne, south Wales, a Mousterian site and Hyaena Den: a report on the University of Cambridge excavations. *Proceedings of the Prehistoric Society* 61: 37–79.

Alexandersen, V. 1988. Description of the human dentitions from the Late Mesolithic grave–fields at Skateholm, southern Sweden, in Larsson, L. (ed.) *The Skateholm Project, I: Man and Environment*. Stockholm: Almqvist & Wiksell International.

Allen, J. R. L. 1991. Saltmarsh accretion and sea level movement in the inner Severn Estuary, southwest Britain: the archaeological and historical contribution. *Journal of the Geological Society* 148: 485–94.

Allen, J. R. L. 2000a. Sea level, saltmarsh and fen: shaping the Severn Estuary Levels in the later Quaternary (Ipswichian–Holocene). *Archaeology in the Severn Estuary* 11: 13–34.

Allen, J. R. L. 2000b. Goldcliff Island: geological and sedimentological background, in Bell *et al.* (eds) 2000: 12–18.

Allen, J. R. L. 2001. Sea level, saltmarsh and fen: shaping the Severn Estuary levels in the Later Quaternary (Ipswichian–Holocene), in Rippon, S. (ed.) *Estuarine Archaeology: The Severn and Beyond. Archaeology in the Severn Estuary* 11: 13–34.

Allen, J. R. L. 2005. Teleconnections and their archaeological implications, Severn Estuary Levels and the Wider Region: The 'fourth' and other mid–Holocene peats. *Archaeology in the Severn Estuary* 16: 17–65.

Allen, J. R. L. and Bell, M. G. 1999. A Late Holocene tidal palaeochannel, Redwick, Gwent: Late Roman activity and a possible early Medieval fish trap. *Archaeology in the Severn Estuary* 10: 53–64.

Allen, J. R. L. and Haslett, S. K. 2006. Granulometric characterization and evaluation of annually banded mid–Holocene estuarine silts, Welsh Severn Estuary (UK): coastal change, sea level and climate. *Quaternary Science Reviews* 25: 1418–46.

Allen, J. R. L. and Rae, J. E. 1987. Late Flandrian shoreline oscillations in the Severn Estuary. *Philosophical Transactions of the Royal Society London* B315: 185–230.

Allen, M. J. and Gardiner, J. 2002. A sense of time: cultural markers in the Mesolithic of southern England? in David, B. and Wilson, M. (eds) *Inscribed Landscapes: Marking and Making Place*: 139–53. Honolulu: University of Hawaii Press.

Alley, R. B. 2000a. *The Two-Mile Time Machine. Ice Cores, Abrupt Climate Change, and Our Future.* Princeton, NJ: Princeton University Press.

Alley, R. B. 2000b. The Younger Dryas cold interval as viewed from central Greenland. *Quaternary Science Reviews* 19: 213–26.

Ames, K. M. 1994. The northwest coast: complex hunter–gatherers, ecology, and social evolution. *Annual Review of Anthropology* 23: 209–29.

Ames, K. M. 2003. The northwest coast. *Evolutionary Anthropology* 12: 19–33.

Anderson, J. 1895. Notice of a cave recently discovered at Oban, containing human remains, and a refuse heap of shells and bones of animals, and stone and bone implements, *Proceedings of the Society of Antiquaries of Scotland* 29, 211–30.

Anderson, J. 1898. Notes on the contents of a small cave or rock–shelter at Druimvargie, Oban; and of three shellmounds in Oronsay, *Proceedings of the Society of Antiquaries of Scotland* 32, 298–313.

Anderson, D. G. 2002. The Evenki of the lower Enisei Valley, in Lee, R. B. and Daly, R. (eds), *The Cambridge Encyclopedia of Hunters and Gatherers*: 142–6. Cambridge: Cambridge University Press. .

Andersson, M., Karsten, P., Knarrström, B. and Svensson, M. 2004. Stone Age Scania: significant places dug and read by contract archaeology. *Riksantikvarieämbetets Förlag Skrifter* 52. Malmö, Sweden: Elanders Berlings.

Andresen, J. M., Byrd, B. F., Elson, M. D., McGuire, R. H., Mendosa, R. G., Staski, E. and White, J. P. 1981. The deer hunters: Star Carr reconsidered. *World Archaeology* 13: 31–46.

Angel, J. L. 1966. Porotic hyperostosis, anemias, malarias, and marshes in the prehistoric eastern Mediterranean. *Science* 153: 760–3.

Armour-Chelu, M. 2007. Animal bones, in Armour-Chelu, M., Bell, M., Bratshay, B., Britnell, W. J., Cameron, N., Caseldine, A. E., Dresser, P. Q., Fancourt, E., Gonzalez, S., Healey, E., Johnson, S., Norris-Hill, J., Schulting, R. and Thomas, D. 2007. Shell middens and their environment at Prestatyn, north Wales, in Bell (ed.) 2007a: 263–317.

Ashton, N., McNabb, J., Irving, B., Lewis, S. and Parfitt, S. 1994. Contemporaneity of Clactonian and Acheulian flint industries at Barnham, Suffolk. *Antiquity* 68: 585–9.

Ashton, N., Healy, F. and Pettitt, P. (eds) 1998. *Stone Age Archaeology: Essays in honour of John Wymer.* Oxford: Lithic Studies Society Occasional Paper 6/Oxbow Monograph 102.

Ashworth, A. C. 1973. The climatic significance of a Late Quaternary insect fauna from Rodbaston Hall, Staffordshire, England. *Entomologica Scandinavica* 4: 191–205.

Backhouse, P. N. and Johnson, E. 2007. Where were the hearths: an experimental investigation of the archaeological signature of prehistoric fire technology in the alluvial gravels of the Southern Plains. *Journal of Archaeological Science* 34: 1367–78.

Bahn, P. and Pettitt, P. 2009. *Britain's Oldest Cave Art: The Ice Age Cave Art of Creswell Crags.* Swindon: English Heritage.

Bailey, G. N. 1987. Shell middens as indicators of postglacial economies, in Mellars, P. (ed.), *The Early Postglacial Settlement of Northern England*: 37–64. London: Duckworth.

Bailey, G. N. and Flemming, N. C. 2008. Archaeology of the continental shelf: Marine resources, submerged landscapes and underwater archaeology. *Quaternary Science Reviews* 27: 2153–65.

Bailey, G. and Spikins, P. 2008. *Mesolithic Europe.* Cambridge: Cambridge University Press.

Balakin, S. and Nuzhinyi, D. 1995. The origins of graveyards: the influence of landscape elements on social and ideological changes in prehistoric communities. *Préhistoire Européenne* 7: 191–202.

Ballin, T. B. 2000. Classification and description of lithic artefacts: a discussion of the basic lithic terminology. *Lithics* 21: 9–15.

Banks, W. E., d'Errico, F., Peterson, A. T., Kageyama, M., Adriana Sima, A. and Sánchez-Goñi, M-F. 2008. Neanderthal extinction by competitive exclusion. *PLoS ONE* 3(12): e3972: 1–8.

Barnard, A. 1983. Contemporary Hunter-gatherers: current theoretical issues in ecology and social organisation. *Annual Review of Anthropology* 12: 193–214.

Barnatt, J. and Edmonds. M. 2002. Places apart? Caves and monuments in Neolithic and earlier Bronze Age Britain. *Cambridge Archaeological Journal* 12(1): 113–29.

Barton, R. N. E. 2000. The Late Mesolithic Assemblages, in Bell, *et al.* (eds), 2000: 39–48.

Barton, N. 2009. The Lateglacial or Latest Palaeolithic occupation of Britain, in Hunter, J. and Ralston, I. (eds), *The Archaeology of Britain: An Introduction for Earliest Times to the Twenty-First Century* (2nd ed.): 18–52. London: Routledge.

Barton, N. and Bell, M. 2000. Mesolithic site conclusions, in Bell *et al.* (eds) 2000: 58–63.

Barton, R. N. E., Berridge, P. J., Walker, M. J. C. and Bevins, R. E. 1995. Persistent places in the Mesolithic landscape: an example from the Black Mountain uplands of south Wales. *Proceedings of the Prehistoric Society* 1: 81–116.

Barton, R. N. E., Jacobi, R. M., Stapert, D. and Street, M. 2003. The Lateglacial reoccupation of the British Isles and the Creswellian. *Journal of Quaternary Science* 18: 631–43.

Bartosiewicz, L., Bonsall, C. and Şişu, V. 2008. Sturgeon fishing in the middle and lower Danube, in Bonsall, C., Boroneant, V. and Radovanović, I. (eds), *The Iron Gates in Prehistory: New Perspectives*: 39–54. Oxford: British Archaeological Report S1893.

Bartosiewicz, L., Zapata, L. and Bonsall, C. 2010. A tale of two shell middens: the natural versus the cultural in "Obanian" deposits at Carding Mill Bay, Oban, western Scotland, in Van Derwarker, A. M. and Peres, T. M. (eds), *Integrating Zooarchaeology and Paleoethnobotany*: 205–25. New York: Springer.

Bateman, M. D., Buckland, P. C., Chase, B., Frederick, C. D. and Gaunt, G. D. 2008. The Late-Devensian proglacial Lake Humber: new evidence from littoral deposits at Ferrybridge, Yorkshire, England. *Boreas* 37: 195–210.

Bateman, M. D., Buckland, P. C., Whyte, M. A., Ashurst, R. A., Boulter, C. and Panagiotakopulu, E. 2011. Re-evaluation of the Last Glacial Maximum typesite at Dimlington, UK. *Boreas* 40: 573–84.

Bayliss, A. and Whittle, A. (eds) 2007. *Histories of the Dead: Building Chronologies for Five Southern British Long Barrows. Cambridge Archaeological Journal* 17(1) supplement.

Bayliss, A. and Woodman, P. 2009. A new Bayesian chronology for Mesolithic occupation at Mount Sandal, Northern Ireland. *Proceedings of the Prehistoric Society* 75: 101–23.

Bayliss, A., Boomer, I., Bronk Ramsey, C., Hamilton, D. and Waddington, C. 2007a. Absolute dating, in Waddington (ed.) 2007a: 65–74.

Bayliss, A., Benson, D., Galer, D., Humphrey, L., McFadyen, L. and Whittle, A. 2007b. One thing after another: the date of the Ascott-under-Wychwood long barrow, in Bayliss and Whittle (eds), 2007: 29–44.

BBC News. 2013. Stone Age carved wooden post found at Rhondda wind farm. dated 17–07–2013 Available online at: http://www.bbc.co.uk/news/uk-wales-23349783

Bell, M. 1995. Field survey and excavation at Goldcliff, Gwent 1994, in Bell, M. (ed.), *Archaeology in the Severn Estuary*: 115–44. Annual Report of the Severn Estuary Levels Research Committee. Lampeter: Welsh Office Highways Agency, CADW and RCHME.

Bell, M. 1999. Prehistoric settlements and activities in the Welsh Severn Estuary, in Coles, B., Coles, J. and Schou Jørgensen, M. (eds), *Bog Bodies, Sacred Sites and Wetland Archaeology*: 17–25. Exeter: WARP Occasional Paper 12.

Bell, M. 2000. Introduction to the Holocene sedimentary sequence (with contributions by J. James and H. Neumann), in Bell *et al.* (eds) 2000: 19–32.

Bell, M. with Allen, J. R. L., Barton, R. N. E., Coard, R., Crowther, J., Cruise, G. M., Ingrem, C. and Macphail, R. 2000. The Goldcliff late-Mesolithic site, 5400–4000 cal BC, in Bell *et al.* (eds) 2000: 33–63.

Bell, M. 2001. Environmental archaeology in the Severn Estuary: progress and prospects, in Rippon, S. (ed.), *Estuarine Archaeology: the Severn and Beyond*: 69–103. *Archaeology in the Severn Estuary* 11.

Bell, M. 2004. Footsteps into past coastal landscapes. *NERC: Planet Earth*: 14–15.

Bell, M. (ed.) 2007a. *Prehistoric Coastal Communities: the Mesolithic in Western Britain*. York: Council for British Archaeology Research Report 149.

Bell, M. 2007b. Mesolithic coastal communities in western Britain: conclusions, in Bell (ed.) 2007a: 318–43.

Bell, M. 2007c. Mesolithic activity at about the time of the lower submerged forest, in Bell (ed.) 2007a: 36–47.

Bell, M. 2007d. Island edge occupation: Site A, in Bell (ed.) 2007a: 57–62.

Bell, M. 2007e. Island edge occupation: Site J, in Bell (ed.) 2007a: 63–82.

Bell, M. 2007f. Conclusions: the Mesolithic/Neolithic transition in the Prestatyn area, in Armour-Chelu *et al.* 2007: 308–17.

Bell, M. and Walker, M. J. C. 2005. *Late Quaternary Environments. Physical and Human Perspectives* (2nd ed.). Harlow, Pearson Prentice Hall/Pearson Education.

Bell, M. G., Caseldine, A. and Neumann, H. (eds) 2000. *Prehistoric Intertidal Archaeology in the Welsh Severn Estuary*. York: Council for British Archaeology Research Report 126.

Bell, M., Allen, J. R. L., Nayling, N. and Buckley, S. 2002. Mesolithic to Neolithic coastal environmental change *c.* 6500–3500 cal BC. *Archaeology in the Severn Estuary* 12: 27–53.

Bell, M., Allen, J. R. L., Buckley, S., Dark, P. and Haslett, S. K. 2003. Mesolithic to Neolithic coastal environmental change: excavations at Goldcliff East, 2002. *Archaeology in the Severn Estuary* 13: 1–29.

Bell, M., Allen, J. R. L., Buckley, S., Dark, P. and Nayling, N. 2004. Mesolithic to Neolithic coastal environmental change: excavations at Goldcliff East, 2003 and research at Redwick. *Archaeology in the Severn Estuary* 14: 1–26.

Bello, S. M., Parfitt, S. A. and Stringer, C. B. 2011. Earliest directly-dated human skull-cups. *PLoS ONE* 6(2): e17026. doi: 10.1371/journal.pone.0017026

Benecke, N. 1987. Studies on early dog remains from northern Europe. *Journal of Archaeological Science* 14: 1–11.

Bennett, K. D. 1986. The rate of spread and population increase of forest tress during the postglacial. *Philosophical Transactions of the Royal Society of London* B 314: 523–31.

Bennett, K. D. and Birks, H. J. B. 1990. Post glacial history of alder (*Alnus glutinosa* (L.) *Gaertn.*) in the British Isles. *Journal of Quaternary Science* 5(2): 123–33.

Berglund, B. E. (ed.) 1986. *Handbook of Holocene Palaeoecology and Palaeohydrology*. Chichester: John Wiley & Sons.

Berndt, C. H. 1981. Interpretations and "facts" in aboriginal Australia, in Dahlberg (ed.). 1981: 153–203.

Bernhard Weninger, B., Schulting, R., Bradtmöller, M., Clare, L., Collard, M., Edinborough, K., Hilpert, J., Jöris, O., Niekus, M., Rohling, E. J., and Wagner, B. 2008. The catastrophic final flooding of Doggerland by the Storegga Slide tsunami. *Documenta Praehistorica* 35: 1–24.

Berridge, P. 1994a. The lithics, in Quinnell and Blockley (eds) 1994: 95–114.

Berridge, P. 1994b. The Mesolithic decorated and other pebble artefacts: synthesis, in Quinnell and Blockley (eds) 1994: 115–31.

Bērziņš, V. 2010. Fishing seasonality and techniques in prehistory: why freshwater fish are special. *Archaeologia Baltica* 13: 37–41.

Bevan, L. and Moore, J. (eds) 2003. *Peopling the Mesolithic in a Northern Environment*. Oxford: British Archaeological Report 1157.

Binford, L. R. 1962. Archaeology as anthropology. *American Antiquity* 28(2): 217–25.

Binford, L. R. 1979. Organisation and formation processes: looking at curated technologies. *Journal of Anthropological Research* 35(3): 255–73.

Binford, L. R. 1980. Willow smoke and dogs' tails: hunter–gatherer settlement systems and archaeological site formation. *American Antiquity* 45(1): 4–20.

Binford, L. R. 1983. *In Pursuit of the Past*. London: Thames and Hudson.

Binford, L. R. 1990. Mobility, housing and environment: a comparative study. *Journal of Anthropological Research* 46(2): 119–52.

Binford, L. R. 2009. Methodological considerations of the archaeological use of ethnographic data, in Lee and DeVore (eds), 2009b: 268–73.

Bird, D. W. and Bliege Bird, R. 2007. Martu Children's Hunting Strategies in the Western Desert, Australia, in Hewlett and Lamb (eds) 2007: 129–46

Birks, H. J. B. 1989. Holocene isochrone maps and patterns of tree-spreading in the British Isles. *Journal of Biogeography* 16(6): 503–40.

Blockley, S. P. E., Donaghue, R. E. and Pollard, A. M. 2000. Radiocarbon calibration and Late-Glacial occupation in northwest Europe. *Antiquity* 74: 112–21.

Blockley, S. P. E., Lowe, J. J., Walker, M. J. C., Asioli, A., Trincardi, F., Coope, G. R., Pollard, A. M. and Donahue, R. E. 2004. Bayesian analysis of radiocarbon chronologies: examples from the European Lateglacial. *Journal of Quaternary Science* 19: 159–75.

Blockley, S. P. E., Blockley, S. M., Donahue, R. E., Lane, C. S., Lowe, J. J. and Pollard, A. M. 2006. The chronology of abrupt climate change and Late Upper Palaeolithic human adaptation in Europe. *Journal of Quaternary Science* 21: 575–84.

Blurton Jones, N. 1976. Rough–and–tumble play among nursery school children, in Bruner, J. S., Jolly, A. and Sylva, K. (eds), *Play: It's Role in Development and Evolution*: 352–63. Harmondsworth: Penguin Books.

Blurton Jones, N., Hawkes, K. and Draper, P. 1994. Foraging returns of !kung adults and children: why didn't !kung children forage? *Journal of Anthropological Research* 50: 217–48.

Bock, J. 2007. What makes a competent adult forager? in Hewlett and Lamb (eds) 2007: 109–28.

Bogaard, A. and Jones, G. 2007. Neolithic farming in Britain and central Europe: contrast or continuity? in Whittle and Cummings (eds) 2007: 357–75.

Bondevik, S., Svendsen, J. I., Johnsen, G., Mangerud, J. and Kaland, P. E. 1997. The Storegga tsunami along the Norwegian coast, its age and runup. *Boreas* 26: 29–53.

Bondevik, S., Mangerud, J., Dawson, S., Dawson, A. and Lohne, Ø. 2005. Evidence for three North Sea tsunamis at the Shetland Islands between 8000 and 1500 years ago. *Quaternary Science Reviews* 24: 1757–75.

Bonsall, C. 1981. The coastal factor in the Mesolithic settlement of North-West England, in Gramsch, B. (ed.), *Mesolithikum in Europa. 2. Internationales Symposium Potsdam 3–8 April 1978 Bericht*: 461–72. Berlin: Deutscher Verlag.

Bonsall, C. 1989a. Ulva Cave, Isle of Ulva, Argyll. *University of Edinburgh Department of Archaeology Annual Report 35*: 23–4.

Bonsall, C. (ed.) 1989b. *The Mesolithic in Europe*. Edinburgh: John Donald.

Bonsall, C. 1990. Ulva Cave excavations. *University of Edinburgh Department of Archaeology Annual Report 36: 15–16*.

Bonsall, C. 1996. The "Obanian" problem: coastal adaptation in the Mesolithic of western Scotland, in Pollard, T. and Morrison, A. (eds), *The Early Prehistory of Scotland*: 183–97. Edinburgh: Edinburgh University Press.

Bonsall, C. 2007. When was the Neolithic transition in the Balkans?, in Spataro, M. and Biagi, P. (eds), *A Short Walk through the Balkans: the First Farmers of the Carpathian Basin and Adjacent Regions*: 53–66. Società Preistoria Protostoria Friuli-V.G., Trieste, Quaderno 12.

Bonsall, C. 2008. The Mesolithic of the Iron Gates, in Bailey, G. and Spikins, P. (eds), *Mesolithic Europe*: 238–79. Cambridge: Cambridge University Press.

Bonsall, C., Anderson, D. E. and Macklin, M. G. 2002. The Mesolithic–Neolithic transition in western Scotland and its European context. *Documenta Praehistorica* 29: 1–19.

Bonsall, C., Macklin, M. G., Payton, R. W. and A. Boroneanţ. 2002. Climate, floods and river gods: environmental change and the Mesolithic–Neolithic transition in southeast Europe. *Before Farming* 3–4(2): 1–15.

Bonsall, C., Cook, G., Lennon, R., Harkness, D., Scott, M., Bartosiewicz, L. and McSweeney, K. 1997. Stable isotopes, radiocarbon and the Mesolithic–Neolithic transition in the iron gates: a palaeodietary perspective. *Journal of European Archaeology* 5(1): 50–92.

Bonsall, C., Cook, G., Lennon, R., Harkness, D., Scott, M., Bartosiewicz, L. and McSweeney, K. 2000. Stable isotopes, radiocarbon and the Mesolithic–Neolithic transition in the Iron Gates. *Documenta Praehistorica* 27: 119–32.

Bonsall, C., Cook, G. T., Hedges, R. E. M., Higham, T. F. G., Pickard, C. and Radovanoviç, I. 2004. Radiocarbon and stable isotope evidence of dietary change from the Mesolithic to the middle ages in the iron gates: new results from Lepenski Vir. *Radiocarbon* 46(1): 293–300.

Bonsall, C., Lennon, R., McSweeney, K., Stewart, C., Harkness, D., Boroneant, V., Bartosiewicz, L., Payton, R. and Chapman, J. 1997. Mesolithic and Early Neolithic in the Iron Gates: a palaeodietary perspective. *Journal of European Archaeology* 5(1): 50–92

Bonsall, C., Radovanović, I., Roksandic, M., Cook, G., Higham, T. and Pickard, C. 2008. Dating burial practices and architecture at Lepenski Vir, in Bonsall, C., Boroneanţ, V. and Radovanović, I. (eds), *The Iron Gates in Prehistory: New Perspectives*: 175–204. Oxford: British Archaeological Report S1893.

Boreham, S., Conneller, C., Milner, N. Taylor, B., Needham, A., Boreham, J. and Rolfe, C. J. 2011. Geochemical indicators of preservation status and site deterioration at Star Carr. *Journal of Archaeological Science* 38: 2833–57.

Borgerhoff Mulder, M. 1999. On pastoralism and inequality. *Current Anthropology* 40(3): 366–7.

Borić, D. 2002. The Lepenski Vir conundrum: reinterpretation of the Mesolithic and Neolithic sequences in the Danube Gorges. *Antiquity* 76: 1026–39.

Bradley, R. 1984. *The Social Foundations of Prehistoric Britain*. Harlow: Longman.

Bradley, R. 2000. *An Archaeology of Natural Places*. London: Routledge.

Bradley, R. S. 1999. *Palaeoclimatology: Reconstructing Climates of the Quaternary* (2nd ed.). Amsterdam: Elsevier Academic Press International Geophysics Series 68.

Brantingham, J. P. 2006. Measuring forager mobility. *Current Anthropology* 47(3): 435–59.

Brassil, K. S., Owen, W. G. and Britnell, W. J. 1991. Prehistoric and early medieval cemeteries at Tandderwen, near Denbigh, Clwyd. *Archaeological Journal* 148: 46–97.

Brayshay, B. and Caseldine, A. E. 2007. Pollen analysis, in Armour-Chelu *et al.* 2007: 287–95.

Bridges, P. S. 1989. Changes in activities with the shift to agriculture in the southeastern United States. *Current Anthropology* 30(3): 385–94.

Brinch Petersen, E. and Meiklejohn, C. 2003. Three cremations and a funeral: aspects of burial practice in Mesolithic Vedbæk, in Larsson *et al.* (eds) 2003: 485–93.

Brooks, S. J. and Birks, H. J. B. 2000. Chironomid-inferred Late-glacial air temperatures at Whitrig Bog, southeast Scotland. *Journal of Quaternary Science* 15(8): 759–64.

Brooks, S. J., Matthews, I. P., Birks, H. H. and Birks. H. J. B. 2012. High resolution Lateglacial and early-Holocene summer air temperature records from Scotland inferred from chironomid assemblages. *Quaternary Science Reviews* 41: 67–82

Brown, A. D. 2004. Late Mesolithic human occupation at the wetland–dryland interface: investigations at Llandevenny. *Archaeology in the Severn Estuary* 14: 49–53.

Brown, A. 2007. Mesolithic to Neolithic human activity and impact at the Severn Estuary wetland edge: studies at Llandevenny, Oldbury Flats, Hills Flats, and Woolaston, in Bell (ed.) 2007a: 249–62.

Brown, T. 1997. Clearances and clearings: deforestation in Mesolithic/Neolithic Britain. *Oxford Journal of Archaeology* 16(2): 133–46.

Brunning, R. 2013. An early Mesolithic cemetery at Greylake, Somerset, UK. Archaeology in the Severn Estuary 2013. Volume 22: 67–70. Annual Report of the Severn Estuary Levels Research Committee.

Brunning, R. and Firth, H. 2012. An early Mesolithic cemetery at Greylake, Somerset, UK. *Mesolithic Miscellany* 22(1): 19–21.

Buckland, P. C. 2002. Conservation and the Holocene record: an invertebrate view from Yorkshire. *Bulletin of the Yorkshire Naturalists' Union* (supplement) 37: 23–40.

Buckland, P. C. 2005. Lowland heathlands: a palaeoentomological view, in Prendergast, D. V. (ed.), *Heathlands – Past, Present and Future*: 57–74. Lewes: East Sussex Council.

Burov, G. M. 1998. The use of vegetable materials in the Mesolithic of Northeast Europe, in Zvelebil *et al.* (eds) 1998: 53–63.

Burrow, S. 2003. *Catalogue of the Mesolithic and Neolithic Collections in the National Museums & Galleries of Wales.* Cardiff: National Museums & Galleries of Wales.

Burrow, S. 2010. Bryn Celli Ddu Passage Tomb, Anglesey; alignment, construction, date and ritual. *Proceedings of the Prehistoric Society* 76: 249–70.

Cannon, A. and Yang, D. Y. 2006. Early storage and sedentism on the Pacific northwest coast: ancient DNA Analysis of salmon remains from Namu, British Columbia. *American Antiquity* 71(1): 123–40.

Canti, M. G. and Linford, N. 2000. The effects of fire on archaeological soils and sediments: temperature and colour relationships. *Proceedings of the Prehistoric Society* 66: 385–95.

Carter, R. J. 2001. New evidence for seasonal human presence at the Early Mesolithic site of Thatcham, Berkshire, England. *Journal of Archaeological Science* 28: 1055–60.

Caseldine, A. 1990. *Environmental Archaeology in Wales.* Lampeter: Department of Archaeology.

Caseldine, A. 2000. The vegetation history of the Goldcliff area, in Bell, *et al.* (eds) 2000: 208–44.

Caulfield, S. 1978. Star Carr – an alternative view. *Irish Archaeological Research Forum* 5: 15–22.

Cauwe, N. 2001. Skeletons in motion, ancestors in action: Early Mesolithic collective tombs in southern Belgium. *Cambridge Archaeological Journal* 11(2): 147–63.

Chambers, F. M. 1982a. Environmental history of Cefn Gwernffrwd, near Rhandirmwyn, Mid-Wales. *New Phytologist* 92: 607–15.

Chambers, F. M. 1982b. Two radiocarbon–dated pollen diagrams from high–altitude blanket peats in south Wales. *Journal of Ecology* 70: 445–9.

Chambers, F. M. 1983. Three radiocarbon–dated pollen diagrams from upland peats North West of Merthyr Tydfil, South Wales. *Journal of Ecology* 71(2): 475–87.

Chambers, F. M. and Price, S.-M. 1985. Palaeoecology of *Alnus* (Alder): Early post-glacial rise in a valley mire, north-west Wales. *New Phytologist* 101(2): 333–44.

Chapman, H. P. and Lillie, M. C. 2004. Investigating "Doggerland" through analogy: the example of Holderness, East Yorkshire (UK), in Flemming (ed.) 2004b: 65–9.

Chapman, J. 1999. The origins of warfare in the prehistory of Central and Eastern Europe, in Carman J. and Harding, A. (eds), *Ancient Warfare: Archaeological Perspectives*: 101–42. Stroud: Sutton.

Chatterton, R. 2003. Star Carr re-analysed, in Bevan and Moore (eds) 2003: 69–80.

Chatterton, R. 2006. Ritual, in Conneller and Warren (eds) 2006: 101–20.

Chisholm, B. S., Nelson, D. E. and Schwarcz, H. P. 1982. Stable carbon ratios as a measure of marine versus terrestrial protein in ancient diets. *Science* 216: 1131–2.

Clark, C. D., Evans, D. J. A., Khatwa, A., Bradwell, T., Jordan, C. J., Marsh, S. H., Mitchell, W. A. and Bateman, M. D. 2004. Map and GIS database of glacial landforms and features related to the last British Ice Sheet. *Boreas*, 33: 359–75.

Clark, J. D. 1968. Studies of hunter-gatherers as an aid to the interpretation of prehistoric societies, in Lee, R. B. and DeVore, I. (eds), *Man the Hunter*. 276–80. Chicago: Aldine Publishing.

Clark, J. G. D. 1938. Mesolithic industries from tufa deposits at Prestatyn, Flintshire and Blashenwell, Dorset. *Proceedings of the Prehistoric Society* 4: 330–4.

Clark, J. G. D. 1939. Further note of the tufa deposit at Prestatyn, Flintshire. *Proceedings of the Prehistoric Society* 5: 201–2.

Clark, J. G. D. 1954. *Excavations at Star Carr, an Early Mesolithic Site at Seamer, near Scarborough, Yorkshire.* Cambridge: Cambrdige University Press.

Clark, J. G. D. 1972. *Star Carr: a Case Study in Bioarchaeology.* US: Addison-Wesley Publishing, Module 10: 1–42.

Clarke, D. 1976. Mesolithic Europe: the economic basis, in Sieveking, G., Longworth, H. and Wilson, K. E. (eds), *Problems in Economic and Social Archaeology*: 449–81. London: Duckworth.

Clarke, D. 1978. *Mesolithic Europe: the Economic Basis.* London: Duckworth.

Clarke, D. 1987. *Mesolithic Europe: The Economic Basis* (2nd ed.). London: Duckworth.

Clarke, S., Bray, J. and Walker, E. A. 2012. A Mesolithic site in Monmouth, SO5113. *Archaeology in Wales* 51: 114–7.

Clutton-Brock, J. and Noe-Nygaard, N. 1990. New osteological and C-isotope evidence on Mesolithic dogs: companions to hunters and fishers at Star Carr, Seamer Carr and Kongemose. *Journal of Archaeological Science* 17: 643–53.

Coard, R. 2000. Large mammal bone assemblage, in Bell *et al.* (eds) 2000: 48–53.

Coard, R. and Chamberlain, A. T. 1999. The nature and timing of faunal change in the British Isles across the Pleistocene/Holocene transition. *Holocene* 9(3): 372–6.

Collcutt, S. N. (ed.). 1986. *The Palaeolithic of Britain and its Nearest Neighbours: Recent Trends*: 59–61. Sheffield: Sheffield University Department of Archaeology & Prehistory.

Coles, B. J. 1998. Doggerland: a speculative survey. *Proceedings of the Prehistoric Society* 64: 45–81.

Coles, B. J. 2000. Doggerland: the cultural dynamics of a shifting coastline, in Pye, K. and Allen, J. R. L. (eds), *Coastal and Estuarine Environments: Sedimentology, Geomorphology and Geoarchaeology*: 393–401. London: Geological Society Special Publication 175.

Coles, B. J. and Coles, J. M. 1986. *The Sweet Track to Glastonbury*. London: Thames and Hudson.

Coles, J. M. 1971. The early settlement of Scotland: excavations at Morton, Fife. *Proceedings of the Prehistoric Society* 37(2): 284–366.

Coles, J. M. 1988. A wetland perspective, in Purdy, B. A. (ed.), *Wet Site Archaeology*: 1–14. Caldwell, NJ: Telford Press.

Coles, J. M. 1989. Prehistoric settlement in the Somerset Levels, in Coles, J. M. (ed.), *Somerset Levels Papers* 15, 14–33.

Conneller, C. 2000. Fragmented space? hunter-gatherer landscapes of the Vale of Pickering, in Conneller (ed.) 2000b: 139–50.

Conneller, C. (ed.) 2000b *New Approaches to the Palaeolithic and Mesolithic. Archaeological Review from Cambridge* 17(1.

Conneller, C. 2008. Lithic technology and the chaîne Opératoire, in Pollard (ed.) 2008: 160–76.

Conneller, C. 2009. Transforming bodies: mortuary practices in Mesolithic Britain, in McCartan *et al.* (eds) 2009: 690–7.

Conneller, C. and Schadla-Hall, T. 2003. Beyond Star Carr: the Vale of Pickering in the 10th millennium BP. *Proceedings of the Prehistoric Society* 69: 85–105.

Conneller, C. and Warren, G. (eds). 2006. *Mesolithic Britain and Ireland: New Approaches*. Stroud: Tempus

Conneller, C., Milner, N., Tayler, B. and Taylor, M. 2012. Substantial settlement in the European Early Mesolithic: new research at Star Carr. *Antiquity* 86: 1004–20.

Cooney, G. 1999. Social landscapes in Irish prehistory, in Ucko and Layton (eds) 1999: 46–64.

Cooney, G. and Grogan, E. 1999. *Irish Prehistory: A Social Perspective*. Dublin: Wordwell (first published 1994).

Coope, G. R. 1994. The response of insect faunas to glacial–interglacial climatic fluctuations. *Philosophical Transactions of the Royal Society of London* (B), 344: 19–26.

Coope, G. R. 2001. Biostratigraphic distinction of interglacial coleopteran assemblages from southern Britain attributed to oxygen isotope stages 5e and 7. *Quaternary Science Reviews* 20: 1717–22.

Coope, G. R. 2002. Changes in the thermal climate in northwestern Europe during Marine Oxygen Isotope Stage 3, estimated from fossil insect assemblages. *Quaternary Research* 57: 401–8.

Coope, G. R. 2004. Several million years of stability amongst insect species because of, or in spite of, Ice Age climatic instability. *Philosophical Transactions of the Royal Society of London* (B), 359: 209–14.

Coope, G. R. 2006 Insect faunas associated with Palaeolithic industries from five sites of pre-Anglian age in central England. *Quaternary Science Reviews* 25: 1738–54.

Coope, G. R. and Brophy, J. A. 1972. Late-Glacial environmental changes indicated by a coleopteran succession from North Wales. *Boreas* 1: 97–142.

Couper, R. 2011. Langstone, Newport (ST 394 912). *Archaeology in Wales* 50: 81–2.

Cowell, R.W. and Innes, J. B. 1994. *The Wetlands of Merseyside*. North West Wetlands Survey. Lancaster: Lancaster Imprints 2 (North West Wetlands Survey).

Cummings, G. 2000. Fire! Accidental or strategic use of fire in the Early Mesolithic of the Vale of Pickering, in Young (ed.) 2000: 75–84.

Cummings, V. 2000. Myth, memory and metaphor: the significance of place, space and the landscape in Mesolithic Pembrokeshire, in Young, (ed.) 2000: 87–95.

Cummings, V. 2007. From midden to megalith? the Mesolithic–Neolithic transition in western Britain, in Whittle and Cummings (eds) 2007: 493–510.

Cummings, V. 2009. *A View from the West: The Neolithic of the Irish Sea Zone*. Oxford: Oxbow Books.

Currant, A. 1986. Man and Quaternary interglacial faunas of Britain, in Collcutt (ed.) 1986: 50–2.

Currant, A. and Jacobi, R. 2001. A formal mammalian biostratigraphy for the Late Pleistocene of Britian. *Quaternary Science Reviews* 20: 1707–16.

Cushing, F. H. 2000. *Exploration of Ancient Key-Dweller Remains on the Gulf Coast of Florida*. Gainsville: University of Florida Press. (First published 1896, *American Philosophical Society Proceedings* 35 (153)).

Czerniak, L. 1998. The Neolithic – what's that?, in Zvelebil *et al.* (eds) 1998: 29–30.

Dahlberg, F. (ed.). 1981. *Woman the Gatherer*. New Haven: Yale University Press.

Dark, P. 1988. Interpretation of the Lake edge sequences, in Mellars and Dark (eds) 1988a: 153–61.

Dark, P. 2003. Dogs, a crane (not duck) and diet at Star Carr: a response to Schulting and Richards. *Journal of Archaeological Science* 30: 1353–6.

Dark, P., Higham, T. F. G., Jacobi, R. and Lord, T. C. 2006. New radiocarbon accelerator dates on artefacts from the early Mesolithic site of Star Carr, North Yorkshire. *Archaeometry* 48(1): 185–200.

Darvill, T. 2010. *Prehistoric Britain* (2nd ed.). London: Routledge.

David, A. E. U. 1989. Some aspects of the human presence in Wales during the Mesolithic, in Bonsall (ed.) 1989b: 241–53.

David, A. E. U. 1990. *Palaeolithic and Mesolithic Settlement in Wales with Special Reference to Dyfed*. Unpublished PhD: University of Lancaster.

David, A. E. U. 1991. Late-Glacial archaeological residues from Wales: a selection, in Barton, N., Roberts, A. J. and Roe, D. A. (eds), *The Late-Glacial in Northwest Europe: Human Adaptation and Environmental Change at the End of the Pleistocene*: 141–59. York: Council for British Archaeology Research Report 77.

David, A. 2007. *Palaeolithic and Mesolithic Settlement in Wales: with special reference to Dyfed*. Oxford: British Archaeological Report 448.

David, A. 2011. Flint, in Crane, P. and Murphy, K., The excavation of a coastal promontory fort at Porth y Rhaw, Solva, Pembrokeshire, 1995–98. *Archaeologia Cambrensis* 159: 53–98.

David, A. and Walker, E. A. 2004. Wales during the Mesolithic period, in Saville, A. (ed.), *Mesolithic Scotland and its Neighbours: The Early Holocene Prehistory of Scotland, its British and Irish Context, and some Northern European Perspectives*: 299–337. Edinburgh: Society of Antiquaries of Scotland.

David, E. 2009. Show me how you make your hunting equipment and I will tell you where you come from: technical traditions, an efficient means of characterizing cultural identities, in McCartan *et al.* (eds) 2009: 362–7.

David, N. and Kramer, C. 2001. *Ethnoarchaeology in Action*. Cambridge: Cambridge University Press.

Davidson, A. (ed.). 2002. *The Coastal Archaeology of Wales*. York: Council for British Archaeology Research Report 131

Davies, B. A. S., Brewer, S., Stevenson, A. C., Guiot, J., COHMAP members. 2003. The temperature of Europe during the Holocene reconstructed from pollen data. *Quaternary Science Reviews* 22: 1701–16.

Davies, M. 1989. Recent advances in cave archaeology in southwest Wales, in Ford, T. D. (ed.), *Limestones and Caves of Wales*: 79–91 Cambridge: Cambridge University Press.

Davies, P., Robb, J. G. and Ladbrook, D. 2005. Woodland clearance in the Mesolithic: the social aspects. *Antiquity* 79. 280–8.

Day, P. 1993. Preliminary results of high–resolution palaeoecological analysis at Star Carr, Yorkshire. *Cambridge Archaeological Journal* 3(1): 129–33.

Day, S. P. 1996. Dogs, deer and diet at Star Carr: a reconsideration of C-isotope evidence from Early Mesolithic dog remains from the Vale of Pickering, Yorkshire, England. *Journal of Archaeological Science* 23: 783–7.

Deith, M. R. 1983. Molluscan calendars: the use of growth–line analysis to establish seasonality of shellfish collection at the Mesolithic site of Morton, Fife. *Journal of Archaeological Science* 10: 423–40.

DeNiro, M. 1985. Postmortem preservation and alteration of *in vivo* bone collagen isotope ratios in relation to palaeodietary reconstruction. *Nature* 317: 806–9.

Detry, C. and Cardoso, J. L. 2010. On some remains of dog (*Canis familiaris*) from the Mesolithic shell-middens of Muge, Portugal. *Journal of Archaeological Science* 37: 2762–74.

Dinnin, M. 1995. Introduction to the palaeoenvironmental survey, in Van de Noort, R. and Ellis, S. (eds), *Wetland Heritage of Holderness: an Archaeological Survey*: 27–48. Hull: Humber Wetlands Project.

Dolukhanov, P. M. 1999. War and peace in prehistoric Eastern Europe, in Carman J. and Harding, A. (eds), *Ancient Warfare: Archaeological Perspectives*: 73–87. Stroud: Sutton.

Donahue, R. E. and Lovis, W. R. 2006. Regional settlement systems in Mesolithic northern England: Scalar issues in mobility and territoriality. *Journal of Anthropological Archaeology* 25: 248–58.

Duday, H. 2006. L'archéoanthatologie ou l'archéologie de la mort, in Gowland, R. and Knüsel, C. (eds), *Social Archaeology of Funerary Remains*: 30–56. Oxford: Oxbow Books.

Duke, P. 1991. Recognising gender in Plains hunting groups: is it possible or even necessary? in Walde, D. and Williams, N. D. (eds), *The Archaeology of Gender: Proceedings of the 22nd Annual Chacmool Conference*: 280–3 Calgary: Archaeological Association of the University of Calgary.

Dupont, C., Tresset, A., Desse-Berset, N., Gruet, Y., Marchand, G. and Schulting, R. 2009. Harvesting the seashores in the Late Mesolithic of northwestern Europe: a view from Brittany. *Journal of World Prehistory* 22: 93–111.

Dyfed Archaeological Trust, 2011. *The Lost Lands of our Ancestors: Exploring the Submerged Landscapes of Prehistoric Wales*. Llandeilo: Dyfed Archaeological Trust.

Edmonds, M. 1999. *Ancestral Geographies of the Neolithic: Landscape, Monuments and Memory*. London: Routledge.

Edmonds, M., Dawson, T., Johnston, R. and Roberts, J. G. 2002. Bardsey Island (SH 117 224). *Archaeology in Wales* 42: 100.

Edmonds, M., Dawson, T., Johnston, R., La Trobe-Bateman, E., Roberts, J. G. and Warren, G. 2003. Bardsey Island (SH 117 224). *Archaeology in Wales* 43: 100–1.

Edmonds, M., Johnston, R., La Trobe-Bateman, E., Roberts, J. G. and Warren, G. 2003. Bardsey Island (SH 117 224). *Archaeology in Wales* 44: 146–7.

Edmonds, M., Johnston, R., La Trobe-Bateman, E., Roberts, J. and Warren, G. 2009. Ynys Enlli: shifting horizons, in McCartan *et al.* (eds) 2009: 385–91, 639–49.

Edwards, K. J. 1999. Palynology and people: observations on the British record. *Quaternary Proceedings* 7: 531–44.

Edwards, R. J. 2006. Mid- to late-Holocene relative sea level change in southwest Britain and the influence of sediment compaction. *Holocene* 16(4): 575–87.

Elliott, B. and Milner, N. 2010. Making a point: a critical review of the barbed point manufacturing process practiced at Star Carr. *Proceedings of the Prehistoric Society* 76: 75–94.

Ellis, C. J., Allen, M. J., Gardiner, J., Harding, P., Ingrem, C., Powell, A., and Scaife, R. G. 2003. An Early Mesolithic seasonal hunting camp in the Kennet Valley, southern England. *Proceedings of the Prehistoric Society* 69: 107–35.

Estioko-Griffin, A. and Griffin, P. 1981. Woman the hunter: the Agta, in Dahlberg (ed.) 1991: 121–51.

Evans, D. J. and Thomson, M. S. 1979. The geology of the central Bristol channel and the Lundy area, south western approaches, British Isles. *Proceedings of the Geologists Association* 90: 1–14.

Evans, J. G. 1975. *The Environment of Early Man in the British Isles*. London: Book Club Associates.

Evans-Pritchard. E. E. 1976. *Witchcraft Oracles and Magic among the Azande*. Oxford: Clarendon Press.

Fahlander, F. 2008. A piece of the Mesolithic: horizontal stratigraphy and bodily manipulations at Skateholm, in Fahlander, F. and Oestigaard, T. (eds), *The Materiality of Death: Bodies, Burials, Beliefs*: 29–46. Oxford: British Archaeological Report S1768.

Finlay, N. 2000a. Microliths in the making, in Young (ed.) 2000: 23–31.

Finlay, N. 2000b. Deer prudence, in Conneller (ed.) 2000b: 67–79.

Finlay, N. 2003a. Microliths and multiple authorship, in Larsson *et al.* (eds) 2003: 167–76.

Finlay, N. 2003b. Cache and carry: defining moments in the Irish later Mesolithic, in Bevan and Moore (eds) 2003: 87–94.

Finlay, N. 2004. E-scapes and E-motion: other ways of writing the Mesolithic. *Before Farming* 2004/1, Article 4: 1–9.

Fisher, A. 2004. Submerged Stone Age – Danish examples and North Sea potential, in Flemming (ed.): 23–36.

Fischer, A., Olsen, J., Richards, M., Heinemeier, J., Sveinbjörnsdóttir, Á. E. and Bennike, P. 2007. Coast–inland mobility and diet in the Danish Mesolithic and Neolithic: evidence from stable isotope values of humans and dogs. *Journal of Archaeological Science* 34: 2125–50.

Fitch, S. and Gaffney, V. 2011. *West Coast Palaeolandscapes Survey*. Birmingham: VISTA, Institute of Archaeology and Antiquity Document Number: WCPS–1997–3B.

Flemming, N. 2002. *The Scope of Strategic Environmental Assessment of North Sea areas SEA3 and SEA2 in Regard to Prehistoric Archaeological Remains*. Department of Trade and Industry, Strategic assessment of parts of the Central and Southern North Sea: SEA3, consultation document. Technical Report. CDROM.

Flemming, N. 2004a. The prehistory of the North Sea floor in the context of Continental Shelf archaeology from the Mediterranean to Nova Zemlya, in Flemming (ed.) 2004b: 11–20.

Flemming, N. C. (ed.). 2004b. *Submarine Prehistory Archaeology of the North Sea: Research Priorities and Collaboration with Industry*: 65–9.. York: Council for British Archaeology Research Report 141.

Flenley, J. R. 1987. The meres of Holderness, in Ellis, S. and Crowther, D. R. (eds), *Humber Perspectives: a Region Through the Ages*: 43–53. Hull: Hull University Press.

Flenley, J. R., Maloney, B. K., Ford, D. and Hallam, G. 1975. *Trapa natans* in the British Isles. *Nature* 257: 39–41.

Formicola, V., Pontrandolfi, A. and Svoboda, J. 2001. The Upper Palaeolithic triple burial of Dolní Věstonice: pathology and funerary behaviour. *American Journal of Physical Anthropology* 115: 372–9.

Frayer, D. W. 1997. Ofnet: evidence for a Mesolithic massacre, in Martin, D. L. and Frayer, D. W. (eds), *Troubled Times: Violence and Warfare in the Past*: 181–216. London: Routledge, War and Society 3.

Frazer, F. C. and King, J. E. 1954. Faunal remains, in Clark. 1954: 70–95.

Fyfe, R. 2006. The importance of local–scale openness within regions dominated by closed woodland. *Journal of Quaternary Science* 22(6): 571–8.

Gaffney, V, Thomson, K. and Fitch, S. 2007. *Mapping Doggerland: the Mesolithic landscapes of the Southern North Sea*. Oxford: Archaeopress.

Gamble, C. 2001. The peopling of Europe 700,000–40,000 years before present, in Cunliffe, B. (ed.), *The Oxford Illustrated History of Prehistoric Europe*: 5–41 Oxford: Oxford University Press.

Garcia-Moncó, C. 2009. Dogs and people, an arising relationship: *Canis familiaris* amongst hunter–gatherer societies in the Iberian peninsula, in McCartan *et al.* (eds) 2009: 675–82.

Gaudzinski-Windheuser, S. and Niven, L. 2009. Hominin subsistence patterns during the Middle and Late Palaeolithic in Northwestern Europe, in Hublin, J.-J. and Richards, M. P. (eds), *The Evolution of Hominin Diets: Integrating Approaches to the Study of Palaeolithic Subsistence* : 99–111. Berlin: Springer Science and Business Media B.V.

Germonpré, M., Sablin, M. V., Stevens, R. E., Hedges, R. E. M., Hotreiter, M., Stiller, M. and Vesprés, V. R. 2009. Fossil dogs and wolves from Palaeolithic sites in Belgium, the Ukraine and Russia: osteometry, ancient DNA and stable isotopes. *Journal of Archaeological Science* 36: 473–90.

Gibson, A. 1999. *The Walton Basin, Powys, Wales: Survey at the Hindwell Neolithic Enclosure*. Powys: Clwyd Powys Archaeological Trust.

Glimmerveen, J., Mol, D., Post, K., Reumer, J. W. F., van der Plicht, H., de Vos, J., van Geel, B., cam Reenen, G. and Pals, J. P. 2004. The North Sea project: the first palaeontological, palynological and archaeological results, in Flemming (ed.): 43–52.

Godwin, H. 1940a. A Boreal transgression of the sea in Swansea Bay. Data for the study of Post-Glacial history, VI. *New Phytologist* 39(3): 308–321

Godwin, H. 1940b. Pollen analysis and forest history of England and Wales. *New Phytologist* 39: 370–400.

Godwin, H. 1960. The Croonian Lecture. *Radiocarbon Dating and Quaternary History in Britain* 153(B): 287–320.

Godwin, H. 1975. *The History of the British Flora: a Factual Basis for Phytogeography* (2nd ed.). Cambridge: Cambridge University Press.

Gooder, J. 2007. Excavation of a Mesolithic house at East Barnes, East Lothian, Scotland: an interim report, in Waddington, C. and Pedersen, K. L. R. (eds), *Mesolithic Settlement in the North Sea Basin and Beyond: Proceedings of a Conference Held at Newcastle in 2003*: 49–59. Oxford: Oxbow Books.

Goodman, A. H., Armelagos, G. J. and Rose, J. C. 1984. The chronological distribution of enamel hypoplasias from prehistoric Dickson Mounds populations. *American Journal of Physical Anthropology* 65: 259–66.

Goodman, A. H., Allen, L. H., Hernandez, G. P., Amador, A., Arriola, L. V., Chavez, A. and Pelto, G. H. 1987. Prevelance and age at development of enamel hypoplasias in Mexican children. *American Journal of Physical Anthropology* 72: 7–19.

Goudie, A. 1996. *Environmental Change: Contemporary Problems in Geography* (3rd ed.). Oxford: Clarendon Press.

Grant, F. 2008. Human impact and landscape change at Moel Llys y Coed in the Clwydian hills, north Wales: the Mesolithic to present day. *Archaeology in Wales* 48: 3–15.

Grant, F. R. 2009. *Analysis of a Peat Core from the Clwydian Hills, North Wales*. Report 0209. Produced for the Royal Commission on the Ancient and Historical Monuments of Wales.

Grasis, N. 2010. A Mesolithic dwelling: evidence interpreting from the Užavas Celmi sie in Latvia. *Baltica* 13: 58–68.

Green, H. S. 1984. *Pontnewydd Cave: a Lower Palaeolithic Hominid Site in Wales*. 1st report. Cardiff: National Museum of Wales.

Green, H. S. 1986. The Palaeolithic Settlement of Wales Research Project: A review of progress 1978–1985, in Collcutt (ed.) 1986: 36–42.

Green, H. S. and Walker, E. 1991. *Ice Age Hunters: Neanderthals and Early Modern Hunters in Wales*. Cardiff: National Museum of Wales.

Grigson, C. and Mellars, P. 1987. The mammalian remains from the middens, in Mellars, P. (ed.), *Excavations on Oronsay. Prehistoric Human Ecology on a Small Island*: 243–89. Edinburgh: University Press.

Grimes, W. F. 1951. *The Prehistory of Wales*. Cardiff: National Museum of Wales (2nd ed.).

Grøn, O. and Skaarup, J. 2004. Submerged Stone Age coastal zones in Denmark: investigation strategies and results, in Flemming (ed.) 2004b: 53–6.

Grønnow, B. 1985. Meiendorf and Stellmoor revisited: an analysis of Late Palaeolithic reindeer exploitation. *Acta Archaeologica* 56: 131–61.

Gumiński, W. 1998. The peat-bog site Dudka, Masurian Lakeland: an example of conservative economy, in Zvelebil *et al.* (eds) 1998: 103–9.

Handa, S. and Moore, P. D. 1976. Studies in the vegetational history of mid Wales. IV. Pollen analyses of some pingo basins. *New Phytologist* 77(1): 205–25.

Hardy, B. L. and Svoboda, J. 2009. Mesolithic stone tool function and site types in northern Bohemia, Czech Republic, in Haslam, M., Robertson, G., Crowther, A., Kirkwood, L. and Nugent, S. (eds), *Archaeological Science Under A Microscope: Studies in Residue and Ancient DNA Analysis in Honour of Tom Loy*: 159–74. Queensland: University of Queensland Press.

Haynes, J. R., Kiteley, R. J., Whatley, R. C. and Wilks, P. J. 1977. Microfaunas, microfloras and the environmental stratigraphy of the Late-Glacial and Holocene in Cardigan Bay. *Geological Journal* 12(2): 129–58.

Healey, E. 2007. Flint and chert lithics, in Armour-Chelu *et al.* 2007: 297–302.

Healy, F. 2004. Hambledon Hill and its implications, in Cleal, R. and Pollard, J. (eds), *Monuments and Material Culture. Paper in Honour of an Avebury Archaeologist: Isabel Smith*: 15–38. East Knoyle: Hobnob Press.

Healy, F., Heaton, M. and Lobb, S. J. 1992. Excavations of a Mesolithic site at Thatcham, Berkshire. *Proceedings of the Prehistoric Society* 58: 41–76.

Hedges, R. E. M. 2004. Isotopes and red herrings: comments on Milner *et al.* and Lidén *et al. Antiquity* 78(299): 23–7.

Hellewell, E. and Milner, N. 2011. Burial practices at the Mesolithic–Neolithic transition in Britain: change or continuity? *Documenta Praehistorica* 38: 61–8.

Hewlett, B. S. and Lamb, M. E. (eds) 2007. *Hunter-Gatherer Childhoods: Evolutionary, Developmental and Cultural Perspectives*. New Jersey: Transaction Publishers.

Hey, G. and Barcley, A. 2007. The Thames Valley in the late fifth and early fourth millennium cal BC: the appearance of domestication and the evidence for change, in Whittle and Cummings (eds) 2007: 399–422.

Heyworth, A. and Kidson, C. 1982. Sea level changes in southwest England and Wales. *Proceedings of the Geological Association* 93(1): 91–111.

Heyworth, A., Kidson, C. and Wilks, P. 1985. Late-Glacial and Holocene sediments at Clarach Bay, near Aberystwyth. *Journal of Ecology* 73(2): 459–80.

Hibbert, F. A. and Switsur, V. R. 1976. Radiocarbon dating of Flandrian pollen zones in Wales and Northern England. *New Phytologist* 77: 793–807.

Hiemstra, J. F., Evans, D. J. A., Scourse, J. D., McCarroll, D., Furze, M. F. A. and Rhodes, E. 2006. New evidence for a grounded Irish Sea glaciation of the Isles of Scilly, U.K. *Quaternary Science Reviews* 25: 299–309.

Higham, T. 2011. European Middle and Upper Palaeolithic radiocarbon dates are often older than they look: problems with previous dates and some remedies. *Antiquity* 85: 235–49.

Hodder, K. H., Bullock, J. M., Buckland, P. C. and Kirby, K. J. 2005. *Large Herbivores in the Wildwood and Modern Naturalistic Grazing Systems*. Peterborough: English Nature Research Report 648.

Hodgetts, L. and Rahemtulla, F. 2001. Land and sea: use of terrestrial mammal bones in coastal hunter–gatherer communities. *Antiquity* 75: 56–62.

Högberg, A. 2008. Playing with flint: tracing a child's imitation of adult work in a lithic assemblage. *Journal of Archaeological Method and Theory* 15: 112–31.

Holliman, S. E. 1991. Health consequences of divisions of labour among the Chumash Indians of south California, in Walde, D. and Williams, N. D. (eds), *The Archaeology of Gender: Proceedings of the 22nd Annual Chacmool Conference*: 462–9. Calgary: Archaeological Association of the University of Calgary.

Housley, R. A., Gamble, C. S., Street, M. and Pettitt, P. 1997. Radiocarbon evidence for the Lateglacial Human recolonisation of northern Europe. *Proceedings of the Prehistoric Society* 63: 25–54.

Hudecek-Cuffe, C. 1996. *Engendering Northern Plains Palaeo-Indian Archaeology: Decision-making and Gender/Sex Roles in Subsistence and Settlement Strategies*. Unpublished PhD thesis: University of Alberta, Canada.

Hughes, P. D. 2009. Loch Lomond Stadial (Younger Dryas) glaciers and climate in Wales. *Geological Journal* 44: 375–91.

Hughes, P. D. M. and Barber, K. E. 2003. Mire development across the fen–bog transition on the Teifi floodplain at Tregaron Bog, Ceredigion, Wales, and a comparison with 13 other raised bogs. *Journal of Ecology* 91: 253–64.

Hyde, H. A. 1940. On a peat bog at Craig–Y–Llyn, Glam. Data for the study of Post–Glacial history. IV. *New Phytologist* 39(2): 226–233.

Ince, J. 1983. Two postglacial pollen profiles from the uplands of Snowdonia, Gwynedd, North Wales. *New Phytologist* 95: 159–72.

Ince, J. 1996. Late-glacial and early Holocene vegetation of Snowdonia. *New Phytologist* 132: 343–53.

Ingrem, C. 2000. Fish, bird and small mammal remains, in Bell *et al.* (eds) 2000: 53–5.

Jackes, M. Lubell, D. and Meiklejohn, C. 1997. Healthy but mortal: human biology and the first farmers of Western Europe. *Antiquity* 71: 639–58.

Jacobi, R. M. 1976. Britain inside and outside Mesolithic Europe. *Proceedings of the Prehistoric Society* 42: 67–84.

Jacobi, R. M. 1978. Northern England in the eighth millennium BC: an essay, in Mellars, P. (ed.), *The Early Postglacial Settlement of Northern Europe: an Ecological Perspective*: 295–332. London: Duckworth.

Jacobi, R. M. 1980. The early Holocene settlement of Wales, in Taylor, J. A. (ed.), *Culture and Environment in Prehistoric Wales*: 131–206. Oxford: British Archaeological Report 76.

Jacobi, R. M. 1987. Misanthropic miscellany: musings on British Early Flandrian archaeology and other flights of fancy, in Rowley-Conwy, P., Zvelebil, M. and Blankholm, H. P. (eds), *Mesolithic Northwest Europe: Recent Trends*: 163–8. Sheffield: Sheffield University Department of Archaeology and Prehistory.

Jacobi, R. 2005. Some observations on the lithic artefacts from Aveline's Hole, Burrington Combe, North Somerset. *Proceedings of the University of Bristol Spelaeological Society* 23(3): 267–95.

Jacobi, R. M. and Higham, T. F. G. 2008. The "Red Lady" ages gracefully: new ultrafiltration AMS determinations from Paviland. *Journal of Human Evolution* 55: 898–908.

Jacobs, K. 1995. Returning to Olenii Ostrov: social, economic and skeletal dimensions of a boreal forest Mesolithic cemetery. *Journal of Anthropological Archaeology* 14: 359–403.

Jacques, D. 2013. Summary of AA309 and U211 students' field work at Vespasian's Camp, near Stonehenge, Wiltshire, 2005–2011. http://www.open.ac.uk/Arts/classical-studies/amesbury/ and http://www.open.ac.uk/Arts/classical-studies/amesbury/discoveries.shtml

Jelsma, J. 2000. *A Bed of Ochre: Mortuary Practices and Social Structure of a Maritime Archaeic Indian Society at Port Au Choix, Newfoundland*. PhD Thesis, Groningen, Rijksunivesiteit.

Jennbert, K. 1998. "From the inside": a contribution to the debate about the introduction of agriculture in Southern Sweden, in Zvelebil *et al.* (eds) 1998: 31–5.

Jennings, S., Orford, J. D., Canti, M., Devoy, R. J. N. and Straker, V. 1998. The role of relative sea level rise and changing sediment supply on Holocene gravel barrier development: the example of Porlock, Somerset, UK. *Holocene* 8(2): 165–81.

Jiang, L. and Liu, L. 2006. New Evidence for the origins of sedentism and rice domestication in the lower Yangzi River, China. *Antiquity* 80: 355–61.

Jochim, M. 2006. Regional perspectives on Early Mesolithic land use in southwestern Germany. *Journal of Anthropological Archaeology* 25: 204–12.

Johnson, S. and Bell, M. 2007. Marine molluscs, in Armour-Chelu *et al.* 2007: 276–8.

Jones, G. 2000. Evaluating the importance of cultivation and collecting in Neolithic Britain, in Fairbairn, A. S. (ed.), *Plants in Neolithic Britain and Beyond*: 79–84. Oxford: Oxbow Books/Neolithic Studies Group Seminar Paper 5.

Jones, N. 2002. Description of the Coast, in Davidson (ed.) 2002: 9–17.

Jones, N. W. 2012. *The Neolithic Chambered Tombs of Breconshire*. Welshpool: Clwyd-Powys Archaeological Trust Report 1126.

Jones, R. L. and Keen, D. H. 1993. *Pleistocene Environments in the British Isles*. London: Chapman and Hall.

Jordan, P. 2003a. Investigating post-glacial hunter gatherer landscape enculturation: ethnographic analogy and interpretative methodologies, in Larsson *et al.* (eds) 2003: 128–38.

Jordan, P. 2003b. Peopling the Mesolithic: insights from ethnographies of landscape and material culture, in Bevan and Moore (eds) 2003: 27–34.

Jordan, P. 2011. Material culture perspectives on the worldview of northern hunter–gatherers, in Cannon, A. (ed.), *Structured Worlds: the Archaeology of Hunter-Gatherer Thought and Action*: 11–31. Sheffield: Equinox.

Karsten, P. 2004. Peak and transformation of a Mesolithic society. 7500–4800 BC, in Andersson, M., Karsten, P., Knarrström and Svensson, M. (eds), *Stone Age Scania: Significant Places Dug and Read by Contract Archaeology*: 71–142. Sweden: National Heritage Board. Riksantikvarieämbetets Förlag Skrifter 52.

Keef, P. A. M., Wymer, J. J. and Dimbleby, G. W. 1965. A Mesolithic site on Iping Common, Sussex, England. *Proceedings of the Prehistoric Society* 31: 85–92.

Kelly, R. L. 1992. Mobility/sedentism: concepts, archaeological measures, and effects. *Annual Review of Anthropology* 21: 43–66

Kelly, R. L. 1995. *The Foraging Spectrum: Diversity in Hunter-gatherer Lifeways.* Washington DC: Smithsonian Institution Press.

Kelly, R. L. 2003. Colonisation of new land by hunter-gatherers: expectations and implications based on ethnographic data, in Rockman, M. and Steele, J. (eds), *Colonisation of Unfamiliar Landscapes: the Archaeology of Adaptation*: 44–58. London: Routledge.

Kenney, J. 2008. Recent excavations at Parc Bryn Cegin, Llandygai, near Bangor, North Wales. *Archaeologia Cambrensis* 157: 9–142

Keith, K. 2006. Childhood learning and the distribution of knowledge in foraging societies. *Archaeological Papers of the American Anthropological Association* 15: 27–40.

Kirby, K. J. 2003. *What Might a British Forest-landscape Driven by Large Herbivores Look Like?* Peterborough: English Nature Research Report 530.

Konduktorova, T. S. 1974. The ancient populations of the Ukraine: from the Mesolithic age to the first centuries of our era. *Anthropologie BRNO* 12(1&2): 5–149.

Koumouzelis, M., Ginter, B., Kozlowski, J. K., Pawlikowski, M., Bar-Yosef, O., Albert, R., Litynska-Zajac, M., Stworzewicz, E., Wojtal, P., Lipecki, G., Tomek, T., Bochenski, Z. M. and Pazdur, A. 2001. The Early Upper Palaeolithic in Greece: the excavations in Klisoura Cave. *Journal of Archaeological Science* 28: 515–39.

Kozłowski, S. K. 2003. The Mesolithic: what do we know and what do we believe? in Larsson *et al.* (eds) 2003: xvii–xxi.

Lamb, M. E. and Hewlett, B. S. 2007. Reflections on hunter-gatherer childhoods, in Hewlett and Lamb (eds) 2007: 407–15.

Lambeck, K. and Chappell, J. 2001. Sea level change through the last glacial cycle. *Science* 292: 679–86.

Lane, P. J. 2008. The use of ethnography in landscape archaeology, in David, B. and Thomas, J. (eds), *Handbook of Landscape Archaeology*: 237–44. Walnut Creek, CA: Left Coast Press.

Lang, A. T. O. and Keen, D. H. 2005. Hominid colonisation and the Lower and Middle Palaeolithic of the West Midlands. *Proceedings of the Prehistoric Society* 71: 63–83.

Larsson, L. 1989. Late Mesolithic settlements and cemeteries at Skateholm, Southern Sweden, in Bonsall (ed.) 1989b: 367–78.

Larsson, L. 1988. The Skateholm Project. Late Mesolithic settlement at a South Swedish Lagoon, in Larsson, L. (ed.) *The Skateholm Project I: Man and Environment*: 9–19. Stockholm: Almqvist & Wiksell.

Larsson, L. 1990a. Dogs in fraction – symbols in action, in Vermeersch, P. M. and van Meer, P. (eds), *Contributions to the Mesolithic in Europe: Papers Presented at the Fourth International Symposium on the Mesolithic in Europe*: 153–60. Leuven: University Press.

Larsson, L. 1990b. The Mesolithic of Southern Scandinavia. *Journal of World Prehistory* 4(3): 257–309.

Larsson, L. 2004. The Mesolithic period in Southern Scandinavia: with special reference to burials and cemeteries, in Saville, A. (ed.), *Mesolithic Scotland and its Neighbours: The Early Holocene Prehistory of Scotland, its British and Irish Context, and some Northern European Perspectives*: 371–92. Edinburgh: Society of Antiquaries of Scotland.

Larsson, L. and Zagorska, I. (eds). 2006. *Back to the Origin. New Research in the Mesolithic–Neolithic Zvejnieki Cemetery and Environment, northern Latvia.* Stockholm: Almqvist & Wiksell, Acta Archaeologica Lundensia 8(52).

Larsson, L. and Sjöström, A. 2010. Mesolithic research in the bog Rönneholms mosse, southern Sweden. *Mesolithic Miscellany* 21(1): 2–9.

Larsson, L., Meiklejohn, C. and Newell, R. R. 1981. Human skeletal material from the Mesolithic site of Ageröd I: HC, Scania, Southern Sweden. *Fornvännen* 76: 161–8.

Larsson, L., Kindgren, H., Knutson, K., Loeffler, D. and Åkerlund, A. (eds) 2003. *Mesolithic on the Move: Papers presented at the Siixth International Conference on the Mesolithic in Europe, Stockholm 2000.* Oxford: Oxbow Books.

Layton, R. and Ucko, P. J.. 1999. Introduction: gazing into the landscape and encountering the environment, in Ucko and Layton (eds) 1999: 1–20.

Leah, M. D., Wells, C. E., Appleby, C. and Huckerby, E. 1997. *The Wetlands of Cheshire*. Lancaster: University Archaeology Unit. Lancaster Imprints 5 (North West Wetlands Survey).

Lee, J. R., Rose, J., Hamblin, R. J. O. and Moorlock, B. S. P. 2004. Dating the earliest lowland glaciation of eastern England: a pre-MIS 12 early Middle Pleistocene Happisburgh glaciation. *Quaternary Science Reviews* 23: 1551–66.

Lee, R. B. 2009. What hunters do for a living, or, how to make out on scarce resources, in Lee and Devore (eds) 2009b: 30–48.

Lee, R. B. and Devore. I. 2009a. Problems in the study of hunters and gatherers, in Lee and Devore (eds), 2009b: 3–12.

Lee, R. B. and Devore, I. (eds) 2009b. *Man the Hunter: the First Intensive Survey of a Single, Crucial Stage of Human Development – Man's Once Universal Hunting Way of Life*. London: Aldine Transaction (2nd Imp.).

Legge, A. J. and Rowley-Conwy, P. 1988. *Star Carr Revisited: a Re-analysis of the Large Mammals*. London: Birbeck College.

Lidén, K., Eriksson, G., Nordqvist, B., Götherström, A. and Bendixen, E. 2004. "The wet and the wild followed by the dry and the tame" – or did they occur at the same time? Diet in Mesolithic–Neolithic southern Sweden. *Antiquity* 79(299): 23–33.

Lillie, M. C. 1998. *The Dnieper Rapids Region of Ukraine: a Consideration of Chronology, Dental Pathology and Diet at the Mesolithic–Neolithic Transition*. Unpublished PhD thesis, Sheffield University.

Lillie, M. C. 2003a. Tasting the forbidden fruit: gender based dietary differences among prehistoric hunter-gatherers of Eastern Europe? *Before Farming* 2(3): 1–16.

Lillie, M. C. 2003b. The fruit and nut case: hunter gatherer subsistence and egalitarianism in the riparian zone, in Bevan and Moore (eds) 2003: 59–68.

Lillie, M. C. 2003c. Cranial surgery: the Epipalaeolithic to Neolithic populations of Ukraine, in Arnott, R., Finger, S. and Smith, C. U. M. (eds), *Trepanation: History – Discovery – Theory*: 175–88. Netherlands: Swets & Zeitlinger.

Lillie, M. C. 2004. Fighting for your life? Violence at the Late-glacial to Holocene transition in Ukraine, in Roksandic, M. (ed.), *Violent Interactions in the Mesolithic: Evidence and Meaning*: 89–96. Oxford: British Archaeological Report S1237.

Lillie, M. C. 2008. Suffer the children: "visualising" children in the archaeological record, in Bacvarov, K. (ed.), *Babies Reborn: Infant/Child Burials in Pre- and Protohistory*. Conference proceedings, UISPP, Lisbon: 33–43. Oxford: British Archaeological Report S1832.

Lillie, M. C. and Budd, C. 2011. The Mesolithic–Neolithic ransition in Eastern Europe: integrating stable isotope studies of diet with palaeopathology to identify subsistence strategies and economy, in Pinhasi, R. and Stock, J. T. (eds), *Human Bioarchaeology of the Transition to Agriculture*: 43–62. Chichester: John Wiley.

Lillie, M. C. and Ellis, S. 2007. Wetland archaeology and environments, in Lillie, M. C. and Ellis, S. (eds), *Wetland Archaeology & Environments: Regional Issues, Global Perspectives*: 3–10. Oxford: Oxbow Books.

Lillie, M. C. and Richards, M. P. 2000. Stable isotope analysis and dental evidence of diet at the Mesolithic–Neolithic Transition in Ukraine. *Journal of Archaeological Science* 27: 965–72.

Lillie, M. C. and Smith, R. 2007. *Understanding Water Table Dynamics and Their Influence on the Buried Archaeological Resource in Relation io Aggregates Extraction*. University of Hull: WAERC Unpublished Report (March 2007).

Lillie, M. C., Budd, C. E. and Potekhina, I. D. 2011. Stable isotope analysis of prehistoric populations from the cemeteries of the Middle and Lower Dnieper Basin, Ukraine. *Journal of Archaeological Science* 38(1): 57–68.

Lillie, M. C., Budd, C. E., Potekhina, I. D. and Hedges, R. E. M. 2009. The radiocarbon reservoir effect: new evidence from the cemeteries of the Middle and Lower Dnieper Basin, Ukraine. *Journal of Archaeological Science* 36(2): 256–64.

Lillie, M. C., Smith, R., Wallace, G., Davison, R. and Garrick, H. 2008. Wetland archaeology, water tables and lowland river systems: assessing aggregate extraction, *in situ* preservation and sustainability, in Kars, H. and van Heeringen, R. M. (eds), *Preserving Archaeological Remains* in situ: *Proceedings of the 3rd conference 7–9 December 2006*: 151–62. Amsterdam: Geoarchaeological and Bioarchaeological Studies 10.

Lillie, M. C., Soler, I. and Smith, R. 2012. Lowland floodplain responses to extreme flood events: long-term studies and short-term microbial community response to water environment impacts. *Conservation and Management of Archaeological Sites* 14(1–2): 125–48.

Liverpool Landscapes. 2012. Lunt Meadows: new Mesolithic settlement found. http://www.liverpool-landscapes.net/2012/11/lunt-meadows-new-mesolithic-settlement-found/ (accessed 21/07/14).

Locock, M. 2000. *Prehistoric Settlement in Southeast Wales: the Lithic Evidence*. Swansea: Glamorgan-Gwent Archaeological Trust Unpublished Report 2000/024.

Locock, M. 2003. The distribution of prehistoric settlement in south-east Wales: fieldwork on lithic scatter sites. *Archaeology in Wales* 43: 59–65.

Lord, J. 1998. The methods used to produce a complete harpoon, in Ashton *et al.* (eds) 1998: 193–5.

Lovis, W. A., Whallon, R. and Donahue, R. E. 2006. Social and spatial dimensions of Mesolithic mobility. *Journal of Anthropological Archaeology* 25: 271–4.

Lowe, S. 1981. Radiocarbon dating and stratigraphic resolution in Welsh lateglacial chronology. *Nature* 293: 210–12.

Lowe, J. J. and Lowe, S. 1989. Interpretation of the pollen stratigraphy of Late Devensian, Lateglacial and Early Flandrian sediments at Llyn Gwernan, near Cader Idris, North Wales. *New Phytologist* 113(3): 391–408.

Lowe, J. J. and Walker, M. J. C. 1984. *Reconstructing Quaternary Environments*. London: Longman.

Lowe, J. J. and Walker, M. J. C. 1997. *Reconstructing Quaternary Environments* (2nd ed.). London: Pearson Education.

Lowe, J. J., Lowe, S., Fowler, A. J., Hedges, R. E. M. and Austin, T. J. F. 1988. Comparison of accelerator and radiometric radiocarbon measurements obtained from Late Devensian Lateglacial lake sediments from Llyn Gwernan, North Wales, UK. *Boreas* 17(3): 355–69.

Lowe, J. J., Coope, G. R., Harkness, D. D., Sheldrick, C. and Walker, M. J. C. 1995. Direct comparison of UK temperatures and Greenland snow accumulation rates 15000–12000 yr ago. *Journal of Quaternary Science* 10: 175–80.

Lukes, A., Zvelebil, M. and Pettitt, P. 2008. Biological and cultural identity of the first farmers: introduction to the Vedrovice bioarchaeology project. *Anthropologie* (Brno) 46(2–3): 117–24.

Lynch, F. 2001. Site B – Mesolithic and Early Neolithic settlement evidence from the area of henge B, in Lynch and Musson 2001: 24–36.

Lynch, F. and Musson, C. 2001. A prehistoric and early medieval complex at Llandegai, near Bangor, North Wales. *Archaeologia Cambrensis* 150: 17–142.

Lynch, F., Aldhouse-Green, S. and Davies, J. L. 2000. *Prehistoric Wales*. Stroud: Sutton.

Macdonald, S. 1997. *Reimagining Culture: Histories, Identities and the Gaelic Renaissance*. Oxford: Berg.

Mackay, A., Battarbee, R., Birks, J. and Oldfield, F. (eds) 2003. *Global Change in the Holocene*. London: Hodder Arnold.

Macklin, M. and Needham, S. 1992. Studies in British alluvial archaeology: potential and prospect, in Needham, S. and Macklin, M. (eds), *Alluvial Archaeology in Britain*: 9–23. Oxford: Oxbow Books.

Malinowski, B. 1922. *Argonauts of the Western Pacific: an Account of Native Enterprise and Adventure in the Archipelagoes of Melanesian New Guinea*. London: Routledge & Kegan Paul.

Malone, C. 2001. *Neolithic Britain and Ireland*. Stroud: Tempus.

Mannino, M. A. and Thomas, K. D. 2011. Intensive Mesolithic exploitation of coastal resources? Evidence from a shell deposit on the Isle of Portland (southern England) for the impact of human foraging on populations of intertidal rocky shore molluscs. *Journal of Archaeological Science* 28: 1101–14.

Marlowe, F. 2002. Why the Hadza are still Hunter–Gatherers, In Kent, S. (ed.), *Ethnicity, Hunter–Gatherers and the "Other": Association or Assimilation in Africa*: 247–75. Washington DC: Smithsonian Institution Press.

Marlowe, F. W. 2005. Hunter–gatherers and human evolution. *Evolutionary Anthropology* 14: 54–67.

Mason, S. L. R., Hather, J. G. and Hillman, G. C. 1994. Preliminary investigation of the plant macro–remains from Dolní Věstonice II, and its implications for the role of plant foods in Palaeolithic and Mesolithic Europe. *Antiquity* 68: 48–57.

Mayewski, P. A. and White, F. 2002. *The Ice Chronicles. The Quest to Understand Global Climate Change*. Lebanon, NH: University of New Hampshire Press.

Mayle, F. E., Bell, M., Birks, H. H., Brooks, S. J., Coope, G. R., Lowe, J. J., Sheldrick, C., Shijie, L., Turney, C. S. M. and Walker, M. J. C. 1999. Climate variations in Britain during the Last Glacial–Holocene transition (15.0–11.5 cal ka BP): comparison with the GRIP ice core record. *Journal of the Geological Society of London* 156: 411–23.

McCartan, S. B. 2003. Mesolithic hunter–gatherers in the Isle of Man: adaptions to an island environment? in Larsson *et al.* (eds), 2003: 331–9.

McCartan, S., Schulting, R. J., Warren, G. and Woodman, P. (eds) 2009. *Mesolithic Horizons: Papers Presented at the Seventh International Conference on the Mesolithic in Europe, Belfast 2005*. Oxford: Oxbow Books

McCarthy, M. 2008. Boundaries and the archaeology of frontier zones, in David, B. and Thomas, J. (eds), *Handbook of Landscape Archaeology*: 202–9. Walnut Creek, CA: Left Coast Press.

McComb, A. M. G. and Simpson, D. 1999. The Wild bunch: exploitation of the hazel in prehistoric Ireland. *Ulster Journal of Archaeology* (3rd Ser.) 58: 1–16.

McGovern-Wilson, R. and Quinn, C. 1996. Stable isotope analysis of ten individuals from Afetna, Saipan, Northern Mariana Islands. *Journal of Archaeological Science* 23: 59–65.

McFadden, L. 2008. Temporary spaces in the Mesolithic and Neolithic: understanding landscapes, in Pollard (ed.) 2008: 121–34.

McFarlane, I. 1995. Llanmelin Wood, Shirenewton (ST 461 966). *Archaeology in Wales* 35: 46.

McLaughlin, R. 2005. Dental microwear, in Schulting 2005: 213–9.

McQuade, M. and O'Donnell, L. 2007. Late Mesolithic fish traps in the Liffey estuary, Dublin, Ireland. *Antiquity* 81: 569–84.

Mears, R. 2010. *Northern Wilderness*. London: Hodder & Stroughton.

Mears, R. and Hillman, G. 2008. *Wild Food*. London: Hodder & Stroughton.

Mein, A. G. 1992. Excavations at Trostrey Castle near Usk, Gwent. *Archaeology in Wales* 32: 11–14.

Mein, A. G. 1996. Trostrey castle, Trostrey (SO 3595 0435). *Archaeology in Wales* 36: 64–6.

Mellars, P. A. 1987. *Excavations on Oronsay: Prehistoric Human Ecology on a Small Island*. Edinburgh: Edinburgh University Press.

Mellars, P. 1998. Introduction: history of research and interpretations at Star Carr, in Mellars and Dark (eds) 1998a: 3–17.

Mellars, P. 2004. Neanderthals and the modern human colonisation of Europe. *Nature* 432: 461–5.

Mellars, P. and P. Dark. 1998a. *Star Carr in Context: new Archaeological and Palaeoecological Investigations at the Early Mesolithic Site of Star Carr, North Yorkshire*. Cambridge: McDonald Institute for Archaeological Research.

Mellars, P. and Dark, P. 1998b. Summary and conclusions, in Mellars and Dark (eds) 1988a: 209–14.

Midgley, M. 1992. *TRB Culture: the First Farmers of the North European Plain*. Edinburgh: Edinburgh University Press.

Mighall, T. M. and Chambers, F. M. 1995. Holocene vegetation history and human impact at Bryn y Castell, Snowdonia, North Wales. *New Phytologist* 130: 299–321.

Meiklejohn, C. 2009. Radiocarbon dating of Mesolithic human remains in Spain. *Mesolithic Miscellany* 22(2): 2–20.

Meiklejohn, C. and Babb, J. 2009. Issues in burial chronology in the Mesolithic of Northwestern Europe, in Crombé, P., Van Strydonck, M., Sergent, J., Boudin, M. and Bats, M. (eds), *Chronology and evolution within the Mesolithic of North-West Europe*: 217–38. Newcastle: Cambridge Scholars Press.

Meiklejohn, C., Merrett, D. C., Nolan, R. W., Richards, M. P. and Mellars, P. A. 2005. Spatial relationships, dating and taphonomy of the human bone from the Mesolithic site of Cnoc Coig, Oronsay Argyll, Scotland. *Proceedings of the Prehistoric Society* 71: 85–105.

Meiklejohn, C., Brinch Petersen, E. and Babb, J. 2009. From single graves to cemeteries: An initial look at chronology in Mesolithic burial practice, in McCartan *et al.* (eds) 2009, 639–49.

Meiklejohn, C., Chamberlain, A. T. and Schulting, R. J. 2011. Radiocarbon dating of Mesolithic human remains in Great Britain. *Mesolithic Miscellany* 21(2): 20–58.

Mensforth, R. P. 1991. Palaeoepidemiology of porotic hyperostosis in the Libben and Bt–5 Skeletal populations. *Kirtlandia* 46: 1–47.

Milner, N. 2006. Subsistence, In Conneller and Warren (eds) 2006: 61–82.

Milner, N. 2007. Fading star. *British Archaeology* 96, 10–14.

Milner, N. 2010. Subsistence at 4000–3700 cal BC: landscapes of change or continuity? in Finlayson, B. and Warren, G. (eds), *Landscapes in Transition*: 46–54. Oxford: Council for British Research in the Levant Suppplementary series 8/Oxbow Books.

Milner, N., Taylor, B. and Conneller, C. 2012. Fieldwork at the Early Mesolithic site of Star Carr. *North Yorkshire Historic Environment News* 2: 18.

Milner, N., Craig, O. E., Bailey, G. N., Pedersen, K. and Andersen, S. H. 2004. Something fishy in the Neolithic? A re–evaluation of stable isotope analysis of Mesolithic and Neolithic coastal populations. *Antiquity* 78(299): 9–22.

Milner, N., Conneller, C., Elliott, B., Koon, H., Panter, I., Penkman, K., Taylor, B. and Taylor, M. 2011. From riches to rags: organic deterioration at Star Carr. *Journal of Archaeological Science* 38(10): 2818–32.

Mitchell, P. 2005. Modeling later Stone Age societies in southern Africa, in Browner Stahl, A. (ed.), *African Archaeology: A Critical Introduction*: 150–73. Oxford: Blackwell Studies in Global Archaeology.

Mithen, S. 1999a. Hunter–gatherers of the Mesolithic, in Hunter, J. and Ralston, I. (eds), *The Archaeology of Britain: an Introduction for Earliest Times to the Twenty-First Century*: 35–57. London: Routledge.

Mithen, S. J. 1999b. Mesolithic archaeology, environmental archaeology and human palaeoecology. *Quaternary Proceedings* 7: 477–83.

Mithen, S. J. and Finlayson, B. 1991. Red deer hunters on Colonsay? The implications of Staosnaig for the interpretation of the Oronsay middens. *Proceedings of the Prehistoric Society* 57(2): 1–8.

Mithen, S., Finlay, N., Carruthers, W., Carter, S. and Ashmore, P. 2001. Plant use in the Mesolithic: Evidence from Staosnaig, Isle of Colonsay, Scotland. *Journal of Archaeological Science* 28: 223–34.

Miyaji, A. 1999. Storage pits and the development of plant food managemenet, in Coles, B., Coles, J. and Schou Jørgensen, M. (eds), *Bog Bodies, Sacred Sites and Wetland Archaeology*: 165–70. Exeter: WARP Occasional Paper 12.

Montelius, O. 1988. *The Civilisation of Sweden in Heathen Times* (2nd ed). London: McMillan and Co. Available to view on–line at: http: //www.archive.org/stream/civilisationswe00montgoog#page/n10/mode/2up

Moore, J. and Scott, E. 1997. *Invisible People and Processes: Writing Gender and Childhood into European Archaeology*. London: Leicester University Press.

Moore, P. D. 1972. Studies in the vegetational history of mid-Wales. III. Early Flandrian pollen data from west Cardiganshire. *New Phytologist* 71(5): 947–59.

Moore, P. D. 1973. The influence of prehistoric cultures upon the initiation and spread of blanket bog in upland Wales. *Nature* 241: 350–3.

Moore, P. D. 1975. Origin of blanket mires. *Nature* 256: 267.

Moore, P. D. 1978. Studies in the vegetational History of mid-Wales. V. Stratigraphy and pollen analysis of Llyn Mire in the Wye Valley. *New Phytologist* 80(1): 281–302.

Moss, M. L. and Erlandson, J. M. 1995. Reflections on North American Pacific coast prehistory. *Journal of World Prehistory* 9: 1–45.

Müldner, G. and Richards, M. P. 2005. Fast or feast: reconstructing diet in later medieval England by stable isotope analysis. *Journal of Archaeological Science* 32: 39–48.

Mulk, I.-M. and Bayliss-Smith, T. 1999. The representation of Sámi cultural identity in the cultural landscapes of northern Sweden: the use and misuse of archaeological knowledge, in Ucko and Layton (eds) 1999: 358–96.

Mulvaney, J. 1987. *The Aboriginal Photographs of Baldwin Spencer*. Victoria: Viking O'Neil.

Murphy, K. 2002. The archaeological resource: chronological overview to 1500 AD, in Davidson (ed.) 2002: 44–64.

Murton, D. K., Pawley, S. M. and Murton, J. B. 2009. Sedimentology and luminescence ages of Glacial Lake Humber deposits in the central Vale of York. *Proceedings of the Geologists' Association* 120: 209–22.

Myers, F. R. 1988. Critical trends in the study of hunter–gatherers. *Annual Review of Anthropology* 17: 261–82.

Nayling, N. 2002. Environmental archaeology, in Davidson (ed.). 2002: 24–32.

Newell, R. R., Constandse-Westermann, T. S. and Meiklejohn, C. 1979. The skeletal remains of Mesolithic man in western Europe: an evaluative catalogue. *Journal of Human Evolution* 8(1): 1–228.

Nicholas, G. P. 1991. Putting wetlands into perspective. *Man in the Northeast* 42: 29–38.

Nicholas, G. P. 1998. Wetlands and hunter gatherers: a global perspective. *Current Anthropology* 39(5): 720–31.

Nicholas, G. P. 2007a. Prehistoric hunter-gatherers in wetland environments: theoretical issues, economic organization and resource management strategies, in Lillie, M. C. and Ellis, S. (eds), *Wetland Archaeology and Environments: Regional Issues, Global Perspectives*: 46–62. Oxford: Oxbow Books.

Nicholas, G. P. 2007b. Prehistoric hunter-gatherers in wetland environments: mobility/sedentism and aspects of socio–political organisation, in Lillie, M. C. and Ellis, S. (eds), *Wetland Archaeology & Environments: Regional Issues, Global Perspectives*: 245–57. Oxford: Oxbow Books.

NSPRMF 2009. *North Sea Prehistory Research and Management Framework*. Amersfoort.

Nilsson, L. 1998. Dynamic cadavers: A field-anthropological analysis of the Skateholm II burials. *Lund Archaeological Review* 4: 5–17.

Nilsson Stutz, L. 2003. Embodied rituals and ritualized bodies. Tracing ritual practices in late Mesolithic burials. *Acta Archaeologica Lundensia* Series 8, 46. Stockholm: Almqvist and Wiksell Intl.

Nilsson Stutz, L. 2009. Coping with cadavers: ritual practices in Mesolithic cemeteries, in McCartan *et al.* (eds) 2009: 657–63.

Nilsson Stutz, L. 2010. The way we bury our dead. Reflections on mortuary ritual, community and identity at the time of the Mesolithic–Neolithic transition. *Documenta Praehistorica* 37: 33–42.

Nuzhnyi, D. 1989. L'utilisation des microlithes géométriques et non géométriques comme armatures de projectiles. *BSPF* 86: 88–96.

Nuzhnyi, D. 1990. Projectile damage on Upper Palaeolithic microliths and the use of the bow and arrow among Pleistocene hunters in the Ukraine, in *Proceedings of the International Conference on Lithic Use-wear Analysis*: 113–24 Sweden: Uppsala.

Nuzhnyi, D. 1993. Projectile weapons and technical progress in the Stone Age. Traces et fonction: les gestes retrouvés. *Colloque International de Liège Éditions*: 41–53. Paris: ERAUL 50.

O'Connell, T. C., Levine, M. A. and Hedges, R. E. M. 2000. The importance of fish in the diet of central Eurasion peoples from the Mesolithic to the early Iron Age, in *Late Prehistoric Exploitation of the Eurasian Steppe: Volume II*: 303–27. Symposium held at the McDonald Institute for Archaeological Research, Cambridge 12–16 January 2000.

O'Shea, J. J. 2006. The origins of lithic projectile point technology: evidence from Africa, the Levant, and Europe. *Journal of Archaeological Science* 33: 823–46.

O'Shea, J. M. and Zvelebil, M. 1984. Oleneostrovski mogilnik: Reconstructing the social and economic organisation of prehistoric foragers in northern Russia. *Journal of Anthropological Archaeology* 3: 1–40.

Oshibkina, S. V. 1989. The material culture of the Veretye-type sites in the region to the East of Lake Onega, in Bonsall (ed.) 1989b: 402–13.

Page, N. 2004. *Prehistoric Undefended Settlements Project, Southwest Wales: a Review of the Lithic Evidence from the Regional SMR*. Cambrian Archaeology Unpublished Report 2004/53, Project Record 50794.

Parfitt, S. A., Ashton, N. M., Lewis, S. G., Abel, R. L., Coope, G. R., Field, M. H., Gale, R., Hoare, P. G., Larkin, N. R., Lewis, M. D., Karloukovski, V., Maher, B. A., Peglar, S. M., Preece, R. C., Whittaker, J. E. and Stringer, C. B. 2010. Early Pleistocene human occupation at the edge of the boreal zone in northwest Europe. *Nature* 466: 229–33.

Parker Pearson, M. 1993. The powerful dead: archaeological relationships between the living and the dead. *Cambridge Archaeological Journal* 3(2): 203–29.

Peeters, H., Murphy, P. and Flemming, N. 2009. *North Sea Prehistory Research and Management Framework*. Amersfoort, Netherlands: Rijksdienst voor het Cultureel Erfgoed and English Heritage.

Pettitt, P. B. 2000. The Paviland radiocarbon dating programme: reconstructing the chronology of faunal communities, carnivore activity and human occupation, in Aldhouse-Green (ed.) 2000b: 63–71.

Pettitt, P. B. 2008. The British Upper Palaeolithic, in Pollard (ed.) 2008: 18–57.

Pettitt, P. B., Bahn, P. and Ripoll, S. 2007. *Palaeolithic Cave Art at Creswell Crags in European Context*. Oxford: Oxford University Press.

Pickard, C. and Bonsall, C. 2004. Deep-sea fishing in the European Mesolithic: fact or fantasy? *European Journal of Archaeology* 7(3): 273–90.

Pickard, C. and Bonsall, C. 2012. A different kettle of fish: food diversity in Mesolithic Scotland, in Collard, D., Morris, J. and Perego, E. (eds), *Food and Drink in Archaeology 3: University of Nottingham Postgraduate Conference 2009*: 76–88. Devon: Prospect Books.

Pike, A., Gilmour, M. and Pettitt, P. 2000. Verification of the age of the Palaeolithic cave art at Creswell Crags using uranium-series disequilibrium dating, in Bahn and Pettitt (eds) 2000: 87–95.

Pitts, M. 1979. Hides and antlers: a new look at the gatherer-hunter site of Star Carr, North Yorkshire. *World Archaeology* 11: 32–42.

Pluciennik, M. 2004. The meaning of "hunter-gatherers" and modes of subsistence: a comparative historical perspective, in Barnard, A. (ed.), *Hunter-Gatherers in History, Archaeology and Anthropology*: 17–29. Oxford: Berg.

Pollard, E. 2011. The Mesolithic maritime landscape on the North Coast of Ireland. *International Journal of Nautical Archaeology* 40(2): 387–403.

Pollard, J. 1999. 'These places have their moments': thoughts on settlement practices in the British Neolithic, in Brück, J. and Goodman, M. (eds). *Making Places in the Prehistoric World: Themes in Settlement Archaeology*: 76–93. London: University College London Press.

Pollard, J. 2000. Ancestral places in the Mesolithic landscape, in Conneller (ed.) 2000b: 123–38.

Pollard, J. (ed.), 2008. *Prehistoric Britain*. Oxford: Blackwell.

Preece, R. C., Gowlett, J. A. J., Parfitt, S. A., Bridgland, D. R. and Lewis, S. G. 2006. Humans in the Hoxnian: habitat, context and fire use at Beeches Pit, West Stow, Suffolk, UK. *Journal of Quaternary Science* 21(5): 485–96.

Price, S. 2009. Wood and wild animals: towards an understanding of a Mesolithic world, in McCartan *et al.* (eds) 2009: 683–9.

Price, T. D. 1989. The reconstruction of Mesolithic diets, in Bonsall (ed.) 1989b: 48–59.

Price, T. D. and Gebauer, A. B. 1995. New perspectives on the transition to agriculture. In Price, T. D. and Gebauer, A. B. (eds), *Last Hunters, First Farmers: New Perspectives on the Prehistoric Transition to Agriculture*: 3–19. Santa Fe, NM: School of American Research Press.

Price, T. D. and Gebauer, A. B. 2005. *Smakkerup Huse: A Late Mesolithic coastal site in Northwest Zealand, Denmark*. Aarhus: Aarhus University Press.

Price, T. D. and Bar-Yosef, O. 2011. The origins of agriculture: new data, new ideas: an introduction to supplement 4. *Current Anthropology* 52(S4): S63–S174.

Quinnell, H. and Blockley, M. R. (eds) 1994. *Excavations at Rhuddlan, Clwyd 1969–73 Mesolithic to Medieval*. York: Council for British Archaeology Research Report 95.

Radovanović, I. 1996. *The Iron Gates Mesolithic*. Michigan: International Monographs in Prehistory Archaeological Series 11.

Reed, L. J. 1991. Women in the sub–arctic: was gathering a viable economic activity?, in Walde, D. and Williams, N. D. (eds), *The Archaeology of Gender: Proceedings of the 22nd annual Chacmool Conference*: 292–6. Calgary: Archaeological Association of the University of Calgary.

Reynier, M. 1998. Early Mesolithic settlement in England and Wales: some preliminary observations, in Ashton *et al.* (eds) 1998: 174–84.

Reynier, M. J. 2000. Thatcham revisited: spatial and stratigraphic analyses of two sub-assemblages from site III and its implications for early Mesolithic typo-chronology in Britain, in Young (ed.) 2000: 33–46.

Richards, M. P. 2000. Human and faunal stable isotope analyses from Goat's Hole and Foxhole Caves, Gower, in Aldhouse-Green, S. (ed.) 2000b: 71–5.

Richards, M. P. 2002. A brief review of the archaeological evidence for Palaeolithic and Neolithic subsistence. *European Journal of Clinical Nutrition* 56: doi: 10.1038/sj.ejcn.160–4.

Richards, M. P. 2009. Stable isotope evidence for European Upper Palaeolithic human diets, in Hublin, J.–J. and Richards, M. P. (eds), *The Evolution of Hominin Diets: Integrating Approaches to the Study of Palaeolithic Subsistence*: 251–7. Berlin: Springer Science and Business Media B.V.

Richards, M. P. and Hedges, R. E. M. 1999. Stable isotope evidence for similarities in the types of marine foods used by Late Mesolithic humans at sites along the Atlantic coast of Europe. *Journal of Archaeological Science* 26: 717–22.

Richards, M. P., Schulting, R. J. and Hedges, R. E. M. 2003. Sharp shift in diet at the onset of Neolithic. *Nature* 425: 366.

Richards, M. P., Jacobi, R., Currant, A., Stringer, C. and Hedges, R. E. M. 2000. Gough's Cave and Sun Hole Cave human stable isotope values indicate a high animal protein diet in the Upper Palaeolithic. *Journal of Archaeological Science* 27: 1–3.

Richards, M. P., Pettitt, P. B., Stiner, M. C. and Trinkhaus, E. 2001. Stable isotope evidence for increasing dietary breadth in the European mid–Upper Palaeolithic. *Proceedings of the National Academy of Sciences* 98(11): 6528–32.

Richards, M. P., Pearson, J. A., Molleson, T. I., Russell, N. and Martin, L. 2003. Stable isotope evidence of diet at Neolithic Çatalhöyük, Turkey. *Journal of Archaeological Science* 30: 67–76.

Richards, M. P., Jacobi, R., Cook, J., Pettitt, P. B. and Stringer, C. B. 2005. Isotope evidence for the intensive use of marine foods by Late Upper Palaeolithic humans. *Journal of Human Evolution* 49: 390–4.

Rippon, S. 2000. *The Transformation of Coastal Wetlands: Exploitation and Management of Marshland Landscapes in North West Europe During the Roman and Medieval periods*. Oxford: Oxford University Press.

Roberts, A. 1994. The scanning electron microcope analysis of the engraved pebbles, in Quinnell and Blockley (eds) 1994: 119–24.

Roberts, M. B., Stringer, C. B. and Parfitt, S. A. 1994. A hominid tibia from Middle Pleistocene sediments at Boxgrove, UK. *Nature* 369: 311–13.

Roberts, M. J., Scourse, J. D., Bennell, J. D., Huws, D. G., Jago, C. F. and Long, B. T. 2011. Late Devensian and Holocene relative sea level change in North Wales, UK. *Journal of Quaternary Science* 26(2): 141–155.

Roberts, N. 1991. *The Holocene: an Environmental History*. Oxford: Blackwell.

Rozoy, J.-G. 1989. The revolution of the bowmen in Europe, in Bonsall (ed.) 1989b: 13–28.

Ross, J. 1999. Proto-historical and historical Spokan prescribed burning and stewardship of resource areas, in Boyd, r. (ed.), *Indians, Fire and the Land in the Pacific Northwest*: 277–91. Corvallis OR: Oregon State University Press.

Rouja, P. M. 1998. *Fishing for Culture: Toward an Aboriginal Theory of Marine Resource Use Among the Bardi Aborigines of One Arm Point, Western Australia*. Unpublished Ph.D. Thesis, University of Durham.

Rouja, P. M., Dewailly, É., Blanchet, C. and the Bardi Community. 2003. Fat, fishing patterns, and health among the Bardi People of North Western Australia. *Lipids* 38(4): 399–405.

Rowley-Conwy, P. 1984. The laziness of the short-distance hunter: the origins of agriculture in western Denmark. *Journal of Anthropological Archaeology* 3: 300–24.

Rowley-Conwy, P. 1998. Cemeteries, seasonality and complexity in the Ertebølle of Southern Scandinavia, in Zvelebil *et al.* (eds) 1998: 193–202.

Rowley-Conwy, P. 2011. Westward Ho! The spread of agriculturalism from Central Europe to the Atlantic. *Current Anthropology* 52 (Supple. 4), S431–S51.

Russell, N. J., Bonsall, C. and Sutherland, D. G. 1995. The exploitation of marine molluscs in the Mesolithic of western Scotland: evidence from Ulva Cave, Inner Hebrides, in Fischer, A. (ed.), *Man and Sea in the Mesolithic:* 273–88. Oxford: Oxbow Books.

Russell-Smith, J., Lucas, D., Gapindi, M., Gunbunuka, B., Kapirigi, N., Namingum, G., Lucas, K., Giuliani, P. and Chaloupka, G. 1997. Aboriginal Resource utilization and fire management practice in Western Arnhem Land, monsoonal northern Australia: notes for prehistory, lessons for the future. *Human Ecology* 25(2): 159–95.

Sargent, H. C. 1923. The massive chert formation of North Flintshire. *Geological Magazine* 60: 168–83.

Saul, H., Madella, M., Fischer, A., Glykou, A., Hartz, S. and Craig, O. E. 2013. Phytoliths in pottery reveal the use of spice in European prehistoric cuisine. PlosOne 8(8)e70583: 1–5.

Saville, A. and Ballin, T. B. 2009. Upper Palaeolithic evidence from Kilmelfort Cave, Argyll: a re–evaluation of the lithic assemblage. *Proceedings of the Society of Antiquaries of Scotland* 139: 9–45.

Scales, R. 2007. Footprint-tracks of people and animals, in Bell (ed.) 2007a: 139–59.

Scaife, R. G. 1992a. Pollen Analysis, in Healy, F., Heaton, M. and Lobb, S. J., Excavations of a Mesolithic site at Thatcham, Berkshire. *Proceedings of the Prehistoric Society* 58: 66–70.

Scaife, R. G. 1992b. Plant Macrofossils, in Healy, F., Heaton, M. and Lobb, S. J., Excavations of a Mesolithic site at Thatcham, Berkshire. *Proceedings of the Prehistoric Society* 58: 64–66.

Scaife, R. 1994. Pollen Analysis and Radiocarbon Dating of the Intertidal Peats at Caldicot Pill, in Bell, M. (ed.), *Archaeology in the Severn Estuary. Annual Report of the Severn Estuary Levels Research Committee*. Lampeter: Welsh Office Highways Agency, CADW and RCHME. 67–80.

Scaife, R. and Long, A. 1994. Evidence for Holocene sea level changes at Caldicot Pill, in Bell, M. (ed.), *Archaeology in the Severn Estuary. Annual Report of the Severn Estuary Levels Research Committee*. Lampeter: Welsh Office Highways Agency, CADW and RCHME. 81–5.

Schadla-Hall, R. T. 1987. Early man in the eastern Vale of Pickering, in Ellis, S. (ed.), *East Yorkshire: Field Guide*: 00–00. Cambridge: Quaternary Research Association.

Schadla-Hall, T. 1989. The Vale of Pickering in the early Mesolithic in context, in Bonsall (ed.) 1989b: 218–24.

Schilling, H. 1997. The Korsør Nor site. The permanent dwelling place of a hunting and fishing people in life and death, in Pedersen, L., Fischer, A. and Aaby, B. (eds), *The Danish Storebælt Since the Ice Age*: 93–8. Copenhagen: A/S Storebælt Fixed Link.

Schoeninger, M. and DeNiro, M. 1984. Nitrogen and carbon isotopic composition of bone collagen from marine and terrestrial animals. *Geochimica et Cosmochimica Acta* 48: 625–39.

Schoeninger, M., DeNiro, M. and Tauber, H. 1983. Stable nitrogen isotope ratios of bone collagen reflect marine and terrestrial components of prehistoric human diet. *Science* 220: 1381–3.

Schofield, A. J. 1994. Lithic artefacts from test-pit excavations on Lundy: evidence for Mesolithic and Bronze Age occupation. *Proceedings of the Prehistoric Society* 60: 423–31.

Schulting, R. 2000. New AMS dates from the Lambourn long barrow and the question of the earliest Neolithic in southern England: repackaging the Neolithic package? *Oxford Journal of Archaeology* 19(1): 25–35.

Schulting, R. 2003. The marrying kind: evidence for a patrilocal postmarital residence pattern in the Mesolithic of southern Brittany, in Larsson *et al.* (eds) 2003: 431–41.

Schulting, R. 2005. "... Pursuing a rabbit in Burrington Combe": New research on the early Mesolithic burial cave of Aveline's Hole. *Proceedings of the University of Bristol Spelaeological Society* 23(3): 171–265.

Schulting, R. 2008. Foodways and social ecologies from the early Mesolithic to the early Bronze Age, in Pollard (ed.), 2008: 90–120.

Schulting, R. 2009. Worm's Head and Caldey Island (south Wales, UK) and the question of Mesolithic territories, in McCartan *et al.* 2009: 354–61.

Schulting, R. 2013. "Tilbury Man" Mesolithic skeleton from the Lower Thames. *Proceedings of the Prehistoric Society* 79: 19–37.

Schulting, R. and Richards, M. P. 2002a. Finding the coastal Mesolithic in southwest Britain: AMS dates and stable isotope results on human remains from Caldey Island, Pembrokeshire, South Wales. *Antiquity* 76: 1011–25.

Schulting, R. J. and Richards, M. P. 2002b. Dogs, ducks, deer and diet: new stable isotope evidence on early Mesolithic dogs from the Vale of Pickering, north-east England, *Journal of Archaeological Science* 29: 327–33.

Schulting, R. and Richards, M. P. 2000c. The use of stable isotopes in studies of subsistence and seasonality in the British Mesolithic, in Young (ed.). 2000: 55–65.

Schulting, R. and Richards, M. P. 2001. Dating women and becoming farmers: new palaeodietary and AMS Dating evidence from the Breton Mesolithic cemeteries of Téviec and Hoëdic. *Journal of Anthropological Anthropology* 20: 314–44.

Schulting, R. and Richards, M. P. 2002. Finding the coastal Mesolithic in southwest Britain: AMS dates and stable isotope results on human remains from Caldey Island, Pembrokeshire, South Wales. *Antiquity* 76: 1011–25.

Schulting, R. and Wysocki, M. 2002. The Mesolithic human skeletal collection from Aveline's Hole: a preliminary report. *Proceedings of the University of Bristol Spelaeological Society* 22(3): 255–68.

Schulting, R., Fibiger, L., Macphail, R., McLaughlin, R., Murray, E., Price, C. and Walker, E. A. 2013. Mesolithic and Neolithic human remains from Foxhole Cave, south Wales. *Antiquaries Journal* 93: 1–23.

Schwarcz, H. P. and Schoeninger, M. 1991. Stable isotope analysis in human nutritionalecology. *Yearbook of Physical Anthropology* 34: 283–321.

Sergant, J., Crombé, P. and Perdaen, Y. 2006. The "invisible" hearths: a contribution to the discernment of Mesolithic non-structured surface hearths. *Journal of Archaeological Science* 33: 999–1007.

Sheenan, I. and Andrews, J. E. (eds) 2000. *Holocene Land-Ocean Interaction and Environmental Change Around the North Sea*. London: Geological Society Special Publication 166.

Sheenan, I., Lambeck, K., Horton, B., Innes, J., Lloyd, J., McArthur, J. and Rutherford, M. 2000a. Holocene Isostacy and relative sea–level changes on the east coast of England, in Sheenan and Andrews (eds) 2000: 275–98.

Sheenan, I., Lambeck, K., Flather, R., Horton, B., McArthur, J., Innes, J., Lloyd, J., Rutherford, M. and Wingfield, R. 2000b. Modelling western North Sea palaeogeographies and tidal changes during the Holocene, in Sheenan and Andrews (eds) 2000: 299–319.

Sheldrick, C., Lowe, J. J. and Reynier, M. J. 1997. Palaeolithic barbed point from Gransmoor, East Yorkshire, England. *Proceedings of the Prehistoric Society* 63: 359–70.

Shi, Z. and Lamb, H. F. 1991. Post–glacial sedimentary evolution of a microtidal estuary, Dyfi Esturay, west Wales, UK. *Sedimentary Geology* 73: 227–46.

Shnirelman, V. A. 2002. The Itenm'i, in Lee, R. B. and Daly, R. (eds), *The Cambridge Encyclopedia of Hunters and Gatherers*, 147–51. Cambridge: Cambridge University Press.

Shreve, D. C. 2001. Differentiation of the British late Middle Pleistocene Interglacials: the evidence from mammalian biostratigraphy. *Quaternary Science Reviews* 20: 1693–1705.

Shreve, D. C. 2006. The taphonomy of a Middle Devensian (MIS 3) vertebrate fauna from Lynford, Norfolk, UK, and its implications for Middle Palaeolithic subsistence strategies. *Journal of Quaternary Science* 21(5): 543–56.

Silvester, R. 2003. The archaeology of the Welsh uplands: an introduction, in Browne, D. and Hughes, S, (eds), *The Archaeology of the Welsh Uplands*: 9–29. Aberystwyth: RCAHMW.

Silvester, B. and Owen, R. 2002. *Early Prehistoric Settlement in Mid and North-East Wales: the Lithic Evidence. Desk Based Assessment.* Welshpool: Clwyd–Powys Archaeological Trust Report 467.

Simmons, I. G. 1996. *The Environmental Impact of Later Mesolithic Cultures*. Edinburgh: Edinburgh University Press.

Simmons, I. G. 2001. *An Environmental History of Great Britain: From 10,000 Years Ago to the Present.* Edinburgh: Edinburgh University Press.

Simmons, I. G. and Tooley, M. J (eds). 1981. *The Environment in British Prehistory*. London: Duckworth.

Simmons, I. G., Dimbleby, G. W. and Grigson, C. 1981. The Mesolithic, in Simmons and Tooley (eds) 1981: 82–124.

Simpson, B. 2003. The humble bead: body adornment and burial practices in the British Palaeolithic and Mesolithic, in Bevan and Moore (eds) 2003: 45–34.

Singer, R., Gladfelter, B. G. and Wymer, J. J. 1993. *The Lower Palaeolithic Site at Hoxne, England*. Chicago: Chicago University Press.

Smith, A. G. 2005. The North-west Wales Lithic Scatters Project. *Lithics* 26: 38–56.

Smith, A. G. and Cloutman, E. W. 1988. Reconstruction of Holocene vegetation history in three dimensions at Waun Fignen Felin, an upland site in South Wales. *Philosophical Transactions of the Royal Society* B, 322: 159–219.

Smith, A. G. and Morgan, L. A. 1989. A succession to ombrotrophic bog in the Gwent Levels, and its demise: a Welsh parallel to the peats of the Somerset Levels. *New Phytologist* 112(1): 145–67.

Smith, A. G. and Pilcher, J. R. 1973. Radiocarbon dates and the vegetational history of the British Isles. *New Phytologist* 72: 903–14.

Smith, C. 1992a. *Late Stone Age Hunters of the British Isles*. London: Routledge.

Smith, C. 1992b. The population of Late Upper Palaeolithic and Mesolithic Britain. *Proceedings of the Prehistoric Society* 58: 37–40.

Society of Antiquaries On-Line Newsletter. 2013. *The Gourmet Diet of Mesolithic Diners*. Salon 307 (27-10-2013).

Speth, J. D. 1989. Early Hominid hunting and scavenging: the role of meat as a resource. *Journal of Human Evolution* 18: 329–43.

Speth, J. D. 1990. Seasonality, resource stress and food-sharing in so-called 'egalitarian' foraging societies. *Journal of Anthropological Archaeology* 9(2): 148–88.

Speth, J. D. and Spielman, K. 1983. Energy source, protein metabolism and hunter gatherer subsistence strategies. *Journal of Anthropological Archaeology* 2: 1–31.

Spikins, P. 2008. "The bashful and the boastful" prestigious leaders and social change in Mesolithic societies. *Journal of World Prehistory* 21: 173–93.

Srejović, D. 1972. *Europe's First Monumental Sculpture: New Excavations at Lepenski Vir*. Aylesbury: Thames and Hudson.

Sternke, F. and Sørensen, M. 2009. The identification of children's flint knapping products in Mesolithic Scandinavia, in McCartan et al. (eds) 2009: 722–9.

Stuart-Macadam, P. 1992. Porotic hyperostosis: a new perspective. *American Journal of Physical Anthropology* 87: 39–47.

Stevens, R. E., Jacobi, R. M. and Higham, T. F. G. 2010. Reassessing the diet of Upper Palaeolithic humans from Gough's Cave and Sun Hole, Cheddar Gorge, Somerset, UK. *Journal of Archaeological Science* 27: 52–61.

Stewart, J. R. 2007. Neanderthal extinction as part of the faunal change in Europe during Oxygen Isotope Stage 3. *Acta Zoologica Cracoviensia*, 50A(1–2): 93–124.

Stig Sørensen, M. L. 2000. *Gender Archaeology*. Malden, MA: Blackwell.

Stiner, M. C., Munro, N. D. and Surovell, T. A. 2000. The tortoise and the hare: Small–game use, the broad–spectrum revolution, and Palaeolithic demography. *Current Anthropology* 41(1): 39–73.

Stonehouse, P. B. 1997. Pule Bents: a possible kill site in the central Pennines. *Yorkshire Archaeological Journal* 69: 1–7.

Street, M., Baales, M., Cziesla, E., Hartz, S., Heinen, M., Jöris, O., Koch, I., Pasda, C., Terberger, T. and Vollbrecht, J. 2001. Final Palaeolithic and Mesolithic research in reunified Germany. *Journal of World Prehistory* 15(4): 365–453.

Stringer, C. 1986. The British fossil hominid record, in Collcutt (ed.) 1986: 59–61.

Stringer, C. 2006. *Homo Britannicus*. London: Allen Lane.

Stringer, C. B., Trinkaus, E., Roberts, M. B., Parfitt, S. A. and Macphail, R. I. 1998. The Middle Pleistocene human tibia from Boxgrove. *Journal of Human Evolution* 34: 509–47.

Switser, V. R. and Jacobi, R. 1979. A radiocarbon chronology for the early postglacial stone industries of England and Wales, in Berger, R. and Suess, H. E (eds), *Radiocarbon Dating: Proceedings of the 9th International Conference Los Angeles and La Jolla*: 41–68. Berkeley and LA: University of California Press.

Taylor, B. and Grey Jones, A. 2009. Definitely a pit; possible a house? Recent excavations at Flixton School House Farm in the Vale of Pickering. *Mesolithic Miscellany* 20(2): 21–6.

Taylor, B., Conneller, C. and N. Milner. 2010. Little house by the shore. *British Archaeology* 115 (Nov/Dec) (online at http: //www.britarch.ac.uk/ba/ba115/feat6.shtml).

Taylor, K. C., Mayewski, P. A., Alley, R. B., Brook, E. J., Gow, A. J., Grootes, P. M., Meese, D. A., Saltzman, E. S., Severinghaus, J. P., Twickler, M. S., White, J. W. C., Whitlow, S. and Zielinski, G. A. 1997. The Holocene–Younger Dryas transition recorded at Summit, Greenland. *Science* 278: 825–7.

Telegin, D. Ya. and Potekhina, I. D. 1987. *Neolithic Cemeteries and Populations in the Dnieper Basin*. Oxford: British Archaeological Reports S383.

Thomas, D. 1993. Nant Hall Road, Prestatyn (SJ070832). *Archaeology in Wales* 33: 50.

Thomas, D. and Britnell, W. J. 2007. Nant Hall Road, in Armour-Chelu *et al.* 2007: 267–9.

Thomas, J. 1999. *Understanding the Neolithic*. London: Routledge.

Thomas, J. 2005. Current debates on the Mesolithic–Neolithic transition in Britain and Ireland. *Documenta Praehistorica* 31: 113–30.

Thomas, K. W. 1965. The stratigraphy and pollen analysis of a raised peat bog at Llanllwch, near Carmarthen. *New Phytologist* 64(1): 101–17.

Thomson, D. F. 1939. The seasonal factor in human culture: illustrated from the life of contemporary nomadic groups. *Proceedings of the Prehistoric Society* 10: 209–21.

Thorpe, I. J. N. 2003. Anthropology, archaeology, and the origins of warfare. *World Archaeology* 35(1): 145–65.

Tilley, C. 1994. *A Phenomenology of Landscape: Places, Paths and Monuments*. Oxford: Berg.

Timofeev, V. I. 1998. The Beginning of the Neolithic in the Eastern Baltic, in Zvelebil *et al.* (eds) 1998: 225–36.

Tipping, R. 1993. A detailed early postglacial (Flandrian) pollen diagram from Cwm Idwal, north Wales. *New Phytologist* 125: 175–91.

Tolan-Smith, C. 2008. Mesolithic Britain, in Bailey, G. and Spikins, P. (eds), *Mesolithic Europe*: 132–57. Cambridge: Cambridge University Press.

Toussaint, M. 2011. Intentional cutmarks on an Early Mesolithic human calvaria from Margaux Cave, (Dinant, Belgium). *American Journal of Physical Anthropology* 144: 100–7.

Tringham, R. 1971. *Hunters, Fishers and Farmers of Eastern Europe, 6000–3000 B.C.* London: Hutchinson.

Trinkaus, E. and Holliday, T. W. 2000. The human remains from Paviland Cave, in Aldhouse-Green, S (ed.) 2000b: 141–204.

Trinkhais, E., Formicola, V., Svoboda, J., Hillson, S. W. and Holliday, T. W. 2001. Dolní Věstonice 15: pathology and persistence in the Pavlovian. *Journal of Archaeological Science* 28: 1291–308.

Tucker, B. and Young, A. G. 2007. Growing up Mikea: children's time allocation and tuber foraging in southwestern Madagascar, in Hewlett and Lamb (eds) 2007: 147–71.

Ucko, P. J. and Layton, R. (eds) 1999. *The Archaeology and Anthropology of Landscape: Shaping your Landscape*. London: Routledge.

van Asch, N., Lutz, A. F., Duijkers, M. C. H., Heiri, O., Brooks, S. J. and Hoek, W. Z. 2012. Rapid climate change during the Weichselian Lateglacial in Ireland: Chironomid-inferred summer temperatures from Fiddaun, Co. Galway. *Palaeogeography, Palaeoclimatology, Palaeoecology* 315–16: 1–11.

Vanderwarker, A. M. 2006. *Farming, Hunting, and Fishing in the Olmec World*. Austin: University of Texas Press.

Van Gennep, A. 1960. *The Rites of Passage*. London: Routledge.

Vera, F. W. M. 2002. A park–like landscape rather than a closed forest. *Vakblad Natuurbeheer (special issue) Grazing and grazing animals* (2000): 13–15.

Waddington, C. (ed.) 2007a. *Mesolithic Settlement in the North Sea Basin and Beyond: a Case Study from Howick, North–East England*. Oxford: Oxbow Books.

Waddington, C. 2007b. Test pits, in Waddington (ed.) 2007a: 28–33.

Waddington, C., Bailey, G. and N. Milner 2007. Howick: Discussion and Interpretation, in Waddington (ed.) 2007a: 189–202.

Waddington, C. in press. A case for a secondary Mesolithic colonisation of Britain following rapid inundation of the North Sea plain, in Ashton, N. (ed.) *No Stone Unturned*. London: British Museum.

Wainwright, G. J. 1963. A reinterpretation of the microlithic industries of Wales. *Proceedings of the Prehistoric Society* 29: 99–132.

Walker, D. and Godwin, H. 1954. Lake stratigraphy, pollen-analysis and vegetation history, in Clark 1954: 25–69.

Walker, E. A. 2000. Burry Holms (SS 4001 9247). *Archaeology in Wales* 40: 88–9.

Walker, E. A. 2001. Burry Holmes (SS 4001 9247). *Archaeology in Wales* 41: 126.

Walker, E. A. 2003. Lithics, in Burrow, S. (ed.), *Catalogue of the Mesolithic and Neolithic Collections in the National Museums & Galleries of* Wales: 10–14 & 21–2.

Walker, M. J. C. 1982a. Early- and Mid-Flandrian environmental history of the Brecon Beacons, south Wales. *New Phytologist* 91(1): 147–65.

Walker, M. J. C. 1982b. The Late-Glacial and Early Flandrian deposits at Traeth Mawr, Brecon Beacons, south Wales. *New Phytologist* 90(1): 177–94.

Walker, M. J. C. 2001. Rapid climate change during the last glacial–interglacial transition; implications for stratigraphic subdivision, correlation and dating. *Global and Planetary Change* 30: 59–72.

Walker, M. J. C. 2005. *Quaternary Dating Methods*. Chichester: John Wiley.

Walker, M. J. C., Coope, G. R. and Lowe, J. J. 1993. The Devensian (Weichselian) Lateglacial palaeoenvironmental record from Gransmoor, East Yorkshire, England. *Quaternary Science Reviews* 12: 659–80.

Walker, M. J. C., Bohncke, S. J. P., Coope, G. R., O'Connell, M., Usinger, H. and Verbruggen, C. 1994. The Devensian? Weichselian Late-glacial in northwest Europe (Ireland, Britain, north Nelgium, the Netherlands, northwest Germany). *Journal of Quaternary Science* 9: 109–18.

Walker, M. J. C., Coope, G. R., Sheldrick, C., Turney, C. S. M., Lowe, J. J., Blockley, S. P. E. and Harkness, D. D. 2003. Devensian Lateglacial environmental changes in Britain: a multi-proxy environmental record from Llanilid, south Wales, UK. *Quaternary Science Reviews* 22: 475–520

Walker, M., Jones, S., Hussey, R. and Buckley, S. 2006. Mesolithic burning in the Welsh uplands: evidence from Esgair Ffraith, near Lampeter, West Wales. *Archaeology in Wales* 46: 3–10.

Walker, P. L. 1997. Wife beating, boxing, and broken bones: skeletal evidence for the cultural patterning of violence, in Martin and Frayer (eds) 1997: 145–79.

Ward, I., Larcombe, P. and Lillie, M. C. 2006. The dating of Doggerland – post-glacial geochronology of the southern North Sea. *Environmental Archaeology* 11(2): 207–18.

Waller, M. (ed.) 1994. *The Fenland Project, Number 9: Flandrian Environmental Change in Fenland*. East Cambridge: Anglian Archaeology 70.

Warren, G. 2003. Life in the trees: Mesolithic people and the woods of Ireland. *Archaeology Ireland* 17(3): 20–3.

Warren, G. 2005. *Mesolithic Lives in Scotland*. Stroud: Tempus.

Warren, G. 2006. Technology, in Conneller and Warren (eds) 2006: 13–34.

Watkins, R., Scourse, J. D. and Allen, J. R. N. 2007. The Holocene vegetation history of the Afron Platform, north Wales, UK. *Boreas* 36: 170–81.

Weerts, H. J. T. 2013. Holocene sea level change, sedimentation, coastal change and palaeogeography in the southern North Sea Basin, in. Thoen, E., Borger, G. J., de Kraker, A. M. J., Soens, T., Tys, D., Vervaet, L. and Weerts, H. J. T. (eds) *Landscapes or Seascapes? The History of the Coastal Environments in the North Sea Area* Reconsidered: 145–73. Belgium: Brepols, CORN Publications Series 13.

Weinstock, J. 2000. Osteometry as a source of refined demographic information: sex-ratios of reindeer, hunting strategies, and herd control in the Late-Glacial site of Stellmoor, Northern Germany. *Journal of Archaeological Science* 27: 1187–95.

Wenban-Smith, F. 2002. *Palaeolithic and Mesolithic Archaeology on the Sea Bed: Marine Aggregate Dredging and the Historic Environment*. Salisbury: Trust for Wessex Archaeology.

Westaway, R. 2011. A re-evaluation of the timing of the earliest reported human occupation of Britain: the age of the sediments at Happisburgh, eastern England. *Proceedings of the Geologists' Association* 122(3): 383–96.

White, M. J. and Jacobi, R. M. 2002. Two sides to every story: Bout Coupe´ handaxes revisited. *Oxford Journal of Archaeology* 21: 109–33.

White, M. J. and Pettitt, P. B. 2011. The British Late Middle Palaeolithic: an interpretive synthesis of Neanderthal occupation at the northwestern edge of the Pleistocene world. *Journal of World Prehistory* 24: 25–97.

White, M. J., Scott, B. and Ashton, N. 2006. The Early Palaeolithic in Britain: archaeology, settlement history and human behaviour. *Journal of Quaternary Science* 21(5): 525–41.

Whittle, A. and Cummings, V. (eds) 2007. *Going Over: The Mesolithic–Neolithic transition in North-West Europe.* Proceedings of the British Academy 144.

Whittle, A. 2007a. The temporality of transformation: dating the early development of the southern British Neolithic, in Whittle and Cummings (eds) 2007: 377–98.

Whittle, A. 2007b. Going over: people and their times, in Whittle and Cummings (eds) 2007: 617–28.

Whittle, A. 2009. The Neolithic period, *c.* 4000–2400 cal BC, in Hunter, J. and Ralston, I. (eds) *The Archaeology of Britain: An Introduction from Earliest Times to the Twenty-first* Century: 78–102.

Wilkinson, R. G. 1997. Violence against women: raiding and abduction in prehistoric Michigan, in Martin and Frayer (eds) 1997: 21–43.

Willoughby, P. R. 1991. Human origins and the sexual division of labour: an archaeological perspective, in Walde, D. and Williams, N. D. (eds), *The Archaeology of Gender: Proceedings of the 22nd Annual Chacmool* Conference: 284–91. Calgary: Archaeological Association of the University of Calgary.

Wolders, S., Zeiler, M. and Bungenstock, F. 2010. Early Holocene environmental history of sunken landscapes: pollen, plant macrofossil and geochemical analyses from the Borkum Riffgrund, southern North Sea. *International Journal of Earth Sciences* (Geol Rundsch) 99: 1707–19.

Woodburn, J. 1982. Egalitarian societies. *Man* (NS) 17: 431–51.

Woodman, J. 2009. An Introduction to Hadza ecology, in Lee and Devore (eds) 2009b: 49–55.

Woodman, P. C. 1978. *The Mesolithic in Ireland.* Oxford: British Archaeological Report 58.

Woodman, P. C. 1985. *Excavations at Mount Sandal, 1973–77.* Belfast: HMSO, Northern Ireland Archaeological Monograph 2.

Woodman, P. C. 1986. Problems in colonization of Ireland, *Ulster Journal of Archaeology* 49: 7–17.

Woodman, P. C. 1987. The impact of resource availability on lithic industrial traditions in prehistoric Ireland, in Rowley-Conwy *et al.* (eds) 1987: 138–46.

Woodman, P., Finlay, N. and Anderson, E. 1999. *Excavations at Ferriter's Cove.* Bray: Wordwell.

Wymer, J. 1962. Excavations at the Maglemosian sites at Thatcham, Berkshire, England. *Proceedings of the Prehistoric Society* 28: 329–61.

Yalden, D. W. 2007. Zoological Perspectives on the Late-Glacial, in Pettitt *et al.* (eds) 2007: 53–60.

Yellen, J. E. 1976. Settlement patterns of the !Kung: An archaeological perspective, in Lee, R. B. and DeVore, I. (eds), *Kalahari Hunter–Gatherers: Studies of the !Kung San and Their* Neighbours: 47–72 . Cambridge, MA/London: Harvard University Press.

Young, R. (ed.). 2000. *Mesolithic Lifeways: Current Research in Britain and Ireland.* Leicester: University of Leicester: Archaeology Monograph 7

Zagorska, I. and Larsson, L. 1994. New data on the chronology of the Zvejnieki Stone Age cemetery. *Mesolithic Miscellany* 15(2): 3–10.

Zaliznyak, L. 1998. The ethnographic record and structural changes in the prehistoric hunter–gatherer economy of Boreal Europe, in Zvelebil *et al.* (eds) 1998: 45–51.

Zendeño, M. N. 2008. The archaeology of territory and territoriality, in David, B. and Thomas, J. (eds), *Handbook of Landscape Archaeology*: 210–17. Walnut Creek, CA: Left Coast Press.

Zhilin, G. 2007a. Mesolithic wetland sites in Central Russia, in Lillie, M. and Ellis, S. (eds), *Wetland Archaeology and Environments: Regional Issues, Global* Perspectives: 65–78. Oxford: Oxbow Books.

Zhilin, M. 2007b. The early Mesolithic of the Upper Volga: selected problems, in Masojć, M., Płonka, T., Ginter, B. and Kozłowski, S. K. (eds), *Contributions to the Central European* Mesolithic: 89–104. Wrocław.

Zhilin, M. G. and Matiskainen, H. 2003. Deep in Russia, deep in the bog. Excavations of Stanovoje 4 and Sahtysh 14, Upper Volga region, in: Larsson *et al.* (eds) 2003: 694–702.

Zhilman, A. L. 1981. Women as shapers of the human adaptation, in Dahlberg (ed.) 1981: 75–120.

Zvelebil, M. 1994. Plant use in the Mesolithic and its role in the transition to farming. *Proceedings of the Prehistoric Society* 60: 35–74.

Zvelebil, M. 1995. *Hunting, Gathering, or Husbandry? Management of Food Resources by the Late Mesolithic Communities of Temperate Europe.* MASCA Research Papers in Science and Archaeology (Supplement) 12.

Zvelebil, M. 1996. Ideology, society and economy of the Mesolithic communities in temperate and northern Europe. *Estratto da Origini Preistoria e Protostoria delle Civiltà Antiche* 20: 39–70.

Zvelebil, M. 1998. Agricultural frontiers, Neolithic origins, and the transtition to farming in the Baltic Basin, in Zvelebil *et al.* (eds) 1998: 9–27.

Zvelebil, M. 2003a. People behind the lithics: social life and social conditions of Mesolithic communities in temperate Europe, in Bevan and Moore (eds) 2003: 1–26.

Zvelebil, M. 2003b. Enculturation of Mesolithic landscapes, in Larsson *et al.* (eds) 2003: 65–73.

Zvelebil, M. 2005. Homo habitus: agency, structure and the transformation of tradition in the constitution of the TRB foraging–farming communities in the North European Plain (*ca.* 4500–2000 BC). *Documenta Praehistorica* 32: 87–101.

Zvelebil, M. 2006. Mobility, contact and exchange in the Baltic Sea basin, 6000–2000 BC. *Journal of Anthropological Archaeology* 25: 178–92.

Zvelebil, M. 2008. Innovating hunter-gatherers: the Mesolithic in the Baltic, in Bailey, G. and Spikins, P. (eds), *Mesolithic Europe*: 18–59. Cambridge: Cambridge University Press.

Zvelebil, M., Dennell, R. and Domańska, L. (eds) 1998. *Harvesting the Sea, Farming the Forest: the Emergence of Neolithic Societies in the Baltic Region.* Sheffield: Academic Press.

APPENDIX

uncal BP	cal BC	uncal BP	cal BC	uncal BP	cal BC
10,300	10,130	8500	7560	6600	5540
10,200	9960	8400	7505	6500	5475
10,100	9750	8300	7395	6400	5400
10,000	9530	8200	7220	6300	5270
9900	9325	8100	7065	6200	5145
9800	9270	8000	6940	6100	5015
9700	9225	7900	7620	6000	4890
9600	8995	7800	6625	5900	4760
9500	8785	7600	6450	5800	4655
9400	8670	7500	6400	5700	4525
9300	8575	7400	6285	5600	4415
9200	8390	7300	6160	5500	4345
9100	8290	7200	6050	5400	4290
9000	8250	7100	5995	5300	4140
8900	8101	7000	5910	5200	4005
8800	7880	6900	5760	5100	3890
8700	7690	6800	5690	5000	3780
8600	7595	6700	5625	4900	3670

General reference guide for correspondence between uncalibrated radiocarbon dates and calendar years BC (10,300–4900 radiocarbon years BP) (*after* Bailey and Spikins 2008: 373). *Note*: these dates are modified slightly when calibrated in OxCal 4.2, but the differences are considered minor in terms of the general overview intended.

INDEX

(Numbers in italics denote pages with illustrations)